ADOPTION, ADAPTION, AND INNOVATION
IN PRE-ROMAN ITALY

ARCHAEOLOGY OF THE MEDITERRANEAN WORLD

VOLUME 3

GENERAL EDITORS

Lin Foxhall, *University of Liverpool*
Peter van Dommelen, *Brown University*

EDITORIAL BOARD

Laurel Bestock, *Brown University*
Andrea De Giorgi, *Florida State University*
Francesca Dell'Acqua, *Università degli Studi di Salerno*
Lieve Donnellan, *University of Melbourne*
Claudia Glatz, *University of Glasgow*
Paul S. Johnson, *University of Nottingham*
Luca Zavagno, *Bilkent Üniversitesi*

Previously published volumes in this series are listed at the back of the book.

Adoption, Adaption, and Innovation in Pre-Roman Italy

Paradigms for Cultural Change

Edited by

JEREMY ARMSTRONG and
AARON RHODES-SCHRODER

BREPOLS

British Library Cataloguing in Publication Data
A catalogue record for this book is available from the British Library.

© 2023, Brepols Publishers n.v., Turnhout, Belgium.

All rights reserved. No part of this publication may be reproduced,
stored in a retrieval system, or transmitted, in any form or by
any means, electronic, mechanical, photocopying, recording,
or otherwise without the prior permission of the publisher.

ISBN: 978-2-503-60232-5
e-ISBN: 978-2-503-60233-2
DOI: 10.1484/M.AMW-EB.5.131520

Printed in the EU on acid-free paper.

D/2023/0095/45

Table of Contents

List of Illustrations	7
Acknowledgements	17
Abbreviations	17

Jeremy Armstrong and Aaron Rhodes-Schroder
1. Rethinking Cultural (Ex)Change in Pre-Roman Italy ... 19

Nicola Terrenato
2. The Paradox of Innovation in Conservative Societies:
Cultural Self-Consistency and Bricolage in Iron Age Central Italy ... 33

Franco De Angelis
3. Mixing up Mediterranean Innovation: The Case of Viticulture and Wine ... 47

Marine Lechenault and Kewin Peche-Quilichini
4. The World Has Changed: Insularity and Tyrrhenian Connectivity
during the Corsican Iron Ages ... 59

John North Hopkins
5. Folding Meaning in an Object: The Ficoroni Cista
and the Heterarchy of Art in Early Italy ... 71

Charlotte R. Potts
6. Virtue in Variety: Contrasting Temple Design in Etruscan Italy ... 85

Aaron Rhodes-Schroder
7. The Demon Is in the Detail: Greek Pottery in Etruscan Funerary Contexts ... 101

Peter Attema, Barbara Belelli Marchesini, and Matthijs Catsman

8. Local Choices in a Networked World: Funerary Practices at
Crustumerium (Lazio) during the Long Seventh Century BCE ... 117

Amanda K. Pavlick

9. From the Ground up: Constructing Monumental Buildings
in Archaic Central Italy ... 147

Gijs Tol

10. The Archaic Countryside Revisited: A Ceramic Approach
to the Study of Archaic Rural Infill in Latium Vetus ... 161

Camilla Norman

11. Ritual Connectivity in Adriatic Italy ... 177

Keely Elizabeth Heuer

12. Face to Face: Isolated Heads in South Italian and Etruscan Visual Culture ... 193

William M. Balco

13. Feasting Transformed: Commensal Identity Expression and
Social Transformation in Iron Age and Archaic Western Sicily ... 221

**Peter Attema, Carmelo Colelli, Martin Guggisberg, Francesca Ippolito,
Jan Kindberg Jacobsen, Gloria Mittica, Wieke de Neef, and Sine Grove Saxkjær**

14. The Deep Past of Magna Graecia's Pottery Traditions:
Adoption and Adaption at Timpone della Motta and in the
Sibaritide (Northern Calabria, Italy) between the
Middle Bronze Age and the Archaic Period ... 235

Index ... 277

List of Illustrations

3. Mixing up Mediterranean Innovation — *Franco De Angelis*

Figure 3.1.   View of the interior of the so-called 'Dionysus Cup' (or *kylix*) by Exekias found at Vulci, Etruria, *c.* 540–530 BCE, depicting the god Dionysos in a ship with vine emerging from the ship's floors and wrapping itself around the mast.   53

Figure 3.2.   View of Side A of the so-called 'Vintaging Amphora' by the Amasis Painter found at Vulci, Etruria, *c.* 530 BCE, showing five satyrs engaged in the production of wine.   53

Figure 3.3.   View of Early Corinthian Eurytios (column) krater found at Cerveteri, dating to the late seventh century BCE.   53

Figure 3.4.   View of Early Corinthian column krater by the Athana Painter found at Cerveteri, Etruria dating to the early sixth century BCE.   53

4. The World Has Changed — *Marine Lechenault and Kewin Peche-Quilichini*

Figure 4.1.   Graffito *KURSIKE* from Populonia.   60

Figure 4.2.   Fibulae from Corsica: a. Snake-form spiral bow fibula from Carbuccia; b. Snake-form wavy bow fibula from l'Ordinacciu; c. Corsican-type fibula from Figa la Sarra.   62

Figure 4.3.   Corsican knife/short sword from Paestum.   64

Figure 4.4.   Map of colonies, Italic-style, and Corsican-type (fortified) settlements in Corsica during the Roman Republican period.   65

Figure 4.5.   Local vessels from Alalia necropolis. Museum of Aleria, CdC.   66

Figure 4.6.   Distribution of Corsican coarse vessels in the Tyrrhenian region, first and second centuries BCE.   67

5. Folding Meaning in an Object — *John North Hopkins*

Figure 5.1.   Ficoroni cista, with view of the Humiliation of Amykos, *c.* 350–315 BCE.   72

Figure 5.2.   Ficoroni cista, detail of foot, *c.* 350–315 BCE.   73

Figure 5.3.   Mirror with Herakles, Hermes, and a third figure.   73

Figure 5.4.   Ficoroni cista, drawing of engraved drum.   74

Figure 5.5.   Ficoroni cista, detail, *c.* 350–315 BCE.   79

6. Virtue in Variety — *Charlotte R. Potts*

Figure 6.1.	Pyrgi and its surroundings along the shore near Caere.	86
Figure 6.2.	General plan of Marzabotto.	87
Figure 6.3.	Plan of the sanctuary of Pyrgi: 'Monumental Sanctuary' with Temples B and A and 'Southern Sanctuary'.	88
Figure 6.4.	Reconstruction of Temple B, Pyrgi, *c.* 510 BCE, without architectural terracottas.	89
Figure 6.5.	Reconstruction of Temple A, Pyrgi, *c.* 470–460 BCE.	89
Figure 6.6.	Plan of the foundations of the Temple of Uni, Marzabotto, late sixth century BCE.	90
Figure 6.7.	Plan of the foundations of the Temple of Tinia, Marzabotto, *c.* 480–470 BCE.	91
Figure 6.8.	Virtual reconstruction of the two urban temples at Marzabotto, viewed from *Plateia* B.	92

7. The Demon Is in the Detail — *Aaron Rhodes-Schroder*

Figure 7.1.	Shapes and decorative techniques of Attic pottery from Tarquinia *c.* 550–450 BCE.	103
Figure 7.2.	Attic black- and red-figure amphora in Tarquinia by quarter century, *c.* 550–450 BCE.	103
Figure 7.3.	Attic black- and red-figure cups in Tarquinia by quarter century, *c.* 550–450 BCE.	103
Figure 7.4.	BAPD data for Attic black- and red-figure amphorae from Vulci, Cerveteri, and Orvieto.	104
Figure 7.5.	BAPD data for Attic black- and red-figure cups from Vulci, Cerveteri, and Orvieto.	104

8. Local Choices in a Networked World — *Peter Attema, Barbara Belelli Marchesini, and Matthijs Catsman*

Figure 8.1.	Location map of Crustumerium within central Tyrrhenian Italy.	119
Figure 8.2.	Crustumerium and its burial grounds.	120
Figure 8.3.	Example of clustering of tombs in the MDB burial ground.	122
Figure 8.4.	The consumption collective affiliations of three objects. A. Spiked *anforetta laziale*. B. *Impasto bruno* Phoenician-Cypriote *oinochoe*. C. Italo-Geometric *oinochoe*.	124
Figure 8.5.	The material consumption collective affiliation network of period IVA, based on the total number of affiliations per tomb and consumption collective; and the percentage of tombs affiliating to a specific consumption collective.	127
Figure 8.6.	Three variants of the same network shown in Figure 8.5, only displaying the central Italian consumption collective affiliations, the Medio-Adriatic consumption collective affiliations and the Italian Peninsular consumption collective affiliations in relation to the gender of the deceased.	128

Figure 8.7.	A variant of the same network shown in Figure 8.6, only displaying the Tyrrhenian hinterland consumption collective affiliations, which mainly concerns the consumption of white-on-red pottery, in relation to the gender of the deceased.	129
Figure 8.8.	The wider socio-cultural consumption collective affiliation network of period IVA, based on the total number of affiliations per tomb and consumption collective; and the percentage of tombs affiliating to a specific consumption collective.	129
Figure 8.9.	The consumption collective affiliation network of period IVB, based on the total number of affiliations per tomb and consumption collective; and the percentage of tombs affiliating to a specific consumption collective.	130
Figure 8.10.	The wider socio-cultural consumption collective affiliation network of period IVB, based on the number of affiliations per tomb and consumption collective; and the percentage of tombs affiliation to a specific consumption collective.	131
Figure 8.11.	Typology of local tombs of Latial periods IVA and B. 1A–B: trench tombs with a niche for the pottery; 1A–C: loculus tombs, housing both the deposition and the pottery and accessible through a shaft; 3A–B: chamber tombs.	132
Figure 8.12.	Orientalizing drinking set. Interpretation based on the association of the shapes used to contain wine.	135
Figure 8.13.	Red impasto shapes taken from the Faliscan area: so-called *scodella crustumina* and deep bowl with a knobbed rim.	136
Figure 8.14.	Latial *pyxis* from tomb MDB196.	136
Figure 8.15.	Selection of red impasto pottery decorated in the white-on-red technique.	136
Figure 8.16.	Huge cylindrical *pyxis* from tomb MDB111.	136
Figure 8.17.	Imported and local Italo-geometric pottery.	136
Plate 8.1.	Objects from Tomb MDB156 (Early Iron Age–Latial periods IIB2–III).	140
Plate 8.2.	Objects from Tomb MDB341 (Latial period IVA2, *c.* 660–630 BCE).	141
Plate 8.3.	Objects from Tomb MDB350 (Latial period IVA2, *c.* 650–630 BCE).	142
Plate 8.4.	Objects from Tomb MDB344 (Latial Period IVB, *c.* 620–580 BCE).	143
Plate 8.5.	Objects from Tomb MDB25 (Archaic period, in use from the beginning to the end of the sixth century BCE).	144
Table 8.1.	A comparative overview of the cultural phases of Latium, Etruria, and Greece.	118
Table 8.2.	The various consumption collectives used in the network analysis.	126

9. From the Ground up — *Amanda K. Pavlick*

Figure 9.1. Locations of known terracotta-roofed buildings constructed in Acquarossa between 640 and 610 BCE. 156

Figure 9.2. Areas of settlement at Tarquinia, Veii, and Gabii in the eighth century BCE as represented by surface scatters. 157

Figure 9.3. Locations of known terracotta-roofed buildings constructed in Acquarossa between 600 and 540 BCE; earlier structures are represented in light grey. 157

Table 9.1. Buildings in Rome with terracotta-tiled roofs, seventh to mid-sixth centuries BCE. 155

Table 9.2. Buildings in Acquarossa with terracotta-tiled roofs, seventh to mid-sixth centuries BCE. 155

10. The Archaic Countryside Revisited — *Gijs Tol*

Figure 10.1. The Pontine region, with areas and sites investigated by the PRP. 162

Figure 10.2. The high-count scenario of ruralization between Satricum and Antium. 165

Figure 10.3. Base fragment of a jar in the augite-rich red-firing fabric. 166

Figure 10.4. Material associations on sites with augite-rich red-firing pottery in the hinterlands of Satricum and Antium. 167

Figure 10.5. Distribution of Archaic sites in the hinterlands of Satricum and Antium. 169

Figure 10.6. Pottery from the Iron Age-Archaic village at site 15088: nos 1–6 and 8 red-firing coarse wares; 7: red-firing loom weight; 9–13: bucchero. 170

Figure 10.7. Material associations on sites with augite-rich red-firing pottery in the hinterland of Norba. 171

Table 10.1. Assemblages recorded for several Archaic (farm) houses. 167

Table 10.2. Archaic sites in the hinterlands of Satricum and Antium. 168

11. Ritual Connectivity in Adriatic Italy — *Camilla Norman*

Figure 11.1. Map showing the find-spots, sites, and regions mentioned in the text. 178

Figure 11.2. Upper half of a female Daunian stele. 179

Figure 11.3. Drawing of the mortar and pestle scene on the lower back of a female Daunian stele, F687. 180

Figure 11.4. Daunian matt-painted *kernos*, provenance unknown. 181

Figure 11.5. North Lucanian matt-painted *askos* from Ripacandida T.46. 181

Figure 11.6. Oenotrian matt-painted *kanthoros* from Guardia Perticara T.115. 181

Figure 11.7. *Aryballos* from Sala Consilina T.B.27, Certosa di Padula. 182

Figure 11.8. Roll-out of the imagery on a Campana *dinos*. 182

Figure 11.9. Drawing of a detail of the Verucchio Throne. 183

Figure 11.10. The Alpago situla, Belluno. 184

Figure 11.11. Hallstatt pot from Sopron, National Museum of Vienna. 185

12. Face to Face — *Keely Elizabeth Heuer*

Figure 12.1. Campanian red-figure bell-krater attributed to the Painter of Oxford 1945 with head of a satyr in profile. New York, Metropolitan Museum of Art, inv. no. 41.162.263, *c.* 360–330 BCE. 195

Figure 12.2. Apulian red-figure skyphos with female head in profile. New York, Metropolitan Museum of Art, inv. no. 76.12.15, *c.* 325–300 BCE. 195

Figure 12.3. Campanian red-figure neck-amphora attributed to the Pilos Head Group. On the neck, head of youth wearing a *pilos*; on the body, a young warrior seated on an altar facing a bearded warrior. New York, Metropolitan Museum of Art, inv. no. X.21.19, *c.* 350–325 BCE. 195

Figure 12.4. Apulian red-figure volute-krater by the Painter of Copenhagen 4223. On the neck, head wearing Phrygian cap; on the body, a youthful warrior and mature male wearing a himation and leaning on a staff in a *naiskos* surrounded by women and youths. Chicago, Art Institute of Chicago, *c.* 340 BCE. 195

Figure 12.5. Lucanian red-figure *nestoris* attributed the Painter of New York 52.11.2. On the neck, head in profile flanked by wings; on the body, a standing youth offering a bird to a seated woman. New York, Metropolitan Museum of Art, inv. no. 52.11.2, *c.* 360–350 BCE. 195

Figure 12.6. Etruscan (Caeretan) red-figure Genucilia plate (name plate of the Genucilia ware) with female head in profile. Providence, Rhode Island School of Design Museum, inv. no. 27.188, *c.* 340–300 BCE. 195

Figure 12.7. Etruscan (Caeretan) red-figure *oinochoe* attributed to the Populonia Torcop Painter. On the neck, female head in profile; on the body, confronted male head wearing wolf-skin cap and female head. Paris, Musée du Louvre, inv. no. K 471, second half fourth century BCE. 195

Figure 12.8. Detail of Hades and Persephone on the Torre San Severo Sarcophagus. Orvieto, Museo Claudio Faina, final decades of the fourth century BCE. 196

Figure 12.9. Campanian red-figure epichysis produced by the Cassandra-Parrish workshop with confronted male and female heads. Bonn, Akademisches Kunstmuseum der Universität Bonn, inv. no. 200, *c.* 380–360 BCE. 196

Figure 12.10. Etruscan (Caeretan) red-figure Torcop Group *oinochoe* with female heads in profile on the neck and body. New York, Metropolitan Museum of Art, inv. no. 91.1.465, *c.* 300 BCE. 196

12 LIST OF ILLUSTRATIONS

Figure 12.11. Campanian red-figure bell-krater by the Seated Nike Painter with female head in profile. Cambridge, Museum of Classical Archaeology, University of Cambridge, inv. no. GR 14/1963, *c.* 380–360 BCE. 196

Figure 12.12. Campanian red-figure stemless *kylix* attributed to the Rhomboid Group with female head in profile surrounded by laurel leaves in the tondo. Edinburgh, National Museum of Scotland, inv. no. 1956.405, *c.* 330–320 BCE. 196

Figure 12.13. Etruscan red-figure Tondo Group skyphos from Chiusi with female heads in floral surround. New York, Metropolitan Museum of Art, inv. no. 07.286.33, *c.* 340–300 BCE. 196

Figure 12.14. Apulian red-figure volute-krater by the Patera Painter. Detail of neck with female head emerging from flower in floral surround. Malibu, J. Paul Getty Museum, inv. no. 77.AE.115, *c.* 330 BCE. 197

Figure 12.15. Attic red-figure hydria attributed to the Herakles Painter with female head flanked by Erotes and satyrs holding pickaxes. Brussels, Musées Royaux d'Art et d'Histoire, inv. no. R 286, *c.* 370 BCE. 201

Figure 12.16. Apulian red-figure *pelike* attributed to the Darius Painter with head emerging from flower gazing at two seated women above. Amsterdam, Allard Pierson Museum, inv. no. 2578, *c.* 340–320 BCE. 201

Figure 12.17. Apulian red-figure volute-krater by the Darius Painter. On the neck, a head wearing a Phrygian cap; on the body, the death of Hippolytos. London, British Museum, inv. no. 1856,1226.1, *c.* 340–320 BCE. 201

Figure 12.18. Apulian red-figure volute-krater attributed to the Darius Painter. On the neck, profile female head emerging from flower in floral surround; on the body, Dionysos visiting Hades and Persephone in the underworld. Toledo, Toledo Museum of Art, inv. no. 1994.19, *c.* 330 BCE. 201

Figure 12.19. Etruscan (Volterran) *kelebe* from the Portone Necropolis at Volterra. On the neck, female head in three-quarter view to left between horse protomes; on the body, pygmy fighting crane. Florence, Museo Archeologico Nazionale, inv. no. 4035, late fourth century BCE. 202

Figure 12.20. Lecce, Ipogeo Palmieri: entry passage frieze with female head in floral setting, late fourth–early third centuries BCE. 202

Figure 12.21a. Vulci, François Tomb: virtual view of the right chamber of the 'atrium' using copies of Carlo Ruspi's reconstruction paintings, *c.* 330–310 BCE. 203

Figure 12.21b. Vulci, François Tomb: female head above central doorway in the right chamber of the 'atrium', *c.* 330–310 BCE. 203

Figure 12.22. Vulci, François Tomb: moulded cement central coffer of the 'tablinum' with the head of Charun, *c.* 330–310 BCE. 203

Figure 12.23. Cerveteri: Tomb of the Reliefs, second half fourth century BCE. 203

Figure 12.24. Sovana: Tomba del Tifone, late fourth–early third centuries BCE. 204

Figure 12.25. Figured capital with isolated heads of the central column in Tomba Campanari at Vulci. Florence, Museo Archeologico Nazionale, inv. no. 75279, late fourth–early third centuries BCE. 204

Figure 12.26.	Perugia, Tomba dei Volumnii: 'tablinum' with two male isolated heads in the gable, third–second centuries BCE.	204
Figure 12.27.	Perugia, Tomba dei Volumnii: coffer with frontal female head in right side-chamber, third–second centuries BCE.	205
Figure 12.28.	Volterra: Porta dell'Arco with sculpted heads on the keystone and imposts, fourth–third centuries BCE.	206
Figure 12.29.	Cinerary urn of Vel Rafi with isolated heads flanking an arched doorway. Perugia, Museo Archeologico Nazionale dell'Umbria, inv. no. 26.291, 150–100 BCE.	206
Figure 12.30.	Sarcophagus of Ramtha Visnai and Arnth Tetnies from Vulci. Boston, Museum of Fine Arts, inv. no. 1975.799, late fourth–early third centuries BCE.	206
Figure 12.31.	Etruscan terracotta cinerary urn with an isolated head with bovine ears and wearing a Phrygian cap with wings, likely produced in Chiusi. New York, Metropolitan Museum of Art, inv. no. 96.9.221a,b, second century BCE.	206
Figure 12.32.	Terracotta female protome from Ospedale Civile necropolis, tomb 67 in Syracuse. Syracuse, Museo Archeologico Regionale 'Paolo Orsi', c. 550–525 BCE.	206
Figure 12.33.	Terracotta tomb slab from tomb 117 at Metaponto, decorated with a mould-made antefix featuring a frontal head wearing a Phrygian cap. Metaponto, Museo Archeologico Nazionale, inv. no. 319201, late fourth century BCE.	207
Figure 12.34.	Terracotta bust of a woman wearing a polos from the rock sanctuary below San Biagio at Agrigento. Syracuse, Museo Archeologico Regionale 'Paolo Orsi', inv. no. 16085, c. 400–350 BCE.	208
Figure 12.35.	Terracotta Etruscan female votive head, possibly from Veii. Chicago, Art Institute of Chicago, inv. no. 1975.342, c. 500 BCE.	208
Figure 12.36a.	Terracotta *pinax* with overlapping male and female profile heads to left from Francavilla di Sicilia. Syracuse, Museo Archeologico Regionale 'Paolo Orsi', inv. no. 85663, c. 475–470 BCE.	208
Figure 12.36b.	Line drawing of the terracotta *pinax*, after Spigo 2000b, 34 fig. 48.	208
Figure 12.37.	Terracotta *arula* from Taranto with a frontal female head surrounded by spiralling tendrils. Taranto, Museo Archeologico Nazionale, inv. no. 208342, second half of the fourth century BCE.	209
Figure 12.38.	Red-figure amphora attributed to the Owl Pillar Group depicting the creation of Pandora in the presence of Hephaistos (?), Zeus (?), and the *pithos*. London, British Museum, inv. no. F 147, c. 450–425 BCE.	212
Figure 12.39.	Terracotta grotto model from Grotto Caruso with female isolated head above cave entrance. Reggio Calabria, Museo Archeologico Nazionale Locri, inv. no. Gr. Car. 356, third–second centuries BCE.	212
Figure 12.40.	Terracotta plaque from Grotta Caruso at Locri depicting three female heads above Euthymos in bull form next to an altar. Reggio Calabria, Museo Archeologico Nazionale, inv. no. 110, fourth century BCE.	212

13. Feasting Transformed — *William M. Balco*

Figure 13.1. Map showing locations of key sites in Iron Age and Archaic western Sicily. 222

Figure 13.2. Illustration of *attingitoio, scodella,* and *capeduncola*. 225

Figure 13.3. Line drawing of *scodella* decorated with *denti di lupo*. Recovered from Salemi. 226

Figure 13.4. Illustration of *capeduncola* with details of exterior, profile, and interior. 227

14. The Deep Past of Magna Graecia's Pottery Traditions — *Peter Attema and others*

Figure 14.1. Map of the Sibaritide with location and toponyms of sites, rivers, and landscape zones mentioned in the text. 236

Figure 14.2. Overview map of Timpone della Motta, Macchiabate, and immediate surroundings. Protohistoric sites without *doli cordonati*; Sites with *doli cordonati*, green areas: fields investigated by the Raganello Archaeological Project. 237

Figure 14.3. Overview map of the site of Timpone della Motta and contexts mentioned in the text (sanctuary, plateaus, excavation areas). 238

Figure 14.4. Example of a complete corded *pithos* from Broglio. 242

Figure 14.5. Grey Ware shapes from Francavilla Marittima and parallels from Broglio di Trebisacce and Torre Mordillo. 243

Figure 14.6. Orthophoto of the lower slopes of Timpone della Motta showing from left to right excavation locations Area Rovitti and Area Aita I–III. 243

Figure 14.7. Early Geometric matt-painted closed vessels from Area Aita. 246

Figure 14.8. Selection of impasto shapes from Francavilla. 247

Figure 14.9. Examples of Italo-Mycenaean open and closed vessels from Area Aita I. 247

Figure 14.10. Wall fragment of a closed shaped vessel decorated by painted spiral motifs from Area Rovitti. 247

Figure 14.11. A possibly imported Mycenaean fragment found in a secondary context in the sanctuary in 2018. 247

Figure 14.12. Proto-Geometric matt-painted fragment from a closed jar from Area Aita I. 248

Figure 14.13. Early Geometric matt-painted biconical jars from Area Aita II. 248

Figure 14.14. Matt-painted pottery decorated in the Middle Geometric 'Undulating Band Style' from Area Aita A. Biconical jar, cup. 251

Figure 14.15.	Matt-painted jar with decoration in the 'Undulating Band Style' with thinner lines.	251
Figure 14.16.	Context US 258 in Area Aita. 1: Imported Euboean Middle Geometric *skyphos*. 2–3: Imported Iapyrgian matt-painted cups. 4: Oinotrian-Euboean *amphora*. 5: Local matt-painted cup. 6: Local matt-painted jar.	252
Figure 14.17.	Examples of indigenous pottery shapes. 1: *Scodella*. 2: Biconical jar.	252
Figure 14.18.	Stand from large vessel in Greek-Euboean style.	253
Figure 14.19.	Euboean-Euboean one-handled cups reproducing the indigenous 'Undulating Band Style'. 1: Cup from the Macchiabate necropolis. 2: Cup from the summit of Timpone della Motta.	253
Figure 14.20.	Imported one-handled bowl with simple matt-painted decoration.	254
Figure 14.21.	Imported, Salentine, matt-painted pottery from Area Aita.	254
Figure 14.22.	Misfired bichrome fragment from structure B, Area Rovitti.	254
Figure 14.23.	Example of bichrome technique applied in the Oinotrian-Euboean production. 1: *Kantharos*. 2: *Scodella*.	257
Figure 14.24.	Ticino Group. 1: Globular *pyxis*. 2: Lidded globular *pyxis*. 3–5: Krater.	257
Figure 14.25.	Lid fragment decorated with a male and a female holding hands related to the Ticino Group.	258
Figure 14.26.	Globular *pyxis* of the Sub-Thapsos class.	258
Figure 14.27.	Horse figures. 1: from Contrada Damale. 2: from Timpone della motta. 3: from Area Rovitti. 4: from Area Aita.	258
Figure 14.28.	Human figurines from Area Aita.	258
Figure 14.29.	1: Misfired *hydriskai* from the sanctuary. 2: Misfired *kernos* from the sanctuary.	261
Figure 14.30.	Colonial pottery. 1: *Kantharos*. 2: *Skyphos*.	262
Figure 14.31.	Longevity of classes of pottery at Timpone della Motta.	263
Figure 14.32.	Actual and circumstantial evidence for pottery production at Timpone della Motta.	263
Table 14.1.	Table showing periodizations as used in the text.	240
Table 14.2.	Table showing similarities in shapes between various classes of pottery during the Bronze Age.	244

Acknowledgements

The volume is a product of the conference 'Exchanging Ideas: Trade, Technology, and Connectivity in Pre-Roman Italy', held at the University of Auckland, New Zealand, 3–6 February 2020. We would therefore like to thank all who were involved in that event — including our co-organizer Sheira Cohen, those whose contributions are contained in this volume, those who contributed to its companion volume (Jeremy Armstrong and Sheira Cohen (eds), *Production, Trade, and Connectivity in Pre-Roman Italy* (London: Routledge, 2022)), and everyone else who presented and participated across those days (including Ashley, Gala, Sally, Gabriele, Marleen, Marian, Alex, Birgit, James, Remco, Doug, and Duncan).

We would also like to thank the Royal Society Te Apārangi of New Zealand Marsden Fund, who supported the overall project ('Blood and Money: The "Military Industrial Complex" in Archaic Central Italy', 17-UOA-136, awarded to Jeremy Armstrong), of which this was a part. Thanks must also go to the anonymous peer reviewers, as well as the wonderful and supportive people at Brepols (esp. Rosie Bonté) and the series 'Archaeology of the Mediterranean World' (esp. Andrea De Giorgi) for helping to bring this volume to fruition. Thanks as well to Gala Morris and Francesca Taylor for their editorial assistance and insight in the final stages.

Most importantly, however, we would like to thank our contributors. The past three years have been dominated by the COVID-19 pandemic, which has wreaked havoc on both the personal and professional lives of all involved. Through it all, our contributors have done a truly heroic job of keeping to deadlines, responding to late-minute queries and requests, and producing what we feel is truly impactful and outstanding work in the process. Thank you all for all of your work.

Finally, thanks must go to our families and immediate support networks — Ashle, William, Theo, Etta, Ashley, and Caspian. Without your time, patience, and encouragement this volume would not have been possible.

Jeremy Armstrong & Aaron Rhodes-Schroder
Auckland, New Zealand

Abbreviations

Abbreviations of ancient works generally follow those in the *Oxford Classical Dictionary*, 4th edition. Modern bibliography abbreviations follow those in *l'Année Philologique*.

BAPD = *Beazley Archive Pottery Database*

CVA = *Corpus Vasorum Antiquorum*

GIA = *Groningen Institute of Archaeology*

LIMC = *Lexicon iconographicum mythologiae classicae*

Nava = Nava, Maria Luisa. 1980. *Stele Daunie*, I (Florence: Sansone)

1. Rethinking Cultural (Ex)Change in Pre-Roman Italy

ABSTRACT For much of the nineteenth and twentieth centuries CE, the ancient Mediterranean basin was thought to have been dominated by large cultural-political entities which operated like expansive 'proto-nation-states'. Described using labels given by the writers of our ancient literary sources (for example 'Greek', 'Roman', and 'Punic' *vel sim*), and considered using early modern and modern frameworks, cultural identity, change, and exchange was thought to operate along the same lines as that suggested for early modern nation-states and empires. However, an ever-increasing archaeological record, increasingly critical and sensitive approaches to the literary evidence, and the impact of postcolonialism (amongst other theoretical shifts) has resulted in a marked change in scholarship over the past half century. The traditional cultural-political monoliths have been replaced by a fluid set of overlapping networks in an ancient Mediterranean basin dominated by microcultures and microhistories. Although a clear step forward, this new model is not without its own problems. While we have gained detail and refinement in some areas, we seem to have lost it in others — especially at the regional level. We have yet to find an appropriate way to connect and structure our microhistories, linking them to their wider Mediterranean context, without falling back on the old, problematic, labels and constructs. This chapter explores some of these issues, discusses possible avenues forward, and outlines the contributions of the present volume to the wider discussion.

This volume explores how and why the peoples of pre-Roman Italy adopted new practices, adapted to new situations, and innovated in response to evolving contexts and relationships. Fifty years ago, this sort of exploration would not have required a volume, because cultural change in early Italy was assumed to be a relatively simple, one-way, externally driven process. As Ogilvie concisely noted, in the introduction of his 1976 *Early Rome and the Etruscans*, 'The advance of Rome [...] was due to the expansion of her mysterious neighbours to the north, the Etruscans' (Ogilvie 1976, 12). The Etruscans, meanwhile, and since Pallottino's classic work (Pallottino 1947), were understood to have been shaped by a 'sudden and intense Orientalization of the culture and taste of the Greek world' (Pallottino 1965, 784). Indeed, as Pallottino, Dräyer, and Hürlimann (1955, 12) suggested, 'In a short time the stagnant backwater of Etruria was transformed into a high and wealthy civilization complete with great buildings, exquisite works of art of its own, as well as goods imported from abroad on a large scale'. While some societies, like the Greeks of the so-called 'Dark Ages', were allowed by scholars to evolve slowly and in seeming isolation, dramatic changes in short periods of time, like that seen in pre-Roman Italy, were thought to have required external impetus. Following models established in the context of early modern empires, cultural change was seen to flow naturally down a slope from 'more advanced and sophisticated' societies to lesser ones (see Nowlin 2021 for discussion). Simple exposure could, and for proponents of the model arguably should, lead to great results.

This broad approach to cultural (ex)change has been largely deconstructed as a result of postcolonialism — although some remnants linger. Increasingly, a more egalitarian 'connected' or 'networked' approach has moved to the fore in ancient Mediterranean studies — pushed into the mainstream by Horden and Purcell's (2000) now seminal work, and expanded on by Broodbank (2013), Pitts and Versluys (2014), and Hodos (2020a) among many others. On the grand scale, the result has been a livelier and more exciting picture, but also one which is far less distinct. Rather than the relatively simple 'passing on' of a discrete set of cultural practices from one 'more advanced' culture to another 'lesser' one,

---

Corresponding author Jeremy Armstrong (js.armstrong@auckland.ac.nz)

scholars have argued for a less context-specific perspective which has resulted in a vibrant and churning Mediterranean basin whereby change seems to be a natural by-product of the energy and connectivity of the system. The end result is a single, networked population, covering the entirety of the basin, featuring a 'Mediterranean-wide bundle of cultural practices' (Padilla Peralta and Bernard 2022, 21) which is the product of an ongoing 'Mediterraneanization' process (Morris 2003, 44–45). On the other end of the spectrum, we have come to grips, as never before, with the unique lived experiences of individuals through detailed, site-specific, archaeologically derived microhistories. The proliferation of data has offered the opportunity not only to discuss local communities in ways which would have been inconceivable fifty years ago, but also to avoid the labels which would have traditionally both defined and obscured them. These connected shifts in approach have been vitally important, as they have broken down the artificial cultural-political monoliths which had previously dominated — and constrained — our thinking, as well as the deeply flawed colonial models of (ex)change. Modern models are more accurate, more dynamic, and more *human* than past models. However, the lack of internal structure has come with concomitant problems. Most notably, while the model makes sense on both the grand scale and in the particular, regional and internal developments have become far more difficult to describe. We struggle to know if our microhistories are indicative of the whole or how they relate to each other — both of which introduce new complications.[1]

It must also be noted that this broad, Mediterranean-wide approach to culture and social groupings (across and between microcultures) does not easily align with the labels and categories expressed by the ancients themselves. From the cultural 'Greekness' (τὸ Ἑλλενικὸν) of Herodotus to Rome's varied socio-political relationships (*civita, civitas sine suffragio, socii*, etc.), larger structures, divisions, and labels seem to have mattered quite a lot to at least some ancient writers — although they obviously did not speak for everyone, and their conceptions were not uncontested. While material culture may suggest new and important connections and groupings, we cannot completely ignore what ancient writers explicitly said on the subject. Something, even if often idealized and theoretical in nature, seems to have existed at the regional level in antiquity. The attempt to define things at this level is not an entirely modern impulse. While those who utilized this 'Mediterranean-wide bundle of cultural practices' may have operated in a mutually comprehensible context, their cultures were neither homogenous nor interchangeable, and at least some ancient writers recognized and expressed these distinctions themselves. While it is clear that modern (and early modern) pseudo-nationalist and ethnic interpretations of labels like 'Greek', 'Roman', or 'Punic' were anachronistic misconceptions, this does not mean the labels themselves, as deployed by the ancients, were wholly without meaning or merit.

Deciding how to describe and define the internal structures of our interconnected ancient Mediterranean, at the regional level, is one of the next great challenges for our discipline. We have rightly broken down and cast aside the old models and approaches but have yet to develop a new methodology or approach which can make sense of, and appropriately structure and categorize, the mass of data, connections, and unique contexts which now confront us. Without this, we cannot tell meaningful stories about this intermediate level. Our microhistories proliferate, as do our grand narratives, but we have no analogous methodology for identity, change, or exchange at the regional level.

The present volume aims to continue, and contribute to, the ongoing conversation around how we approach cultural identity and interaction in the ancient Mediterranean basin, and especially in pre-Roman Italy.[2] While its companion volume (Armstrong and Cohen 2022) highlighted ways in which we might reconsider and reidentify social and cultural groups in pre-Roman Italy on their own terms, albeit also through the lens of connectivities and production, this volume explores the ways in which these groups engaged with cultural change and exchange. Central to this is an interrogation of the cultural interaction which has traditionally dominated the first half of the first millennium BCE in this region: that between the peoples of Italy and those of the 'Greek East' (see De Angelis 2020 for recent discussion and bibliography). Although now recognized as only one of many sets of interactions occurring in the peninsula, this particular relationship continues to have an outsized importance

---

1   It is worth noting that those who work with microhistories might not view this as an issue, as this approach often deliberately adopts a theoretical posture against 'universal laws of human behaviour' and other types of grand narrative history.

---

2   The bibliography on this subject is vast (and growing). McInerney's Blackwell volume *A Companion to Ethnicity in the Ancient Mediterranean*, as well as volume 21 of *Archaeological Dialogues*, together provide a useful summary up until 2014. For more recent discussion see also Clackson and others 2020 and Balot 2021, but particularly the excellent summary and discussion in Hodos 2020b.

in our models due to its visibility in our extant evidence. Beyond the traditional importance of 'the East' in the development of Italic culture, one can also look to the north, and long-standing connections which existed between the Italian peninsula and continental Europe — largely running through the Alps. Perhaps most visible in the material remains of metallurgical trade and technology (Iaia 2005), it is clear that Italy and the continent were involved in a dynamic set of cultural interactions which stretched from the Early Bronze Age through the Classical period. Looking south and west also reveals vibrant connectivities. From contacts with the Nuragic culture of Sardinia, to Corsica, Sicily, north Africa, and Iberia, the western Mediterranean is now known to have featured a strong social, cultural, and economic network from at least the Neolithic (Blake 2001). Of arguably greater importance are Italy's internal networks, nurtured and facilitated by a mobility which has increasingly come to the fore in modern studies (esp. Isayev 2017). The cultures of pre-Roman Italy were not simply 'reheated Hellenism', or even the sum of their various networked parts, but rather a combination of influences channelled through a unique Italic context. The present volume will explore, through its various case studies, how and why the cultures of pre-Roman Italy changed the way they did with the goal of highlighting how we might understand cultural change and exchange within the wider Mediterranean world.

Moving from 'the East'

No discussion of cultural (ex)change in pre-Roman Italy, even now, can begin without some discussion of 'the East'. Although they were clearly not the only factors which shaped Italic society during the first millennium BCE, it is impossible to deny that connections with the eastern Mediterranean played a significant, or at least overt, role. The dominant paradigm for understanding cultural change and development in pre-Roman, Iron Age Italy has traditionally been *ex oriente lux* for a reason, supported by the explicit statements of the ancients and seemingly corroborated by mountains of archaeological evidence. Going back to the sixteenth and seventeenth centuries CE, exposure to eastern civilization and culture, even if just through trade, was thought to be the primary driver behind most, if not all, of the social and cultural developments of the period (famously, see Boardman 1999; see Nowlin 2021 for discussion, critique, and bibliography). This was particularly true for Etruria, where the massive increase in the number of items originating in the Greek East, visible in the

archaeological record, was often seen to be responsible for the emergence and development of civilization during the so-called 'Orientalizing' and Archaic periods (for example Pallottino 1947). Etruria was traditionally seen as a key gateway for civilization and culture into Italy, helping to reshape and 'educate' Italian society in a way which laid the foundations for later Roman society (especially Alföldi 1965; see also Scullard 1967; Ogilvie 1976; etc.). While it was always debatable whether the Etruscans were ever properly 'Hellenized', it was taken for granted that contact with the Greeks, and other cultures from the eastern Mediterranean like that of the Phoenicians, was key to their success in the pre-Roman period. At the same time, the Etruscans' seeming failure to properly adopt Greek practices was also seen to have played a role in their perceived downfall (Torelli 1986; and more recently Cerchiai 2017). While the Etruscans were considered consumers *par excellence* of Greek culture, their own versions were often seen as cheap imitations — clumsy, unskilled, and decidedly 'un-Greek' (see Izzet 2007 for discussion). While clearly able to recognize 'high culture', and deploy certain aspects of it adeptly, they were thought to be somehow inherently incapable of producing it themselves. Thus, when their connection with Greece was supposedly severed after the Battle of Cumae in 474 BCE (Diod. Sic., XI. 51; Pindar, *Pyth.*, I. 71–75), they fell into decline as a result (Meyer 1980; Torelli 1986).

Similar forces were also often seen to be at play elsewhere in Italy, albeit to a lesser extent, whereby the rate of civilization and development was roughly equivalent to the extent to which a region adopted the, supposedly, more advanced Greek cultural practices. One can see this, for instance, in Rome, where Greek culture was often seen to be mediated by the Etruscans (famously through the Tarquin monarchs) or occurred as part of specific embassies — for instance in the mid-fifth century BCE when the Romans supposedly sent an embassy to study Greek laws before crafting their own legal code (Livy, III. 31. 7–8; Dion. Hal., *Ant. Rom.*, X. 52. 3). Alternatively, one could look to Campania, where there was always a perceived tension between the 'civilized' (and often Greek) communities and the local, 'barbarian', Italian tribes (see Dench 1995 for discussion). The Italian tribes were thought to be militarily superior, raiding or even capturing communities, only to be ultimately conquered and converted by the civilizing practices they found there. Cicero's 'vincabamur a victa Graecia' ('we have been conquered by the conquered Greeks', Cic., *Brut.*, 254) and Horace's 'Graecia capta ferum victorem cepit et artis intulit agresti Latio' ('Captive Greece then captured its uncivilized victor and brought the arts to rustic Latium', Horace, *Epist.*, II. 1. 156–57) are still often interpreted to long predate the conquest of Greece proper.[3] Shifts in the society of pre-Roman Italy, and particularly the emergence and development of urban centres along with agriculture, the alphabet, architecture, art, etc., have often been seen to be driven by, and indeed to have been dependent upon, the energy and ideas coming from the east.

Edward Said's 1978 book *Orientalism* marked one of the first major challenges to this paradigm. Part of the wider postcolonial debate, it highlighted the importance of the concept of 'the East' in modern conceptions of 'the West' and challenged the perceived dichotomy. The relationship between 'East' and 'West' in the ancient Mediterranean has remained contested ever since, and particularly in the past twenty-five years.[4] In particular, works noted above, like Horden and Purcell's *The Corrupting Sea* (2000) and Broodbank's (2013) *The Making of the Middle Sea*, have emphasized how interconnected the ancient Mediterranean was in antiquity. These works are part of a wider discourse which has suggested that, rather than being limited to a few distinct periods and only occurring in one direction, we should see much more complicated, multi-directional, and heterogenous cultural engagement and entanglement (van Dommelen 1998; De Angelis 2013). Indeed, as noted at the outset of this chapter, the idea of a fluid and fundamentally interconnected Mediterranean is now a mainstream part of most conceptions of antiquity. Alongside this, cultural imperialism, particularly in the contexts of both 'Romanization' and 'Hellenization', has given way to a more balanced dialogue discussed in terms of 'creolization', 'hybridity', and 'globalization' (Hodos 2010; Versulys 2014; Hodos 2020b).

Yet, when it comes to pre-Roman Italy, the Greek East retains a surprisingly strong hold on our understanding of local culture. Despite the developments in scholarship noted above, alongside the emergence of more nuanced conceptions of the preceding Bronze Age (for example Blake 2014) and into the Iron Age (for example Hodos 2020a), the broad idea of 'Hellenization' (if not the explicit term) is still frequently invoked to explain the spread of Greek-looking material remains, cultural practices, or artistic styles in pre-Roman Italy (see Robinson 2020, especially 9–11, for discussion). Contact and com-munication with the Greek East also still forms the primary backdrop for cultural (ex)change and differentiation in the region. As Padilla Peralta and Bernard (2022, 20–21) recently noted when exploring how we might approach Roman society in the middle Republic:

> One driving force in the rise of this [central Italic cultural] *koiné* was the adoption up and down the peninsula of philhellenism as a flexible and capacious rubric for internal and external differentiation [...] To the same or perhaps even to a greater extent than the imperial Republic itself, other communities in Italy and throughout the Mediterranean bought into and quickly capitalised on philhellenic discourses. The phenomenon is well known from its outcomes in material culture: among recent discoveries, we have already noted those monumental aristocratic tombs from nearby south Etruria that seem to show Etruscan elites employing models of Macedonian palatial architecture, and perhaps even a similarly styled monument from the Capitoline at Rome. Additionally, through historical or semi-historical encounters with Greek philosophy (the Samnite Herennius Pontius comes to mind), active incorporation of practices marked as or perceived to be 'Greek' into their political systems, or the creative interpretation and retrofitting of Greek heroic mythologies to suit their aetiological needs, elites in multiple Italic polities took to philhellenism enthusiastically during our period.

From religion and architecture, to industry and economy, to commensality and commemoration, Iron Age Italians are still seen by scholars to be looking 'elsewhere' — most often to the east — for inspiration. This is especially true during the period from the eighth through sixth centuries BCE. Although the arguments are more nuanced, and connectivity emphasized, the basic principles still underpin large aspects of our modern scholarly framework.

To be clear, this is not to say that such analyses are inaccurate. In their discussion quoted above, Padilla Peralta and Bernard are almost certainly correct in their assessment of the utility of 'Greek' culture for central Italians. We would also note, and support, their use of the term 'philhellenism' to describe this phenomenon, which gives a significant agency to the Italians in this relationship, as well as their use of 'central Italic cultural *koiné*' — points we will return to later. Indeed, looking at the wider archaeological picture, it is difficult to argue that the so-called 'Orientalizing period' did not mark at least a change in Italy's relationship with the eastern Mediterranean, given the massive increase in archaeo-

---

3   The site of Poseidonia/Paestum, and the scholarly tradition relating to the site, offer up a prime example of this phenomenon. See Torelli 1988; Pedley 1990; and Greco and others 2001.

4   See Nowlin 2021 for a recent overview, as well as Riva and Vella's excellent 2006 volume.

logical evidence for trade and exchange with the east in this period. In particular, it is the predominance of Greek ceramic material in Italian archaeological contexts, coupled with the widespread adoption of Greek artistic motifs and decorative styles in local Italian material remains, that facilitates interpretations of this influence as being (at least largely) one-way. This is only reinforced by the corresponding lack of any such indicators of Italian influence, either material or otherwise, in Greek contexts (Hodos 2020a, 95–146). While Broodbank and others may be able to demonstrate connectivity going back to the Bronze Age, it is clear that it was not always evidenced uniformly.

What is problematic about this situation is not the detail, data, or even the specific arguments. The issue is the context within which they have all been placed. While we have copious evidence from a range of contexts supporting connections between Italy and the eastern Mediterranean, and a grand narrative which suggests that this was normal, we have yet to create an appropriate set of constructs which equate to regional entities or cultures which do not have the colonial overtones of the previous models. The regional culture of Greece remains an attractive and exportable 'Hellenism', seemingly separate and distinct from the peoples who lived it. It has been increasingly emancipated from its overt colonial baggage, but it remains a product of that system. We also lack an understanding of how these entities or groups might have interacted with each other, and other cultural assemblages, on a regional stage. We have been let down by the continued lack of regional structures and labels in our new, pan-Mediterranean approaches, and so have reverted to traditional terminology and constructs. While the relationships and players have been reframed in less culturally imperialist ways, the language and dynamics we use to describe them continue to reinforce the idea that the cultural influence was largely one-way, from east to west, and operating in a remarkably — and worryingly — early modern way. Despite our best efforts, the traditional cultural monoliths seem to return.

To move on, we must recognize that the arrival of merchants and colonists from Greece, Asia Minor, and Phoenicia in the eighth and seventh centuries BCE was not at all like the arrival of Europeans in the Americas, which brought cultures and populations together for the first time (Hodos 2020a, 20–22). In the ancient Mediterranean, the peoples of Greece and Italy had been in contact and regular communication since at least the Bronze Age, and even the 'shrinking horizons' of the early first millennium BCE — the Greek Dark Ages and the Mediterranean-wide unrest which coincided with them — did not fully sever

the connection (on early connections, see Vagnetti 1996; Peroni and others 1998). As a result, colonists and merchants from the eastern Mediterranean did not bring a wholly new culture with them to Italy in the eighth and seventh centuries BCE, but rather reinvigorated and expanded an existing connection, which was in turn part of a wider, shared cultural network. These were peoples and societies which knew each other and had developed within a shared cultural context and broadly shared environment. They were contacts, neighbours, friends, and maybe even relatives. While they brought regionally distinctive styles, practices, and technologies, these all existed within a broadly shared cultural *koiné*, which is likely one reason why some Greek variations proved popular. We need to shift our approach and language to account for this situation.

Moving towards a New Paradigm

How we approach cultural identity and (ex)change in the ancient Mediterranean basin is a fast-moving conversation. In particular, archaeology is both shining a light on rich local cultures and shifting emphasis away from the eastern Mediterranean. As noted earlier, superficially, and traditionally, the archaeological record has been seen to support both the sudden appearance and dominance of Greek culture in Italy in the eighth and seventh centuries BCE, based largely on a sudden influx of imported pottery — which survives remarkably well in the archaeological record. As our knowledge of the archaeological record has increased, and our models have become more sophisticated and nuanced, the importance of this imported pottery has slowly waned. First, as explored by several chapters in this volume, it is clear that the Italians were not mindless consumers of these items, but selected items carefully for incorporation into distinctly local practices. Additionally, different types and classes of items reveal different sets of connections. For instance, as suggested above, it is increasingly clear from metallurgical evidence that Greece was not the only region that Italy was connected to, and indeed there were strong connections between Italy and continental Europe going back to at least the Bronze Age. Bronzeworking in Italy during this period, and especially in the north, seems to have existed as part of a European network of production, sharing not only material networks, but also styles, forms, and techniques (Iaia 2005 and 2013). This continued into the Early Iron Age, and is particularly well attested in military equipment finds, with a distinctive type of crested helmet appearing everywhere from Villanovan contexts in Italy to Ukrainian contexts in the far north-east (Iaia 2022). By the middle of the first millennium BCE, the focus of this network seems to have shifted, and we can see the movement of new types of iron weapons — and their productive techniques — entering Italy from the north-west. While south Italic bronzeworking certainly showed evidence of connections within a Mediterranean context, with aspides, muscled cuirasses, and Corinthian-style helmets being produced, it is clear that craftspeople in Italy were not only, or even predominantly, looking in this direction for inspiration. The East/West binary is clearly flawed, but even models emphasizing 'Mediterraneanization' may be incomplete.

None of this is to say that the arrival of people from Greece, in large numbers, in the eighth and seventh centuries BCE did not change Italy and Italian culture. It most certainly did. However, our traditional models, largely based on examples from the early modern period, have been revealed to be entirely unsuited to the task — as, indeed, they are likely unsuited to even the early modern empires upon which they were initially based. This is not a situation where two previously unconnected societies suddenly connected, but rather a shifting relationship between sprawling, overlapping networks with long-standing connections within a broadly shared region and context. The peoples of Greece and Italy were not identical in the early first millennium BCE. As will be discussed below, and in this volume, they clearly differed in some key areas. But they were also not so different as often supposed, and the labels 'Greek' and 'Italian' — with their modern national associations — are probably unhelpfully divisive.

The present volume explicitly aims to continue the deconstruction of colonial models of cultural change and engagement. Instead of seeking evidence of the penetration of external (especially 'Greek') culture and elements into the Italian peninsula, we (following in the footsteps of Hodos amongst others) would like to emphasize the ways in which the peoples of Italy seem to have approached cultural contact and exchange on their own — particularly, although not exclusively, with the eastern Mediterranean. Rather than highlight the agency of the outsiders and their ability to dominate Italian markets and influence tastes, we seek to join those exploring how and why the Italians allowed, accepted, and integrated certain aspects of, or inspirations from, external culture into their own. This acknowledges the possibility, however remote, that the ancient Italians could have chosen *not* to integrate *any* aspects of an outsider's culture.

We would also suggest that one way of moving away from the traditional, colonially embedded mod-els is to shift our terminology towards a set of cultural labels which lack strong, pseudo-nationalist, and ethnic overtones — at least for periods which lack strong state-based structures which can be used as a notional proxy for networks of other types. One possible step in this direction would be the gradual adoption of stable, geographically determined terminology, which describes the cultures common in a region and the connections which they maintain without the possibility of cultural imperialism. Here we would return to Padilla Peralta and Bernard's terminology touched on above, and their use of the phrase 'central Italic cultural *koiné*' as a way to describe the cultures of this region (Padilla Peralta and Bernard 2022, 20). Although they did not push for the wider use of this sort of model in their text, we would suggest this is an incredibly useful paradigm to describe the mix of cultures in a region or subregion, which centres their identity in their local area. While less distinct than the traditional labels, it offers more structure than the current situation, and can be used to reflect both material culture and connective networks present within a region. One would not have 'Greek culture' in central Italy, but rather a 'central Italic cultural *koiné*' which exhibits connections to, and influences from, the east. Indeed, on this latter aspect, one would still need a way to indicate the myriad links and connections which bound these networks together. Here, Padilla Peralta and Bernard's use of 'philhellenism' also represents a useful path to explore (Padilla Peralta and Bernard 2022, 20–21). Although this particular word is obviously loaded with quite a bit of colonial baggage, most notably from the nineteenth century CE and the movement towards Greek independence, it has tremendous utility when applied to antiquity. It centres the receiving society as the active participant in the relationship, and highlights desire-based connections on the part of recipients. Three large concerns remain. The first is the acknowledged ambiguity over what this 'Hellenism' represented. While there are certain resonances, it seems clear that the received culture was somewhat different from that which actually existed in Greece. Hellenism, and philhellenism, seem to occupy a liminal and somewhat idealized or theoretical space between two lived cultures. The second worry is that both the term philhellenism and the power dynamics which underpin it remain rather one-sided, perhaps indicative of an unrequited love. It may be useful to consider philhellenism operating synergistically with a concomitant 'philitalicism' of the Greeks, although the lack of data to support and elucidate this is problematic. Third, as noted above, the term also comes loaded with its own colonial baggage — although less, perhaps, than other labels. Most notably, 'phil-hellenism', whether applied to nineteenth-century CE Europeans or third- and second-century BCE Romans, is typically used to reflect the desire of members of a more powerful state for the traditional culture of a society perceived to be weaker or in decline. It is, therefore, more the reverse of 'Hellenization' than an entirely distinct phenomenon. However, and the above being noted, a conscious emphasis on the desire-based relationships, on both sides of an interaction, may help to move beyond our current roadblock.

It should also be acknowledged that all of these influences were ultimately based on social relationships which operated between real people, with complicated and unique identities, and not theoretical constructs or idealized cultures. While it is apparent that ancient trade and interaction could occur where other forms of communication were largely absent — consider Herodotus's (IV. 196) famous story of Carthaginian traders relying on 'silent' trade with peoples living beyond the Pillars of Herakles — this was evidently the exception and not the norm. Throughout our ancient sources (for example Hdt. IV. 24) it is also clear that Mediterranean traders generally preferred to rely on existing connections and translators.[5] Trade was generally social. It was relational. It required trust, and this is especially true of the sort of deeply embedded trade relationships which seem to have been present between merchants from around the Mediterranean and Italians during this period. If we are to discard the principle of overt Greek cultural supremacy, a key feature of any model intended to explain this sort of regional, transcultural interaction must therefore explain how Italians negotiated meaningful relationships with people outside of their normal social and cultural networks. As noted earlier, Italian culture was more than just the sum of its networked parts. The Italians themselves brought an important set of elements to this relationship.

While the peoples of the ancient Mediterranean may have shared some broad characteristics due to their shared context, which likely provided a certain foundation for interaction, they were certainly different in many ways. The same is true, albeit to a lesser extent, amongst the peoples of Italy them-

selves. The Italian peoples of the Early Iron Age were not homogenous (Bourdin 2012; Farney and Bradley 2018). They had clear material cultural and linguistic differences. And yet, the way in which they engaged with foreign cultures bear some remarkable similarities. While it is impossible to encapsulate the myriad complexity of the cultures of pre-Roman Italy in a few short paragraphs, we would suggest that two key, pan-Italic structuring principles had a profound impact on the peoples of pre-Roman Italy in transcultural interactions: the importance of kinship, and a potential for mobility. Obviously, neither of these two principles are unique to pre-Roman Italy, but their importance in personal and communal interaction is particularly marked in this context.

Kinship has long been identified as a vital structuring aspect of early Italian society. It is connected to descent and lineage, and yet not rigidly so. Family was not solely defined by blood. It was thus rather different from more restrictive conceptions, like that found in Classical Athens (Blok 2017), which was traced through one and later both parents.[6] In Italy, kinship was based on a set of relationships which did not necessarily require a shared culture or society (Isayev 2017, 95). In fact, across the ancient Mediterranean, institutions of intermarriage consciously allowed for, and worked to bridge, social and cultural divides (Smith 2006, 30–50). This is most evident amongst the upper socio-economic and political echelons, where alliances between powerful, rival families and kingdoms were often sealed through marriage. However, it is evident at lower levels as well. The movement of pottery styles, generally associated with female-oriented, household production, between present-day Albania and Apulia, hint at the movement of women, perhaps through intermarriage, across the Adriatic in antiquity (Bernardo-Ciddio 2022). Although one would hesitate to give them a label, it seems clear that they were not part of the ruling class. Additionally, as touched on above, many Italian communities and lineages developed mythical kinship relationships connected to local figures, or epic heroes. While it is debatable whether these lineages were ever considered real in practical terms, they certainly had real implications, and played an important role in helping populations relate to one another in Italy (Dench 2005). As a result, while kinship in Iron Age

---

5   *Tesserae hospitales*, like the famous ivory one from S'Omobono in Rome bearing the Etruscan personal name *araz silqetenas spurianas* or the ivory boar found in Carthage with *Mi puinel karthazie els q*[---]*na* ('I (am) Puinel from Carthage', written in Etruscan), provide physical evidence of this sort of behaviour. See also Plaut., *Poen.*, V. 1. 25; 2. 87–99 for later use. See Nicols 2015 for discussion.

6   It is worth noting that adoption of children was allowed in both Greek and Roman society, thus allowing some fluidity and control (see Lindsay 2009), although adoption was arguably more important and more widely practised amongst the Romans. It is uncertain how widely adoption was practised amongst other Italian peoples.

Italy is certainly not unique as a structuring principle in the ancient Mediterranean, the way in which it functioned to encourage and facilitate integration seems to have worked, alongside other factors, to stimulate a uniquely Italian approach to intercultural contact. While concepts of citizenship and other community-based types of identity slowly emerged to complement (and complicate) these kinship identifiers in the eastern Mediterranean, in Italy kinship seems to have remained the most important structuring element for a while longer. In fact, the importance of the *gens* and powerful elite families in recent models of Roman expansion (Terrenato 2019), hint that this predominance may have even survived the emergence of urban centres and states. While the continued primacy of kinship may have made certain types of integration more difficult, for instance those associated with simple co-location, it may have opened the door for other types, which may have suited more mobile populations.

The importance of mobility in early Italy for large segments of the population must be acknowledged. This feature of Italian society has also been emphasized in a number of recent studies (see especially Isayev 2017 and Hodos 2020a). While few would suggest that any of Italy's peoples were truly nomadic, or anywhere close to it, a certain amount of mobility — often seasonal in nature — seems to have been part of the normal rhythm of life for many of pre-Roman Italy's inhabitants (Cohen 2022; Heitz 2022). The implications of this mobility are only just being explored. As Bradley has argued, the possible mobility of urban populations may have altered the dynamics of early urban states — including Rome (Bradley 2020, 245–54). Evolving populations and resultant agricultural and pastoral practices may have also resulted in unique approaches to land and territory (Fulminante 2014). From a cultural perspective, however, there would have been a regular dialogue in Italy between various groups on a regional, and likely interregional, level. Italians would have been used to interacting with people from outside their own immediate social group, either as travellers themselves, as hosts to travellers, or preying upon travellers. Contact, communication, acceptance, and integration (at least in some form) with those who thought and behaved differently was common. Again, to reiterate, none of these factors are unique to pre-Roman, Iron Age Italy. Family and mobility were important in Greece as well, as they were to those elsewhere in the ancient Mediterranean world, and in continental Europe. However, when coupled with Italy's location in the centre of the Mediterranean and its unique geography, marked by

the spine of the Apennines and various river valleys and crossings, they may have facilitated the emergence of a set of populations which was both primed and ideally prepared to serve as cultural mediators (Isayev 2017, 74).

The peoples of Italy seem to have carried a very strong, and yet flexible, sense of identity when it came to cultural interaction and entanglement. This is, arguably, epitomized by the later Roman example, which famously promoted both their own conservatism *and* adaptiveness. In the *Ineditum Vaticanum*, a first-century BCE/CE text referring to events at the start of the First Punic War, the Roman Kaeso (possibly Kaeso Fabius, cos. 269 BCE) noted:

'ἡμεῖς' εἶπεν 'οὕτως πεφύκαμεν (ἐρῶ δέ σοι ἔργα ἀναμφισβήτητα, ἵνα ἔχηις ἀπαγγέλλειν τῆι πόλει)· τοῖς πολεμοῦσιν εἰς τὰ ἐκείνων ἔργα συγκαταβαίνομεν, κἂν τοῖς ἀλλοτρίοις ἐπιτηδεύμασι περίεσμεν τῶν ἐκ πολλοῦ αὐτὰ ἠσκηκότων. Τυρρηνοὶ γὰρ ἡμῖν ἐπολέμουν χαλκάσπιδες καὶ φαλαγγηδόν, οὐ κατὰ σπείρας μαχόμενοι· καὶ ἡμεῖς μεθοπλισθέντες καὶ τὸν ἐκείνων ὁπλισμὸν μεταλαβόντες παρετατόμεθα αὐτοῖς, καὶ τοὺς ἐκ πλείστου ἐθάδας τῶν ἐν φάλαγγι ἀγώνων οὕτως ἀγωνιζόμενοι ἐνικῶμεν. οὐκ ἦν ὁ Σαυνιτικὸς ἡμῖν θυρεὸς πάτριος, οὐδ' ὑσσοὺς εἴχομεν, ἀλλ' ἀσπίσιν ἐμαχόμεθα καὶ δόρασιν· ἀλλ' οὐδ' ἱππεύειν ἰσχύομεν, τὸ δὲ πᾶν ἢ τὸ πλεῖστον τῆς Ῥωμαϊκῆς δυνάμεως πεζὸν ἦν. ἀλλὰ Σαυνίταις καταστάντες εἰς πόλεμον, καὶ τοῖς ἐκείνων θυρεοῖς καὶ ὑσσοῖς ὁπλισθέντες ἱππεύειν τε αὐτοὺς ἀναγκάσαντες, ἀλλοτρίοις ὅπλοις καὶ ζηλώμασιν ἐδουλωσάμεθα τοὺς μέγα ἐφ' ἑαυτοῖς πεφρονηκότας. οὐδὲ πολιορκεῖν, ὦ Καρχηδόνιοι, ἐγινώσκομεν· ἀλλὰ παρὰ τῶν Ἑλλήνων μαθόντες, ἀνδρῶν τοῦ ἔργου πεπειραμένων, κἀκείνων τῶν ἐπιστημόνων καὶ πάντων ἀνθρώπων ἐν πολιορκίαι δεδυνήμεθα πλέον. μὴ δὴ Ῥωμαίους ἀναγκάσητε ἅψασθαι τῶν θαλαττίων· εἰ γὰρ ἡμῖν δεήσει ναυτικοῦ, πλείους μὲν καὶ ἀμείνους ὑμῶν ἐν ὀλίγωι χρόνωι κατασκευασόμεθα ναῦς, κρεῖττον δὲ ναυμαχήσομεν τῶν ἐκ πλείστου ναυτικῶν.' καὶ οὐκ ἐψεύσατο ὁ Καίσων· βιασθέντες γὰρ ὑπὸ Καρχηδονίων ναυμαχῆσαι, εὐθὺς τῆι πρώτηι περιεγένοντο ναυμαχίαι, Δουιλίου στρατηγοῦντος.[7]

> (We have flourished in this way (I'll tell you most unambiguous things, so that you may report them back to your city): in war, we agree with our enemies to fight on their terms, and in foreign skills we surpass those who have practised them for a long time.

---

7 *Ineditum Vaticanum* (839) 3.

For instance, the Etruscans made war upon us with bronze shields and in phalanx formations, not fighting in maniples. And we, changing our armour and equipping ourselves with theirs, drew ourselves in formation against them, and contending thus we defeated men who had long been accustomed to phalanx warfare. Similarly, the Samnite rectangular shield was not among our traditional weapons, nor did we use javelins, but instead we fought with round shields and spears. And neither were we strong in cavalry warfare, all or nearly all of Rome's strength laying in infantry. But when engaging with the Samnites in war, we equipped ourselves with their shields and javelins, and fought against them with cavalry, and by emulating the use of foreign weaponry we became masters of those who thought such a great deal about themselves. And, Carthaginians, we had no clue as to how to stage a siege. But learning from the Greeks, people who were very knowledgeable in siegecraft, and indeed we flourished to become superior to the most able of all men in siege warfare. Do not force the Romans to set upon the sea! For if we need a fleet, we shall build more numerous and better ships than yours in no time at all, and we shall prevail in sea battle over people who have so long engaged in seafaring.)[8]

Although written in a later period than that focused upon in this volume, when the idea of 'Romanitas', as well as other cultural designations, had become much more solid (Dench 2005), the basic narrative seems to have been based on earlier materials and reflects a widely held set of central Italian beliefs (Sall., *Cat.*, LI. 37–38; Tact., *Ann.*, III. 27. 1; see Cornell 1995, 170). The Romans, although deeply conservative in their adherence to the *mos maiorum*, were also very happy to change the outward accessories of their culture, even in something as core to their identity as warfare. Thus, by the time historical writing appears *c.* 200 BCE, there seems to have been an established idea of being 'Roman' which not only allows for, but promotes, adaptability and cultural borrowing. Whether this borrowing actually occurred or not is beside the point (Armstrong 2016, 111–26). The ability to adopt the physical trappings of another culture was seen to be a positive part of what it meant to be 'Roman'. Indeed, it should not be limited to physical trappings alone, as the Romans readily adopted foreign cults and religious practices as well (Orlin 2010). This adaptability seemingly had no impact on their own, pre-existing cultural identification; it arguably reinforced it.

Further, the passage above highlights three key factors which may be useful when thinking about pre-Roman (and Roman) Italy. First, we must be very careful how far we push the meaning and importance of aspects of material culture which were adopted by Italians. Although a late and singular example, it is clear that the Romans in the text of the *Ineditum Vaticanum* did not view the adoption of key aspects of military tactics and equipment as part of a wider cultural assimilation or dependency. Second, the Romans and other ancient Italians were likely very conscious and aware of the principle of cultural borrowing. While it is probable that the passage over-emphasizes the cultural differences, given its context in the lead up to war, it is clear that the Romans were not unaware of broad cultural differences and the associations that particular aspects of material culture and practice may have had. While Italians may not have felt as if they were 'becoming Greek' through purchasing pottery from Greece, they likely did not disassociate the pottery from its Greek origin or context either. Artefacts and practices could exist in both cultural contexts simultaneously. Third, an appreciation and adoption of particular aspects of a foreign culture did not indicate a sense of cultural superiority or inferiority. As the *Ineditum Vaticanum* indicates, the Romans felt they were able to display their overall superiority by deploying aspects of another culture against itself.

Case Studies

Using specific case studies, the present volume argues that we have far more to learn about the way in which the peoples of pre-Roman Italy interacted with cultures and societies both inside and outside of the peninsula — most notably those of Greece. Nicola Terrenato, in his chapter 'The Paradox of Innovation in Conservative Societies: Cultural Self-Consistency and Bricolage in Iron Age Central Italy' highlights one of the core tensions in the modern debate around cultural change in pre-Roman Italy: How do we reconcile the highly conservative and traditional kinship-based societies of Early Iron Age Italy with the radical changes typically argued for during the 'Orientalizing' and Archaic periods? Terrenato suggests that a key factor in the seeming adaptiveness of early Italians was their ability to 'scale-up' traditional elements of their society to meet new challenges. This scaling-up clearly involved massive change for all involved, but also offered a stable and con-

---

8 Trans. Beck 2011.

servative foundation for them to conceptualize the change within.

Franco De Angelis, in his chapter on viticulture in early Italy, offers another possible solution to the tension highlighted by Terrenato. While viticulture is often argued, by both ancient and modern writers, to be one of the many Greek innovations picked up by the Italians, De Angelis demonstrates that this is oversimplifying a very complex situation; viticulture had a long tradition in Italy which predates the traditional mass influx of Greek culture. Linking to later chapters, like that by Attema and others on Timpone della Motta (discussed below), De Angelis points to a much wider shared culture, with connections going back centuries, which suggest that some traditional aspects of Italy's 'Hellenization' may therefore be 'mirages'.

Another key feature of Italy's engagement with the wider Mediterranean world was its variability, even within relatively small regions. This point is emphasized by Marine Lechenault and Kewin Peche-Quilichini's discussion of Corsica in the Iron Age, where different parts of the island seem to have engaged quite differently with both the Italian mainland and the wider Mediterranean. The island formed a vital nexus point in Mediterranean trade and movement at the northern end of the Tyrrhenian Sea, linking Sardinia, mainland Italy, and the coast of Gaul. However, each side of the island seems to have experienced this set of connections slightly differently. We should not assume that connections mean networks, nor should we assume that networks mean archaeologically visible change.

John Hopkins, Charlotte Potts, Aaron Rhodes-Schroder, Keely Heuer, and Camilla Norman all tackle the thorny issue of how cultural exchange and interaction played out in the sphere of art — an area long thought to have been dominated, or at least more extensively influenced, by the peoples of Greece. While each chapter explores a different medium (bronze vessels, temple decoration, the use of imported pottery, the production of pottery domestically, and ritual iconography), and asks different questions of it, all emphasize the impact and agency of the various actors involved. Art production was collaborative, and the product of a complex dialogue. As Norman in particular suggests, it was also an area which was not exclusively beholden to cultural influences from Greece, but where other regional connections, especially to the north, seem to have played significant roles.

Peter Attema, Barbara Belelli Marchesini, Matthijs Catsman, Amanda Pavlick, and Gijs Tol explore the nature of urban centres in pre-Roman, Iron Age Italy. Urban zones have traditionally been given an outsized importance in our interpretations as the source of much of our evidence (both literary and archaeological). The rise of urban zones in Italy also generally coincides with increased evidence for contact with the eastern Mediterranean. Attema and others, focusing on the site of Crustumerium, consider the complex interplay between local traditions and foreign elements at the site between the ninth and sixth centuries BCE. Pavlick, discussing monumental building in Archaic central Italy, investigates the role which the built environment of settlements had in regional interactions, and not just with locals and foreign visitors as is sometimes supposed. Tol, on the other hand, highlights how we may be over-emphasizing the importance of urban zones and should consider the wider region. Taking the Pontine region as an example, Tol suggests that rural infill around settlements may have been much less than commonly supposed, meaning that these settlements may not have served as the central hub of vast productive zones as commonly suggested.

Peter Attema, Carmelo Colelli, Martin Guggisberg, Francesca Ippolito, Jan Kindberg Jacobsen, Gloria Mittica, Wieke de Neef, Sine Grove Saxkjær, and Bill Balco then bring the discussion to southern Italy and Sicily, the nexus of the interaction between Greeks and Italians, and introduce two final case studies. Balco discusses the use of different vessels amongst the indigenous Elymian populations of western Sicily, and explores how their use can be interpreted in a local and conservative context — highlighting the continuing functions which new wares served. Attema and others close the volume with a discussion of the situation at Timpone della Motta, near the Greek colony of Sybaris, highlighting both the continuity and change visible in the pottery record at the site. While it is clear that the arrival of a large number of Greek colonists changed the local dynamics, the pottery record reveals how this impact has been largely misunderstood until now. The Greeks who founded Sybaris were not an alien population, but a reinvigoration and expansion of a long-standing connection which is evidenced well into the Bronze Age. Far from being overwhelmed by a cultural invasion, the local population adopted and adapted to the changing context, as did the new arrivals.

Thinking about Cultural (Ex)Change in Italy

The ways in which we approach the issue of cultural (ex)change in pre-Roman, Iron Age Italy has profound implications for the types of questions we ask and the answers we arrive at. Traditionally, the emphasis had been on the eastern Mediterranean (especially the 'Greek world') and its ability to penetrate, or culturally colonize, the peoples of Italy. It is evident that cultural (ex)change was occurring, but it was traditionally — and colonially — conceived of in terms of a 'cultural, gravitational flow', whereby cultural elements naturally moved from 'high culture' populations towards 'low culture' zones. This one-sided explanation missed the tremendous complexity which existed on both the Italian *and* Greek sides, as well as the dynamic nature of the relationship and exchange which occurred in the middle. As recent scholarship has begun to reveal, for Italians, the influx of items and ideas from 'the Greek East' formed but a part of an existing cultural palette which could be utilized in a range of different ways — albeit always in service of a series of what might often have been much more tightly held beliefs and structuring principles. A more interesting and productive line of questioning might therefore be how and why Italians were able to adapt and adopt as much as they did. As we have suggested here, it is likely that some of the broad structuring principles of Italian society (especially kinship and mobility), coupled with Italy's unique location and geography, helped to promote adaptability and openness amongst the peoples who lived there. However, this is but the tip of the iceberg. Far more than offering answers, this volume intends to provoke questions, and push the discussion of cultural change away from passive recipients and towards networked agents.

Works Cited

Alföldi, Andreas. 1965. *Early Rome and the Latins* (Ann Arbor: University of Michigan Press)

Armstrong, Jeremy. 2016. *War and Society in Early Rome: From Warlords to Generals* (Cambridge: Cambridge University Press)

Armstrong, Jeremy, and Sheira Cohen (eds). 2022. *Production, Trade, and Connectivity in Pre-Roman Italy* (London: Routledge)

Balot, Ryan. 2021. 'Epilogue: Identity, Politics, Power: From Classical Antiquity to the 21st Century', *Polis: The Journal for Ancient Greek and Roman Political Thought*, 38: 127–33

Beck, Hans. 2011. 'Ineditum Vaticanum (839)', in *Brill's New Jacoby*, ed. by Ian Warmington (Leiden: Brill) <https://www.doi.org/10.1163/1873-5363_bnj_a839>

Bernardo-Ciddio, Leah. 2022. '"The Potter Is by Nature a Social Animal": A Producer-Centred Approach to Regionalisation in the South Italian Matt-Painted Tradition', in *Production, Trade, and Connectivity in Pre-Roman Italy*, ed. by Jeremy Armstrong and Sheria Cohen (London: Routledge), pp. 99–128

Blake, Emma. 2001. 'Constructing a Nuragic Locale: The Spatial Relationship between Tombs and Towers in Bronze Age Sardinia', *American Journal of Archaeology*, 105: 145–61

——. 2014. *Social Networks and Regional Identity in Bronze Age Italy* (Cambridge: Cambridge University Press)

Blok, Josine. 2017. *Citizenship in Classical Athens* (Cambridge: Cambridge University Press)

Boardman, John. 1999. *The Greeks Overseas* (London: Thames & Hudson)

Bourdin, Stéphane. 2012. *Les peuples de l'Italie préromaine: identités, territoires et relations interethniques en Italie centrale et septentrionale* (Rome: École française de Rome)

Bradley, Guy. 2000. *Ancient Umbria: State, Culture, and Identity in Central Italy from the Iron Age to the Augustan Era* (Oxford: Oxford University Press)

——. 2020. *Early Rome to 290 BC: The Beginnings of the City and the Rise of the Republic* (Edinburgh: Edinburgh University Press)

Broodbank, Cyprian. 2013. *The Making of the Middle Sea: A History of the Mediterranean from the Beginning to the Emergence of the Classical World* (Oxford: Oxford University Press)

Cerchiai, Luca. 2017. 'Urban Civilization', in *Etruscology*, ed. by Allesandro Naso (Berlin: De Gruyter), pp. 617–44

Clackson, James, Patrick James, Katherine McDonald, Livia Tagliapietra, and Nicholas Zair (eds). 2020. *Migration, Mobility and Language Contact in and around the Ancient Mediterranean* (Cambridge: Cambridge University Press)

Cohen, Sheira. 2022. 'Mechanisms of Community Formation in Pre-Roman Italy: A Latticework of Connectivity and Interaction', in *Production, Trade, and Connectivity in Pre-Roman Italy*, ed. by Jeremy Armstrong and Sheira Cohen (London: Routledge), pp. 226–43

Cornell, Tim. 1995. *The Beginnings of Rome: Italy and Rome from the Bronze Age to the Punic Wars (c.1000–264 BC)* (London: Routledge)

De Angelis, Franco. 2013. 'Introduction: Approaches to the Movement of Ancient Phenomena through Time and Space', in *Regionalism and Globalism in Antiquity: Exploring their Limits*, ed. by Franco De Angelis (Leuven: Peeters), pp. 1–12

—— (ed.). 2020. *Blackwell Companion to Greeks across the Ancient World* (London: Wiley-Blackwell)

Dench, Emma. 1995. *From Barbarians to New Men: Greek, Roman, and Modern Perceptions of Peoples of the Central Apennines* (Oxford: Oxford University Press)

——. 2005. *Romulus' Asylum: Roman Identities from the Age of Alexander to the Age of Hadrian* (Oxford: Oxford University Press)

Dommelen, Peter van. 1998. *On Colonial Ground: A Comparative Study of Colonialism and Rural Settlement in First Millennium BC West Central Sardinia* (Leiden: University of Leiden)

Farney, Gary, and Guy Bradley (eds). 2018. *The Peoples of Ancient Italy* (Berlin: De Gruyter)

Fulminante, Francesca. 2014. *The Urbanization of Rome and Latium from the Bronze Age to the Archaic Era* (Cambridge: Cambridge University Press)

Greco, Emanuele, Giovanna Greco, and Angela Pontrandolfo. 2001. *Da Poseidonia a Paestum* (Rome: Ingegneria per la cultura)

Heitz, Christian. 2022. 'A Mobile Model of Cultural Transfer in Pre-Roman Southern Italy', in *Production, Trade, and Connectivity in Pre-Roman Italy*, ed. by Jeremy Armstrong and Sheira Cohen (London: Routledge), pp. 204–25

Hodos, Tamar. 2010. 'Local and Global Perspectives in the Study of Social and Cultural Identities', in *Material Culture and Social Identities in the Ancient World*, ed. by Shelley Hales and Tamar Hodos (Cambridge: Cambridge University Press), pp. 3–31

——. 2020a. *The Archaeology of the Mediterranean Iron Age* (Cambridge: Cambridge University Press)

——. 2020b. 'Greeks and Cultural Development in the Pre-Roman Mediterranean', in *Blackwell Companion to Greeks across the Ancient World*, ed. by Franco De Angelis (London: Wiley-Blackwell), pp. 483–97

Horden, Peregrine, and Nicholas Purcell. 2000. *The Corrupting Sea: A Study of Mediterranean History* (Oxford: Oxford University Press)

Iaia, Cristiano. 2005. *Produzioni toreutiche della prima età del ferro in Italia centro-settentrionale: stili decorativi, circolazione, significato* (Rome: Poligrafici Internazionali)

——. 2013. 'Metalwork, Rituals and the Making of Elite Identity in Central Italy at the Bronze Age-Iron Age Transition', in *Exchange Networks and Local Transformations: Interactions and Local Changes in Europe and the Mediterranean between Bronze and Iron Age*, ed. by Maria Emanuela Alberti and Serena Sabatini (Oxford: Oxford University Press), pp. 102–16

——. 2022. 'Bronzesmiths and the Construction of Material Identity in Central Italy (1000–700 BCE)', in *Production, Trade, and Connectivity in Pre-Roman Italy*, ed. by Jeremy Armstrong and Sheira Cohen (London: Routledge), pp. 129–51

Isayev, Elena. 2017. *Migration, Mobility and Place in Ancient Italy* (Cambridge: Cambridge University Press)

Izzet, Vedia. 2007. 'Greeks Make It; Etruscans Fecit: The Stigma of Plagiarism in the Reception of Etruscan Art', *Etruscan Studies*, 10: 223–37

Lindsay, Hugh. 2009. *Adoption in the Roman World* (Cambridge: Cambridge University Press)

McInerney, Jeremy. 2014. *A Companion to Ethnicity in the Ancient Mediterranean* (London: Blackwell)

Meyer, Jeremy C. 1980. 'Roman History in Light of the Import of Attic Vases to Rome and South Etruria in the 6th and 5th Centuries B.C.', *Analecta Romana Instituti Danici*, 9: 47–68

Morris, Ian. 2003. 'Mediterraneanization', *Mediterranean Historical Review*, 18.2: 30–55

Naso, Alessandro (ed.). 2015. *Etruscology* (Berlin: De Gruyter)

Nicols, John. 2015. 'The Rituals of *hospitium*: The *tesserae hospitales*', in *Ancient Documents and their Contexts: First North American Congress of Greek and Latin Epigraphy (2011)*, ed. by John Bodel and Nora Dimitrova (Leiden: Brill), pp. 190–98

Nowlin, Jessica. 2021. *Etruscan Orientalization* (Leiden: Brill)

Ogilvie, Robert Maxwell. 1976. *Early Rome and the Etruscans* (London: Collins)

Orlin, Eric. 2010. *Foreign Cults in Rome: Creating a Roman Empire* (Oxford: Oxford University Press)

Padilla Peralta, Dan-el, and Seth Bernard. 2022. 'Middle Republican Connectivities', *Journal of Roman Studies*, 112: 1–37

Pallottino, Massimo. 1947. *L'origine degli Etruschi* (Rome: Studium Urbis)

——. 1965. 'Orientalizing Style', in *Encyclopedia of World Art*, x (New York: McGraw-Hill), pp. 782–96

Pallottino, Massimo, Walter Dräyer, and Martin Hürlimann. 1955. *Art of the Etruscans* (New York: Vanguard)

Pedley, John. 1990. *Paestum, Greeks and Romans in Southern Italy* (London: Thames & Hudson)

Peroni, Renato, Alessandro Vanzetti, and Stefania Bagella. 1998. *Broglio di Trebisacce 1990–1994: elementi e problemi nuovi dalle recenti campagne di scavo* (Soveria Mannelli: Rubbettino)

Pitts, Martin, and Miguel Versluys (eds). 2014. *Globalisation and the Roman World: World History, Connectivity and Material Culture* (Cambridge: Cambridge University Press)

Robinson, Elizabeth. 2020. *Urban Transformation in Ancient Molise: The Integration of Larinum into the Roman State* (Oxford: Oxford University Press)

Scullard, Howard Hayes. 1967. *The Etruscan Cities and Rome* (London: Thames & Hudson)

Smith, Christopher. 2006. *The Roman Clan: The 'gens' from Ancient Ideology to Modern Anthropology* (Cambridge: Cambridge University Press)

Terrenato, Nicola. 2019. *The Early Roman Expansion into Italy: Elite Negotiation and Family Agendas* (Cambridge: Cambridge University Press)

Torelli, Mario. 1986. 'History: Land and People', in *Etruscan: Life and Afterlife*, ed. by Larissa Bonfante (Detroit: Wayne State University Press), pp. 19–47

——. 1988. 'Paestum romana', in *Poseidonia-Paestum: atti del ventisettesimo convegno di studi sulla Magna Grecia; Taranto-Paestum, 9–15 ottobre 1987* (Taranto: Istituto per la storia e l'archeologia della Magna Grecia), pp. 33–115

Vagnetti, Lucia. 1996. 'Espansione e diffusione dei Micenei', in *I Greci: storia cultura arte società, II.1: Una storia greca: formazione*, ed. by Salvatore Settisn (Turin: Einaudi), pp. 133–72

Versluys, Miguel. 2014. 'Understanding Objects in Motion. An Archaeological Dialogue on Romanization', *Archaeological Dialogues*, 21: 1–20

NICOLA TERRENATO

2. The Paradox of Innovation in Conservative Societies

Cultural Self-Consistency and Bricolage in Iron Age Central Italy

ABSTRACT There is an apparent paradox in our narratives about the emergence of state organizations in Iron Age central Italy: on the one hand, we describe these societies as highly conservative and traditional, and, on the other, we have no problem imagining that they underwent a wholesale cultural revolution when states and cities were formed. Implicit teleological assumptions, rooted in what was called the 'western tradition', have rendered it unremarkable that self-replicating kin groups would blithely abandon centuries of relatively uneventful village life to merge into a citizen body agitated by new value systems and ideologies. When we instead make the effort to imagine their limited horizon and their deeply rooted world-views, it becomes much less obvious to understand why, and especially how, these changes took place without irretrievably shattering the cultural self-consistency of these groups. Building on visionary work by Fustel de Coulanges and other sociologists, the chapter argues that strategies of scaling-up and refunctionalization of traditional elements were deployed to adapt to, and cope with, the ongoing transformations. A sort of bricolage, in which established concepts were reworked to serve new and larger purposes, can help us conceptualize choices and responses in the time of the earliest Italian state formation. Some broader theoretical repercussions, which could potentially be applied to other comparable contexts, are also explored.

The emergence of complex, urban societies in first-millennium BCE central Italy has been considered utilizing a variety of angles and theoretical frameworks. It would be beyond the scope of this chapter to review them here extensively.[1]

There is, however, one salient element common to most approaches: postulating that the participants in the process would have had no doubts about its desirability and direction. Seeing urbanization in an endogenous perspective, most scholars have tended to assume that the benefits of cities and states would have been self-evident to everyone, even if Italy had no precedent whatsoever for polities of that kind. This line of thinking has rendered unremarkable that self-replicating kin groups would blithely abandon centuries of relatively uneventful village life to merge into, or bond with, a citizen body agitated by new value systems and ideologies. A surprisingly small amount of thinking has gone into figuring out how the actual actors would have made sense and adapted to the radically changed socio-political circumstances (on innovation in general, Sluiter 2017). Even the motivations that led the key decision makers to move in the way they did are seldom investigated in any sustained and context-appropriate ways. In comparison with, say, the precise chronology of urbanization at Rome and elsewhere, or with defining the signature traits of the state formation process, the cultural aspects have often been downplayed and taken for granted. There is very clearly a strong assumption underpinning most of the discourse, one that boils down to a form of teleology that is particularly common when it comes to describing transitions towards greater complexity in terms of standard social theory. In these narratives the state is such an obvious attractor, a natural goal for striving leaders, that there is no need to question their choices or wonder how they explained them to themselves (for a recent overview, Jennings and Earle 2016). In this respect, the discourse on Italian state formation appears still closely aligned with the framework that characterized the social anthropology and archaeology in the 1960s and 1970s (for example, Service 1975; Wright 1977).

---

1 Overviews include Smith 1996; Pacciarelli 2001; Fulminante 2014; Bradley 2020.

Corresponding author Nicola Terrenato (terrenat@umich.edu)

Adoption, Adaption, and Innovation in Pre-Roman Italy: Paradigms for Cultural Change, ed. by Jeremy Armstrong and Aaron Rhodes-Schroder, AMW 3 (Turnhout, 2023), pp. 33–46 · BREPOLS ∰ PUBLISHERS · 10.1484/M.AMW-EB.5.133264

The present chapter has a limited scope: that of directly addressing the ways in which the participants in the process might have conceptualized it, making an effort to couch it within the mentality of the time. Rather than endowing them with foresight and political knowledge that were not available to them, or with a flexibility that is rare in traditional societies, the agents are evoked here in the form that can be imagined based on what had happened up to that point in time. Such a reconstruction can only be conjectural, given the complete lack of any textual or artistic documents from the period. Cultural traits are inferred from socio-economic conditions, inevitably relying on comparisons with similar, but better-known, periods. Further elements are derived from aspects of long-term Italian mentality, as known from later periods. While this may seem like another form of the teleology criticized above, it focuses on those underlying ideas that do not seem to change much over time, rather than on the rapidly evolving forms of government or of economic integration (an approach exemplified by MacMullen 2011). Precisely the traditionalism that has often been ascribed to central Italian culture in the early first millennium BCE provides an opportunity and, at the same time, poses a challenge to our understanding of how complex polities came together in this period. On the one hand, the deep world-view underpinning later cultural manifestations, for instance in the religious or institutional sphere, has been used to arrive at some foundational pillars (for example Momigliano 1963; Wiseman 2008). On the other, the same resistance to change makes it far from obvious how entirely new polities were created without irretrievably shattering the cultural self-consistency of these groups.

The approach taken here to investigate these complex questions ultimately is rooted in the work of nineteenth-century French classicist Numa-Denys Fustel de Coulanges (1830–1889). His dissertation book, *La cité antique: étude sur le culte, le droit, les institutions de la Grèce et de Rome* (1864), explored how a new form of government could have emerged within the context of a traditional kin-based society. Lacking any archaeological support, his reconstruction remained abstract and essentially timeless, and so ended up being mostly ignored by later Roman historians.[2] Some of Fustel's insights, however, resonate deeply today for those who look at the early central Italian mentality with the theoretical tools offered by post-structuralism (discussed

below; overview in Flynn 2005, 61–82). As we shall see, Fustel identified strategies of scaling-up and refunctionalization of traditional elements that were deployed to adapt to and cope with the ongoing transformations. Building on his visionary ideas, it may be possible to flesh out, in much greater detail, how the process might have worked. A sort of cultural bricolage, in which established concepts were reworked to serve new and larger purposes, would have helped the participants conceptualize choices and responses in the time of the earliest Italian state formation.

A Conservative Background

Independently from the study of their political complexity, early first-millennium BCE central Italian societies have been widely regarded as profoundly traditional. Without a doubt, the origins of this pervasive idea can be traced to the later Romans themselves, who frequently exalted long-standing conservatism, mostly in the context of deploring its supposed incipient demise in the culture of their own time. The custom of the ancestors, the *mos maiorum*, never lost its aura of authority and was constantly invoked, including by politicians entirely unfettered by it (for example Gruen 1974; Rosenstein 2006). It is, of course, nearly impossible for us to trace with certainty any specific cultural element from late Republican Rome back to the Iron Age (and the same was true for the Romans themselves). It is, however, not far-fetched to imagine central Italian culture as underpinned by self-replicating mechanisms, on the strength of a number of indirect and comparative indications that can be briefly summarized here.

Especially in the realm of religion (rather than, say, morality), the exaltation of conservatism appears to be rooted in some realities. Roman observances involved prayers that were so old that they could not be understood anymore, or rituals that had become incomprehensible and even repugnant, to name just two examples (North 1976). Throughout the region, and not only in Rome, cults were valued precisely because their origins were lost in the mists of time, and their foundation narratives reached back to mythical eras, regardless of how reliable such connections to antiquity might have been. This has led most historians of religion to trace the lineage of the essential, defining elements of central Italian beliefs to a high antiquity, not often precisely defined, but certainly reaching the Bronze Age and beyond. Georges Dumézil and his school notoriously connected them with the spread of Indo-European lan-

---

2 Even if it was foundational for sociologists like Durkheim, who studied with him; Chamboredon 1984; Héran 1987.

guages, which may go as far back as the Neolithic — a framework that Dumézil ultimately had derived from Fustel and the ideas developed at their common institution, the École Normale Supérieure in Paris (Macé 2019).

It has also been remarked that the deep-seated familism that characterized the entire region was inherently conservative. Authority within extended lineages resided with senior males whose function was, amongst other things, to guard tradition and preserve the constituted order (Di Fazio and Paltineri 2019). Indeed, the political power in the early polities in question here seems to have been tightly associated with councils of elders, as indicated by the etymology of the word senate. It should also be remarked that a traditionalism of this kind is entirely typical of societies like the ones we can reconstruct for Iron Age central Italy. One does not need to adhere to the strictures of classic functionalist anthropology to recognize that cultural self-replication tends to be the norm in most pre-urban, non-literate, small-scale agricultural communities. In the historical and ethnographic cases, for which we are better informed, a certain cultural viscosity (not to be confused with timelessness) has often been described from a variety of points of view (for example Johnson and Earle 2000, 123–243). The value of these formulations is simply to provide a context of verisimilitude (rather than probation) for the generally held view that central Italian societies displayed a considerable reluctance to rapid and radical changes in their mentality.

The relevant archaeological record, admittedly, cannot do much by itself to reconstruct complex cognitive elements, as it entirely lacks either texts or figurative art. What we do have, however, is certainly compatible with a culture along the lines outlined so far. The period covering the Middle and Late Bronze Age (roughly corresponding to 1600–900 BCE, in the traditional chronology) cannot be described as eventful by any stretch of the imagination. This is particularly true in comparison with other not-too-distant regions, such as Sardinia, Sicily, the Po plain, the Adriatic coast, Malta, and parts of coastal southern Italy, not to mention Crete or mainland Greece, which all had exhibited significant dynamism (Coles and Harding 2014). Over a span of some seven hundred years, while elsewhere monumental settlements spectacularly rose and collapsed, central Italian settlements maintained their modest nature. For the most part, they were long-lived defended villages, not over a hectare in area, dotted by wattle-and-daub huts of similar size (Di Gennaro 1986; Bietti Sestieri 2010). Even locational turnover was very limited, with most sites being occupied for the entire period.[3] Crafts, architecture, and even the rare acquisition of exotic prestige items showed very little variance, both over time and across space. Impasto pottery styles mercifully allow the definition of a periodization, but do not display much else in terms of changes in foodways or technology.

Throughout this period, wealth accumulation appears very limited, and almost exclusively evidenced by caches of assorted bronze pieces, often fragments of discarded finished objects. No real sign of economic transformation or intensification over time is discernible (Di Gennaro 1999; Cardarelli 2018). The existence of elites and of inherited rank therefore must be inferred primarily on the strength of the funerary record. Richer, multigenerational family burials, in chambers or clusters, attest to the continued presence of aristocratic lineages, perhaps a single one in each village (Barbaro 2010). Such nucleation is, however, all but invisible in the settled area, where there is no evidence of communal areas or projects, aside from the rudimentary fortifications. Cult appears entirely circumscribed to domestic ancestor worship, which is also confirmed by the absence of recognizable shrines.

Understanding the nature of the elite lineages should be essential to any study of the emergence of political complexity, since it is accepted by most scholars that they were the primary agents in the process. This is certainly the approach taken here. Unfortunately, the scarcity of direct archaeological evidence forces us to piece together a tentative picture that has to rely, also, on later religious and legal elements, as well as on comparative approaches. It has been proposed elsewhere that Levi-Strauss's House Society model is the most useful to describe the kind of social units at the top of each community (Naglak and Terrenato 2019; 2020; see also González-Ruibal and Ruiz-Gálvez 2016). Profound group identity and loyalty, combined with rivalry and diffidence towards other Houses, are some of the key traits that would characterize cultures of this kind. It is within this framework that the complex transition to larger and more structured settlements must be investigated and understood, making a sustained effort at imagining how a culture of this kind would cope with the unprecedented challenge.

---

3 Significantly, a few dozen of them later become major cities, and quite a few of them are still inhabited today.

A Marked Discontinuity

It is at this point archaeologically well established, and widely accepted in the literature, that the long central Italian slumber ended with a start sometime after 900 BCE (in the traditional chronology). A few of the existing fortified villages emerged as aggregation points for the future cities that grew on them, while many (but not all) of the others were abandoned. The newly coalesced settlements were much larger (in the 80–150 ha range), but for centuries they went on being occupied very patchily. In each of them, about ten to thirty hut clusters were created, with considerable empty space between them (Pacciarelli 2001; 2017). While it cannot be proven that each cluster represented a resettled village community, their individual size and nucleation are comparable. Recent discoveries at Gabii are elucidating the structure of one of these entities, which had a clear spatial and social differentiation between an elite lineage and what might be described as 'commoners' who lived with them (Evans and others 2019; Mogetta 2020). Once again, there is not much in the overall settlement that can be considered public or communal, with the possible exception of the fortifications, whose circuit is defined from the beginning and keeps being improved and updated, down into the historical period.[4] The connected exclusion of adult burials from the same perimeter is one of the few undeniable instances of site-wide decision-making, in the form of a rule that applies to all the habitation units within the fortification (Bettelli 1997). Claims concerning the gradual emergence of new, communal cult places, perhaps connected with civic functions, have been advanced in a few cases;[5] while quite credible, they are far from unassailable. In any case, very little else archaeologically indicates the presence of any kind of central authority, which, however, must have been there, at least to coordinate fortifications, defence, and burial exclusion.

When seen against the background of the previous half-millennium, the transition to larger settlements was sudden and quite revolutionary, despite some aspects of continuity. The reasons behind such a dramatic break with the past have been endlessly debated (together with its precise chronology), especially since they are generally linked with the origins of all-important developments represented by cit-

ies and states (Carandini 1997; Guidi 1998). In fact, they have often hijacked the conversation. To avoid that risk, they will be entirely sidestepped here in favour of focusing instead on a virtually unexplored angle, the ways in which the participants would have made sense of the marked disjunction that was taking place. There was so much in it that would have been unprecedented and disruptive for the kind of traditional mentalities that we posit for them. The list of shocking novelties is in fact very long, especially when we consider that it is based only on what little is visible to us. It includes: 1) a settlement size two orders of magnitude larger than anything that existed before; 2) albeit embryonic, a level of authority above that of the Houses; 3) rules that applied to the whole community; 4) potentially, a jurisdiction of higher order than that of the individual Houses; 5) incipient non-domestic communal cult places, worshiping non-ancestral deities; 6) instantiations of military action, presumably mostly defensive ones, in which the entire community fought together.

It is hard to underestimate the profound impact that these changes, happening all at once, would have wreaked on any community, but especially for members of a traditional, conservative society of the kind we have described. If we make the effort of imagining their limited horizon, combined with the memory of centuries of self-replication, then the transition comes into light in all its momentousness — truly a revolution, although not one yet displaying every one of the traits that Childe (1950) had defined. Not only was there no local precedent for what was happening, but it is unlikely that they even had the concepts or the language to describe them. One essential element was that objects, goods, and spaces (later buildings) that did not belong to any House or individual were coming into existence for the very first time. Collectively, they formed a new abstraction that would have been challenging to conceptualize or define in existing terms. These stark material novelties somehow had to be connected to a level of power and of rule-setting, whose presence and import had never been felt before. Even if we, regrettably, are unable to conduct ethnographic interviews, it should be evident what a 'culture shock' the emergence of larger settlements in central Italy must have been. Only modern teleological thinking could normalize such an upheaval, conceiving it instead as inevitable and non-traumatic.

At the risk of making a simplistic observation, it should be kept in mind that all the features listed above have been commonplace in the life of almost all the scholars who have participated in the debate about Italian state formation. Especially considering the foundational role attributed to Rome in so-called

---

4   Fontaine and Helas 2016; it is not inconceivable that initially fortifications might have been created through collective action rather than top-down directive; this does not change the terms of the present argument.

5   Most notably at Tarquinia and Satricum; Bonghi Jovino and Bagnasco Gianni 2012; Kleibrink 1997.

'western culture', it was natural to assume, unquestioningly, that early Italians would have jumped at the opportunity of finally getting started on the great unilinear progression that had modern states as its perceived culmination (critique in Scott 1998; Yoffee 2005; Graeber and Wengrow 2021; see also Woolf 2020). The manifest destiny of the Eternal City has always been such a strong icon that it was difficult to imagine that it could not be prophetically obvious a thousand years prior. Such unspoken teleological assumptions have pervaded the entire discourse, producing what can be provocatively termed 'the fallacy of Aeneas's shield'. As is well known, in the *Aeneid* the Trojan hero is divinely endowed with a shield engraved with imagery preconizing the future greatness of Augustan Rome (Harrison 1997). Vergil's long digression serves obvious purposes of contemporary political flattery and propaganda, but it is also a powerful symbol of the impossible need to know the future in order to make sense of the present. Thus, the divine shield conveniently illustrates to a Late Bronze Age leader what the consequences of his actions will be in the long run, obfuscating, for Roman as well as modern readers, that the perspective of ancient peoples was just as limited as our own. We may find some significance in the fact that such a connoisseur of Italian traditions as Vergil felt that even a refugee from a monumental Anatolian city would have benefited from a glimpse of the future, to help him navigate such a radical transformation. Even having an urban background, his civilizing mission could be positively reinforced by a robust foreshadowing of its glorious ending.

The reality, as best we can reconstruct it, was instead that no teleological shields of any kind were available to Iron Age central Italians. Not only could they not have any inkling of their future urban accomplishments, but neither is there tangible evidence of any input from the much older political experiences of the eastern Mediterranean. Especially at the time the transition happened, in the early ninth century BCE, attested cultural contacts with the Levant were minimal, and no other urban entity existed in between (Thomas 2009). So, the conclusion must be reached that the transformation was initiated and directed internally. Unlike the case of Carthage,[6] there was no imperial or commercial power that was guiding and shaping the process. No pre-existing state power was behind the scenes, no oracle was there to provide directions, however confusing. Indeed, it is hard to imagine that anyone else in the

Mediterranean remotely cared what a few unremarkable central Italians did with their own non-coastal settlements, provided that they remained interested in the occasional purchase of exotic goods, which they certainly did. Ideas would have circulated, bundled, as it were, with those tchotchkes, despite the barriers posed by different languages and mentalities. Being exposed to a new concept, however, would not automatically involve adopting it. Finally, even if the innovation of much larger settlements had been imported from the East, this would still have required coping with the disruption to the traditional order.

Along the Adriatic or Ionian coasts, communities that were just as (if not more) prosperous, sophisticated, and well connected (and bought the same exotic objects) did not undergo political developments similar to those in Etruria and Latium and seem to have lived just as happily (Camporeale 2003). This indicates that no universal pressure forced the transition. Its actors elected to engage in it and were under no material obligation to do so. Since we are arguing that the phenomenon was essentially an endogenous one, we have to look for its protagonists within the communities that created the larger settlements, and in particular for their leadership. For this key question, there is only limited evidence, predominantly from the funerary record, which shows elite burials in central positions, presumably created by the same lineages that had previously extended the family tombs built in the Middle Bronze Age. After the spread of urn-field-like cemeteries, around the eleventh century BCE, the same kind of individuals are prominently buried at the centre of clusters that can at times be vast. A similar warrior ideology pervades the entire funerary record of the region (Bietti Sestieri 1992; Pacciarelli 2017). The reasons that led these elites to move to larger settlements were varied and complex, and have been discussed elsewhere (Terrenato 2019, 51–70). For the present discussion, it is enough to accept that there were immediate, tangible benefits for the leadership that put the new polities together. What is in question here is instead how they (and the rest of the community) might have conceptualized them.

Reconstructing the mental processes of historical actors is always a fraught endeavour, even when textual materials abound. It is positively daunting for a period like the early Italian Iron Age. So, perhaps it is fair to recognize that scholars could have been dissuaded by more than just teleological assumptions. And yet, for heuristic reasons, the question must at least be formulated, if only to declare it unsolvable. At the very least, some obvious impossibilities can be excluded, and other reflections may help posit connections not seen before. Even if we can never

---

6 Whose foundation was probably somewhat later in any case; Docter 2009; Miles 2010.

inhabit the mentality of the time, just by considering what it might have been, we can at least make sure to avoid anachronistic retrojections. There are certain facts of life that can be safely taken for granted, for instance that that no power holder ever started a revolution that would certainly result in eroding or even destroying their own paramountcy, regardless of what the pictures on a shield might have encouraged them to do. The transformation they spontaneously initiated must have made political and cultural sense in terms that can reasonably be attributed to individuals with their mindset.

What needs to be understood is how Bronze Age village leaders, whose power (although certainly limited in absolute terms) was the dominant one in their little settlement, would have agreed to live within the same fortifications with dozens of their peers, thus necessarily becoming smaller fishes in a much larger pond. Their position was primarily underpinned by custom and tradition, since they had little besides their symbolic capital to assure them of their leadership roles. So, what guaranteed that it would safely migrate with them to the new settlement? Their challenge was paradoxical: a lot had to change for a new polity to emerge, and yet enough had to stay the same so that the foundation of their power remained rock-solid. Even if they could have foreseen the future glory of the larger settlements (whose appearance was for the time quite uninspiring) they were putting together, this would benefit them little, if a completely different class of rulers were to reap the urban triumphs to come.

Some political theorists, such as Werner Sombart or Max Weber, do not seem to have a real problem with their actors committing political suicide, so that entirely different leaders can conquer the Mediterranean five hundred years later (Finley 1977; Brennan 1997). This behaviour is not only hard to attribute to real people like us, instead of, say, state-obsessed bots, but it is actively disproven by the evidence of social continuity. The archaeological record proves that, wittingly or not, the central Italian elites *did* survive their adventurous somersault. Judging from the burial record, the same kind of warrior aristocracy seems to have been in power once the transformation was complete. Indeed, over time, the larger pond they went to swim in seems to have agreed with them. The tombs became fabulously rich in the seventh century BCE and true palaces were being built by the end of the sixth (Terrenato 2001; Fulminante 2003). It is, of course, impossible to trace actual family descent across these early periods, despite the wild claims to great antiquity that some Italian families were making much later. Incidentally, these inventions attest to the value placed on conti-

nuity and conservatism in central Italian elite mentality. The real issue, at any rate, is the survival of the social order, rather than of individual lineages. In any period, it is in the nature of these noble Houses to come and go, to fission and re-aggregate. The vested interest of these groups is instead in the permanence of a social structure that guarantees their leadership role over other components.

It has been argued elsewhere, although by no means to the satisfaction of all other scholars, that by the time reliable historical records are consistently available, for instance in the fourth century BCE, central Italian states were still primarily ruled by traditional landed aristocrats, who were still firmly clinging to many of their customary prerogatives (Terrenato 2014; 2019, 155–93). These customary rights protected them as a social group vis-à-vis new emergent groups, but also from impingement by the state government and its jurisdiction. What would instead signal true disruption of that order would be any sort of political drift toward a more 'democratic' power, skewed towards urban trading and artisanal factions of the kind that had prevailed in some Greek cities to the south (Giangiulio 2015, chs 5–7; see also Terrenato 2019, 144–45), which is precisely what is not only absent in most of the cities in question, but what was actively repressed as a key component of the Roman expansion in central Italy. In what follows, the survival of the aristocratic system will be postulated, in favour of examining how the transition might have been accomplished in terms of culture and mentality.

A Strategy of Cultural Adaptation

A Tutelary Ancestor

The time has come to face the central question that the present chapter means to address: How did the participants in the transition to much larger settlements in central Italy adapt to it? More specifically, how did they think about it? How was their culture changed, and how much of their traditional mindset could be preserved? Questions like these, pertaining as they do to the history of mentalities, are difficult to answer for any period, and nearly impossible for one lacking textual material entirely. There is always a heuristic value in wondering which song the Sirens might have sung, however, and perhaps some lines of approach can be fruitfully explored. This was a belief firmly maintained by the tutelary ancestor that is deliberately chosen as an inspiration for this effort. Fustel de Coulanges was certainly the scholar that, to date, went further in exploring the mental processes connected with the creation of the ancient city than anyone else, even if he wrote over 150 years ago. All his insights are contained in his dissertation book, since after that, for patriotic and other reasons, he turned to medieval French history for the rest of his career (Hartog 1988). Combining early Greek, Roman, and Indian texts, he advanced a model for the emergence of urban centres, clearly intended to have specific reference to speakers of Indo-European languages. As is already evident from this choice, Fustel positioned himself in the sphere of ancient mentality (which he called *âme*, soul), rather than in that of precise historical reconstruction. *The Ancient City* inhabits the same chronologically vague world of religiousness and collective psychologies as *The Golden Bough* (Frazer 1890), *Totem und Taboo* (Freud 1920), or *Das Mutterrecht* (Bachofen 1861). Certainly, it could never have been written once the obsession with establishing series of punctual events had taken an unshakeable hold over the classical historical discourse.

Significantly, Fustel operated in that mid-1800s scholarly Garden of Eden in which so-called classicists could be full participants in the broader intellectual debate animating the social sciences dealing with all periods and all contexts. At the École Normale in Paris, E. Durkheim was Fustel's star student, and thus the seeds of the interdisciplinary approach known as structuralism were planted. It was only in the second half of the nineteenth century that German philology somehow managed to get itself expelled from that paradise, just as the Prussians had driven Fustel away from his first university chair at Strasbourg after the war of 1870. Since then, Fustel's lesson has been regarded as little more than an obsolete curio in the study of Greek and Roman history (for example Finley 1977), while many sociologists, anthropologists, and social psychologists continue to recognize its foundational contribution (Isin 2003; Yoffee and Terrenato 2015). The level of discourse that it contributed to, which could roughly be described as non-philological, lost its citizenship almost entirely in Graeco-Roman studies, only surviving in the rare *maître a penser* free-minded enough to defy the norms.[7]

Reading Fustel today, as an archaeologist of early central Italy trying to break free from the circumscribed intellectual discourse of the discipline, traditionally defined, is an inspiring experience. Not only is his range of action wonderfully broad, but many of his insights appear to be highly relevant to a redefinition of ancient history in terms that finally transcend those set by Mommsen (whom Fustel personally detested). While a full conceptualization of a neo-Fustelian approach to Italian antiquities would go far beyond the scope of this chapter, there are a few key themes of *The Ancient City* that are particularly relevant here. A central one is that religious thinking was the primary tool used to make sense of reality, especially for those cultures that were not yet conceptualizing politics and laws in abstract terms. This is not to say that politics was simply driven by the religious concerns, but rather that political relationships, and especially evolving ones, were easiest to understand when expressed in religious terms. Another crucial insight is that the mental architecture in these communities was built on the extended family group, the *foyer*, to which everyone's primary loyalty was directed.[8] To this central concern, individual identities and the public sphere were equally foreign.

Finally, and somewhat miraculously, Fustel was able to sense that scaling-up and metaphor had been indispensable tools that participants had deployed to make sense of the unprecedented political developments. Thinking of a new thing as a larger version of a very familiar one — no matter if the thought is accurate or not — could be of enormous help in adapting to a disconcerting reality. The same applied to metaphors that, both conceptually and linguistically, defined new objects with well-established words, transferring them to a different context where they would acquire a novel and yet more reassuring meaning than entirely unheard-of concepts. All these strategies were required because the participants in the process entirely lacked the cultural tools that elsewhere, for instance in the eastern Mediterranean, were being used to guide and describe political complexity, thanks to the millennia of experience with states and cities. Fustel's *anciennes* are not exactly traditionalists who are wary of excessive change, and thus stubbornly resisting it; they are actively initiating a radical transformation, but, at the same time, it is essential that they couch it in terms that will remain understandable and not too disruptive for their overall world-view. Having been the first to pose questions of this kind, Fustel ransacked his fragmentary textual record to explore a possible model that would answer it.

---

7 An obvious example would be fellow Normalien Paul Veyne; Le Goff 2016. Also very significant is the work of Arnaldo Momigliano (e.g., Momigliano 1977, 325-43) and Carmine Ampolo (e.g., Ampolo 1980).

8 Fustel de Coulanges 1864, 39–130; these are essentially equivalent to the entities defined here as Houses, a term defined in Lévi-Strauss 1975.

A Role for Cultural Bricolage and Ecology of Mind

The way in which Fustel's insights are contextualized here owes much to later theorizations, which have emphasized how cultures, and especially traditional ones, are tightly woven together and have distinctive forms of conceptual architecture. Perhaps most influential in this sense is Gregory Bateson's brilliant insight that the human mind, both individually and collectively, shares some properties with ecosystems (Bateson 1972). Following a different path, structuralist anthropology arguably arrived at similar formulations, when it reconstructed the internal cohesion and balance of traditional mindsets.[9] Diverging in one essential aspect from classic structuralism, however, the ecosystem analogy implies that there is no universal balance, but instead variability across space and time. Just like in nature, there are, and have been, an infinite variety of ecological balances — the same is true of cultural ones. What they have in common is simply that they have internal interconnections, they tend to self-replicate and, to some extent, to right themselves again. Thus, altering one element affects all the others in complex ways, and some changes — as the settlement expansion in our case — have the potential to upset the entire cultural coherence, at least temporarily. Given time, change can be absorbed, and a new homeostatic equilibrium point can be reached. It is for this reason that, even when they initiate it themselves, actors in a traditional culture will tend to defend it from being completely subverted, for the sake of their own collective sanity (Terrenato 2000).

Returning to Iron Age central Italy, the leaders that put together the much larger settlements can be imagined to have at least two layers to their conservatism: to the above-mentioned need to preserve their customary power and privilege, we must add the instinct of maintaining a measure of ecological balance to their culture. It cannot have been an easy circle to square. They were aggregating their communities in an entirely novel way, but the rest needed be disrupted as little as possible. Most importantly, the new elements should not clash with and undermine the old ones; a new harmonization must be somehow arrived at. It is at junctures like these that the ideas and the words used to make sense of new realities can make all the difference. Inasmuch as is possible, the elements that are absolutely unprecedented must be conceptualized in terms that already have a place in the traditional culture, so that they will feel familiar and reassuring, and their impact will be mitigated. A key strategy in this sense can be termed 'cultural bricolage', and it has been employed at various junctures in the study of first-millennium BCE Italy (Terrenato 1998; 2013). Based on the work of scholars as disparate as Lévi-Strauss (1962), Monod (1970), and Moretti (1996), bricolage refers to the refunctionalization of existing elements for new purposes. In the cultural realm, this means that innovations tend to be processed making recourse to existing ideas, which are applied to a new context, often in a scaled-up or in a metaphorical sense. The goal, once again, is to protect the balance of one's cultural ecosystem, or to smooth the transition to a new equilibrium.

A Case Study

Perhaps ironically, Fustel's insights ended up influencing the sociological analysis of nineteenth-century France or the anthropological study of Amazon tribes far more than the Indo-European early urban societies for which they had been originally conceived. For sure, very little of his daring framework can be found in the mainstream scholarship on Iron Age central Italy (for an exception, Ampolo 1980). In what follows, some of his key insights will be experimentally applied to the case study in question, through the lens of bricolage and with the benefit of a reliable archaeological dataset. Funerary practices, which were central to Fustel's reconstruction, can offer a convenient point of departure, specifically the earliest site-wide rule and the aforementioned exclusion of adult burials from a newly defined perimeter (Smith 2020). Since a similar taboo existed in Bronze Age villages, it is not hard to imagine that it could be recycled and scaled up, making it much bigger and more relative to an area that also contained vast empty spaces. It was, however, the same basic principle, perhaps rooted in beliefs about death impurity and/or afterlife, and this made the novel idea much easier to adapt to and understand. The cultural bricolage, significantly, took place in the sphere of established religion and ritual, rather than in the unprecedented one of abstract political concepts.

The perimeter of exclusion coincided with the line of defence of the settlement, which later, typically, became the official boundary of the city and was reinforced by stone walls. However, the transition to a settlement boundary two orders of magnitude larger than before presented inherent challenges,

---

9 C. Lévi-Strauss's ideas about mental structures (for example Lévi-Strauss 1962), in this reading, can be seen as having deep roots in Fustel's vision; this gives substance to their intellectual line of descent at the École through Durkheim, who was Fustel's student and Lévi-Strauss's teacher; Héran 1986; 1987.

despite the best sense-making efforts. One, certainly, was a generational discontinuity in family tombs: with the relocation, there would necessarily be a generation of children who could not be buried next to their parents. Moreover, in those settlements, like Rome, that had initially allowed burials in-between the hut clusters, existing tombs would be paved over, so to speak, as those areas became part of the habitation area (Bettelli 1997; De Santis 2003). The flipside of this was that outside the perimeter, much larger necropoleis than ever before were coming into existence (which often lasted into historic times, like the one on the Esquiline). In these, ancestors from different groups, together with their relative cults, would be intermingling in ways that never happened before. It cannot have been easy for them to rub scapulas, as it were, with complete strangers. The clusters of family tombs that have been identified (Bietti Sestieri 1992) are presumably attempts at mitigating the uncomfortable proximity and maintaining the group identity that was quintessential to individuals at this time.

The new fortifications themselves posed interesting issues. It is likely that, in a world of endemic raiding warfare, the tactical benefit of pooling defensive resources was one of the key benefits that the much larger settlements could offer, especially over the long term. Once again, these perimeters could be thought of as a scaled-up version of the village defences that had existed for many centuries. In their vastly expanded form, however, they would necessarily have engendered concerns about trust and fair share. Communal defence required counting on a more disparate group of people, including distant acquaintances and even former feud enemies. Over time, as the fortifications required a bigger investment of resources, there must have been doubts about the fair subdivision of the burden of construction and maintenance. Here, a key coping element must have resided in jealously preserving the sovereign right of each group to conduct raids individually or in whichever configuration they saw fit (a prerogative that later Romans called *imperium*; Drogula 2007; Armstrong 2016). Having a military footprint as a House within the larger settlement surely counterbalanced the novelty represented by joint defence. At the same time, if there was a prohibition against inter-House warfare within the settlement (a rule that admittedly can only be projected back from later evidence), this would make fighting together less problematic. In this hypothetical scenario, it has been suggested that what was used for bricolage was the existing concept of the temporary truce (Terrenato 2011).

There can be little doubt that, of all the complex transitions that the larger settlements entailed, the most momentous was the form that power itself would take within them. The leaders who assembled them were literally putting it all on the line. If a radically different and pre-eminent form of authority emerged in the new polity, their own power would be trumped, their customs subverted, and their own House control weakened. Ultimately, the familiar (pun intended) reality would cease to exist, to be replaced by a disconcerting, unprecedented new power structure that made them irrelevant. Once again, while we cannot know for sure what these people were thinking, it seems unwise to imagine they would choose such a self-defeating course. Instead, they must somehow have finessed creating a central power that had never existed before and without undermining centuries of House authority. This was not just a problem that required a political solution, but also a cultural shift that could make sense of the transition, suggesting that social life as it had been known until then was not at an end. It was a balancing act and a leap of faith that must have been terrifying. It is no surprise that many other similar Houses, for instance on the eastern coast of Italy, decided to avoid it altogether.

A central idea of *La cité ancienne* is that human groups came together in a 'federation' that preserved its constituent entities, and that was itself modelled on them. Fustel expressed this idea in fascinating terms:

> Ainsi la société humaine [...] n'a pas grandi à la façon d'un cercle qui s'élargirait peu a peu, gagnant de proche en proche. Ce sont, au contraire, de petits groups qui, constitués long temps à l'avance, se sont agrégés les uns aux autres. Plusieurs familles ont formé la phratrie, plusieurs phratries la tribu, plusieurs tribus la cité. *Famille, phratrie, tribu, cité, sont d'ailleurs des sociétés exactement semblables entre elles et qui sont nées l'une de l'autre par une série de fédérations.*[10]

> (Thus, human society [...] did not grow like a circle, which expanded little by little, gaining a bit at a time. Instead, it was long-preexisting little groups that coalesced together. Several families formed the phratria, several phratrias the tribe, several tribes the city. Family, phratria, tribe, city are in any case exactly similar societies, which were born one from the other by means of a series of federations.)[11]

---

10 Emphasis not original.
11 Fustel de Coulanges 1864, 143.

The key here is the claim of similarity, indeed of identity, between the various forms of human aggregation. We would perhaps say today that the new entities were conceptualized as a scaled-up version of existing ones, which continued to operate. So, the constituent hut clusters remained spatially discrete and partially autonomous, while the larger settlement encompassing them was imagined as the larger version of one of them. It was a village of villages, and its leadership was modelled accordingly. To make sense of a new level of power, reference was made to well-known forms of it. It could be said that the cultural bricolage operated here by means of a metaphor, and at a different scale. The emerging political complexity, for which almost certainly there was no abstract word (like state or city) yet, was arguably conceived as a sort of House of Houses.[12] In this way, the new concept is defined by a combination of existing ones.

About the leadership of the larger settlement, we know little that is certain, 'kings' (*reges*) only being reliably attested from the sixth century BCE at Rome. Given the long-term nature of aristocratic power in central Italy, it is appealing, however, to hypothesize that its relationship to the Houses that led each component unit was analogous to that of the House leader to the House members. If the new polity was understood as a House of Houses, its leaders should be scaled-up versions of House leaders. This not only helped explain the nature of power at all levels, but it also defined some clear expectations for the participants. In the new aggregation, for instance, the Houses should have maintained their identity, just as House members did. More, it placed a customary constraint on the authority of the leadership, embedding it with the traditional rules of the paternalistic mentality. As is the case for the House leader, the power of life and death was conferred, but it had to be used wisely and with restraint. A leader who instead became superb or insane (*furiosus*, to use the term of the XII Tables; Guarino 1973, 244–53) would have to be removed from power.

While Fustel believed in a perfect symmetry between 'family, tribe, and city', the evidence, albeit scant, suggests instead that there were significant differences, and that the analogy was deployed in a context of cultural bricolage, to make sense of the new by assimilating it with the old. The metaphor of the House of Houses, as all metaphors do, also obfuscates differences. A macroscopic difference is that the Houses maintained far more power than individuals would have within each House. Indeed, Houses not only survived in the larger settlement but, arguably, only devolved enough power to its site-wide leadership to keep it afloat, jealously guarding most of their prerogatives and jurisdictions. As the frequent breakdowns of the legal order indicate, Houses would always reserve the right to temporarily revoke the state's monopoly on violence. These are all things that ordinarily House members could not do, even if instability and strife within Houses certainly existed (Terrenato 2019, 49, with references). At the end of the day, after the creation of the larger settlements, the authority that would prove more long-lived, even in the face of political change, was precisely that of the Houses — an outcome that in any case Fustel himself emphasized.

Another important insight that permeates Fustel's entire work is that religion provided the primary tool to conceptualize the transformation. As an example, he stressed how the king was the main priest of the city, thus assuming the same role as the *pater* within each family. For Rome, Fustel referenced the cult of Vesta; in modern archaeological terms, it has been independently observed how the whole complex of the Regia, Vesta, the House of Vestals, and the Domus Publica can be seen as a scaled-up version of an elite House compound (Coarelli 1983, 55–79). Once again, the analogy can help in making sense of unprecedented site-wide roles and, at the same time, define certain customary expectations about their prerogatives and behaviours. In terms of our current discourse, this translates into a focus on the introduction of the earliest cults that were truly communal to the whole settlement. While the precise forms and chronologies are still hotly debated, there is a general agreement that this emergence is a signature indicator of communal identity and beliefs (Potts 2015). In Fustelian terms, the new cults were to the city what ancestor cults had been (and continued to be) to each House. At both levels, they provided cohesion and loyalty, reinforcing and making sense of each other, but they remained separate. Indeed, we do know that in Italy ancestor worship would never be entirely replaced by public cults. More, the Houses would long maintain control even of some non-ancestral cults (the so-called gentilicial cults; Fiorentini 1988; 2005), thus continuing to play out the tension between their power and that of the government on the religious plane. Other aspects of the new settlement could be considered under the same lens, but perhaps enough examples have been provided to clarify the approach propounded here.

---

12 A semantic device similar to the eastern king of kings, or the *capo di tutti i capi* in Mafia organization; Beale 1985; Bolzoni and D'Avanzo 2011.

An Afterword

As will be clear to those who have read so far, this is an attempt to reframe the key transition to larger settlements in central Italy within the context of a history of mentalities, rather than in the prevailing archaeological and historical terms. The value of such an exercise (for those willing to believe there is one) is heuristic, before anything else. As has been the case for other periods, posing questions pertaining to the cognitive sphere, however difficult to answer reliably at the moment, must necessarily be the first step to make any progress in that direction (Abramiuk 2012). What is essential, of course, is to be clear about the epistemological status of these considerations, and, above all, to be explicit about the postulates on which the edifice is built. It may therefore be appropriate to offer a few essential clarifications about the assumptions underpinning the present discourse. At the same time as the ancient collective mentality is conceptualized as an ecosystem that seeks to regain its balance or arrive at a new one, the same model must necessarily be applied to our own.[13] With reference to the questions at hand, this means that whatever we think of the past can only be part of our own present-day sense-making and rebalancing efforts. It is in this reflexive sense that the hypotheses about ancient actors have to be considered. The only possible standard of proof is whether they contribute to a self-consistent and well-balanced mindset, or not. *Pace* both Mommsen and Binford, the past does not exist outside us. We can only talk about it together, trying to arrive at a picture that is satisfactory for the greatest possible number of participants in the discourse.

On the strength of what is at once an interpretive model and an epistemological stance, it is proposed here that cultural bricolage — the refunctionalization of traditional elements in new forms — is a fundamental concept to understand how participants in a major transformation could adapt to it. More specifically, the application of a familiar concept to a much bigger scale or its metaphorical use in a different context are strategies that we see applied in the transition to larger settlements and, later, to greater political complexity in central Italy. Even if the novelty is sometimes misrepresented, at least in part, by the analogy with the old element, the whole operation serves to make sense of what is happening, but also to prevent it from catastrophically upending the ecological balance of the cultural make-up. It interprets and it refrains at the same time. One aspect that has not been considered here is the possibility of clashing views within the same community about how to process a new development. Sense-making is an eminently political activity, and different groups should be expected to assert the interpretation of reality that suits them and their interests best. In the case in question, unfortunately, the very scant record does not allow any further breaking down of the discourse that may have happened at the time.

Yet another inspiration that is drawn from Fustel's work concerns the broader value that reconstructions of this kind might have. Unlike Morgan (1877), Frazier, or Freud, to name just a few, Fustel was careful never to claim any universal applicability of his reconstruction, beyond the trimurti of Vedic India, Homeric Greece, and Dionysian Rome (in the sense of based on Dionysius of Halicarnassus, of course). But it is also clear that his sweeping narrative was offered (and, outside the Classics, was read) as containing a lesson about how human cultures *might* work. A similar hope is expressed here, albeit, humbly, in scaled-down terms. The present reconstruction is deliberately presented in somewhat abstract (and certainly non-*événementielles*) terms, that find validation in Fustel's timelessness — a trait that Classics has come instead to abhor. While the challenge of adapting to larger settlements that had no precedent was peculiar, but not unique, to central Italians, the cultural strategies that they deployed might serve as useful examples in other contexts. This is not based on any assumption about the universality of mind structures, but simply on the observation that the juxtaposition of disparate human stories and discourses often broadens the spectrum of interpretive possibilities that we are capable of considering.

Acknowledgements

I am thankful to the organizers for the invitation to contribute, and to the anonymous readers for their comments. John Hopkins and Carmine Ampolo kindly read a draft and offered their impressions. All the mistakes, and especially the unorthodox ideas, remain my own.

---

13 A similar equation, it can be noted in passing, allowed Durkheim to apply Fustel's view of ancient cities to contemporary France; Isin 2003.

Works Cited

Abramiuk, Marc A. 2012. *The Foundations of Cognitive Archaeology* (Boston: MIT Press)

Ampolo, Carmine. 1980. 'Le origini di Roma e la "cité antique"', *Mélanges d'archéologie et d'histoire de l'École française de Rome: antiquité*, 92: 567–76

Armstrong, Jeremy. 2016. *War and Society in Early Rome: From Warlords to Generals* (Cambridge: Cambridge University Press)

Bachofen, Johan Jakob. 1861. *Das Mutterrecht: Eine Untersuchung über die Gynaikokratie der alten Welt nach ihrer religiösen und rechtlichen Natur* (Stuttgart: Krais & Hoffmann)

Barbaro, Barbara. 2010. *Insediamenti, aree funerarie ed entità territoriali in Etruria meridionale nel Bronzo finale* (Florence: Insegna del giglio)

Bateson, Gregory. 1972. *Steps to an Ecology of Mind* (New York: Ballantine)

Beale, Gregory K. 1985. 'The Origin of the Title "King of Kings and Lord of Lords" in Revelation 17. 14', *New Testament Studies*, 31: 618–20

Bietti Sestieri, Anna Maria. 1992. *The Iron Age Community of Osteria dell'Osa: A Study of Socio-political Development in Central Tyrrhenian Italy* (Cambridge: Cambridge University Press)

——. 2010. *L'Italia nell'età del bronzo e del ferro: dalle palafitte a Romolo (2200–700 a.C.)* (Rome: Carocci)

Bettelli, Marco. 1997. *Roma, la città prima della città: i tempi di una nascita; la cronologia delle sepolture ad inumazione di Roma e del Lazio nella prima età del ferro* (Rome: L'Erma di Bretschneider)

Bolzoni, Attilio, and Giuseppe D'Avanzo. 2011. *Il capo dei capi* (Milan: Rizzoli)

Bonghi Jovino, Maria, and Giovanna Bagnasco Gianni. 2012. *Tarquinia: il santuario dell'Ara della Regina; i templi arcaici* (Rome: L'Erma di Bretschneider)

Bradley, Guy. 2020. *Early Rome to 290 BC: The Beginnings of the City and the Rise of the Republic* (Edinburgh: Edinburgh University Press)

Brennan, Catherine. 1997. *Max Weber on Power and Social Stratification: An Interpretation and Critique* (London: Ashgate)

Camporeale, Giovannangelo (ed.). 2003. *I Piceni e l'Italia medio-adriatica* (Pisa: Istituti editoriali e poligrafici internazionali)

Carandini, Andrea. 1997. *La Nascita di Roma* (Turin: Einaudi)

Cardarelli, Andrea. 2018. 'Before the City: The Last Villages and Proto-urban Centres between the Po and the Tiber Rivers', *Origini*, 42: 359–82

Chamboredon, Jean-Claude. 1984. 'Émile Durkheim: le social objet de science. Du moral au politique', *Critique*, 40.445–46: 460–531

Childe, V. Gordon. 1950. 'The Urban Revolution', *The Town Planning Review*, 21: 3–17

Coarelli, Filippo. 1983. *Il foro romano* (Rome: Quasar)

Coles, John M., and Anthony F. Harding. 2014. *The Bronze Age in Europe: An Introduction to the Prehistory of Europe c. 2000–700 B.C.* (London: Routledge)

De Santis, Anna. 2003. 'Le sepolture di età protostorica a Roma', *Bullettino comunale*, 102: 269–80

Di Fazio, Massimiliano, and Silvia Paltineri (eds). 2019. *La società gentilizia nell'Italia antica tra realtà e mito storiografico* (Bari: Edipuglia)

Di Gennaro, Francesco. 1986. *Forme di insediamento tra Tevere e Fiora dal bronzo finale al principio dell'età del ferro* (Florence: Olschki)

——. 1999. 'Indizi archeologici di élites nell'età del bronzo dell'Italia mediotirrenica', in *Eliten in der Bronzezeit: Ergebnisse zweier Kolloquien in Mainz und Athen*, I (Mainz: Römisch-Germanischen Zentralmuseums), pp. 185–96

Docter, Roald F. 2009. 'Carthage and its Hinterland', in *Phönizisches und punisches Städtewesen*, ed. by Sophie Helas and Dirce Marzoli (Mainz: Von Zabern), pp. 179–89

Drogula, Fred K. 2007. '*Imperium, potestas*, and the *pomerium* in the Roman Republic', *Historia: Zeitschrift für Alte Geschichte*, 56: 419–52

Evans, J. Marilyn, J. Troy Samuels, Laura Motta, Matthew Naglak, and Mattia D'Acri. 2019. 'An Iron Age Settlement at Gabii: An Interim Report of the Gabii Project Excavations in Area D, 2012–2015', *Etruscan Studies*, 22: 6–38

Finley, Moses I. 1977. 'The Ancient City: From Fustel de Coulanges to Max Weber and Beyond', *Comparative Studies in Society and History*, 19: 305–27

Fiorentini, Mario. 1988. *Ricerche sui culti gentilizi* (Rome: La Sapienza)

——. 2005. 'Culti gentilizi, culti degli antenati', *Scienze dell'antichità*, 14: 987–1046

Flynn, Thomas R. 2005. *Sartre, Foucault, and Historical Reason*, II: *A Poststructuralist Mapping of History* (Chicago: University of Chicago Press)

Fontaine, Paul, and Sophie Helas (eds). 2016. *Le fortificazioni arcaiche del Latium vetus e dell'Etruria meridionale (IX–VI sec. a.C.): stratigrafia, cronologia e urbanizzazione* (Brussels: Institut historique belge de Rome)

Frazer, James G. 1890. *The Golden Bough: A Study in Comparative Religion* (London: Macmillan)

Freud, Sigmund. 1920. *Totem und Tabu: Einige Übereinstimmungen im Seelenleben der Wilden und der Neurotiker* (Leipzig: Internationaler Psychoanalyscher Verlag)

Fulminante, Francesca. 2003. *Le sepolture principesche nel Latium Vetus: tra la fine della prima età del ferro e l'inizio dell'età orientalizzante* (Rome: L'Erma di Bretschneider)

——. 2014. *The Urbanisation of Rome and Latium Vetus: From the Bronze Age to the Archaic Era* (Cambridge: Cambridge University Press)

Fustel de Coulanges, Numa-Denys. 1864. *La cité antique: étude sur le culte, le droit, les institutions de la Grèce et de Rome* (Paris: Hachette)

Giangiulio, Maurizio. 2015. *Democrazie greche: Atene, Sicilia, Magna Grecia* (Rome: Carocci)

González-Ruibal, Alfredo, and Maria Luisa Ruiz-Gálvez. 2016. 'House Societies in the Ancient Mediterranean (2000–500 BC)', *Journal of World Prehistory*, 29: 383–437

Graeber, David, and David Wengrow. 2021. *The Dawn of Everything* (New York: Farrar, Straus and Giroux)

Gruen, Erich S. 1974. *The Last Generation of the Roman Republic* (Berkeley: University of California Press)

Guarino, Antonio. 1973. *Le origini quiritarie: raccolta di scritti romanistici* (Naples: Jovene)

Guidi, Alessandro. 1998. 'The Emergence of the State in Central and Northern Italy', *Acta archaeologica*, 69: 139–61

Harrison, S. J. 1997. 'The Survival and Supremacy of Rome: The Unity of the Shield of Aeneas', *Journal of Roman Studies*, 87: 70–76

Hartog, Francois. 1988. *Le XIXe siècle et l'histoire: le cas Fustel de Coulanges* (Paris: Presses universitaires de France)

Héran, François. 1986. 'Le rite et la croyance', *Revue française de sociologie*, 27: 231–63

——. 1987. 'L'institution démotivée. De Fustel de Coulanges à Durkheim at au-delà', *Revue française de sociologie*, 28: 67–97

Isin, Engin F. 2003. 'Historical Sociology of the City', in *Handbook of Historical Sociology*, ed. by Gerard Delanty (London: SAGE), pp. 312–25

Jennings, Justin, and Timothy K. Earle. 2016. 'Urbanization, State Formation, and Cooperation: A Reappraisal', *Current Anthropology*, 57: 474–93

Johnson, Allen W., and Timothy K. Earle. 2000. *The Evolution of Human Societies: From Foraging Group to Agrarian State* (Stanford: Stanford University Press)

Kleibrink, Marianne. 1997. 'L'organizzazione spaziale dei culti a Satricum', *Mededelingen van het Nederlands Instituut te Rome*, 56: 139–64

Le Goff, Alice. 2016. 'Don, autorité et reconnaissance dans la sociologie de l'évergétisme de Paul Veyne', in *Donner, reconnaître, dominer: trois modèles en philosophie sociale*, ed. by Louis Carré and Alain Loute (Villeneuve d'Ascq: Presses du Septentrion), pp. 169–72

Lévi-Strauss, Claude. 1962. *La pensée sauvage* (Paris: Plon)

——. 1975. *La voie des masques* (Paris: Skira)

Macé, Arnaud. 2019. 'Renan et Fustel: le comparatisme indo-européen et la science des origines', *Romantisme*, 185: 96–105

MacMullen, Ramsay. 2011. *The Earliest Romans: A Character Sketch* (Ann Arbor: University of Michigan Press)

Miles, Richard. 2010. *Carthage Must Be Destroyed: The Rise and Fall of an Ancient Mediterranean Civilization* (London: Allen Lane)

Mogetta, Marcello (ed.). 2020. *Elite Burial Practices and Processes of Urbanization at Gabii: The Non-adult Tombs from Area D of the Gabii Project Excavations* (Portsmouth, RI: Journal of Roman Archaeology)

Momigliano, Arnaldo. 1963. 'An Interim Report on the Origins of Rome', *Journal of Roman Studies*, 53: 95–121

——. 1977. *Essays in Ancient and Modern Historiography* (Oxford: Blackwell)

Monod, Jacques. 1970. *Le hasard et la nécessité: essai sur la philosophie naturelle de la biologie moderne* (Paris: Seuil)

Moretti, Franco. 1996. *Modern Epic* (London: Verso)

Morgan, Lewis Henry. 1877. *Ancient Society, or Researches in the Lines of Human Progress from Savagery, through Barbarism to Civilization* (New York: Holt)

Naglak, Matthew, and Nicola Terrenato. 2019. 'A House Society in Iron Age Latium? Kinship and State Formation in the Context of New Discoveries at Gabii', in *La società gentilizia nell'Italia antica tra realtà e mito storiografico*, ed. by Massimiliano Di Fazio and Silvia Paltineri (Bari: Edipuglia), pp. 1–21

——. 2020. 'Central Italian Elite Groups as Aristocratic Houses at Gabii in the Ninth to Sixth Centuries BCE', in *Roman Law before the Twelve Tables: An Interdisciplinary Approach*, ed. by Paul Du Plessis and Sinclair Bell (Edinburgh: Edinburgh University Press), pp. 25–40

North, John A. 1976. 'Conservatism and Change in Roman Religion', *Papers of the British School at Rome*, 44: 1–12

Pacciarelli, Marco. 2001. *Dal villaggio alla città: la svolta protourbana del 1000 a.C. nell'Italia tirrenica* (Florence: All'insegna del giglio)

——. 2017. 'Society, 10th cent.–730 BCE', in *Etruscology*, ed. by Alessandro Naso (Berlin: De Gruyter), pp. 818–28

Potts, Charlotte R. 2015. *Religious Architecture in Latium and Etruria, c. 900–500 BC* (Oxford: Oxford University Press)

Rosenstein, Nathan Stewart. 2006. 'Aristocratic Values', in *A Companion to the Roman Republic*, ed. by Nathan Stewart Rosenstein and Robert Morstein-Marx (Oxford: Blackwell), pp. 149–66

Scott, James C. 1998. *Seeing Like a State: How Certain Schemes to Improve the Human Condition Have Failed* (New Haven: Yale University Press)

Service, Elman Rogers. 1975. *Origins of the State and Civilization: The Process of Cultural Evolution* (New York: Norton)

Sluiter, Ineke. 2017. 'Anchoring Innovation: A Classical Research Agenda', *European Review*, 25: 20–38

Smith, Christopher J. 1996. *Early Rome and Latium* (Oxford: Oxford University Press)

——. 2020. 'The Laws of the Kings – A View from a Distance', in *Roman Law before the Twelve Tables: An Interdisciplinary Approach*, ed. by Paul Du Plessis and Sinclair Bell (Edinburgh: Edinburgh University Press), pp. 111–32

Terrenato, Nicola. 1998. 'The Romanization of Italy: Global Acculturation or Cultural Bricolage?', *Theoretical Roman Archaeology Journal*, 97: 20–27

——. 2000. 'Coerenza culturale e origini della modernità', in *Archeologia teorica*, ed. by Nicola Terrenato (Florence: Insegna del Giglio), pp. 281–91

——. 2001. 'The Auditorium Site in Rome and the Origins of the Villa', *Journal of Roman Archaeology*, 14: 5–32

——. 2011. 'The Versatile Clans. The Nature of Power in Early Rome', in *State Formation in Italy and Greece*, ed. by Nicola Terrenato and Donald C. Haggis (Oxford: Oxbow), pp. 231–44

——. 2013. 'Patterns of Cultural Change in Roman Italy. Non-elite Religion and the Defense of Cultural Self-Consistency', in *Religiöse Vielfalt und soziale Integration*, ed. by Martin Jehne, Bernhard Linke, and Jörg Rüpke (Heidelberg: VerlagAntike), pp. 43–60

——. 2014. 'Private *vis*, Public *virtus*. Family Agendas during the Early Roman Expansion', in *Roman Republican Colonization: New Perspectives from Archaeology and Ancient History*, ed. by Tesse Dieder Stek and Jeremia Pelgrom (Rome: Palombi), pp. 45–59

——. 2019. *The Early Roman Expansion into Italy: Elite Negotiation and Family Agendas* (Cambridge: Cambridge University Press)

Thomas, Carol G. 2009. 'The Mediterranean World in the Early Iron Age', in *A Companion to Archaic Greece*, ed. by Kurt A. Raaflaub and Hans van Wees (Malden: Wiley-Blackwell), pp. 25–40

Wiseman, Peter T. 2008. *Unwritten Rome* (Exeter: University of Exeter Press)

Woolf, Greg. 2020. *The Life and Death of Ancient Cities: A Natural History* (Oxford: Oxford University Press)

Wright, Henry T. 1977. 'Recent Research on the Origins of the State', *Annual Review of Anthropology*, 6: 379–98

Yoffee, Norman. 2005. *Myths of the Archaic State: Evolution of the Earliest Cities, States and Civilizations* (Cambridge: Cambridge University Press)

Yoffee, Norman, and Nicola Terrenato. 2015. 'Introduction: A History of the Study of Early Cities', in *The Cambridge World History*, III: *Early Cities in Comparative Perspective*, ed. by Norman Yoffee (Cambridge: Cambridge University Press), pp. 1–24

FRANCO DE ANGELIS

3. Mixing up Mediterranean Innovation

The Case of Viticulture and Wine

ABSTRACT Viticulture and wine played well-known, important roles in elite interaction and many other aspects of ancient life. Less well known are the origins of viticulture and wine in pre-Roman Italy and the western Mediterranean in general. Recent scholarship contains contradictory views as to whether or not Phoenician and Greek migrants introduced viticulture and wine to Italy. Positions slot into one of the two polarized options: indigenous versus introduced. In this chapter, I offer a case study on viticulture and wine as a re-examination of the question of cultural and economic transfers in the pre-Roman western Mediterranean between the ninth and third centuries BCE. My approach entails bridging scholarly divides and presenting more complex and nuanced arguments. In the case of viticulture and wine, the picture is much more mixed than currently imagined. To arrive at this conclusion, I use an interdisciplinary approach that is multilateral and draws on all available forms of evidence, including archaeological science, ecological approaches, iconography, and a broader range of theory. With this chapter, I attempt not only to present a case study in its own right, but also to sketch out a larger framework on how we might think of indigenous versus introduced features more generally in the crucial centuries before the creation of the Roman Empire.

It almost goes without saying that most critical re-evaluations of the purported Hellenization of the western Mediterranean have come from scholars whose research focuses mainly on the non-Hellenic peoples whom ancient Greeks encountered. This is a logical and natural reaction, because the impact of the Greeks on the western Mediterranean has traditionally been regarded as both profound and transformative in all spheres of life. In this regard, it is essential to remind ourselves of the now long-forgotten *locus classicus* of this Hellenocentric framework. In 1899, the great Swedish archaeologist Oscar Montelius (1899, 1) wrote as follows in the opening paragraphs of his groundbreaking synthesis *Der Orient und Europa*:

> Zu einer Zeit, wo die Völker Europas so zu sagen noch aller Civilisation baar waren, befand sich der Orient, und besonders das Euphratgebiet und das Nilthal, im Besitz einer blühenden Cultur. Diese Cultur begann schon früh Einfluss auf unseren Weltheil zu üben, und da gewährt es ein eigenes Schauspiel zu sehen, wie die wichtige Culturelemente empfangende, vorhistorische Europa sich dem Orient in ähnlicher Weise verhielt, wie heutzutage die Länder 'der Wilde', ja der einst so hoch civilisirte Orient selbst, Europa gegenüber stehen.
>
> Die Civilisation, welche allmälig in unserem Weltheil in Erscheinung trat, war lange nur ein schwacher Widerschein der Cultur des Ostens. Dies gilt selbst von den am meisten vorgeschrittenen Ländern – Griechenland und Italien – bis um die Mitte des letzten vorchristlichen Jahrtausends, wo die Griechen ihre überlegene Begabung dadurch bethätigten, dass sie dasjenige, was sie empfangen, umarbeiteten und veredelten und zwar in einer Weise, welche zeigt, dass das Lehrling den Meister überholt hatte.

> (At a time when the peoples of Europe were, so to speak, devoid of all civilization, the Orient, and especially the Euphrates and the Nile Valley, was in possession of a flourishing culture. This culture began to exercise an early influence on our part of the world, and there it offers its own spectacle to see how prehistoric Europe receiving the important cultural elements behaved similarly to the Orient, just as nowadays 'Savage' lands do when faced against Europe, as indeed once it did vis-à-vis the civilized Orient itself.

Corresponding author Franco De Angelis (franco.de_angelis@ubc.ca)

Adoption, Adaption, and Innovation in Pre-Roman Italy: Paradigms for Cultural Change, ed. by Jeremy Armstrong and Aaron Rhodes-Schroder, AMW 3 (Turnhout, 2023), pp. 47–58 · BREPOLS PUBLISHERS · 10.1484/M.AMW-EB.5.133265

Civilization, which gradually appeared in our part of the world, was for a long time but a feeble reflection of the culture of the East. This is true even of the most advanced countries — Greece and Italy — until the middle of the last millennium, when the Greeks exerted their superior gifts by reworking and refining what they received, in a manner that shows that the apprentice had overtaken the master.)[1]

This explicitly colonialist framework is unidirectional and gives priority to the incoming populations, who are regarded as inherently superior. It has a top-down approach that we have become accustomed to, that smothers and conquers local cultures and agency, and that assimilates and acculturates them in terms of the outsiders. In consequence, this framework generally ignores the study of these local cultures and defines issues, like social complexity, in terms of the eastern cultures. Pyramids and writing systems, for example, are set as the pinnacle of 'civilization'. Although the Bronze Age civilizations of the Euphrates and Nile Valley are initially singled out, Montelius ends by crediting the Iron Age Greeks with their magical touch of reworking and disseminating civilization from the eastern to the western Mediterranean. Notably absent are Phoenicians and any other Levantine peoples. The tenor of the time in which Montelius was writing is crucial to bear in mind. The 1890s represented a watershed moment for anti-Semitism in the world, which greatly impacted scholarly attitudes to all Semitic-speaking populations in all periods of history (Bernal 1987, 337–99). Since then, modern scholarship has been playing catch-up with restoring the role of Phoenicians and other Levantine peoples in the ancient history of the western Mediterranean (see now López-Ruiz 2021). This may help to explain, at least in part, why so many of the discussions of cultural transfer and innovation in the western Mediterranean usually engage only, or primarily, with Greeks. One must bear in mind that the intellectual framework against which scholarship has been reacting has not only been long-standing, but it has also been tightly coiled around a very extreme spring from the start. Once released, this spring logically and naturally recoils from its contained energy. The result, perhaps inevitably, has been a polarizing framework that currently characterizes interpretations of pre-Roman technology and culture in the western Mediterranean in two diametrically opposed ways: the first sees all central features as being introduced from outside

(largely by Greeks), whereas the second sees these very same features as being of indigenous origin.

The outcome has led, and is leading, to all kinds of laudable, new developments in research. While it may be thought that no scholars in their right mind think along the drastic lines that Montelius long ago sketched out, or that research regarding pre-Roman technology and culture has uniformly advanced across all categories of topics and evidence, this is simply not true. A case in point concerns viticulture and wine, the focus of this chapter. This is what one reads in the standard work on the domestication of plants in the Old World, now in a fourth edition from 2012 (Zohary and others 2012, 126): 'Viticulture was apparently introduced to the west Mediterranean basin by Phoenician and Greek colonists (Stager 1985; Buxó 1997). The Romans brought this crop to temperate Europe (Loeschke 1933; König 1989).' These two sentences represent fewer than thirty words from a chapter subsection that runs for more than five full pages of text and images. The reader, however, leaves these pages with the impression that our leading lights on Old World plant domestication have a 'gut-feeling' that something may be awry with their pithy conclusion. Their choice of the word 'apparently' is the obvious clue, but throughout their standard work they attempt to draw on the latest developments in molecular biology, archaeology (which they define broadly), and other relevant historical, linguistic, and circumstantial sources, such as geological probability (Zohary and others 2012, 9–19). Nevertheless, when it comes to viticulture and wine, they feel compelled to state the standard narrative. This can only mean one thing: that we archaeologists and historians of the pre-Roman Mediterranean have given them little reason to say otherwise. We have come to believe in the rock-solid foundations of the canonical picture that has been built up over successive generations of scholarship since Montelius. With some notable exceptions, discussions of viticulture and wine continue to be framed, even by scholars who are otherwise theoretically sensitive, in terms of Greeks and Phoenicians bringing viticulture and wine to peoples previously wholly ignorant of it (Hodos 2010, 87–88; Riva 2017, 253; though Hodos 2020, 128 with n. 169 now has it right). If the impetus for change cannot come from within the field itself, then we should not expect anything more from specialists in Old World plant domestication. The onus, in other words, rests with those of us who work on the pre-Roman and Roman Mediterranean to supply the impetus for this change.

We are at the stage in which the devil is in the details. This language is shared by another con-

---

1 Author's own translation, from the German.

tributor and editor of this volume, Aaron Rhodes-Schroder, who has independently been thinking along the same lines, with his very clever title 'The Demon Is in the Detail'. We can all no doubt agree that, while there has been much excellent research undertaken in the last generation on showing how the top-down, all-encompassing Hellenization model is fundamentally wrong, what has been lacking for Italy, and the western Mediterranean as a whole, is the development of a new, more evidence-based view, warts and all, of the role played by Greeks (and other incoming peoples for that matter). The onus rests on us Hellenists too, in other words, to question the assumptions and practices of our own field as formulated by earlier generations of scholars, and to add to the new view.

In this chapter, my purpose is twofold. First, I will begin by sketching out a larger framework on how we might think of indigenous versus introduced features more generally in the crucial centuries before the creation of the Roman Empire. Second, I will present a case study on viticulture and wine, revealing how the picture of Mediterranean innovation is considerably more mixed than has generally been imagined.

Sketching out a Larger Framework

Anyone who has followed developments in the study of the pre-Roman western Mediterranean over the last generation knows that Etruria, Sardinia, and Iberia stood out in the Early Iron Age for their advanced social development and interregional connections by the time Phoenicians and Greeks encountered them (Bietti Sestieri 1997; Guidi 1998; 2008; Dietler and López-Ruiz 2009a; Celestino and López-Ruiz 2016; Webster 2016). The western Mediterranean was hardly backwards and passively waiting to be civilized (De Angelis 2022, where the apparent backwardness of Etruria is fully tested and challenged). This new picture has come about through the growth and interpretation of archaeological data, accompanied by a revolution in absolute chronology supported by the scientific dating techniques of radiocarbon and dendrochronology (Bartoloni and Delpino 2005; Nijboer 2005; Brandherm and Trachsel 2008). The decolonization of this absolute chronology from its original Hellenocentric base has also contributed significantly to the question of indigenous versus introduced features in the pre-Roman western Mediterranean. These scholarly developments, and the many case studies that have accumulated over this same time, are all inescapable and present us with facts that cannot be denied or ignored. Their

deployment, however, in new historical narratives, that seek to replace the old *Ex Oriente Lux* diffusionist theories that linger on and to reconfigure how we imagine the ancient Mediterranean to have worked in the Early Iron Age, has happened more slowly, and rather haphazardly, to date.

The concepts of microregionalism and microecology need to be drawn upon more in discussions of the pre-Roman western Mediterranean (Horden and Purcell 2000). While, admittedly, this is not an entirely new idea (see Riva and Vella 2006, 10), these concepts have not been articulated enough and become mainstream in scholarly discussions. As Peregrine Horden and Nicholas Purcell (2000, 53) note in their classic work *The Corrupting Sea*:

> We can never hope to come to an understanding of what can usefully be said of the Mediterranean-wide human or physical landscape until we are fully sensitive to the enormous variety and diversity of environments within the basin of the sea, not just to the constants that apparently underline the chaos.

Environmental fragmentation at all scales and for all variables (geology, relief, soils, hydrology, climate, resources, and so on) defines this variety and diversity (Horden and Purcell 2000, 78–79). The relationships human societies (and other living organisms) have with their environments must be included not only to avoid environmental determinism but also to establish historical ecology as the methodological framework needed to achieve the understanding of the Mediterranean envisaged by Horden and Purcell (2000, 45–49, 392). The paradox of the Mediterranean's fragmentation is particularly overcome by the Mediterranean Sea's relative ease of maritime communications and mobility it offers (Horden and Purcell 2000, 549). Such connectivity can potentially link microregions together and in turn create a kaleidoscope of microecologies, defined as a 'locality' (a 'definite place') with a distinctive identity derived from the set of available productive opportunities and the particular interplay of human responses to them found in a given period' (Horden and Purcell 2000, 80). It is well worth observing that southern Etruria, of direct relevance to this paper, is one of four 'definite places' used by Horden and Purcell (2000, 59–65) to illustrate microregionalism and microecology.

As we increasingly define the Mediterranean as microregional and microecological, it only follows that we should keep pace with viewing the ancient world as decentred and, consequently, polycentric. Some comparative reading suggests that we might think instead of a system of overlapping regional trajectories that could be linked together by heightened levels of mobility and connectivity, as can be found in the map from Janet Abu-Lughod's (1989, 34) classic book *Before European Hegemony: The World System A.D. 1250–1350*. This map provides food for thought, in that it makes us think about how regional systems could develop and exist on their own in the pre-Roman western Mediterranean and elsewhere, while at the same time allowing for polycentrism and the linking together of wide swathes of space through a kind of 'Venn Diagram framework' in which the various regional systems could overlap and be integrated into a larger global whole. Interestingly, two regional systems overlapped in central Italy in the fourteenth century CE, just as they did in the ninth century BCE. At the same time, however, just because increased social development (Morris 2013) can be established for Etruria or any other western Mediterranean region (like Sardinia or Iberia), does not necessarily make all of the western Mediterranean just as socially developed as them. In fact, this point also applies to the eastern Mediterranean, since it shared the same microregionalism (Liverani 2017). While connectivity is usually highlighted when using a microregional perspective, ecology, as just discussed, is the other integral element in this paradigm. If we seriously want to include this element, it only follows that Mediterranean ecology needs to be treated as part of the more level playing field that is, in theory, common to all of the basin's inhabitants, providing them with their own agency. For me, this also means that more of us need to become economic historians to some degree, since ecology and economy do go hand in hand.

It also follows from this that movement and interaction in the Mediterranean occurred, not only in the traditional east to west manner, but also in a west to east manner, and in a north to south manner. Some distinguished scholars have begun to recognize the possible implications of these advances in research and have hypothesized that some western Mediterranean actors may have initiated interaction with Dark Age Greece and ultimately stimulated social developments there (Bietti Sestieri and others 2002, 425–26; Osborne 2009, 121). In effect, the western Mediterranean acted as a magnet that attracted the eastern Mediterranean immigrants. Such a view represents, unwittingly, a modified form of *Ex Medio Lux* ('from the middle, light'), developed in 1930s fascist Italy in the context of Neolithic Malta, and its claimed centrist role in the formation of Mediterranean civilization (De Francesco 2013, 187). In a similar vein, and more recently, the editors of an important volume on ancient Iberia have spoken of *Ex Occidente Lux* ('from the west, light') adding that 'This state-

ment is more than a whimsical inversion of an old trope; it is an assertive claim of considerable significance in view of the traditional marginalization of the Western Mediterranean in classical studies' (Dietler and López-Ruiz 2009b, vii). They are absolutely correct: the pre-Roman western Mediterranean, as a historical entity in its own right, is still either not at all included in global historical narratives, or at best treated as an appendix of the Aegean Sea basin and eastern Mediterranean more generally. There is no longer any good reason to deny or ignore this fact in our new historical narratives that reconfigure how we imagine the ancient Mediterranean to have worked in the Early Iron Age. Once again, the devil is in the details. However, in order to avoid swinging the pendulum from one extreme to another, a more careful and nuanced approach can be advanced that thinks in terms of regional hubs all across the ancient world. To quote Horden and Purcell (2000, 549) once again: '"Hubs"' are not determined by geography but by their place in the overall "system" which may well change from one period to another as the component microecologies alter'.

Let me conclude the first part of my chapter by emphasizing how regional and interregional interactions in the western Mediterranean supplied, on their own, the conditions for complexity to emerge without ignition by Phoenicians and Greeks. Microregions and microecologies had already developed to a significant degree there, and this stands in stark contrast to the traditional viewpoints of modern scholarship that think in terms of a backward western Mediterranean eager to be civilized by outsiders. Our historical narratives must keep pace with the new approaches and evidence that have emerged. In this new scenario, Phoenicians and Greeks were drawn to the existing attractions that the western Mediterranean had to offer. With their arrival, the world of the western Mediterranean became even more complicated and entangled in a further series of interactions and networks, providing the 'fantastic cauldron of expanding cultures and commerces' (as Jean-Paul Morel (1984, 150) long ago so astutely characterized this region during the pre-Roman period) in which the Roman Empire was ultimately forged. This complicated entanglement can be illustrated by my case study on viticulture and wine in the second part of my paper.

Viticulture and Wine, a 'Mixed Picture'

My methodology for this case study seeks to be as robust as possible, and to employ all available forms of evidence: molecular biology and archaeobotany, material and visual culture, literary and epigraphic sources, and a greater range of interpretative tools. Part of the problem of research has been the division between prehistoric and classical archaeology, and their different emphases. Some scholars have long been calling for the bridging of this divide, in order to more effectively study ancient situations that knew no such artificial divisions of labour and competencies. I have myself called for the creation of a proper 'contact archaeology' to rectify this problem (De Angelis 2009, 57; 2016, 99–100). The place to begin our case study is with recent developments in archaeological science and archaeobotany.

Specialists in plant domestication always aim to establish whether indigenous wild ancestors can be found in the same regions where cultivars thrive. Zohary, Hopf, and Weiss (2012, 121–24), whom I quoted earlier, are no exception to this rule. In the case of the vine, it has long been known that wild ancestors existed in Italy, across the coastal regions of the western Mediterranean, and some inland parts of temperate Europe. Recent research in molecular biology and archaeobotany has added to that picture, demonstrating that microregionalism in the ancient Mediterranean also extended to plants (Arroyo-García and others 2006; Marvelli and others 2013). An independent variety of the vine has been identified for the western Mediterranean, something which challenges the traditional view that the vine had a single place of origin in Transcaucasia and gradually spread westwards through successive transplanting of cultivated grape cuttings. That does not mean, however, that I dismiss altogether any role for diffusionism in my methodological framework (see below).

While the presence of an independent variety of vine in the western Mediterranean provides a theoretical basis for the development of viticulture there, painstaking work by archaeobotanists over the last generation has produced convincing direct and indirect evidence of the cultivated vine, and wine produced from it, before Greeks and Phoenicians began to frequent the western Mediterranean in the ninth century BCE (Cicirelli and others 2008; Brun 2011, 103–06; de'Siena 2012, 34–35). Some of the most secure evidence, which has clinched the argument, comes from Poggiomarino, located about 10 km north-north-east of Pompeii. Here, exceptional waterlogged conditions allowed for the controlled retrieval of well-preserved organic material, including the cultivated vine, along with wood samples dated dendrochronologically to between 905 and 864 BCE (Cicirelli and others 2008; see Brun 2011, 105–06 on the significance of this evidence). This evidence, once and for all, requires us to temper previous arguments regarding the wholesale importation of the vine and viticulture into the western Mediterranean by Greeks and Phoenicians starting in the second half of the ninth century.

Once the possibility of independent viticultural traditions evidenced in some parts of pre-Roman Italy, before the arrival of Greeks and Phoenicians, is admitted, other evidence comes into clearer view and can be used as further support for these arguments. Basic planting techniques provide some notable insights. The Italic method was to support the vine by attaching it to a live tree; the Greeks, by contrast, staked the vine to a short wooden post. This difference may be due to climate; the Italic method, using live trees, was better suited to wetter and marshier areas (Braconi 2006, 57–58; de'Siena 2012, 36–37), but it could also have been due to polycropping practices that sought greater efficiency with labour (Van Limbergen and others 2017, 361). Perhaps not surprisingly, the Italic practice is found most in areas with Etruscan civilization (Braconi 2006, 56–57; Komar 2021, 246–47). Ancient terminology also exists for this difference (Braconi 2006). The ancient technical word for the Italic practice, *arbustum*, survives in Latin and medieval texts, and the Greek writers Theophrastus, Polybios, and Hesychios mention it, and use a version of the word *anadendras* (*ampelos*), or the Etruscan word *ataison* in Hesychios's case, to describe attaching the vine to a live tree. The Latin texts use another word, *vinea*, for the Greek method. There is also a difference in ancient terminology for wine (Torelli 2006, 35). The usual focus on *oinos-vinum/vinun* has obscured the existence of an older indigenous culture of wine, altogether independent of the Greek tradition. In old Latin, the word for wine is *temetum*, to be drunk is *temulentus*, and to be sober is *abstemius*. These differences in vocabulary are also undergirded by Indo-European linguistics, in which an Italic, Celtic, Germanic, and Balto-Slavic subgroup for wine can be distinguished from a central subgroup made of up Greek, Armenian, and Albanian (Gorton 2017, 9).

The apparent dissonances between Greek and Etruscan viticultural practices, known from the literary and epigraphic sources, also become intelligible. One thinks of, in particular, the Etruscan practice of non-professional women, such as wives, responsible for the mixing of wine, as well as consuming it in such family contexts as funerary rituals (Colonna 1980; Martinelli 1984; Ford Russell 2003, 80–82; Iaia 2006; de'Siena 2012, 74–83). Such practices are not to be regarded as abnormalities or misunderstandings of Greek practices, and are instead to be explained as social and cultural practices strongly rooted in Etruscan identity. The association of particular pottery shapes with these female roles, as well as male roles, is also well established from the evidence for pre-existing viticultural practices. A group of Villanovan pottery shapes have been associated with the consumption of wine (Torelli 2006, 36–39; de'Siena 2012, 76–77). One is a cup with a single looped handle used for drawing and drinking liquids of all kinds; it is found associated with both males and females at all social levels. A second shape is the amphora with spirals, which was made at first in impasto, and then in bucchero from the mid-seventh to the second half of the sixth centuries. It is thought to have been used to store and serve liquids. When the Villanovan ceramic repertoire comes into contact with the Phoenician and Greek ones, these identifications, based on the modern observer's hindsight, are corroborated (Bartoloni and others 2012). It is interesting to observe that even though the earliest Phoenician and Greek imports are made up of drinking cups, wine jugs, kraters, and amphorae (Fletcher 2007, 23–28), many Phoenician and Greek pottery shapes already had a rough equivalency in the pre-existing Villanovan repertoire. The only exception is the oenochoe, for which no close equivalency existed, and which filled a clear need in the serving of wine. Local agency drove this selective adoption, which was discerning (de'Siena 2012, 81). We are not witnessing the wholesale adoption of new ceramic practices, as might be inferred if we take a classical archaeological perspective and overlook the pre-contact situation. It, instead, becomes clear that any decision to adopt a new shape was made with a view to slotting it into an established practice of consumption, and that Phoenician and Greek imports respond to a pre-existing local demand (cf. Hodos 2020, 132).

In general, this seems to have been what happened: the arrival of Phoenicians and Greeks simply resulted in the conjunction of cultural and economic traditions and trajectories, bringing the expansion and acceleration of viticulture and wine in this and other parts of the Mediterranean (Ampolo 1980, 32; de Cazanove 1991, 175; de'Siena 2012, 31, 36, 42; Mitterlechner 2021). At first, in the ninth, eighth, and first half of the seventh centuries BCE, the so-called 'Oriental' cultural model was dominant over the Greek one, in terms of amphorae, wine, and additions to wine, like green onions (Torelli 2000, 386–88; de'Siena 2012, 79). From the mid-seventh century, the Greek cultural model gained the upper hand, again in terms of similar things, but it also included reclined banqueting. This occurs, still, in a two-way dialogue, and can be illustrated through pottery production, where Greek appeal also extended (Torelli 2006, 37–39; de'Siena 2012, 71–72, 76–77). The Italic spiral amphora and handled cup were imitated, as is well known, in Athenian workshops, especially that

of Nikosthenes, for the Etruscan market. The imitation of pottery shapes from Greece to Etruria came in the form of the *kantharos*, likely from Boeotia. The shape started to be imitated in bucchero from the mid-seventh century BCE and was in turn exported from Etruria to many parts of the Mediterranean, including Greece.

The iconography on the Greek exports also made reference to local Etruscan features, a point recognized in previous discussions (see most recently Bundrick 2019), but the subject can be further developed. From Athenian workshops, there are two specific, previously unrecognized, examples of relevance that I would like to highlight. One is the black-figure cup (*kylix*) by Exekias depicting Dionysos, found at Vulci and dating to around 540–530 BCE (Fig. 3.1). The vine emerges from the ship's floors and wraps itself around the mast. The vine extends beyond the mast and branches out into various directions, to produce an overall effect that is reminiscent of a tree, much in the same way as the Italic planting technique discussed earlier, which marries the vine to a live tree. The other possible representation of this planting technique may appear on an amphora by the Amasis Painter, who also worked in Athens in the same period and whose amphora was also found at Vulci (Fig. 3.2). In the most recent work on this scene known to me, the supporting structure is described as a trellis and usually taken as an example of how grapes were crushed in ancient Greece (McGovern and others 2013, fig. S6). The trellis idea is plausible, but it can also be used, judging from numerous later depictions from Italy, in connection with marrying a vine to a tree (see Braconi 2006, 57 for one such illustration).

While we might have become preconditioned to think that Athenian potters and painters were blazing a trail of innovation here (recently, Riva 2017, 252), it may be argued that they may well have been following along the lines already established by their Corinthian predecessors. The latter seem to have composed new pottery shapes and images to satisfy Etruscan demand by targeting particular Etruscan social and cultural practices. These social and cultural practices include the role of wives and daughters who were responsible for the mixing of wine, as mentioned above. Two Corinthian column kraters found at Cerveteri, and that are both now in the Louvre, provide the food for thought as to this targeting by Corinthian potters and painters.

Louvre E635 is the Early Corinthian Eurytios krater, dating to the late seventh century BCE (Fig. 3.3). It depicts Herakles at a banquet with the royal family at Oechalia, in the kingdom of Eurytos. The princess Iole stands between Herakles and her

3. MIXING UP MEDITERRANEAN INNOVATION   53

Figure 3.1. View of the interior of the so-called 'Dionysus Cup' (or *kylix*) by Exekias found at Vulci, Etruria, c. 540–530 BCE, depicting the god Dionysos in a ship with vine emerging from the ship's floors and wrapping itself around the mast. Munich, Antikensammlungen, inv. no. 8729.

(Exekias (Public domain), via Wikimedia Commons from Wikimedia Commons, <https://commons.wikimedia.org/wiki/File%3AExekias_Dionysos_Staatliche_Antikensammlungen_2044_n2.jpg> [accessed 24 January 2023]).

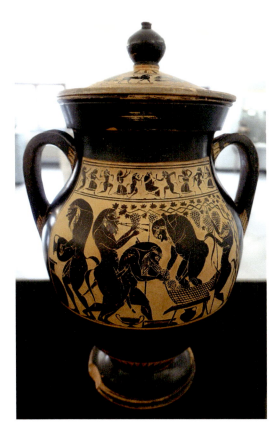

Figure 3.2. View of Side A of the so-called 'Vintaging Amphora' by the Amasis Painter found at Vulci, Etruria, c. 530 BCE, showing five satyrs engaged in the production of wine. The trellis is depicted in the top right above the three satyrs involved in the treading of the grapes. Würzburg, Universität, Martin von Wagner Museum, inv. no. 265.

(Daderot [Public domain], via Wikimedia Commons from Wikimedia Commons, <https://commons.wikimedia.org/wiki/File:Belly_amphora_with_satyrs_at_the_grape_harvest,_Amasis_Painter,_540-530_BC,_L_265_-_Martin_von_Wagner_Museum_-_W%C3%BCrzburg,_Germany_-_DSC05615.jpg> [accessed 24 January 2023]).

Figure 3.3. View of Early Corinthian Eurytios (column) krater found at Cerveteri (Louvre E635), dating to the late seventh century BCE. The scene depicts Herakles at banquet with the royal family at Oechalia, the kingdom of Eurytos. The princess Iole stands on the right-hand side close to her brother Iphitos who is reclining on a couch. Paris, Musée du Louvre, inv. no. E635.

(Louvre Museum/CC BY (<https://creativecommons.org/licenses/by/2.5>; <https://commons.wikimedia.org/wiki/File:Eurytios_Krater_Louvre_E635_n1.jpg> [accessed 24 January 2023]).

Figure 3.4. View of Early Corinthian column krater by the Athana Painter found at Cerveteri, Etruria (Louvre E629) dating to the early sixth century BCE. The scene shows women reclining alongside men on banqueting couches. Paris, Musée du Louvre, inv. no. E629.

(This work is out of copyright, with photographic rights held by the Bridgeman Art Library. <https://www.bridgemanimages.com/en-US/> [accessed 24 January 2023]).

brother Iphitos. This is perhaps a banquet before the archery contest for the hand of Iole between Eurytos and his sons and Herakles. From the usually one-sided perspective of Greek art historians, Iole is literally taken to be a Greek woman who rather passively 'attends' at the banquet and 'waits upon' the men (Carpenter 1991, 133 and fig. 221 caption). But if this scene is Etruscanized, it becomes likely that an Etruscan woman may have been able to relate to the images depicted without any of these overtones. The other krater, catalogued as Louvre E629, is a black-figure krater by the Athana Painter that dates to the early sixth century BCE (Fig. 3.4). It is not as good for my argument, since it is impossible to tell with absolute certainty the status of the women who recline with the men. Darrell Amyx (1988, II, 386), in his *magnum opus* on Archaic Corinthian pottery, describes these women as naked. I would not go as far as that; at most, we have fully clothed women who have one exposed breast. I find more appealing Fiona Hobden's (2013, 3–4) discussion of this very krater, which is used to illustrate her more general point about looking for literal truths in depictions of the symposium. She would rather view this space as rhetorical and discursive. If I tease out that point further within Hobden's interpretative framework, then it is possible to think that the Corinthian painter was playing with Etruscan men and women to be a little more fun and flirty on the occasions in which they consumed wine together. In both cases, therefore, the kraters and their images acted like the Athenian ceramic behaviour of later times, in being targeted at and composed for Etruscan audiences. It is not too far-fetched to think that, while couched in Greek myth and iconography, the Etruscan women involved in mixing and consuming wine may have self-identified with the women depicted. The column kraters, the imagery, and the reclined drinking on them would have been novel to the Etruscans (Amyx 1988, II, 378; de'Siena 2012, 61), and for that reason readily adoptable, but the rest happened in an otherwise unchanged Etruscan world. It is also worth noting that these kraters and their images have long been in the public domain and can be found in the classic work of, for instance, Humfry Payne (1931) on Corinthian art. What has changed since then are the concerted efforts to enter our material into a two-way dialogue, instead of imposing and assuming top-down Hellenization as was common in the Oxford and elsewhere of Payne's time. The iconography on Greek exports that make reference to Etruscan and Italic features is certainly a subject that can be developed even further within the larger framework sketched out in this study, in particular to establish how frequent the phenomenon was.

These two Corinthian kraters in the Louvre provide more fodder for the argument that the arrival of Phoenicians and Greeks in the western Mediterranean resulted in the conjunction of cultural and economic traditions and trajectories, bringing the expansion and acceleration of viticulture and wine in this and other parts of the Mediterranean. This is not the birth of viticulture and wine in the western Mediterranean, as the Hellenocentric line has long wanted us to believe. Instead, what the Italic material demonstrates is that what we are witnessing, in our archaeological, epigraphic, and literary sources of the Early Iron Age and Archaic period, is a change in elite behaviour in an increasingly interconnected world. In the case of Archaic Rome, as Michel Gras (1983) has long ago convincingly argued, *temetum*, the word for wine discussed earlier, is used to refer to religious contexts and therefore restricted to specific rituals handled by specially charged priests (see also de Cazanove 1991, 174–78; Ford Russell 2003; Komar 2021, who specifically comes out in favour of Gras after considering the arguments that have appeared since). Imported wine was outside this internally dictated religious realm, and the appearance of imported, transport amphorae in women's tombs at Castel di Decima and Laurentina, and other banqueting paraphernalia, can best be seen in this light. Elite women and men found a new outlet offered to them to express themselves and to emphasize their differences with non-elite members of their communities.

Viticulture and wine allows us also to illustrate some other theoretical thinking that has been little applied to questions of innovation in pre-Roman Italy and the western Mediterranean. A distinction can be made between complete and conceptual transfers (Frankel 2012), or 'engrafted innovation', as it has more recently been dubbed (Helwing 2017, 162); this term is particularly appropriate in the context of viticulture and wine, although I will continue with the more standard wording. While we usually think in terms of complete transfers, better known as diffusionism, concepts alone could also be transferred and applied to local conditions. Let me illustrate with examples which contain both complete and conceptual transfers at the same time, as well as on their own.

For Sardinia, distinguished Dutch archaeobotanist Corrie Bakels (2002) has hypothesized two viticultural traditions: an imported one in the Phoenician coastal zone, using imported vines, and another, pre-Phoenician, Nuraghic one in the island's interior using local vines. Interestingly, the Phoenicians may have imported archaic types of vines with seeds morphologically close to those of wild vines found on Sardinia. The Phoenicians seem not only to have worked with Sardinia's ecology, but also to have generated a synergy with a pre-existing viticultural economy at Sant'Imbenia in north-western Sardinia (Botto 2016, 88–93). The so-called Sant'Imbenia amphorae originated in the last decades of the ninth century BCE in several different parts of Sardinia; they are inspired by Levantine shapes and show interactions between Levantine and Sardinian potters, the former possibly resident at Sant'Imbenia, at least on a seasonal basis, judging from the high incidence of domestic wares. The arrival of Phoenicians there accelerated the production of these amphorae, which were still produced with local Nuragic techniques and technology, namely hand-forming with slow wheel shaping, and local materials (established via archaeometric means). They are found as far west as Atlantic Andalusia and in the central Mediterranean, from northern Etruria to Carthage, where a high percentage of them appear in Carthage's earliest archaeological layers. The amphorae were probably used to store food products, including wine, from Sardinia for Phoenician sailors. The likelihood that some contained wine has been argued for indirectly through their frequent association with the Sardinian *askoid* jug (Botto 2016, 89–90). The Sardinian *askoid* jug, moreover, was exported to Iberia in the Late Bronze Age, long before this synergy at Sant'Imbenia occurred, suggesting to Massimo Botto (2016, 79–88) that Sardinians initiated and were involved in promoting wine consumption in Iberia as part of a social strategy to seal exchange transactions before the Phoenicians did so there. The Phoenicians in Iberia latched on to this long-standing social practice and extended it by planting their own vines at Huelva and elsewhere (Pérez Jordà 2015; Echevarría Sánchez and Vera Rodríguez 2015; González de Canales and others 2020). In the sixth century BCE, the Phoenicians took over the entire economic and social networks in Iberia established by Sardinians. This represents a kind of reverse conceptual transfer.

In France's Rhone Valley, Gallic wine production is attested in the fifth and fourth centuries BCE using local vines, but surely adopting a conceptual transfer from nearby Greek Massalia, by then famed for its wine (Bouby and Marinval 2001). However, while the Greeks of Massalia are usually thought to have brought viticulture and wine to Mediterranean France, a point reaffirmed at the start of this century in an important collection of essays by leading specialists (Brun and Laubenheimer 2001), chemical analyses on ancient organic compounds absorbed into the Etruscan amphorae found at Lattara (modern-day Lattes, to the north-west of Marseilles) published a dozen years later now provides the earliest biomolecular archaeological evidence for grape wine and viticulture in modern France (McGovern and others 2013). The authors have also hypothesized that the Etruscans may have brought their own vines for transplantation, supporting their argument with the evidence from the Grand Ribaud F shipwreck found in waters east of Marseilles (McGovern and others 2013, 10151). The wreck is dated to about 515–475 BCE, and its hold was filled with grapevines originally identified by its excavators as, essentially, cushioning placed between the 700 and 800 amphorae stacked as cargo. The authors also argue that the idea of transplantation can be supported in a general way by the fourth-century BCE Punic shipwreck found in the waters of Majorca at El Sec, in which grapevines on board were transported embedded in soil in the cool hull for later transplantation. In that case, too, the wreck's cargo mainly consisted of numerous transport amphorae, cups, and other shapes used in the transport and mixing of wine. If both these hypotheses are correct, then they would also provide evidence of diffusionism. Moreover, the Massaliot Greeks seem to have eventually taken over the Etruscan viticultural networks in France through competition and conflict, judging from the ample signs of destruction and conflict at Lattara, which date to about 475 BCE (Gailledrat 2015, 38–41), and slot in nicely to the wider comparative context of competition and conflict in the western and eastern Mediterranean around this time. Massaliot transport amphorae only started to be produced in the mid-sixth century BCE, some fifty years after the foundation of Massalia. The earliest archaeological layers of Massalia have revealed a dominance of Etruscan transport amphorae, in the range of 80–90 per cent of all identifiable finds of this class of material (Bats 2012, 146–47). Clearly, the Massaliot Greeks arrived second when it came to viticulture and wine, but they went from followers to leaders by adopting a conceptual transfer in reverse. Perhaps Montelius, quoted at the outset, was right after all about Greeks reworking and refining what they received from others, though certainly not in the way that he and others had imagined for the western Mediterranean. Nevertheless, a role here for Greeks cannot be denied, but imagining an exclusively Greek origin for viticulture and wine in Gaul, as recorded in our surviving Greek and Latin sources, must again be considered alongside the pre-contact situation.

Conclusions

My mini case studies on viticulture and wine could have been expanded with others,[2] but the argument would still be the same. The case studies chosen serve to illustrate my methodology and the new framework I am putting forth concerning innovation in the pre-Roman western Mediterranean as a whole. This methodology is robust and employs all available forms of evidence: molecular biology and archaeobotany, material and visual culture, literary and epigraphic sources, and a greater range of interpretative tools. My methodology also pays serious attention to local cultures and inserts the Phoenicians and Greeks into them, in order to be cross-cultural and interdisciplinary. The result is a mixed picture of Mediterranean innovation that represents a more complex and nuanced reconstruction of viticulture and wine. It is this mixed picture that helps us understand better later Roman conditions and decisions regarding viticulture and wine in Italy, which had both indigenous and introduced traditions to choose from (Aversano and others 2017; Van Limbergen and others 2017).

---

2 For example, Apulia: see Colivicchi 2004; 2014, 216–17; Bianco and others 2015.

Works Cited

Abu-Lughod, Janet. 1989. *Before European Hegemony: The World System A.D. 1250–1350* (Oxford: Oxford University Press)

Ampolo, Carmine. 1980. 'Le condizioni materiali della produzione. Agricoltura e paesaggio agrario', *Dialoghi di archeologia*, n.s., 2: 15–46

Amyx, Darrell A. 1988. *Corinthian Vase-Painting of the Archaic Period*, 3 vols (Berkeley: University of California Press)

Aversano, Riccardo, Boris Basile, Mauro Paolo Buonincontri, Francesca Carucci, Domenico Carputo, Luigi Frusciante, and Gaetano Di Pasquale. 2017. 'Dating the Beginning of the Roman Viticultural Model in the Western Mediterranean: The Case of Chianti (Central Italy)', *PLoS ONE*, 12.11: e0186298

Arroyo-García, Rosa, Leonor Ruiz-Garcia, Laurence Bolling, R. Ocete, M. Lopez, Claire Arnold, A. Ergul, G. Söylemezoğlu, Ibrahim Uzun, F. Cabello, Javier Ibáñez, Malli Aradhya, Atanas Atanassov, Ivan Atanassov, S. Ballintt, Jose L. Cenis, Laura Costantini, S. Goris-Lavets, M. S. Grando, Benjamin Y. Klein, Patrick E. McGovern, Didier Merdinoglu, Ivan Pejic, Pelsy Frédérique, N. Primikirios, V. Rrisovannaya, Kalliopi Roubelakis-Angelakis, Hager Snoussi, P. Sotiri, Shubhada Tamhankar, Patrice This, L. Troshin, J. M. Malpica, François Lefort, and J. M. Martinez-Zapater. 2006. 'Multiple Origins of Cultivated Grapevine (*Vitis vinifera* L. ssp. *sativa*) Based on Chloroplast DNA Polymorphisms', *Molecular Ecology*, 15: 3707–14

Bakels, Corrie. 2002. 'Plant Remains from Sardinia, Italy, with Notes on Barley and Grape', *Vegetation History and Archaeobotany*, 11: 3–8

Bartoloni, Gilda, and Filippo Delpino (eds). 2005. *Oriente e Occidente: metodi e discipline a confronto; riflessioni sulla cronologia dell'età del ferro in Italia; atti dell'incontro di studi, Roma, 30–31 ottobre 2003* (Pisa: Istituti editoriali e poligrafici internazionali)

Bartoloni, Gilda, Valeria Acconcia, and Silvia ten Kortenaar. 2012. 'Viticoltura e consumo del vino in Etruria: la cultura materiale tra la fine dell'età del Ferro e l'Orientalizzante Antico', in *Archeologia della vite e del vino in Toscana e nel Lazio: dalle tecniche dell'indagine archeologica alle prospettive della biologia molecolare*, ed. by Andrea Ciacci, Paolo Rendini, and Andrea Zifferero (Florence: Edizioni all'Insegna del Giglio), pp. 201–75

Bats, Michel. 2012. 'Les Phocéens, Marseille et la Gaule (VIIe-IIIe s. av. J.-C.)', in *Les diasporas grecques du VIIIe à la fin du IIIe siècle av. J.-C.*, ed. by Laurianne Martinez-Sève, Pallas, 89 (Toulouse: Presses universitaires du Midi), pp. 145–56

Bernal, Martin. 1987. *Black Athena*, I: *The Fabrication of Ancient Greece* (New Brunswick: Rutgers University Press)

Bianco, Giuliana, Sara Ganafei, Fabio Colivicchi, Tommaso Cataldi, and Alessandro Buchicchio. 2015. 'Ancient Pottery from Archaeological Sites in Southern Italy: First Evidence of Red Grape Product Markers', *European Journal of Mass Spectrometry*, 21: 693–99

Bietti Sestieri, Anna Maria. 1997. 'Italy in Europe in the Early Iron Age', *Proceedings of the Prehistoric Society*, 63: 371–402

Bietti Sestieri, Anna Maria, Alberto Cazzella, and Alain Schnapp. 2002. 'The Mediterranean', in *Archaeology: The Widening Debate*, ed. by Barry Cunliffe, Wendy Davies, and Colin Renfrew (Oxford: Oxford University Press for the British Academy), pp. 411–38

Botto, Massimo. 2016. 'La produzione del vino in Sardegna tra Sardi e Fenici: lo stato della ricerca', *Rivista di storia dell'agricoltura*, 56: 79–96

Bouby, Laurent, and Philippe Marinval. 2001. 'La vigne et les débuts de la viticulture en France: apports de l'archéobotanique', *Gallia*, 58: 13–28

Braconi, Paolo. 2006. 'La vite maritata all'albero', in *Vino: tra mito e cultura*, ed. by Maria Grazia Marchetti Lungarotti and Mario Torelli (Milan: Skira), pp. 55–62

Brandherm, Dirk, and Martin Trachsel (eds). 2008. *A New Dawn for the Dark Age? Shifting Paradigms in Mediterranean Iron Age Chronology* (Oxford: Archaeopress)

Brun, Jean-Pierre. 2011. 'La produzione del vino in Magna Grecia e in Sicilia', in *La vigna di Dionisio: vite, vino e culti in Magna Grecia; atti del quarantanovesimo convegno di studi sulla Magna Grecia, Taranto, 24–28 settembre 2009*, ed. by Mario Lombardo and others (Taranto: Istituto per la storia e l'archeologia della Magna Grecia), pp. 95–142

Brun, Jean-Pierre, and Fanette Laubenheimer (eds). 2001. 'La viticulture en Gaule', *Gallia*, 58: 1–260

Bundrick, Sheramy D. 2019. *Athens, Etruria, and the Many Lives of Greek Figured Pottery* (Madison: University of Wisconsin Press)

Carpenter, Thomas. 1991. *Art and Myth in Ancient Greece: A Handbook* (London: Thames & Hudson)

Cazanove, Olivier de. 1991. 'Θεὸς ἐν ἀσκῷ. Osservazioni sui meccanismi di trasmissione della figura di Dionysos all'Italia centrale arcaica', in *Dionysos: mito e mistero; atti del convegno internazionale Comacchio 3–5 novembre 1989*, ed. by Fede Berti (Ferrara: Liberty House), pp. 171–84

Celestino, Sebastián, and Carolina López-Ruiz. 2016. *Tartessos and the Phoenicians in Iberia* (Oxford: Oxford University Press)

Cicirelli, Claudia, Claude Albore Livadie, and Karl-Uwe Heussner. 2008. 'Stato delle ricerche a Longola di Poggiomarino: quadro insediamentale e problematiche', in *Nuove ricerche archeologiche nell'area vesuviana (scavi 2003–2006): atti del convegno internazionale, Rome 1–3 febbraio 2007*, ed. by Pier Giovanni Guzzo and Maria Paola Guidobaldi (Rome: L'Erma di Bretschneider), pp. 473–91

Colivicchi, Fabio. 2004. 'L'altro vino. Vino, cultura e identità nella Puglia e Basilicata anelleniche', *Siris*, 5: 23–68

——. 2014. '"Native" Vase Shapes in South-Italian Red-Figure Pottery', in *The Italic People of Ancient Apulia: New Evidence from Pottery for Workshops, Markets, and Customs*, ed. by Thomas H. Carpenter, Kathleen M. Lynch, and Edward G. D. Robinson (Cambridge: Cambridge University Press), pp. 213–42

Colonna, Giovanni. 1980. 'Graeco more bibere: l'iscrizione della tomba 115 dell'Osteria dell'Osa', in *Archeologia Laziale*, III: *Terzo incontro di studio del Comitato per l'archeologia laziale*, ed. by Stefania Quilici Gigli, Quaderni del Centro di studio per l'archeologia etrusco-italica, 4 (Rome: Consiglio nazionale delle ricerche), pp. 51–55

De Angelis, Franco. 2009. 'Colonies and Colonization', in *The Oxford Handbook of Hellenic Studies*, ed. by George Boys-Stones, Barbara Graziosi, and Phiroze Vasunia (Oxford: Oxford University Press), pp. 48–64

——. 2016. '*E pluribus unum*: The Multiplicity of Models', in *Conceptualising Early Colonisation*, ed. by Lieve Donnellan, Valentino Nizzo, and Gert-Jan Burgers, Contextualising Early Colonisation, 2 (Turnhout: Brepols), pp. 97–104

——. 2022. 'New Data and Old Narratives: Migrants and the Conjoining of the Cultures and Economies of the Pre-Roman Western Mediterranean', in *Homo migrans: Modeling Mobility and Migration in Human History*, ed. by Megan J. Daniels (Albany: State University of New York Press), pp. 95–109

De Francesco, Antonino. 2013. *The Antiquity of the Italian Nation: The Cultural Origins of a Political Myth in Modern Italy, 1796–1943* (Oxford: Oxford University Press)

de'Siena, Stefano. 2012. *Il vino nel mondo antico: archeologia e cultura di una bevanda speciale* (Modena: Mucchi)

Dietler, Michael, and Carolina López-Ruiz (eds). 2009a. *Colonial Encounters in Ancient Iberia: Phoenician, Greek, and Indigenous Relations* (Chicago: University of Chicago Press)

——. 2009b. 'Ex Oriente Lux: A Preface', in *Colonial Encounters in Ancient Iberia: Phoenician, Greek, and Indigenous Relations*, ed. by Michael Dietler and Carolina López-Ruiz (Chicago: University of Chicago Press), pp. vii–xiii

Echevarría Sánchez, Alejandra, and Juan Carlos Vera Rodríguez. 2015. 'Los inicios de la viticultura en la Península Ibérica a partir de las huellas de cultivo', in *Historia y arqueología en la cultura del vino*, ed. by Rafael Francia Verde (Logroño: Instituto de Estudios Riojanos), pp. 57–68

Fletcher, Richard N. 2007. *Patterns of Imports in Iron Age Italy*, British Archaeological Reports, International Series, 1732 (Oxford: Archaeopress)

Ford Russell, Brigette. 2003. 'Wine, Women, and the *polis*: Gender and the Formation of the City-State in Archaic Rome', *Greece & Rome*, 50: 77–84

Frankel, Rafael. 2012. 'Ancient Technologies: Complete vs. Conceptual Transfer', *Tel Aviv*, 39: 115–26

Gailledrat, Eric. 2015. 'New Perspectives on Emporia in the Western Mediterranean: Greeks, Etruscans and Native Populations at the Mouth of the Lez (Hérault, France) during the Sixth-Fifth Centuries BC', *Journal of Mediterranean Archaeology*, 28: 23–50

González de Canales, Fernando, Aurelio Montaño, and Jorge Llompart. 2020. 'The Beginnings of Grape Cultivation in the Iberian Peninsula: A Reappraisal after the Huelva (Southwestern Spain) Archaeological Finds and New Radiocarbon Datings', *Revista Onoba*, 8: 35–42

Gorton, Luke. 2017. 'Revisiting Indo-European "Wine"', *Journal of Indo-European Studies*, 45: 1–26

Gras, Michel. 1983. 'Vin et société à Rome et dans le Latium à l'époque archaïque', in *Modes de contacts et processus de transformation dans les sociétés anciennes: actes du colloque de Cortone (24–30 mai 1981)*, ed. by Pierre Lévêque and Georges Vallet (Rome: École française de Rome), pp. 1067–75

Guidi, Alessandro. 1998. 'The Emergence of the State in Central and Northern Italy', *Acta archaeologica*, 69: 139–61

——. 2008. 'Archeologia dell'Early State: il caso di studio italiano', *Ocnus*, 16: 175–92

Helwing, Barbara. 2017. 'A Comparative View on Metallurgical Innovations in South-Western Asia: What Came First?', in *Appropriating Innovations: Entangled Knowledge in Eurasia, 5000–1500 BCE*, ed. by Philipp W. Stockhammer and Joseph Maran (Oxford: Oxbow), pp. 161–70

Hobden, Fiona. 2013. *The Symposion in Ancient Greek Society and Thought* (Cambridge: Cambridge University Press)

Hodos, Tamar. 2010. 'Globalization and Colonization: A View from Iron Age Sicily', *Journal of Mediterranean Archaeology*, 23: 81–106

——. 2020. *The Archaeology of the Mediterranean Iron Age: A Globalising World c. 1100–600 BCE* (Cambridge: Cambridge University Press)

Horden, Peregrine, and Nicholas Purcell. 2000. *The Corrupting Sea: A Study of Mediterranean History* (Oxford: Blackwell)

Iaia, Cristiano. 2006. 'Servizi cerimoniali e da simposio in bronzo del primo Ferro in Italia centro-settentrionale', in *La ritualità funeraria tra età del ferro e orientalizzante in Italia: atti del convegno, Verucchio 26–27 giugno 2002*, ed. by Patrizia von Eles (Pisa: Fabrizio Serra), pp. 103–10

Komar, Paulina. 2021. 'Wine Taboo regarding Women in Archaic Rome, Origins of Italian Viticulture, and the Taste of Ancient Wines', *Greece & Rome*, 68: 239–54

Liverani, Mario. 2017. 'Conservative versus Innovative Cultural Areas in the Near East ca. 800–400 BC', in *Eurasia at the Dawn of History: Urbanization and Social Change*, ed. by Manuel Fernández-Götz and Dirk Krausse (Cambridge: Cambridge University Press), pp. 198–210

López-Ruiz, Carolina. 2021. *Phoenicians and the Making of the Mediterranean* (Cambridge, MA: Harvard University Press)

Marchetti Lungarotti, Maria Grazia, and Mario Torelli (eds). 2006. *Vino: tra mito e cultura* (Milan: Skira)

Martinelli, Maurizio. 1984. 'Per il dossier dei nomi etruschi di vasi: una nuova iscrizione ceretana del VII secolo a.C.', *Bollettino d'arte*, 27: 49–54

Marvelli, Silvia, S. de'Siena, Elisabetta Rizzoli, and Marco Marchesini. 2013. 'The Origin of Grapevine Cultivation in Italy: The Archaeobotanical Evidence', *Annali di botanica*, 3: 155–63

McGovern, Patrick, Benjamin Luley, Nuria Rovira, Armen Mirzoian, Michael Callahan, Karen Smith, Gretchen Hall, Theodore Davidson, and Joshua Henkin. 2013. 'Beginning of Viniculture in France', *Proceedings of the National Academy of Sciences of the United States of America*, 110.25: 10147–52

Mitterlechner, Tina. 2021. *Das Bankett: Ein Bildmotiv zwischen Diesseits und Jenseits im vorrömischen Italien (8.-2./1. Jh. v. Chr.)* (Vienna: Holzhausen)

Montelius, Oscar. 1899. *Der Orient und Europa: Einfluss der orientalischen Cultur auf Europa bis zur Mitte des letzten Jahrtausends v. Chr.*, trans. by Johanna Mestorf (Stockholm: Kungl. Hofboktryckeriet)

Morel, Jean-Paul. 1984. 'Greek Colonization in Italy and the West (Problems of Evidence and Interpretation', in *Crossroads of the Mediterranean*, ed. by Tony Hackens, Nancy D. Holloway, and R. Ross Holloway (Providence: Brown University, Center for Old World Archaeology and Art), pp. 123–61

Morris, Ian. 2013. *The Measure of Civilization: How Social Development Decides the Fate of Nations* (Princeton: Princeton University Press)

Nijboer, Albert J. 2005. 'The Iron Age in the Mediterranean: A Chronological Mess or "Trade before the Flag", Part II', *Ancient West and East*, 4: 255–77

Osborne, Robin. 2009. *Greece in the Making, 1200–479 BC*, 2nd edn (London: Routledge)

Payne, Humfry. 1931. *Necrocorinthia: A Study of Corinthian Art in the Archaic Period* (Oxford: Oxford University Press)

Pérez Jordà, Guillem. 2015. 'El cultivo de la vid y la producción de vino en la Península Ibérica durante el I milenio ane', in *Historia y arqueología en la cultura del vino*, ed. by Rafael Francia Verde (Logroño: Instituto de Estudios Riojanos), pp. 47–55

Riva, Corinna. 2017. 'Wine Production and Exchange and the Value of Wine Consumption in Sixth-Century BC Etruria', *Journal of Mediterranean Archaeology*, 30: 237–61

Riva, Corinna, and Nicholas C. Vella. 2006. 'Introduction', in *Debating Orientalization: Multidisciplinary Approaches to Change in the Ancient Mediterranean*, ed. by Corinna Riva and Nicholas C. Vella (London: Equinox), pp. 1–20

Torelli, Mario. 2000. 'I Greci nel Tirreno: un bilancio', *Scienze dell'antichità*, 10: 383–93

——. 2006. 'Vino greco e vino etrusco, vini speziati e vini indigeni', in *Vino: tra mito e cultura*, ed. by Maria Grazia Marchetti Lungarotti and Mario Torelli (Milan: Skira), pp. 33–39

Van Limbergen, Dimitri, Patrick Monsieur, and Frank Vermeulen. 2017. 'The Role of Overseas Export and Local Consumption Demand in the Development of Viticulture in Central-Adriatic Italy (200 BC–AD 150). The Case of the Ager Potentinus and the Wider Potenza Valley', in *The Economic Integration of Roman Italy: Rural Communities in a Globalising World*, ed. by Tymon C. A. de Haas and Gijs Tol, Mnemosyne Supplement, 404 (Leiden: Brill), pp. 342–66

Webster, Gary S. 2016. *The Archaeology of Nuragic Sardinia*, Monographs in Mediterranean Archaeology, 14 (London: Equinox)

Zohary, Daniel, Maria Hopf, and Ehud Weiss. 2012. *Domestication of Plants in the Old World*, 4th edn (Oxford: Oxford University Press)

4. The World Has Changed

Insularity and Tyrrhenian Connectivity during the Corsican Iron Ages

ABSTRACT 'No man is an island', wrote John Donne in his famous poem arguing against isolationism. But what about being an island in a connected and multipolar world? This chapter explores such a situation. The last few decades have seen a marked shift in the perception of Bronze and Iron Age Corsica in the context of the Tyrrhenian Sea, where external connections had previously been seen to be limited to Alalia/Aleria. The recent analyses of existing data from economic areas, settlements, various kinds of craftsmanship, mines, and metal artefacts, coupled with new metallurgical data from neighbouring regions (Etruria, Elba, and Phoenician settlements), have raised significant questions about the role of Corsican communities in the dynamic Tyrrhenian landscape between the fourth and third centuries BCE. Indeed, an increasing number of archaeological surveys relating to the Iron Age have occurred since 2000, as well as the revisiting of previous findings and data from former work (mostly unpublished), which have shed new light on these insular, yet not isolated, societies. Moreover, the current globalization of scientific thinking has played a significant role in the development of new approaches (including such scholars as Rainbird, Purcell, and Horden). As a result, innovative perspectives about the concepts of fragmentation and Mediterranean connectivity have been offered. This chapter aims to explore these issues in relation to Corsica through the investigation of material and immaterial transmission.

Early Iron Age Corsica sits at a metaphorical crossroads in more ways than one. Physically, it was situated at a key nexus of communication and movement, at the northern end of the Tyrrhenian Sea. As such, although an island and thus (at least theoretically) prone to a degree of insularity and isolation, it also served as a vital part of the wider connective, maritime networks which bound the ancient Mediterranean together. Conceptually, Iron Age Corsica also occupies a liminal space. Long thought to represent either a harsh cultural backwater or the nadir of the transition between the more well-known and attested cultures of the Bronze Age and the Classical periods, new data is increasingly challenging these notions — although the resultant picture is arguably no less confusing.

A few introductory remarks are needed, before going further in this brief attempt to define the relationships between Corsican communities and the wider region (especially Italy) during the Iron Age. First, this research builds upon a long tradition of related studies. In particular, the present chapter relies upon the seminal work of Fernand Braudel, and specifically his 1985/1986 *Méditerranée*, which brilliantly demonstrated that an environment can be described according to the highest standards in Humanities and Social Sciences without losing its poetry (Braudel 1985; 1986). With regards to the archaeology of islands in the ancient Mediterranean, this study is indebted to Michel Gras's *Trafics tyrrhéniens archaïques*, which has shown the significant role played by Sardinia and Sicily in the dynamic and connected Mediterranean Sea (Gras 1985). Between them, these studies have laid the foundations of the connected approach, fully relevant for these chronological and cultural areas. However, together with a renewed scientific approach for the archaeological and historical data, there is still much to be done, most notably with regards to the perception of an 'island' itself (Evans 1977; Boomert and Bright 2007; Broodbank 2018). In addition to sharing similar Latin roots, notions of 'island' and 'isolation' often carry negative associations, even subconsciously. The words may suggest disconnected, constricted, impoverished, and lonely or deserted worlds; modern European literature likely

Corresponding author Marine Lechenault (Marine.Lechenault@univ-lyon2.fr)

Adoption, Adaption, and Innovation in Pre-Roman Italy: Paradigms for Cultural Change, ed. by Jeremy Armstrong and Aaron Rhodes-Schroder, AMW 3 (Turnhout, 2023), pp. 59–70

has much to do with this. This trend in literature has been well identified and analysed (Rainbird 1999) and must be taken into account when considering Bronze and Iron Age island archaeology. However, there is hope. Over the past two decades, island studies (especially in the Mediterranean) have benefited immensely from the recent shift in focus towards maritime connectivity, which was pushed into the mainstream by Horden and Purcell's 2000 volume *The Corrupting Sea*. Twenty years later, Corsica, in particular, is ready for a reinterpretation.

Context, Sources, Search History, and Scientific Challenges

Corsica is the fourth largest island in the Mediterranean in terms of area (8722 km²). It is located in the western Mediterranean, 164 km south of the Côte d'Azur, 40 km west of Elba Island, 83 km west of Tuscany, and 13 km north of Sardinia. Due to its mountainous topography (2706 m above sea level at Monte Cintu), and depending on the weather conditions, reciprocal visibility can exist between Corsica, Tuscany, and Sardinia. Travel time is a single day when sailing from Corsica to Liguria or Tuscany. Corsica is located at a closing point for the north-western Tyrrhenian basin, which is formed by the western coast of Italy, the Calabrian peninsula, Sicily, and Sardinia. The Tyrrhenian Sea exists as a discrete maritime area, with localized phenomena, and represented a privileged area for exchange dynamics from the Bronze Age, reaching a peak during the Iron Age (Peche-Quilichini 2015; forthcoming (b)). Consequently, Corsica's role and importance must first be understood through a maritime perspective, in both ancient and modern times (Taddei 2003, 18).

The island of Corsica is mentioned by ancient Greek authors using the name Kurnos (e.g. Hecataeus of Miletus, XL; Hdt. I. 164–67; Pseudo-Scylax, *Periplus*, VI. 7), and by the Romans, using the name Kursikè or Corsica (e.g. Diod. Sic. V. 60; Strabo V. 2. 7; Plin., *HN*, III. 6. 80; Paus. XVII. 8 and XVII. 11). Written sources generally describe Corsica as a tough land, populated by tough people. Diodorus, Strabo, and Seneca — to list only the major commentators — mention scarce resources, an outdated economy, and savage behaviours. In brief, Corsica is described as a hostile and uninteresting land, which struggled to connect with the rest of the ancient world. This distorted picture, although increasingly common from the reign of the emperor Augustus, goes against the efforts made by the Greeks, the Etruscans, the Carthaginians, and the Romans themselves to 'conquer' Corsican coasts. During times of exploration,

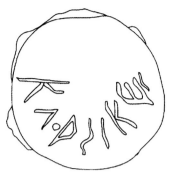

Figure 4.1. Graffito KURSIKE from Populonia (after Maggiani 1999).

networking, and colonization, controlling trading points and strategic gateways, like those located on and around Corsica, would have been crucial. The economy stands as the main driving force of this attention, although always imbued with strong social and cultural resonances, forming the solid indigenous bedrock of local Iron Age communities. Indeed, the more one looks, the more evidence that can be found which problematizes the bleak perspective of Corsica found in explicit descriptions. For instance, there are foundation myths that link the Corsicans to the Etruscans, including one which attributes the settlement of Populonia to Corsicans. On this point, it is interesting to note this graffito (Fig. 4.1), discovered in Populonia, where the word KURSIKE appears (Maggiani 1999, 55). Although not conclusive, its presence is suggestive of a long-standing relationship.

The Corsican Iron Age has remained obscure and undefined for a long time, stuck between two 'Golden Ages' of Corsican archaeology: the Bronze Age 'Torrean civilization' on the one hand, and Alalia/Aleria's early antiquity on the other hand. Sandwiched between these two periods, the Corsican Iron Age has been reduced to a transitional period, characterized by a degradation of the previous features as well as bringing the first signs of the next period's initiatives. This denigration, which was partly based on the interpretations of ancient literary sources, has only recently begun to be revised in the aftermath of work carried out in the 1990s and 2000s. During this period, new research programmes explored questions such as settlement (Peche-Quilichini 2014a, 5–6; Milanini 2017, 42), necropoleis (Milanini 1998, 11; 2004, 238–39), and production/consumption (especially pottery and metal goods, see Peche-Quilichini 2014b, 185; Lechenault 2020, 24–28). The result of this work has been a complete rejection of the previous model, and a new interpretative framework which emphasizes the original and complex character of the Corsican Iron Age. However, with this new model comes new questions, including those related to the settlement strategy, exploitation modes, and territorial organization, architecture, funerary practices, production *modus operandi*, economic processes, etc. The rest of this chapter will explore how these new questions are shaped by Iron Age Corsica's relationship with peninsular Italy, focusing on the mechanisms and consequences of exchanges: the convergence, transfer of tradition, and circulation of materials or finished products, that make the Tyrrhenian area such a dynamic space.

The Early, or 'First', Iron Age (900–550 BCE) and the North/South Divergences

The Corsican Iron Age, which lasted from *c.* 900 to 100 BCE, has been subdivided into a number of periods based on radiometric and stylistic data. In general, the beginning of the Early Iron Age, or First Iron Age, in Corsica is usually placed between 900 BCE (based on evidence in the north) and 850 BCE (based on evidence in the south), following the last stages of the Final Bronze Age, which was mostly evidenced in the valleys of southern Corsica. Recent models have tried to split the Early/First Iron Age into still more periods (EIA-A and EIA-B), especially in the south (Peche-Quilichini 2014a, 209). The middle of sixth century BCE, marked by the establishment of Alalia's colony and the sea battle that led to the Phoceans' departure, stands as the division between the First and Second Corsican Iron Ages. The Second Corsican Iron Age is split into three stages (A: 550–400 BCE; B: 400–250 BCE; C: 250–100 BCE). Stage C, in particular, is seen as something of a transitional period, with Corsica existing under a wider Roman hegemony during this period, and so also equates to both the Hellenistic and late Republican periods of Greek and Roman chronologies. Most notably, this final stage coincides with the First Punic War (264–241 BCE) and with the moving of Marius's veterans to the new Roman colony, Mariana (*c.* 100/99 BCE), on the island — marking a phase of massively increased interaction and influence between the island and the mainland.

For a long time, the so-called 'survival' or perseverance of Final Bronze Age features on the island has been highlighted to characterize the conservative and traditional nature of Early Iron Age Corsican society (Jehasse and Jehasse 1982, 13; Camps 1999, 29). However, this conception is heavily influenced by gaps in the record for indigenous contexts from the ninth to sixth centuries BCE, making change difficult to see. Revisiting legacy data, notably from funerary contexts, and exploring domestic contexts through new archaeological surveys have allowed us to revise our models.

Regarding Early Iron Age settlements in southern Corsica, there is no denying that second-millennium fortifications were abandoned in favour of a new model, based on open villages, composed of seven–ten houses (maximum twenty-five), settled on plateaus, such as at Curciupula, Nuciaresa, or Cozza Torta. The middle of these EIA settlements almost always included a circular structure (*c.* 14 m diameter), which has been dubbed a *rotonde*. This kind of building, none of which has been excavated so far, may have played a public or civic role. The houses of this period have elliptical shapes, visible in the massive, raised blocks used for their foundations. They are designed with two lengthwise naves covered by a peaked roof. The load-bearing posts suggest one or more storeys in height. The internal area is then further organized into two or three rooms, which include, systematically, a circular fireplace. This kind of house shows a clear connection and evolution from earlier architectural models present at the end of the Bronze Age.

These settlement strategies show that new socio-economic considerations were emerging (Peche-Quilichini and Cesari forthcoming). Although continuity can be demonstrated by typologies, architecture, and domestic organization, the reduced average footprint (*c.* 20 m²) and increased number of houses show that significant change occurred in the nature of domestic structures within settlements (Salvà and Peche-Quilichini forthcoming). Our picture is, admittedly, far from complete though. Much of our evidence for this period comes from southern Corsica. In central and northern Corsica, it has been observed that settlements were focused on more defensive sites (e.g. E Mizane). Additionally, the shapes of houses and architecture are largely unknown. This absence of evidence may be explained by the generalized use of perishable materials, such as unbaked earth. Still, in certain cases, substructures made of massive blocks have been found.

While evidence for settlements is variable, one type of evidence which appears consistently throughout the microregions of Corsica during the Early Iron Age is mortuary evidence, and especially that which uses natural cavities (for example at l'Ordinacciu, Teppa di Lucciana, Cagnano, Acciola, etc.). At this stage, it is important to specify that the notion of 'microregion' here means a subdividing of the regional, insular area into smaller territorial entities that can be defined according to geographical, historical, and cultural (including linguistic) criteria. This idea aligns with Horden and Purcell's idea of Mediterranean connectivity, and many of the principles outlined by Armstrong and Rhodes-Schroder in the Introduction to this volume. It implies an

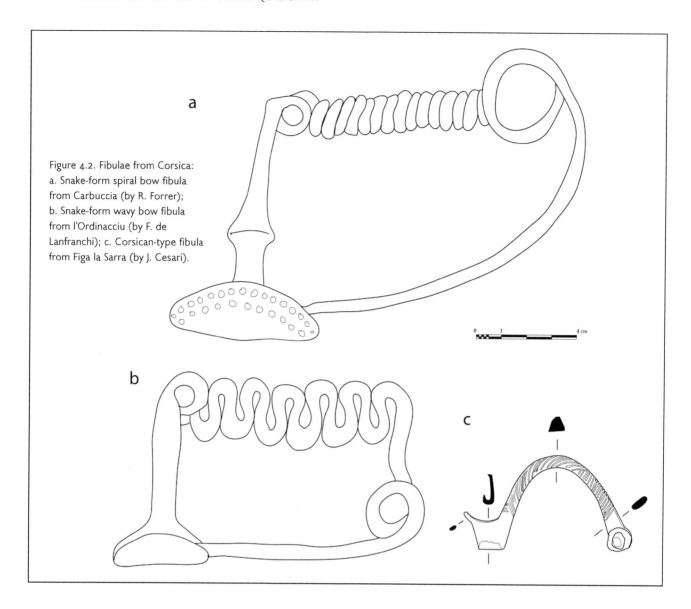

Figure 4.2. Fibulae from Corsica: a. Snake-form spiral bow fibula from Carbuccia (by R. Forrer); b. Snake-form wavy bow fibula from l'Ordinacciu (by F. de Lanfranchi); c. Corsican-type fibula from Figa la Sarra (by J. Cesari).

in-depth understanding of local forces before proposing further global interpretations. Through the rest of the chapter, we hope to demonstrate how far this kind of approach may be relevant in Corsica.

In the north, sepulchral sets include pottery and bronze artefacts, including fibulae (Fig. 4.2). These fibulae consistently show an Italic typology, most often related to Villanovan models, or connected with what is commonly considered to be the 'orientalizing', and then 'Etruscan', types: fibulae with *occhielli*, snake-shaped type, *a gomito*, *a navicella*, *a sanguisuga*, Certosa, etc., aligning with contemporary customs in mainland Italy. The other categories of metallic objects, such as dishes and *simpula*, are more infrequent, but also show connections with Etruscan society. There is also evidence for trade with Carthaginians or Phoenicians, mainly in the form of glass beads. Local Corsican products are also well represented. In the south, pottery is also found in graves but, interestingly, fibulae are completely absent, as are any objects corresponding to either Villanovan or Etruscan typologies. The rare bronze artefacts which are found are all of local manufacture and style, or evoke the repertoires of late Nuragic Sardinia, like the conical bronze buttons.

In the Early Iron Age there is, therefore, across a range of evidence types, a north–south divide. This distinction is visible in both costume and practice, and especially in the influence of exogenous traditions, where the north seems to be oriented towards Etruria, while the south was both more autonomous and oriented towards Sardinia. In this context, it is also important to emphasize that Sardinia maintained direct and privileged relations with Villanovan Italy, as evidenced by the numerous Nuragic *bronzetti* present in mainland Italian necropoleis — although this does not seem to have been transmitted, via Sardinia, to Corsica. In all cases, metallurgy is the main, and often only, type of evidence which seems to have been influenced by connections with Etruria, while pottery is almost completely absent from Corsica — except, as will be discussed below, in Alalia.

Given this interesting set of connections and influences, another striking fact is that the number of fibulae in Sardinia declines throughout the first millennium BCE, whereas Corsican fibulae can be found in ever-increasing numbers, despite fewer archaeological explorations in the latter (Lechenault 2012, 104–05). In the beginning of the Iron Age, fibulae are often the only metallic good found in the funeral sets. Furthermore, many local types of fibulae have been identified in Corsica from the eighth to fifth centuries BCE, in marked contrast to the situation in Sardinia. Corsican fibulae are also found outside of Corsica itself (see below). That suggests fundamental differences between Sardinian and Corsican communities and their external relationships, despite both existing on islands in the Tyrrhenian Sea. Some have also theorized that fibulae were used as identity markers, and may have been openly worn so that an individual's geographic origins could be understood by all.

It must be noted, however, that our knowledge of funerary practices will always be limited by the acidity of Corsican soils and its impact on preservation. Some contexts preserve human remains buried in decubitus positions, often surrounded by reductions located in the cavity's corners. A few cremations are also suspected (Milanini 1998, 28–29). Even if assemblages show commonalities with continental Italy's funerary practices, the cremations which form one of the hallmarks of Villanovan society seem to be missing here. In addition, no real equivalent to the numerous and more recent Etruscan *hypogea* can be found on the island, except of course in the fifth-century graves of Alalia, which are the most significant Etruscan funerary assemblage discovered outside Italy. In the Second Corsican Iron Age (550–100 BCE), few changes occur in the funerary practices, especially in the north, and natural cavities are still used for this purpose. However, a major evolution is visible in southern Corsica. From this period, a fibula is often included within graves. As noted above, this kind of ornament was usually missing during the First Iron Age.

Pottery, so often the mainstay of these sorts of studies, is generally less important in Corsica due to its relative paucity. However, in general, the evidence that does exist follows the same basic patterns outlined above. The material production can be defined by significant regionalization of processes.

Indeed, this is more visible for pottery than other artefact types, as the typological distribution shows a deep dichotomy between northern and southern areas (Peche-Quilichini and others forthcoming). Influences from mainland Italy, especially Etruria, are visible in Final Bronze Age pottery practices (Peche-Quilichini forthcoming (a)), while Early Iron Age pottery shows a fundamentally local stylistic evolution, without evidence of any external influence. The Early Iron Age pottery is, however, related to the technical and stylistic Final Bronze Age tradition, as shown by the recurrence of low specimens or flared neck jars. In southern Corsica, typical Nuciaresa pottery derives from the Final Bronze Age Apazzu-Castidetta-Cucuruzzu style (Peche-Quilichini 2014b, 210–11). From the eighth century BCE, types change rapidly in this region: profiles' segmentations get smoother, low specimens get rarer, closed vessels get more numerous, and decoration appears. Among the latter, the most significant are little incisions (so-called 'rice grain' incisions), placed in rows. The occurrence of figurative items, such as handles in the shape of animal heads (notably cattle, rams, or *mouflon* sheep), are also evident. The pottery that carries such decoration is only evidenced in ritually charged contexts, such as foundation deposits and graves. Interestingly, then, from a metaphorical and cultural point of view, Early Iron Age Corsica should not be considered as a single island but as a closed archipelago with two or three distinct zones.

Finally, we should consider metals and mineral deposits. 'Metals make the world go round', Christopher Pare (2000) wrote. This is particularly relevant in the case of the island of Elba. Despite its small size, Elba may have appeared as a giant iron mine, rising from the waves, from Etruscan and Roman points of view, providing the raw materials for the production of tools, architectural materials, or arms and armour. Both funerary practices and material culture suggest an exploration of the role of metals in northern Corsica is warranted (esp. Cape, Nebbiu, Balagna, Castagniccia, Niolu). Northern Corsica was connected to the Etruscan metallurgical systems and networks from as early as the eighth century BCE (Lechenault 2020, 56). As the Iron Age progressed, Corsica arguably developed a true 'culture of metals', with a significant increase in the production and storage of metallic goods. According to the evidence available to date, however, southern Corsica does not seem to have joined this movement. The metal goods well-known in the north, such as fibulae and annular jewellery, were either largely absent or late in arriving in the south. Political and economic divergences have been proposed to explain

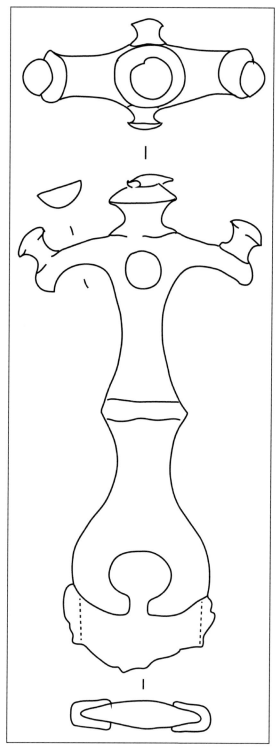

Figure 4.3. Corsican knife/short sword from Paestum (by S. Verger).

dem with that. Frustratingly, however, the contexts of production are largely unknown. Only the beginning of the period offers up any evidence for crucibles and stone or baked earth casting moulds, and there is some limited evidence of slag, revealing the presence of workshops. Throughout the First Iron Age, several pieces hint at the introduction of lost wax techniques (Milanini 2013, 757–59), perhaps from Sardinia, to produce weapons and ornaments. In this framework, it must also be noted that the first iron artefacts known are dated to the second half of eighth century BCE (Cuciurpula). These artefacts are mostly tools (knives), but we also see changes in technical elements. According to the current state of knowledge, the introduction of this new metal to the island, and its related *chaînes opératoires*, seems to occur far later than in Etruria.

Finally, moving on to metallurgy from this period, the lack of work in this area limits what can be said. However, as previously explained, the 'culture of metals' seems to have reached northern Corsica by the very first stages of Iron Age, with an increase in the production of metal artefacts shaped by both local and external influences. Both hammering and lost wax techniques are visible in the bronze production. Regarding the Early Iron Age, red-toned items have led scholars to wonder whether arsenic was included in copper alloys, especially as a substitute for tin (Lechenault 2020, 21). If correct, this may shed new light on western European and Mediterranean metal routes. In any case, this feature seems to disappear from the artefacts in the following centuries. The Early Iron Age is also marked by the introduction of iron, in small quantities, in artefacts, for instance in the knife from Cagnano (*c.* eighth century BCE). Still in Cagnano, iron is later evidenced in the barb of a Certosa fibula (fifth century BCE).

Refining the typology and definition of Corsican artefacts and assemblages more accurately also allows us to recognize such objects outside of the island. We have seen it for Aleria. The same goes for Corsican fibulae in Populonia and Vetulonia (Maggiani 1979, 99; 1982, 62; Cygielman and Millemaci 2007, 350 sq., fig. 4, 151), in addition to the Corsican short sword identified from a sanctuary at Paestum (Verger 2000, 43–47). This eighth-century BCE blade (Fig. 4.3) belongs to a well-known Corsican series. The fibulae belong to later types, not before the fifth century BCE. Together with the *KURSIKE* inscription, these personal goods raise once again the question of human mobility in the Tyrrhenian Sea and, more specifically, in the mining sectors of Etruria. It encourages us to explore these connections further, and to compare Elban and Corsican datasets.

those different developments. A strong relationship does seem to have been built between northern Corsica and Etruria during the Early Iron Age and, as a result, the material culture of the north, as well as its social structure and practices, evolved in tan-

The Case of Alalia: The Meeting Point between Local and Overseas Populations

The testimony of Herodotus (1. 165–67) offers tantalizing hints about the political history of the island in the middle of the first millennium BCE. The historian of Halicarnassus recounted the founding of Alalia, located in the middle of the eastern coast of Corsica, by the Greeks of Phocaea in 565/563 BCE and their subsequent departure following a naval battle against a coalition of Etruscans and Carthaginians around 540 BCE. After this event, Alalia is known as an Etruscan settlement for almost three centuries. At the same time, written sources agree upon a fairly strong Carthaginian political influence, which has never been evident in the archaeology, until Roman colonization.

With the exception of some ancient levels that have been detected under the Roman town (Jehasse and Jehasse 2004, 98–100), the character of Alalia's early settlement remains unknown. Only the rich necropolis has been studied in any detail. The excavation data show a quite intensive colonization of this small coastal territory. The tombs appear as *hypogea* with *dromoi*. The majority of the known graves were discovered and excavated in the 1960s and 1970s (Jehasse and Jehasse 1973; 2001). A large number of rich tombs show clear evidence of influence from Etruscan funeral practices which seems to align with the literary narrative suggesting Etruscan domination.

Together within this wider Etruscan cultural context, however, some fifth-century graves show features that should be highlighted here: piles of rocks in front of the doors, yellow or red ochre, and reductions of bodies are described. These features are reminiscent of earlier funerary practices, well attested in southern Corsica (Milanini 1998, 20; 2004, 242). Moreover, social features like the Etruscan banquet, broadly recorded in the wider iconography of the necropolis, are never illustrated in these graves. Although far from conclusive, this hints that there may have been a far more heterogenous culture utilizing the necropolis, which not only contained the known Etruscan elements but, perhaps unsurprisingly, also contained local aspects.

It is clear there were strong connections between Etruria and Aleria. Indeed, at first sight, the city may seem to constitute an entity — at least partly — disconnected from the economic and cultural Corsican networks which were in evidence at the beginning of the Second Corsican Iron Age. On the other hand, indigenous practices and material culture, now that they are becoming better known, can

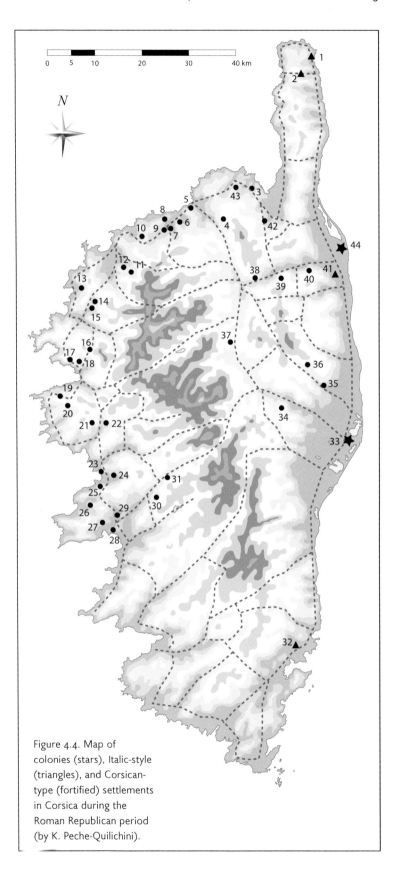

Figure 4.4. Map of colonies (stars), Italic-style (triangles), and Corsican-type (fortified) settlements in Corsica during the Roman Republican period (by K. Peche-Quilichini).

Figure 4.5. Local vessels from Alalia necropolis. Museum of Aleria, CdC.

clearly be identified in the city. It must be noted that, as the now axiomatic saying goes, 'pots are pots, not people', and these observations push the limits of what archaeology can offer in terms of ancient identity. The question of defining Aleria's communities remains fully open. However, there are clearly distinct material culture traditions in evidence, which at least challenges the existing models. The same issues surround quantifying the impact of the town, along with its Etruscan influences and connections, on the indigenous communities inland, which were typically measurable, amongst other methods, based on the amount of imported pottery found. Subtly present from the second half of the seventh century BCE, Greek, Sicilian, and Etruscan products were found in both land and sea contexts, mostly on the southern and northern Corsican coasts. Very few examples come from the mountainous regions (Nuciaresa). The rhythm of exchanges becomes quicker and richer only from 580/540 BCE, probably in connection with Tyrrhenian networks and Alalia's development. However, the true nature of the dynamic and its importance is entirely uncertain.

Late Iron Age (550–250 BCE) and Roman Republican Era (250–100 BCE): Global Flows and Microregional Discrepancies

According to all our extant ancient authors, the political situation on Corsica remained broadly unchanged until the third century BCE, when the island was annexed by Rome in the aftermath of the First Punic War, resulting in the creation of the province of *Corsica et Sardinia* (Zucca 1996, 27–31). The level of Roman influence seems to have increased during the course of the third century, most notably during and after the First and Second Punic Wars. Frustratingly, archaeology offers very little to fill in the narrative. Little is known about fifth-/fourth-century BCE Corsican settlements (and, thus, about a significant part of the economy). Information becomes richer and clearer only for the period starting from the middle of third century BCE, aligning with its annexation by Rome, and mainly for eastern and northern Corsica.

The third century BCE was an important period in the history of the island and would have had a strong impact on local populations. From the point of view of settlement patterns, it is necessary to note a strong Roman influence on the regions of the eastern coast, where small communities suddenly began to show an Italic-type urbanism. This is especially visible in the shape and the organization of rectangular domestic structures, reachable from streets and squares (I Palazzi). In the northern regions, as the map shows (Fig. 4.4), the proliferation of hillforts (Capu Mirabù, Cima à I Mori, Pulveraghja, Monte di Morta, Castellu di Luri, etc.) is evident (Peche-Quilichini forthcoming (b)).

The changing settlement patterns on the northern and eastern coasts is suggestive of a period of economic and social tension which can be related to ancient texts. It is likely that indigenous groups may have found themselves caught between more traditional Punic elements and new Roman arrivals during the third century. According to the written sources, the revolts were numerous and severely punished by Rome, which imposed executions, exile, and financial penalties levied in wood, honey, wax, and slaves (Livy XIIL.7; Diod. Sic. V.13). In the south, the situation remains unknown. The hillforts, common in earlier periods disappear, as do the coastal colonial establishments. The Carthaginian influence may have been stronger there because of the proximity to Punic Sardinia, resulting in a greater decline after Roman conquest.

At the same time that we see these clear social and cultural differences, the entire island of Corsica seems to have been within a single economic network which distributed products from mainland Italy, notably the Graeco-Italic amphorae. Black varnish pottery, in particular, seems to represent a significant and important class of imported item. Coinage also appeared in indigenous contexts during this time. The integration of Corsica into the Tyrrhenian economic space, organized from Rome, seems to begin in this period and would last for nearly seven centuries. Excavating indigenous settlements, such as I Palazzi, offers important insight into this evolution. This particular settlement flourished from 150 BCE, but was confronted only fifty years later with the establishment of the Mariana colony, located a few kilometres farther into the lowland. It is particularly interesting to notice that the ratio of local pottery to imported ware, which began at about 60 per cent of the total before the Roman veterans' arrival, goes continually down until the site's eventual abandonment at the beginning of the Augustan period. Additionally, the discovery of many imported glass beads in the Second Iron Age Corsican graves offers another example for the progressive integration of Corsica into the broad cultural and commercial Tyrrhenian ensemble.

In contrast to this growing foreign influence, other data attest to the liveliness of indigenous traditions until the beginning of the Imperial era. This is particularly the case for local ceramic production, which was still produced without the use of a potter's wheel. These vessels are made from clay mixed with asbestos and decorated with a comb (Fig. 4.5), and are believed to have served as containers for honey and beeswax (Piccardi and Peche Quilichini 2013, 706). However, due to the lack of analysis, it must be noted that these interpretations remain uncertain. The most well-known items are pitchers with

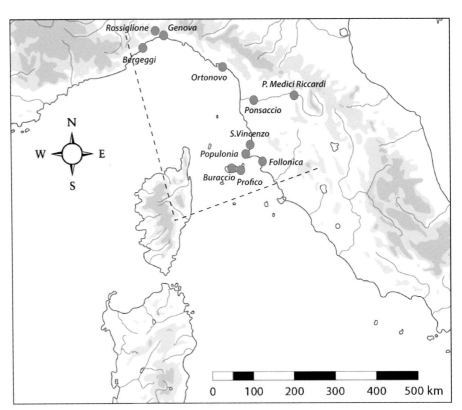

Figure 4.6. Distribution of Corsican coarse vessels in the Tyrrhenian region, first and second centuries BCE (by K. Peche-Quilichini).

a single handle, truncated bowls, flat dishes, and jars. Salt production is evidenced by one example of a bricklaying pillar. Some items carry Latin graffiti informing about their volume capacities. These rough vessels can also be found on the island of Elba, as well as all along the Etruscan and Ligurian coasts (Fig. 4.6), which probably illustrates the presence of Corsican sailors associated with the movement of freight between Corsica and the mainland. Petrographic analyses show also a production of pottery with Elban and Tuscan clays, which may reveal the presence of Corsican individuals in Etruscan trading posts (Populonia, Pisa) in the first century BCE. This aspect is reinforced by their presence in necropoleis, notably in Elba (Buraccio and Profico).

Conclusions

The relationship between ancient Corsica and Italy reveals a complex, but still not entirely understood, set of relationships and dynamics. From the human colonization of the island in the Mesolithic until the French annexation at the end of the eighteenth century, Corsican people have maintained contact with their Tyrrhenian neighbours, mainly the populations of Liguria, Tuscany, and Sardinia. Intermittent in the Neolithic, and frequent but somewhat variable in the Bronze Age, this relationship became more structured during the Iron Age, before the island was inexorably intertwined in Rome's Italic systems during the Classical period. The indigenous inhabitants of the island have variously integrated Italic initiatives and innovations, adopting, adapting, transforming, or ignoring them according to their own needs.

In the early periods, the archaeological evidence for these contacts hints that they were initially based on the desire for various raw materials and, quickly thereafter, a taste for novelty and finished items may have emerged as a means of signalling social status. From the end of the seventh century BCE, the economy of the entire island was increasingly shaped by what would now be called commercial relations. These are stronger in the eastern part of Corsica, facing Etruria. However, here again is another feature of Corsica; despite being a single island, it regularly displays a striking range of microregional discrepancies. Various causes and consequences seem to come as a result of the interest shown by these cultural and economic Italic dynamics. The few Corsican exporta-

tions known so far are not enough to explain them. In fact, more than its resources, Corsica's geographical position, in the heart of the Mediterranean's maritime networks, may be the main reason for Greek, Carthaginian, Etruscan, and, finally, Roman interest in and presence on the island. This interest and presence seem to have focused on the eastern side, with limited impact on the inland and western populations. In southern Corsica, the primary contacts with Sardinia were characterized by specific dynamics that have been less exposed here.

Due to its insular nature and the difficulties of navigation, more accentuated from one microregion to another, but also because of a topography which limits internal movement, and also because the population was sparse and dispersed there, Corsica never constituted a homogeneous land or population, and the external cultural and economic influences received a contrasted evolution there. Indeed, significant Corsican and Sardinian diasporas still exist nowadays. Archaeological analysis highlights these local specificities and offers an image of a connected and adaptive territory on the outskirts of the Tyrrhenian dynamics.

Works Cited

Boomert, Arie, and Alistair J. Bright. 2007. 'Island Archaeology: In Search of a New Horizon', *Island Studies Journal*, 2.1: 3–26

Braudel, Fernand. 1985. *La Méditerranée*, I: *L' espace et l'histoire* (Paris: Flammarion)

——. 1986. *La Méditerranée*, II: *Les hommes et l'héritage* (Paris: Flammarion)

Broodbank, Cyprian. 2018. 'Does Island Archaeology Matter?', in *Regional Approaches to Society and Complexity: Studies in Honor of John F. Cherry*, ed. by Alex R. Knodell and Thomas P. Leppard (Sheffield: Equinox), pp. 188–206

Camps, Gabriel. 1999. 'La Corse à l'Âge du fer', in *Archéologie des Celtes: mélanges offerts à la mémoire de René Joffroy*, ed. by Bruno Chaume, Jean-Pierre Mohen, and Patrick Périn (Montagnac: Mergoil), pp. 29–40

Cygielman, Mario, and Giovanni Millemaci. 2007. 'Vetulonia, via Garibaldi (Castiglione della Pescaia, GR): scavi 2003–2006', *Materiali per Populonia*, 6: 345–86

Evans, John Davies. 1977. 'Island Archaeology in the Mediterranean: Problems and Opportunities', *World Archaeology*, 9.1: 12–26

Gras, Michel. 1985. *Trafics tyrrhéniens archaïques*, Bibliothèque des Écoles françaises d'Athènes et de Rome, 258 (Paris: École française de Rome)

Horden, Peregrine, and Nicholas Purcell. 2002: *The Corrupting Sea: A Study of Mediterranean History* (Oxford: Blackwell)

Jehasse, Jean, and Laurence Jehasse. 1973. *La nécropole préromaine d'Aléria*, Supplément à Gallia, 25 (Paris: Centre national de la recherche scientifique)

——. 1981–1982. 'L'âge du Fer et les débuts de l'urbanisation en Corse', *Archeologia Corsa*, 6–7: 11–17

——. 2001. *Aléria, nouvelles données de la nécropole* (Lyon: Maison de l'Orient et de la Méditerranée)

——. 2004. *Aleria métropole: les remparts préromains et l'urbanisation romaine* (Ajaccio: Journal de la Corse)

Lechenault, Marine. 2012. 'Les fibules de l'âge du Fer corse: aspects méthodologiques et état des recherches', in *L'âge du Fer en Corse: acquis et perspectives; actes de la table ronde de Serra-di-Scopamène*, ed. by Kewin Peche-Quilichini (Ajaccio: Cuciurpula), pp. 96–106

——. 2020. *Kursikè: Traffics tyrrhéniens dans l'âge du Fer corse*, La Corse archéologique, 4 (Ajaccio: Orma)

Maggiani, Adriano. 1979. 'Urna cineraria con corredo dalla Val di Cornia. Contributo alla definizione del territorio volterrano in età ellenistica', in *Studi in onore di Enrico Fiumi* (Pisa: Pacini), pp. 99–108

——. 1982. 'Qualche osservazione sul fegato di Piacenza', *Studi etruschi*, 50: 53–88

——. 1999. 'Nuovi etnici e toponimi etruschi', in *Incontro di studi in memoria di Massimo Pallottino* (Pisa: Istituti editoriali e poligrafici internazionali), pp. 47–62

Milanini, Jean-Louis. 1998. 'La sépulture à l'Âge du Fer: acquis et problèmes', *Bulletin de la Société des sciences naturelles et historiques de la Corse*, 682–683–684: 9–31

——. 2004. 'Lieux et pratique des cultes en Corse à l'âge du Fer', *Documents d'archéologie méridionale*, 27: 237–49

——. 2013. 'Découverte de moules non permanents sur le site du premier âge du Fer de Cozza Torta (Porto-Vecchio, Corse-du-Sud)', *Bulletin de la Société préhistorique française*, 110.4: 757–60

——. 2017. 'Cozza Torta (Porto-Vecchio, Corse-du-Sud): un site indigène majeur dans les échanges méditerranéens au Premier âge du Fer', *Bulletin de la Société des sciences historiques et naturelles de la Corse*, 758–59: 41–67

Pare, Christopher. 2000. *Metals Make the World Go Round: The Supply and Circulation of Metals in Bronze Age Europe* (Oxford: Oxbow)

Peche-Quilichini, Kewin. 2014a. *Cuciurpula, un village protohistorique en Alta Rocca*, La Corse archéologique, 2 (Ajaccio: Orma)

——. 2014b. *Protohistoire d'une île: vaisselles céramiques du Bronze final et du premier âge du Fer de Corse (1200–550 av. J.-C.)*, Monographies d'archéologie méditerranéenne, 34 (Montpellier-Lattes: Édition de l'Association pour le développement de l'archéologie en Languedoc-Roussillon)

——. 2015. 'Influences, inspirations ou transferts? La question des affinités corso-toscanes dans les productions matérielles protohistoriques', in *La Corsica e Populonia: atti del XXVIII Convegno di studi etruschi ed italici*, ed. by Giovanni Camporeale and Dominique Briquel (Rome: L'Erma di Bretschneider), pp. 227–39

Peche-Quilichini, Kewin. Forthcoming (a). 'What We Did to Father. Impatto e grado di assimilazione dei repertori stilistici italici e sardi nella produzione materiale corsa dell'età del Bronzo', in *Italia tra Mediterraneo ed Europa: mobilità, interazioni e scambi; atti della LI Riunione scientifica dell'Istituto italiano di preistoria e protostoria*

Peche-Quilichini, Kewin. Forthcoming (b). 'Un pas en avant, trois pas en arrière … Les formes de l'habitat corse à la fin du second âge du Fer', in *De l'âge du Fer à l'Antiquité dans les îles-sœurs*, ed. by Kewin Peche-Quilichini and Joseph Cesari (Ajaccio: Patrimoine d'une île)

Peche-Quilichini, Kewin, and Joseph Cesari. Forthcoming. 'Sò elli è simu noi, macchjaghjoli è cappiaghji. Habitats, habitations et utilisations du territoire dans le sud de la Corse à l'âge du Bronze et au premier âge du Fer: historiographie, terminologie et résultats', in *Méthodologie et interprétation des habitats: approches multiscalaires des types et formes d'occupation du territoire dans l'Europe du nord-ouest de la fin du Néolithique à La Tène ancienne*, ed. by Yann Lorin and Emmanuelle Leroy-Langelin (Actes du XLIVᵉ colloque d'HALMA, PCR HABATA)

Peche-Quilichini, Kewin, Nadia Ameziane-Federzoni, and Jean-Philippe Antolini. Forthcoming. 'Le faciès Tuani-Mizane et la géographie céramique de la Corse au premier âge du Fer', in *Six millénaires en Centre Cors* (Actes du colloque du LRA)

Piccardi, Eliana, and Kewin Peche-Quilichini. 2013. 'Production, Trading and Imitation of Pottery in the Northern Tyrrhenian Sea Area in the Second Iron Age: Potential Evidence of Identity', in *Identity and Connectivity: Proceedings of the XVIth Symposium on Mediterranean Archaeology*, ed. by Luca Bombardieri, Anacleto d'Agostino, Guido Guarducci, Valentina Orsi, and Stefano Valentini, British Archaeological Reports, International Series, 2581 (Oxford: Archaeopress), pp. 705–14

Rainbird, Paul. 1999. 'Islands out of Time: Towards a Critique of Island Archaeology', *Journal of Mediterranean Archaeology*, 12.2: 216–34

Taddei, Dominique. 2002. *USS Corsica: L'île porte-avions* (Ajaccio: Albiana)

Verger, Stéphane. 2000. 'Un poignard corse à Paestum', *Annali di archeologia e storia antica*, 7: 43–47

Zucca, Raimondo. 1996. *La Corsica romana* (Oristano: S'Alvure)

JOHN NORTH HOPKINS

5. Folding Meaning in an Object

The Ficoroni Cista and the Heterarchy of Art in Early Italy

ABSTRACT Perhaps more than any other object, the Ficoroni cista has stood out as an example of artistic production and consumption in central Italy during the fourth century BCE. Yet those who invoke it usually trace its significance to one end: as evidence either for Roman art and expansion, Praenestine families and luxury consumption, or the enduring sophistication of Etruscan craftwork. It is, rather, an indexical object that conflates and amplifies its contexts, generating multiple realities; in doing so, it dissolves boundaries, both within its historical context and in the modern disciplinary fields of art history, archaeology, and material studies. This chapter presents an argument for an object that militates against typological or categorical study in the assessment of early cultures, and which complicates the study of a 'Roman art'.

Over the past half century, the relationship between Greek and Roman art has seen fundamental reconsideration on several fronts. Chief among them has been a concern for how a person living under Roman rule might understand and use Archaic, Classical, and Hellenistic forms, iconographies, typologies, and other visual elements for their own purposes, and how a clearer sense of the complexity of such use might reveal more about a person's encounter with works of art. Among the most important contributions are those that underscore the significance of alteration and creative agency in Roman works tied (in differing ways) to the tradition of Greek 'ideal' sculptures, as well as the socially and culturally constructed visualities — the 'Roman eyes' — through which people experienced objects and understood visual- and material-based encounters with the world around them.[1] Much of this work has focused on

the late Republic and Empire, and, problematically, assumes that a meaningful visual system incorporating 'Greek' elements appeared in the late third or second centuries BCE, alongside a recurring artistic interest throughout the Mediterranean in retrospectivism.[2]

Yet, in the past few decades, scholars have begun to question such a paradigm, as the art and architecture of early central Italy, Rome included, has seen renewed attention for its complex ties to the wider Mediterranean world and for its historical value independent of such ties and outside of the hierarchical linearity of traditional art historical narratives. As difference within Greek and Mediterranean visual cultures of the eighth to third centuries BCE has seen wider recognition, and as the study of connections across the Mediterranean has seen subtler treatment (testimony of which can be found in the contributions and bibliography of this volume), scholars have highlighted the expressive visual potentials already in Rome and across the Italic peninsula well before the third century, which engaged purposefully with forms, iconographies, and other elements from local, regional, and wider Mediterranean communities to materially and visually generate meaning-filled experiences that could be uneven in their effects.[3]

---

especially 9–13; Hölscher 2004, with comments by Elsner and an updated bibliography; Perry 2005; Elsner 2007; Kousser 2008; Marvin 2008; Trimble 2011.

2 Hölscher is explicit and many have followed his cue.

3 On Rome, some seminal examples and selections with important bibliographies include Aa. Vv. 1973; Heurgon and Pallottino 1981; Coarelli 1990; Cristofani 1990; Pallottino 1993; Warden 2013; Coarelli 2016. Far more work has been done on Roman architecture, but the questions are somewhat different here. The subtlest work on art and visual experience has been achieved by scholars working on 'Etruscan' art (really work that goes far beyond Etruscan areas) and the art and cultures of the Greek and Punic west: for example Bonfante 1989; Ridgway 2000; Torelli 2000; Malkin 2002; Hall 2004; Ridgway 2010; De Angelis 2015; Bundrick 2019. Three recent companion volumes on Etruscan culture (Turfa 2015; Bell and Carpino 2016; Naso 2017) incorporate much of the most innovate scholarship and good

---

1 Some seminal works and works with extensive bibliography include Hölscher 1987; Zanker 1990; Gazda 2002; Clarke 2003,

---

Corresponding author John North Hopkins (jnh1@nyu.edu)

Figure 5.1. Ficoroni cista, with view of the Humiliation of Amykos, c. 350–315 BCE. Rome, Museo Nazionale Etrusco di Villa Giulia a Roma, inv. 24787 (by permission of the Museo Nazionale Etrusco di Villa Giulia).

the potential for multiple, coexisting, meaning-filled object engagements, which belie the centring of any one feature or object in a canon or taxonomy of art and culture. It also suggests that cultural change, a primary theme of this book, is often possible within single works, in the meeting of traditions in a single object and in its exchange and encounter. Indeed, in compound objects, one can sometimes find the substances of sociocultural shift.

An Object of Change

The Ficoroni cista lies at the meeting-place of these uneven potentials and these often-segregated branches of the field (Fig. 5.1). A work of skilled bronze casting — in the feet and handle — and incised cold-work decoration on a rolled and assembled bronze drum and lid, it is three-quarters of a metre tall. The intricate decorative floral bands and central register of complex mythology on the drum are some of the best examples of Italic engraved bronzework, a hallmark of cistae and mirrors typically associated with Etruscan workshops, but also produced in Praeneste, Rome, and elsewhere in the region. Its manufacture is dated between c. 350 and 315 BCE, and an inscription on the handle — DINDIA MACOLNIA FILEAI DEDIT — states that it was a gift by one of the Dindii clan to her daughter.[5] The Dindii were among the most prominent families in Praeneste, where the cista was found in 1738, presumably deposited in a grave, though its provenience within the polity is unclear (Ficoroni 1745; Dohrn 1972, 7–9 with references).[6] Such lavish cylindrical cistae, tall and engraved around the drum and on

Shared or common visual features would meet with opposing ones and with different artefact types, different applied uses, different contexts, and differing viewer experiences. In such situations, an object's elements could become heterarchical — none more commanding or important than the other in a user's experience, each bearing discrete communicative and experiential opportunities.[4] This situation created

bibliographies in chapters on 'Etruscan' art by some of the pre-eminent scholars writing at the moment.

4 This takes Crumley's (1995) heterarchical understanding of complex societies and applies it to elements of material culture, what Sonia Hazard (2013, 65) has summarized as 'unruly tangles of heterogeneous things that we usually regard as discrete or dialectically opposed entities'. Essential to this view: For example, Mol and Law 1994; 2002; Massey 2006; Feldman 2015; De Landa 2016.

5 Among the latest dates is that given by Dohrn, based on his analysis of styles (some of which seem too late) and on Beazley's suggestion of a post-336 date based on the type of boxing gloves: Dohrn 1972. Since then, Adam (1980) argued for a much earlier date c. 380–360, but this seems too early. Massa-Pairault and Corelli place its date c. 350 largely based on Adam's suggestion: Coarelli 2016, 207–08; Massa-Pairault 1992, 129; and see Gilotta and Baglione 2007, 32; Del Chiaro among others, agrees with a date closer to 325 following Beazley's argument and the styles and comparanda for several figures: Del Chiaro 1955, 285. Indeed, mid-late fourth-century styles of several figures (see below) suggest a date between c. 350 and 330, and although the gloves may not provide a definitive *terminus post quem* as Beazley argued, they do suggest the date could not be much before c. 336 and may belong afterward.

6 On the Dindii a summary of their record in Praeneste can be found in Šašel 1981.

the lids, their current dull green-brown patina belying an original brilliant lustre, are an established hallmark of elite Praenestine culture.[7] Part of the daily toilet, they held combs, mirrors, pins, cosmetics, and other objects. On the opposite side of the handle, however, another well-known inscription, *NOVIOS PLAUTIOS MED ROMAI FECID*, complicates the cista's history. It bears the name of the artist or patron initially responsible for the work, Novios Plautius, and it clarifies that the cista was made in Rome.

The components of the cista are all well studied, and its assembly from diverse artistic communities is clearly recognizable.[8] The handles and feet immediately unsettle its nature as a simplistically understood 'Roman' or 'Praenestine' piece. They are most often tied to Etruscan style and manufacture, imported perhaps from Vulci to be added to the body. Indeed, the composition of the figures on the handle, the terpsichorean position of the feet, and the specific ponderation and posture, namely the application of a naturalistic relaxed stance found widely in the classical Mediterranean but with foot forward, chest out, and a presentational frontality, is a hallmark of art tied predominantly — though not exclusively — to artisans working in Etruria. An undeciphered Etruscan inscription on one of the feet identifies their linguistic culture of production, and the composition of the three figures (Hermes at centre, Herakles to his left, and a third figure) is recognizable in a copy on a mirror from Bologna (Figs 5.2–5.3).[9] The body carries a scene that was

Figure 5.2. Ficoroni cista, detail of foot, c. 350–315 BCE (by permission of the Museo Nazionale Etrusco di Villa Giulia).

Figure 5.3. Mirror with Herakles, Hermes, and a third figure. Bologna, Museo Civico di Bologna, inv. It. 1072, coll. Universitaria No. 278 (after Gerhard, *ES* 2.CXXXI).

---

7   The bibliography on them is extensive. Some important studies include Bordenache Battaglia and others 1979–1990; Massa-Pairault 1992; Menichetti 1995; see Serra Ridgway 1998. The Toscanella Cista at the British Museum is from the Campanari property in northern Lazio (s. Etruria), and many of the 'Praenestine' cistae come from the art market and lack a provenience.

8   The masterful study by Dohrn (1972) on the object provides a comprehensive analysis of most of its elements. See citations in n. 4 above and in discussion below.

9   On the inscription: Schneider 1886, 4; Wachter 1987, 124; Massa-Pairault 1992, 123; Franchi De Bellis 2005, 141. On the iconography: Del Chiaro 1955, 285; Dohrn 1972, 24, pl. 27; Sassatelli 1981, 106; van der Meer 2016b, 75–76. The copy is exact except for the caduceus, which Hermes holds in his left hand by the snakes in the mirror and in his right hand by the staff (with the third figure clasping the top) on the feet of the cista. What Erika Simon believed to be a liver in Hermes' left hand may be so: quoted in de Grummond 2002, 71 n. 30. It is unclear whether the feet were created by an artist who misunderstood the original, where Hermes held the caduceus in the left hand, or whether the artist of the mirror misunderstood the object in that hand as the caduceus. It is uncommon for Hermes to hold it by the entwined snakes, and his right hand on the mirror hangs at his side in a position that wants the pole of the caduceus.

Figure 5.4. Ficoroni cista, drawing of engraved drum (after Bröndsted 1847, pl. 2a–b).

well illustrated in other works from the Italic peninsula by the mid-late fourth century BCE: the myth of Pollux humiliating Amykos, son of Poseidon and king of the Bebryces, after his failed attempt to best the demigod in boxing, while his fellow Argonauts watch, relax, and prepare for voyage after their stop in Bithynia, which prompted the agonistic event (Weis 1982; Fig. 5.4).[10]

Much of the earliest scholarship on the piece focused on its Praenestine find-spot, its Roman manufacture, and what was then understood as its Greek source (for example Winckelmann 1776, 291; Overbeck 1869, II, 386; Brunn 1889, 531; but also Ducati 1927, 517; Ryberg 1940, 442; Beazley 1949; Romanelli 1967, 26; Robertson 1975, 444; Bianchi Bandinelli 1976, 17; Brendel 1978, 355). In these studies, the object fell into an historiographical narrative that pitted cultures against one another and made Roman craft a dependent artistic tradition. As much as the art history of the Empire indicated Greek roots for Roman art, scholarship on the Republic pointed to Etruscan roots, and the Ficoroni cista appeared through the mid–late twentieth century as a culmination of that trend.[11] Described as an example of Etruscan or Praenestine art, which itself was understood to derive from a tradition in engraved mirrors that originated in Etruscan influence, the Ficoroni cista was recognized as Roman by way of other artistic origins. Much of this was surgically questioned and repositioned in the work of Tobias Dohrn (1972), who methodically treated each element of this cista in his monograph of the piece. Dohrn acknowledged the Etruscan manufacture of the handle and feet — a consensus that remains widely acknowledged in scholarship — but he made the astute argument for a Roman pre-eminence in the art world of the late fourth century BCE: the artist of this cista clearly situated his workshop in Rome, signalling its cultural authority, and the Praenestine Dindii sought a Roman workshop (rather than a Praenestine one) for their prized possession, going as far as to permanently mark the object's place of manufacture in inscription. Dohrn's argument has been repeated since as an indication of Rome's surpassing visual culture already in the late fourth century BCE.[12] Yet, for Dohrn, Rome did not stand on its own feet. The greatest element of the object, its primary frieze bearing a megalographic quality in its soaring mythology and meticulous — almost scholastic — attention to individual characters, literary detail, and subtle late classical composition and posture, was, for Dohrn, a variation of an Athenian painting, perhaps by Mikon, of the fourth century (Dohrn 1972, 34–35). The Roman artist, in this telling, is extraordinary for his adaptation of that genius Greek masterpiece to a local need, but *Kopienkritik* ruled this study.

Since the 1970s, much of this has seen reconsideration through much of the same criticism levelled against scholarship on the Roman Empire.[13]

Both objects appear to be working from a third model, unless the liver or rock in Hermes hand on the cista's foot bears some meaning to the scene, as yet unrecognized.

10 Weis corrects the assumption of a heroic Greek iconography in Dohrn 1972, 24–40.

11 It is still occasionally presented this way, under the rubric of Etruscan art. See n. 3 and 11.

12 The assertion is repeated in most of the scholarship, including Rouveret 1996; Coarelli 2016; Haumesser 2017.

13 Some important reassessments can be found in Weis 1982; Bordenache Battaglia and others 1990, 217; Massa-Pairault 1992; Menichetti 1995; Schneider 1995; Rouveret 1996; Serra Ridgway 1998; van der Meer 2016b. See other references throughout this essay.

In brief, the motif of Amykos's humiliation, which Dohrn placed in the works of Mikon or Nikias, has been tied instead to the comedy of Sicily and the subject matter of vases and engraved art produced in Italy, especially Apulia, Lucania, Etruria, and Latium (Weis 1982). Scholars have highlighted that specific compositions of figures are identifiable chiefly in the same painted and engraved objects, again from Lucanian, Etruscan, and Latin sites; Dohrn recognized these, but tied them unnecessarily to Greek roots through the master painters of Athens and especially the sculpture of Lysippus.[14] In light of the reassessments, most scholars working on the cista have sought recently to explain its value in understanding Praenestine social and visual culture or a Roman artistic centre that was aware of Greek art but independent of it.[15]

Yet, as much of this scholarship has succeeded in decoupling visual acuity from artistic dependency in the use of styles, techniques, or subject matter, it has also continued to situate the cista in one cultural milieu — as an Etruscan object or a Praenestine one, as a Roman object that participates (for unclear reasons) in a vaguely defined Mediterranean artistic *koine*, or as a work that indicates an early Roman productive centre (and supersession) over Etruscan or other Italic arts. Although certain aspects of these explanations have value, they neglect a necessary element of its use as an object — one of the few extant in the corpus of ancient art that so explicitly speaks to such a purpose — that was created specifically to communicate across cultural, socio-political, linguistic, and visual boundaries and especially as a means to facilitate social interaction beyond one cultural milieu. In this light, the function and experience of the cista is vital and a reconsideration of its meaning in fourth-century BCE central Italy must begin with the context of its use.

Engagement in Exchange

In some ways, a close reading of the cista's intended function, or of a viewer's encounter with it, is not possible. Scholars agree that Praenestine cistae were part of the daily toilet, and that similar cistae come from female graves. Yet many cistae first reappeared on the art market and exist now without a sound — or even reported — archaeological context. That some were found in female graves is an important fact to keep in mind, but only through circular argument can such an observation be applied categorically as a means to determine that all cistae are feminine objects and that, for example, their iconology was a celebration through *paideia* of marriage as an ordering phenomenon (Menichetti 1995; contra: Serra Ridgway 1998; van der Meer 2016a). Many other objects, once assumed to be exclusive to women and interpreted through that lens (including the closely related category of engraved mirrors) have since been recognized in male burials, exposing problematic anachronisms in some interpretive scholarship (for example Curti and others 1996; Carpino 2008; Allison 2015; Esposito and Pollini 2021; van Oppen 2021, 22–23). With such uncertainty, it is best to consider the function of the cista in the terms that are widely agreed upon: it was an object made in Rome and given by a mother to her daughter, likely at her marriage, when such luxury items were often betrothed; it was later interred in her grave, if the story of its discovery is accurate. Within this broad description of its function, and against the specifics of the dedicatory inscription, there is enough to better situate the vessel not just as a work of art in a comparative world of visually connected objects, but as one of the very finest and most expertly crafted works of luxury bronze personal items in a central Italic milieu characterized by a culture of elite gift exchange.[16]

The inscription on the handle holds several keys, none of which is as straightforward as is typically reported. The primary inscription is frequently translated 'Novios Plautius made me in Rome', a clear artist's signature, which most read in the manner of Greek vases signed *epoiesen*. In this sense, Novios Plautius is understood to have overseen production.[17] He is not the artist of the handle where the text was inscribed, and although he may have been responsible for the primary engraved decoration, the inscription's location and word choice implies he was responsible for more than that; rather than

---

14 Dohrn 1972, but updated in the bibliography cited in n. 12. See below as well.

15 Del Chiaro 1955; Mansuelli 1964; Weis 1982; Massa-Pairault 1992; Haumesser 2017. Others foreground this mixture but essentially reclaim the work as a symbol of one dominant cultural, Praenestine/Roman (Bordenache Battaglia and others 1990, xxxvii; Menichetti 1995; Coarelli 2016; van der Meer 2016b) or Etruscan (Brendel 1978; Gilotta and Baglione 2007).

---

16 On objects of elite exchange, see Warden 2013. A recent summary of the phenomenon and its significance (with extensive bibliography) can be found in Terrenato 2019. Bernard (2018) who highlights the important of elite exchange and the social role of such interaction between elites specifically across political lines before the introduction of coinage.

17 Mansuelli 1964, 133; Dohrn 1972, 27; Bianchi Bandinelli 1976, 17. Repeated in Coarelli 1990; Massa-Pairault 1992; and most scholarship to date; for a recently discovered comparanda: Nicosia and others 2012; Sacco and others 2013; Ferrandes 2014; Colonna 2016; Ferrandes 2017, 33.

cailavit, used on works, such as the mirror of Vibis Pilipus, to indicate the engraver, a more general sense of making is implied in the inscription on the cista (Della Seta 1918, 484; Mansuelli 1964, 134; Dohrn 1972, 27). In fact, several artists seem to have been involved in production: multiple styles are distinguishable between the primary figural scene on the body and the framing motifs of heraldic sphinxes and anthemion decoration with medusa heads (themselves both markedly different in manner), and scholars recognize variable depth in different registers of the engraving, a mark of multiple makers at work (Bordenache Battaglia and others 1979–1990, I.1, 111–26). This is to say nothing of the engraved lid, which carries a style closer to the sphinxes, but still different, or the technical work involved in rolling the bronze and welding its seams. Plautius seems either to be the workshop leader responsible for overseeing assembly of the elements (and perhaps creating some of the engraved decoration), or for overseeing the sourcing of materials, artisans, and designs from a managerial position.

Although the version offered above is the most commonly repeated translation and understanding of the inscription, this is not its only interpretation. Another reading of this very public-facing text suggests that *fecid* be read in the sense of *faciendum curavit*: Novios Plautius had me made in Rome. Peter Kruschwitz points to a third-century BCE bronze vase from Amiternum inscribed *Q(uintus) Lainio(s) Q(uinti) f(ilius) praifectos pro trebibos fecit*, the construction of which indicates that Quintius Lainios had the vase made for a tribe, presumably as a donation or gift (Kruschwitz 2002, 29).[18] Such an implication in the use of *fecid* becomes common on inscriptions later in the Republic, and it appears to be one possible meaning by at least the third century BCE. Later textual descriptions of luxury objects and public dedications often assume such a meaning. The example from Amiternum, a small inscription on a luxury bronze object presented to an elite group, provides a near exact parallel for the circumstance of the Ficoroni cista. The second dedication on the cista, by an elite matron to her daughter, would thus render the full inscription one of notoriety, meant to impress and call attention to the individuals involved in its exchange.[19]

Neither reading is more definitive than the other. The assumption that *fecid* should be read like *epoiesen* derives from the rare but consistent uses of the word on inscriptions and dipinti in central Italy from the seventh to the fourth centuries BCE, and that the Ficoroni cista bears an accusative *med*, following a traditional formula for a *titulus loquens* that names an artist (examples in Wallace 2005). Still, not all early Latin artist signatures and *tituli loquentes* carry the accusative *med* (for example, those from Cales), making such a determination arbitrary, and before the second century BCE the construction is so rare and sporadic (just seven examples over five centuries) that it is hardly certain (Wallace 2005 and see also Warmington 1940, IV, 196–215). Many of these are understood to be artist signatures only through circular reasoning. The majority of scholarship on the Ficoroni cista has been written by art historians and archaeologists, and nearly all of that literature repeats the translation of an artist's signature in assessing centres of production. Yet scholarship on early Latin epigraphy and on middle Republican Latin suggests the translation as a commission, and underscores that *fecid/fecit* does not bear a meaning that restricts its use to physical manufacture. In short, either possibility must be taken seriously.

It is not my purpose to argue conclusively for one reading or another, but rather to underscore that both are possible, and to examine how this object might be understood in either context. Merely in recalling the public-facing nature of this inscription, the possibility of a mark of patronage, and the interest in signalling exchange, I hope to have shifted the focus from questions about artistic centres and the cista's value as an *objet d'art* to the context of the inscription — its rare, deliberate, indelible mark on an object that was exchanged between families. In each situation, the inscription recalls the broad functionality of the object, as a masterful luxury item exchanged among elites, who wished to signal the names of those involved in its production *and* exchange. At the very least, a mother gave the cista to her daughter, who would have married a member of another clan, in whose home the object would be used and where it would proclaim the Roman manufacture and luxury status as a gift from the Dindii and Magolnii families of Praeneste.[20] If the primary inscription names a patron, then it provides yet another point of contact, from a Plautius of Rome to the Dindii (and Magolnii) of Praeneste, who wished not only

---

18 I am grateful to Brent Vine for highlighting this line of scholarship and to Wolfgang de Melo for discussing it further with me.

19 The dependence of the second inscription on the first is generally understood by the same hand being used for both inscriptions and owing to the absence of a direct object in the second part: Dohrn 1972, 27 with references.

20 Whether Dindia Magolnia is the mother or Dindia the mother and Magolnia the daughter (two equally possible readings of the inscription), the use of both names suggests marriage between the families.

to signal their own gift to a daughter, but also the family's reception of a gift from the Plautii. Indeed, such a scenario could also explain why the object appears to art historians and archaeologists to date to the mid-fourth century BCE (when it would be given by Plautius to the Dindii), but the inscription appears to epigraphers to date to the late fourth century or early third century BCE (when it would be given by the mother and engraved to commemorate its origins and the act of gift giving).

If Plautius is the artist rather than the patron, the inscription remains significant beyond the narrow concern for artist names and artistic centres. In his analysis of the inscription, Mommsen proposed that Plautius may be understood as an artisan who was granted a place in the noble *gens* Plautia as a former slave or client.[21] That an object bearing the name 'Plautius' should be tied to the historical Plautii, who emigrated from the region around Tibur or Praeneste in the early fourth century and held multiple consulships and a censorship at Rome between *c.* 358 and 312 BCE, may seem excessive conjecture.[22] Yet, as Terrenato (2019, 174–81) has recently explained at length, the Plautii who immigrated to Rome were important members of an expanded elite family that specifically connected Rome, Tibur, Praeneste, and Caere, and the cista is not the only occasion where their cognomen is found in connection with Praeneste, and specifically these families. Two burials of the third and second centuries BCE in Praeneste bear the names of Plautii who had intermarried with the Dindii (*Dindi Plauti C. ux*: CIL I² 2460 p. 870) and Magolnii (*L. Magolnio Pla. f.*: T. Mommsen, *Römische Geschichte* 450; see also Pensabene 1982, 42, 76, 96). The consequential intermarriage of the Plautii in each polity, and their entry into the highest echelons of society across the region, underscores the real possibility that this object was made by a member of the extended *gens* Plautia, further entangling — perhaps with some socio-political intention — the fortunes of the two polities and these elite families.[23] Whatever clan he belonged to, if he is understood to be the artist, Plautius should not be seen as a humble artisan; if he was not a member of the famous and noble branch of the Plautii, he

nonetheless had both a praenomen and cognomen, indicating a degree of social status. In this sense, one should situate Plautius alongside Fabius Pictor — an artist of an elite family whose name appeared next to his own work of the same era in Rome (Massa-Pairault 1992, 144). For the Dindii to choose a cista from a Roman workshop, and for that workshop to produce such a rare and exceptional piece, would indicate their desire to highlight Rome as a centre of production. Yet they did not only specify the Roman origin; they chose to indelibly carve the elite artist's name into the piece.

This is to say that either interpretation of the inscription calls to mind the desire in an elite owner to signal her ties to a specific elite patron or artist in Rome — to signal her family's ties to that workshop or that political lineage — and to pass tangible and legible testimony of those connections on to her daughter and her daughter's new family and home. As an exceptional luxury object, made for the most prominent of families, and as an object fabricated in Rome for a Praenestine home in the midst of one of the most complex periods of socio-political relations between the two polities, the cista verbally specifies a transcendent context of visual communication, wherein cultural and political boundaries and hierarchies are superseded.

Compound Object Encounters

With this in mind, the assemblage of visual elements in the cista gains meaning.[24] The frieze is by far the most commanding visual element of the chest and it is an ideal lens through which to recognize a compound visual encounter with the piece overall. The subject matter derives from a Greek myth, and an eastern setting, beyond doubt. No element of the myth of the Argonauts' encounter with Amykos fits in a western Mediterranean geographical context, and the artist has not attempted to reset the event. Yet this specific scene, the humiliation, has a lengthier tradition in visual and comic representation in the Italic peninsula and on Sicily (Weis 1982). Indeed, the earliest examples of the iconography are found on Apulian, Etruscan, Lucanian, Roman, and Latin art. The scene may derive from the Sicilian playwright, Epicharmos's, late fifth-century BCE comedy, *Amykos*, and the iconography on most examples from the late fifth and fourth centuries BCE include Dionysiac imagery and in some cases (including the Ficoroni cista) a Papposilenus (Köhnken 1965,

---

21 CIL 154 (= CIL I² 561, p. 430). Massa-Pairault (1992) extends this analysis further; Terrenato (2014, 48; 2019, 175) follows.

22 Not unlike the dedication by an Avile Vipiiennas at Veii, which is sometimes linked to Aulus Vibenna: Cornell 1995, 135 n. 50 with references. On the Plautii and their roots: Münzer 1920, 45–46; Taylor 1956; Farney 2007, 43 n. 15.

23 On intermarriage as a means of networking among the Plautii especially: Terrenato 2019, especially 155–93. On intermarriage and similar relationship with elite at Caere: Cornell 1995, 321.

24 Assemblage, *sensu* De Landa 2016.

90–91; Weis 1982, 26). The comic setting specific to the version of the myth distinguishes it from the elevated heroic tale that Dohrn suggested in the putative Athenian masterwork from which it would be copied. The visual diffusion of the Amykos myth in Italic wares seems to stem from the Italic tradition of comedy and the popularity of Dionysiac scenes (Rouveret 1996; Wiseman 1988, 5–7; Weis 1982; Denoyelle 2014). Within this thoroughly Italic milieu of such an eastern Greek myth, the artist has further placed very local familiarizing elements, from the characteristic central Italic footwear of Minerva and the figure seated next to her to the specific vessel shapes held in the hands of Pollux's attendant at the base of the tree and in the hands of the shipman descending the ladder to the bulla worn on the figure in recline, mirrored as it swings around the dancing Dionysus in the handle (Dohrn 1972).

Yet, the frieze is neither an exclusively local or regional image. Broader Mediterranean traditions are present, for example, in the composition of the figures, which pull from elements of certain types sometimes rooted in Greek examples but adapted in Italic contexts already before the cista or contemporaneously with it. A palpable care for *kalokagathia* is recognizable in the figures to Minerva's left; their idealized musculature, profiles, and properly manicured bodies visibly contrasting with the hairy bodies, unkempt beards and unidealized facial features of the eastern, humiliated Amykos and the two eastern figures next to Pollux, identified as Mygdon (Amykos's brother) and the winged figure Boreas, Sosthenes, or Calchas (compare Fig. 5.1 and Fig. 5.4).[25] Though a visual and conceptual formula well established in Greek art and culture, the use of such ideals has been tied increasingly to Roman and central Italic art and elite culture of the fourth and third centuries as well (Rouveret 1996, with extensive references). Furthermore, the play with posture and ponderation — the expert selection of meaningful body compositions — throughout the frieze speaks equally to interests that had comparison around the Mediterranean, but which were selected and deployed in highly specific ways in central Italic contexts, with respect to narrative meaning in each figure and in the subject as a whole.[26] Minerva — stylistically erect, almost statue-like in her fifth–early fourth-century frontal typology — wears an ornate Italic garment

as she watches over the primary scene in her role as the austere patron goddess of the Greek Argonauts. Meanwhile, suitable to their narrative function, the Argonauts are less commanding and less rigid. A figure in a *pilos*, sometimes identified as Jason, bears a composition that pulls from and yet substantially adjusts (in reverse) the mid–late fourth-century BCE Sandal Binder type. He leans over a bent knee, but rather than being set alone, he is in conversation with a companion, who shows his back to the viewer (Fig. 5.5).[27] Other figures engage more actively, bringing energy to the scene. The crossed bodies and torsion of the boxer and the helmsman, his hair swept back in the manner of middle and late fourth-century BCE central Italic painting and sculpture, play expertly with the three-quarter and twisting views of fourth–third-century BCE figures and enliven the otherwise mundane activities of the Argonauts.[28] In each, their ponderation and position bears an appropriately casual, carefree demeanour, imbuing the figures and the protagonists of the scene overall with the dignity, authority, and idealization appropriate to their roles.

The extraordinary precision and complexity of the piece means that each figure bears elements that are mixed within them. No single cultural or visual tradition dominates the work; rather, in the considered actions of craft and composition, a maker has changed, adjusted, and juxtaposed many forms and features. And no element can hold focus over others. Although the iconography, mixed styles, and sophisticated use of individual typologies are commonly associated with Greek art, many can be found more easily in central and southern Italy. At the same time, those figures that might seem at first to privilege a fourth-century BCE type that is best known in Greek art history is adjusted by garments, positions, pairings, and the scene as a whole, pulling attention away from the elements of any Mediterranean or Greek visual tradition. Even the subject seems to be hierarchical, its megalographic quality suggestive of heroic scenes from the mainland, but with a comic twist that would render it out of place in such an environment. In short, each element seems to have been worked into a single, compound piece with equal care for the use of multiple cues to convey narrative meaning.

---

25 None of the winged figures mentioned play a role in the myth of Amykos, which has presented problems. See Williams 1945, 340 with references; Dohrn 1972, 17; Coarelli 2016, 217. On *kalokagathia* in Greek art, see Stewart 1986; Zinserling 1975.

26 For a succinct exploration of this subtlety, with excellent bibliography: De Angelis 2016.

---

27 See Dohrn (1972, 19) for *Kopienkritik* that is hard to contradict here; the Sandal Binder type is known from later Roman versions in Munich, in the Louvre and Lansdowne collections.

28 Good comparanda for the helmsman's hair can be seen in the Aurora Painter's name vase and the sculpture of Leukothea from Pyrgi, from the middle and late fourth century.

The same entanglement of production centres, iconographies, typologies, accoutrements, and narratives affects the cista as a whole, from the Dionysiac handles, Caledonian iconography of the lid, the embossed feet, and elsewhere. As an object it is, consequently, not identifiable as any single cultural product. Though typologically closest to other engraved Praenestine cistae, to speak of it as a Praenestine object is to ignore the production of the feet in Etruria, and the composition of several elements that are found more prominently in specific Etruscan, Attic, or Lucanian contexts, not to mention its stated manufacture in Rome. To call it Roman is to ignore the same Etruscan, Italic, and Greek elements, as well as the typically Praenestine object type. To ignore the Hellenicity of the myth or the styles and individual figural types, with models and paradigmatic examples in some of the most famous Greek sculptures of the period, is to be wilfully blind to their significance beyond Italy and to the manner in which Italic artists outside of the Greek-speaking centres adapted these types to their own visual purposes. To call it an 'Italic' piece is no more helpful, because such a cultural designation is both too specific (the object bears visual cues and stories that are significant and stem from eastern Greek artistic and narrative contexts) and not specific enough (the technique of engraving on this type of vessel is not especially suited to a south Italian context or even a Campanian or northern Etruscan one — such engraved vessels predominate in Latium and occasionally in south Etruria).

To ignore, diminish, or disproportionately embrace any one of these elements is to obscure the very meaningfulness of its multivalence: this object would speak discretely across boundaries and to multiple cultural audiences. The broad Italic style and character of the iconography is important as a sign of its broad communicative potential; seen by a visitor from Tarentum, Paestum, or Vulci, the object would carry recognizable visual meaning and artistic sophistication. The Greek mythology and the currency of the styles and iconography is crucial to such communicative and social value. At the same time, the Praenestine and Latin vessel type and accoutrements in the iconography, for example, localized its meaning for its immediate audience of daily use, as would its Latin inscription.

So, the cista is extraordinary not because of the artist's ability to merely adapt a style and iconography, or produce such technical excellence (though certainly the engraved scene of Amykos is among the most admirable produced anywhere in central Italy during the fourth century), but because of his ability to seamlessly combine these elements

Figure 5.5. Ficoroni cista, detail, c. 350–315 BCE
(by permission of the Museo Nazionale Etrusco di Villa Giulia).

(and many others) in an object that could speak — not through a vague *koine* or by aping Greek or Etruscan art, but through specific visual elements — to a Praenestine, Lucanian, Apulian, Roman, Sicilian, Latin, or Etruscan audience, each with its own associations, each interpreting and understanding it through their own eyes, and each recognizing meaningful elements in its composition in differing — possibly divergent — ways. This visual complexity set the object not in a confined, overly traditional or restricted local milieu, and not in a meaningless 'Mediterranean' context, but instead in a heterarchical cultural sphere.[29] Although some elements would have been recognizable across cultures, many of these cues would be specifically meaningful to a restricted audience, namely the Roman, Praenestine,

---

29 Arguing for a similarly precise use of visual elements, and also eschewing a vague *koine*: De Angelis 2016, 370, and see n. 3.

and Latin patrons, users, and visitors who might recognize the cachet of its traditional typology and local attributes as well as be able to recognize and appreciate the declaratory social significance of the inscription. These same familiarizing traits would render the object exotic to visitors from afar who would, nonetheless, appreciate its style and subject. Some of those viewers might distinguish the subtle stylistic elements of posture and ponderation and the sophisticated intercultural character of the piece; others might not. The owner, who had the most time with the object, could penetrate its entangled meanings most deeply; a visitor from southern Italy or northern Etruria less so. Many of these visual elements would, for the occasional visitor, root it in her or his own traditions, and through the subject matter, specific iconography, style, and other components, it might mean something quite different than it would for the local elite. Hardly a *koine* (spoken and understood by all), the visual assemblage could speak in radically different terms to its many viewers, even for the Roman creator and Praenestine owner, the mother and her daughter's new family. In this way, the cista participates in multiple specific cultural traditions that intersected socially, politically, militarily, and visually in the high-stakes elite culture of an expanding Roman, Praenestine, and central Italic world.

As an object of elite exchange — either from the Plautii to the Dindi-Magolni and within the family to their daughter as she joined a new clan, or simply among the Dindi-Magolni to their daughter and her new family — the artists and assembler of the cista harnessed an extraordinarily heterogenous mix of established tradition and innovative style, locally meaningful, and distributed visual elements. The same is true, to a certain extent, for many such objects — cistae, candelabra, ceramic vessels, sarcophagi; the Ficoroni cista stands in here as an example. Other cistae have handles and engraved iconography that seem to compete in their traditions or maker communities much like this one; or they participate clearly in the Praenestine cylindrical form and its function for grooming while their artistry seems strikingly different. In a way, the Ficoroni cista is itself an outlier, odd in its landscape: it is enormous by comparison to others, and the scholasticism of its primary decoration is unlike most. So, even in a Praenestine landscape of cista-sameness, each one might remake cultural practice — or adjust it.

As a vessel of elite exchange, the cista embodies the formlessness of art and objects in the milieu of engagement and expansionism.[30] The desire to hold objects within canons and systems can be comforting and useful, but such works also broke down frames and, in their fluidity, contributed to change and difference. Neither Roman nor Praenestine, Etruscan nor Greek, Italic nor Latin, the cista highlights an art that reached across boundaries, communicating discretely based on a viewer's own visual acuities. Beyond language and political markers, such objects bound people across lines at the same time that they bore the heterarchical potential to communicate differently, to pull viewers and users in different directions, signalling cultural sameness and difference, and perhaps provoking change.

---

30 Formlessness *sensu* Bataille 1929, 382. See also Bois and Krauss 1997.

Works Cited

Aa. Vv. 1973. *Roma medio repubblicana: aspetti culturali di Roma e del Lazio nei secoli IV e III a.C.* (Rome: Assessorato antichità, belle arti e problemi della cultura)

Adam, Richard. 1980. *Recherches sur les miroirs prénestins* (Paris: Presses de l'École normale supérieure)

Allison, Penelope. 2015. 'Characterizing Roman Artifacts to Investigate Gendered Practices in Contexts without Sexed Bodies', *American Journal of Archaeology*, 119.1: 103–23

Bataille, Georges. 1929. *Documents (Paris, France: 1929)* (Paris: Jean-Michel Place)

Beazley, John. 1949. 'The World of the Etruscan Mirror', *Journal of Hellenic Studies*, 69: 1–17

Bell, Sinclair, and Alexandra Ann Carpino (eds). 2016. *A Companion to the Etruscans* (Chichester: Wiley-Blackwell)

Bernard, Seth. 2018. 'The Social History of Early Roman Coinage', *Journal of Roman Studies*, 108: 1–26

Bianchi Bandinelli, Ranuccio. 1976. *Roma, l'arte romana nel centro del potere* (Milan: Rizzoli)

Bois, Yve-Alain, and Rosalind E. Krauss. 1997. *Formless: A User's Guide* (New York: Zone Books)

Bonfante, Larissa. 1989. 'Nudity as a Costume in Classical Art', *American Journal of Archaeology*, 93: 543–70

Bordenache Battaglia, Gabriella, Adriana Emiliozzi, and Fritzi Jurgeit. 1979–1990. *Le Ciste prenestine*, I.1–2 (Rome: Consiglio nazionale delle ricerche)

——. 1990. *Le Ciste prenestine*, II.1.1 (Rome: Consiglio nazionale delle ricerche)

Brendel, Otto. 1978. *Etruscan Art* (New York: Penguin)

Bröndsted, Peter O. 1847. *Den Ficoroniske Cista* (Copenhagen: Dorph)

Brunn, Heinrich von. 1889. *Geschichte der Griechischen Kunst* (Stuttgart: Verlag von Ebner & Seubert)

Bundrick, Sheramy D. 2019. *Athens, Etruria, and the Many Lives of Greek Figured Pottery* (Madison: University of Wisconsin Press)

Carpino, Alexandra. 2008. 'Reflections from the Tomb: Mirrors as Grave Goods in Late Classical and Hellenistic Tarquinia', *Etruscan and Italic Studies*, 11.1: 1–34

Clarke, John R. 2003. *Art in the Lives of Ordinary Romans: Visual Representation and Non-Elite Viewers in Italy* (Berkeley: University of California Press)

Coarelli, Filippo. 1990. 'Cultura artistica e società', in *Storia di Roma*, II.1: *L'impero mediterraneo* (Turin: Einaudi), pp. 159–85

——. 2016. *Le origini di Roma* (Milan: Jaca)

Colonna, G. 2016. 'Iscrizioni latine arcaiche dal santuario romano delle Curiae Veteres', *Scienze dell'Antichita*, 22.1: 93–109

Cornell, Tim. 1995. *The Beginnings of Rome: Italy and Rome from the Bronze Age to the Punic Wars 1000–264 B.C.* (London: Routledge)

Cristofani, Mauro. 1990. *La Grande Roma dei Tarquini* (Rome: L'Erma di Bretschneider)

Crumley, Carole L. 1995. 'Heterarchy and the Analysis of Complex Societies'. *Archeological Papers of the American Anthropological Association*, 6: 1–5

Curti, Emanuele, Emma Dench, and John R. Patterson. 1996. 'The Archaeology of Central and Southern Roman Italy: Recent Trends and Approaches', *Journal of Roman Studies*, 86: 170–89

De Angelis, Francesco. 2015. *Miti greci in tombe etrusche* (Rome: Giorgio Bretschneider)

——. 2016. 'Etruscan Bodies and Greek Ponderation: Anthropology and Artistic Form', in *Companion to the Etruscans*, ed. by Sinclair Bell and Alexandra A. Carpino (Oxford: Wiley), pp. 368–87

de Grummond, Nancy T. 2002. 'Mirrors, Marriage, and Mysteries', in *Pompeian Brothels, Pompeii's Ancient History, Mirrors and Mysteries, Art and Nature at Oplontis, and the Herculaneum 'Basilica'*, ed. by Tom McGinn, Nancy T. de Grummond, Bettina Bergmann, and T. Najbjerg, Journal of Roman Archaeology Supplement, 47 (Portsmouth, RI: Journal of Roman Archaeology), pp. 62–86

——. 2004. 'For the Mother and for the Daughter: Some Thoughts on Dedications from Etruria and Praeneste', in *ΧΑΡΙΣ: Essays in Honor of Sara A. Immerwahr*, ed. by Anne P. Chapin, Hesperia Supplements, 33 (Athens: American School of Classical Studies), pp. 351–70

De Landa, Manue. 2016. *Assemblage Theory* (Edinburgh: Edinburgh University Press)

Del Chiaro, Mario. 1955. 'Two Etruscan Mirrors in San Francisco', *American Journal of Archaeology*, 59.4: 277–86

Della Seta, Alessandro. 1918. *Museo di Villa Giuli* (Rome: Danesi)

Denoyelle, Martine. 2014. 'Hands at Work in Magna Graecia: The Amykos Painter and his Workshop', in *The Italic People of Ancient Apulia: New Evidence from Pottery for Workshops, Markets, and Customs*, ed. by Edward Guy D. Robinson, Kathleen M. Lynch, and Tom H. Carpenter (Cambridge: Cambridge University Press), pp. 116–30

Dohrn, Tobias. 1972. *Die Ficoronische Ciste in der Villa Giulia in Rom* (Berlin: Mann)

Ducati, Pericle. 1927. *Storia dell'arte etrusca* (Florence: Rinascimento del libro)

Elsner, Jaś. 2007. *Roman Eyes: Visuality & Subjectivity in Art & Text* (Princeton: Princeton University Press)

Esposito, Arianna, and Airton Pollini. 2021. 'Gender, Identities, and Material Culture in the Italic Peninsula: Burial Practices and Loom Weights in Perspective', *Etruscan Studies*, 24.1–2: 18–35

Farney, Gary D. 2007. *Ethnic Identity and Aristocratic Competition in Republican Rome* (Cambridge: Cambridge University Press)

Feldman, Marian H. 2015. 'Beyond Iconography: Meaning-Making in Late Bronze Age Eastern Mediterranean Visual and Material Culture', in *The Cambridge Prehistory of the Bronze and Iron Age Mediterranean*, ed. by A. Bernard Knapp and Peter van Dommelen (Cambridge: Cambridge University Press), pp. 337–51

Ferrandes, Antonio. 2014. 'Circolazione ceramica e approvvigionamento urbano a Roma nel I secolo a.C. Nuovi dati dall'area degli Horti Lamiani', *Rei Cretariae Romanae Fautorum Acta*, 42: 68–78

——. 2017. 'Gli artigiani e Roma tra alta e mediaetà repubblicana', in *Gli artigiani e la città*, ed. by Maria Cristina Biella, Roberta Cascino, Antonio F. Ferrandes, and Martina Revello-Lami (Rome: Quasar), pp. 21–53

Ficoroni, Francesco de. 1745. *Le memorie ritrovate nel territorio della prima e seconda città di Labico e i loro giusti siti* (Rome: Nella stamperia di Girolamo Mainardi)

Franchi De Bellis, Annalisa. 2005. *Iscrizioni prenestine su specchi e ciste* (Alessandria: Edizioni dell'Orso)

Gazda, Elaine K. (ed.). 2002. *The Ancient Art of Emulation: Studies in Artistic Originality and Tradition from the Present to Classical Antiquity* (Ann Arbor: University of Michigan Press)

Gilotta, Fernando, and Maria Paola Baglione. 2007. *Corpus speculorum Etruscorum: Italia, VI.1: Roma: Museo nazionale etrusco di Villa Giulia* (Rome: L'Erma di Bretschneider)

Hall, Jonathan M. 2004. 'How "Greek" Were the Early Western Greeks?', in *Greek Identity in the Western Mediterranean: Papers in Honour of Brian Shefton*, ed. by Kathryn Lomas (Leiden: Brill), pp. 35–54

Haumesser, Laurent. 2017. 'Hellenism in Central Italy', in *Etruscology*, ed. by Alessandro Naso (Berlin: De Gruyter), pp. 645–64

Hazard, Sonia. 2013. 'The Material Turn in the Study of Religion', *Religion and Society*, 4.1: 58–78

Heurgon, Jacques, and Massimo Pallottino. 1981. *Gli Etruschi e Roma* (Rome: Giorgio Bretschneider)

Hölscher, Tonio. 1987. *Römische Bildsprache als semantisches System: Vorgetragen am 16. Juni 1984* (Heidelberg: Winter)

——. 2004. *The Language of Images in Roman Art*, trans. by Anthony Snodgrass and Annemarie Künzl-Snodgrass (Cambridge: Cambridge University Press)

Köhnken, Adolf. 1965. *Apollonios Rhodios und Theokrit* (Göttingen: Vandenhoeck & Ruprecht)

Kousser, Rachel Meredith. 2008. *Hellenistic and Roman Ideal Sculpture: The Allure of the Classical* (Cambridge: Cambridge University Press)

Kruschwitz, Peter. 2002. 'Carmina Saturnia epigraphic: Einleitung, Text und Kommentar zu den Saturnischen Versinschriften' (unpublished doctoral thesis, Freie Universität Berlin)

Malkin, Irad. 2002. 'A Colonial Middle Ground: Greek, Etruscan and Local Elites in the Bay of Naples', in *The Archaeology of Colonialism*, ed. by Claire L. Lyons and John K. Papadopoulos (Los Angeles: Getty Research Institute), pp. 151–81

Mansuelli, Guido Achille. 1964. 'Novios Plautios Med Romai Fecid', *Athenaeum*, 42: 131–35

Marvin, M. 2008. *The Language of the Muses: The Dialogue between Roman and Greek Sculpture* (Los Angeles: Getty Publications)

Massa-Pairault, Françoise-Hélene. 1992. 'Aspetti e problemi della società prenestina tra IV e II sec. A.C.', in *La necropoli di Praeneste: periodi orientalizzante e medio repubblicano* (Palestrina: Comune di Palestrina, assessorato alla cultura), pp. 109–45

Massey, Doreen. 2006. 'Landscape as a Provocation: Reflections on Moving Mountains', *Journal of Material Culture*, 11.1–2 (1 July): 33–48

Meer, L. Bouke van der. 2016a. 'On the Imagery of Pear-Shaped Mirrors and Cistae', *BABESCH: Annual Papers on Mediterranean Archaeology*, 91: 105–28

——. 2016b. 'Reevaluating Etruscan Influences on the Engravings of Praenestine Pear-Shaped Mirrors and Cistae', *Etruscan Studies*, 19.1: 68–86

Menichetti, Mauro. 1995. *… Quoius forma virtutei parisuma fuit… : Ciste prenestine e cultura di Roma medio-repubblicana* (Rome: Giorgio Bretschneider)

Mol, Annemarie, and John Law. 1994. 'Regions, Networks and Fluids: Anaemia and Social Topology', *Social Studies of Science*, 24.4: 641–71

——. 2002. *Complexities: Social Studies of Knowledge Practices* (Durham, NC: Duke University Press)

Naso, Alessandro (ed.). 2017. *Etruscology* (Berlin: De Gruyter)

Nicosia, Emanuele, Dante Sacco, and Manuela Tondo. 2012. 'Das Schwert von San Vittore Del Lazio, Provinz Frosinone', in *Waffen für di Götter: Krieger Trophäen Heiligtümer*, ed. by Wolfgang Meighörner (Innsbruck: Tiroler Landesmuseum), pp. 71–74

Oppen, B. W. van. 2021. 'Radiant Bodies: Living with Etruscan Bronze Candelabra' (unpublished doctoral thesis, Columbia University)

Overbeck, Johannes Adolf. 1869. *Geschichte der griechischen Plastik für Künstler und Kunstfreunde* (Leipzig: Hinrichs)

Pallottino, Massimo. 1993. *Origini e storia primitiva di Roma* (Milan: Rusconi)

Pensabene, Patrizio. 1982. 'Sulla tipologia e il simbolismo dei cippi funerari a pigna con corona di foglie d'acanto di Palestrina', *Archeologia classica*, 34: 38–97

Perry, Ellen. 2005. *The Aesthetics of Emulation in the Visual Arts of Ancient Rome* (Cambridge: Cambridge University Press)

Ridgway, David (ed.). 2000. *Ancient Italy in its Mediterranean Setting: Studies in Honour of Ellen Macnamara* (London: Accordia Research Institute)

——. 2010. 'Greece, Etruria and Rome: Relationships and Receptions', *Ancient West & East*, 9: 43–61

Robertson, Martin. 1975. *A History of Greek Art* (Cambridge: Cambridge University Press)

Romanelli, Pietro. 1967. *Palestrina* (Cava dei Tirreni: Di Mauro)

Rouveret, Agnès. 1996. 'La ciste Ficoroni et la culture romaine du milieu du IVᵉ siècle av. J.-C.', *Bulletin de la Société nationale des antiquaires de France*, 1994, 1996 (26 October): 225–42

Ryberg, Inez S. 1940. *An Archaeological Record of Rome from the Seventh to the Second Century B.C.* (Philadelphia: University of Pennsylvania Press)

Sacco, Dante, Manuela Tondo, and Emanuele Nicosia. 2013. 'Il santuario di Fondo Decina. Materiale votivo e forme di culto. La spada di San Vittore', in *Lazio e Sabina*, IX: *Atti del convegno*, ed. by Giuseppina Ghini and Zaccaria Mari (Rome: Quasar), pp. 483–86

Šašel, Jaro. 1981. 'I Dindii: vicende ed economia di una famiglia di Preneste', *Zeitschrift für Papyrologie und Epigraphik*, 43: 337–42

Sassatelli, Giuseppe (ed.). 1981. *Corpus speculorum Etruscorum*, 1.1: *Bologna Museo Civico* (Rome: L'Erma di Bretschneider)

Schneider, Engelbert. 1886. *Dialecti Latinae priscae et Faliscae inscriptiones* (Leipzig: Teubner)

Schneider, Rolf Michael. 1995. 'Gegenbilder und Verhaltensideal auf der Ficoronischen Ciste', *Studi etruschi*, 60: 106–23

Serra Ridgway, Francesca R. 1998. 'Menichetti (Mauro). … Quoius forma virtutei parisuma fuit … Ciste prenestine e cultura di Roma medio-repubblicana', *Revue belge de philologie et d'histoire*, 76.1: 275–77

Stewart, Andrew F. 1986. 'When Is a Kouros Not an Apollo? The Tenea "Apollo" Revisited', in *Corinthiaca: Studies in Honour of Darrell A. Amyx*, ed. by Mario Del Chiaro (Columbia: University of Missouri Press), pp. 54–70

Taylor, Lily Ross. 1956. 'Trebula Suffenas and the Plautii Silvani', *Memoirs of the American Academy in Rome*, 24: 2–30

Terrenato, Nicola. 2014. 'Private *vis*, Public *virtus*. Family Agendas during the Early Roman Expansion', in *Roman Republican Colonization: New Perspectives from Archaeology and Ancient History*, ed. by Tesse D. Stek and Jeremia Pelgrom, Papers of the Royal Netherlands Institute in Rome, 62 (Rome: Palombi), pp. 45–59

——. 2019. *The Early Roman Expansion into Italy Elite Negotiation and Family Agendas* (Cambridge: Cambridge University Press)

Torelli, Mario. 2000. *The Etruscans* (Milan: Bompiani)

Trimble, Jennifer. 2011. *Women and Visual Replication in Roman Imperial Art and Culture* (Cambridge: Cambridge University Press)

Turfa, Jean MacIntosh. 2015. *The Etruscan World* (London: Routledge)

Wachter, Rudolf. 1987. *Altlateinische Inschriften: Sprachliche und epigraphische Untersuchungen zu den Dokumenten bis etwa 150 v. Chr.* (Bern: Lang)

Wallace, Rex. 2005. 'A Faliscan Inscription in the Michael and Judy Steinhardt Collection', *Zeitschrift für Papyrologie und Epigraphik*, 153: 175–82

Warden, Gregory. 2013. 'The Importance of Being Elite', in *A Companion to the Archaeology of the Roman Republic*, ed. by Jane DeRose Evans (Oxford: Blackwell), pp. 354–68

Warmington, Eric H. (trans.). 1940. *Remains of Old Latin*, IV: *Archaic Inscriptions* (Cambridge, MA: Harvard University Press)

Weis, Anne. 1982. 'The Motif of the Adligatus and Tree: A Study in the Sources of Pre-Roman Iconography', *American Journal of Archaeology*, 86.1: 21–38

Williams, Phyllis L. 1945. 'Note on the Interpretation of the Ficoroni Cista', *American Journal of Archaeology*, 49.3: 348–52

Winckelmann, Johann Joachim. 1776. *Johann Winkelmanns Geschichte der Kunst des Altertums* (Vienna: Im Akademische Verlage)

Wiseman, Timothy Peter. 1988. 'Satyrs in Rome? The Background to Horace's *Ars poetica*', *Journal of Roman Studies*, 78: 1–13

Zanker, Paul. 1990. *The Power of Images in the Age of Augustus*, trans. by H. A. Shapiro (Ann Arbor: University of Michigan Press)

Zinserling, Verena. 1975. 'Zum Bedeutungsgehalt des archaischen Kuros', *Eirene*, 13: 19–33

CHARLOTTE R. POTTS

6. Virtue in Variety

Contrasting Temple Design in Etruscan Italy

ABSTRACT This chapter will consider why temples with variants of peripteral and Tuscan plans were built side by side in select central Italic sanctuaries during the Etruscan Archaic period (*c.* 580–480 BCE). The collocation of temples with starkly different plans, as exemplified at Pyrgi and Marzabotto, has often been read as a sign that a site underwent a phase of Hellenization in architecture, religion, or culture more generally. The juxtaposition has also been ascribed to the demands of unknown rituals. As excavations uncover more similarities between the sanctuaries of Pyrgi and Regio I at Marzabotto, however, potential explanations for this phenomenon should now evolve to include factors that connect both sites as well as other examples. This chapter will consequently suggest that the collocation of temple plans reflects a central Italic affinity for visual variety and competition, comparable to the delight in contrasting designs displayed later at sites like Largo Argentina in Rome. The result is a model in which the use of 'Greek' architectural styles in Etruria and Latium is explained with reference to local aesthetic preferences.

The importance of external stimuli for the development of Etruscan architecture is a matter of ongoing debate. Some accounts hold that exposure to 'Oriental', 'Hellenic', and 'Roman' cultures in turn was a catalyst for change and innovation, and are part of a wider scholarly tradition in which the external connections that were always characteristic of Etruscan life are seen as signs of acculturation.[1]

In contrast, other (largely recent) studies have stressed the role of local forces in driving aesthetic and technical change.[2] In these analyses, factors such as demography, economics, ideology, and cultural conventions play a significant role in shaping the adoption and adaptation of practices from elsewhere. While all of these influences are most likely to have operated in concert in different ways at various times, the balance between them contributes to broader reconstructions of identity, connectivity, and power, and as such is as relevant for histories of Etruria as its buildings.

This chapter contributes to the debate by reassessing the interplay of Greek and Etruscan elements in the construction of Archaic temples. More specifically, it offers close readings of the 'Greek' and 'Tuscanic' temples built next to one another at Pyrgi and Marzabotto, both as individual structures and as pairs, and considers possible reasons for their juxtaposition. Although the heterogeneity of Etruscan sites means they are often studied individually, Pyrgi and Marzabotto offer complementary case studies of design: both have adjacent temples with starkly different plans, built decades apart, and thereby show how two communities responded to architectural choice. The first part of the chapter summarizes broad trends in Archaic temple architecture in Etruria and neighbouring Latium to contextualize the evidence of the four temples that is set out next.

Potts 2014–2015, among others. On the broader tradition see Riva 2018.

2   Architectural terracottas were one of the first areas in which scholars challenged models of one-way Hellenic influence: see, for example, Bianchi Bandinelli 1972; Edlund Gantz 1972, 188–94; Rystedt 1983, 159–64; Phillips Jr. 1984, 416–17. On temples see Potts 2015; on domestic architecture see Colantoni 2012 (on Latium but with wider relevance) and Miller 2017; and on urban planning see Govi 2014. Important examples outside the field of architecture include Spivey 1991; Riva 2006; Izzet 2007; Riva 2009; Bundrick 2019; cf. also Ridgway 2012.

---

1   For example: Torelli 1985, 27–32; Cifani 2008, 269–72, on central Italy rather than just Etruria; Torelli 2000, 72–73, 77 (Near Eastern influence); Ampolo 1971; Pallottino 1975, 174; Drews 1981, 154–57; Colonna 1986, 464; Ridgway 1988, 666–67; Owens 1991, 96, 104–05 (Hellenic influence); and for discussions and critique of Roman influence see Edlund-Berry 2013, 695–99;

| **Corresponding author**: Charlotte R. Potts (charlotte.potts@classics.ox.ac.uk)

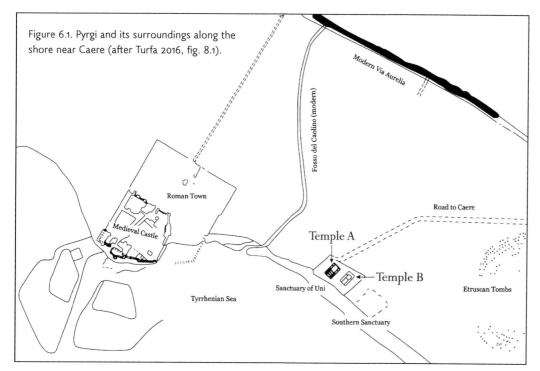

Figure 6.1. Pyrgi and its surroundings along the shore near Caere (after Turfa 2016, fig. 8.1).

These buildings are then analysed in three dimensions, rather than solely from plans, and are, lastly, evaluated for what their proximity suggests about the timing and prestige of 'Hellenic' forms. The results suggest that temples of the time were designed with a local frame of reference as much as, or even more than, a Greek one.

Archaic 'Hellenization'

Architectural histories recognize that many of the first temples built in central Italy incorporate elements more familiar in the Greek world. When the first monumental temples appear in Etruria and Latium during the Archaic period (c. 580–480 BCE), seemingly in dialogue with one another, many have features such as peristyles, crepidomas, and decorations that show figures and scenes from Greek myths. Some of the temples built at Satricum, Pyrgi, Marzabotto, and Rome, for example, have peripteral and semi-peripteral plans. The first Temple of Mater Matuta in Rome has a closed pediment rather than the open gables common on other buildings and is laid out on axis with an external altar. Terracotta sculptures of Herakles, Athena, and gorgons ornament many temples in Etruria and Latium, and a bull-headed man or minotaur is part of the decorated roof of the building beneath the later Regia in Rome (Downey 1995, 9–10, 19–30; Lulof 2000; 2016). Scholars have argued that the Attic foot is used in the design of temples at Pyrgi and Marzabotto, and possibly also the Capitoline temple in Rome (Colonna 1970c, 289; Melis 1985, 130; Cifani 2008, 239 n. 684, 240, 293; Govi 2017b, 157), while technical connections between the Capitoline temple and the Samian Heraion are suggested by the way in which their foundations include a transverse wall between the cella and the frontal colonnade and the longitudinal internal walls are bound to those of the perimeter (Hopkins 2016, 113–15, 118–19). Some temples at Veii, Orvieto, and Tarquinia are even oriented eastwards (Pernigotti 2019).[3] Together these features indicate that central Italian builders and audiences were familiar with components of Hellenic art and architecture and were willing to use them in the enhancement of their own cult sites.

Explanations for the number of elements that these temples share with their Greek counterparts are slowly changing. Traditional models argue that religious architecture in central Italy was partly 'Hellenized' in the Archaic period, through changes in building practice, cult, or society more generally (for example Colonna 1984, 405; Torelli 2000a, 280–84; Cifani 2008, 293, 300; Mura Sommella 2009, 348; Haack 2017, 1008–09; Govi 2017b, 172; cf. Boethius and others 1978, 36, 164). Such claims are often informed by theories of diffusionism or acculturation, with a belief that people in central Italy sought Hellenic glamour and authority, be it achieved through imitation of a certain polity, or through the practices of a less differentiated Greek world.[4] Other studies, however, have suggested that concurrences in temple construction in many areas around the Mediterranean are unsurprising in a connected world, and particularly at a time when increased investment in cult sites turned select temples into monumental statements of wealth and piety. The construction of these temples, on a new scale and with new techniques, likely required external expertise; in time, the result may have been mobile or international

---

3 Pernigotti 2019 identifies five out of twenty-eight Etruscan temples that were oriented east.

4 For critiques of Hellenization as a concept, including the notion of a monolithic type of Hellenic or Greek culture, see Hall 1997; Malkin 2001; Hall 2002; Dougherty and Kurke 2003; Wallace-Hadrill 2008; Skinner 2012.

communities of practice that facilitated common elements (Potts 2022). In this situation, temple building may not merely reflect connectivity, but actively drive it. Furthermore, at Ephesus, Samos, Rome, Naukratis, and Pyrgi, among others, the resultant buildings have architectural and religious points of convergence to the point where they can be considered part of a network (Davies 2006; Potts 2015, 114–20; Hopkins 2016, 17–18, 176). At the same time, each has local details in its décor, elevation, proportions, and resident deity. Newer interpretations of this phenomenon range far from the centre–periphery model found in standard accounts of Hellenization, and instead draw on approaches used in studies of globalization, where convergence finds a corollary in the resurgence of local differences (Hodos 2017, 4–5), as well as studies of economics and different types of network theories. Such conceptual changes prompt scholars to reassess the design of these buildings and the motivations of societies that produced them.

Against this backdrop of sanctuaries as entities that can represent wider attitudes and relationships, the following analysis explores how site-specific and broader architectural practices — both cultural and multicultural — may have been balanced in the creation of temples at two Etruscan settlements.

Pyrgi and Marzabotto

Pyrgi and Marzabotto offer unusual insight into Etruscan architecture through the mutual possession of paired, or juxtaposed, temples. As well as having adjacent temples with markedly different plans, sanctuaries at both sites appear to have been created with designs that made use of the Attic foot; excavations at both have yielded inscriptions that hint at the historical conditions of construction; and both have been subject to many years of study that allow their temples to be put into wider contexts. They also have important differences. One site lies on the coast and the other inland, and one is flanked by other cult sites while the other stands amidst a city (Figs 6.1 and 6.2).[5] Furthermore, they lie over 260 km apart. Given that Etruscan art and architecture often diverge markedly over short distances, to the point that heterogeneity is a key feature of much Etruscan material culture, commonalities between these sites may thus hint at factors that went beyond one locale or setting, and were instead cultural. Before studying any trends, however, it is useful to review the data for each building.

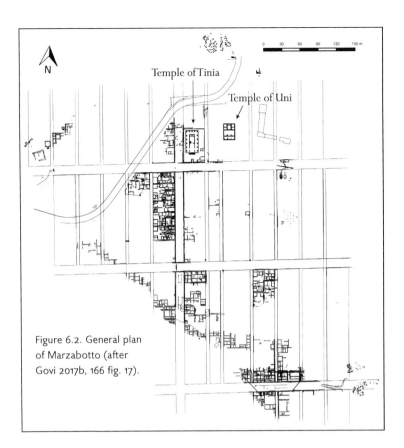

Figure 6.2. General plan of Marzabotto (after Govi 2017b, 166 fig. 17).

Pyrgi: Temples B and A

In *c.* 510 BCE, the ground of the monumental sanctuary at Pyrgi was artificially raised by a clay embankment on top of which builders erected Temple B. The foundations of the temple, built of large blocks of tufo imported from the surroundings of Caere, measured approximately 29.65 × 20.10 m and comprised an internal rectangle, divided by a transverse wall, and connected to an outer rectangle by minor walls at one end (Fig. 6.3) (Melis 1985b, 130; Michetti 2016, 79). Spoliation of the blocks hampers full knowledge of the original height of the base, but there are suggestions that the outer rectangle may have narrowed at the two upper levels to produce a stepped crepidoma and stylobate (Melis 1985b, 130). Four fragments of stone columns suggest that the superstructure included smooth-shafted columns with a lower diameter of 1 m that were covered in plaster. The walls appear to have been built with tufo blocks that were plastered and painted with red and white pigments, and fragments of a tapering terracotta doorframe with a moulded floral design suggest an impressive entrance (Melis 1970b, 380–87). The excavators propose that the temple had a single cella and a pronaos open to the south-west, surrounded by a perimeter colonnade with four columns across the front and two columns immediately behind, with the entire structure facing the sea (Colonna 1970e, 286). They

---

5 For recent overviews of the topography of Pyrgi see Michetti 2016; Baglione 2017, and for Marzabotto see Govi 2017a and 2017b.

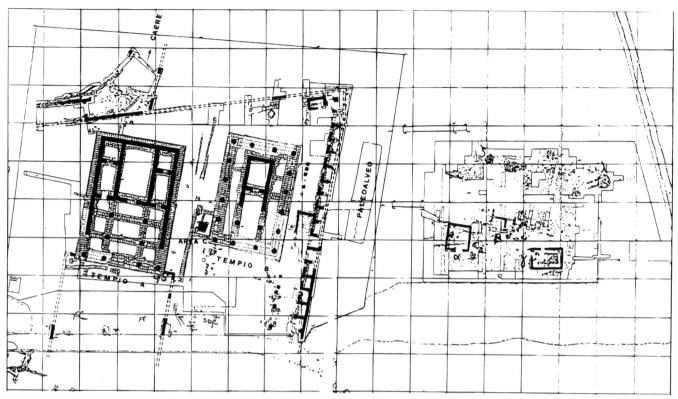

Figure 6.3. Plan of the sanctuary of Pyrgi: 'Monumental Sanctuary' with Temples B and A (left) and 'Southern Sanctuary' (right) (Michetti 2016, 78 fig. 7.5, courtesy of Sapienza Università di Roma, Dipartimento di Scienze dell'Antichità, Archivio Etruscologia).

also suggest that the plan was designed according to the Attic foot of 29.6 cm and used a module of three Attic feet (Colonna 1970e, 289; Melis 1985b, 130). Alternatively, archaeologists not connected with the excavation have read the wide porticoes and short cella as indications that the building may have had one cella and two alae instead of a peristyle, and thus could have resembled a more traditional Tuscanic temple (Nielsen and Poulsen 1992, 78, 131).

Excavations have yielded additional evidence about the roof, setting, and possible historical context of Temple B. Architectural terracottas show that the inclination of the roof was approximately 15 degrees and the use of large antepagmenta imply a recessed gable (Colonna 1985, 130). Acroteria include statues of women, Amazons, horses, and riders, as well as a possible central acroterion featuring Herakles and Athena; revetments depict horses, riders, men, women, felines, a hydra, and ornamental decoration; and there are antefixes in the form of the heads of men, women, and satyrs (Colonna 1970a; 1970d; Melis 1970a; 1970b; Colonna 1985, 130–33; Lulof 2016, 137 n. 53). The trabeation is usually reconstructed with queen posts and collar beams, while the need for trusses has been debated (Fig. 6.4) (Melis 1985, 131 fig. 7.1 B; Turfa and Steinmayer 1996, 18–19 n. 27; Damgaard Andersen 1998, I, 123–24). At the time of its construction, the temple appears to have been surrounded by a wall on at least three sides — the western side of the sanctuary has been lost to erosion and the shifting coastline — with an opening to the east that allowed visitors approaching from Caere to access the back of Temple B, and a series of roofed rooms along the south wall (Colonna 1989–1990, 209–12; Baglione 2017, 110–12). Between the north side of the temple and the wall there was a small, enclosed space, now called Area C, containing a well, two or three altars, and animal bones (Cardini 1970; Colonna 1970b). When Temple B was dismantled centuries later, some of its blocks were used to fashion a space within Area C to hold three gold sheets or tablets with Punic and Etruscan inscriptions and eight bronze nails with gilded heads. The tablets record that a ruler of Caere named Thefarie Velianas gave a holy item to a goddess named Astarte in Punic and Uni in Etruscan, in return for her favour. The excavators date the tablets to the late sixth century BCE, and believe that the nails were used to fasten the tablets to the doorjamb of the cella of Temple B at the time that it was dedicated, thereby giving the building a named actor and a resident god.[6]

---

[6] The bibliography on the tablets is vast. Key contributions include Colonna 1965; 1970e; 2000, 294–309, but see also Heurgon 1966, 7 on debated dating, and Pfiffig 1965, 42 and Heurgon 1966,

In c. 470–460 BCE the sanctuary was nearly doubled in size with a construction programme that included expanding the embankment to the north, building Temple A, extending the boundary wall, and creating a new monumental entrance to the east.[7] Two longitudinal walls, three full-width latitudinal walls, and two shorter latitudinal walls in the inner part of the foundations of Temple A suggest a plan of approximately 34.33 × 23.98 m in which the rear of the building had three cellas, with the lateral cellas divided into front and back areas and both smaller than the single-roomed central space (Fig. 6.5) (Colonna 1970d, 46–47; Melis 1985a, 134). Fragments of stone drums and a partial capital found to the west indicate a columned porch, and have led to the reconstruction of antae and three rows of columns on the western side of the building, including a central intercolumniation wider than those at the sides (Fig. 6.5) (Colonna 1970d, 42–44; Melis 1985a, 136). The excavators believe that the building was designed with the Attic foot again (Melis 1985a, 134). Spoliation of the blocks in the substructure means there are no traces of features such as stairs, but two remnants of a stone moulding have been read as signs of a decorated podium (Colonna 1970d, 40–43; Melis 1985a, 134). Traces of walls extending from the front of the temple, either side of wells, may outline a large terrace (Melis 1985a, 134). Stone blocks with white plaster have been interpreted as remains of the external walls of the temple while mud bricks with plaster and polychrome paint may have been used for interior walls; a third type of plaster is thought to have covered the underside of the roof tiles (Colonna 1970d, 44–46). As a whole, the building is larger than Temple B and, although it may have followed the alignment of the earlier building, it stands noticeably forward from it.

The roof decorations from Temple A are masterpieces of Etruscan terracotta art. The rear of the building had several antepagmenta that indicate a roof slope of 18 degrees and are large enough to suggest a recessed gable, possibly as part of a roof built with cypress beams arranged in tie-beam trusses (Melis 1985a, 136; Colonna 1988–1989, 111 fig. 88). All of the antepagmenta at the rear of the building may illustrate episodes from the myth of the Seven against Thebes: the column plaque shows Zeus/Tinia throwing a lightning bolt towards Capaneus/Capne, as Athena/Menrva watches Tydeus/Tute eating the

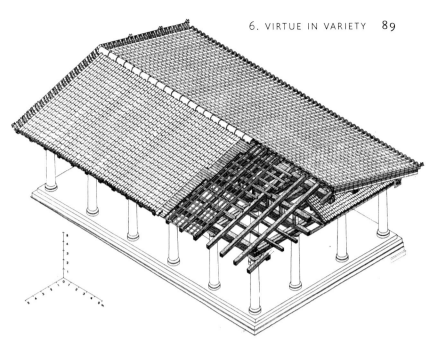

Figure 6.4. Reconstruction of Temple B, Pyrgi, c. 510 BCE, without architectural terracottas (Melis 1985, 131 fig. 7.1 B, courtesy of Archivio di Etruscologia, Dipartimento di Scienze dell'Antichità, Sapienza Università di Roma).

Figure 6.5. Reconstruction of Temple A, Pyrgi, c. 470–460 BCE (Colonna 2000, 310 fig. 34, courtesy of Archivio di Etruscologia, Dipartimento di Scienze dell'Antichità, Sapienza Università di Roma).

brains of his opponent; a plaque to the left depicts four or six warriors, who Colonna theorizes may be Argives; and a plaque to the right includes a male helmeted head that could, according to Colonna, be part of a depiction of the fratricide of Eteocles and Polynices (Colonna 1970b; 2000, 311–25; Baglione 2017, 115 n. 72). The original reliefs from the front of the building have been lost, but seem to have been replaced in the late fifth century BCE with scenes of Herakles and Amazons, judging by fragments preserved in wells. A third redesign in the fourth century

---

6–7 for alternative hypotheses about the structure to which the tablets refer.

7 An alternative dating of Temple A to c. 490–480 BCE has also been proposed: Damgaard Andersen 1998, IV, 88 n. 487; countered by Colonna 2000, 311–12.

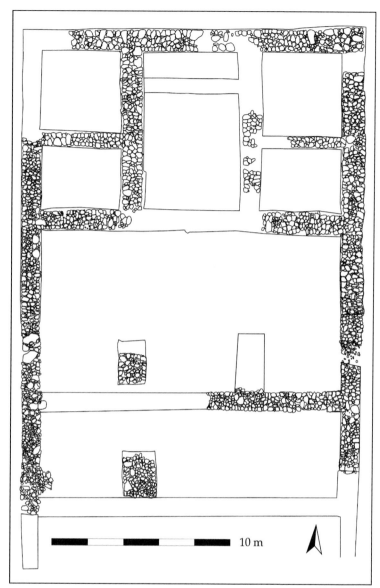

Figure 6.6. Plan of the foundations of the Temple of Uni, Marzabotto, late sixth century BCE (from Govi 2017b, 147 fig. 2).

BCE may have shown Ino/Leucothea and Palemone being received by Herakles, perhaps at Pyrgi itself given Herakles' possible role in the mythical foundation of the site (Colonna 2000, 304–05, 325–33). Colonna (2000, 326–27, 331) has argued that the successive decorations on the front of the temple stress Herakles not as a solitary hero but as a champion of civil society, opposing the disorder represented by the Amazons and promoting the right of asylum. Scholars have also suggested that the scenes on the front and the back of the temple may be connected to one another on two levels: as allusions to political events, either in connection with Syracuse or with Caere, the latter as a condemnation of the recent tyrannical rule of Thefarie Velianas through references to the dangers of hubris and the reassertion of order; or alternatively as hopes for salvation after death, reflecting concerns in contemporary Etruscan and Greek religion.[8] The possible use of Greek figurative language to express Etruscan values will be explored further below.

Marzabotto: The Temples of Uni and Tinia

Excavations carried out from 2013 to 2015 in Regio I at Marzabotto uncovered a Tuscanic temple previously known only from geophysics and archaeological surveys (Govi 2017b, 146–58). The remains are largely those of the foundations, formed of medium-sized pebbles arranged in up to seven layers with a height of approximately 1.10 m in the best-preserved areas, and include sandstone boulders up to 1 m long placed predominantly at corners (Fig. 6.6). The foundations sink into virgin soil and appear to date to the late sixth century BCE and thus roughly the same time that the town was substantially rebuilt. Above the pebbles lie larger quadrangular stones thought to mark the base of the podium, and a layer of travertine workings that suggest the shaping of blocks onsite. The remaining walls indicate a plan measuring 19.14 × 25.7 m in total, perhaps following the Attic foot (Govi 2017b, 157); although the arrangement at the front of the building is unclear, traces of two walls extending either side to the south may have bounded stairs (Garagnani, Gaucci, and Gruška 2016, 79; Govi 2017b, 150–51). The back part of the building appears to have had three cellas, each divided internally into a front and back room, with the largest front room located in the central cella. A deep porch preserves two supports on the western side that suggest two rows of columns, possibly four in front and two behind, laid against two transverse walls in the substructure. Based on materials used elsewhere in the settlement, it has been suggested that the walls of the superstructure were made of mud brick, supported by beams, while the columns could have been made of wood or stone with bases and capitals of local travertine (Sassatelli and Govi 2005, 26; Govi and Sassatelli 2010, I, 213–18; Garagnani, Gaucci, and Gruška 2016, 79). Palaeobotanical studies indicate the presence of oak trees that may have supplied the roof beams, thought to have been arranged in a pseudo-truss system (Garagnani, Gaucci, and Gruška 2016, 79–80). Few roof decorations have survived,

---

[8] Allusion to politics: Pairault Massa 1992, 72–75; Colonna 2000; Haynes 2000, 180–81; Jannot 2005, 111; Baglione 2013, 619–20; Smith 2014, 83; Michetti 2016, 79; Baglione 2017, 113–15; Haack 2017, 1003. Salvation: Colonna 2000, 334–35.

but some come from palmette antefixes (Garagnani, Gaucci, and Gruška 2016, 80; Govi 2017b, 163).

Finds in and around the temple may offer a political context for construction. Two pieces of a bucchero amphora placed in one of the south-west foundation walls are inscribed with the Etruscan words *kainu*[...] and *śpural*[...] (Govi 2017b, 158–63). The term *Kainua* is known from other inscriptions at Marzabotto and appears to be the ancient name of the settlement. *Śpura* is thought to be the genitive of a word referring to the city as a politically organized community, akin to *civitas* in Latin. The fragments may record the dedication of the temple on behalf of the city (the *śpura*) rather than an individual, and their concealment in the walls is reminiscent of a foundation ritual (Govi 2017b, 160–63). The discovery of another, later inscription in the vicinity of the temple refers to the goddess Uni and makes it possible that the building was dedicated to her (Govi 2017b, 163–65).

A few decades later a second temple was built near the first. It was larger and closer to the road than its neighbour, had a peristyle, and as discussed below appears to have been dedicated to Uni's consort, Tinia. A small street between the two buildings formalized their distinct identities (Govi 2017a, 92; 2017b, 171–72). The new temple stood above, and partially reused, the pebble walls of a pre-existing structure with a different orientation; the presence of a fragmentary rim of a bucchero chalice from the last decades of the sixth century BCE dates this structure to the same era as the adjacent temple (Sassatelli and Govi 2010, 33). The fifth-century BCE temple faced south, like its neighbour, but was built with a different technique that provides an unusually clear plan (Sassatelli and Govi 2005; 2010) (Fig. 6.7). The foundations consisted of two or three layers of pebbles beneath blocks of local stone, and up to four layers of cobbles beneath columns, indicating that the placement of columns was planned from the start. L-shaped walls at the front indicate a staircase measuring 10.60 m wide and 3.80 m deep and a podium at least 1.20 m high likely decorated with moulded stone revetments given their presence in a well to the north-east (Sassatelli and Govi 2010, 31–32). Visible column bases record the use of a peristyle with four columns at the front, five at the back, and six either side, in a plan of 35.5 × 21.9 m. A single cella in the middle was subdivided into a bipartite rear space and a pronaos with anta walls. The excavators believe that the roofing system did not use a truss, and tiles found in the well to the north-east differ in shape and size from those currently recognized in the rest of the settlement (Sassatelli and Govi 2010, 32). The measurements of the tem-

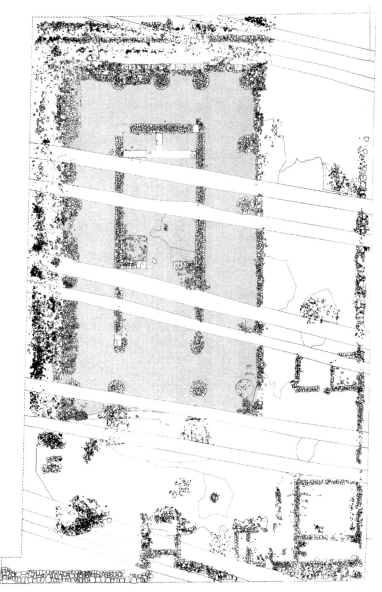

Figure 6.7. Plan of the foundations of the Temple of Tinia, Marzabotto, c. 480–470 BCE (from Sassatelli and Govi 2005, 14 fig. 5).

ple are again thought to correspond with the Attic foot (Sassatelli and Govi 2005, 26–30; 2010, 32). The recovery of a small bucchero *olla*, inscribed with the word *tins* after firing, has seen the temple assigned to Tinia (Sassatelli and Govi 2005, 38–47; 2010, 34).

In a striking parallel with the temple at Pyrgi, an inscribed bronze tablet was found between the western wall of the temple and its enclosure (Govi 2015; 2017b, 169–71). The text is incomplete, but the extant portion has five lines in Etruscan and a nail hole that suggests it was displayed. The first two lines appear to refer to an action performed by one or two people, and the other three lines contain the verb *hecce*, meaning to build, construct, or make, in an act involving an additional two people. The tablet has been dated to the second quarter of the fifth century

Figure 6.8. Virtual reconstruction of the two urban temples at Marzabotto, viewed from *Plateia* B (after Garagnani, Gaucci, and Govi 2016).

BCE, like the adjacent building, and the excavators propose that the whole text was a record of activities related to the foundation of the temple. In such a scenario, the people mentioned could be priests or magistrates and the use of the word *śpura* in the second line again evokes an institutional framework. The way in which the temple occupies a whole block of the newly reorganized city, lying at the intersection of two of its most important roads and on the route to the acropolis (Fig. 6.2), also reinforces the sense that its construction should be understood as part of a systematization of urban life encompassing architecture, topography, and public performance (Govi 2017b, 172–74). In this way, the temple can be placed within a larger socio-political context much like Temple B at Pyrgi, paving the way for discussion of connections between architecture and culture.

From Plans to Buildings

Although the data presented so far are relatively straightforward, the buildings they generate challenge the cultural labels used in traditional architectural typologies. A significant part of the problem lies in the habit of studying buildings on the basis of their plans alone. Recourse to plans is arguably justifiable when the remains of many central Italian structures comprise little more than foundations, but it effectively reduces a building to two dimensions. A plan is only one element of architecture: elevations, décor, and setting all shape how structures look and are perceived, as do patterns of use, sensory stimuli, and more abstract factors such as memory and time. When the temples under consideration here are explored as three-dimensional entities with an everyday, lived reality, it complicates the idea that a peripteral plan produces a 'Greek' temple and a plan with a closed rear and frontal columns creates an 'Tuscanic' or 'Etrusco-Italic' one. This, in turn, affects assessments of cultural influence and rationales for particular choices.

The Temple of Tinia at Marzabotto is a prime example of the need to avoid reading the presence of a peristyle as shorthand for 'Greek' sacred design. The excavators have pointed out that the Temple of Tinia has multiple features that are characteristic of local, not Greek, architecture. The peristyle has five columns at the rear but only four in front, and those at the front are aligned with the cella walls to give a wider central intercolumniation that highlights the facade (Sassatelli and Govi 2010, 32). The frontal emphasis is strengthened by the staircase, itself part of a monumental podium that raises the floor and restricts access to those approaching from the south. The asymmetrical use of columns in the plan has comparanda in Campania and Sicily, seen, for example, in the basilica at Paestum and the

Olympeion at Agrigento, and also at Ionian sites such as Ephesus, but the way in which it is part of a design marked by frontality and axiality at Marzabotto may find a closer parallel in the Capitoline temple at Rome, where a peristyle or *peripteros sine postico* arrangement is thought to have stood atop a high podium (Cifani 2008, 105, 107; Mura Sommella 2009; Hopkins 2012); the excavators have noted that the association of the Marzabotto temple with Tinia, the Etruscan equivalent of Jupiter, may not be coincidental (Sassatelli and Govi 2010, 32; Govi 2014, 97). When the elevation, deity, and unusual peristyle are considered together, the result is a building that embodies central Italian architectural preferences as much as Greek ones.

A similar blurring of the architectural grammars usually read as 'Greek' and 'Tuscanic' occurs at Pyrgi. As mentioned above, the use of a peristyle in Temple B at Pyrgi is less secure than in the Temple of Tinia at Marzabotto, but the temple ostensibly displays Greek connections on its roof as well through imagery connected with Herakles. Scenes from myths featuring the hero appear to have decorated the gables and eaves, and a central acroterion depicting Herakles with Athena is likely to have crowned the whole edifice. Such subjects were not uncommon in Etruscan art, and similar acroteria appear to have decorated at least twelve other central Italian temples in the Archaic period (Lulof 2000; 2016, n. 36; Lulof and Smith 2017, 7–9). At Pyrgi, the choice of these seemingly Greek subjects has been partly explained by Hellenic analogies: the conjunction of Boardman's theory that Peisistratos used Herakles imagery to bolster his rule in sixth-century Athens and the high number of tyrants in Archaic Greece has seen Thefarie Velianas, the ruler of Caere named in the tablets, interpreted as a comparable tyrant who used Temple B to assert his power (Boardman 1972; Colonna 2000, 283–94; Baglione 2017, 112–14). The theory that Herakles and Athena acroteria were popular in Etruria and Latium because they represent a male leader bolstered by the support of a female deity, a legitimizing concept traceable in sources from the Pyrgi tablets to accounts of early Roman kings (for example Dion. Hal., *Ant. Rom.*, IV. 27. 7; IV. 40. 7; Plut., *Quaest. Rom.*, XXXVI, LXXIV; Plut., *De fort. Rom.*, X, describing Fortuna's favouring of Servius Tullius), dovetails with this perception (Coarelli 1988, 253–55, 301–28; Pairault Massa 1992, 60–63; Cornell 1995, 146–47; Linke 2010, 188 92; Lulof 2016, 136–37). The dedication of the building to the Punic goddess Astarte adds a cosmopolitan dimension, as does the possibility that Herakles could be assimilated to Melqart (Colonna 2000, 304–05; Malkin 2011, 119–41), fur-

ther bridging multiple cultural frameworks. Again, however, these elements are combined with features more characteristic of the Etruscans. The front of the temple is emphasized by a double row of four columns. Terracotta decorations are held up by a roof with a recessed gable and perhaps tie-beam trusses, while the original wall around the temple and the construction of Area C impose an axial experience. Finally, the equivalence of Astarte and the Etruscan goddess Uni in the tablets likely represents assimilation with a local goddess. The result is a temple with 'Greek-Italian' features (Colonna 2000, 304–05; cf. Mertens 1980, 49–50), with references to Punic and Etruscan cults, in an Etruscan sanctuary. The reality is that this is far from a simple Greek temple.

The nearby Temple A at Pyrgi also has a dense layer of mythological imagery, but this time placed over a classic Tuscanic plan. Scenes from the Theban mythological cycle appear on the rear of the building, while Herakles has a starring role at the front. As outlined in the previous section, the Greek material on Temple A has been read as another commentary on local events, this time the end of Thefarie Velianas's rule. The imagery on the rear gable that faced visitors approaching Pyrgi from Caere has also encouraged interpretations that link the narratives with the Etruscan city (Jannot 2005, 111; Bonfante and Swaddling 2006, 23; Baglione 2013, 619–20; Carpino 2016, 412–13). However, explanations in this vein do not have to centre on Thefaire Velianas. The Theban cycle was popular in Etruscan art (Krauskopf 1974; von Vacano and von Freytag gen Löringhoff 1982, 34–46), and is it possible that the display of myths connected with Thebes, on a symbol of Caere's piety and wealth, was as much about equating the Etruscan city with its counterparts in Greece as it was an attempt to elevate the building through Hellenic-inspired décor.

At this point, one can also question the extent to which patrons, builders, and worshippers saw the myths illustrated at Pyrgi as Greek rather than Etruscan, or alternatively as part of a common heritage. The Pyrgi tablets suggest that the same goddess could simultaneously be known as Uni and Astarte, or at least worshipped by visitors under different names in the same place. It is thus plausible that Herakles, celebrated in the sculptural decoration of both Temples B and A, may also have been understood to be Etruscan Hercle, and perhaps even the Roman Hercules or Phoenician Melqart, by those using the sanctuary. Etruscan Hercle is far from a carbon copy of the Greek Herakles. Etruscan artists show Hercle in exploits unknown in Greek myth, such as the abduction of the lady Mlacuch, or performing deeds that in Greece are ascribed to other heroes, such as the slaying of the Minotaur.[9] In another disparity with Greek tradition, artworks show him attaining immortality by being breastfed by Uni in adulthood, perhaps reflecting an Etruscan belief in the transformative power of bodily fluids.[10] With his own mythology and cult, he appears to have been worshipped in Etruria as a god rather than a hero (de Grummond 2006, 182). Hercle may also have had special status at Pyrgi itself. Colonna notes that the connection between Hercle and sacred waters in Etruscan religion mean it is not inconceivable that Hercle was once worshipped at the freshwater spring that flowed east of the monumental sanctuary at Pyrgi, and likely accounts for the original siting of the port; his cult may therefore predate the worship of multivalent goddesses there (Colonna 2000, 274–75, 292–93). It is thus debatable to what extent the Herakles/Hercle imagery is 'Greek' rather than 'Etruscan' or even multicultural. Looking beyond the Herakles/Hercle scenes, the wielding of a lightning bolt on the columen plaque of Temple A may also chime with Etruscan reverence for such portents (Turfa 2012, 61). There are thus grounds to acknowledge that Etruscan visitors may have understood the decoration of the temples at Pyrgi differently from their Greek equivalents.

Another issue in quantifying the 'Greek' elements of the four temples in this study relates to claims that they were built with designs that utilized the Attic foot. Damage to blocks, and the hypotheses involved in reconstructing temple plans, mean that precise measurements always risk giving a misleading sense of accuracy (Turfa and Steinmayer 1996, 1), and while the use of an empirical or relative building module can be identified at some sites — for instance, between roof tiles and other elements — the recognition of fixed, independent units is open to challenge. Notwithstanding these caveats, metrologists call a foot of 29.6 cm both 'Attic' and 'Attic-Roman', as the unit was widely used in Archaic and Republican Italian architecture and in time became the standard 'Roman' foot (Robertson 1969, 82 n. 3, 149 n. 1; Turfa and Steinmayer 1996, 2 n. 3; Jones 2000, 73–74 fig. 1; Maras 2013, 486); a chronological

marker for when the measure passed from being a hallmark of building in Greece to building in Italy must be arbitrary and overlooks shared practice. If one accepts that a temple was built with a module of 29.6 cm, that does not automatically make the result a Greek temple.

All of the above suggests that at least three of the four paired temples at Marzabotto and Pyrgi combine elements that, in isolation, can be mapped onto cultural categories ranging from Greek and Etruscan to Punic, central Italian, and even Roman. Yet dissecting buildings in this way overlooks the reality to which each element contributed, as does trying to describe the end product with just one of these labels based on anything other than its location (cf. the arguments by John North Hopkins elsewhere in this volume). One should also be aware of imposing ethnic and cultural classifications which contemporaries may have deemed less relevant than ideas held by local inhabitants and external visitors (Riva 2009, 91). Regardless of their forms, these temples stood in sanctuaries in Etruria, and helped Etruscans to communicate with their gods. This is not to deny that people from other cultures used these sanctuaries, nor to side-line features more characteristic of Punic, Greek, or Roman culture, but to emphasize that the primary frame of reference for viewers and visitors of these temples was their location in Etruria. Here, visible and invisible geographies could establish an Etruscan frame of reference. For instance, the reorganization of the urban plan at Marzabotto at the end of the sixth century BCE appears to have been guided by solar and religious precepts, which saw the paired temples in Regio I located in the north-east part of the city just as Tinia and Uni and were thought to reside in the north-east part of the Etruscan heavenly *templum* (Malgieri 2007b; Morpurgo 2007; Govi 2017b). Such a scenario reinforces that the intrinsic function of these temples was to facilitate the worship of gods in Etruria. Calling two of the results 'Greek' would prioritize style over location, setting, and cults identified epigraphically, or, more accurately, would make the peristyle the typological determinant in a typology that is moreover purely visual.

Subsequently, the use of peristyles and Greek myths — and perhaps also anthropomorphic deities who enjoyed monumental houses — in Etruria needs justifying. If local needs were important, why incorporate such features at all? The traditional answer is acculturation, arguing that builders and worshippers believed Greek features were superior. An alternative answer, just as speculative as the traditional one, is that there was little or no change in the underlying concepts that shaped Etruscan reli-

---

9 Note that these representations appear after the Archaic period, for example the abduction of Mlacuch is shown on a mirror from *c.* 480–470 BCE now in the British Museum, and the image of Hercle as Minotaur-slayer appears on a mirror from Civita Castellana of *c.* 300 BCE, present location unknown: see de Grummond 2006, 180–88.

10 As shown on a bronze mirror of *c.* 400–375 BCE now in the Museo Civico Archeologico in Bologna, and on another mirror from Volterra, *c.* 325 BCE, now in the Museo Archeologico Nazionale in Florence: de Grummond 2006, 84–85. On the belief more generally see Brandt 2015, 125–31.

gion or its architecture, but instead a selective, superficial change that worked to local advantage. Here the pairing of temples becomes significant, and it is to this that I now turn.

Paired Temples

The sequence of decisions that produced adjacent temples at Pyrgi and Marzabotto differs enough between sites to challenge the notion that Hellenic features, or more specifically peristyles, were always preferable for temple designs in Etruria. While the temple with the peripteral plan was the first of the two built at Pyrgi, at Marzabotto it was the second. The chronological gap between the construction of the first and second temples at both sites accordingly suggests that the use of a peripteral plan should not be attributed to a fastmoving trend in Etruria in either the late sixth century or early fifth century BCE. The relative prominence of each plan in the pair is also dissimilar. At Pyrgi, the peripteral temple is the smaller of the two and is set back in the sanctuary; the Tuscanic temple is physically and visually dominant (Baglione 2017, 114–15). At Marzabotto, however, the peripteral temple is significantly larger and placed forward of its neighbour, obscuring the smaller temple from visitors approaching from the south or west (Fig. 6.8) (Govi 2017a, 92; 2017b, 172). The divergent sizes indicate that there was no inherent drive to make temples with a peripteral plan larger or smaller than those without. The comparison therefore suggests there was no perception that peristyles belonged in temples that were bigger, somehow better, or first.

Nonetheless, there are similarities between the sites that hint at larger trends. Both communities appear to have wanted the second temple to be larger than the first, reflecting an increase in resources or confidence. More importantly, both seem to have believed that temples with different plans were desirable. This went beyond having a variety of temples spread across a sanctuary or settlement. The juxtaposition was deliberate, emphatic, and not an isolated case. One can therefore theorize, albeit cautiously, that the decision to duplicate, but not replicate, an existing structure may represent a preference that transcended one city and one part of Etruria.

One explanation for diversified temple exteriors is that the visual culture of Archaic Etruria included an aesthetic that could be termed 'eclectic'. Although this adjective has been used pejoratively in regard to Roman art history, the term is gradually being rehabilitated through recognition of the connoisseurship that can be involved in selecting creations to create new meanings and serve new functions. Heterogeneity is being recognized increasingly in Roman rhetoric, literature, and other intellectual endeavours, suggesting that a delight in *varietas* was not merely a feature of Roman art, but one characteristic of Roman culture (Tronchin 2012; Fitzgerald 2016, 47–83). It therefore does not have to have a negative connotation when applied to the culture of neighbouring Etruria, nor contribute to what are now outdated views about the stylistic unity, and therefore superiority, of Hellenic visual culture; indeed, the concept of *poikilia* in Archaic Greek aesthetics may be comparable (Grand-Clement 2015, 410). As has been noted, however, it is not enough to view eclecticism as a valid aesthetic and go no further; scholars should attempt to understand how and why such a style arose and what it may convey about those who celebrated it (Tronchin 2012, 275; Petersen 2012). In terms of architecture, one could propose that the eclectic designs of the four adjacent temples in the Largo Argentina sanctuary at Rome at the end of the second century BCE derive from a tendency fostered centuries earlier by examples such as the paired temples at Pyrgi and Marzabotto.[11] This inevitably returns focus to the Archaic period and the question of why such variety may have been cultivated by Etruscan communities.

An eclectic aesthetic has the potential to denote authority. A varied assemblage can signal the ability to source items of different provenance, informed by knowledge of what is available and the resources to acquire it (Elsner 2006, 272; Tronchin 2012, 280). The application and interweaving of elements of different origin, style, type, iconography, and narrative to a unified end can also demonstrate the imposition of meaning and thereby its command. It is thus possible to see architectural design as an exercise in curation. By investing in the collection of columns, myths, and gods, the sanctuaries at Pyrgi and Marzabotto may exemplify the ability to select and subordinate elements of multiple entangled cultural spheres, and to manipulate them to engage a variety of viewers and achieve their own ends (cf. Potts 2015, 111–17). The construction of temples that integrated

---

11 I am grateful to Janet DeLaine for this suggestion. Interestingly, support for the idea that there was a desire for architectural variation in Etruria may be found elsewhere even within Marzabotto. Remains of at least five buildings lie on the acropolis: structures B and D were roofless and appear to be altars, while structures A, C, and E are likely to be the foundations of temples. The substructure of building C suggests a triple cella-plan with frontal columns but building A, in contrast, has been reconstructed with a peripteral plan above a podium, akin to the Temple of Tinia on the valley floor below. See Vitali 1985; Vitali and others 2001; Malgieri 2007; Gilotta 2017, 1050.

varied elements and put them to local service can thus be seen as monumental declarations of power, not of Greece over Etruria, but by Etruscan communities in their own right. It may not be coincidental that the Archaic period represents the high point of Etruscan urbanism: the exploration of different ways to mark and celebrate related forms of socio-political organization and status might be discernible here in the built environment.

This suggestion, offered with due caution, is far from traditional Hellenizing tropes. It now remains to consider the religious dimension of these temples as a potential rationale for their designs. This aspect has not been analysed in depth earlier in this chapter because much about the relationship between gods and temples in Etruria remains unclear and tends to be hypothesized on the basis of later or external written sources and other classical Mediterranean comparanda. For example, when votive inscriptions establish that a certain god was worshipped at an Etruscan temple, as at Marzabotto where the *olla* inscribed with the name of Tinia was excavated close by, it is uncertain if worship there was restricted to that god (or a pair or triad). The phenomenon of 'visiting gods' in Greece opens the possibility that a number of cults could be observed at an ancient temple, even if it was dedicated to a certain one or ones, meaning that votive inscriptions may identify only a subset of cults performed in the vicinity (Alroth 1987, 9 n. 4; 1989–1990, 303 n. 5; Maras 2009, 95–96). Comparing the location or orientation of a temple with reconstructions of the Etruscan *templum* suffers the same problem.[12] Theoretically, a plan with one cella could suggest that a temple was dedicated to one god and a plan with a triple cella to three, but that leaves open the question of whether other gods could also be approached there, as well as the issue of how syncretic gods were housed, conceptualized, and worshipped. These uncertainties about the nature of deities and communication with them limit our understanding of connections between the form and religious function of temples at present and mean there is little secure ground for rationalizing particular choices; one should be wary of any claim that architectural style offers a window onto religious mentality in the absence of contemporary, emic evidence. Reconstructing the relationship between architecture and society thus remains contingent on both data and models for its interpretation, and changes in either element will undoubtedly spur new considerations.

Conclusions

This chapter has suggested that religious architecture in Archaic Etruria did not incorporate Greek elements either unthinkingly or in slavish imitation of Hellenic examples. Instead, Etruscan communities may have drawn on skills and fashions circulating in the Mediterranean to create buildings in accord with local architectural, ritual, and visual preferences. The idea that the collocation of temples with different plans may reflect a central Italian affinity for visual variety and competition, comparable to the delight in contrasting designs later connected with Roman eclecticism, also redirects the study of connections between the architecture of Etruria and other cultures to those within Italy rather than Greece. The result is a proposed reorientation of agency and effect.

Reframing discussions of Archaic architecture in this way permits greater acknowledgement that Etruscan religious buildings, as well as the activities they supported, assimilated features from elsewhere throughout the first millennium BCE. From this broader perspective, growth in overt connections with Greece in the sixth and fifth centuries BCE appear to be less a step change than a temporary intensification. Evaluating what is cosmetic and what is deep-seated about these changes is not simple, but greater contextualization — in three-dimensions, in setting, in the region, and in time — may be a useful start. The relationship between Etruria and external cultures has long reflected prevailing intellectual trends as much as ancient evidence, and as such is far from settled; remodelling, now as in antiquity, can be worthwhile.

---

12 On different reconstructions of the *templum* see Stevens 2009.

Works Cited

Alroth, Brita. 1987. 'Visiting Gods – Who and Why?', in *Gifts to the Gods: Proceedings of the Uppsala Symposium 1985*, ed. by Tullia Linders and Gullög Nordquist (Uppsala: University of Uppsala), pp. 9–19

——. 1989–1990. 'Visiting Gods', *Scienze dell'antichità*, 3–4: 301–10

Ampolo, Carmine. 1971. 'Analogie e rapporti fra Atene e Roma arcaica. Osservazioni sulla *Regia*, sul *rex sacrorum* e sul culto di Vesta', *La parola del passato*, 26: 443–60

Baglione, Maria P. 2013. 'The Sanctuary of Pyrgi', in *The Etruscan World*, ed. by Jean M. Turfa (London: Routledge), pp. 613–31

——. 2017. 'Tra Caere e Pyrgi. I grandi santuari costieri e la politica di Caere', in *La città etrusca e il sacro: santuari e istituzioni politiche; atti del convegno, Bologna 21–23 gennaio 2016*, ed. by Elisabetta Govi (Bologna: Bononia University Press), pp. 97–120

Bianchi Bandinelli, Ranuccio. 1972. 'Qualche osservazione sulle statue acroteriali di Poggio Civitate (Murlo)', *Dialoghi di archeologia*, 6: 236–47

Boardman, John. 1972. 'Herakles, Peisistratos, and Sons', *Revue archéologique*, 1: 57–72

Boethius, Axel, Roger Ling, and Tom Rasmussen. 1978. *Etruscan and Early Roman Architecture* (Harmondsworth: Penguin)

Bonfante, Larissa, and Judith Swaddling. 2006. *Etruscan Myths* (London: British Museum Press)

Brandt, Johan Rasmus. 2015. 'Passage to the Underworld. Continuity or Change in Etruscan Funerary Ideology and Practices (6th–2nd Centuries BC)?', in *Death and Changing Rituals: Function and Meaning in Ancient Funerary Practices*, ed. by J. Rasmus Brandt, Marina Prusac, and Håkon Roland (Oxford: Oxbow), pp. 105–83

Bundrick, Sheramy D. 2019. *Athens, Etruria, and the Many Lives of Greek Figured Pottery* (Madison: University of Wisconsin Press)

Cardini, Luigi. 1970. 'Area C: Il riempimento del pozzo. Materiale osteologico', in *Pyrgi: scavi del santuario etrusco (1959–1967)*, ed. by Giovanni Colonna, Notizie degli scavi di antichità, Supplement, 2 (Rome: Accademia Nazionale dei Lincei), pp. 610–25

Carpino, Alexandra A. 2016. 'The "Taste" for Violence in Etruscan Art: Debunking the Myth', in *A Companion to the Etruscans*, ed. by Sinclair Bell and Alexandra A. Carpino (Chichester: Wiley-Blackwell), pp. 410–30

Cifani, Gabriele. 2008. *Architettura romana arcaica: edilizia e società tra monarchia e repubblica* (Rome: L'Erma di Bretschneider)

Coarelli, Filippo. 1988. *Il foro boario: dalle origini alla fine della repubblica* (Rome: Quasar)

Colantoni, Elizabeth. 2012. 'Straw to Stone, Huts to Houses: Transitions in Building Practices and Society in Protohistoric Latium', in *Monumentality in Etruscan and Early Roman Architecture: Ideology and Innovation*, ed. by Michael Thomas and Gretchen E. Meyers (Austin: University of Texas Press), pp. 21–40

Colonna, Giovanni. 1965. 'L'identificazione del tempio di Astarte e la questione dello 'ŠR QDŠ', *Studi etruschi*, 33: 201–09

——. 1970a. 'Il tempio B: le terrecotte eseguite a mano. Gli acroteri', in *Pyrgi: scavi del santuario etrusco (1959–1967)*, ed. by Giovanni Colonna, Notizie degli scavi di antichità, Supplement, 2 (Rome: Accademia Nazionale dei Lincei), pp. 300–11

——. 1970b. 'L'area sacra C: le strutture', in *Pyrgi: scavi del santuario etrusco (1959–1967)*, ed. by Giovanni Colonna, Notizie degli scavi di antichità, Supplement, 2 (Rome: Accademia Nazionale dei Lincei), pp. 587–97

——. 1970c. 'Il tempio A: l'altorilievo mitologico', in *Pyrgi: scavi del santuario etrusco (1959–1967)*, ed. by Giovanni Colonna, Notizie degli scavi di antichità, Supplement, 2 (Rome: Accademia Nazionale dei Lincei), pp. 48–82

——. 1970d. 'Il tempio A: le strutture', in *Pyrgi: scavi del santuario etrusco (1959–1967)*, ed. by Giovanni Colonna, Notizie degli scavi di antichità, Supplement, 2 (Rome: Accademia Nazionale dei Lincei), pp. 23–47

——. 1970e. 'Il tempio B: le strutture', in *Pyrgi: scavi del santuario etrusco (1959–1967)*, ed. by Giovanni Colonna, Notizie degli scavi di antichità, Supplement, 2 (Rome: Accademia Nazionale dei Lincei), pp. 275–89

——. 1970f. 'Il tempio B: le terrecotte eseguite a stampo. Le antefisse a figura intera', in *Pyrgi: scavi del santuario etrusco (1959–1967)*, ed. by Giovanni Colonna, Notizie degli scavi di antichità, Supplement, 2 (Rome: Accademia Nazionale dei Lincei), pp. 311–32

——. 1970g. 'L'area sacra C: il recinto delle lamine', in *Pyrgi: scavi del santuario etrusco (1959–1967)*, ed. by Giovanni Colonna, Notizie degli scavi di antichità, Supplement, 2 (Rome: Accademia Nazionale dei Lincei), pp. 597–604

——. 1984. 'I templi del Lazio fino al V secolo compreso', *Archeologia Laziale*, 6: 396–411

——— (ed.). 1985. *Santuari d'Etruria* (Milan: Electa)

——. 1986. 'Urbanistica e architettura', in *Rasenna: storia e civiltà degli Etruschi*, ed. by Giovanni Pugliese Carratelli (Milan: Libri Scheiwiller), pp. 371–530

——. 1988–1989. 'Gli oggetti lignei', in *Pyrgi: scavi del santuario etrusco (1969–1971)*, ed. by Giovanni Colonna, Notizie degli scavi di antichità, 42–43, Supplement, 2 (Rome: Accademia Nazionale dei Lincei), pp. 111–21

——. 1989–1990. '"Tempio" e "santuario" nel lessico delle lamine di Pyrgi', *Scienze dell'antichità*, 3–4: 197–216

——. 2000. 'Il santuario di Pyrgi dalle origini mitistoriche agli altorilievi frontonali dei Sette e di Leucotea', *Scienze dell'antichità*, 10: 251–336

Cornell, Tim. 1995. *The Beginnings of Rome: Italy and Rome from the Bronze Age to the Punic Wars (c. 1000–264 BC)* (London: Routledge)

Damgaard Andersen, Helle. 1998. 'Etruscan Architecture from the Late Orientalizing to the Archaic Period (c. 640–480 B.C.)', 5 vols (unpublished doctoral thesis, University of Copenhagen)

Davies, Penelope J. E. 2006. 'Exploring the International Arena: The Tarquins' Aspirations for the Temple of Jupiter Optimus Maximus', in *Common Ground: Archaeology, Art, Science, and Humanities; Proceedings of the XVIth International Congress of Classical Archaeology, Boston, August 23–26, 2003*, ed. by Carol C. Mattusch, Alice A. Donohue, and Amy Brauer (Oxford: Oxbow), pp. 186–89

de Grummond, Nancy T. 2006. *Etruscan Myth, Sacred History, and Legend* (Philadelphia: University of Pennsylvania Museum of Archaeology and Anthropology)

Dougherty, Carol, and Leslie Kurke (eds). 2003. *The Cultures within Ancient Greek Culture* (Cambridge: Cambridge University Press)

Downey, Susan B. 1995. *Architectural Terracottas from the Regia* (Ann Arbor: University of Michigan Press)

Drews, Robert. 1981. 'The Coming of the City to Central Italy', *American Journal of Ancient History*, 6: 133–65

Edlund-Berry, Ingrid. 2013. 'The Architectural Heritage of Etruria', in *The Etruscan World*, ed. by Jean M. Turfa (London: Routledge), pp. 695–707

Edlund Gantz, Ingrid. 1972. 'The Seated Statue Akroteria from Poggio Civitate (Murlo)', *Dialoghi di archeologia*, 6: 167–235

Elsner, Jas. 2006. 'Classicism in Roman Art', in *Classical Pasts: The Classical Traditions in Greece and Rome*, ed. by James Porter (Princeton: Princeton University Press), pp. 270–97

Fitzgerald, William. 2016. *Variety: The Life of a Roman Concept* (Chicago: University of Chicago Press)

Garagnani, Simone, Andrea Gaucci, and Elisabetta Govi. 2016. 'ArchaeoBIM: dallo scavo al Building Information Modeling di una struttura sepolta. Il caso del tempio tuscanico di Uni a Marzabotto', *Archeologia e calcolatori*, 27: 251–70

Garagnani, Simone, Andrea Gaucci, and Bojana Gruška. 2016. 'From the Archaeological Record to ArchaeoBIM: The Case Study of the Etruscan Temple of Uni in Marzabotto', *Virtual Archaeology Review*, 7: 77–86

Gilotta, Fernando. 2017. 'Late Classical and Hellenistic Art, 450–250 BCE', in *Etruscology*, ed. by Alessandro Naso (Berlin: De Gruyter), pp. 1049–78

Govi, Elisabetta. 2014. 'Etruscan Urbanism at Bologna, Marzabotto and in the Po Valley', in *Papers on Italian Urbanism in the First Millennium B.C.*, ed. by Elizabeth C. Robinson (Portsmouth, RI: Journal of Roman Archaeology), pp. 81–111

——. 2015. 'Una nuova iscrizione dal tempio urbano di Tinia a Marzabotto', *Studi etruschi*, 77: 109–47

——. 2017a. 'Kainua-Marzabotto: The Archaeological Framework', *Archeologia e calcolatori*, 28.2: 87–97

——. 2017b. 'La dimensione del sacro nella città di *Kainua*-Marzabotto', in *La città etrusca e il sacro: Santuari e istituzioni politiche; atti del convegno, Bologna 21–23 gennaio 2016*, ed. by Elisabetta Govi (Bologna: Bononia University Press), pp. 145–79

Govi, Elisabetta, and Giuseppe Sassatelli (eds). 2010. *Marzabotto: La Casa 1 della Regio IV, Insula 2*, 2 vols (Bologna: Ante Quem)

Grand-Clement, Adeline. 2015. 'Poikilia', in *A Companion to Ancient Aesthetics*, ed. by Pierre Destress and Penelope Murray (Chichester: Wiley-Blackwell), pp. 406–21

Haack, Marie-Laurence. 2017. 'Ritual and Cults, 580–450 BCE', in *Etruscology*, ed. by Alessandro Naso (Berlin: De Gruyter), pp. 1001–11

Hall, Jonathan M. 1997. *Ethnic Identity in Greek Antiquity* (Cambridge: Cambridge University Press)

——. 2002. *Hellenicity: Between Ethnicity and Culture* (Chicago: University of Chicago Press)

Haynes, Sybille. 2000. *Etruscan Civilization: A Cultural History* (London: British Museum Press)

Heurgon, Jacques. 1966. 'The Inscriptions of Pyrgi', *Journal of Roman Studies*, 56: 1–15

Hodos, Tamar. 2017. 'Globalization: Some Basics. An Introduction to the *Routledge Handbook of Archaeology and Globalization*', in *The Routledge Handbook of Archaeology and Globalization*, ed. by Tamar Hodos (London: Routledge), pp. 3–11

Hopkins, John N. 2012. 'The Capitoline Temple and the Effects of Monumentality on Roman Temple Design', in *Monumentality in Etruscan and Early Roman Architecture: Ideology and Innovation*, ed. by Michael Thomas and Gretchen E. Meyers (Austin: University of Texas Press), pp. 111–38

——. 2016. *The Genesis of Roman Architecture* (New Haven: Yale University Press)

Izzet, Vedia. 2007. *The Archaeology of Etruscan Society* (Cambridge: Cambridge University Press)

Jannot, Jean-René. 2005. *Religion in Ancient Etruria* (Madison: University of Wisconsin Press)

Jones, Mark Wilson. 2000. 'Doric Measure and Architectural Design 1: The Evidence of the Relief from Salamis', *American Journal of Archaeology*, 104.1: 73–93

Krauskopf, Ingrid. 1974. *Der thebanischen Sagenkreis und andere griechische Sagen in der etruskischen Kunst* (Mainz: Von Zabern)

Linke, Bernhard. 2010. 'Kingship in Early Rome', in *Concepts of Kingship in Antiquity: Proceedings of the European Science Foundation Exploratory Workshop, Held in Padova, November 28th–December 1st, 2007*, ed. by Giovanni B. Lanfranchi and Robert Rollinger (Padua: S.A.R.G.O.N.), pp. 181–96

Lulof, Patricia S. 2000. 'Archaic Terracotta Acroteria Representing Athena and Heracles: Manifestations of Power in Central Italy', *Journal of Roman Archaeology*, 13.1: 207–19

——. 2016. 'New Perspectives on the Acroteria of Caeretan Temples', in *Caere*, ed. by Nancy T. de Grummond and Lisa C. Pieraccini (Austin: University of Texas Press), pp. 131–40

Lulof, Patricia, and Christopher Smith. 2017. 'The Age of Tarquinius Superbus. History and Archaeology', in *The Age of Tarquinius Superbus: Central Italy in the Late 6th Century; Proceedings of the Conference 'The Age of Tarquinius Superbus, A Paradigm Shift?' Rome, 7–9 November 2013*, ed. by Patricia S. Lulof and Christopher J. Smith (Leuven: Peeters), pp. 3–13

Malgieri, Angelalea. 2007a. 'The Acropolis', in *Marzabotto: An Etruscan Town*, ed. by Elisabetta Govi (Bologna: Ante Quem), pp. 20–22

——. 2007b. 'The Urban Temple of *Tinia*', in *Marzabotto: An Etruscan Town*, ed. by Elisabetta Govi (Bologna: Ante Quem), pp. 23–25

Malkin, Irad (ed.). 2001. *Ancient Perceptions of Greek Ethnicity* (Cambridge: Center for Hellenic Studies, Trustees for Harvard University)

——. 2011. *A Small Greek World: Networks in the Ancient Mediterranean* (Oxford: Oxford University Press)

Maras, Daniele F. 2009. *Il dono votivo: gli dei e il sacro nelle iscrizioni etrusche di culto* (Pisa: Farbizio Serra)

——. 2013. 'Numbers and Reckoning: A Whole Civilization Founded upon Divisions', in *The Etruscan World*, ed. by Jean M. Turfa (London: Routledge), pp. 478–91

Melis, Francesca. 1970a. 'Il tempio B: le terrecotte eseguite a stampo. Le altre antefisse (tipi B: 1 – B: IV)', in *Pyrgi: scavi del santuario etrusco (1959–1967)*, ed. by Giovanni Colonna, Notizie degli scavi di antichità, Supplement, 2 (Rome: Accademia Nazionale dei Lincei), pp. 332–46

——. 1970b. 'Il tempio B: le terrecotte eseguite a stampo. Le terrecotte non figurate (tipi B: 1 – B: 9)', in *Pyrgi: scavi del santuario etrusco (1959–1967)*, ed. by Giovanni Colonna, Notizie degli scavi di antichità, Supplement, 2 (Rome: Accademia Nazionale dei Lincei), pp. 346–402

——. 1985a. 'Modello di ricostruzione del Tempio A', in *Santuari d'Etruria*, ed. by Giovanni Colonna (Milan: Electa), pp. 134–36

——. 1985b. 'Modello di ricostruzione del Tempio B', in *Santuari d'Etruria*, ed. by Giovanni Colonna (Milan: Electa), pp. 130–31

Mertens, Dieter. 1980. 'Parallelismi strutturali nell'architettura della Magna Grecia e dell'Italia centrale in età arcaica', in *Attività archeologica in Basilicata, 1964–1977: Scritti in onore di Dino Adamesteanu*, ed. by Mauro Padula (Matera: Edizioni Meta), pp. 37–82

Michetti, Laura M. 2016. 'Ports: Trade, Cultural Connections, Sanctuaries, and Emporia', in *Caere*, ed. by Nancy T. de Grummond and Lisa C. Pieraccini (Austin: University of Texas Press), pp. 73–86

Miller, Paul M. 2017. *Continuity and Change in Etruscan Domestic Architecture* (Oxford: Archaeopress)

Morpurgo, Giulia. 2007. 'The Urban Layout', in *Marzabotto: An Etruscan Town*, ed. by Elisabetta Govi (Bologna: Ante Quem), pp. 11–13

Mura Sommella, Anna. 2009. 'Il tempio di Giove Capitolino: una nuova proposta di lettura', in *Gli Etruschi e Roma: fasi monarchica e alto-repubblicana; atti del XVI convegno internazionale di studi sulla storia e l'archeologia dell'Etruria*, ed. by Giuseppe M. Della Fina, Annali Faina, 16 (Orvieto: Quasar), pp. 333–72

Nielsen, Inge, and Birte Poulsen (eds). 1992. *The Temple of Castor and Pollux*, I: *The Pre-Augustan Temple Phases with Related Decorative Elements* (Rome: De Luca)

Owens, E. J. 1991. *The City in the Greek and Roman World* (London: Routledge)

Pairault Massa, Françoise-Hélène. 1992. *Iconologia e politica nell'Italia antica: Roma, Lazio, Etruria dal VII al I secolo a.C.* (Milan: Longanesi)

Pallottino, Massimo. 1975. *The Etruscans* (London: Allen Lane)

Pernigotti, Antonio Paolo. 2019. 'A Contribution to the Study of the Orientation of Etruscan Temples', in *Archaeoastronomy in the Roman World*, ed. by Giulio Magli, Antonio C. González-García, Juan Belmonte Aviles, and Elio Antonello (Cham: Springer), pp. 3–15

Petersen, Lauren H. 2012. 'Collecting Gods in Roman Houses: The House of the Gilded Cupids (VI.16.7, 38) at Pompeii', *Arethusa*, 45.3: 319–32

Pfiffig, Ambros J. 1965. *Uni-Hera-Astarte: Studien zu den Goldblechen von S. Severa-Pyrgi mit etruskischer und punischer Inschrift*, Osterreichische Akademie der Wissenschaften, Philosophisch-Historische Klasse, 88 (Vienna: Böhlau)

Phillips Jr., Kyle Meredith. 1984. 'Protective Masks from Poggio Civitate and Chiusi', in *Studi di antichità in onore di Guglielmo Maetzke*, II (Rome: Bretschneider), pp. 413–17

Potts, Charlotte R. 2014–2015. 'Vitruvius and Etruscan Design', *Accordia Research Papers*, 14: 87–99

——. 2015. *Religious Architecture in Latium and Etruria, c. 900–500 BC* (Oxford: Oxford University Press)

——. 2022. 'Introduction: Building Connections', in *Architecture in Ancient Central Italy*, ed. by Charlotte R. Potts (Cambridge: Cambridge University Press), pp. 1–30

Ridgway, David. 1988. 'The Etruscans', in *The Cambridge Ancient History*, IV: *Persia, Greece and the Western Mediterranean c. 525 to 429 BC*, ed. by John Boardman (Cambridge: Cambridge University Press), pp. 634–75

——. 2012. 'Demaratus of Corinth and the Hellenisation of Etruria', in *From the Pillars of Hercules to the Footsteps of the Argonauts*, ed. by Antoine Hermary and Gocha R. Tsetskhladze (Leuven: Peeters), pp. 207–22

Riva, Corinna. 2006. 'The Orientalizing Period in Etruria: Sophisticated Communities', in *Debating Orientalization*, ed. by Corinna Riva and Nicholas C. Vella (London: Equinox), pp. 110–34

——. 2009. 'Ingenious Inventions: Welding Ethnicities East and West', in *Material Culture and Social Identities in the Ancient World*, ed. by Shelley Hales and Tamar Hodos (Cambridge: Cambridge University Press), pp. 79–113

——. 2018. 'The Freedom of the Etruscans: Etruria between Hellenization and Orientalization', *International Journal of the Classical Tradition*, 25: 101–26

Robertson, Donald S. 1969. *Greek and Roman Architecture* (Cambridge: Cambridge University Press)

Rystedt, Eva. 1983. *Acquarossa*, IV: *Early Etruscan Akroteria from Acquarossa and Poggio Civitate (Murlo)* (Stockholm: Aström)

Sassatelli, Giuseppe, and Elisabetta Govi. 2005. 'Il tempio di *Tina* in area urbana', in *Culti, forma urbana e artigianato a Marzabotto: nuove prospettive di ricerca* (Bologna: Ante Quem), pp. 9–62

——. 2010. 'Cults and Foundation Rites in the Etruscan City of Marzabotto', in *Material Aspects of Etruscan Religion*, ed. by L. Bouke van der Meer (Leuven: Peeters), pp. 27–37

Skinner, Joseph E. 2012. *The Invention of Greek Ethnography: From Homer to Herodotus; Greeks Overseas* (Oxford: Oxford University Press)

Smith, Christopher. 2014. *The Etruscans: A Very Short Introduction* (Oxford: Oxford University Press)

Spivey, Nigel. 1991. 'Greek Vases in Etruria', in *Looking at Greek Vases*, ed. by Tom Rasmussen and Nigel Spivey (Cambridge: Cambridge University Press), pp. 131–50

Stevens, Natalie L. C. 2009. 'A New Reconstruction of the Etruscan Heaven', *American Journal of Archaeology*, 113.2: 153–64

Torelli, Mario. 1985. 'Introduzione', in *Case e palazzi d'Etruria*, ed. by Simonetta Stopponi (Florence: Regione Toscana), pp. 21–32

——. 2000a. 'Etruscan Religion', in *The Etruscans*, ed. by Mario Torelli (Milan: Bompiani), pp. 273–89

——. 2000b. 'Le *regiae* etrusche e laziali tra orientalizzante e arcaismo', in *Principi etruschi: tra Mediterraneo ed Europa*, ed. by Gilda Bartoloni, Filippo Delpino, Cristiana Morigi Govi, and Giuseppe Sassatelli (Venice: Marsilio), pp. 67–78

Tronchin, Francesca C. 2012. 'Introduction: Collecting the Eclectic in Roman Houses', *Arethusa*, 45.3: 261–82

Turfa, Jean M. 2012. *Divining the Etruscan World: The Brontoscopic Calendar and Religious Practice* (Cambridge: Cambridge University Press)

——. 2016. 'Prisoners and Plagues', in *Caere*, ed. by Nancy T. de Grummond and Lisa C. Pieraccini (Austin: University of Texas Press), pp. 87–94

Turfa, Jean M., and Alwin G. Steinmayer, Jr. 1996. 'The Comparative Structure of Greek and Etruscan Monumental Buildings', *Papers of the British School at Rome*, 64: 1–39

Vacano, Otto W. von, and B. von. Freytag gen Löringhoff. 1982. *Talamone: il mito dei Sette a Tebe; catalogo della mostra, Firenze, Museo Archaeologico, 19 febbraio – 3 ottobre 1982* (Florence: Vision)

Vitali, Daniele. 1985. 'L'acropoli di Marzabotto', in *Santuari d'Etruria*, ed. by Giovanni Colonna (Milan: Electa), p. 91

Vitali, Daniele, Anna M. Brizzolara, and Enzo Lippolis. 2001. *L'acropoli della città etrusca di Marzabotto* (Imola: University Press Bologna)

Wallace-Hadrill, Andrew. 2008. *Rome's Cultural Revolution* (Cambridge: Cambridge University Press)

7. The Demon Is in the Detail

Greek Pottery in Etruscan Funerary Contexts

ABSTRACT The dominance of Greek figure-decorated pottery in Etruscan contexts has traditionally been ascribed to a profound level of Hellenization in pre-Roman central Italy. In such models, the local significance of the Greek imagery found on these vases is often subordinated to the practical use of the vessels' shapes in the banquet itself. However, more recent studies have highlighted the degree to which polysemy can explain the roles of certain Greek themes in Etruscan contexts, whereby the Etruscan consumers of these images could simultaneously recognize the Greek episodes depicted while also finding resonance with local themes and ideas. This is particularly apparent in the funerary sphere, where many of the Greek scenes can be seen to be resonating with local beliefs regarding the afterlife, although these differed from the original Greek meanings. This chapter will examine the ways in which the trade and diffusion of Greek figure-decorated pottery in Etruria served to provide basic iconographical models from which the Etruscans first adopted, and then actively adapted imagery in their own art to present their own eschatological beliefs during the Archaic period. A quantitative analysis of the types of scenes which predominate on Attic figure-decorated pottery imports into Tarquinia, and their relationship with local funerary art, will provide evidence of this process and help to explain the patterns of the apparent popularity of particular Greek mythical episodes in Etruria.

The question of why Greek vases appealed to the Etruscans is one that has recently re-emerged as a point of discussion (Avramidou 2011; Bundrick 2019; Tsingarida 2020). Traditional approaches minimized Etruscan agency, often relegating them to the status of uncivilized barbarians besotted with a superior Greek culture (Boardman 1964: 210–11). Developments in the late twentieth century began to reverse these colonial approaches, however, by recognizing the active selection of particular shapes that was evident in distribution data for these pots (de La Genière 1986; 2006; Langridge-Noti 2013; Lynch 2017). Despite the strong evidence for this selectivity on the part of the Etruscans, many still maintained that this agency was limited to the functional aspects of the vases' shapes, and that there was no similar selectivity at play in the choice of imagery that decorated the vases (Reusser 2002). Yet here too, recent studies have challenged such views, and consistently shown that in a number of case studies the scenes painted on these vases can be interpreted from an Etruscan perspective in ways that resonated with their own beliefs and world-views, particularly in the funerary sphere (Bundrick 2020). Fundamental to these recent approaches is the recognition that such readings need not be the only possible reading of a scene; they do not deny the original Greek intentions and meanings of these images, but assert that, alongside these, a different, Etruscan reading can be proposed that is just as valid in the new cultural context within which many of these vases were ultimately destined to be viewed.

This paper will examine the ways in which the trade and diffusion of Greek figure-decorated pottery in Etruria served to provide basic iconographical models from which the Etruscans first adopted, and then actively adapted imagery in their own art to present their own eschatological beliefs during the Archaic period. A quantitative analysis of the types of scenes which predominate on Attic figure-decorated pottery imports into Tarquinia, and their relationship with local funerary art, will provide evidence of this process and help to explain the patterns of the apparent popularity of particular Greek mythical episodes in Etruria.

Corresponding author: Aaron Rhodes-Schroder (arho009@aucklanduni.ac.nz)

The Attic Vase Trade in Tarquinia

Among the sites of Etruria, Tarquinia offers one of the best opportunities for a quantitative analysis of Greek pottery from funerary contexts. Tarquinia, like all major Etruscan cities, suffers from extensive issues associated with the early excavations of the eighteenth and nineteenth centuries, with the concomitant issues of decontextualization and loss of exact details of provenience. However, the local collections housed in the Museo Archeologico Nazionale di Tarquinia did not suffer the same fate of dispersion that occurred in sites like Vulci or Cerveteri, retaining a significant body of artefacts that, despite the loss of exact archaeological details, are known to have largely derived from the ancient city's necropoleis (Leighton 2004, 25). The extensive publication of the museum's Attic pottery in a series of catalogues over the last four decades, regardless of its quality or attribution, goes a long way to ameliorating the issues involved in relying solely upon Beazley's lists of pottery provenances that plagued many of the early quantitative studies of this class of material in Etruria (Small 1994; Hannestad 1988). As such, the *Materiali del Museo Archeologico Nazionale d Tarquinia* (MMAT) series will form the basis of the data collated for this study, supplemented by the data provided by the expanded and digitized *Beazley Archive Pottery Database* (BAPD), and Marroni's recent *Vasi Attici a Figure Rosse da Tarquinia* which completes the publication of the Tarquinian Attic red-figure from the Classical period.[1]

As noted above, scholars have recognized the Etruscans' selectivity in regard to vase shape for some time now, and the preliminary analysis of the collated material from Tarquinia confirms these trends (Fig. 7.1). Most notably, there is a clear preference for two main shapes of the imported Attic pottery that is evident in the data (Figs 7.2 and 7.3). Over the course of *c.* 550–450 BCE cups and amphorae stand out as the dominant shapes that were preferred for funerary deposition at this site: of the 520 vases catalogued for Tarquinia, 175 are amphorae, and 176 are cups; these two shapes alone count for 68 per cent of all Attic pottery deposited in the graves of this site between *c.* 550–450 BCE, with the remaining 32 per cent comprising the other twenty vase shapes attested, of which no single shape accounts for more than 5 per cent of the total amount of pottery.

Among these two prominent shapes of Attic pottery there is a further disparity to be noted: while the cups are nearly evenly split between the earlier black-figured production and the later red-figure vases, the amphorae are nearly exclusively comprised of black-figured vessels from the second half of the sixth century BCE. The presence of a great number of red-figure cups from the later period demonstrates that Tarquinia had access to pottery decorated in this newer technique in the first half of the fifth century BCE, and were happy to substitute the earlier black-figure cups in their funerary depositions. The same, however, is clearly not true of the larger format vases, and particularly the amphorae, for which we only have five red-figure examples evident in the recorded material, as opposed to the 170 black-figure vases in this shape. This disparity in the shapes of Attic pottery appearing in different decorative techniques points to a far more complex situation of selectivity that has yet to be recognized in scholarship. Very few of the statistical studies of Attic pottery in Etruria have made any attempt to evaluate each of these techniques on their own terms, many simply assuming that, as in Athens, the 'superior' red-figured technique simply superseded the less technical black-figured. It appears, however, that in Tarquinia the decorative technique mattered, particularly when it came to the larger format vases which were selected for deposition in funerary contexts. And this may also be the case for the other Etruscan cities of southern Etruria if the data from the BAPD is representative. For Vulci, Cerveteri, and Orvieto both cups and amphorae are the dominant shapes: while cups appear in both decorative techniques (Figs 7.4 and 7.5), there is a greater tendency toward red-figure in the latter two sites; for all three sites amphorae in black-figure outnumber those in red-figure in a similar fashion to the data from Tarquinia.[2]

This Etruscan preference for large format Attic black-figured vases has serious implications for how we view the vase trade in Etruria in the fifth century BCE. Most accounts of this trade assert that the decline of Attic pottery in the archaeological record in the fifth century BCE in Etruria is part of the wider 'crisis' affecting central Italy following the Battle of Cumae in 474 BCE (Torelli 1986). Indeed, the quantity of Attic pottery recovered from Etruscan graves is one of the central pillars of evidence that is routinely cited in support of this theory. However,

---

1 See Campus 1981; Tronchetti 1983; Pierro 1983; Ferrari 1988; Nati 2012; Marroni 2017; *Beazley Archive Pottery Database* (BAPD).

2 Based upon the totals for all subshapes of amphorae and cups at each site (excluding fragments) from the BAPD as of 30 January 2021. Vulci: 752 amphorae (84 per cent black-figure (= bf), 16 per cent red-figure (= rf)); 724 cups (43 per cent bf, 57 per cent rf). Cerveteri: 134 amphorae (87 per cent bf, 13 per cent rf); 129 cups (12 per cent bf, 88 per cent rf). Orvieto: 67 amphorae (87 per cent bf, 13 per cent rf); 164 cups (18 per cent bf, 82 per cent rf).

7. THE DEMON IS IN THE DETAIL

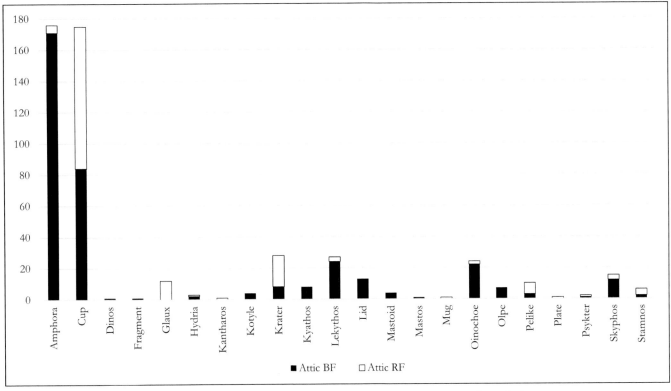

Figure 7.1. Shapes and decorative techniques of Attic pottery from Tarquinia c. 550–450 BCE (by author).

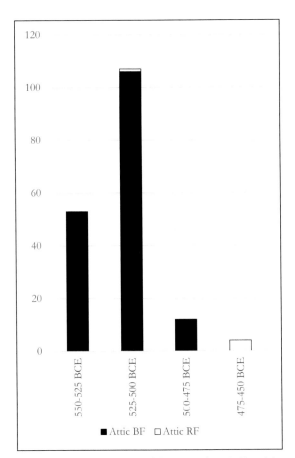

Figure 7.2. Attic black- and red-figure amphora in Tarquinia by quarter century, c. 550–450 BCE (by author).

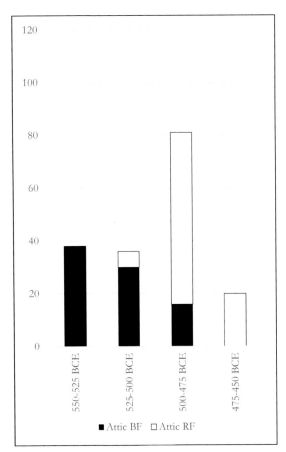

Figure 7.3. Attic black- and red-figure cups in Tarquinia by quarter century, c. 550–450 BCE (by author).

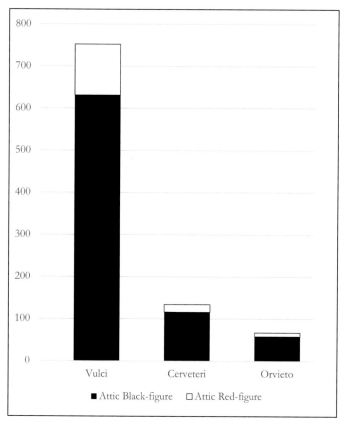

Figure 7.4. BAPD data for Attic black- and red-figure amphorae from Vulci, Cerveteri, and Orvieto (by author).

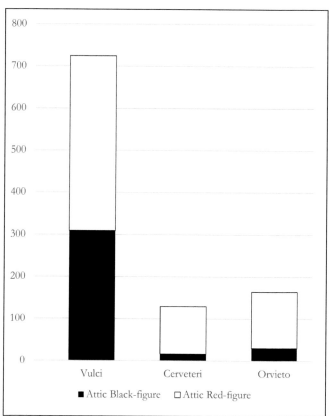

Figure 7.5. BAPD data for Attic black- and red-figure cups from Vulci, Cerveteri, and Orvieto (by author).

Reusser (2002) has conclusively demonstrated that Attic pottery continued to be imported and used in non-funerary contexts throughout the fifth century BCE; it is only in specifically funerary contexts where the decline in Attic pottery is most marked. While specialists have generally moved away from the idea of a 'crisis' in this period, the idea is still often repeated in general studies.

The evidence from the analysis here may point to a different situation, one which is rooted not in the Etruscans' ability (or lack thereof) to purchase such vases, but in changes in the Athenian potteries' production which affected their ability to supply vases which suited Etruscan funerary needs. The decline of pottery in Etruscan funerary contexts occurs within a few decades of a major shift in production at Athens, when the workshops of the *keramaikos* largely shifted away from producing high-quality black-figure vases in favour of the newer red-figure technique. Most scholars consider this a natural progression to a more advanced and refined artistic method which allowed for greater detail in the scenes depicted on these vases (Boardman 2001). Other changes also took place at this time too, notably in the types of scenes which were being produced on the vases. There is a distinct shift away from producing mythological scenes in favour of genre scenes, or scenes of everyday life, and with it a decline in the number of vases which were being produced that depicted narrative scenes involving mythical protagonists and their supernatural adversaries. While these changes in production have been well studied in the art-historical investigations of Attic vase-painting, the impact that these changes in production had on the export markets has yet to be considered. Indeed, these changes in the decorative technique of Attic pottery, and the shifts in the prevalent types of imagery produced on these vases, coincide with the changes in pottery deposition in Etruscan tombs. Prior to this point, large format Attic black-figure vases, and amphorae in particular, are the most dominant type of pots chosen for deposition as grave goods. Afterwards, however, these vases are no longer being produced in the same quantity and quality, and it is shortly after this that we see the decline of Attic pottery in Etruscan funerary contexts.

The implicit assumption that underlies many studies of the export market to Etruria is that the consumers ought to be just as willing to accept the newer, more advanced technique as the old one without question. While the Etruscans seem to happily fit such a model in the case of cups, it certainly was not so with the larger format vases, and especially amphorae, where the Attic black-figured production of the late sixth century BCE was clearly preferred to the red-figured counterparts in the early fifth. This discrepancy is likely tied to the ways in which these vase shapes were used within Etruscan graves.

Attic cups, both black-figure and red-figure, seem to have been utilized in a number of different ways in funerary depositions. Their obvious capacity is that for which they were initially designed: as drinking vessels for the consumption of wine. Indeed, this is generally the explanation for all Attic pottery in Etruscan contexts, as symbolic markers of the adoption of Greek wine-drinking practices, principally the symposium (Cerchiai 2015; Osborne 2007). However, a comparison of the depictions of this vase shape in Tarquinian tomb painting reveals that they were seldom shown used in this way (Jannot 1995). The basic shape of the cup/*kylix* is held by a number of figures in these frescoes, but they are often either metallic versions, or plain black clay (Reusser 2002). When figure-decorated cups are clearly shown, they are never used, instead sitting on the *kylikeia* along with other vases, or hung on the walls above them (Wiel-Marin 2005). Instead, it is the *phialai* that are more commonly shown held in the hand of the banqueters on these paintings, a shape that in Greece is more closely associated with rituals. There are, however, other uses for these cups that are evident in both the iconographical and archaeological record. There are indications that these cups were used for libations, liquid offerings for, or on behalf of, the dead to ensure their arrival in the afterlife (Bundrick 2019, 67). Cups also appear to have served a different function in some Italian contexts, holding food offerings in the tomb, which indicates a transformation of their functional use (Peruzzi 2016; see Tonglet 2018 on Etruscan contexts). Finally, while most of the archaeological contexts of vases in Tarquinia has been irrevocably lost, there are some details to be gleaned from the original excavation reports as well as some of the more recent discoveries. Among these, a number of finds reported that many cups were recorded as being used as lids for larger vases, whether kraters, *hydriai*, or amphorae where they were turned upside down and placed over the top of the larger vessel. This is a practice which harks back to the earlier Villanovan cremation burials in biconical urns which sometimes used drinking vessels as lids too (de La Genière 1986). Evidently, the basic form of the Attic cup was a shape which lent itself to an array of different uses in Etruria, and as such, the decorative schemes of this particular vase shape could perhaps have been more diverse, allowing for

the adaptability of the shape to a number of different functional uses within the funerary deposition.

By contrast, the amphorae seem to have a much more specific use in Etruscan funerary contexts, particularly at Tarquinia, where they are frequently recorded to have been used as cinerary urns for the cremated remains of the deceased. Palmieri (2003) notes that, of the sixty-seven recorded cremation burials known from Tarquinia, 70 per cent of these are contained within an amphora. While initially associated with wealthy burials, by the final quarter of the sixth century, these vessels appear to have served as cineraria for a much wider cross section of society (Reusser 2002), with many *tomba a bucca* featuring only a cremation in an Attic amphora with few or no other associated grave goods. Given the poor state of recording in many of the earlier excavations of Etruscan necropoleis, de La Genière suggested that prevalent use of these vases as cinerary urns in Tarquinia could likely be extended to the many other Attic amphorae from this site where the details of their find context were not recorded. It is likely that the strong preference for these amphorae to be decorated in the black-figure technique was closely related to this specific use to which these vases were put. An argument that it was only the colour of the decorative technique that mattered is insufficient, as we have clearly seen that the Tarquinians were equally willing to deposit red-figure cups in the same contexts.

The question that remains, therefore, is that of the imagery presented on these Attic black-figure amphorae. Scholarship of Greek vase-painting has documented the clear changes of decoration that occur alongside the transition from black-figure to red-figure in the Athenian workshops (Boardman 2001; Osborne 2018). In general, there is a pronounced shift away from the active, mythological scenes of black-figure — especially those which focus on the monstrous and fantastical elements — towards a more ponderous presentation of everyday genre scenes of Greek daily life. This change is well recognized among scholars of Greek vase-painting, and yet the impact of this shift has never been considered in the context of the vase trade to Etruria. When it comes to these large format vases, the amphorae chief among them, it is likely that the more mundane types of images that the Athenians chose to depict on the red-figure vases in the fifth century BCE no longer appealed to the Etruscans in the same way as the earlier, mythologically rich, black-figure imagery had. In light of this, we turn now to an analysis of the mythological scenes which are evident on the black-figure amphorae from Tarquinia to assess the types of scenes portrayed, and to consider, from an

Etruscan perspective, how these might have had significance in an Etruscan funerary setting.

The Imagery of Attic Black-Figure Amphorae from Tarquinia

The analysis of the Attic black-figure amphorae from Tarquinia reveals that of the 170 vases catalogued for this site, 140 (76 per cent) of them feature at least one mythological scene, with fifty-six of these (33 per cent) featuring a mythological scene on both sides. Taken together, there are a total of 187 different mythological scenes found upon these vases. Within this range of Attic black-figure amphorae, a definite pattern emerges of particular mythological figures who frequently appear: Apollo is depicted in 11 per cent of the scenes; Hermes on 19 per cent; Athena on 26 per cent; Herakles on 30 per cent; while Dionysian themes appear on 32 per cent.[3] The Dionysian scenes are here categorized as any scene featuring Dionysos, satyrs, and/or maenads, and the appearances of each occurs as follows: Dionysos himself appears in 27 per cent of scenes, while satyrs occur on 25 per cent, and maenads on 20 per cent. Only one other identifiable figure occurs on more than 5 per cent of these vases, and that is Iolaos, who exclusively appears alongside Herakles.

While the popularity of Herakles and Dionysos have been well studied by Etruscologists (most recently Cerchiai 2015; Bundrick 2020 with references), their appeal is often seen to have been substantially similar in Etruria as it was in Greece, with little consideration for the changed cultural contexts into which these images were received. By contrast, the first three figures, Apollo, Hermes, and Athena, have rarely warranted extended discussion in considerations of Attic iconography in Etruria, likely because they tend to appear in compositions with other figures. Hermes, in particular, regularly features as a supporting figure in a plethora of mythological contexts, where he is rarely central to the narrative. Athena, likewise, in nearly 60 per cent of her appearances is alongside Herakles; Apollo, too, most often occurs in the contexts of other figures, either with Artemis and Leto, or in chariot procession scenes alongside Hermes, Dionysos, and/or Athena. Again, interpretations here have regularly been based upon Hellenocentric approaches, pri-

oritizing Greek, and particularly Athenian, understandings of these figures.

However, if we begin our approach to these figures from what we know of Etruscan eschatological concepts, we can see a definite pattern which relates to the majority of black-figure amphorae that were deposited in Etruscan tombs. The choice of Tarquinia as a case study here is strengthened by the fact that this site holds the largest body of Etruscan funerary art, in the form of the painted chamber tombs, that is contemporary with the height in the deposition of Attic vases in the graves of the southern Etruscan cities (Steingräber 2006; Marzullo 2016). This therefore allows us to evaluate the kinds of iconographies which the Etruscans themselves considered to be important in these contexts, and to compare these to the images we find depicted on the vases that the Etruscans chose for the same purposes. When we consider the images depicted on the imported Attic vases in light of what the Etruscans themselves prioritized in their own funerary art, we find that the images presented on the Attic pottery resonates with specifically Etruscan eschatological themes on a number of levels.

Apollo

The majority of the depictions of Apollo on the Attic black-figure amphorae depict the god with his characteristic attribute: the kithara. This is highly significant from a Tarquinian perspective as depictions of musicians are among the most popular themes to be depicted on their tomb paintings, only being surpassed by what Brandt (2015) terms the 'heraldic animals'.[4] The popularity of musicians on these frescoes, particularly on those from the Archaic period, indicates that this was a central aspect of their funerary concerns, whether this involved the funerary ritual itself or expectations for the afterlife. When we consider the imagery from the Attic black-figure amphorae, Apollo stands out as the most common figure to be depicted as a musician, befitting his status as the god of music. Indeed, of Apollo's twenty-one appearances on these vases, he is only depicted four times without a musical instrument.

Nearly half of the scenes featuring Apollo as a musician add a further layer of significance for an Etruscan audience. These are the chariot procession scenes that depict some combination of Apollo,

---

3 These percentages do not add up to 100, as there is considerable crossover in these figures appearing alongside each other in the same scene. This is particularly the case with Apollo, Hermes, and Athena, who often appear alongside other mythological figures in their depictions.

---

4 Although it is significant that Brandt does not collate the data for musicians in his analysis. Altogether, depictions of figures playing musical instruments occur on fifty-three tombs, or 44 per cent of all tomb paintings in Tarquinia.

Hermes, Dionysos, and/or Athena, in conjunction with an unidentified couple in or mounting a chariot. Such scenes are not specifically tied to particular mythological episodes, and they are often seen by scholars of Greek vase-painting as evoking Athenian wedding processions. However, the basic composition of these scenes, of a chariot procession featuring musicians and attendants, is strongly echoed in many Etruscan tomb paintings where, instead of a wedding procession, the depictions are focused on portraying the journey of the deceased in a chariot to the afterlife. This parallel can clearly be seen on the left wall of the T. d. Demoni Azzurri, where the deceased male is preceded by musicians and attendants as he progresses toward the eternal banquet on the rear wall (Roncalli 2015).

Further significance of depictions of Apollo in Etruscan funerary contexts may be deduced from the assimilation of this Greek god with the local deity Suri (Colonna 1996). Whereas the Greek Apollo is rarely shown in association with death in the Classical period, his local Etruscan counterpart seems to have had a clear chthonic aspect with afterlife associations (Krauskopf 1984; de Grummond 2006). The inclusion of these Attic black-figure amphorae in graves with imagery that evoked the prominent funerary themes of music, often in association with eschatologically significant chariot processions, and where the musician himself was syncretized with a significant local chthonic deity, would result in a multilayered reading of these vases by any Etruscan who viewed them within the context of a grave assemblage. The initial Greek design of these images therefore counts for little when these vases were redeployed in an entirely new way by the Etruscans, whereby a far more complex and nuanced reading of the imagery can be seen to be at play.

Hermes

Hermes rarely appears as the central focus of either the scenes or the narrative contexts in which he is depicted, instead generally being a supporting figure of other identifiable mythological characters. There is only one vase bearing an episode in which Hermes plays a pivotal role: the single Judgement of Paris scene.[5] Hermes' most common appearances on the black-figure amphorae from Tarquinia is either as a supporting figure in Heraklean scenes, or in chariot procession scenes where he stands on the edge of the scene at the heads of the horses. His role is often described as one of attending upon heroic or divine affairs, without explicitly becoming involved (Boardman 1991), and thus he can easily be inserted into a number of different scenes by the Athenian painters without affecting the narrative. It would therefore be easy to discount the frequency of his appearances on the vases from Etruria as not having any significance; this precept changes, however, if we consider the significance of Hermes first from an Etruscan perspective.

Hermes was recognized in Etruria as Turms, though he does not seem to have been the recipient of any cult there (Jannot 2005, 152). The Etruscans' own depictions of Turms reproduce his role as the messenger of the gods, and he is frequently found fulfilling the same roles as we find in Greek iconography. One of the more distinctive aspects of the Etruscan Turms, however, is the emphasis placed upon his chthonic aspect: Turms Aitas, the 'Hermes of Hades', which emphasizes the role of Turms as a psychopompos, leading the deceased on their journey to the afterlife (de Grummond 2006). In a number of examples in Etruscan art, we find that the figure of Turms is duplicated to show both his celestial and chthonic aspects interacting with each other.[6] This pluralization of gods is a feature not uncommon for many divine figures from Etruscan religion, and it is particularly well attested for the later death demons who largely take over the role of Turms Aitas from the fourth century BCE onwards.

In the preceding Archaic period, however, these demons are relatively rare in Etruscan art. Their iconographies had yet to be firmly established, though we can see early attempts in local vase-painting and a clear development by the time of the T. d. Demoni Azzurri in the second half of the fifth century BCE. What is notable is that depictions of Turms often feature a number of attributes that would characterize these later demons, particularly Charu(n): he can be winged, bear the characteristic hammer of Charu, and as noted above is depicted as a plural deity on more than one occasion (Harari 1997). It therefore seems that iconographically, Turms fulfilled an important role as a representation of the psychopompos figure for the Etruscans while they were still developing their own pictorial model for the demons who would later dominate in this function. Therefore, when Attic vases were chosen for deposition within funerary contexts, the presence of Hermes in a scene would likely, from an Etruscan point of view, facilitate an eschatological interpreta-

---

5   Tarquinia 630, BAPD 320087.

---

6   Ferrara 12127; *LIMC*, VIII, 107 no. 115; Vatican 14963 (Z 83), *LIMC*, VIII, 106, no. 97.

tion. In this respect, it is suggestive that he frequently occupies a position that is most often taken by the death demons in later Etruscan funerary art: at the edges of the main decorative zone.

Athena

As with Hermes, Athena has not received much attention in scholarship on imported Attic vases in Etruria, despite the frequency with which she appears. The reason for this is amply demonstrated by the material from Tarquinia: of the forty-nine black-figure amphorae which depict Athena, twenty-nine of these are Heraklean episodes where the titular hero is the central focus of the scene, and therefore often where scholarly discussion is concentrated. In Etruscan art, too, the bulk of Menrva's appearances occur alongside Hercle, particularly on temple acroteria, where at least twelve different groups are known from across south Etruria and Latium (Lulof 2000). These sculptural groups in particular are often interpreted as depictions of the Apotheosis of Hercle, at the point where Menrva introduces the hero to the gods, and the widespread proliferation of this theme in decorative art attests to the importance of this episode in Etruscan thought (Colonna 1984; Schwarz 1990).

However, rather than simply being included by association with this episode, it may be her role in facilitating this transformation of Hercle from hero to god that is the reason for her prominence in the material from funerary contexts. Hercle's standing as one of the few, and certainly the most popular, figures from Greek myth to undergo apotheosis as a result of his achievements in life, is often counted among the reasons for his popularity in Etruria. There are indications that the exact relationship in Etruria between Hercle and Menrva differs from the Greek Herakles and Athena, yet Menrva still retains a central aspect in facilitating Hercle's apotheosis. She is the goddess who oversees Hercle's transition from mortal life to divine, and she is known from other mythical episodes, namely the Seven Against Thebes illustrated so clearly on the temple pediment from Pyrgi, to have the power to bestow immortality. Furthermore, as with both Hermes and Apollo, the Etruscan counterpart to Athena had clear chthonic aspects associated with her worship, evidenced by the *bothroi* associated with her altars in the sanctuaries of both Santa Marrinella and Veii (Jannot 2005, 148).

These aspects are therefore likely to have played a significant role in the Etruscans' choice of vases depicting her for funerary depositions. Athena's place as the most commonly appearing female deity on Attic vases in Tarquinia can be understood to be relevant within the framework of Etruscan eschatological beliefs, particularly when she appears in conjunction with Herakles. She is not seen simply as a patron of the hero in his deeds, offering passive support at the edges of the scene. Instead, Athena foreshadows Herakles' ultimate fate and transition which she herself will facilitate. The fact that on these vases she is frequently depicted as a bystander at the edges of the scenes does not change this interpretation. Indeed, as we have seen with Hermes, the scene margin was the prime position occupied by death demons on later sarcophagi and cinerary urns, and so such positioning could have carried similar connotations.

Herakles

As noted above, Herakles accounts for a significant proportion of the mythological scenes found on the Attic black-figure amphorae from Tarquinia: fifty-six individual scenes feature this hero-god, making him one of the most popular figures on these vases. The popularity of Herakles has been a point of discussion among scholars. Initially, it was believed that he was seen as an exemplar for the aristocratic Etruscans, to whom many of these vases were believed to have belonged (d'Agostino and Cerchiai 1999). In particular, it is Herakles' reward of apotheosis by means of his own *virtus* and achievements which are claimed to have been at the heart of his appeal to the upper echelons of Etruscan society (Spivey and Stoddart 1990). There are, additionally, indications in the ancient sources of the Etruscan belief that their dead were in some way deified, echoing again the fate of Herakles (Arnobius, *Adv. nat.*, II. 62). Furthermore, the observation is often made that Herakles' journey to the underworld to retrieve Kerberos makes him particularly fitting for vases used as grave goods, regardless of whether or not this particular episode was depicted (Brizzolara and Baldoni 2010). While the recognition in recent years that these pots were used by a wide range of Etruscan society, and not just a restricted elite, has discredited the exclusivity of Heraklean imagery, it has not fundamentally shifted current understanding of the appeal of these images in Etruscan contexts, and particularly in funerary contexts (Reusser 2002). In general, these same explanations are simply extended out to the wider populace.

However, there is more that can be said of the appeal of Herakles to Etruscan funerary concerns. While Bundrick has recently emphasized the resonance of Herakles' apotheosis scenes with Etruscan, and particularly Vulcian, funerary beliefs, only one such scene may be identified among the Attic pottery from Tarquinia (Bundrick 2020).[7] As such it is necessary to consider the other Heraklean episodes represented on pottery found at this site before exploring their relevance to local funerary needs. Two particular aspects can be highlighted among these vases which have parallels in the Tarquinians' own funerary art: the journey to the afterlife, and the encounters with monstrous creatures.

The location of the afterlife in Etruscan beliefs is nowhere specifically indicated. The closest we get are depictions of funerary banquets taking place in the presence of Aita and Phersipnei as in the T. d. Golini I in Orvieto. More often we find depictions of the journey undertaken by the deceased to reach the afterlife, sometimes culminating with the arrival at the doors that are generally understood to mark the threshold to the beyond. While many scholars are content to simply equate the Etruscan afterlife with the Greek conception of an underworld, claiming a direct adoption of later Hellenic ideas, there are in fact more indications that the ultimate destination may be more similar to earlier Greek conceptions of locations like the Isles of the Blessed, Erythiea, or the Gardens of the Hesperides. What is notable is that Herakles travels to two of these in the course of his labours after a long journey by both land and sea. Such a journey is evocative of the Etruscans' own conceptions of the journey to the afterlife. When taken together with the retrieval of Kerberos and his ultimate apotheosis, Herakles travels beyond the limits of mortal life on no less than four separate occasions.

A further resonance between Heraklean iconography and Etruscan funerary art can be seen in the many monstrous creatures which are depicted in association with both. Herakles is well known to have been the Greek monster slayer *par excellence*, and many of his labours and *peregra* revolve around his encounters with creatures or beings who are somehow extraordinary in nature. Such monstrous creatures are also frequently depicted in Etruscan funerary art without Herakles: the Lernean hydra, centaurs, Kerberos, Tritons, and Geryon, for example, are all attested on a number of different monuments. Further examples of monstrous creatures proliferate in Etruscan funerary art too, and among the most notable are the large felines: panthers, leopards, and lions are among the most dominant funerary motifs in tomb painting from Tarquinia,

and tomb statuary from Vulci. Here again, a strong resonance can be found in Herakles' fight with the Nemean Lion, and it is perhaps no coincidence that at Tarquinia it is this labour in particular which is the most commonly depicted Heraklean scene on the Attic black-figure amphorae.

Dionysos

Dionysian themes stand out as the most commonly occurring among the mythological scenes depicted on the Attic black-figure amphorae from Tarquinia: they occur on sixty scenes on fifty-one separate amphorae, accounting for 32 per cent of all mythological scenes. The focus here on Dionysian scenes rather than just the figure of Dionysos himself is because, firstly, this god can appear in a number of different contexts which do not pertain to his own specific myths. So, for example, we can find Dionysos depicted in *gigantomachia*, chariot procession scenes, or assemblies of gods where he is not central to the narrative, but just one of a number of participating deities. Secondly, his regular attendants, satyrs and maenads, regularly appear in Dionysian contexts without the god present. These Dionysian contexts regularly centre on key themes: consumption of wine, music, and dancing; all of which are central aspects of his worship in the Greek world.

While many scholars have argued that this is a sign of a pervasive spread of Dionysian cults, and particularly mystery cults associated with salvation, throughout Etruria in the Archaic period, we have no certain evidence of this so early (Colonna 1991; d'Agostino and Cerchiai 1999; 2015). That these cults existed later seems assured, not only from Livy's account of the Bacchanalia affair in 186 BCE (Livy XXXIX. 8), but also from inscriptional evidence from at least three stone sarcophagi that attest to a cult of Bacchus/Pachies dating to the third century BCE (Colonna 1991). The earliest indications of the syncretization of these two gods comes from three inscribed Attic vases from Vulci dating from the mid–late fifth century BCE (Colonna 1991; Maras 2019). The rapid spread of Dionysian imagery a century earlier, however, is not certainly associated with the later spread of these cults. Indeed, Puritani (2015) has noted that the local depictions of Dionysos/Fufluns at this early point seems to focus much more on the original associations of Fufluns with vegetation, rather than the more well-known Greek associations, which only develop in Etruscan art over the course of the fifth century BCE.

As with all of the mythological figures examined so far, there is more that can be said of the relevance

---

7 Tarquinia RC6976 (BAPD 320197).

of Dionysos/Fufluns to Etruscan funerary contexts than simply explaining it by way of Hellenizing influences. The key Dionysian themes depicted on these Attic amphorae are wine consumption and dancing, often to the accompaniment of music. All three of these find numerous parallels in Tarquinian tomb painting without explicit reference to Dionysos or his world, where banquets often dominate the rear walls and revellers dance and play music along the side walls. Indeed, aside from the heraldic animals which grace the tympanum zones of these painted tombs, the themes of banqueting, music, and dance are the most commonly depicted in the frescoes from the late sixth century BCE down to the early fourth (Brandt 2015).[8] These themes clearly held great importance for the Etruscan funerary beliefs, whether as a part of actual funerary rituals or as a representation of ideal pursuits hoped for in the afterlife.

From a practical perspective, however, if an Etruscan wished to deposit a Greek vase depicting any of these themes in their tomb, the most likely context to find them on Attic black-figured amphorae would be in a Dionysian scene: both wine consumption and dancing are rarely depicted outside of Dionysian or *komast* scenes in black-figure; musical instruments are more widely represented on the black-figured amphorae from Tarquinia, appearing in the hands of Apollo, or in a few examples of Herakles Kitharodes, yet they are only found in combination with dancing and or wine consumption in Dionysian scenes. And it is precisely the combination of these themes which resonates with the depictions in Etruscan funerary art. Any desire on the part of the Tarquinians to deposit Attic vases bearing a combination of these themes would virtually necessitate the choice of a Dionysian scene, regardless of whether or not adherence to any Dionysian cult was at play.

There are also elements of Dionysos's myths which lend themselves to an Etruscan eschatological context. Namely, Dionysos's journey to retrieve his mother Semele from the underworld and raise her to Olympos, and possibly also his similar actions in regard to Ariadne that are reported in some accounts (Apollod. III. 5. 3). As with Herakles, Dionysos undertakes the journey to the afterlife, and as with Athena, he takes an active role in facilitating Semele's apotheosis. The raising of the status of these women to godhood may also be echoed in Dionysos's role in the Return of Hephaistos. Here, the wine god's cen-

tral role in leading Hephaistos on his journey back to Olympos may be read as a re-apotheosis of sorts accompanied by a procession of dancing revellers. This is fundamentally similar in composition to the funerary processions we find depicted in many Etruscan tombs. What is key here is that Dionysos's central role in transforming the status of these individuals to that of deities once again echoes the central element remembered by Arnobius that the Etruscan dead were somehow deified.

Monstrous Beasts and Hybrid Creatures

The popularity of Dionysian and Heraklean scenes on the Attic black-figured amphorae in Tarquinia can be explained by the elements of their respective myths which resonate with the Etruscans' own eschatological concepts. They are both capable of crossing the threshold to the afterlife, and both are associated with apotheosis. Etruscan funerary art reveals a central concern with the safe journey to the afterlife and the deification of the deceased. Elements of this can be detected in local art from the Villanovan period, long before the adaptation of Greek imagery and ideas. As such, both Heraklean and Dionysian imagery would have been highly relevant in an Etruscan funerary context. Yet there is another common feature in the scenes depicting both of these figures, one which is directly evocative of themes which are central in Etruscan funerary art, one which again finds precedent among the earliest phases of Etruscan art, and one which persists until Etruscan culture was subsumed under Rome: both Herakles and Dionysos are the two figures from the Attic black-figure repertoire who are the most commonly depicted in association with monstrous beasts and hybrid creatures.

As we have seen for Herakles, these monstrous beasts are often the adversaries faced by the hero-god in the course of his labours. Yet these same creatures find ample representations without Hercle in numerous Etruscan funerary monuments, indicating that they were not conceived of as only relating to Hercle, but that they had a significant place in the Etruscans' eschatological conceptions independent of him. That such fantastic beasts appealed to the Etruscans on Greek pottery has long been recognized: they were, after all, one of the most characteristic aspects of the Corinthian pottery that first indicated the importance of the Etruscan market for Greek vases (Haynes 2000). Indeed, it is precisely the early Attic painters' adoption of the friezes of fantastical animals and hybrid creatures which many scholars attribute to their being able to edge into this

---

8 This is echoed in other funerary art from throughout Etruria, particularly in the relief sculptures from Chiusi, see Jannot 1984 and De Angelis 2015.

market in the early sixth century BCE. This is also one of the most prominent features of the Tyrrhenian amphorae which were tailored to the Etruscan market (Boardman 1991, 36–37; Lubtchansky 2014). However, over the course of the sixth century these decorative friezes were eventually dropped by the workshops in the Kerameikos in favour of a single large decorative panel on the body of the vases. By the final quarter of the sixth century BCE, the most likely place of finding such creatures depicted on these vases was when they were the focus of the main narrative decoration. Herakles' interactions with a wide variety of these creatures, and his general popularity, meant that depictions of him were the most likely place to find depictions of these beasts. As with wine, dancing, and music considered above, an Etruscan's desire to include a vase depicting such a creature would nearly always result in the inclusion of a Heraklean scene, as these were the most common narrative context to find them depicted in the Athenian black-figure amphorae production in the second half of the sixth century BCE.

For Dionysos, his chief interactions with monstrous creatures come in the form of his most closely associated followers: the half-human half-equine satyrs that feature in forty-eight scenes on these black-figure amphorae from Tarquinia. These hybrid creatures are not only Dionysos's most common companions in Greek art, but they are almost always depicted in association with the Dionysian sphere in Greek contexts, with the result that they have largely become synonymous with Dionysian ideas. This is the lens with which they have largely been viewed in Etruria too, where many have taken them as one of the chief signs of the widespread wholesale adoption of Dionysian cult (d'Agostino and Cerchiai 1999; Fiorini 2007; Cerchiai 2015). However, when we consider the evidence for their depiction in central Italian contexts, there is one factor which may caution us against this: while the iconography of the satyr was readily adopted in Etruscan art, they are rarely depicted with Dionysos/Fufluns. Indeed, the god himself is only rarely depicted in Etruscan art until the middle of the fifth century BCE, especially outside of the medium of local figure-decorated pottery. By contrast, we find depictions of satyrs on a wide range of media, and in a number of different contexts: from temple acroteria, bronze appliques, figure-decorated pottery, and funerary art (Simon 1994).

There are also some good indications that satyrs had some different associations in Etruria that were distinct from their Dionysian roles known in Greece. De Grummond (2006, 34–35) has highlighted that a number of alternative depictions of these creatures on Etruscan mirrors seem to indicate their important powers in the realm of prophecy. Jannot (1984, 345) has further noted that satyrs, or people dressed in satyr costume, appear to have had an important role in Etruscan processions and sacrifice rituals, echoing the descriptions of Roman *pompa* recorded by Dionysius of Halicarnassus. Furthermore, Govi (2008) has shown that in the fifth century BCE the Felsine stelae of Etruria Padana frequently depict satyrs in the role of psychopompoi, a role that would be replaced with representations of death demons in the fourth century. It is this funerary aspect in particular which is of relevance to the preponderance of satyr imagery found on Attic vases in Tarquinia, especially given the prominence of black-figure amphorae featuring these beings that found their way into funerary depositions. Satyrs share a number of iconographic features with later depictions of Charu(n): their grotesque faces, animal ears, snub noses, and wild appearance bear striking similarities. The existence of some Felsine stelae depicting satyrs holding attributes that would come to be associated with Charu(n) further reinforces this association.

The Demon in the Detail

The role of the satyrs and the five gods discussed above share a common feature: they all represent beings who have power over the transitional space between life and the afterlife. The motif of the journey through this space is a prominent one in Etruscan eschatology, one which is evident since at least the Orientalizing period, with elements which perhaps originate even earlier. It is also a role that, from the mid–late fifth century BCE, comes to be increasingly represented in the company of the uniquely Etruscan death demons. The T. d. Demoni Azzurri presents the first unequivocal example of these demons in Etruscan funerary art, and by the fourth century BCE, they had been further refined and developed so that we can clearly recognize the two chief demons associated with the funerary sphere: Charu(n) and Vanth. These demons were not new; both are attested in inscriptional evidence, with a dedication to Charu(n) on a cup by Oltos dating to the end of the sixth century BCE, and a dedication to Vanth from the late seventh (Maras 2019). Their depiction, however, was, at least as far as we can recognize it, new, emerging clearly over the course of the fourth century BCE to become some of the most regularly depicted Etruscan mythological figures.

Why did this imagery not emerge earlier? It is well recognized that most of the Etruscan iconography for their mythological figures was derived from external stimuli; beginning with the Phoenician influences in the Orientalizing period, and increasingly marked by Hellenic influences in the Archaic period, the Etruscans adopted, and adapted, iconographies from these cultures to represent their own divine beings, but only when they recognized their own gods in these foreign prototypes. The principal gods who were readily syncretized to the Greek Olympians are clear examples of this adoption, but there are a number of Etruscan deities with no known Greek equivalent that are known by name but never depicted in art (de Grummond 2006).

Charu(n) and Vanth fit this pattern seamlessly, being uniquely Etruscans and having no direct Greek equivalents (Jannot 1991). Yet, in a culture that was clearly concerned with representing eschatological ideas on their funerary monuments, this presents a problem. While there is evidence for some early attempts by the Etruscans to depict demons in the sixth century BCE (Klinger 2013), they were clearly not confident in inventing figures from nothing at this early date, preferring instead to adapt existing foreign models to their needs. We can see this process at play in the Felsine stelae, where the iconographies of satyrs are redeployed to serve as psychopompoi in funerary contexts. While not exactly matching the depictions of the later Charu(n), the satyrs were the closest figures from the available iconographic models at the time, and so were refunctionalized to serve in that role. It is likely that a similar process was at play in southern Etruria too, where satyr imagery proliferates, especially on the imported Attic vases that were chosen to serve as grave goods. The fact that satyrs are connected with the Dionysian sphere would only strengthen the eschatological associations for an Etruscan viewer, where the associations of wine, dancing, and music were already intimately associated with the funerary sphere.

Conclusions

The hybrid creatures and fantastic beasts found upon Attic black-figure amphorae show a strong resonance with the funerary imagery of the Etruscans that had been established long before the importation of Attic vases began. This is most markedly apparent in those scenes associated with Heraklean and Dionysian imagery in the second half of the sixth century BCE. Of all of the different mythological scenes painted by the Athenian craftsmen, it was these two broad categories which were most likely to have involved such fantastic creatures. Other figures from Greek myth who interacted with monstrous beings are not depicted on Attic vases in the

sheer quantity that these two are. The changing preference of the vase painters away from the subsidiary, decorative friezes of animals and hybrids over the course of the sixth century in favour of a single large narrative zone on each side of the vase by the end of the century meant that the number of vases featuring such creatures would be limited to those few mythological figures who regularly interacted with them. Herakles and Dionysos stand out among the corpus of Greek mythological figures who not only are frequently depicted with these beings, but also as those whose scenes were most likely to be depicted by the vase painters.

They were, as such, the most commonly available scenes for the Etruscans to choose from when selecting which vases to use as either grave offerings or, indeed, as cinerary urns. There is clear agency at play in the Etruscans' choice of vase shape. The analysis here suggests that this is the case also with the mythological scenes painted on these vases: the most commonly occurring figures on these vases are those whose Etruscan counterparts have strong eschatological associations. Apollo/Suri and Athena/Menrva have well attested chthonic associations in Etruria; both Dionysos/Fufluns and Herakles/Hercle are figures who traverse the journey between the mortal realm and the afterlife on more than one occasion; Hermes/Turms and the satyrs have clear functions as psychopompoi leading the dead on their final journey.

That it was the depictions on these vases that held significance for the Etruscans in the sixth century may be further asserted based upon what happens in the fifth century BCE: these vases decline drastically in funerary depositions, particularly from c. 475 BCE. This decline in the presence of Attic pottery in Etruscan graves has traditionally been explained by the fifth-century 'crisis'. However, another explanation can readily be deduced from the changes in production at Athens. This is precisely the same time when the Athenian potteries largely shifted their technique of decoration from black-figure to red-figure. Concurrent with this shift in decorative technique was a change in the types of scenes which were depicted on the vases, whereby mythological scenes where far less likely to be depicted in favour of genre scenes, or scenes of mundane Greek life. Even among the mythological scenes that continued to be depicted, there is a notable decline in the number of episodes that feature fantastic beasts and hybrid creatures, with Boardman (1975, 215) noting that there is a 'tendency [...] to expunge the monstrous and exotic'.

As we have seen, the monstrous and exotic were exactly the types of scenes which held significant resonance with Etruscan funerary ideas that are clearly evident from the Orientalizing period. The general decline in the number of large format Attic vases bearing images which resonated with Etruscan eschatological concepts is equally apparent, and this likely lies behind the sharp decline of Attic vases from funerary contexts immediately after this shift in production at Athens. Simply put, Athens was no longer producing vases bearing imagery that was deemed suitable by the Etruscans for their funerary needs. It should therefore follow that the Etruscans would not deposit unsuitable vases in their graves, and this is exactly what we see happening in southern, coastal Etruria from *c.* 475 BCE onwards. It is also possible that the decline in the vase trade led to the stimulation of Etruscan artists: the rapid development of local Etruscan depictions of death demons in the mid-fifth century BCE coincides with the cessation of Attic pottery deposition in tombs. No longer provided with ready-made vases which they could simply adapt to their own funerary needs, they set about creating their own iconographies for these beings. Iconographies which drew upon the attributes of different figures from Greek art, combined in new ways to present their own uniquely local conceptions of their guides to the afterlife.

Works Cited

Avramidou, Amalia. 2011. *The Codrus Painter: Iconography and Reception of Athenian Vases in the Age of Pericles* (Madison: University of Wisconsin Press)

'Beazley Archive Pottery Database (BAPD)' <www.beazley.ox.ac.uk> [accessed 12 January 2019]

Boardman, John. 1964. *The Greeks Overseas* (Middlesex: Penguin)

——. 1975. *Athenian Red Figure Vases the Archaic Period* (London: Thames & Hudson)

——. 1991. *Athenian Black Figure Vases* (London: Thames & Hudson)

——. 2001. *The History of Greek Vases* (London: Thames & Hudson)

Brandt, J. Rasmus. 2015. 'Passage to the Underworld: Continuity or Change in Etruscan Funerary Ideology and Practices (6th–2nd Century BC)?', in *Death and Changing Rituals, Function and Meaning in Ancient Funerary Practices*, ed. by J. Rasmus Brandt, Marina Prusac, and Håkon Roland (Oxford: Oxbow), pp. 105–84

Brizzolara, Anna Maria, and Vincenzo Baldoni. 2010. 'Eracle nella ceramica Attica in Etruria padana: la ricezione delle immagini', *Bollettino di archeologia online*, special volume: *International Congress of Classical Archaeology: Meetings between Cultures in the Ancient Mediterranean (Rome, 22–26 September 2008)*: 1–14 <https://bollettinodiarcheologiaonline.beniculturali.it/wp-content/uploads/2019/05/2_Brizzolara_Baldoni_paper.pdf> [accessed 7 March 2023]

Bundrick, Sheramy D. 2019. *Athens, Etruria, and the Many Lives of Greek Figured Pottery*, Wisconsin Studies in Classics (Madison: University of Wisconsin Press)

——. 2020. 'Herakles on the Move: A Greek Hydria's Journey from Athens to Vulci', *Memoirs of the American Academy in Rome*, 63–64 (2018/2019): 85–136

Campus, Lucrezia. 1981. *Ceramica attica a figure nere mel Museo di Tarquinia: piccoli vasi e vasi plastici*, Materiali del Museo archeologico nazionale di Tarquinia, 2 (Rome: Giorgio Bretschneider)

Cerchiai, Luca. 2015. 'Il dionisismo nell'immaginario funebre degli Etruschi', in *La viaggio oltre la vita*, ed. by Giuseppe Sassatelli and Alfonsina Russo Tagliente (Bologna: Bononia University Press), pp. 37–44

Colonna, Giovanni. 1984. 'Menerva', in *LIMC*, II, pp. 1050–74

——. 1991. 'Riflessioni sul dionisismo in Etruria', in *Dionysos: mito e mistero*, ed. by Fede Berti and Carlo Gasparri (Ferrara: Liberty House), pp. 117–56

——. 1996. 'L'Apollo di Pyrgi', in *Magna Grecia, Etruschi, Fenici: atti del trentatreesimo convegno di studi sulla Magna Grecia, Taranto, 8–13 Ottobre 1993* (Taranto: Istituto per la storia e l'archeologia della Magna Grecia), pp. 345–75

d'Agostino, Bruno, and Luca Cerchiai. 1999. *Il mare, la morte, l'amore: gli Etruschi, i Greci, e l'immagine* (Rome: Donzelli)

De Angelis, Francesco. 2015. *Miti greci in tombe etrusche: le urne cinerarie di Chiusi*, Monumenti antichi, serie monografica, 73 (Rome: Giorgio Bretschneider)

de Grummond, Nancy T. 2006. *Etruscan Myth, Sacred History, and Legend*, 1st edn (Philadelphia: University of Pennsylvania Museum of Archaeology and Anthropology)

Ferrari, Gloria. 1988. *I vasi attici a figure rosse del periodo arcaico nel Museo archeologico di Tarquinia*, Materiali del Museo archeologico nazionale di Tarquinia, 11 (Rome: Giorgio Bretschneider)

Fiorini, Lucio. 2007. 'Immaginario della tomba. Retaggi arcaici e soluzioni ellenistiche', *Ostraka*, 16.1: 131–47

Govi, Elisabetta. 2008. 'Le stele di Bologna di V Sec. a.C.: modelli iconografici tra Grecia ed Etruria', *Bollettino di archeologia online*, special volume: *International Congress of Classical Archaeology: Meetings between Cultures in the Ancient Mediterranean*: 36–47 <https://bollettinodiarcheologiaonline.beniculturali.it/wp-content/uploads/2019/05/5_Govi_paper.pdf> [accessed 12 February 2023]

Hannestad, Lise. 1988. 'Athenian Pottery in Etruria *c.* 550–470 BC.', *Acta archaeologica*, 59: 113–30

Harari, Maurizio. 1997. 'Turms', in *LIMC*, VIII, pp. 98–111

Haynes, Sybille. 2000. *Etruscan Civilization* (London: British Museum Press)

Jannot, Jean-René. 1984. *Les reliefs archaïques de Chiusi* (Rome: Ecole française de Rome)

——. 1991. 'Charon et Charun: à propos d'un démon funéraire étrusque', *Comptes rendus des séances de l'Académie des inscriptions et belles-lettres*, 135.2: 443–64

——. 1995. 'Les vases métalliques dans les représentations picturales étrusques', *Revue des études anciennes*, 97.1–2: 167–82

——. 2005. *Religion in Ancient Etruria*, Wisconsin Studies in Classics (Madison: University of Wisconsin Press)

Klinger, Sonia. 2013. 'Underworld Demons on an Early Fifth Century BCE Etruscan Black-Figure Stamnos from Vulci Now in Berlin', *Etruscan Studies*, 16.1: 39–74

Krauskopf, Ingrid. 1984. 'Aplu', in *LIMC*, II, pp. 335–63

La Genière, Juliette de. 1986. 'Rituali funebri e produzione di vasi', in *Tarquinia: ricerche, scavi e prospettive*, ed. by Maria Bonghi Jovino and Cristina Chiaramonte Treré (Rome: L'Erma di Bretschneider), pp. 203–08

—— (ed.). 2006. *Les clients de la céramique grecque: actes du colloque de l'Académie des inscriptions et belles-lettres, Paris, 30–31 Janvier 2004* (Paris: Académie des inscriptions et belles-lettres)

Langridge-Noti, Elizabeth. 2013. 'Consuming Iconographies', in *Pottery Markets in the Ancient Greek World (8th–1st Centuries B.C.): Proceedings of the International Symposium Held at the Université libre de Bruxelles, 19–21 June 2008*, ed. by Athena Tsingarida and D. Viviers (Brussels: CreA-Patrimone), pp. 61–72

Leighton, Robert. 2004. *Tarquinia: An Etruscan City* (London: Duckworth)

Lubtchansky, Natacha. 2014. '"Bespoken Vases" tra Atene e Etruria? Rassegna degli studi e proposte di ricerca', in *Artisti, committenti e fruitori in Etruria tra VIII e V secolo a.C.: atti del XXI convegno internazionale di studi sulla storia e l'archeologia dell'Etruria*, Annali della Fondazione per Il Museo 'Claudio Faina', 21 (Rome: Quasar), pp. 357–87

Lynch, Kathleen M. 2017. 'Reception, Intention, and Attic Vases', in *Theoretical Approaches to the Archaeology of Ancient Greece*, ed. by Lisa Nevett (Ann Arbor: University of Michigan Press), pp. 124–42

Maras, Daniele F. 2019. *Il dono votivo: gli dei e il sacro nelle iscrizioni etrusche di culto*, Biblioteca di 'Studi etruschi', 46 (Rome: Fabrizio Serra)

Marroni, Elisa. 2017. *Vasi attici a figure rosse da Tarquinia* (Pisa: Edizioni ETS)

Marzullo, Matilde. 2016. *Grotte cornetane: materiali e apparato critico per lo studio delle tombe dipinte di Tarquinia*, I, Tarchna, 6 (Milan: Ledizioni)

Nati, Danilo. 2012. *Ceramica attica a figure nere nel Museo archeologico nazionale di Tarquinia*, I.1: *La collezione Bruschi Falgari*, Materiali del Museo archeologico nazionale di Tarquinia, 20 (Rome: Giorgio Bretschneider)

Osborne, Robin. 2007. 'What Travelled with Greek Pottery?', *Mediterranean Historical Review*, 22.1: 85–95

——. 2018. *The Transformation of Athens: Painted Pottery and the Creation of Classical Greece* (Princeton: Princeton University Press)

Palmieri, Alessandro. 2003. 'Il repertorio tipologico dei cinerari tarquiniesi di VI e V Sec. a.C.', *Bollettino della Società tarquiniese di arte e storia*, 32: 55–72

Peruzzi, Bice. 2016. 'Eggs in a Drinking Cup: Unexpected Uses of a Greek Shape in Central Apulian Funerary Contexts', in *The Consumers' Choice: Uses of Greek Figure-Decorated Pottery; Selected Papers on Ancient Art and Architecture*, II, ed. by Thomas H. Carpenter, Elizabeth Langridge-Noti, and Mark Stansbury-O'Donnell (Boston: Archaeological Institute of America), pp. 65–81

Pierro, Elena. 1983. *Ceramica 'Ionica' non figurata e coppe attiche a figure nere nel Museo di Tarquinia*, Materiali del Museo archeologico nazionale di Tarquinia, 6 (Rome: Giorgio Bretschneider)

Puritani, Laura. 2015. 'Fufluns und seine Pflanzen in der archaischen Vasenmalerei des 6. Jhs. v. Chr.', in *ΦΥΤΑ ΚΑΙ ΖΩΙΑ: Pflanzen und Tiere auf griechischen Vasen; Internationales Symposion, Graz, 26.–28. September 2013*, Corpus vasorum antiquorum, Österreich, Beiheft, 2 (Vienna: Verlag der Österreichischen Akademie der Wissenschaften), pp. 139–46

Reusser, Christoph. 2002. *Vasen für Etrurien*, 2 vols (Zürich: Akanthus), I

Roncalli, Freancesco. 2015. 'L'Aldilà: dall'idea al paesaggio', in *La viaggio oltre la vita*, ed. by Giuseppe Sassatelli and Alfonsina R. Tagliente (Bologna: Bononia University Press), pp. 53–60

Schwarz, S. J. 1990. 'Hercle', in *LIMC*, v.2, pp. 196–253

Simon, Erika. 1994. 'Silenoi', in *LIMC*, VII, pp. 1108–33

Small, Jocelyn Penny. 1994. 'Scholars, Etruscans, and Attic Painted Vases', *Journal of Roman Archaeology*, 7: 34–58

Spivey, Nigel, and Simon Stoddart. 1990. *Etruscan Italy* (London: Batsford)

Steingräber, Stephan. 2006. *Abundance of Life: Etruscan Wall Painting* (Los Angeles: J. Paul Getty Trust)

Tonglet, Delphine. 2018. 'A Useful Melting-Pot: Towards a Definition of Etruscan Banquet Sets in Funerary Contexts', paper presented at the 19th International Congress of Classical Archaeology (AIAC), Cologne/Bonn, 22–26 May 2018, in panel 5.15: 'Greek and Etruscan Vases: Shapes and Markets'

Torelli, Mario. 1986. 'History: Land and People', in *Etruscan: Life and Afterlife*, ed. by Larissa Bonfante (Detroit: Wayne State University Press), pp. 19–47

Tronchetti, Carlo. 1983. *Ceramica attica a figure nere nel Museo archeologico di Tarquinia*, Materiali del Museo archeologico nazionale di Tarquinia, 5 (Rome: Giorgio Bretschneider)

Tsingarida, Athena. 2020. 'Oversized Athenian Drinking Vessels in Context: Their Role in Etruscan Ritual Performances', *American Journal of Archaeology*, 124.2: 245–74

Wiel-Marin, Federica. 2005. 'Vasi reali e vasi raffigurati nelle tombe dipinte di epoca arcaica di Tarquinia', in *Pittura parietale e pittura vascolare: ricerche in corso tra Etruria e Campania (giornata di studio Santa Maria Capua Vetere (Caserta) 2003)*, ed. by Fernando Gilotta (Naples: San Biagio dei Librai), pp. 9–17

PETER ATTEMA, BARBARA BELELLI MARCHESINI,
AND MATTHIJS CATSMAN

8. Local Choices in a Networked World

Funerary Practices at Crustumerium (Lazio)
during the Long Seventh Century BCE

ABSTRACT The long-term investigations of the burial grounds of ancient Crustumerium in northern Latium Vetus, located on the Tiber just north of Rome, have resulted in a wealth of information on the use of material culture by its community. To date, over four hundred tombs have been excavated, spanning four centuries between the mid-ninth century and the turn of the sixth century BCE. The data recovered from the burial grounds reflect profound changes in the social structure of the community that lived at Crustumerium and highlight specific material cultural connections within the wider region. Material culture expressions shared with other regions were, however, embedded in the distinctly local, social, and cultural context associated with the communities of northern Latium Vetus, and of Crustumerium itself. To study this dynamic, the present chapter offers a pilot network analysis of the material culture of a subset of Crustumerium's tombs dating to Latial periods IVA and IVB (720–580 BCE) revealing regional cultural connections and affiliations. The results of this study indicate how funerary architectural models and material culture objects of the long seventh century BCE, also known as the 'Orientalizing period', were adapted to local usage and interpretations, creating the distinct material funerary cultural context of Crustumerium.

In line with the aim of this volume, this chapter grapples with the tangled question of indigenous and introduced features in the material culture in pre-Roman Italy by exploring material culture changes in the funerary record of Crustumerium, a Latin settlement located on the west bank of the Tiber, just north of Rome (Fig. 8.1). Covering the Latial IIB2 period to

the end of the Archaic period, Crustumerium's burial record includes the so-called 'Orientalizing period' — in Latial cultural chronology represented by periods IVA and IVB (Table 8.1). While, at some settlements, the 'orientalizing' phenomenon in central Italy resulted in extremely rich find contexts, stimulated by interregional trade, with material manifestations linked to elite networks, at Crustumerium, and in comparable settlements in Latium Vetus, the effects of the increased cultural transmission that pervaded the Mediterranean basin were subtler and more strongly embedded in the local context of the Iron Age origins of the settlement and, as far as Crustumerium is concerned, the wider cultural environment of the early Latin, Etruscan, Falisco-Capenate, and Sabine peoples.

To highlight regional interconnectivity within the funerary culture of Latial periods IVA and IVB in Latium, we will discuss the relationships between objects from a sample of fifty well-preserved tombs from Crustumerium with funerary material from tombs of the surrounding regions. In this, we will use a type of network analysis suited to map cultural affiliations which, rather than focus on the question of the origin of objects, focuses instead on the shared adoption of certain objects in local repertoires by groups of communities termed 'consumption collectives'.[1]

Consumption collectives are heuristic constructs, not unlike communities of practice. The latter are defined by Wenger and Wenger-Trayner (2015) as

---

1 The network analysis was carried out by the third author within the framework of his research master thesis in archaeology at the University of Amsterdam entitled 'Connected through Death, the application of consumption collective affiliation networks in the study of seventh century BCE funerary cultural interconnectivity in Latium Vetus'; see also Catsman 2020.

Corresponding author: Peter Attema (p.a.j.attema@rug.nl)

Adoption, Adaption, and Innovation in Pre-Roman Italy: Paradigms for Cultural Change, ed. by Jeremy Armstrong and Aaron Rhodes-Schroder,
AMW 3 (Turnhout, 2023), pp. 117–146   BREPOLS ▩ PUBLISHERS   10.1484/M.AMW-EB.5.133270

Table 8.1. A comparative overview of the cultural phases of Latium, Etruria, and Greece. Column 1 gives the traditional dating (all dates BCE), accepted by most Etruscologists and Classical scholars; column 2 gives the dating based on dendrochronology (after Cascino and others 2012, table 3.2).

Traditional Chronology	Dendrochronology	Conventional Periods	Latium	Etruria	Greece
1200–1000				Tolfa	Proto-Geometric
1000–900	Final Bronze Age 3 1050–950	Final Bronze Age Protovillanovan Culture	Latial period I 1000–900	Allumiere	
	Early Iron Age I 950–850	Early Iron Age Villanovan I 900–820	Latial period II 900–770	Tarquinia I 900–800	Early Geometric 900–850
900–770	Early Iron Age II 850–750	Intermediate Villanovan		Tarquinia II 800–700	Middle Geometric 850–750
770–720		Late Iron Age Villanovan II 770–720	Latial period III 770–725/720		Late Geometric Early Proto-Corinthian 750–700
720–670		Etruscan	Latial period IVA1 720–680	Early Orientalizing 730/20–670	Middle and Late Proto-Corinthian 700–640
670–630			Latial period IVA2 680–625	Middle Orientalizing 670–630	Early Corinthian 640–600
630–580			Latial period IVB 625–580	Late Orientalizing 630–580	Archaic 610–450
580–480			Regal 580–509	Archaic	
			Early Republican		Classical
480–320				Classical	

groups of people 'who share a concern or a passion for something they do and learn how to do it better as they interact regularly'. Just as with communities of practice, consumption collectives can cover different scales ranging from the local, to the intraregional, to the Mediterranean-wide. Different to communities of practice, however, consumption collectives are based on shared consumption patterns and consumption preferences that exist without the need for repeated and intensive contacts. The concept of consumption

collectives we use in this paper is based on the idea of 'serial collectives' as discussed by Fahlander (2003).[2]

2 This concept, ultimately based on work by Sartre, entails the idea that heterogenous agents might intermittently come together engaging in certain practices binding them in a situational 'collective' which creates relatedness between them. Depending on the type of practice, the actions involved, the context of the practice as well as the frequency or 'seriality' of the practice on which the situational collective is based (see below), the ensuing collectives might or might not become socially significant in the identity of the participating agent (Fahlander 2003, 31–40).

We define a consumption collective as an etically defined situational group of individuals or community based on the archaeologically visible shared consumption of one or multiple specific objects and/or consumption preferences for specific object shapes, ware types, or decoration types. As such, consumption collectives can reflect a wider range of types of interconnectivity between communities than communities of practice, ranging from single exchanges and local adoptions to more intense forms of interconnectivity and adaption of meaning and values. As situational constructs, these consumption collectives do not necessarily need to result in shared meaning and value systems, although a consumption collective may show overlap with a community of practice. If the latter is the case, the consumption collective may also include shared practices and value systems. In order to discern the characteristics of interconnectivity of a consumption collective, contextual analyses of the shared material culture and practices are necessary. The use of consumption collectives thus forms a first step in the analysis of interconnectivity, and is a bottom-up approach for reflecting on local adoptions, adaptions, and even the creation of related practices and meanings. At Crustumerium, the adoption of specific objects in the funerary set related to drinking, such as the *oinochoe* and *kotyle*, is an example of participation in a Mediterranean-wide consumption collective, pointing to the local adoption of practices and meanings.

To study the significance of the changes in the material record of Crustumerium's burial grounds during Latial periods IVA and IVB, in terms of the adoption and adaption of novel objects in the funerary rituals, we place the outcome of the network analysis of consumption collectives of this cultural phase within the wider chronological frame of the Early Iron Age (Latial periods IIB2, IIIA, and IIIB) and the Archaic period. In both these periods, the quantity of objects per tomb was more limited and less variegated compared to the often abundant and diverse grave gifts present in the tombs of the Latial periods IVA and IVB. But while the observation of the changing consumption collective affiliations, as provided by the pilot network analysis, is insightful on the level of interconnectivity, it does not *explain* the changes in the preference for certain objects. To interpret the significance of preference, we need to study changes in the social structure of individual communities and explore how they might be mirrored by object related funerary practices. We reiterate here that only detailed contextual studies can inform us on how participation in consumption collectives relates to communities of practice and the local adoption or adaption of social practices.

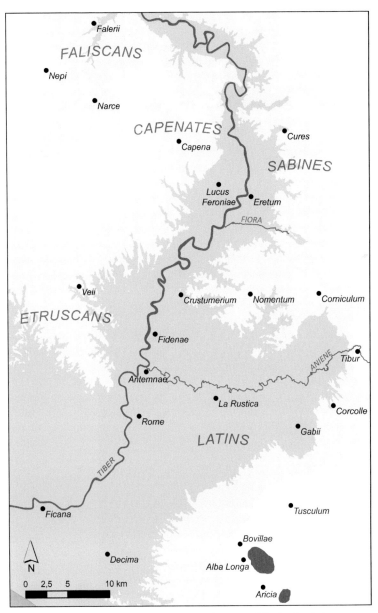

Figure 8.1. Location map of Crustumerium within central Tyrrhenian Italy (by R. Bronkhorst and S. Boersma / GIA-RuG).

While Mediterranean-wide consumption collective affiliations are certainly traceable in the Early Iron Age, they become much more evident in the following periods.[3] In contrast with the Early Iron Age burial record, that of Latial periods IVA and IVB must be placed in a context of growing population numbers, increasingly pronounced social differentiation, labour specialization, and increasing interregional interaction and trade. Rapid demographic, socio-economic, and cultural changes in this period

---

3   See Cifani (2021, 37–81) for an overview of local production and regional and extra-regional importation in Latial periods II, III, IVA, and IVB.

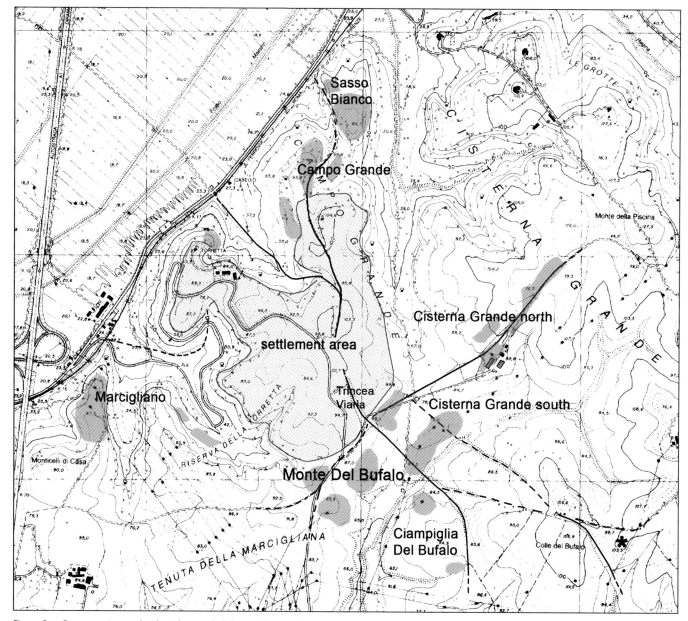

Figure 8.2. Crustumerium and its burial grounds (after Belelli Marchesini 2020, fig. 1).

resulted in the introduction of new forms of material expression in tomb architecture, grave gifts, and burial ritual, providing a means to express social status (Bartoloni 2003). A new 'lifestyle', initially embodied and exemplified through elite behaviour, gradually trickled down in the funerary practices of communities.

At Crustumerium, the material manifestation of the 'orientalizing lifestyle' gradually ended with the introduction of chamber tombs meant for collective, multiple generation burial practices. These likely came into fashion as a reflection of the greater role of high-status families within the now fully urban community, and material manifestation in the tombs is gradually reduced. In some chamber tombs of the early sixth century BCE, the inventory consists of but a few bucchero and Etrusco-Corinthian vases and an occasional piece of weaponry. Even the presence of chamber tombs at Crustumerium with a grave inventory is, however, quite unique in Latium Vetus as there is only scarce published evidence for this period from elsewhere in the region. This reflects Crustumerium's continued cultural affiliation with Etruria and the Faliscan area, where chamber tombs, of the types adopted at Crustumerium, occur. It warns us that any analysis of material culture affiliations should take into account tomb typology and that defining a cultural *koine* based on objects only can be misleading and always needs the study of context in which objects were used.

Below we first discuss the general chronological and spatial development of Crustumerium's burial ground, its main cultural characteristics, and social context. Then we will discuss the methodological background of the network analysis that the third author performed. This is followed by an interpretation of the graphs resulting from the analysis. Finally, we discuss the interpretation of adopted and adapted objects in the local funerary context of Crustumerium and their significance in the funerary ritual, followed by a conclusion and recommendations.

Chrono-Spatial Development of Crustumerium's Burial Ground, Cultural Characteristics, and Social Context

The settlement of Crustumerium is surrounded by several burial grounds (Fig. 8.2) with tombs covering Latial period IIB2 to the end of the Archaic period (Table 8.1).[4] To date, the burial ground of Monte Del Bufalo (MDB) has received the most attention with four hundred tombs, partly looted and partly intact, having been documented since the first formal excavation in 1987.[5] On account of the large number of tombs excavated at MDB, an adequate insight has been obtained into its chronological and spatial development.[6] The dating of the earliest tombs, twenty-eight in total, is in line with the earliest traces of habitation on the settlement plateau (di Gennaro, Belelli Marchesini, Nijboer 2016). This implies that, from its very foundation in the mid-ninth century BCE, the inhabitants conceived of the hill-system of Crustumerium as a unitary settlement, with demarcated domains for the living and the dead (Attema and others 2014). Our recent, as of yet unpublished, excavation of a huge artificial mound erected on top of a section of the MDB burial ground has confirmed that the dating of the latest tombs at Crustumerium is in line with the

abandonment phase of the settlement in the early fifth century BCE. This means that we can view the development of the MDB burial ground as reflecting the socio-cultural development of the community over a period of almost four centuries, always taking into account ideological filters that may have operated in representing the deceased (Willemsen 2014, 13–14; Nizzo 2015).

While it is generally accepted that Latin society went through a profound cultural transformation between the Early Iron Age and the Archaic period, as part of a Mediterranean-wide process of increased connectivity, contextual analyses are still few.[7] From this perspective, the burial grounds of Crustumerium offer a unique possibility to analyse the changes in a local social and cultural context. Before presenting the network analysis and discussing local choices, we give a concise overview of the chronological and spatial development of the burial grounds of MDB, an overview of the social and cultural characteristics of each period represented (Early Iron Age, Orientalizing, and Archaic periods), and introduce aspects of tomb architecture and the types of objects that testify to regional connectivity.

As noted above, Crustumerium was surrounded by several burial areas that extended over the slopes of the urban plateau and the adjacent hills.[8] The earliest tombs align with the foundation date of the settlement (Latial period IIB2), but so far the evidence is scanty. This may be due to a restriction on formal burial at an early stage, but it is also likely that erosion by agricultural activities has affected the preservation of such tombs, which were only slightly cut in the bedrock. Apart from a ploughed-out tomb at Sasso Bianco (and ploughed-out sherds from Campo Grande), the vast majority of the Early Iron Age tombs at the site are found at MDB. Their spatial distribution shows two different patterns that highlight social transformation. The first is the use of delineated areas in which the tombs are spatially distributed at regular intervals, respecting a ritual orientation to the north-east. The second pattern is the location of isolated early tombs inside plots that were subsequently exploited, probably by the members of a particular clan or family (Fig. 8.3). Available data also suggest that tombs of this period were pos-

---

4   Excavation campaigns conducted since 1987 have also provided information about the cemeteries on the northern (Sasso Bianco, Campo Grande), eastern (Cisterna Grande), and south-eastern (Monte Del Bufalo) sides of the settlement and about a small cluster of infant tombs located along the Road Trench climbing up the settlement from the south. Some sepulchral areas (Marcigliano, Ciampiglia Del Bufalo) are only known from the illegal activity of tomb robbers (Crustumerium 2016, 79–110).

5   Between 2006–2017, MDB was excavated by the Superintendency of Rome (SSABAP) in collaboration with the Groningen Institute of Archaeology

6   Data obtained from burial grounds other than MDB, even if still limited, suggests apart from resemblances also significant differences regarding the nature and chronology of tomb clusters.

7   For example, Osteria dell'Osa (Bietti Sestieri 1992), Marino-Riserva del Truglio (Taloni 2013), and Satricum (Waarsenburg 1995). For an overview of the development of Latin cemeteries between the seventh and sixth centuries, based on the available data, see Bartoloni and others 2009.

8   Belelli Marchesini 2020 for a preliminary analysis of the MDB burial ground with references to earlier publications; more in general see contributions in Crustumerium catalogue 2016.

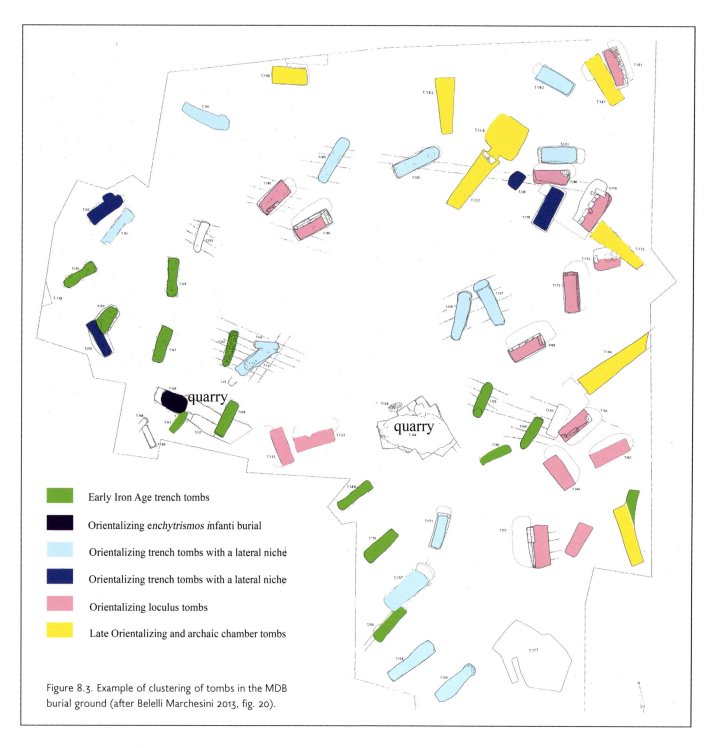

Figure 8.3. Example of clustering of tombs in the MDB burial ground (after Belelli Marchesini 2013, fig. 20).

sibly clustered according to gender. Tombs dating from the Latial periods IVA and IVB are mainly documented in the cemeteries to the north (Sasso Bianco, Campo Grande) and south-east (MDB) of the settlement, whereas a loose distribution of Archaic chamber tombs exists in the northern district of the Cisterna Grande burial ground.

At MDB, the distribution of tombs shows that the totality of the cemetery was not in use during Latial periods IVA and IVB and the Archaic period, and that the burial areas were separated by empty strips of land. The spatial distribution of tombs within the different clusters seems to mirror aspects of social development. At first, individual tombs with identical ritual orientation were distributed in rows, but during the seventh century BCE progressive clustering takes place. The process begins with the formation of small groups of two or three tombs close to each other, and ends with the appearance of chamber tombs suitable to be used by several generations.

The development of Crustumerium is in line with the main transformations occurring in the Tyrrhenian area starting from the eighth century BCE, connected with increasing cultural and commercial contacts with the eastern Mediterranean, but its social and peculiar cultural characteristics are influenced by its local geographic position. Located on the left bank of the Tiber, Crustumerium falls in the northern district of the Latin territory, well delimited to the south by the River Aniene (Fig. 8.1). Its frontier position, with respect to the Etruscan (Veii), Falisco-Capenates, and Sabine territories, and its location along a long-distance track, crossing the Tiber and connecting Etruria with Latium and Campania, has favoured the passage of people and goods, as well as the reception of different external influences and the consequent elaboration of an original material culture. However, its peripheral position in the northern portion of the Latin territory, and in respect to Rome, may have affected the development of social stratification as reflected in the apparent lack of really outstanding tombs in all periods, compared with nearby Fidenae and other Latin settlements.[9]

In the Early Iron Age, the limited repertoire of impasto shapes and their decoration, consisting of zig-zag, double-angle, or N-shaped motifs traced with single incised lines (Pl. 8.1), fit the cultural characteristics of pottery production of the trans-Tiberine region, including the Etruscan town of Veii and the Latin area delimited to the south by Rome and Gabii (di Gennaro and Iaia 2000). However, in the course of the Iron Age, Crustumerium would develop its own material identity.

The cultural change at the transition from Early Iron Age to the Orientalizing periods is marked by the appearance of individual tombs of remarkable architectural engagement, the renovation of the pottery repertoire, and the adoption of ceremonial habits and new burial rituals. The individual tomb types used during Latial periods IVA and IVB are the result of the adoption, and sometimes adaption, of models from the opposite bank of the Tiber. As far as pottery production is concerned, the introduction of several new shapes is coeval with the appearance of different specialized workshops that drew upon the Latin, Etruscan, and Faliscan repertoires. In funerary contexts dated from the late eighth to the end of the seventh centuries, pottery assemblages (Plates 8.2–8.4) reflect ceremonial banqueting habits in which the consumption of wine played a central role in line with the

general cultural trends of the Orientalizing period in Etruria and Latium Vetus (Bartoloni and others 2012).

The social development of the community, and the emergence of family groups, is reflected in the introduction of architectural models suitable to be used by several generations. We will return to this below. Chamber tombs occur between the third and last quarter of the seventh century BCE in tandem with a change in ritual behaviour marked by a gradual decline of funerary objects (Pl. 8.5). This change in ritual behaviour regarding the use of objects, as well as the final disappearance of grave goods from the middle of the sixth century BCE, reflect the deep social and political transformations in Latium Vetus leading to the more isonomic character of the social organization of the Archaic towns.

In sum, while we see an overall tendency for the adoption and adaption of (new) architectural forms throughout the period, Latial periods IVA and IVB in particular betray a preoccupation with the adoption and adaption of new objects in Crustumerium's funerary practices, both in a quantitative (tombs may now contain over sixty objects) and a qualitative sense (now outstanding and unique objects are found in some tombs). Access to new objects in the orientalizing fashion was promoted by increased trade of objects on a Mediterranean-wide scale, and in central Italy led to local interpretations of foreign production techniques and to specific morphological, functional, and stylistic traits of objects. Increased interconnectivity between Etruria and Latium Vetus, and indeed beyond, functioned as a motor for the creation of new consumption collectives, sharing innovations in material culture that might be given local meanings. In the following section, we present affiliation network graphs visualizing the cultural interconnectivity and consumption collective affiliations of fifty tombs from the MDB burial ground at Crustumerium dating to Latial periods IVA–IVB (720–580 BCE) with representative grave inventories preserved.[10]

Mapping Relatedness and Material Culture Entanglements

The affiliation network graphs presented below are based on objects from fifty tombs dated to Latial periods IVA and IVB, and serve to visualize relatedness between different archaeological contexts based on the concurring consumption of material

---

9 See Nijboer 2018 for an in-depth discussion of the variegated material expressions of social reality in death in central Tyrrhenian Italy.

10 This method builds on an exemplary network methodology developed by Lieve Donnellan in her study of Pithecusae (Donnellan 2016).

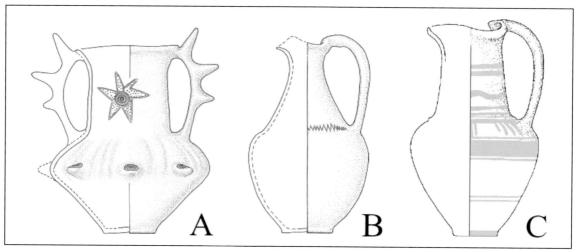

Figure 8.4. The consumption collective affiliations of three objects (by M. Catsman).
A. Spiked *anforetta laziale*. B. *Impasto bruno* Phoenician-Cypriote *oinochoe*. C. Italo-Geometric *oinochoe*.

culture: when two contexts share the consumption of a specific object a relationship — or affiliation — is drawn between them (Brughmans 2013, 638; Donnellan 2016).[11] However, in this specific network, the Crustumerium funerary contexts are not directly affiliated to other tomb contexts, as this would make the network too difficult to read.[12] Instead, funerary assemblages are affiliated to various (cultural) consumption collectives.

As mentioned in the introduction, a consumption collective is a group of individuals or communities which share the consumption of one or multiple specific objects and/or consumption preferences, as visible in specific shared material elements of consumed objects (for example object shape, ware type, or decoration). Depending on the (number of) shared elements, the shared consumption of an object might reflect a strong connection and high degree of interconnectivity, for example when sharing the consumption of exactly the same object, or a more indirect adaption and lower degree of interconnectivity, for example when the connection to a consumption collective is only based on a single element, such as a ware or decoration type. The concept is based on the notion of serial collectives, which is itself based on the idea that heterogenous agents might share certain actions — in this instance, the consumption of a specific object or specific consumption preferences — which binds them in a situational (etic) collective and creates relatedness, without *a priori* assuming that the shared consumption of a specific object had the same significance for the participants (Fahlander 2003, 31–34).

In theory, a consumption collective includes all individuals or communities which participated in an exchange network through which an object was traded or through which knowledge about material culture was shared which influenced local consumption preferences. In contrast to the much more common focus on direct interconnectivity with the area of production, the concept of consumption collectives allows us to analyse how a local community participated within networks of various scales within the wider Mediterranean world.[13]

As stated, in heuristic terms a consumption collective can be regarded as a weaker form of a community of practice: the social and cultural meaning of the object or practices related to its consumption do not need to be the same, as is the case with a community of practice. Nor does the concept of a consumption collective necessitate repeated and intensive contact, as communities of practice do (Wenger and Wenger-Trayner 2015). Consumption collectives can also be related to a much wider range of types of interconnectivity, from occasional and low degree to a much higher and more intense degree of interconnectivity. In this way, the use of consumption collectives allows us to investigate the interconnectivity of individuals and communities even when practices and value systems involved might

---

11 For more on networks in general and their applicability and popularity in archaeology see foremost Brughmans and Peeples 2017; Brughmans and others 2016; and Collar and others 2015.

12 This would mean including hundreds of nodes representing funerary contexts both at Crustumerium and many other sites throughout Italy and the wider Mediterranean area.

13 This seems all the more paramount when we realize that we often do not know exactly how objects reached a site, that is to say directly or indirectly from the area of production.

have been heterogenous. In short, the construction and analyses of consumption collective affiliations forms a bottom-up, heuristic approach to investigate a community's participation in possibly heterogeneous and contextual constellations of interconnected communities and allows us to explore the effects of this interconnectivity on a local culture.

In compiling the affiliation data, each item within the funerary assembly was provided with two affiliations. The first concerns an affiliation based on the shared consumption of the object in its specific material form and focuses on the area where this object occurs. The second affiliation concerns how the object might reflect the sharing of wider socio-cultural consumption preferences and practices. These affiliations often concern less direct material similarities between objects, and are concerned with adaptions of more widely shared consumption preferences.

The attribution of these affiliations is in turn based on the many highly detailed contextual studies of single object types of the material culture of Latium Vetus and the central Tyrrhenian area in the literature. The analysis of the material culture recovered from Crustumerium's funerary contexts resulted in the delineation of different consumption collectives in which the community of Crustumerium participated during the seventh century BCE. Largely overlapping object consumption collectives were combined into overarching collectives (Table 8.2, left column) operating at different scales (Table 8.2, central and left column) and constructed on the basis of the attributed affiliations per subperiod (Latial period IVA and IVB, Table 8.1).

As an example we provide consumption collective affiliations of three objects:

1. The *anforetta laziale* with spiked handles (Fig. 8.4, A) only occurs at Crustumerium in its specific material form; therefore the object is attributed to a Crustumerium-affiliated consumption collective. However, the *anforetta laziale* object type, as well as the *impasto bruno* ware and incised decoration, reflect wider socio-cultural consumption preference of communities throughout Latium Vetus. Therefore, the object is also attributed a Latial consumption collective affiliation.

2. The *impasto bruno* Phoenician-Cypriote *oinochoe* (Fig. 8.4, B) in its specific material form occurs throughout the entire central Tyrrhenian area and it is consequently attributed a central Tyrrhenian consumption collective. However, the object shape reflects socio-cultural consumption preferences for this type of pouring vessel, in various material forms, shared throughout a wider Mediterranean area. As such it is also attributed a Mediterranean consumption collective affiliation.

3. The Italo-Geometric *oinochoe* (Fig. 8.4, C) occurs throughout the entire central Tyrrhenian area and is consequently attributed an affiliation with a central Tyrrhenian consumption collective. However, the object shape, ware type, and decoration reflect central Tyrrhenian preferences for Hellenic-inspired material elements, which result from the region's interconnections with a Mediterranean-wide exchange network. As such it is attributed a second Greek Mediterranean consumption collective affiliation.

The advantage of working with these different types of affiliations and the construction of these graphs is that it allows us to think about the entanglement of local material culture on the scale level of an entire community and start to explore how this material culture might have included the adoption or adaption of wider circulating cultural influences (Stockhammer 2013). Finally, the fact that the various tomb contexts remain visible in the graph, as distinct entities, means that this kind of graph is well suited for performing multivariate comparative analyses of intracommunal variation in interconnectivity through the use of various colorizations indicating different characteristics of these contexts (for example, date of the tomb, gender of the deceased, etc.). Below we present the main results of this comparative affiliation network analysis.

Results of the Affiliation Network Analysis

The affiliation analysis results in the recognition of various consumption patterns related to synchronic variations and diachronic changes in the cultural interconnectivity of the local buried community.

Period IVA

In period IVA, the funerary assemblages usually consist of a banqueting set and a strictly personal set (that is, jewellery, weaving-related objects, and/or weaponry). The differentiation between these two elements of the funerary assemblage is also clearly visible in the cultural interconnectivity.

The banqueting set mainly displays a central Tyrrhenian affiliated material culture, with strong regional and local elements. This is reflected within the material affiliation network in the central position of the central Tyrrhenian, Latial, and Crustumerium's

Table 8.2. The various consumption collectives used in the network analysis (by M. Catsman).

Consumption collective	Scale level	Related areas
Crustumerian	Local	Crustumerium and its direct surrounding areas
Latial	Regional	Latium Vetus
Tyrrhenian hinterland	Interregional	Part of central Tyrrhenian area concerning the more inland areas of Faliscan-Capenate area, the Tiberine-Sabine area and several sites in southern Etruria
Central Tyrrhenian	Interregional	Etruria, Latium Vetus, the Faliscan-Capenate and Tiberine-Sabine area
Medio-Adriatic	Interregional	Area more or less coinciding with the central Tyrrhenian Apennines and Adriatic coastal area
Central-Italian	Interregional	The combined area of the central Tyrrhenian areas and Medio-Adriatic areas
Italian peninsula	Interregional	Central and southern Italy
Mediterranean Greek	Global	Areas throughout the Mediterranean basin in which (im)material culture affiliated to the Greek (colonial) world was spread
Mediterranean Phoenician	Global	Areas throughout the Mediterranean basin in which (im)material culture affiliated to the Phoenician (colonial) world was spread
Mediterranean Etruscan	Global	Areas throughout the Mediterranean basin in which (im)material culture related to the sixth-century Etruscan trade networks was spread
Unknown	n.a.	No related area can be discerned

consumption collectives (Fig. 8.5). The types of objects involved are consumed by communities throughout Latium Vetus, as well as in the south Etruscan and Falisco-Capenate areas, and indicate a *koine* of material culture (i.e. consumption collective), possibly including associated banqueting practices (i.e. mirrored by a community of practice). The dataset used for the network analysis does not include tombs with bucchero objects, which do appear at Crustumerium at the end of this period, in spite of early contacts with Etruscan production centres (Caere, Veii). This phenomenon might be explained as a specific choice of ritual conservatism, preferring the broad local production of impasto pottery (Interdonato and others 2008; Interdonato 2013).[14]

Latial affiliated objects, exclusive to the material culture consumed by communities within Latium Vetus in this period, occur in roughly two-thirds of the tombs (Fig. 8.5). This mainly concerns the ubiquitous inclusion of the *anforetta laziale* within the banqueting set (Pl. 8.2, objects 2, 3 and Pl. 8.3, objects 1–5).[15] The strong local character of some objects

within the banqueting sets, as reflected in the local Crustumerium collective's size and central position in the network, is fascinating. In fact, approximately 78 per cent of all grave assemblages within the dataset contain at least one or two distinct local objects, making this the second most commonly affiliated consumption collective.[16] These local, material affiliations are mainly reflected in objects relating to drinking practices — such as the *anforette laziali* and cups with spiked handles (Pl. 8.2, objects 5, 6 and Pl. 8.3, objects 7, 11), but also the krater-cup, which is consistently of smaller dimensions than usual in Latium Vetus. These distinctly local objects, most of which are local adaptions of Latial and central Tyrrhenian object types, indicate that a local element was deemed important in funerary practices and the construction of funerary identities.

Whereas the banqueting set shows a central Tyrrhenian character, the more personal set of items seems to fit within a wider Italic context, and more widely shared central Italian socio-cultural consumption preferences. These are reflected in the network graph through affiliations with the Medio-Adriatic, central Italian, and Italian peninsular collectives. Many of these affiliations seem to have been regulated by gendered patterns (Fig. 8.6). Whereas the male personal items mainly show socio-cultural affiliations with the Medio-Adriatic and central Italian

---

14 De Puma (2010, 96) suggested that the lack of bucchero objects might be due to the low number of early tombs excavated at the time. Given the high number of tombs which have been excavated by now a possible data bias no longer seems to be the reason.

15 This is one of the few object types which can be distinguished as a truly Latial object, as most of the other banqueting objects are also consumed in the regions of southern Etruria and the Faliscan-Capenate area (i.e. the central Tyrrhenian consumption collective).

---

16 Most of these objects can be considered as localized versions of either Latial or central Tyrrhenian material culture.

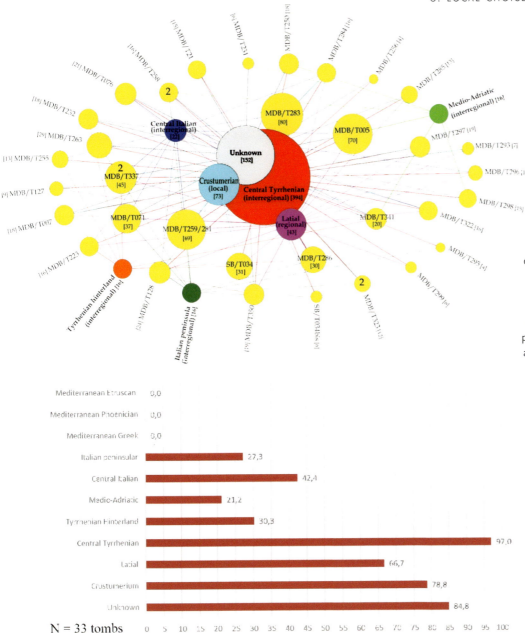

Figure 8.5. The material consumption collective affiliation network of period IVA on the left, based on the total number of affiliations per tomb and consumption collective; and the percentage of tombs affiliating to a specific consumption collective on the right (by M. Catsman).

consumption collectives, through the presence of specific dagger and spear types (Pl. 8.2, objects 10, 11), female personal grave objects show affiliations with the central and Italian peninsular consumption collective through the inclusion of specific jewellery, such as bronze bracelets and amber beads.[17] These affiliations illustrate that the mainly local and (inter)regional funerary culture of Crustumerium fits within wider Italic socio-cultural consumption patterns and preferences, which probably have their roots in earlier periods of Italic interconnectivity. At the same time, some of these affiliations, such as the ones related to the presence of specific dagger types in male tombs, show the site's unique participation amongst the Latial communities in interregional exchange networks with the Faliscan and Medio-Adriatic regions of central Italy. This is likely a result of the site's position in the north-eastern district of Latium Vetus along the upper Tiber River (Weidig 2008; Nijboer and Attema 2010).

Throughout the dataset of period IVA, access to the various consumption collectives seems to be reasonably egalitarian: the community is not characterized by strong qualitative differences in the number of various consumption collectives tomb assemblages are affiliated with (Fig. 8.5). Only the

---

17 The participation in the consumption of non-figurative amber beads is a good example of how Crustumerium participated in wider Italic peninsular consumption patterns and shows the importance of not neglecting peninsular exchange networks in the seventh century BCE.

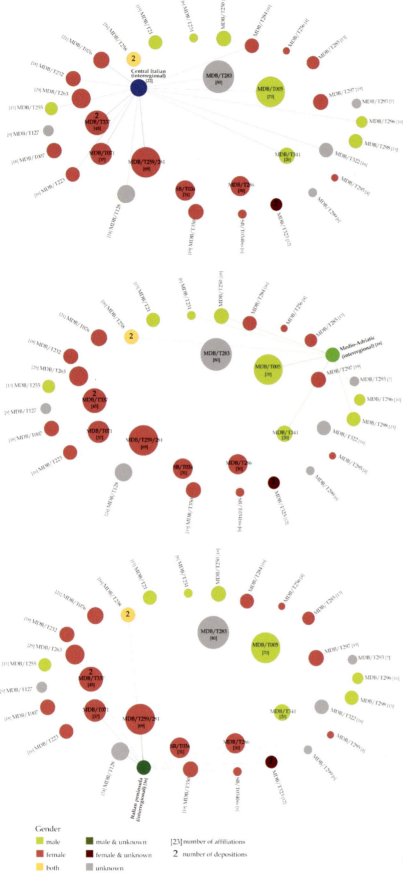

Figure 8.6. Three variants of the same network shown in Figure 8.5, only displaying the central Italian consumption collective affiliations (upper), the Medio-Adriatic consumption collective afiliations (middle), and the Italian Peninsular consumption collective affiliations (bottom) in relation to the gender of the deceased (by M. Catsman).

Tyrrhenian hinterland collective seems to be related to status differences, which is mainly based on the consumption of white-on-red pottery. Affiliations with this consumption collective are limited to tombs with larger funerary assemblages. This is visible in the close placement of the Tyrrhenian hinterland node amongst larger tombs in the lower left corner of the network (Fig. 8.7).

The community at Crustumerium does not seem to have participated in the consumption of objects exchanged on a Mediterranean-wide scale level (such as imported objects) in this period, at least as reflected in the funerary practices and assemblages of this dataset. It did, however, share specific consumption preferences related to Mediterranean-wide cultural models. This is mostly reflected in specific consumption preferences for novel object types related, almost exclusively, to drinking practices (for example, Hellenic types of drinking cups such as the *kotyle* and *skyphos*, and the Phoenician-Cypriote *oinochoe*) which are adapted into the local range of impasto objects, but also in the consumption of central Tyrrhenian 'Mediterraneanized' depurated wares inspired by Hellenic examples (such as Italo-geometric wares). These consumption collective affiliations (Fig. 8.8) thus reflect the influence of objects circulating on a Mediterranean scale and resulting in central Tyrrhenian regional or even local adaptions of material aspects.

The earliest occurrence of such Mediterranean consumption preferences at Crustumerium dates as early as the end of the eighth century BCE. However, these early occurrences are rather rare in the dataset and only become more common during period IVA2 (650–625 BCE).[18] Similar to the consumption of bucchero, these data suggest that the community either did not have direct access to the exchange networks through which this central Tyrrhenian Mediterraneanized material culture was being exchanged early on, due to socio-economic reasons, or for some ideological consideration did not choose to consume it as part of the funerary ritual. In line with the former hypothesis, is the fact that the majority of the Mediterraneanized object types within the dataset (*c.* 60 per cent) are produced in impasto wares, possibly indicating a more economical or localized participation in Mediterraneanized central Tyrrhenian consumption collectives. Nonetheless,

---

18 Out of the thirteen tombs containing Mediterranean-affiliated objects executed in impasto ware three predate 650 and eight postdate 650 with certainty (two tombs having too wide a date range). Out of thirteen tombs dating before 650 with certainty, only one contains depurated ware. Out of eleven tombs dating after 650 with certainty, six contain depurated ware.

8. LOCAL CHOICES IN A NETWORKED WORLD 129

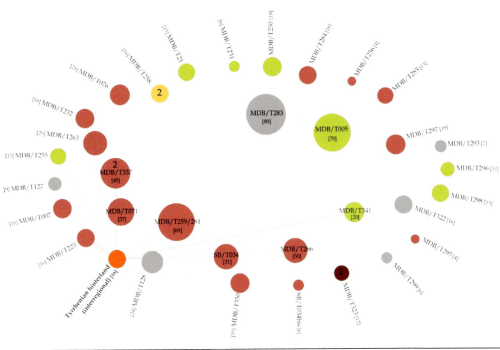

Figure 8.7. A variant of the same network shown in Figure 8.5, only displaying the Tyrrhenian hinterland consumption collective affiliations, which mainly concerns the consumption of white-on-red pottery, in relation to the gender of the deceased (by M. Catsman).

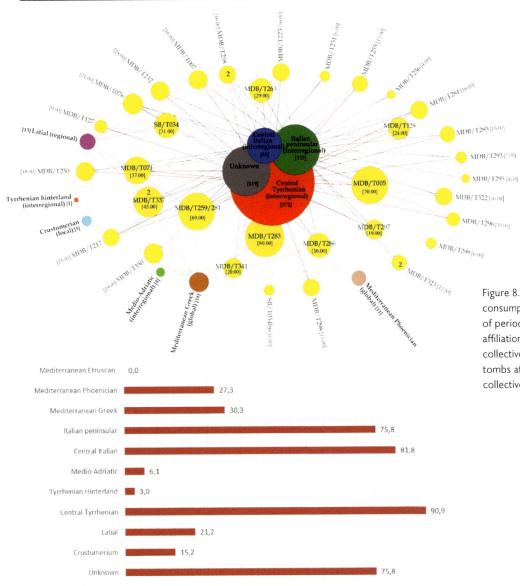

Figure 8.8. The wider socio-cultural consumption collective affiliation network of period IVA, based on the number of affiliations per tomb and consumption collective (top); and the percentage of tombs affiliation to a specific consumption collective (bottom) (by M. Catsman).

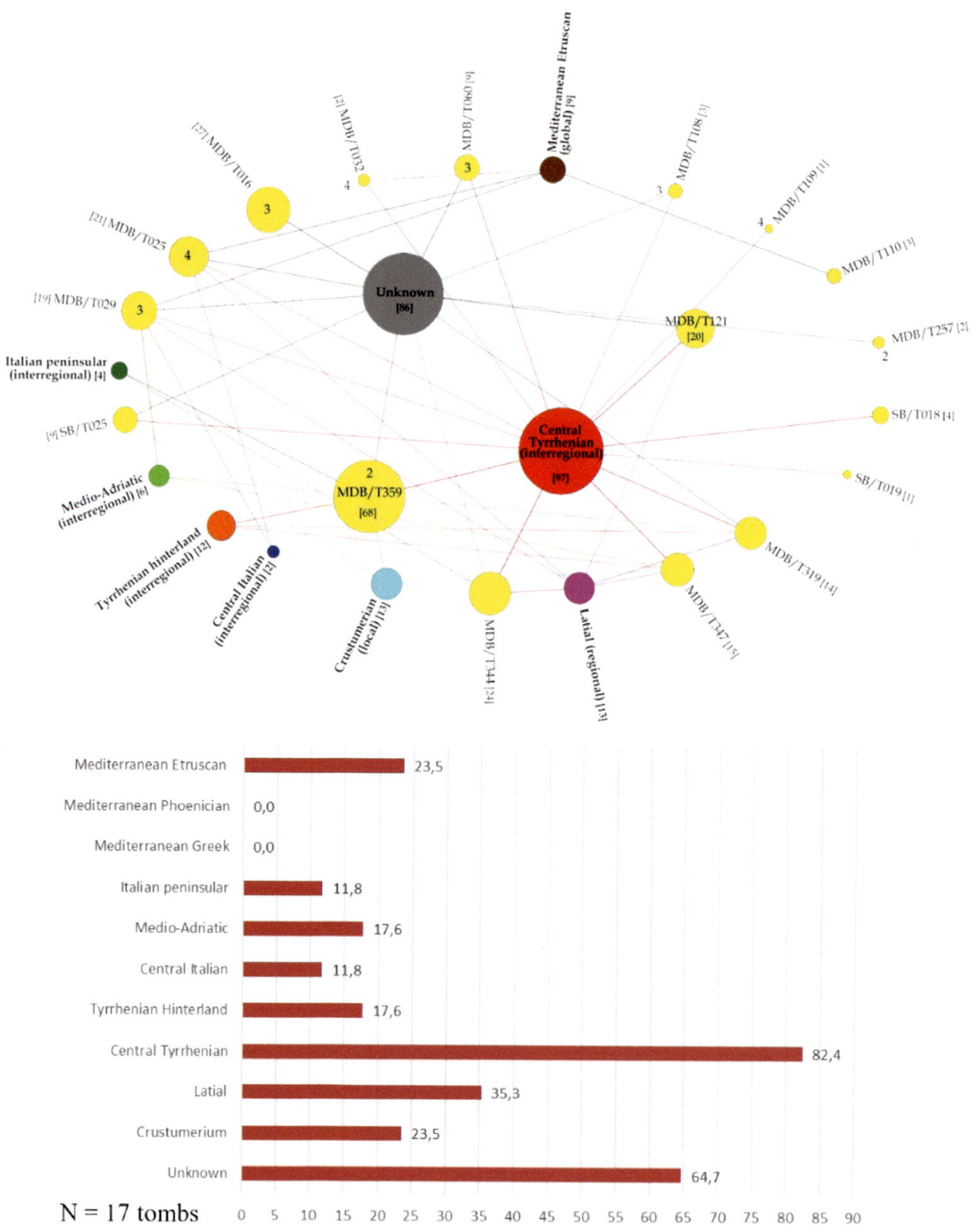

Figure 8.9. The consumption collective affiliation network of period IVB (top), based on the number of affiliations per tomb and consumption collective; and the percentage of tombs affiliating to a specific consumption collective (bottom). (by M. Catsman).

we can conclude that, over the entire period of IVA, a wide section of the buried community seems to have participated in 'orientalizing' Mediterranean consumption preferences, as just under half of the tombs within the dataset display affiliations with the Greek or Phoenician Mediterranean consumption collective (fifteen out of thirty-three tombs).

Period IVB

The networks of period IVB show that the consumed funerary material culture of this period at Crustumerium is characterized by both continuity and change. In fact, the network seems to contain two groups of tombs. In the lower half of the network is a group of tombs whose affiliations are similar to the tombs of period IVA, and which show a similar diversity in the number of consumption collectives they affiliate to (Fig. 8.9). Some of the qualitative trends visible towards the end of period IVA also characterize the object sets of these tombs. For example, following on the increased demand in period IVA2 for the consumption of Mediterraneanized objects executed in depurated ware, period IVB sees a sharp decline in Mediterranean-affiliated objects executed in the local impasto ware (Pl. 8.4). A new trend in the object sets of this group of tombs is the participation in the central Tyrrhenian-wide consumption of bucchero objects, to which the community now clearly has either gained access or whose funer-

8. LOCAL CHOICES IN A NETWORKED WORLD   131

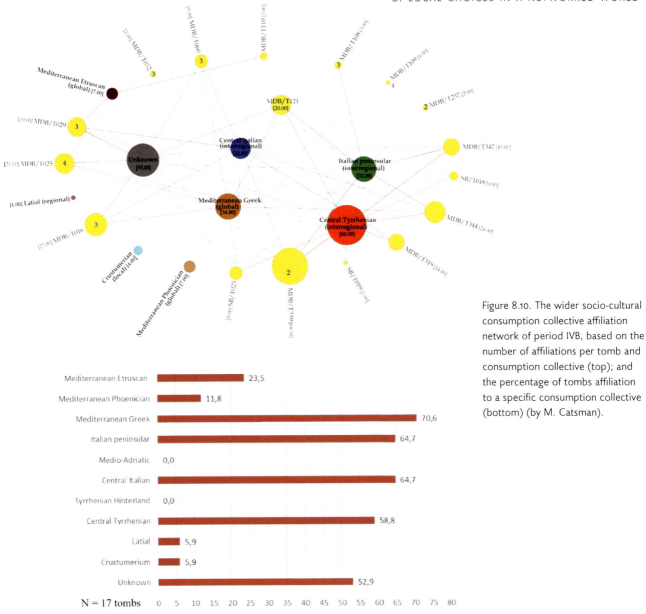

Figure 8.10. The wider socio-cultural consumption collective affiliation network of period IVB, based on the number of affiliations per tomb and consumption collective (top); and the percentage of tombs affiliation to a specific consumption collective (bottom) (by M. Catsman).

ary consumption was now ideologically accepted (Pl. 8.4, object 8).

The group of tombs in the upper half of the network has much smaller object sets — as visible in the smaller size of the nodes — and shows a much lower number of consumption collectives they affiliate with. In most cases, these tombs only affiliate with one central Tyrrhenian consumption collective. Though this might be a result of a quantitative trend characterizing this group (i.e. the reduction in grave gifts in period IVB), it also seems to be accompanied by a qualitative pattern of change. The strong, local element and regional Latial elements become more limited in these tombs (Pl. 8.4). This is mainly caused by the fact that certain object types, such as the 'traditional' *anforetta laziale* and cups/ladle-cups of period IVA, are no longer popular in this period.[19] Pouring shapes such the *oinochoe/olpe* are now mainly included in the repertoire (Pl. 8.4, objects 2–4).[20] Towards the beginning of the sixth

---

19 In period IVA twenty-five out of thirty-three tombs (75.8 per cent) contain the *anforetta laziale* and twenty-nine tombs (87.9 per cent) contain a ladle-cup or a double-handled cup. In period IVB only five out of seventeen tombs contain an *anforetta laziale* (29.4 per cent), three of which certainly date before 600 BCE. Of the seventeen tombs only three contain a ladle-cup, a double-handled cup, or a bowl (17.6 per cent).

20 In period IVA eight out of thirty-three tombs (24.2 per cent) contain an *oinochoe*. In period IVB eight out of seventeen tombs contain an *oinochoe* (47.1 per cent). The fact that Greek-affiliated cup types do not see a similar increase as the *oinochoe* is mainly caused by the fact that the central Tyrrhenian *kantharos* is a more

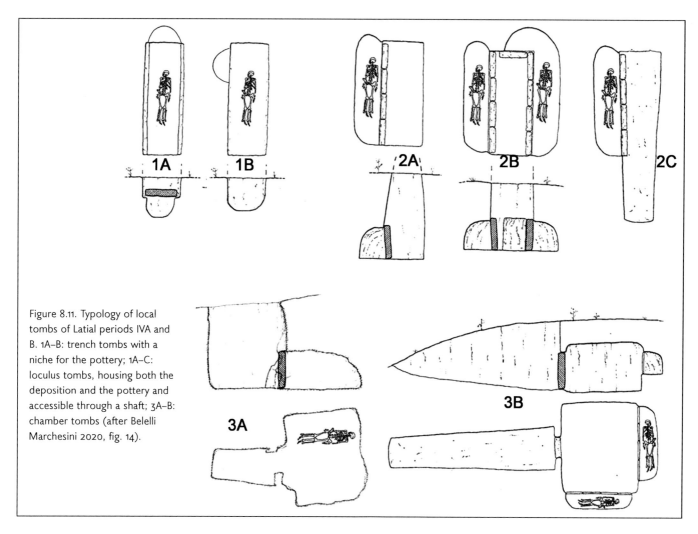

Figure 8.11. Typology of local tombs of Latial periods IVA and B. 1A–B: trench tombs with a niche for the pottery; 1A–C: loculus tombs, housing both the deposition and the pottery and accessible through a shaft; 3A–B: chamber tombs (after Belelli Marchesini 2020, fig. 14).

century BCE, there appears to be a preference for a more Mediterraneanized central Tyrrhenian drinking set, which replaces the more traditional Italic drinking sets with their strong local and regional cultural affiliations. As a result of this shift in the consumption collective affiliations, the Greek Mediterranean consumption collective becomes the most common wider socio-cultural collective, which is affiliated within period IVB, resulting in its central position in the network (Fig. 8.10).

Though it cannot be proven with full certainty, due to wide date ranges of some of the period IVB tombs in the dataset, the developments highlighted above seem to indicate a diachronic development in period IVB, with tombs following more traditional period IVA patterns before the turn of the seventh century, and newly emerging patterns after

popular cup type in period IVB. If this is included in the category of non-traditional cups, nine tombs out of seventeen period IVB tombs (52.9 per cent) contain a new cup type vs. eight out of thirty-three period IVA tombs (24.2 per cent).

c. 600 BCE. This would be in line with earlier conclusions about the funerary customs in the transition to the Archaic period (di Gennaro and others 2007, 139; Belelli Marchesini 2013; Willemsen 2014, 45).

Local Choices: Adoption and Adaption of Architectural Models and Funerary Objects

As exemplified by the pilot network analysis discussed in the previous section, and based on a sample of tombs, the consumption patterns of the local community of Crustumerium throughout the seventh century BCE perfectly align with the changes that occurred in the funerary record of other settlements in Latium Vetus in the same period. This is evident from the progressive decrease of objects included in the grave inventory, and a broader presence of fine wares and closed shapes ending in the final disappearance of funerary gifts (Bartoloni and others 2009). Noticeable is the shift from early drinking sets mainly based on the traditional black impasto pottery to a much more variegated assemblage of objects, implying a changing attitude towards the burial. At the same time, the choice of specific shapes and additional objects (for example, the Cypriot-Phoenician *oinochoe*) highlights cultural preferences of specific families within a seemingly quite egalitarian social context. Our perception of the social asset is, of course, based on the available data from the cemeteries, showing the lack of princely tombs: so far, the only status symbol from Crustumerium is the bronze footstool from the robbed tomb MDB40 (Belelli Marchesini 2013, 104 fig. 12). Elaborate ornamental *parures* and peculiar personal ornaments are also rarely documented. On the other hand, the functional analysis of the pottery shows that during the IVA period the most outstanding grave inventories include entirely different categories of vessels related to the preparation, presentation, and consumption of drinks and food, and that the drinking set featured in all tombs is sometimes emphasized through the duplication of some shapes (*anforette*, cups, and ladle-cups). Some outstanding female and male tombs, dating throughout the seventh century, also contain a large number of ladle-cups (up to forty-three) that are placed around the wine container, hinting at collective ceremonial drinking (*circum-potatio*). In the second half of the seventh century, the changing ritual implies that the relationship between the number of different shapes and their selection does not follow specific rules (Willemsen 2014, 45–52); in some grave inventories (for example, tomb MDB350: Pl. 8.3), the lack of the container of wine (jar) in the drinking set, the very symbol of the symposium, is noticeable. But while the network analysis helps to place clustered individual burials within a wider cultural framework and network of interactions, it does not, as stated earlier, describe how objects of this shared material culture were used, adapted, and given meaning in specific contexts. Below we will go into this aspect.

As outlined in the introduction, due to its geographical position, Crustumerium was receptive to cultural models from the surrounding regions (di Gennaro and others 2007; Amoroso 2012; De Puma 2012; Nijboer, and Attema 2012). From the early formation of the settlement, such influences likely played an important role in the definition of a decidedly local material culture. In the Early Iron Age, the pottery production of Crustumerium (Pl. 8.1), and to a lesser extent its funerary architecture, fit the cultural characteristics of a wide territorial district that includes both sides of the Tiber, notably the Etruscan town of Veii and the Latin area delimited to the south by Rome and Gabii (di Gennaro, Nijboer, and Belelli Marchesini 2016, 131–34) (Fig. 8.1). In

the subsequent period, the changes in the funerary material culture and associated rituals reflect adherence to a local interpretation of the new 'orientalizing life-style' and the altered meaning of the burial as a social event. We note at Crustumerium the introduction of new tomb types, while adaptions in pottery production point to increasing technological skills, and the passage from household industry to the public control of productive activities and emergence of specialized workshops.[21] Below we discuss examples from Crustumerium that give insight into the local choices, based on the full evidence from MDB cemetery.[22]

Funerary Architecture

Examples of the adaption of cultural influences are, in the first place, found in the sphere of funerary architecture. While in the Early Iron Age the only architectural model was the simple trench tomb, in which the deceased was buried inside a wooden coffin or tree-trunk surrounded by grave objects, in Latial periods IVA and IVB bodies and grave inventories are ritually placed in different locations. Two different tomb models are now adopted, both from the other bank of the Tiber. Their architectural engagement, together with the increased number of grave gifts, stress the social status and economic power of the emergent families.

The first model is the trench tomb holding the deposition, its personal ornaments, and the objects conveying the social status of the deceased, and is provided with a niche cut-out in the bedrock (a so-called, 'votive loculus', housing the grave inventory). At Veii and in the Faliscan area, this model appears in the third quarter of the eighth century BCE and is characterized by the presence of a niche in a central position along the lateral side of the trench that is slightly elevated with respect to the deposition. At MDB, trench tombs with a lateral niche similar to the Etruscan and Faliscan examples are relatively rare (twenty-one examples) but in the extant examples the niche is always beside the head of the deceased and at the same level (Fig. 8.11, 1B). Indeed, typical of Crustumerium and Fidenae (the settlements within northern Latium), is a new ver-

---

21 As regards the economic and social implications of this shift, see Nijboer 1998.

22 For a general discussion about the local development of funerary architecture, the composition of grave inventory, and the funerary rituals from the Early Iron Age to the Archaic period, see di Gennaro and Belelli Marchesini 2012; Belelli Marchesini 2013; Willemsen 2014; and Belelli Marchesini 2020.

sion of the trench tomb where the 'votive' niche is carved out on the short side of the trench behind the head of the deceased; in the most elaborated examples of such tombs, the coffin is protected by a row of horizontal tuff slabs (Fig. 8.11, 1A).

The second architectural model is the so-called 'loculus tomb', accessible through a deep rectangular shaft (Fig. 8.11, 2A). The loculus contains the deposition and the funerary gifts and, in the earliest examples, is closed using upright tuff slabs. The model was elaborated at Veii and became widespread in the Faliscan area and the inner Etruscan region up to Poggio Buco; also a few examples are known from Capena (di Gennaro 2007). While only a few late examples of this type are known from Latium Vetus, dating to the Archaic period, at Crustumerium and Fidenae it was already fashionable from Latial period IVA on. In this case, the architectural model was adopted without meaningful changes. Nevertheless, the location of the deposition and the grave inventory inside the loculus follows the same ritual choice as in the trench tombs. The pottery was usually placed behind the head of the deceased and inside some kind of connected niche which was, in fact, a prolongation of the loculus. Both models of the tomb type use tuff slabs of roughly modular size, either extracted from the local bedrock while digging the tombs or transported from some distance. The latter is the case with the red tuff, which comes from the territory of the nearby town of Fidenae (the so-called tufo di Fidene). The now standardized dimensions of the tombs point to the normalization of quarrying activities and the evolution of building techniques. The latter aspect is mirrored by the adoption of roof tiles in the closing system of sepulchral loculi from around 600 BCE.

Another case of adaption, or rather local evolution, of architectural models is the introduction of chamber tombs. Some loculus tombs had already been used for multiple depositions by either reusing the same loculus or adding a second loculus on the opposite side of the shaft (Fig. 8.11, 2B). In the Latial period IVB and the Archaic period the use of large chamber tombs became widespread, to house depositions belonging to more generations (Fig. 8.11, 3B). Noticeably, at MDB, there are a few chamber tombs of small dimensions that have an ellipsoid plan and a shaft entrance, and which are meant as individual tombs (Fig. 8.11, 3A): their overall character suggests their possible evolution from trench tombs with an axial niche. Now the trench is turned into a shaft and the body is transferred inside an enlarged niche. This suggestion is based on a similar phenomenon that is well documented at Veii, in the burial ground of Macchia della Comunità (Neri

2014). There, small individual chamber tombs, accessible through a transversal shaft, seem to derive from trench tombs with a lateral niche. But, while underground chamber tombs appeared at an early stage and became widespread on the opposite bank of the Tiber, they are scarcely recorded in the Latin territory, maybe because of the poor quality of local bedrock. At Crustumerium, the high number of chamber tombs in all cemeteries is therefore exceptional, even though the local geology is at most places not conducive to the development of really monumental architecture. In fact, their modest layout is in contrast with the careful representation of architectural details of some exceptional capstones in red tuff, which could be considered as proper house models. They surmounted the tombs in the eighth and seventh centuries BCE and are a local evolution of the more schematic ones that were fashionable on the opposite bank of the Tiber and only hinted at the house by representing the roof.

Pottery

Having discussed the funerary architecture, as the context of the deposition and the objects, we will now briefly discuss examples of local adoption/adaption of objects and shapes at Crustumerium that characterize the material culture of the middle Tyrrhenian area.

As stated above, the drinking set exhibited by the tombs in the Latial period IVA mainly includes impasto pottery. The main black impasto shapes are taken from the Latin repertoire, but typical of Crustumerium (and Fidenae) is the addition of spikes to the handles of cups and *anforette laziali* (Fig. 8.12, h, b). From a technical point of view, the latter shape is manufactured with a combination of hand modelling, moulds, and wheeling, reflecting its evolution from early local pottery production. Typical of the female tombs is a rather big cup (krater-cup) provided with a monumental handle (Fig. 8.12, d), that is always associated with the wine container and the cups and therefore points to the direct involvement of women in the preparation of ceremonial drinks, in contrast with the Greek habit;[23] this is a less monumental version compared to the huge krater-cups exhibited by eminent tombs of other Latin settlements (for example Acqua Acetosa Laurentina), but is similar to exemplars from the Faliscan area

---

23 For the difference between the Greek and Etrusco-Italic women, see Kruta Poppi 2015. For an overview of female depositions at Crustumerium, see Belelli Marchesini and di Gennaro 2011.

8. LOCAL CHOICES IN A NETWORKED WORLD   135

Figure 8.12. Orientalizing drinking set. Interpretation based on the association of the shapes used to contain wine (the red impasto jar: a) and water or other liquids (the *anforetta laziale*: b–c), to mix and prepare drinks (the big cup with a monumental handle: d), to pour (Cypriot-Phoenician *oinochoe*: l), and to drink (chalice, ladle-cups, and cups of different sizes: e–h). The *kotyle* (m) was a drinking cup but was maybe used for food as well, whereas the function of the spiral amphora (i) is uncertain (by B. Belelli Marchesini, photographs courtesy of Crustumerium photo archive).

and Etruria.[24] *Anforette laziali* and cups of different size endowed with elaborated stamped and incised decorative patterns feature the most outstanding depositions.

---

24 For example, some big cups from Veii: Bartoloni and others 2012, 218 tav. VIII:2–1.

Typical of both Crustumerium's male and female depositions, throughout Latial periods IVA and IVB, is a lid-bowl with a deeply incised geometric pattern, the so-called *scodella crustumina* (Fig. 8.13, a): this shape seems to have been adopted from the Faliscan area (Narce: Tabolli 2013, 280), where it is documented by a few exemplars only, dating to the third quarter of the eighth century.

Figure 8.13. Red impasto shapes taken from the Faliscan area: a) so-called *scodella crustumina* and b) deep bowl with a knobbed rim (by B. Belelli Marchesini).

Figure 8.14. Latial *pyxis* from tomb MDB196.

Figure 8.15. Selection of red impasto pottery decorated in the white-on-red technique (by B. Belelli Marchesini).

Figure 8.16. Huge cylindrical *pyxis* from tomb MDB111.

Figure 8.17. Imported (a–b) and local (c) Italo-geometric pottery.

All photographs on this page courtesy of Crustumerium photo archive.

The inclusion of some peculiar *impasto bruno* shapes in the grave inventory of a limited number of depositions is noteworthy. At MDB, no more than four female tombs dating from the middle of the seventh century BCE are accompanied by a Latial *pyxis* (Fig. 8.14), a richly decorated shape, covered with a lid and probably meant to contain hot food, that should be considered a highly symbolic object featuring in both outstanding female and male Latin depositions and ceremonial domestic contexts (Rathje 2017). No more than twenty-five female and male tombs dating from around 650 BCE to the end of the seventh century are accompanied by the Cypriot-Phoenician *oinochoe* (Fig. 8.12, l), a shape of Phoenician origin that spread all over the Mediterranean and was broadly imitated by local workshops; after its introduction in Italy at the beginning of the seventh *c.* BCE, this shape is found in rich tombs as a personal object of the deceased, whereas starting from the second quarter of the seventh century it is documented both in settlements and funerary contexts in relation to a larger number of graves (Taloni 2012, 45–87). At Crustumerium, Cypriot-Phoenician *oinochoai* are often associated with the *kotyle* (Fig. 8.12, m), a drinking cup that is considered to be a status symbol. The choice for the spiral amphora (Fig. 8.12, i), a shape widespread in Latium, south Etruria, and the Faliscan area from the last quarter of the eighth century,[25] features no more than fifteen depositions throughout the seventh century; the function of this shape, which was manufactured in bucchero starting from the second quarter of the seventh century, is unknown, but probably connected to purification rituals (Torelli 1986, 231). Red impasto pottery from MDB tombs exhibit shapes and painted decorative techniques adopted from the other bank of the Tiber.[26] As far as shapes are concerned, it is noticeable that the deep bowl with knobs on the upper rim, a peculiar Faliscan shape that imitates metallic objects, is well documented at Crustumerium (Fig. 8.13, b) and Fidenae, both in the cemeteries and the settlement areas (di Gennaro and others 2009, 158–59 fig. 10). The amount of red impasto pottery bearing a white-on-red painted decoration from Crustumerium is exceptional compared with the overall evidence from Latium for this ware, and points to the existence of local highly specialized workshops (Fig. 8.15). This technique is typical of the south Etruscan (Caere) and Faliscan areas and was most probably transmitted early on through

imported objects (for example, the only example of a *holmos* is from Crustumerium tomb 232: Nijboer and Attema 2012, 270 fig. 9) and migrant craftsmen (Micozzi 2014). However, the local production of red impasto ware includes an innovative shape, the so-called *olla a coppette* (Fig. 8.15, c). This is a ceremonial vase which was elaborated by adding three or four cups around the rim of the jar, and was evidently intended to emphasize the meaning of the jar as the main wine container in symposia (*circumpotatio*), in association with a set of ladle-cups (Belelli Marchesini and di Gennaro 2021). With regards to the function of the cups around the rim, the best explanation is that they were used to hold the ladle-cups after scooping the wine and to prevent dripping. In spite of its sporadic occurrence at Rome, Lavinium, and also Capena, as well as the many exemplars from the illegal market, this shape can be surely attributed to Crustumerium: in this respect, it is also meaningful that the body of the big jar from tomb 344 (Pl. 8.4), is identical to the ribbed *olla a coppette*, but lacking the additional cups.

Regarding the importation or adoption of foreign shapes, noteworthy are five monumental *pyxides* (Fig. 8.16) from four tombs dating to the last quarter of the seventh century BCE. Such huge cylindrical *pyxides* are, in fact, typical of the Caeretan production (Micozzi 1994 25–27), but the Etruscan exemplars are always found featuring a stemmed foot or supported by three props. The ones from Crustumerium, however, have different proportions and a flat base.

Cultural connections with the Etruscan and Faliscan areas can be traced for the production of Italo-geometric wares.[27] Some of the few *oinochoai* and deep bowls on a stemmed foot, included in the grave inventory of tombs dating to the first half of the seventh century, may be considered as imports, such as the ones from tomb MDB5 (Fig. 8.17, a–b) attributed to the Painter of Narce (Conti and Giuliani 2016, 104–05). Whereas sometimes it is difficult to discriminate between imported and local pottery, some shapes are recurrent in all tombs starting from the early seventh century and were certainly locally manufactured, such as the small bowls with a horizontal rim, decorated with horizontal strips (Fig. 8.17, c). It is noteworthy that at Crustumerium this typically Italo-geometric shape (Neri 2010, 127–33 pl. 23) is also manufactured in red impasto ware and decorated in the white-on-red and, exceptionally, in the

---

25 For the elaboration at Veii and the development of this shape, see Mottolese 2021.

26 For an overview about the production of red ware in southern Etruria and Latium, see ten Kortenaar 2011.

27 For the Etruscan production and its diffusion in the Faliscan area, see Neri 2010. For the existence of workshops at Rome and the way of transmission of Greek pottery, see Colonna 1988, 298–300, 306–07.

red-on-white technique and that both versions are associated in most tombs.

In the second half of the seventh century, the introduction of new shapes and wares, such as the bucchero and the Etrusco-Corinthian pottery, gives way to a progressive change of the grave assemblage as well as the location of the objects in the tombs that beforehand were tendentially associated according to their function. It is meaningful that the new shapes are sometimes adapted to the local rituals. Typical of the earlier tombs of the seventh century BCE is the inclusion of a ladle-cup inside one of the cups, maybe signifying the participation of the deceased at the banquet; this ritual seems to be respected when impasto cups are replaced by bucchero *kantharoi*. A meaningful change affects the ritual of purification of the burial area or the corpse itself: in the Latial period IVA this was performed with a mug (by using water or wine?) that was deposited next to, and sometimes underneath, the body; in the following periods the mug is replaced by Etrusco-Corinthian *aryballoi* and *alabastra*, implying the use of ointments. So far, we have not been able to point out comparable adaptions in the Archaic period apart from the adoption of strict rules regarding the burial leading to a severe decrease in grave gifts.

From the beginning of sixth century, the earliest depositions inside chamber tombs feature the red impasto jar, but there is also a typical association with bucchero jugs/*oinochoai* and cups (Pl. 8.5), sometimes with depurated wares. The drastic reduction of grave goods, including no more than three pieces of pottery, gives way to the final disappearance of grave inventories from roughly 560–550 BCE onwards. This phenomenon occurs at Veii, Rome, and the Latin settlements that were most influenced by Rome, such as Crustumerium and Fidenae north of the Aniene River. It implies the adoption of strict rules or norms in the performance of the burials, probably meant to convey investments from the private sphere to the public domain (Smith 1996, 187–88). There is indeed scanty but meaningful evidence at Crustumerium of public buildings and their roofing systems, including some painted in the white-on-red technique and moulded terracottas comparable with evidence from the other bank of the Tiber (Nijboer and Attema 2020, 160–63).

These sumptuary rules would then later have been codified in the Twelve Tables in the middle of the fifth century BCE. It is noteworthy that the Twelve Tables specifically forbade collective drinking (*circumpotatio*), the kind of ceremonial aspect which is typical of eminent 'orientalizing' tombs at Crustumerium, but which is absent in the burials from the beginning of the sixth century.

In this section, we have shown how many features of the funerary architecture, grave inventory, and personal adornments in the tombs at Crustumerium — whether locally conceived, adopted and adapted from models elsewhere, or imported — were strongly embedded in local funerary traditions and rites that required certain combinations of those features. These combinations not only depended on what was in vogue and available in the period, but also on gender, status, and adherence to either traditionalist or newly accepted funerary habits. We also outlined how changes in the funerary practices were related to meaningful societal changes through time. It appears that the room for manoeuvring, in terms of funerary expenditure and choice in the use, adoption, and adaption of material culture to perform certain rituals, was relatively broad until in the midsixth century when strict rules and norms were evidently imposed on funerary practices.

Conclusions: Linking Material Symbols, Ritual, and Social Structure at Crustumerium

In this chapter, we have first explored the cultural consumption collectives in which Crustumerium participated, and to which it had access, during the Latial periods IVA and IVB when a new 'orientalizing lifestyle' spread over the Mediterranean basin, reflected in the emergence of elite networks and iconic material culture. Next, we looked into the reception of these influences in the material record linked to funerary practices at Crustumerium and its elaboration into a unique material signature, merging traditional and new features. A major innovation was the adoption and adaption of new banqueting practices as a consequence of commercial and cultural contacts with the eastern Mediterranean, which had a great effect on the material culture and funerary practices in central Italy. While ritual drinking, as part of funerary practice, was already clear from the material culture present in the Early Iron Age tombs, the ceremonial consumption of wine became central to the aristocratic ideology in the seventh century BCE. This is evidenced by outstanding contexts in nearby urban areas (Bartoloni and others 2012, 201–06). In the same way, the introduction of new shapes, wares, and production techniques (first of all, the potter's wheel) was the result of the progressive and experimental acquisition of technical skills through early central Tyrrhenian contacts with the Levantine and the Greek world: for example, the few early examples of pottery coated with a red slip, dating even before the foundation of Pithecusae, seem to anticipate the broad adoption of the Phoenician-type, red-slip ware in the Orientalizing period (Drago Troccoli 2009). At Crustumerium, the funerary material culture during Latial periods IVA and IVB was the result of the adoption of different models and decorative techniques from the surrounding cultural districts with an exceptionally strong regard for both local/traditional and innovative elements contributing to the material identity of this community. While the consumption collective analysis shows that Crustumerium was part of regional central Tyrrhenian material networks, as well as wider Mediterranean networks through which the new cultural models were exchanged, this was mediated by larger hubs, such as the nearby centres of Veii and Rome, but also Caere and Faliscan towns. Increased interconnectivity between Etruria and Latium Vetus, and beyond, functioned as a motor for the creation of new 'consumption collectives' sharing innovations in material culture that might be given local meanings. Clearly Crustumerium's crucial geographic position made its community receptive to external influences of those towns that were directly involved in trade and cultural exchanges at a Mediterranean scale. All of this being noted, we must also emphasize that archaeometric analysis is needed to discrim-

inate imported from locally manufactured objects, in order to increase our understanding of local choices highlighting the progressive acquisition of specific 'foreign' wares/shapes by local workshops. When considering the mapping of single shapes and pottery wares in the burials throughout this period, it is crucial that we increase our knowledge of the mechanism of transmission and the discrimination between imported and locally manufactured objects, also taking into account the participation of migrant specialized craftsmen. While such discrimination is, at least most of the time, possible through autoptic analysis and the rare occurrence of specific shapes, a greater investment in archaeometrical studies is needed to arrive at more detailed conclusions. Such research, as well as expanding the network analysis to comprise all tombs from all periods excavated at Crustumerium, will certainly reveal more detailed social patterns than is possible now. However, we hope to already have shown that an approach which embeds the analysis of the adoption and adaption of funerary architecture and objects on the local level by individual communities to regional, interregional, and global consumption collectives is capable of highlighting human agency in funerary practices.

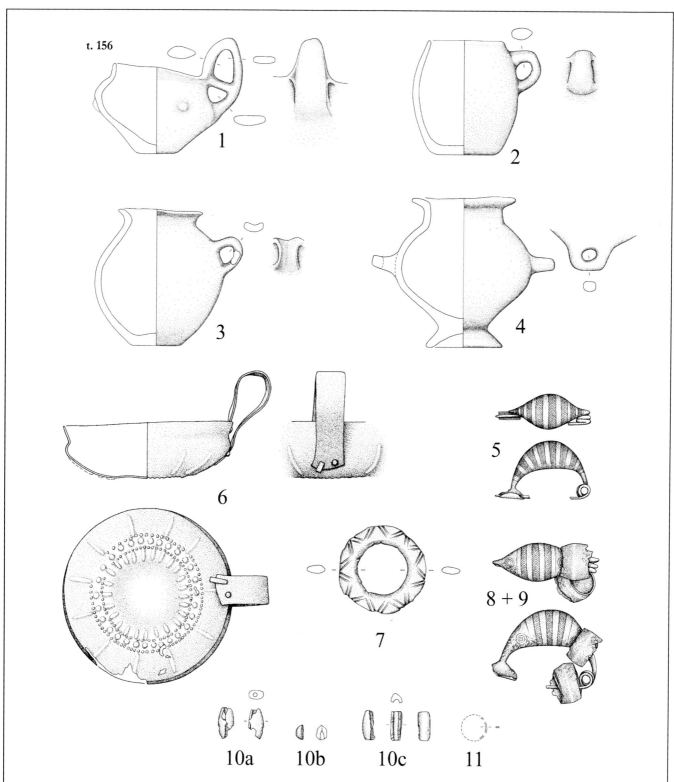

Plate 8.1. **Objects from Tomb MDB156.** This trench tomb, oriented to NE-SW, is 65–70 cm wide and 270 cm long. In spite of the poor preservation of the skeleton (restricted to fragments of a femur), it can be attributed to an adult woman. The position of the deposition was marked by the ornaments, including a couple of fibulae, one of them holding two rings (5, 8), a suspension ring (7) a necklace consisting of 3 amber beads (10) and fermatrecce (11). Objects pointing to the social role are not present. This tomb included four undecorated different impasto shapes: a cup (1) was placed beyond the head and the other three objects — a mug (2), a jug (3) and a double-handled bi-conical neck-jar (4) — were aligned along the right side of the body. The prestige of the deposition is highlighted by the presence of a bronze cup (6), that was placed next to the feet. The pottery from this tomb can be dated between Latial phases IIA2 and IIB, whereas the ornaments suggest a chronology to the early Latial Period III. (Early Iron Age, Latial periods IIB2-III). Figure assembled by B. Belelli Marchesini, drawings by S. Boersma.

8. LOCAL CHOICES IN A NETWORKED WORLD 141

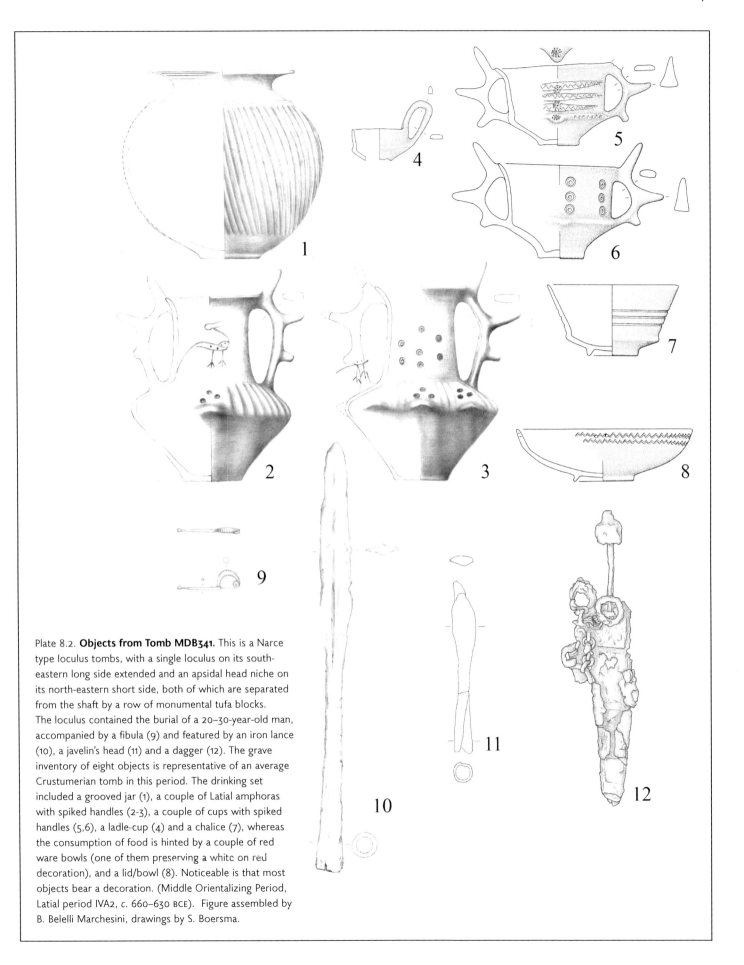

Plate 8.2. **Objects from Tomb MDB341.** This is a Narce type loculus tombs, with a single loculus on its south-eastern long side extended and an apsidal head niche on its north-eastern short side, both of which are separated from the shaft by a row of monumental tufa blocks. The loculus contained the burial of a 20–30-year-old man, accompanied by a fibula (9) and featured by an iron lance (10), a javelin's head (11) and a dagger (12). The grave inventory of eight objects is representative of an average Crustumerian tomb in this period. The drinking set included a grooved jar (1), a couple of Latial amphoras with spiked handles (2-3), a couple of cups with spiked handles (5,6), a ladle-cup (4) and a chalice (7), whereas the consumption of food is hinted by a couple of red ware bowls (one of them preserving a white on red decoration), and a lid/bowl (8). Noticeable is that most objects bear a decoration. (Middle Orientalizing Period, Latial period IVA2, c. 660–630 BCE). Figure assembled by B. Belelli Marchesini, drawings by S. Boersma.

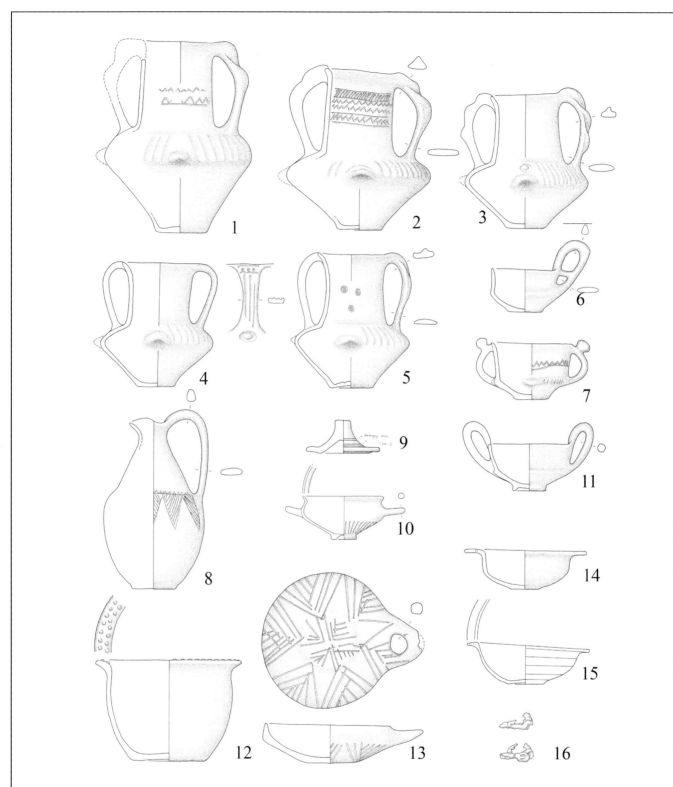

Plate 8.3. **Objects from Tomb MDB350.** This is a trench tomb with a sizeable lateral niche, located along the southern side of the fossa which had been closed off with an irregular small tufa blocks. The trench housed the deposition of a 40-50 years old man, accompanied by a fibula and an iron object, maybe a spear head. The niche contained a banqueting set of 16 objects. The drinking set lacks the jar (wine container) and is represented by black impasto several Latial amphoras (1-5), a handled cup (7) and a ladle-cup (6), associated with a Phoenician-cypriote oinochoe (8) and a impasto kantharos (11). The grave inventory also include objects in italo-geometric ware such as the skyphos (10), a lid (9) and small bowls. Noticeable is the inclusion of the so called scodella crustumina (13) featured by the deeply incised decoration and the deep bowl with the knobbed decoration(12), both shapes which also occur in the Faliscan area. (Middle Orientalizing period, Latial period IVA2, c. 650–630 BCE). Figure assembled by B. Belelli Marchesini, drawings by S. Boersma.

8. LOCAL CHOICES IN A NETWORKED WORLD 143

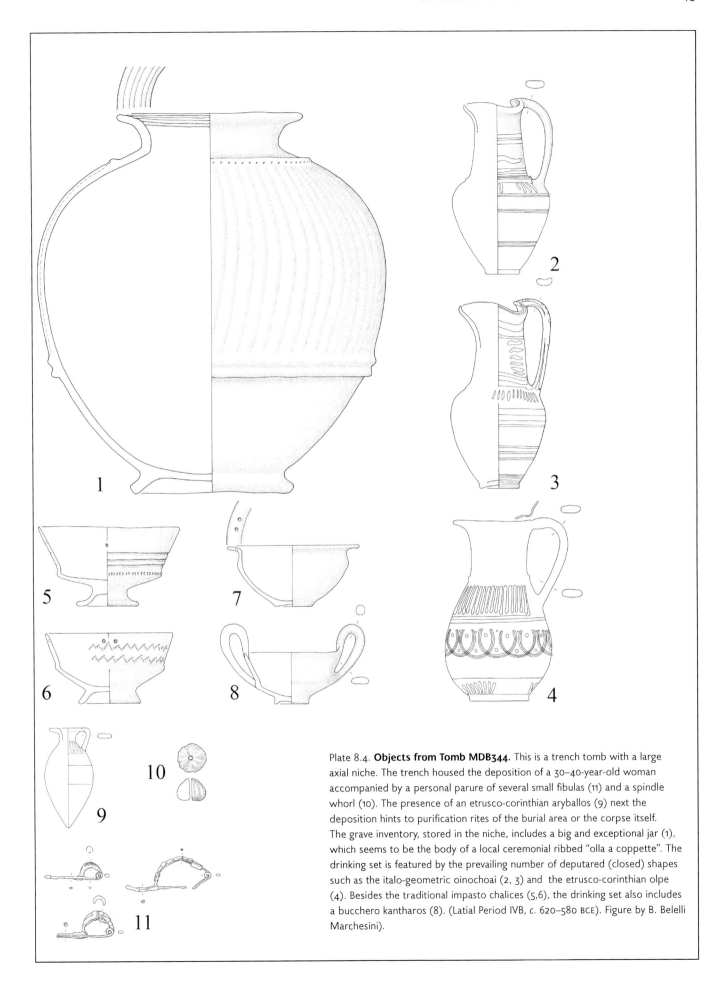

Plate 8.4. **Objects from Tomb MDB344.** This is a trench tomb with a large axial niche. The trench housed the deposition of a 30–40-year-old woman accompanied by a personal parure of several small fibulas (11) and a spindle whorl (10). The presence of an etrusco-corinthian aryballos (9) next the deposition hints to purification rites of the burial area or the corpse itself. The grave inventory, stored in the niche, includes a big and exceptional jar (1), which seems to be the body of a local ceremonial ribbed "olla a coppette". The drinking set is featured by the prevailing number of deputared (closed) shapes such as the italo-geometric oinochoai (2, 3) and the etrusco-corinthian olpe (4). Besides the traditional impasto chalices (5,6), the drinking set also includes a bucchero kantharos (8). (Latial Period IVB, *c.* 620–580 BCE). Figure by B. Belelli Marchesini).

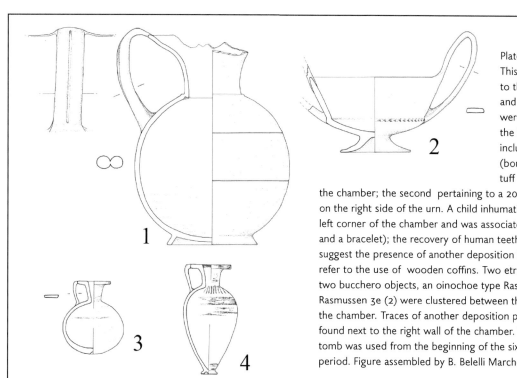

Plate 8.5. **Objects from Tomb MDB25.** This badly eroded chamber tomb, oriented to the NW, is roughly trapezoidal in shape and is lacking sepulchral loculi. Depositions were clustered against the rear wall and the left rear corner of the chamber. They include two cremation burials, the first (bones to be examined) inside a cinerary tuff urn leaning against the rear wall of the chamber; the second pertaining to a 20–40-year-old man, placed on the floor on the right side of the urn. A child inhumation burial was placed next to the rear left corner of the chamber and was associated with some ornaments (two fibulas and a bracelet); the recovery of human teeth pertaining to an adult individual suggest the presence of another deposition in the same area. Scattered iron nails refer to the use of wooden coffins. Two etrusco-corinthian unguentaria (3, 4) and two bucchero objects, an oinochoe type Rasmussen 7f (1) and a kantharos type Rasmussen 3e (2) were clustered between the infant deposition and the left wall of the chamber. Traces of another deposition pertaining to an adult individual were found next to the right wall of the chamber. The grave inventory suggests that the tomb was used from the beginning of the sixth century BCE and through the archaic period. Figure assembled by B. Belelli Marchesini, drawings by M. Sabatini.

Works Cited

Amoroso, Angelo. 2012. 'Caratteri degli insediamenti del Latium Vetus settentrionale', *Bullettino della Commissione Archeologica Comunale di Roma*, 113: 193–214

Attema, Peter A. J., Francesco di Gennaro, Jorn Seubers, Barbara Belelli Marchesini, and Burkart Ullrich. 2014. 'Early Urbanization at Crustumerium (9th–5th c. B.C.)', in *Papers on Italian Urbanism in the First Millennium B.C.*, ed. by Elizabeth C. Robinson, Journal of Roman Archaeology, Supplement, 97 (Portsmouth, RI: Journal of Roman Archaeology), pp. 175–96

Attema, Peter A. J., Jorn Seubers, Sarah Willemsen, Remco Bronkhorst, Paola Filippini, Barbara Belelli Marchesini, Anselmo Malizia, and Anne Marie Nielsen (eds). 2016. *Crustumerium Catalogue: Death and Afterlife at the Gates of Rome; Catalogue to the Exhibition in the Ny Carlsberg Glyptotek* (Copenhagen: Narayana)

Bartoloni, Gilda. 2003. *Le società dell'Italia primitiva: lo studio delle necropoli e la nascita delle aristocrazie* (Rome: Carocci)

——. 2010. 'Il cambiamento delle pratiche funerarie nell'età dei Tarquini', in *La grande Roma dei Tarquini: atti del XVII Convegno internazionale di studi sulla storia e l'archeologia dell'Etruria*, ed. by Giuseppe M. Della Fina (Rome: Quasar), pp. 159–85

Bartoloni, Gilda, Valeria Acconcia, and Silvia ten Kortenaar. 2012. 'Viticoltura e consumo del vino in Etruria: la cultura materiale tra la fine dell'età del Ferro e l'Orientalizzante antico', in *Archeologia della vite e del vino nella Toscana e nel Lazio: dalle tecniche dell'indagine archeologica alle prospettive della biologia molecolare*, ed. by Andrea Ciacci, Paola Rendini, and Andrea Zifferero (Florence: All'Insegna del Giglio), pp. 201–75

Bartoloni, Gilda, Valentino Nizzo, and Maria Taloni. 2009. 'Dall'esibizione al rigore: analisi dei sepolcreti laziali tra VII e VI sec. a.C.', in *Tra Etruria, Lazio e Magna Grecia: indagini sulle necropoli (atti dell'incontro di studio, Fisciano 5–6 marzo 2009)*, ed. by Raffaella Bonaudo, Luca Cerchiai, and Carmine Pellegrino, Tekmeria, 9 (Paestum: Pandemos), pp. 65–86

Belelli Marchesini, Barbara. 2013. 'La necropoli di Crustumerium: bilancio delle acquisizioni e prospettive', in *Crustumerium: ricerche internazionali in un centro latino; Archaeology and Identity of a Latin Settlement near Rome*, ed. by Peter A. J. Attema, Francesco di Gennaro, and Eero Jarva (Groningen: Groningen Institute of Archaeology), pp. 95–112

——. 2020. 'Data from the Burial Grounds', in *The People and the State: Material Culture, Social Structure and Political Centralisation in Central Italy (800–450 BC) from the Perspective of Ancient Crustumerium (Rome, Italy)*, ed. by Peter Attema and Remco Bronkhorst, Corollaria Crustumina, 4 (Groningen: Groningen Institute of Archaeology), pp. 95–138

Belelli Marchesini, Barbara, and Francesco di Gennaro. 2011. 'Qualche osservazione sulla componente femminile della comunità laziale di Crustumerium (IX–V sec. a.C.)', *Medicina nei secoli*, 23: *Essere donna tra protostoria e tardo antico: archeologia, medicina e antropologia; atti del convegno internazionale*: 315–34

——. 2021. 'Le libagioni di gruppo dei Latini settentrionali', in *Preistoria del cibo: l'alimentazione nella preistoria e protostoria*, ed. by Isabella Damiani, Alberto Cazzella, and Valentina Copat, Studi di preistoria e protostoria, 6 (Florence: Pacini editore), pp. 833–38

Bietti Sestieri, Anna Maria (ed.). 1992. *La necropoli laziale di Osteria dell'Osa* (Rome: Quasar)

Brughmans, Tom. 2013. 'Thinking through Networks: A Review of Formal Network Methods in Archaeology', *Journal of Archaeological Method and Theory*, 20: 623–62

Brughmans, Tom, Anna Collar, and Fiona Coward. 2016. 'Network Perspectives on the Past: Tackling the Challenges', in *The Connected Past: Challenges to Network Studies in Archaeology and History*, ed. by Tom Brughmans, Anna Collar, and Fiona Coward (Oxford: Oxford University Press), pp. 3–19

Brughmans, Tom, and Matthew A. Peeples. 2017. 'Trends in Archaeological Network Research: A Bibliometric Analysis', *Journal of Historical Network Research*, 1: 2–24

Cascino, Roberta, Helga Di Giuseppe, and Helen L. Patterson. 2012. *Veii: The Historical Topography of the Ancient City; A Restudy of John Ward-Perkins's Survey*, Archaeological Monographs of the British School at Rome, 19 (London: British School at Rome)

Catsman, Matthijs. 2020. 'Verbonden in de dood: een netwerkmethode voor funerair onderzoek naar Centraal-Italische interconnectiviteit in de zevende eeuw voor Christus', *Tijdschrift voor Mediterrane Archeologie*, 62: 21–30

Cifani, Gabriele. 2021. *The Origins of the Roman Economy: From the Iron Age to the Early Republic in a Mediterranean Perspective* (Cambridge: Cambridge University Press)

Collar, Anna, Fiona Coward, Tom Brughmans, and Barbara J. Mills. 2015. 'Networks in Archaeology: Phenomena, Abstraction, Representation', *Journal of Archaeological Method and Theory*, 22: 1–32

Colonna, Giovanni. 1988. 'La produzione artigianale', in *Storia di Roma*, 1: *Roma in Italia*, ed. by Arnaldo Momigliano, Aldo Schiavone, and Carmine Ampolo (Turin: Einaudi), pp. 291–316

Conti, Alessandro, and Biagio Giuliani. 2016. 'Rileggendo un holmos in white-on-red da Narce. Suggestioni tiberine', in *I Falisci attraverso lo specchio (Atti della giornata di studi per festeggiare Maria Anna De Lucia Brolli, Mazzano Romano, 31 ottobre 2015)*, ed. by Maria Cristina Biella and Jacopo Tabolli (Rome: Officina edizioni), pp. 93–116

De Puma, Richard. 2010. 'Crustumerium and Etruria', *Bollettino di archeologia online*, special volume: *International Congress of Classical Archaeology: Meetings between Cultures in the Ancient Mediterranean (Rome, 22–26 September 2008)*: 96–101 <http://www.bollettinodiarcheologiaonline.beniculturali.it/documenti/generale/8_DEPUMA.pdf> [accessed 28 June 2013]

——. 2012. 'Rapporti tra Crustumerium e l'Etruria. La ceramica', *Bullettino della Commissione Archeologica Comunale di Roma*, 113: 279–84

di Gennaro, Francesco. 2007. 'Le tombe a loculo di età orientalizzante di Crustumerium', in *Tusculum: storia, archeologia, cultura e arte di Tuscolo e del Tuscolano (atti del primo incontro di studi, 27–28 maggio e 3 giugno 2000)*, ed. by Franco Arietti and Anna Pasqualini (Rome: Comitato nazionale per le celebrazioni del millenario della fondazione dell'Abbazia di S. Nilo a Grottaferrata), pp. 163–76

di Gennaro, Francesco, and Cristiano Iaia. 2000. 'Elementi culturali della prima età del ferro nell'area di cerniera tra Sabina, Etruria e Latium Vetus', in *Preistoria e protostoria in Etruria: atti del quarto incontro di studi, Manciano, Montalto di Castro, Valentano 12/14 Settembre 1997; l'Etruria tra Italia, Europa e mondo mediterraneo; ricerche e scavi*, ed. by Nuccia Negroni Catacchio (Milan: Centro studi di preistoria e archeologia), pp. 245–53

di Gennaro, Francesco, Paolo Togninelli, and Richard De Puma. 2002. 'Crustumerium e l'Etruria', *Etruscan Studies*, 9: 45–62

di Gennaro, Francesco, Angelo Amoroso, and Paolo Togninelli. 2007. '*Crustumerium* e *Fidenae* tra Etruria e ColliAlbani', in *Tusculum: storia, archeologia, cultura e arte di Tuscolo e del Tuscolano; atti del primo incontro di studi (27–28 maggio e 3 giugno 2000)*, ed. by Franco Arietti and Anna Pasqualini (Rome: Comitato nazionale per le celebrazioni del millenario della fondazione dell'Abbazia di S. Nilo a Grottaferrata), pp. 135–62

di Gennaro, Francesco, and Barbara Belelli Marchesini. 2012. 'Scavi 1987–2011 nel sepolcreto crustumino di Monte Del Bufalo', *Bullettino della Commissione Archeologica Comunale di Roma*, 113: 229–43

di Gennaro, Francesco, Barbara Belelli Marchesini, and Albert J. Nijboer. 2016. 'Early Iron Age Tombs at Crustumerium (Rome), ca. 850–725 BC', *Palaeohistoria*, 57/58: 117–36

di Gennaro, Francesco, Federica Bartoli, Elena Foddai, Beatrice Giorgetta, Cristiano Iaia, Manuela Merlo, Sara Pasquarelli, and Silvia ten Kortenaar. 2009. 'Contesti e materiali della prima età del ferro, di età orientalizzante, arcaica e tardo-arcaica da Fidene', in *Ceramica, abitati, territorio nella bassa valle del Tevere e Latium Vetus*, ed. by Marco Rendeli, Collection de l'École française de Rome, 425 (Rome: École française de Rome), pp. 137–210

Donnellan, Lieve. 2016. 'A Networked View on "Euboean" Colonisation', in *Conceptualising Early Colonisation*, ed. by Lieve Donnellan, Valentino Nizzo, and Gert-Jan Burgers (Brussels: Belgisch Historisch Instituut te Rome), pp. 149–66

Drago Troccoli, Luciana. 2009. 'Il Lazio tra la I Età del Ferro e l'Orientalizzante. Osservazioni sulla produzione ceramica e metallica tra il II e il IV periodo, l'origine dell'impasto rosso e i rapporti tra Greci, Fenici e Sardi', in *Il Lazio dai Colli Albani ai Monti Lepini tra preistoria ed età moderna*, ed. by Luciana Drago Troccoli (Rome: Quasar), pp. 229–88

Fahlander, Fredrik. 2003. 'The Materiality of Serial Practice. A Microarchaeology of Burial' (unpublished doctoral dissertation, Göteborg University)

Interdonato, Carmelo. 2013. 'Studi archeometrici su ceramica di impasto. Crustumerium: prospettive e primi risultati', in *Crustumerium: ricerche internazionali in un centro latino*, ed. by Peter A. J. Attema, Francesco di Gennaro, and Eero Jarva (Groningen: Groningen Institute of Archaeology), pp. 117–25

Interdonato, Carmelo, Angela Baldanza, Marcella Di Bella, Francesco di Gennaro, Giuseppe Sabatino, and Maurizio Triscari. 2008. 'Materiali ceramici da Crustumerium (Roma): primi dati archeometrici', in *V Congresso nazionale di archeometria (A.I.A.R. 2008)*, ed. by Anna Gueli (Siracusa: Morrone), pp. 317–28

Kortenaar, Silvia ten. 2011. *Il colore e la materia: tra tradizione e innovazione nella produzione dell'impasto rosso nell'Italia medio-tirrenica (Cerveteri, Veio e il Latium vetus)* (Rome: Officina edizioni)

Kruta Poppi, Luana. 2015. 'La donna etrusco-italica e quella greca: due mondi a confronto', in *Donne dell'Etruria padana dall'VIII al VI sec.: tra gestione domestica e produzione artigianale*, ed. by Luana Kruta Poppi and Diana Neri (Florence: All'Insegna del Giglio), pp. 22–28

Micozzi, Marina. 1994. *'White-on-red': Una produzione vascolare dell'orientalizzante etrusco* (Rome: Gruppo Editoriale Internazionale)

——. 2014. 'Vingt ans après. Retour sur la diffusion des styles "white-on-red"', in *Les potiers d'Étrurie et leur monde: contacts, échanges, transferts; hommages à Mario A. Del Chiaro*, ed. by Laura Ambrosini and Vincent Jolivet (Paris: Armand Colin), pp. 109–21

Mottolese, Chiara. 2021. 'Elaborazione e sviluppo dell'anfora a doppia spirale', in *Leggere il passato, costruire il futuro: gli Etruschi e gli altri popoli del Mediterraneo; scritti in onore di Gilda Bartoloni*, ii, ed. by Valeria Acconcia, Alessandra Piergrossi, and Iefke van Kampen, Mediterranea, 18 (Rome: Quasar), pp. 163–71

Neri, Sara. 2010. *Il tornio e il pennello: ceramica depurata di tradizione geometrica di epoca orientalizzante in Etruria meridionale* (Rome: Officina edizioni)

——. 2014. 'The Orientalizing Necropolis of Macchia della Comunità – Veii: Some Observations on its Development', in *Research into Pre-Roman Burial Grounds in Italy*, ed. by Albert J. Nijboer, Sarah L. Willemsen, Peter A. J. Attema, and Jorn F. Seubers, Caeculus, 8 (Paris: Leuven), pp. 121–38

Nijboer, Albert J. 1998. *From Household Production to Workshops: Archaeological Evidence for Economic Transformations, Pre-monetary Exchange and Urbanisation in Central Italy from 800 to 400 BC* (Groningen: University of Groningen, Department of Archaeology)

——. 2018. 'Diversity in Death: A Construction of Identities and the Funerary Record of Multi-ethnic Central Italy from 950 to 350 BC', in *Papers in Italian Archaeology*, vii: *The Archaeology of Death; Proceedings of the Seventh Conference of Italian Archaeology Held at the National University of Ireland, Galway, April 16–18, 2016*, ed. by Edward Herring and Eoin O'Donoghue (Oxford: Archaeopress), pp. 107–27

Nijboer, Albert J., and Peter A. J. Attema. 2010. 'Cultural Characteristics of the Ancient Community Living at Crustumerium and the Excavations of the Groningen Institute of Archaeology at the Monte Del Bufalo Necropolis', *Bollettino di archeologia online*, special volume: *International Congress of Classical Archaeology: Meetings between Cultures in the Ancient Mediterranean (Rome, 22–26 September 2008)*: 23–38 <www.bollettinodiarcheologiaonline.beniculturali.it> [accessed 24 January 2023]

——. 2012. 'Tratti culturali della comunità antica di *Crustumerium* dagli scavi dell'Istituto d'Archeologia di Groningen a Monte Del Bufalo', *Bullettino della Commissione Archeologica Comunale di Roma*, 113: 263–78

——. 2020. 'Crustumerium in Context', in *The People and the State: Material Culture, Social Structure, and Political Centralisation in Central Italy (800–450 BC) from the Perspective of Ancient Crustumerium (Rome, Italy)*, ed. by Peter A. J. Attema and Remco Bronkhorst (Eelde: Barkhuis), pp. 153–70

Nizzo, Valentino. 2015. *Archeologia e antropologia della morte: storia di una idea; la semiologia e l'ideologia funeraria dellesocietà di livello protostorico nellariflessione teorica tra archeologia e antropologia* (Bari: Edipuglia)

Rathje, Annette. 2017. 'Pissidi orientalizzanti da Ficana. Una nota', in *Scritti per il decimo anniversario di Aristonothos*, ed. by Enrico Giovannelli, Aristonothos: scritti per il Mediterraneo antico, 13.1 (Milano: Ledizioni), pp. 167–81

Smith, Christopher. 1996. *Early Rome and Latium, Economy and Society c. 1000 to 500 BC* (Oxford: Clarendon)

Stockhammer, Philipp W. 2013. 'From Hybridity to Entanglement, from Essentialism to Practice', *Archaeological Review from Cambridge*, 28: 11–28

Tabolli, Jacopo. 2013. *Narce tra la prima età del Ferro e l'Orientalizzante antico: l'abitato, i Tufi e la Petrina* (Pisa: Fabrizio Serra)

Taloni, Maria. 2012. 'Le oinochoai cosiddette fenicio-cipriote: origine, rielaborazione e trasformazione di una forma vascolare', in *Mode e modelli: fortuna e insuccesso nella circolazione di cose e idee*, ed. by Carlo Regoli, Officina Etruscologia, 7 (Rome: Officina edizioni), pp. 77–98

——. 2013. *Le tombe da Riserva del Truglio al Museo Pigorini di Roma*, Officina Etruscologia, 8 (Rome: Officina edizioni)

Torelli, Mario. 1986. 'La religione', in *Rasenna: storia e civiltà degli Etruschi*, ed. by Massimo Pallottino (Milan: Schweiller), pp. 159–237

Waarsenburg, Demetrius. 1995. *The Northwest Necropolis of Satricum, an Iron Age Cemetery in Latium Vetus* (Amsterdam: Thesis)

Weidig, Joachim. 2008. 'I pugnali a stami. Considerazioni su aspetti tecnici, tipologici, cronologici e distribuzione in area Abruzzese', in *Ricerche di archeologia Medio-Adriatica: atti dell'Incontro di studio Cavallino-Lecce, 27–28 maggio 2005*, i: *Le necropoli: contesti e materiali*, ed. by Gianluca Tagliamonte (Galatina: Congedo), pp. 105–41

Wenger, Etienne, and Beverly Wenger-Trayner. 2015. *Communities of Practice: A Brief Introduction* <https://wenger-trayner. com/introduction-to-communities-of-practice/> [accessed 24 January 2023]

Willemsen, Sarah L. 2014. *Into the Light: A Study of the Changing Burial Customs at Crustumerium in the 7th and 6th Centuries BC* (Groningen: Groningen Institute of Archaeology)

AMANDA K. PAVLICK

9. From the Ground up

Constructing Monumental Buildings in Archaic Central Italy

ABSTRACT Terracotta roof tiles have long been used as proxies for buildings that have otherwise been largely or entirely lost. The study of these tiles has served many purposes, ranging from the minute details of their raw materials to the broad strokes of the adoption of monumental architecture across Archaic central Italy. Yet we have often left unexamined the issues that the first adopters of this new architectural technology faced in the seventh century BCE. These people broke with centuries of tradition to employ a complex and wholly new architectural form, and this paper seeks to examine some of the problems they encountered in the process. By examining issues such as the mobilization of labour, investment of natural resources, and choice of building site, this paper seeks the perspective of the seventh-century building commissioner and, in turn, the insights that seeking such a point of view may bring to our understanding of urban development in central Italy.

The period from the eighth to the fifth centuries BCE has been called the 'flowering of Italy' (Pallottino 1991, 59); a time of increasing social complexity, emerging urbanism, and multifaceted processes of both growth and contraction. A key part of these changes was the adoption of a new style of architecture: stone-founded rectilinear buildings with terracotta-tiled roofs, built in Italy as early as *c.* 650 BCE, which facilitated a revolution in terms of the functionality, capacity, and external appearance of such structures. All of these were significant factors in the increasing urban complexity of the time.

The importance of these structures has never been in doubt, though the nature of their survival in the archaeological record has led us to study them in particular ways.[1] Their primary, and sometimes only, surviving element are the terracottas that made up their roof tiles and architectural decorations, and it is these, therefore, which are foremost in our examination of such ancient structures. Traditionally, study of these buildings has focused more on the facts of their existence — their dating, locations, and visual elements, for example — rather than the circumstances that led to their creation and use. While some attention has been paid to these topics,[2] they have rarely been brought to the forefront, nor given attention as a unified process of creation. Therefore, what actually went into building a tile-roofed structure is underrepresented, hampering our understanding of this crucial aspect of urban development. I argue that by focusing on the decision-making process of those individuals who commissioned and built these structures, we gain new insights.

In this chapter, I examine these buildings as a series of questions, focusing, when possible, on those who conceived of the idea to construct them in the first place and the methods by which they carried out their plan. I am particularly interested in quantifying the construction process, utilizing volumetrics and architectural energetics to shed light on the full complexity of building such a structure. Using this approach, I problematize terracotta-tile roofed

---

1   Wikander and Wikander (2006, 42) called for increased focus on the production of, and economic questions surrounding, this material, rather than the 'custom of stylistic analysis' which had dominated up until that point.

2   Notably, the work of Charlotte and Örjan Wikander has shed much light on the production, final products, and use of terracotta tiles; cf. C. Wikander 1981; 1988, Ö. Wikander 1986; 1993. Additionally, holistic work done by Knoop (1987) at Satricum; Turfa and Steinmayer on comparative Greek and Italian structures (1986); Winter's (2009) *magnum opus* of Archaic architectural terracottas from central Italy; and Hopkins (2016) on the development of architecture in Archaic Rome have all been significant contributions.

Corresponding author Amanda K. Pavlick (pavlicka@xavier.edu)

structures by looking at the earliest of these in Italy, dating to the mid-seventh century into the first half of the sixth century BCE, when construction using durable materials was just beginning, in order to question why this change may have occurred and what it can potentially tell us about contemporary society. My argument here will focus on the roofs, as the most well-known and securely quantifiable portion of these buildings, but discussion will consider all elements of the structures in question.

This chapter, therefore, is about a moment of creation that led to a great shift in the built environment. Investigating the decisions that created these structures — the problems, challenges, and new circumstances they created — reorients our perspective from the buildings themselves to their commissioners and labourers. Why did these people engage in this process? And what can asking this, and other related questions, tell us about this point in the Italian past?

From Huts to Houses

We will begin with the environment within which rectilinear buildings with stone foundations and terracotta roofs were first constructed. In the mid-seventh century BCE, a tradition of building lightweight, generally curvilinear huts (often referred to by the Italian *capanne*) had existed in Italy for hundreds of years,[3] traceable at least to the tenth century (Karlsson 2017). Building such huts was part of the inherited knowledge of generations; their materials, their maintenance, and their sustainability within the local landscape would have been well known. Their construction was likely the product of the household; by observing traditional building methods for huts in the Roman campagna in the early twentieth century, Erixon (2001, 451) noted that the framing for a rounded hut with a single, central post could have been completed by one man. Abrams states that residents of Copan, Honduras, who built single-family homes of wattle and daub using methods similar to those of the Classic Maya, often had a construction crew of one to five people, consisting of the homeowner and friends or family members.[4] Thus we can presume that such structures in early Italy were

also achievable for a family on an as-needed basis, their construction and maintenance taking minimal labour and time away from other, more necessary tasks. This then leads us to the first question from the perspective of a new building's commissioner: Why opt out of this tradition, and instead opt into something labour intensive, untested, and untried?

Furthermore, the advent of terracotta-tile roofed structures represents a socio-economic shift. Terracotta tiles indicate the presence of skilled labourers to create such a product, and thus, a shift from household- to market-oriented production (Rystedt 2001, 26). The building's commissioner would have to determine how to achieve the construction of something much more complex — requiring the aforementioned skilled labour, specialized production locations, and an increased workforce — which we know would also require specific economic change for the settlement in question. We cannot speak in broad terms here about the nature of that change, as the number of building projects — for example, if only one building was desired, or if multiple structures would be built over a longer period of time — would dictate the scale of that change, and the patterns were different at various settlements during the seventh to fifth centuries.[5] Whatever the specific circumstances at a given location, though, this decision was a significant one.

This moment of decision is therefore an inflection point in the Italian past which deserves full examination, something it has not yet received. Some have described this change as a simple matter of emulation and acculturation — that is, passive receptivity to what is perceived to have been a superior construction style, adopted without question from the Greeks.[6] This is perhaps owing in part to modern biases that assume that huts should be less desirable than the more respectable 'houses',[7] and that building a stone-founded house with a durable roof would simply be a matter of upgrading one's quality of life. However, this assumption does not engage with the motivating factors behind the decision for the seventh- or sixth-century builder, nor with the

---

3 While most of the known *capanne* are oval or rounded, some rectilinear huts have been found, such as phase 1 of House 1 at San Giovenale, Area F (Karlsson 2006, 142–54), and Villanovan rectilinear huts at Tarquinia (Linington 1978).

4 Of fifteen homes surveyed, five were built solely by the owner. Homes consisted of a raised, beaten-earth platform, wattle and daub walls, and roofs of either grass, palm, tile, or corrugated steel sheeting (Abrams 1994, table 2).

---

5 See Winter (2009) for known roofs from sites throughout central Italy dating from *c.* 650 to 510 BCE.

6 Boethius 1978, esp. 34; Brown 1961, esp. 12. Izzet (2001, 45) argues that claiming the Greeks were solely responsible for terracotta-tiled roofs in Italy is ethnocentric and inadequate.

7 Huts/*capanne* and houses/*case* are terms often used as shorthand for architecture of the time period, referring to lightweight buildings with thatch roofs vs. stone-founded structures with terracotta roofs. cf. *Case e palazzi d'Etruria*, a 1985 exhibition later published as a standalone volume (Stopponi 1986), and the 1997 *From Huts to Houses* symposium on early Italian architecture (Brandt and Karlsson 2001).

realities of construction. It also overlooks the fact that there was no quick or linear shift from huts to houses at any central Italian site; huts continued to be built and used alongside stone-founded rectilinear structures for generations afterward.[8] Both types of structure had pros and cons to its construction and its use, which should be examined first.

Choosing to build a terracotta-roofed structure led to an entirely novel process. From the beginning, this would require new ideas,[9] training, more skilled labour — possibly involving workers who were foreign to the site or region — and the increased exploitation of natural resources, including stone, clay, and wood. This significantly increased cost as compared to traditional building methods demonstrates this structure was an investment. Additionally, as with anything new, there was the risk of failure — ranging from smaller issues like tiles that warp during firing, to larger ones such as a structurally unsound building — which should not be overlooked in hypothesizing this phase of the project.

What, then, was the perceived return on that investment? The architecture itself, and its possible benefits, are thus the first thing to question. We might assume that using stone-founded buildings and rectilinear architecture allowed for the creation of larger structures; where the size of curvilinear huts was often restricted by the height of the trees used for their roof beams,[10] rectilinear buildings, on the other hand, could be more easily enlarged owing to more complex roofs, roof trusses, and the presence of interior, load-bearing walls (Torelli 1985, 25; Cornell 1995, 101).[11] Large structures naturally draw attention, particularly when they are rare; one defi-

nition of monumentality is a structure that is simply larger than its function requires (Trigger 1990, 119), so this is an important element. It is, however, not adequate as a sole explanation. The first buildings to use terracotta roofing tiles in Greece were temples, of significant size and built at great cost. Wikander (1990, 289) notes that the need to protect such a building from weather and potential fire with a durable roof was a motivator for the development of terracotta tiles in that location. Early scholarship on Italian tiled roofs presumed their buildings were also temples;[12] however, the earliest of these structures in Italy appear instead to have been residences, of varying sizes.[13] Furthermore, Izzet (2001, 43) has pointed out that some rectilinear buildings at Acquarossa were actually smaller than contemporary huts, which should make us question if size was a primary motivator.[14]

Practicalities may have also been attractive factors for such a building; weatherproofing, increased durability, and an environment more advantageous for health and hygiene would have been desirable benefits. Huts of any shape or size were made with non-durable materials — pisé or wattle and daub walls, often with a clay or plaster covering, and thatch or reed roofs — which would need regular maintenance and rebuilding, depending upon the particular materials used and weather conditions.[15] Thatch

---

8   Considering the earliest stone-founded structures at Rome, built over the course of up to seventy years, numbered in the single digits (see Table 9.1), we must assume that there were huts still in use for the vast majority of the population.

9   Ridgway and Ridgway (1994, 7–8) argued for this as less of a major pivot and more of a progression of indigenous architectural traditions. They propose that the invention of terracotta roofing systems could have begun with wooden roofs weatherproofed with pitch and covered in clay that would bake in the sun for added protection. This would then be the jumping-off point 'to the heavier and more permanent [roofs] fitted with baked terracotta tiles and ornaments', the design of which would likely be the purview of Etruscan potters at the outset.

10   On average, 2.4–3.6 m, and with a maximum height of 4.2 m used in huts; Izzet 2001, 43; Potts 2015, 31, with references.

11   For example, Karlsson (2006, 155) describes the roof of House I at San Giovenale as being so heavy as to have 'required internal supports' and that internal columns would have supported the ridge of the roof above; similarly, House II had postholes that would accommodate large (c. 30 cm thick) columns beneath the ridge, as well as 'larger, stylobate blocks, strong enough to support wooden columns' along the house's portico (2006, 158). Further, see Turfa and Steinmayer (1996) on the importance

of the invention of the tie-beam truss for Archaic Italian architecture.

12   Andrén's pioneering work on Italian architectural terracottas from 1940 was entitled *Architectural Terracottas from Etrusco-Italic Temples*, and while he does discuss residential structures as well, he classes them as 'supplementary evidence' for 'a complete reconstruction of an Etrusco-Italic temple' (Andrén 1940, xxi). The excavation of sites such as Poggio Civitate (Murlo) and Acquarossa, beginning decades after Andrén's book, added significant residential architecture to our knowledge base and supplanted the idea that only temples in Italy had terracotta tiles.

13   Of seventh-century buildings with known functions, the exceptions to this generalization are the three structures at Poggio Civitate (one of which may have been a residence (OC1), but also including a tripartite structure (OC3) and a workshop (OC2); see Tuck 2021, esp. 20–23), and the buildings in Rome which will be discussed below. For the difference in building function between early Greek and Italic structures, cf. Wikander 1990, 290.

14   Winter (2009, 527) notes that the span of many of the buildings in her catalogue were modest in size, ranging from 3 to 7.5 m (at Acquarossa) to 12.4 m (the north flank of the Upper Building (Roof 3-8) at Poggio Civitate).

15   Noble (2007, 151) states that thatch may require annual rebuilding, as seen primarily in tropical climates, but also elsewhere such as in the Hebridean Islands in Scotland, or every few rainy seasons, as recorded in New Guinea by Meggitt (1957). Wind, as opposed to rain, is a major challenge for such a light material, though thatch roofs also lose their ability to hold out rainwater over time. Beyond roofing concerns, wattle and daub

roofs may harbour insects and other pests, potentially bearing zoonotic diseases, impacting most significantly those who spend the majority of their time in the home, such as women and dependents.[16] On the contrary, any building finished with terracotta roof tiles would improve on these conditions. First, covering the roof and capping the beams with terracotta would help keep out damp and extend the life of the roof and walls, decreasing the need for regular maintenance.[17] The roof itself would also be fireproof and the building overall would therefore be more (albeit not entirely) fire-resistant, as it relied less on flammable elements (Wikander 1990, 289).[18] Stone foundations would provide a stronger barrier at ground level, and the thicker walls — though still often of wattle and daub and the like — required to support the weight of the roof would offer increased insulation from the extremes of weather outside. With all of these factors combined, not only would the comfort and health of the people inside increase, but also the durability and lifespan of the building itself.

Therefore, we can theorize that the person who desired to build a terracotta-roofed structure would have had several practical reasons for embarking on this project. However, *capanne* were not abandoned by any means; in fact, terracotta-tile roofed structures remained rare through the fifth century in central Italy; of the known roofs at twenty-six sites, eighteen of these only had one or two buildings with such roofs in total, six sites had between three and ten, and only two sites had more than ten: Rome had twelve in total from 650–520 BCE, and Acquarossa had at least thirty-nine from 640–520 BCE.[19] Thus

we may assert that pure pragmatism was not behind this change, or surely the numbers would be higher. The potential ideological reasons behind this decision will be discussed toward the end of this paper.

A Consequential Choice

The next question for our theoretical building commissioner is how to actually get the structure built if they are the first, or one of the first, to do so in central Italy. Embarking upon a construction project which includes both a new architectural style and technological innovation is no small feat; nearly every aspect of this new building would require different or increased labour and materials.

First, site preparation and the substructure would require more effort than traditional building models; wider foundation trenches were required to accommodate stone foundations to support the weight of the superstructure. Where preserved, such foundations are commonly of tuff chips or ashlar blocks, the latter of which would require a significant outlay of labour to create.[20] The additional investment in quarrying, transporting, and laying the ashlars would be a dramatic uptick in work from the foundation of any hut. Moving on to the superstructure, the walls themselves would need to be thick enough to support the weight of the roof that would cap it;[21] mud brick, wattle and daub, and pisé walls are all found in Italy when traces of the architecture are preserved, though some — such as Houses I, II, and III at San Giovenale,[22] and at least one building

---

huts also could not be constructed in areas that would be subject to seasonal flooding, such as in low-lying areas in Rome, as pointed out by Hopkins (2016, 28).

16 Various types of insects have been recorded with relation to thatch roofs, such as triatomine bugs (commonly known as assassin or kissing bugs) in Central and South America (Abrams 1994), which can spread Chagas Disease (Klotz and others 2016), as well as fleas, as demonstrated in New Guinea (Meggit 1957, 161). Other issues include fungi and mould, as noted in southern England (Kirby and Rayner 1989), and globally, vermin (Noble 2007, 151).

17 Winter (2009, 519 and 521) says that most roof elements with exposed surfaces were slipped, likely to provide waterproofing. Many terracotta-tile roofed buildings at this time in central Italy still had walls of pisé and similar, but a tiled roof would ostensibly protect those walls more thoroughly than a thatched roof.

18 A fire that was intentionally set for observation by scholars to a modern wattle and daub, thatch-roofed hut in Serbia reached the roof within three minutes and within another three 'was described as an inferno' (Kruger 2015, 898).

19 This includes known roofs from 650–510 BCE; not all structures were contemporaneous. Figures take into account sites from as far south as Satricum and as far north as Castelnuovo Berardegna; data derived from Winter 2009. See below for a

discussion of the known buildings from Acquarossa with regards to the extent of excavations at the site.

20 While not directly applicable here, the labour requirements for the ashlar blocks of tuff used in Rome provide some idea of how much work quarrying required; DeLaine estimated a crew of three workmen (one skilled, two unskilled) could extract a single block in a workday of a harder tuff such as *tufo giallo*, a figure backed up by Abrams's work in Honduras. A softer stone such as *tufo del Palatino* could allow up to three complete blocks per day by a similar crew (see Bernard 2018, 233–34). Both figures require additional time for finishing the block, transport, and installation. The specific hardness of the local stone, tools used, distance from quarry to building site, and method of transportation available, all impact the specific amount of labour required, so explicit numbers will not be given here as this is beyond the scope of this paper.

21 Guaitoli (1984, 378–79) noted the compression ratio of a tile roof on walls of various materials, and the need for a wooden framework supporting the wall in some circumstances.

22 Karlsson 2006, 155–63. Though Winter (2009, 11) groups these tiles into one roof (number 1-3), she notes that they may have made up one roof or multiple; all date to Period 3 of the site (c. 625–550/530 BCE), but the excavators believe Houses II and III to be contemporary owing to the fact that they share a bonded wall (Karlsson 2006, 159).

at Acquarossa, Portico Building C, Zone F[23] — had walls entirely of tuff blocks.

All of this supported a complicated roof made up of multiple types of tiles, the successful creation of which required specific technical knowledge: this is including, but not limited to: the various roof elements, their dimensions and shapes, and the process required to craft them with enough precision so as to make the work efficient and the roof functional.

The mass of the finished roof also posed a challenge to the overall structure, hence the durability of the walls and foundations. The weight of a tiled roof is estimated to be *c.* 60 kg per square metre (Wikander 1993, 130), meaning even a small building would have a roof of considerable bulk.[24] As an example, among the smallest sixth-century buildings known is House A, Zone B at Acquarossa (*c.* 550–530 BCE) (Winter 2009, 14–15),[25] with foundations measuring 9.5 × 6 m.[26] Each roof would have overlapped the walls by an estimated 0.5 m to protect them from rain, giving us a roof measuring 10 × 6.5 m. Therefore, this roof would have weighed *c.* 3900 kg when dry. Though slipped, in part for weatherproofing, Wikander (1993, 130) states that, over time, this slip wore away and the tiles would hold rather than repel rainwater, increasing the weight to *c.* 70 kg per m^2 when wet and bringing the total weight up to 4.55 (metric) tonnes. Further, this assumes a relatively simplistic roof without ridge tiles and lateral or raking simas;[27] therefore, buildings employing these elements and other decorative features would

have had additional weight (Wikander 1993, 130),[28] and none of these figures include the weight of the beams that made up the frame, nor the potential wooden backing upon which the tiles themselves rested.[29] Therefore, even these basic calculations are an underestimate, and a single, complete roof for even a modestly sized structure would weigh multiple tonnes, placing significant stress on the walls and foundation, and on those engineering the cap for this new type of building. In sum, the structure supporting even the lightest terracotta-tiled roofs had to reliably hold a weight unprecedented in any earlier architecture — a problem not posed by the lighter, commonplace thatch.

The difficulties the decision to build would pose were clearly not insurmountable obstacles; unfortunately, the reasons behind such decisions are sadly ephemeral without documentary evidence. However, if we then take a step back and look at where these buildings appear, when, and in what number, the resulting pattern may provide new insights into the intriguing question of why.

My argument is based around the mobilization of labour, which the application of architectural energetics can help to reveal. This method, brought to full fruition by Abrams (1994), quantifies architectural remains via the labour 'cost' required to create them, and thus allows us to speculate on the organization of practicalities employed in the project. Abrams and McCurdy (2020, 3) argue this is 'the most direct means of inferring political, social, and economic power relations in the archaeological past'. Building on the volumetric data of tiles, above, I will consider labour costs for the roofs of two representative structures. For reasons of space, I focus on the roof because that is the most securely quantifiable element of many of these buildings, and here may stand as a representative sample of some of the work invested in their creation.

---

23 Winter 2009, 235. Additionally, the Southeastern House, Zone J has three preserved ashlar blocks of tufa (Winter 2009, 13), though it is unclear to me whether these are the superstructure or part of the foundation.

24 Wikander (1993, 128) notes that an assumption of a perfect roof of neat, straight tiles of identical shape and size was likely not the case for many private homes, and that instead 'we should rather try to visualize ancient tile-roofs in accordance with those encountered today […] some "correctly" laid rows of pan and cover tiles, tiles placed upside-down or obliquely, broken tiles […] *Mutatis mutandis*, this is presumably the reality'. All weights here are an estimate for the purpose of providing a framework for discussion.

25 Wikander (1993, 138) says that this is roughly the average size of a house at Acquarossa (citing 10 × 6 m). However, of the known terracotta roofs from this time period, few are associated with foundations well-preserved enough to provide a secure indication of size, so while Wikander asserts that this is an average house from Acquarossa, there are few other examples from central Italy that are, in fact, smaller.

26 A potential addition comprising a room (room 6) and a porch (indicated by postholes) may have extended this house to 9.5 × 8.5 in a later phase (Winter 2009, 14); however, only the first phase is considered here for the purpose of the example.

27 This particular roof was made up of pan tiles, cover tiles, ridge tiles, antefixes, and possibly eaves tiles (Winter 2009, 15).

28 Wikander notes that the Acquarossa roofs weighed less than other contemporary roofs, citing examples up to 94 kg per m^2 (the Temple of Apollo on Temple Hill, Corinth).

29 Beam weight would be dependent upon the wood employed, which cannot be known with certainty for Acquarossa. Abrams (1994, 68) notes, for example, that a fragment of hardwood was recovered for one building at ancient Copan, and this type of wood was specifically used for beams and lintels. For beam weight estimates, see Turfa and Steinmayer 1996, 3. Examining the Portonaccio Temple at Veii, they estimate the weight of the complete roof to have been 85 kg per m^2. Some roofs likely had a wooden backing, adding even more weight overall, though Wikander (1993, 122) states that he does not believe, but cannot prove, that roofs at Acquarossa had this backing, and rather rested directly on the beams and rafters.

Generating these roof tiles would require skilled labour to plan, mould, and fire the tiles before they could be assembled on site. For the earliest structures, this labour was likely drawn from — and would divert the time and attention of — the settlement's potters, as was the case in seventh-century Corinth, at Phari on Thasos (Perreault 1990), and may have been for Acquarossa as well.[30]

How much time would this have required of these artisans? Thanks to experiments done in recreating Archaic tiles, we can begin to quantify some of their labour. Here, I rely particularly on Sapirstein's research on the process of tile making for the Old Temple at Corinth (*c.* 680 BCE).[31] This roof's tiles were of the complex Proto-Corinthian system, featuring pan and cover tiles with rabbeted and bevelled sections to allow one tile to interlock with the next in the sequence. This is quite different from the flat, flanged pan tiles (also known by the Latin *tegulae*) and curved cover tiles (*imbrices*) used in central Italy,[32] but Sapirstein's experiment gives us a way to come closer to concrete figures.[33] He indicates that a crew of four men, minimum,[34] working on gathering the raw materials, making moulds, and producing the tiles, would work an average of 2.2 hours per square metre of finished roof,[35] indi-

cating that a roof the size of House A, Zone B at Acquarossa (again, *c.* 10 × 6.5 m), might require 143 working hours — that is, roughly 14.3 working days,[36] or a minimum of two weeks of active work to create just the tiles, not including transporting them to the building site, installing them on the roof, or any of the labour involved in creating the structure upon which the roof rested.

One must also consider the context. This structure was built *c.* 550–530 BCE, nearly a century after the earliest buildings were erected at this site, and at a time when so many were being built that Wikander has estimated *c.* 11,000 tiles were produced per year (Wikander 1993, 137–39). The commissioner, therefore, had an established local tile industry to utilize — as one surely existed to create such an output — making his individual task the simpler one of purchasing something already in mass production nearby.[37] But what of someone who sought to commission such a structure when no such industry existed — indeed, when their building was the first, or among the first, in Italy?

Groundbreaking Architecture?

To explore this question, I turn to Rome, and one of the first known terracotta-roofed structures in Italy: the Residence along the Sacra Via,[38] dating to *c.* 650–625 BCE.[39] This edifice, the fourth phase of the building, measured 33 × 15 m, significantly larger than the later structure at Acquarossa and thus requiring that much more of an investment.[40] No other build-

---

30 Wikander (1993, 137) highlights the similarities between contemporary pottery and tiles found at Acquarossa, from the clay and temper to the slip and paint, as well as saying that some of the animal protomes were clearly worked on a potter's wheel. This leads him to speculate that the potters may have also worked as tile makers.

31 Sapirstein 2008, especially ch. 8. See also Winter 1993, 12–18 on this roof (here called the early Temple of Apollo) and the Protocorinthian system.

32 On *tegulae*, including terminology and typology, see Wikander 1993, 25–45; on *imbrices*, Wikander 1993, 45–58. Roofs from Archaic central Italy generally included a ridge tile to cover the join at the apex of the roof, for which no Latin name has been preserved; they are now called ridge tiles or *kalypteres* (Wikander 1994, 58–73).

33 The production of a Proto-Corinthian tile involves the cutting of the bevels while the tile was in leather-hard stage, a process done by hand (Sapirstein 2018, 218, with images). Removing this time from the figures is a starting point, though the ideal would of course be an experimental production of the types of tiles used in Archaic central Italy.

34 Sapirstein (2008, 252) states that the minimum effective crew to maintain an efficient work schedule is four crewmen plus one donkey, though this could be as few as two to three men, and as many as six.

35 The Old Temple at Corinth measured 20 × 70 m, which would have required 1491 tiles. Sapirstein (2008, 231–64, but especially 260–63) estimates that thirty moulds would have been required to keep work moving efficiently and includes the creation of these in his figures. Allowing for a reasonable failure rate for cracked or warped tiles, he estimates 3100 person-hours for making the tiles and moulds, or 3300 if a separate kiln needed to be built.

36 A ten-hour workday is the common unit used for activities of moderate manual labour (generally twelve hours with two hours for breaks throughout), cf. DeLaine 1997, 106. This estimate is confirmed by ethnographic parallels of potters and tile- and brick-makers by Sapirstein 2008, esp. 240.

37 No workshops have been found at Acquarossa, but the areas where one might expect to find such workshops were not excavated, so this is unsurprising (Wikander 1993, 138). Wikander also reports that multiple clay sources were exploited for the Acquarossa tiles, possibly indicating multiple workshops in various locations.

38 Winter 2009, 8–9; Filippi 2004. This building has also been called the Domus Regia and Domus Publica (Filippi 2004).

39 The dating is preliminary and may be revised in the future; Ammerman and others 2008, 26 and n. 54 expresses reservation about the date but does not dispute it.

40 It is worth noting that both roofs, however, belong to Winter's group 1, Undecorated or Modestly Decorated Roofs, 650–530 BCE (Winter 2009, 7–47) and thus share the stylistic aspect of being somewhat austere in their design. However, the roof from Rome (Roof 1-1) belongs to a group of some of the earliest in Italy, whereas the house from Acquarossa (Roof 1-13) is perhaps a century later and belongs to a group where a change has been made *away* from decoration — which, at this point, was

ing in Rome dates this far back — if even the latest possible date for this building is accurate, it would still predate the next known building in Rome with a tiled roof (the first phase of the Regia) by at least five years.[41] So the commissioner of this structure possibly required a one-off roof, and was able to marshal the labour and technical skill required to achieve it. Based on the calculations above for the person-hours invested in a roof,[42] the time for the tiles alone would have been *c*. 115 days. Further, we can speculate on whether the process was more laborious owing to its newness;[43] the way by which terracotta roof tiles were first realized in Italy is highly speculative,[44] but we can say at least that tile making was not a well-established Roman endeavour at this time. This leads us to the next question: How was this labour marshalled, and who had the social standing to do so?

Recent explorations of the Roman Forum and surrounding areas have given us new information to add to this overall scenario. Petrography and neutron activation analysis have shown that the clay source exploited for the tiles on the Residence was in the Velabrum (Ammerman and others 2008), located *c*. 200 m away from the building site. With the quarry and building site both nearby, we can presume that the kiln(s) for the project were likely here as well. This is striking; we tend to see potter's quarters located outside of the city proper, such as at Corinth and Athens, yet here we may have one very much within the ancient settlement, just between the Forum and the Tiber, in proximity to residences on the nearby hills.[45] Yet with a quarry and kilns close by, we can imagine this location as a smoky,[46] cluttered,[47] and potentially dangerous industrial area. So the person who had the tiles made for the structure that would become the Residence along the Sacra Via had the power — be it political, social, economic, or some combination thereof — to initiate a complicated process of producing a roof, heretofore likely unknown in both Rome and in Italy, the industrial production of which would take place in a populous area for all nearby residents to take auditory and olfactory note of for several months, if not longer.

It is also worth noting that the person doing this may have been involved in the project that raised the ground level by *c*. 2 m to extend the Roman Forum. This amount of levelling would have required a minimum of 10,000, or as much as 23,000 cubic metres of soil — an incredible amount of work both to generate and to move.[48] The soil from this fill includes the overburden that covered the clay beds in the Velabrum (Ammerman 2011, 261). Unfortunately, it is not possible to securely date the land reclamation project; the difficulty of dating the strata from Boni's deep sounding, re-examined by Gjerstad, leaves this

---

reserved for monumental buildings at Acquarossa — and toward unadorned roofs for private homes (Wikander 1993, 158).

41 Winter (2009, 9–11), following Brown (1974–1975, 21–26) puts this phase of the building at 620 BCE; Brocato and Terrenato (2016, 12), however, have instead put forth the end of the seventh to the beginning of the sixth centuries as a date in their preliminary publication of their work on Brown's Regia excavations.

42 Abrams (1984) first advocated for the replacement of man-hours/days as the standard unit with person-hours/days to account for the participation of adolescents, women, and children (Abrams and McCurdy 2020). Though DeLaine (1997, 106) and Lancaster (2020, 97) are among those who advocate for the use of man-days for their specifically male-dominated workforces (in imperial Rome and Archaic Syracuse, respectively), considering our lack of detailed knowledge for Archaic Italy on this matter, I join Abrams in using person-hours/days.

43 For example, Wikander (1993, 157–58) divides the earliest roofs at Acquarossa up into three phases, noting that the first (phase 1A, *c*. 640/620 BCE) was made up of experimental roofs, and that standardization in tiles did not appear until *c*. 620/600 with the beginning of his phase 1B. If this was the time it took for the Acquarossa tile makers to standardize their craft, we might assume the work of the earliest Roman tile makers was similarly not yet streamlined.

44 Ridgway and Ridgway (1994, 7–8) argue for the local invention of terracotta tiles in Italy, building on the evolution of indigenous building traditions (above, n. 9); while I find their argument compelling, it is currently without secure proof. Ancient documentarians provided a story of an individual originator of tile making in Italy, which derives in part from Pliny the Elder (*HN*, XXXV. 42. 12), who says the art of *plastica* was imported to Italy from Greece via a Bacchiad from Corinth, Demaratus, along with three artisans skilled in different media (see also Dion. Hal. III. 46. 3–5 and Livy I. 34. 2). Some build on this story (see Ridgway 2002, 29–31; Winter 2002, with an argument for connections between Corinth, Corfu, and Rome as seen through temple construction and decoration), though fitting the story with dating and details via archaeological material is problematic (cf. Sapirstein 2008, 350–53, with references).

---

45 While this urban kiln is speculative, kilns in residential areas are not unprecedented; they have been found at places such as Kainua (Marzabotto), dating to the sixth and fifth centuries BCE (Mattioli 2023), and at Kassope (Tsakirgis 2005, 78), dating to the third century BCE.

46 Ammerman and others 2008, 26. Hasaki (2005, 144) records the desire of residents near to the potter's quarter of Moknine, Tunisia to relocate the potters owing to the 'hanging clouds of smoke'.

47 Hasaki 2011 notes the potters of Moknine using exterior spaces for storing wood for fuelling the kilns (21), discard of failed items (24, stating the material was often recycled or reused rapidly), and stacking of finished products awaiting distribution (22), with very little interior space in a workshop dedicated to any type of storage (22).

48 Ammerman (1990, 641–42) estimates 10,000–20,000 m³ of soil, but Hopkins (2016, 34 n. 53) argues for 23,000 m³.

an open question.[49] However, there may have been a link between these two projects, possibly underscoring the power of the building's commissioner.

Regardless of the specific sequence, this land reclamation project and subsequent new construction in the area indicates this is a period when the Forum was becoming a focal point of the growing city.[50] The next known structures built were in the Forum (see Table 9.1): the Regia (its first phase,[51] and its later third-phase rebuild),[52] and a building near the Lapis Niger (590–580 BCE; Winter 2009, 144), hypothesized by Colonna (1988, 312) to be the earliest iteration of the Curia Hostilia. Solid buildings with brightly coloured terracotta caps would make for an impressive spectacle, and some were likely visible from the river. It is not until *c.* 590–580 BCE that temples were first built; a possible temple to Jupiter Feretrius on the Capitoline (Winter 2009, 148) — the first use of high ground for such architecture in Rome — and the Archaic temple in the Forum Boarium (Winter 2009, 149–50), each built one or several generations after the first Forum structures. The first buildings in Rome were thus used for a variety of purposes, but all adorned the growing urban core, drawing the eye from the port on the Tiber, and elevating the appearance of the early city.

The Individuals behind the Actions

Who, then, is our hypothetical Roman building commissioner? Someone who could have knowledge that something like this was possible to construct, who could locate and then bring in craftspeople — foreigners, possibly, to the site and even Italy itself — and initiate a project that would dominate part of the heart of Rome for several months while raw materials were extracted and turned into finished products, the sum of which resulted in what was the largest structure in Rome to date. This individual held significant social power; yet their name and title escape us.

It is well known that the historical record for this time is problematic at best, written by authors

such as Livy and Dionysius of Halicarnassus whose sources are lost or unnamed. Most of the sites in central Italy that are of archaeological note at this time, with the exception of Rome, are given either scant reference or none at all by these authors. Therefore, while it is tempting to mine historical accounts for the glimpses of the people and their motivations that they might provide, there are as many pitfalls, if not more, in using them in this way. Instead, I follow here a model proposed by Terrenato (2011), who sees Rome outside of the teleology of imperial documentary sources and instead as part of a continuum of activity of the landed elite, as demonstrated through material culture from the city's earliest periods into the Republic. Terrenato's argument forefronts the agency of individuals, specifically clan heads, within a heterogeneous power structure. He argues that the account of the creation of the Roman state in which the heads of clans, dominant since the Late Bronze Age (Peroni 1990), willingly and immediately allowed themselves to be superseded by a 'king' (*rex*) in an untested form of government, at a time when states were few and fledgling in the Mediterranean, only makes sense if these men were able to see the future pay-off for their actions; that is, knowing that the stable Roman state of centuries to come would be worth the contemporary sacrifice of the supremacy of their clans and ancestral cults to the newly formed state and state gods (Terrenato 2011, 235). Terrenato (2011, 236) proposes, instead, that these clan leaders acted as strong men within a 'weak' state which they manipulated to work for their own purposes. Essentially, he argues for continuity — seeing the activity of big men in the Late Bronze Age and Early Iron Age and the persistence of that activity through the early years of the Roman state, forefronting the actions of powerful individuals as seen in the archaeological record, rather than the events of a textual record written hundreds of years later.

The structures built in Rome mentioned above need not exist in opposition to a tradition of kings — indeed, there is nothing in this statement that argues *against* the Residence on the Sacra Via as having been built by 'royalty' — so this should not be seen as contradicting the ancient historians or modern scholarship which utilizes their writing. Instead, I argue that by taking this view of Rome we are able to then create a next step; to not simply read a textual record that fails to speak of the internal political structure of, for example, Acquarossa or Poggio Civitate and reach a dead end, but to instead see the power dynamics inherent in the building activity in Rome and then look at other sites through this same lens.

---

49 Ammerman 2016. See also Hopkins 2016, 30 and n. 41 for further comment on the dating dispute.

50 Hopkins (2016, 36–37) rightly points out that our knowledge of seventh- and sixth-century Rome is sparse at best, and that there were many other desirable locations for community growth beyond the Forum area, including the Esquiline, Viminal, Oppian, and Quirinal.

51 See above, n. 39.

52 Winter 2009, 144–48. The second phase of the Regia, as determined by Brown, was an extension of the courtyard and thus considered by Brocato and Terrenato (2016, 13) to be a subphase of the first rather than its own full structure.

Table 9.1. Buildings in Rome with terracotta-tiled roofs, seventh to mid-sixth centuries BCE. Data from Winter 2009 unless otherwise noted.

Roof no.	Name	Construction Date
1-1	Residence along the Sacra Via in the Roman Forum	650–625
1-2	First-Phase Building below the Later Regia in the Roman Forum	620 BCE[53] or end of the seventh century–beginning of the sixth century[54]
3-1	Building Near the Lapis Niger in the Roman Forum	590 or 590–580
3-2	Third-Phase South Building on the Site of the Later Regia in the Roman Forum	590–580
3-3	Temple of Jupiter Feretrius? on the Capitoline Hill	590–580
3-6	First-Phase Temple of Mater Matuta at S. Omobono in the Forum Boarium	580

Table 9.2. Buildings in Acquarossa with terracotta-tiled roofs, seventh to mid-sixth centuries BCE. Data from Winter 2009.

Roof no.	Name	Construction Date
2-4	Zone G, House B, Room F, Roof G:1	640–620
2-5	Zone M, Northern House, Roof M:1	640–620
2-6	Zone F, House D, Roof F:2	640–620
2-7	Zone F, House J, Roof F:1	640–620
2-12	Zone B, from Building Earlier than, and in between, House C and E; Roof B:1	620–610
2-8	Zone F, Building below Building C, Southern Room, Roof F:6	620–600
2-9	Zone F, Building below the Eastern Courtyard, Roof F:7	620–600
2-10	Campo dei Pozzi, Roof Sp:1	620–600?
2-11	Zone F, House G, Roof F:4	620–600
2-17	Zone O, Roof O:1	620–580?
2-13	Zone B, House E, Roof B:2	610–600
2-18	Zone F, House E, Roof F:11	600–580
2-19	Zone A, Roof A:2	600–580
2-20	Zone N, Building below House E, Roof N:4	600–580?
2-23	Zone A, Roof A:1	600–580
2-24	Zone F, Building(s) to West of Courtyard, Roof F:10	600–580
2-25	Zone G, Building below House A, Roof G:3	600–580
2-15	Zone F, Early Portico Building below Building C, Roof F:3	c. 600
2-16	Zone F, Building below House B, Roof F:5	c. 600
2-14	Zone B, From Buildings below House D, Roof B:3	600
2-28	Building in Northern Part of Zone G, Roof G:2	580–560
2-29	Zone H, House A, Roof H:1	580–560
2-30	Area 80, Roof SP:3	580–560
4-4	Unknown Building	570–560
1-10	Zone L, House A, Roof L:1	560–540
1-11	Zone L, House B, Roof L:2	560–540
1-12	Zone L, House C, Roof L:3	560–540
1-9	Zone J, Southeastern House, Roof J:1	560–540
4-5	Portico Building A in Zone F, Roof F:8	560

---

53 Brown 1974–1975, 19–21.
54 Brocato and Terrenato 2016, 12.

To illustrate the utility of this model I will discuss, briefly, just one other site as a case study in order to demonstrate the benefits of this approach; namely, that it allows us to more clearly see the patterns of socio-political dynamics across central Italy at a time when our information is rich, and yet still frustratingly incomplete.

The building activity in seventh-century Acquarossa is significantly different from that of Rome, so as to present an intriguing counterpoint to the types of political machinations that the historical sources discuss. As with Rome, the terracotta-tile roofed structures at Acquarossa are among the earliest known in Italy; a twenty-year window of construction begins in 640 BCE and sees four buildings constructed (see Table 9.2). These structures, labelled 'houses' by the excavators, are in three separate archaeological zones, but all on the tuff plateau, also called the acropolis, where the main settlement was located (Fig. 9.1); one in Zone G, one in Zone M, and two in Zone F. A fifth structure, built *c.* 620–610, was placed in Zone B, and another twenty-year wave of building added three more structures to Zone F while including structures also at Zone O and the Campo dei Pozzi, on the opposite end of the acropolis.

What we may find in this activity is a pattern similar to that seen in the coalescing of Early Iron Age sites; small groupings of activity on hills and plateaus, in a leopard-spot pattern (Naglak and Terrenato 2020), seemingly indicative of clan groups forging their own discrete locations even within what must have been a single settlement (Fig. 9.2). That the earliest buildings at Acquarossa, from a period that spans just a bit more than a single generation, show us this same pattern, but at a later time and utilizing this new, grander style of architecture, is something as yet unseen elsewhere in Italy at this time.

The years *c.* 610–530 see the creation of twenty-five more roofs (Fig. 9.3; Table 9.2). Many of these are their own new structures, some are repairs or partial replacements, and a few have no architecture with which to connect them, but the flurry of activity is significant. We can perhaps trace the development of this urban settlement; earlier huts being replaced by rectilinear houses, generally with one appearing in different 'neighbourhoods' first and then, over time, growing in number and contributing to the development of the built landscape of a rapidly growing settlement.

Further, we can speculate about a possible construction industry; surely, to support the *c.* 11,000 tiles produced per annum, as estimated by Wikander, there would have had to have been at least a semi-per-

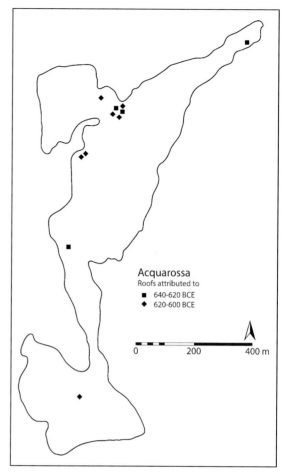

Figure 9.1. Locations of known terracotta-roofed buildings constructed in Acquarossa between 640 and 610 BCE (by D. Diffendale).

manent infrastructure to create such an output.[55] Indeed, Wikander (1993, 138) estimates that, based on the fact that only *c.* 4 per cent of the site has been excavated, there may have once been 1200 tiled buildings standing at Acquarossa at one time, and a total of 1700 built during the lifespan of the site, which had a total population of *c.* 4000–7000 people (Persson 1986, 43).[56] Though many other archaeological sites suffer from the same paucity of excavation, tiles appear in many contexts and *in-situ* architecture need not be uncovered in order to find traces of its roof; therefore, the evidence does not currently suggest that any other site in central Italy

---

55 No trace of any workshops has been found at Acquarossa, though the likely locations for where one might find such structures — often on the outskirts of a settlement and not within the main habitation area — have not been systematically explored (Wikander 1993, 137–38).

56 *Contra* this, Harris (1989, 378–79) states 'no less than 1250' residents would be expected for a settlement of Acquarossa's size, but Wikander (1993, n. 283) refutes this, saying *c.* 50 people per hectare was a very low estimate.

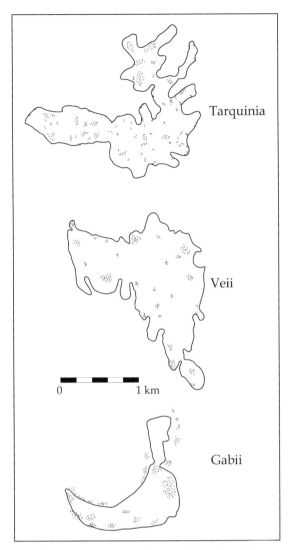

Figure 9.2. Areas of settlement at Tarquinia, Veii, and Gabii in the eighth century BCE as represented by surface scatters (after Terrenato 2019).

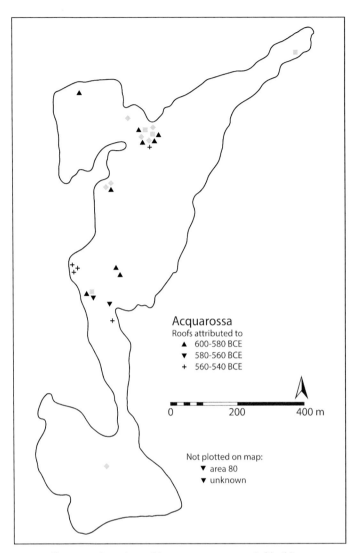

Figure 9.3. Locations of known terracotta-roofed buildings constructed in Acquarossa between 600 and 540 BCE; earlier structures are represented in grey (by D. Diffendale).

in the seventh or sixth centuries BCE had this same multitude of terracotta-roofed structures.

What, then, might we see in this activity? Rome's earliest structures are all in the Forum and its immediate environs. These are locations where we can be relatively sure that not just anyone might build. Such activity could fit within a monarchical government, be it a strong or a weak state; buildings constructed to amplify the possessors and places of power as perceived by the king or big men. But at Acquarossa, we instead see domestic structures built in discrete locations across the acropolis, and those structures then multiplying, with other locations being filled in as the decades progressed. Over the course of c. 110 years, over thirty structures were built, and the vast majority of these were domestic, seemingly without a temple or recognizable civic building — structures which we might expect as expressions of growing urbanism.[57]

It is probable that this pattern is therefore one of a plurality of powerful families, utilizing new architectural advances as a way to not only improve their quality of life but also to make certain statements. Internally, the statement would be about their wealth and power; surely the families who could opt into this activity were not only affluent but among the

---

57 While no temple has been identified so far, the excavators note the likely location of one which has gone unexcavated (Persson 1985, 42). Some structures are built c. 560 that appear to have a public function, such as Portico Building A in Zone F (Strandberg Olofsson 1986, 81; Winter 2009, 229–31) with elaborate architectural decoration, but the precise use of this structure is not known.

most affluent of that society, and a physical demonstration of that via architecture would be advantageous to them within the confines of said society. The process of construction we see continuing after the first generation or so of this phenomenon would then indicate more families participating in this new activity: a trend of conspicuous consumption. Externally, the statement made to the wider world would be dramatic: hundreds of red-painted terracotta roofs covering a raised plateau, among fertile fields, at the delta of two rivers, and likely with an as-yet unknown extension of the settlement off the acropolis, including the smoking, bustling, industrial area nearby. This view of an active, prosperous, and populous settlement with its monumentalized acropolis would speak of the collective power of the community as a whole; a potent message at an uncertain time.

Conclusions

I present here only two examples, but I believe they exemplify a pattern of activity in the seventh and early sixth centuries BCE. Tile roofs are simply one way to trace deployment of new technologies and the expansion of urbanism in central Italy, but there is much more to be found in this rich archaeological material than we have previously sought. Seeing these buildings as a series of problems and challenges, faced in various ways, in different places and at different times, allows us to gain more information. They tell us of the social, political, and economic contexts of the settlements where these roofs were employed and allow us to shed light on the needs and motivations of the individuals who created them. How buildings were utilized, not only as functional spaces for a growing population and an increasingly complex political apparatus, but also as visual statements for the communities that they adorned, is important to keep in mind. These sites purposely manipulated their appearance, mindful of their interactions — positive and negative — with neighbouring settlements, crafting statements for their contemporaries that, for us, are valuable elements of reconstructing the past.

Works Cited

Abrams, Elliot M. 1994. *How the Maya Built their World: Energetics and Ancient Architecture* (Austin: University of Texas Press)

Abrams, Elliot M., and Leah McCurdy. 2020. 'Massive Assumptions and Moundbuilders: The History, Method, and Relevance of Architectural Energetics', in *Architectural Energetics in Archaeology: Analytical Expansions and Global Explorations*, ed. by Leah McCurdy and Elliot M. Abrams (New York: Routledge), pp. 1–25

Ammerman, Albert J. 1990. 'On the Origins of the Forum Romanum', *American Journal of Archaeology*, 94.4: 627–45

——. 2011. 'Relocating the Center: A Comparative Study', in *State Formation in Italy and Greece: Questioning the Neoevolutionist Paradigm*, ed. by Nicola Terrenato and Donald C. Haggis (Oxford: Oxbow), pp. 265–72

——. 2016. 'On Giacomo Boni, the Origins of the Forum, and Where We Stand Today', *Journal of Roman Archaeology*, 29: 293–311

Ammerman, Albert J., Ioannis Iliopoulos, Federica Bondioli, Jill Hilditch, Alessandra Manfredini, Licio Pennisi, and Nancy A. Winter. 2008. 'The Clay Beds in the Velabrum and the Earliest Tiles in Rome', *Journal of Roman Archaeology*, 21: 7–30

Andrén, Arvid. 1940. *Architectural Terracottas from Etrusco-Italic Temples* (Lund: Gleerup)

Bernard, Seth. 2018. *Building Mid-Republican Rome: Labor, Architecture, and the Urban Economy* (Oxford: Oxford University Press)

Boëthius, Axel. 1978. *Etruscan and Early Roman Architecture*, 2nd integrated edn rev. (New Haven: Yale University Press)

Brandt, J. Rasmus, and Lars Karlsson (eds). 2001. *From Huts to Houses: Transformations of Ancient Societies; Proceedings of an International Seminar Organized by the Norwegian and Swedish Institutes in Rome, 21–24 September 1997*, Skrifter utgivna av Svenska institutet i Rom, 4°; Acta Instituti romani Regni Sueciae, 4°, 56 = 56 (Stockholm: Aström)

Brocato, Paolo, and Nicola Terrenato. 2016. 'Nuove ricerche sugli scavi dell'Accademia Americana alla Regia', in *Nuovi studi sulla Regia di Roma*, ed. by Paolo Brocato and Nicola Terrenato, Paesaggi antichi, 2 (Cosenza: Luigi Pellegrini), pp. 9–22

Brown, Frank E. 1961. *Roman Architecture* (New York: Braziller)

——. 1974. 'La protostoria della regia', *Atti della Pontificia Accademia Romana di Archeologia*, 47: 15–36

Colonna, Giovanni. 1988. 'La produzione artigianale', in *Storia di Roma*, ed. by Arnaldo Momigliano, Aldo Schiavone, and Carmine Ampolo (Turin: Einaudi), pp. 292–316

Cornell, Tim. 1995. *The Beginnings of Rome: Italy and Rome from the Bronze Age to the Punic Wars, c. 1000–263 BC* (London: Routledge)

Damgaard Andersen, Helle, and Judith Toms. 2001. 'The Earliest Tiles in Italy?', in *From Huts to Houses: Transformations of Ancient Societies; Proceedings of an International Seminar Organized by the Norwegian and Swedish Institutes in Rome, 21–24 September 1997*, ed. by J. Rasmus Brandt and Lars Karlsson, Skrifter utgivna av Svenska institutet i Rom, 4°; Acta Instituti Romani Regni Sueciae, 4°, 56 = 56 (Stockholm: Aström), pp. 263–68

DeLaine, Janet. 1997. *The Baths of Caracalla: A Study in the Design, Construction, and Economics of Large-Scale Building Projects in Imperial Rome*, Journal of Roman Archaeology, Supplement, 25 (Portsmouth, RI: Journal of Roman Archaeology)

Erixon, Sigurd. 2001. 'The Shepherd Huts in the Roman Campagna and the Characteristics of their Construction', in *From Huts to Houses: Transformations of Ancient Societies; Proceedings of an International Seminar Organized by the Norwegian and Swedish Institutes in Rome, 21–24 September 1997*, ed. by J. Rasmus Brandt and Lars Karlsson, Skrifter utgivna av Svenska institutet i Rom. 4°; Acta Instituti Romani Regni Sueciae. 4°, 56 = 56 (Stockholm: Aström), pp. 451–58

Filippi, Dunia. 2004. 'La domus Regia', *Workshop di archeologia classica: paesaggi, costruzioni, reperti*, 1: 101–22

Guaitoli, M. 1984. 'Le città latine fino al 338 a.C.: urbanistica', *Archeologia Laziale*, 8.6: 364–81

Hasaki, Eleni. 2005. 'The Ethnoarchaeological Project of the Potters' Quarter at Moknine, Tunisia. Seasons 2000, 2002', *Africa: nouvelle série des séances scientifiques*, 3: 137–80

——. 2011. 'Crafting Spaces: Archaeological, Ethnographic and Ethnoarchaeological Studies on Spatial Organization in Pottery Workshops in Greece and Tunisia', *Pottery in the Archaeological Record: Greece and Beyond; Acts of the International Colloquium Held at the Danish and Canadian Institutes in Athens, June 20–22, 2008*, ed. by Mark L. Lawall and John Lund (Aarhus: Aarhus University Press), pp. 11–28

Hopkins, John North. 2016. *The Genesis of Roman Architecture* (New Haven: Yale University Press)

Izzet, Vedia. 2001. 'Putting the House in Order: The Development of Etruscan Domestic Architecture', in *From Huts to Houses: Transformations of Ancient Societies; Proceedings of an International Seminar Organized by the Norwegian and Swedish Institutes in Rome, 21–24 September 1997*, ed. by J. Rasmus Brandt and Lars Karlsson, Skrifter utgivna av Svenska institutet i Rom, 4°; Acta Instituti Romani Regni Sueciae, 4°, 56 = 56 (Stockholm: Aström), pp. 41–49

——. 2007. *The Archaeology of Etruscan Society* (Cambridge: Cambridge University Press)

Karlsson, Lars (ed.). 2006. *San Giovenale, IV.1: Area F East: Huts and Houses on the Acropolis*, Skrifter utgivna av Svenska institutet i Rom, 4°, 26 (Stockholm: Åström)

——. 2017. 'Hut Architecture, 10th cent.–730 BCE', in *Etruscology*, ed. by Alessandro Naso (Berlin: De Gruyter), pp. 723–38

Kirby, Jolyon J. H., and Alan D. M. Rayner. 1989. 'The Deterioration of Thatched Roofs', *International Biodeterioration*, 25.1–3: 21–26

Klotz, Stephen A., Mazda Shirazi, Keith Boesen, Norman L. Beatty, Patricia L. Dorn, Shannon Smith, and Justin O. Schmidt. 2016. 'Kissing Bug (*Triatoma* spp.) Intrusion into Homes: Troublesome Bites and Domiciliation', *Environmental Health Insights*, 10.1: 45–49

Knoop, Riemer R. 1987. *Antefixa Satricana: Sixth-Century Architectural Terracottas from the Sanctuary of Mater Matuta at Satricum (Le Ferriere)*, Satricum, 1 (Assen: Van Gorcum)

Lancaster, Jerrad. 'To House and Defend: The Application of Architectural Energetics to Southeast Archaic Greek Sicily', in *Architectural Energetics in Archaeology: Analytical Expansions and Global Explorations*, ed. by Leah McCurdy and Elliot M. Abrams (New York: Routledge), pp. 95–113

Linington, Richard E. 1978. 'Alle origini di Tarquinia: scoperta di un abitato villanoviano sui Monterozzi', *Studi etruschi*, 46: 3–14

Mattioli, Chiara. 2023. 'From Clay to Vases: Operative Workflow', in *Kainua (Marzabotto)*, ed. by Elisabetta Govi (Austin: University of Texas Press), pp. 135–44

McCurdy, Leah, and Elliot M. Abrams (eds). 2020. *Architectural Energetics in Archaeology: Analytical Expansions and Global Explorations* (New York: Routledge)

Meggitt, Mervyn J. 1957. 'House Building among the Mae Enga, Western Highlands, Territory of New Guinea', *Oceania*, 27: 161–78

Naglak, Matthew C., and Nicola Terrenato. 2020. 'Central Italian Elite Groups as Aristocratic Houses in the Ninth to Sixth Centuries BCE', in *Roman Law before the Twelve Tables: An Interdisciplinary Approach*, ed. by Sinclair W. Bell and Paul J. duPlessis (Edinburgh: Edinburgh University Press), pp. 25–40

Noble, Allen G. 2007. *Traditional Buildings: A Global Survey of Structural Forms and Cultural Functions* (London: Tauris)

Pallottino, Massimo. 1991. *A History of Earliest Italy*, trans. by Martin Ryle and Kate Soper (Ann Arbor: University of Michigan Press)

Peroni, Renato. 1996. *L'Italia alle soglie della storia*, Collezione storica (Rome: Laterza)

Perreault, Jacques Y. 1990. 'L'atelier de Potier Archaïque de Phari (Thasos) la production de Tuiles', *Hesperia*, 59.1: 201

Persson, Claes B. 1986. 'Urbanistica: Acquarossa', in *Architettura etrusca nel viterbese: ricerche svedesi a San Giovenale e Acquarossa 1956–1986* (Rome: De Luca), pp. 40–46

Potts, Charlotte R. 2015. *Religious Architecture in Latium and Etruria, c. 900–500 BC* (Oxford: Oxford University Press)

Ridgway, David. 2002. *The World of the Early Etruscans* (Jonsered: Aström)

Ridgway, David, and Francesca R. Ridgway. 1994. 'Demaratus and the Archaeologists', in *Murlo and the Etruscans: Art and Society in Ancient Etruria* (Madison: University of Wisconsin Press)

Rostoker, William, and Elizabeth Gebhard. 1981. 'The Reproduction of Rooftiles for the Archaic Temple of Poseidon at Isthmia, Greece', *Journal of Field Archaeology*, 8.2: 211–27

Rystedt, Eva. 1986. 'Introduzione topografica e storia degli scavi e delle ricerche: Acquarossa', in *Architettura etrusca nel viterbese: ricerche svedesi a San Giovenale e Acquarossa 1956–1986* (Rome: De Luca), pp. 30–33

——. 2001. 'Huts vis-à-vis Houses: A Note on Acquarossa', in *From Huts to Houses: Transformations of Ancient Societies; Proceedings of an International Seminar Organized by the Norwegian and Swedish Institutes in Rome, 21–24 September 1997*, ed. by J. Rasmus Brandt and Lars Karlsson, Skrifter utgivna av Svenska institutet i Rom, 4°; Acta Instituti Romani Regni Sueciae, 4°, 56 = 56 (Stockholm: Aström), pp. 23–27

Sapirstein, Philip. 2008. *The Emergence of Ceramic Roof Tiles in Archaic Greek Architecture* (New York: Cornell University)

——. 2009. 'How the Corinthians Manufactured their First Roof Tiles', *Hesperia*, 78.2: 195–229

Stopponi, Simonetta (ed.). 1985. *Case e palazzi d'Etruria* (Milan: Electa)

Strandberg Olofsson, Margareta. 1986. 'L'area monumentale di Acquarossa', in *Architettura etrusca nel viterbese: ricerche svedesi a San Giovenale e Acquarossa, 1956–1986; Viterbo, Museo archeologico nazionale, Rocca Albornoz dal 19 Settembre 1986* (Rome: De Luca), pp. 81–92

Terrenato, Nicola. 2011. 'The Versatile Clans: Archaic Rome and the Nature of Early City-States in Central Italy', in *State Formation in Italy and Greece: Questioning the Neoevolutionist Paradigm*, ed. by Nicola Terrenato and Donald C. Haggis (Oxford: Oxbow), pp. 231–44

Torelli, Mario. 1985. 'Introduzione', in *Case e palazzi d'Etruria*, ed. by Simonetta Stopponi (Milan: Electa), pp. 21–32

Trigger, Bruce G. 1990. 'Monumental Architecture: A Thermodynamic Explanation of Symbolic Behaviour', *World Archaeology*, 22.2: 119–32

Tsakirgis, Barbara. 2005. 'Living and Working around the Athenian Agora: A Preliminary Case Study of Three Houses', in *Ancient Greek Houses and Households: Chronological, Regional, and Social Diversity*, ed. by Bradley A. Ault and Lisa C. Nevett (Philadelphia: University of Pennsylvania Press), pp. 67–82

Tuck, Anthony. 2021. *Poggio Civitate (Murlo)* (Austin: University of Texas Press)

Turfa, Jean MacIntosh, and Alwin G. Steinmayer. 1996. 'The Comparative Structure of Greek and Etruscan Monumental Buildings', *Papers of the British School at Rome*, 64: 1–39

Wikander, Charlotte. 1981. *Acquarossa, I.1: The Painted Architectural Terracottas: Catalogue and Architectural Context*, Skrifter utgivna av Svenska institutet i Rom, 4°, 38.1.1 (Stockholm: Aström)

——. 1988. *Acquarossa, I.2: The Painted Architectural Terracottas: Typological and Decorative Analysis*, Skrifter utgivna av Svenska institutet i Rom, 4°, 38.1.1 (Stockholm: Aström)

Wikander, Charlotte, and Örjan Wikander. 2006. 'Architectural Terracottas in Theory and Practice: Reflections on Thirty Years of Experience', in *Deliciae fictiles*, III, ed. by Ingrid E. M. Edlund-Berry, Giovanna Greco, and John Kenfield (Oxford: Oxbow), pp. 42–44

Wikander, Örjan. 1986. *Acquarossa: The Roof Tiles, I: Catalogue and Architectural Context*, Skrifter utgivna av Svenska institutet i Rom (Stockholm: Aström)

——. 1990. 'Archaic Roof Tiles: The First Generations', *Hesperia*, 59.1: 285–90

——. 1993. *Acquarossa: The Roof Tiles, II: Typology and Technical Features*, Skrifter utgivna av Svenska institutet i Rom, 6.2 (Stockholm: Aström)

Winter, Nancy A. 1993. *Greek Architectural Terracottas: From the Prehistoric to the End of the Archaic Period*, Oxford Monographs on Classical Archaeology (Oxford: Clarendon)

——. 2009. *Symbols of Wealth and Power: Architectural Terracotta Decoration in Etruria and Central Italy, 640–510 B.C.* (Ann Arbor: University of Michigan Press)

GIJS TOL

10. The Archaic Countryside Revisited

A Ceramic Approach to the Study of Archaic Rural Infill in Latium Vetus

ABSTRACT In the last decades, many field survey projects carried out in Latium have reconstructed a flourishing Archaic countryside that matches the strong urban development in this period (sixth century BCE). Recently, the nature and density of this Archaic rural infill was called into question by Attema and others (2017) in a contribution to the proceedings of the conference 'The Age of Tarquinius Superbus'. A crucial point emerged: that identification of phases of Archaic activity has often been based on pottery types and wares with long chronologies, pre- and postdating the Archaic period, and we poorly understand what a central Italian rural Archaic assemblage looks like. This chapter will add to this discussion by establishing the material fingerprint for a number of rural sites relating to this period — both published and unpublished (originating from the collection of the *antiquarium di Nettuno*) — and evaluate its implications by re-examining the evidence for Archaic occupation and state formation in several parts of southern Latium.

In Latium Vetus, as in wider Tyrrhenian central Italy, the Archaic period — roughly corresponding to the sixth century BCE — saw the culmination of a centuries-long process of settlement nucleation that resulted in a system of regularly spaced city-states boasting impressive fortifications and monumental public buildings. Traditionally, this process of 'urbanization' has been associated with a concomitant 'ruralization' of the hinterlands of these city-states, in response to the growing food demands of the expanding centres. The material reflection of this ruralization process has been found in a dense system of farmsteads that have been identified during decades of topographical work and intensive field surveys throughout the region. This sudden and wholesale rural infill provides a clear break with previous, centralized modes of rural settlement (with people residing in rural villages) and is generally thought to indicate the birth of a system of dispersed isolated rural settlement that would become characteristic of the later Roman countryside.

In this chapter I will critically re-examine the evidence for Archaic ruralization in Latium Vetus and its use as one of the indicators for (central) Italian state formation, mainly drawing on data collected within the Pontine Region Project (henceforth PRP), a long-running landscape archaeological project set in the Pontine region in southern Latium.[1] The long research focus on a single region has allowed the gradual building of an intimate knowledge of the material culture and settlement history of the region between protohistory and the Middle Ages, and has recently led to a phase of reflexivity, in which we have started to review earlier interpretations. One of the periods that has been most severely affected by this re-evaluation is the Archaic period, stimulated by the realization that — in line with criteria adopted by other projects active in Latium Vetus — the identification of rural activity belonging to that period has often been based on pottery types and wares with long chronologies, pre- and postdating the Archaic period, and that we actually have a poor understanding of what a rural Archaic assemblage is supposed to look like. Based on this realization, I will review the uncertainties in identifying Archaic rural occupation and attempt to get onto somewhat

---

1 This paper has benefitted greatly from discussions with other PRP members, including Peter Attema, Tymon de Haas, and, in particular, Jorn Seubers. The views expressed, however, are the author's own and do not necessarily reflect those of my project colleagues.

Corresponding author Gijs Tol (gijs.tol@unimelb.edu.au)

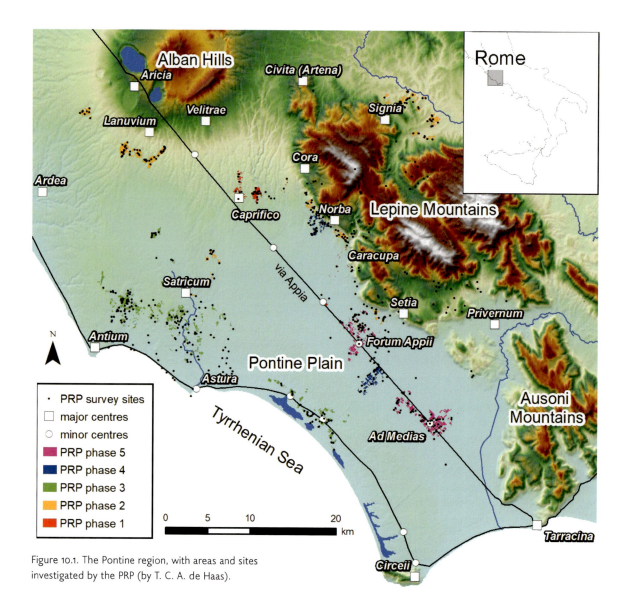

Figure 10.1. The Pontine region, with areas and sites investigated by the PRP (by T. C. A. de Haas).

more solid ground regarding the nature and scale of Archaic rural occupation. This review will initially be based on PRP work in the hinterlands of Antium and Satricum, two of the main Archaic centres in the Pontine region, but is subsequently extended to other parts of the region and Latium Vetus more widely.

Background

The Pontine region is situated in central Italy, some 50 km south of Rome. It consists of a coastal plain bounded to the west by the Tyrrhenian Sea, and to the north and east by the Alban Hills and Lepine Mountains. The plain itself can be divided into a higher system of marine terraces and, further inland, a lower area that is generally known as the Pontine marshes or Palude Pontine, a former wetland area that was reclaimed for large-scale habitation and agricultural exploitation in the 1920s and 1930s under Mussolini's fascist regime.

In this region, the PRP has been active for over four decades. Initially, the project aimed to provide a regional context for the University of Groningen excavations at the Latin town of Satricum, but it subsequently extended its scope to the study of human settlement and land use on a regional scale. Since the mid-1980s it has gone through several subphases (usually coinciding with five-year funding cycles), each with a distinct geographical and topical focus and by now some 40 km² of the region have been studied, mainly through systematic and intensive field surveys (Fig. 10.1).[2] In recent years it has devel-

---

[2] On the methodological development of the project see De Haas and Tol forthcoming. Critical output of the project includes Attema 1993; Attema and others 2010; De Haas 2011 and Tol 2012.

oped into an international and multi-institutional partnership, including the Universities of Leiden and Melbourne.

Historically, the Pontine region forms a particularly interesting area to study processes of early centralization and settlement nucleation, which are apparent from the Late Bronze Age and Early Iron Age onwards, and culminated in a system of regularly spaced settlements with urban characteristics by the Archaic period (Bouma and van 't Lindenhout 1997; Fulminante 2014). PRP investigations have targeted the immediate surroundings of several of these towns, both in the inland and coastal parts of the region.[3] In this contribution, the focus will be chiefly on the area between the Latin towns of Antium and Satricum. The first reason for this is that this area covers parts of the hinterlands of two well-documented Archaic centres, rendering it a good case study to investigate the effects that these developing towns had on surrounding rural areas. The second reason is that the available data for this area are of comparatively high quality, and have provided the foundation for several successive studies, leading to the continuous scrutinization and review of earlier results in light of expanding knowledge of regional pottery traditions and settlement development. We have high-resolution site and ceramic data from our own field surveys carried out here between 2003 and 2005,[4] supplemented by data from revisits and selective hyper-intensive site surveys carried out in the period 2006–2007.[5] Moreover, these field data were successfully combined with information acquired during an earlier large-scale topographic survey carried out in the late 1960s and early 1970s by Fabio Piccarreta (1977) for one of the *Forma Italiae* volumes, and with a large collection of objects brought together by a local amateur archaeologist — in most cases with precise provenance — that is housed in the *antiquarium* of Nettuno (Tol 2012, 134–211).

State Formation in Tyrrhenian Central Italy

Sometime between the end of the Final Bronze Age and the beginning of the Early Iron Age, communities in Tyrrhenian central Italy — previously organized in dispersed villages situated in open positions or small hilltops — shifted towards the occupation of large natural plateaux with good access to natural resources.[6] Although occupation of these plateaux initially appears to have been characterized by different settlement clusters (so called 'leopard-skin settlements') speaking against the presence of a unified community, in subsequent centuries these centres, almost without exception, exhibit clear signs of settlement nucleation and centralization, and the simultaneous foundation of smaller satellite villages (in sizes ranging from a few to as much as 15 ha), often placed at the edges of hypothesized territories.[7] By the Archaic period (roughly the sixth century BCE), 'urbanization' in Tyrrhenian central Italy reached a clear peak. Towns, throughout Etruria and Latium, demonstrate the presence of substantial defensive and infrastructural works, and the construction of large private residences, whilst many of the previously small sanctuaries increased in size and became monumentalized with stone foundations and elaborately decorated tiled roofs. The votive deposits associated with these large complexes are rich, emphasizing the accumulation of wealth within the settlement. Although the parameters to assess the transition towards larger and more complex settlements are thus well established, discussion continues about its motivations. Traditionally seen as an eastern innovation, Nicola Terrenato (2019, and in this volume) has recently argued for the emergence of urban societies in Italy based on endogenous socio-political transformations that were carefully mediated by contemporary elites.

The two Archaic towns in our case study area at first sight provide good examples of early Italian states. Although the evidence for Antium is a bit sketchy, as it is largely covered by the modern town of Anzio, it is clear that the Archaic settlement was concentrated on the Vignacce plateau, which boasted

---

3   For an overview of the different phases of the PRP see De Haas and Tol forthcoming.

4   These surveys were published in two preliminary reports (Attema and others 2008 and Attema and others 2010) and synthesized in Attema and others 2011. A further elaboration of the same data is presented in De Haas 2011. Additional data for the hinterlands of both towns was acquired during small-scale field surveys around Campoverde and in the Padiglione area (van Loon and others 2014).

5   Tol 2012, chs 3 (revisits) and 5 (hyper-intensive site surveys).

---

6   From the long list of literature on early state formation and urbanization in central Italy see two recent monographs: Fulminante 2014 and Terrenato 2019. For the possible mentalities behind the shift towards urban societies in central Italy see Terrenato (this volume).

7   On these secondary centres see, for example, Fulminante 2014, ch. 2 and Amoroso 2016.

impressive earthwork defences.[8] At Satricum, impressive fortifications were built as well, and on the acropolis houses and the main temple were constructed on stone foundations and with tiled roofs, replacing the traditional wattle and daub hut structures with thatched roofs. These buildings on the acropolis were aligned according to the same orientation, demonstrating overall planning, and paved streets connected the acropolis to the lower town.

State formation theory assumes that the development of these urban centres came with increasing levels of territoriality, with towns taking control over well-defined territories that became intensively exploited, stimulated by the food demands of the expanding centre. Whereas the direct surroundings of these centres would most likely be cultivated by farmers living in those centres, areas at further distance would undergo a process of ruralization, during which they became settled by farmers that, although living in the countryside, were socio-economically bound to the town, as such giving birth to the system of open settlement (consisting of isolated farmsteads).

Over the past decades, topographic studies and systematic field surveys have targeted the countryside surrounding many Etruscan and Latin communities, including Rome, and provided the quantitative evidence to assess the scale of ruralization in Tyrrhenian central Italy. These studies, almost without exception, record a strong peak in rural infill during the late seventh, and especially the sixth centuries BCE that has been considered the product of the expansion of the primary urban centres. For example, in the northern Suburbium of Rome, Carandini and his colleagues documented an increase from sixty rural sites during the seventh century BCE to 150 sites for the Archaic period, whilst the Tiber Valley Project recorded a degree of rural infill that would not be surpassed until the early Imperial period.[9] A similar trend is noted for the countryside of several large Etruscan centres; to name just one, around Cerveteri, an enormous jump in settlement from twenty-one to 330 sites has been recorded.[10] At the same time, the excavation of several important rural sites of Archaic date in the 1980s and 1990s (the

Auditorium villa, the farm at Podere Tartuchino (and two other Archaic sites) in the Albegna Valley in northern Tuscany, and the excavation of houses at Torrino and Acqua Acetosa Laurentina, among others) provide us with valuable insights into the variety of farmhouses belonging to this period, ranging from small, rectangular one-room structures at one end of the scale to larger buildings with a sequence of rooms around a central courtyard at the other end.[11]

The Ruralization of Antium and Satricum

Similar trajectories towards a rapid intensification of the exploitation of the countryside between the Orientalizing and Archaic periods have been mapped for several parts of the Pontine region, and the hinterlands of Antium and Satricum were initially thought to constitute the clearest examples of this process. Based on systematic and intensive field surveys carried out between 2003–2005, a dense and well-articulated system of rural infill was reconstructed (Attema and others 2011, 53–56), comprising both small, isolated farmsteads and several larger hamlets/villages clustering around later roads and river courses, whilst on the coast — based on earlier small-scale excavations carried out in 2001–2002 — a large, specialized site involved in the production of salt was situated (Fig. 10.2).[12]

It is important to clarify the material foundation adopted for this reconstruction of Archaic rural infill. Pottery of the Archaic period circulating in Tyrrhenian central Italy is rather well documented. It is characterized by an extensive repertoire of wares and shapes that — despite obvious local variations — shows remarkable similarities across this area.[13] However, our current knowledge of Archaic material culture is almost exclusively based on the study of urban (mainly religious) and funerary contexts.[14]

---

8   For the fortifications at Antium see Egidi and Guidi 2009; for the overall development of the town see Tol 2012, 1–7.

9   For the Roman Suburbium see Caradini and others 2006, 511–57; for the Tiber Valley Project see Patterson and others 2020, 109.

10 Cifani (2002) brings together evidence for rural infill around many Archaic centres. See also Carandini and others 2007, 563–64 for the area immediately north of Rome. It reconstructs a densely occupied landscape with individual farms located 150–200, or sometimes 300–500 m apart.

11 For the Auditorium villa see Terrenato 2001 and Carandini and others 2007. For Torrino see Bedini 1984. For Podere Tartuchino: Perkins and Attolini 1992. For Acqua Acetosa Laurentina see Bedini 1981.

12 The production of salt along the coastal stretch south of Antium has been attested as early as the Middle Bronze Age (Attema and others 2003; Nijboer and others 2006) and continued on a large scale until at least Archaic times as is indicated by excavations at the site of Depuratore (Tol and others 2012). See also Alessandri and others 2019.

13 These include a wide variety of characteristic coarse ware shapes (see Carafa 1995), and distinctive fine wares such as (Etrusco-) Corinthian pottery (Szilágy 1992) and bucchero (see Rasmussen 1979).

14 For the Pontine region see for example van Loon 2018 (for the cult place of Laghetto del Monsignore near

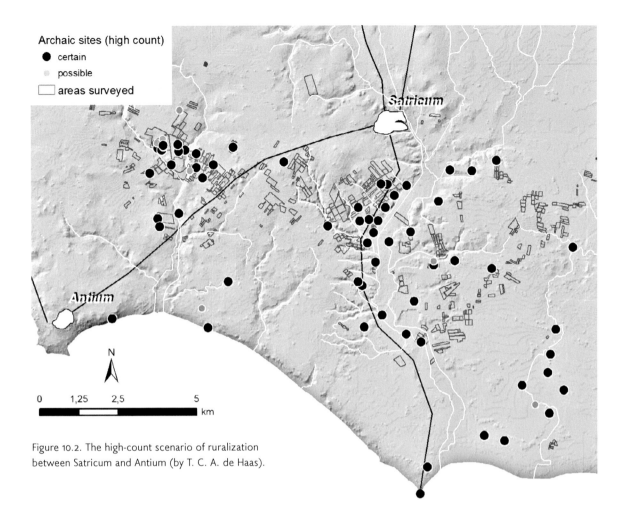

Figure 10.2. The high-count scenario of ruralization between Satricum and Antium (by T. C. A. de Haas).

In contrast, there is little evidence for what an Archaic rural assemblage looks like and, relevant for our region, to date there are no published examples of excavated Archaic farm sites for the entire Pontine region. In mapping Archaic activity during field surveys by the Pontine Region Project, it was assumed that material evidence for the period would be relatively difficult to identify compared to that of later periods on the basis of a few assumptions (Attema and others 2017, 196). First, that the period was characterized by low pottery consumption levels, especially when compared to the later Roman Republic and Imperial periods. Second, that consumed pottery would be of relatively poor quality (again compared to the highly standardized high-fired pottery of later periods), negatively impacting its survival in the archaeological surface record. And third, that the highly diagnostic and well-recognizable fine wares of this period — such as bucchero, impasto rosso, and (Etrusco-) Corinthian pottery — constituted 'luxury materials' that hardly circulated outside urban networks, with rural sites predominantly consuming a conservative repertoire of indistinct coarse ware shapes. These factors, which were thought to negatively impact the capacity of identifying Archaic rural activity, were further exacerbated by the assumption that the sixth century BCE saw the birth of the system of open settlement, meaning that much of the material evidence for the supposed Archaic agricultural boom (the actual farm buildings and their associated materials) would be buried under centuries of successive Roman occupation, giving Archaic materials a comparatively smaller chance of surfacing through ploughing. To compensate for these factors, from the outset the PRP adopted flexible criteria for the identification of Archaic-period settlements: 'certain' occupation was not only indicated by the presence of diagnostic pottery shapes and well-studied wares such as bucchero, but also by fragments — diagnostic and undiagnostic — of red-firing augite-rich pottery and tile, which are abundant in Archaic strata at Satricum (and other contemporary urban settlements), and occur

Campoverde) and Ginge 1996 (for one of the sanctuaries at Satricum).

Figure 10.3. Base fragment of a jar in the augite-rich red-firing fabric (photo by T. van Loon).

frequently on rural sites in the Pontine region (and wider Tyrrhenian central Italy — see Fig. 10.3).[15] In adopting these criteria, the PRP followed the example of many other central Italian field survey endeavours, which also strongly relied on the presence of red-firing tiles and pottery for the identification of Archaic rural settlement (see below).

Issues in Interpretation

During subsequent work in the same area, we found more and more reasons to critically approach the foundation on which these reconstructions of the process of ruralization for the hinterlands of Antium and Satricum were based. A prominent role in this has been played by a progressive increase in our knowledge of local ceramic traditions. Most importantly, we came to realize that the production of red-firing augite-rich ceramics, previously thought to be exclusively associated with Archaic-period activity, continued well into the period of the Roman Republic (e.g. Borgers and others 2018a and 2018b). Based on this realization the scale of rural infill for the area between Satricum and Antium has been revised in several different stages. First, De Haas used stricter criteria for the identification of Archaic activity in the area, although maintaining a strong reliance on fabric data,[16] resulting in a lowering of the number of Archaic sites recorded. In 2006–2007, systematic revisits to all known rural sites in the area were carried out by the author in the context of his PhD research (Tol 2012, 50–133). The resulting data further exposed issues of chronology: sites of supposed Archaic date consistently lacked diagnostic wares and shapes that could be securely dated to this period; a strong correlation was recorded between sites with red-firing augite-rich pottery and mid-Republican fine wares (black gloss ware); and numerous shapes that could be typologically ascribed to the early and mid-Republican period (including cooking jars and lids, *teglie* and *tegame*) appeared to be made in the same red-firing fabric. Based on these observations, even more restrictive criteria were adopted for the identification of Archaic rural activity, most notably rejecting the use of fabric data (apart from obvious categories, such as bucchero). On the other hand, red-firing tiles were still used as a good indicator for Archaic occupation. The adoption of these criteria resulted in a further, and more substantial, decrease in the number of recorded Archaic sites in the study area. To summarize then, by the adoption of different qualitative and quantitative criteria, we, in the timespan of only a few years, ended up with three completely different reconstructions of rural infill for the territories of the Archaic towns of Antium and Satricum, that range from a high-count scenario suggestive of significant agricultural intensification to a more conservative model evocative of much more limited rural infill.[17]

Archaic Domestic Assemblages

In the remainder of this chapter, I would like to look even more closely at the available data and outline a fourth scenario of even more restricted rural infill based on the following premise: that there is no reason to expect repetitive, impoverished, and undiagnostic assemblages on rural sites of Archaic date, and that sites on which no clear Archaic materials occur are therefore unlikely to be of Archaic date.

To begin with, we can critically question whether Archaic wares, both fine wares like bucchero and impasto rosso and the many distinct utilitarian pottery shapes documented in urban contexts, should be considered rare in rural assemblages. In a scenario of

---

15 For this fabric see Attema and others 2002.
16 De Haas 2011. For the identification of certain Archaic activity, he adopted both qualitative (presence of clear Archaic wares such as bucchero, as well as the presence of red-firing tile) and quantitative (at least ten fragments of red-firing pottery) criteria. Sites on which the qualitative markers were absent and on which less than ten fragments of red-firing pottery were recorded, were identified as 'possible' Archaic sites.
17 These three different scenarios were discussed in Attema and others 2017.

Table 10.1. Assemblages recorded for several Archaic (farm) houses.

	Coarse Ware	*Impasto chiaro sabbioso*	Depurated Ware	Bucchero	Impasto rosso	Other
Podere Tartuchino Late 6th/Early 5th c. BCE (N = 1382)	70.2%	22.9%	—	6.8%	—	0.1%
Auditorium, Period 1 2nd half 6th c. BCE (N = 100)	53.0%	21.0%	4.0%	6.0%	11.0%	3.0%
Auditorium, Period 2 500–c. 350 BCE (N = 285)	63.9%	15.1%	5.6%	5.6%	6.7%	2.9%
Centocelle, structure A	79.3%	14.6%	3.3%	2.8%	—	—
Centocelle, structure B	52.4%	40.8%	4.2%	2.5%	—	—

ruralization, we would expect ceramic assemblages of urban centres and rural sites to be of roughly similar composition, as the relationship between city and country presumes reciprocity. The foundation of rural farmsteads can be seen as a response to increasing food demands by the city, whilst rural sites, in turn, depend on the urban centre for protection and access to a wide range of goods and services. Bucchero in particular was produced in many different centres in Latium and Etruria, and local production of the ware has been hypothesized for Satricum itself, as well as for nearby Ardea.[18] To emphasize the ease of circulation of this ware, one only has to look at quantified data from excavated rural farm buildings in central Italy (see Table 10.1),[19] recording varied domestic assemblages that include the same distinctive utilitarian pottery shapes documented at, for example, Rome, and containing healthy percentages of bucchero, ranging from 2.5 per cent to as much as 6.8 per cent of all collected pottery.[20]

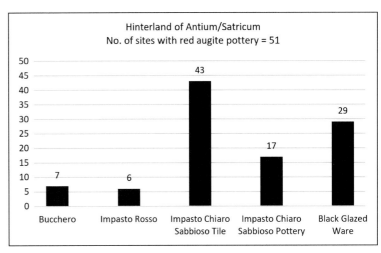

Figure 10.4. Material associations on sites with augite-rich red-firing pottery in the hinterlands of Satricum and Antium (by G. Tol).

Although we might argue that both the farmhouses at Podere Tartuchino and the Archaic phase of the later Auditorium villa are not representative for rural sites more generally — especially because the latter is at the top end of the settlement scale — this is much less true for the structures at Centocelle, whilst similar varied domestic assemblages are found on other excavated rural settlements all the way down to the small (4 m²), one-room structures constructed largely in perishable materials recovered at Casal Brunori south of Rome.[21]

Our survey work around Antium and Satricum, however, shows that the assemblages of rural sites, previously thought to be of Archaic date, can only rarely be matched with the convincingly Archaic assemblages that we know from both urban settle-

---

18 Gran-Aymerich (1993) lists Satricum as a production site for bucchero. Nijboer, however, argues that current evidence for local production is insufficient and that if bucchero was produced at Satricum, it was on a limited scale (Nijboer 1998, 83). For bucchero production at Ardea see Ceccarelli 2019.

19 For Podere Tartuchino see Perkins and Attolini 1992; for the Auditorium villa Carandini and others 2007; for the structures at Centocelle Volpe and others 2009. In Table 10.1, the class 'coarse ware' groups impasto/coarse ware counts with those for *dolia* (separately recorded for Podere Tartuchino — 15.5 per cent of all pottery and the Auditorium villa — respectively 2 per cent and 1.1 per cent for periods 1 and 2). Impasto rosso was only recorded separately for the Auditorium villa and is likely to have been grouped with 'impasto/coarse wares' for the three other structures. Contained in the 'other' category are two fragments of amphorae for Podere Tartuchino; one fragment of Laconian pottery, a loom weight, and a *fornello* fragment for Auditorium period 1; one loom weight, two fragments of *fornelli*, two fragments of Attic pottery, one fragment of Etrusco-Corinthian pottery, one fragment of *ceramica etrusca a vernice nera*, and one black gloss fragment for Auditorium period 2.

20 This contrasts with contemporary (Etrusco-)Corinthian pottery, which does appear to be extremely rare outside of votive and burial contexts.

21 This goes for the fortified settlement of Acquafredda between Veii and Rome (Carandini and others 2007, 511–20), for small rural buildings in the territory of Fidene (Cifani 2008, 185) and Ficana (Cifani 2008, 217–18), for the structures recorded at Acqua Acetosa Laurentina (Bedini 1981) and for the small structures at Casal Brunori (Bedini 1993; Buonfiglio and D'Annibale 2009).

Table 10.2. Archaic sites in the hinterlands of Satricum and Antium.

Sites	Location	Site type	Bibliography
15141	4 km north-west of Satricum	Farmstead	Van Loon and others 2014
11330	5.8 km south of Satricum	Farmstead/pottery production site?	Tol 2012, ch. 3
15108	5 km north-east of Antium	Farmstead	Attema and others 2010
15143	7.5 km north-west of Satricum	Hamlet	Van Loon and others 2014
15126	4.8 km east of Antium	Salt production site/nearby hamlet?	Tol and others 2014
11202	12.5 km south-east of Antium; 11.7 km south of Satricum	Unknown — finds at location of later villa of Torre Astura, close to mouth of the river	Tol and others 2012, ch. 3
15005	6.9 km south-west of Satricum; 7.2 km north-east of Antium	Farmstead	Tol 2012, ch. 3
11369	9 km south-east of Satricum	Farmstead	Attema and others 2008
15088 (Riserva Tallone)	8.6 km south-east of Satricum	Hamlet	—
15019	5.8 km north-east of Antium	Unknown	Tol 2012, ch. 4
15262	2 km north-east of Antium	Tombs?	Tol 2012, ch. 4
15072	1.4 km north-east of Antium	Tombs?	Tol 2012, ch. 4
15076	5.5 km south of Satricum	Farmstead	Tol 2012, ch. 4

ments and the excavated rural sites mentioned above. Where the red-firing coarse wares and tiles in these cases are consistently associated with substantial numbers of impasto rosso and bucchero that supports an early date of the find context, during PRP work they are generally found together with *impasto chiaro sabbioso* tiles and pottery, both of which date anywhere between the sixth and the third centuries BCE, as well as mid-Republican coarse and fine wares (black gloss) (Fig. 10.4).

Out of the fifty-one sites on which such red-firing wares were recorded during PRP surveys, these were found together with clear Archaic materials on only seven sites: six of these yielded both impasto rosso and bucchero fragments, and an additional one recorded bucchero only. Interestingly, it is precisely on these same seven sites that we also find diagnostic fragments of red-firing coarse wares and *dolia* of clear Archaic date, as well as in some cases small quantities of *fornelli*, weaving utensils, and some miniature pottery. This picture is reinforced by the evidence for five more Archaic rural sites that were identified through the study of the collection of the *antiquarium di Nettuno*, again demonstrating a mix of distinct wares and shapes. Moreover, the generally good state of preservation of all recovered materials militates against an adverse chance of recovery of Archaic materials (because of their supposed friability), although the generally small quantities of material recorded do suggest lower overall pottery consumption rates compared to later phases.

Based on the above analyses of Archaic material assemblages, from both excavated and non-excavated sites, it appears possible to pinpoint the ceramic fingerprint of an Archaic-period rural site. This fingerprint is largely similar to what we know from both urban sites and excavated rural contexts, consisting of a mix of fine wares, cooking and storage pottery, and occasional evidence for weaving. This leads to the conclusion that the majority of sites on which no Archaic wares or diagnostic materials were collected — and where the only supposedly Archaic materials are undiagnostic fragments of red-firing pottery and/or tile — do not date to the Archaic period at all, but are more likely, based on their frequent association with black gloss and other Republican wares and fabrics, to be of predominantly early or mid-Republican date.[22] Further substantiation of the likely exaggeration of Archaic rural occupation in the area comes from hyper-intensive site surveys on two sites that, during the initial PRP surveys, were thought to have been founded during the Archaic period based on the presence of red-firing augite-rich pottery and tile. Subsequent full surface coverage and total collection (yielding totals of 1875 and 29,229 fragments

---

22 There is no reason to assume a sudden and complete transition from roofs made of red-fired roof tiles to ones employing light-coloured roof tiles in *impasto chiaro sabbioso* at the transition from the Archaic to the early Republican period. At excavated sites, such as Acquafredda, healthy amounts of *rosso-bruno* tiles continue to be found in strata dating up till the early fourth century BCE, although over this period increasing amounts of ICS tile are recorded (see Carandini and others 2007, 511–24).

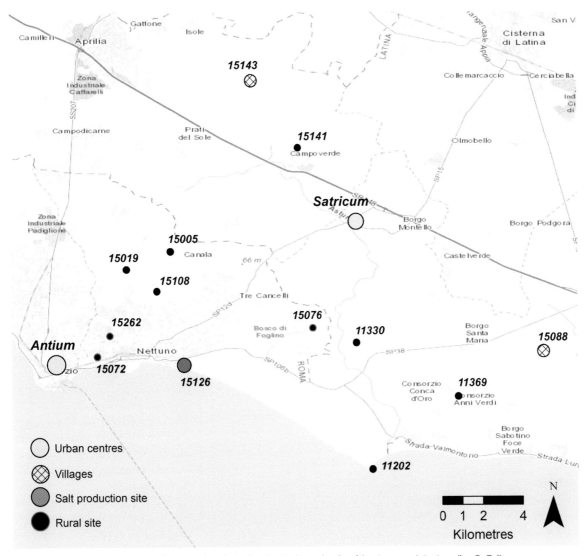

Figure 10.5. Distribution of Archaic sites in the hinterlands of Satricum and Antium (by G. Tol).

respectively) failed to identify a single ceramic fragment of secure Archaic date and rather suggested an origin in, respectively, the early and mid-Republican periods for these two sites (Tol 2012, 212–97; sites 15034 and 15106).

Reassessing Rural Infill in the Territories of Antium and Satricum

Although, in the above, I have questioned the degree of Archaic rural infill in the hinterlands of Antium and Satricum suggested by earlier research, this certainly does not mean that I am contesting that ruralization, in tandem with the strong development of these two towns, took place. The material reflection of their expansion and success is notable and, in a way, a revised reconstruction of Archaic rural infill — considering the problems outlined earlier — still provides a good fit with state formation theory (see Fig. 10.5; Table 10.2).

Although much of the immediate surroundings of Antium nowadays is heavily urbanized, two contexts from the collection of the *antiquarium di Nettuno* suggest the presence of graves in close proximity (*c.* 2 km) to the town. Three other small rural sites — two of which can be identified as isolated farmsteads based on their ceramic assemblages, comprising building materials, fragments of storage vessels and fine wares — are situated within a 5–7 km radius north-east of the town. Satricum nowadays still sits amidst a predominantly agricultural landscape, allowing us to better trace the process of Archaic ruralization. Interestingly, and mirroring observations around Antium, there is no rural settlement evidence until around 4 km from Satricum, perhaps indicative of the farming of these nearby fields by the town's inhabitants. On the other hand, the 'low

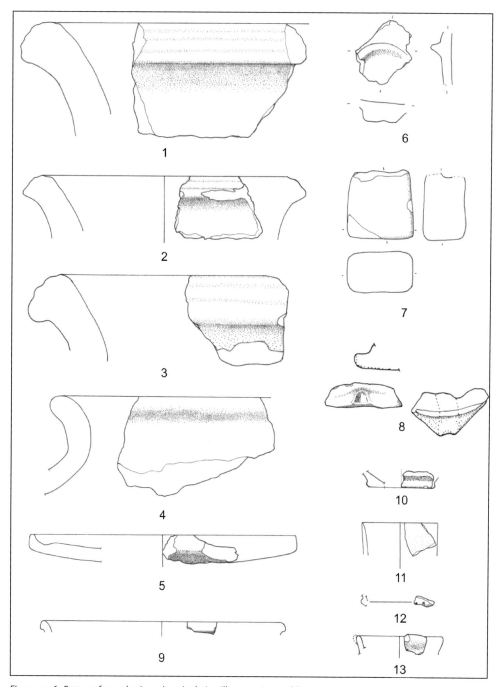

Figure 10.6. Pottery from the Iron Age-Archaic village at site 15088: nos 1–6 and 8 red-firing coarse wares; 7: red-firing loom weight; 9–13: bucchero.

Interesting too is the presence of at least two hamlets. The first, mapped during PRP investigations as a dense surface scatter measuring at least 4 ha (site 15143), can be found approximately 7.5 km north-west of Satricum and contained an abundance of *grumo*, red-brown tile, a wide variety of coarse ware shapes (including *dolia*), and weaving utensils. The other (site 15088) is presently unpublished but was recorded c. 8.6 km southwest of Satricum by the old director of the *antiquarium di Nettuno* as a dense and large spread of materials, including red-brown tile, a wide range of utilitarian pottery (including *dolia*), a loom weight, and large amounts of bucchero (Fig. 10.6). Both of these sites appear to originate in the Early Iron Age — roughly contemporary with the initial settling of Antium and Satricum — and fit a wider pattern of satellite villages that may have grown up in tandem with the emerging primary centres to exert (and extend) the latter's control over farming territories.[23] Another indication for the importance of satellite centres for the control of territories and resources is the large industrial site of Depuratore, approximately 4.8 km east of Antium, that was probably dedicated to the production of salt (Attema and others 2003; Tol and others 2012). The importance of this commodity and the scale of production attested (with remains scattered over a length of at least 100 m) strongly suggests that it was controlled from a nearby village in a system similar to that reconstructed for coastal Etruria (Pacciarelli 2009; Iaia and Mandolesi 2010). Further confirmation for the presence of a nearby settlement was provided by the find of a seventh/

count' model presented here places several small rural sites within a 4–9 km radius, both to the north-west and the south of Satricum, so within the supposed territory of the town. These rural sites display clear domestic assemblages consisting of table wares, pottery for cooking and storage, and loom weights that mirror those encountered in urban contexts, indicating the strong economic ties between town and countryside that one would expect in a scenario of mutual dependence.

---

23 A similar pattern can for example be identified for the area between the towns of Ardea and Antium, where smaller centres such as L'Altare and Colle Rotondo developed from the Early Iron Age onwards and remained active until at least the Archaic period. See, for example, Amoroso 2016.

sixth-century BCE *fibula sanguisuga*, probably part of a burial, just south of the site.[24]

Wider Implications

This stark revision towards a much more moderate degree of Archaic rural infill might be a localized phenomenon specific to the areas around Antium and Satricum, and it is entirely possible that other parts of Tyrrhenian central Italy demonstrate completely different settlement trajectories. Indeed, the varying degrees of settlement nucleation and ruralization in ancient Latium have been expertly discussed by Gabriele Cifani (2010, 2015) in several of his articles on state formation in central Italy. However, looking in detail at the actual material evidence that underlies the reconstruction of Archaic rural infill in other parts of Latium suggests, at the very least, that the reservations outlined above might have broader validity.

When looking at PRP data first, several of the issues in the identification of Archaic ruralization in the hinterlands of Antium and Satricum are echoed in other parts of the Pontine region. For example, during the Ninfa survey in the early 1990s, a densely settled Archaic landscape was mapped, indicating 'a strong intensification of settlement and land use with respect to previous phases' with a three-tier settlement system consisting of a large central site (Caracupa/Valvisciolo), a single smaller nucleated settlement and a dense landscape of isolated small farmsteads (van Leusen 1998). The identification of Archaic rural activity was based on the occurrence of 'coarse red firing pottery with augite temper, occurring in thick (*dolium*) and thin (*olla*) forms' on all sites and all fields surveyed. At the same time, there was a conspicuous absence of diagnostic shapes of Archaic date in this fabric, as well as of other decidedly Archaic wares (such as bucchero). Moreover, it was noted that although post-Archaic materials were hard to identify (a general problem in Tyrrhenian central Italy), Republican sites (indicated by black gloss ware fragments) generally occurred in the same locations as Archaic ones. Likewise, during systematic surveys in the western slopes of the Lepine Mountains, around the town of Norba, nineteen locations yielded red-firing tile and pottery, fourteen of which were interpreted as certain (five) or possible (nine) Archaic (farm) sites.[25] Also here, however, not

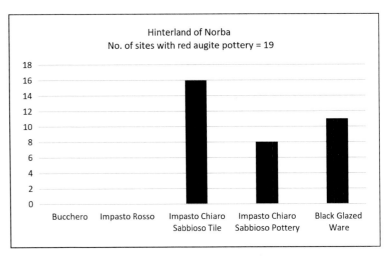

Figure 10.7. Material associations on sites with augite-rich red-firing pottery in the hinterland of Norba (by G. Tol).

a single diagnostic fragment of undisputable Archaic date was collected, and — like in the area between Antium and Satricum — there is a strong association between these red-firing fabrics and *impasto chiaro sabbioso* tile and pottery, and mid-Republican black gloss ware (Fig. 10.7).

If we move to other parts of central Italy, often similarly equivocal criteria have been adopted for the identification of Archaic rural activity. For example, many of the Latium Vetus surveys carried out around important Archaic centres just north of Rome in the 1970s and 1980s mapped a notable increase of dispersed settlement in their respective hinterlands during the sixth century BCE, interpreted by Quilici as the reflection of a booming regional rural economy during this period.[26] This reconstruction, however, hinges mostly on sites where the presence of *rosso-bruno* tiles, impasto and coarse wares was recorded, and there is again a notable scarcity of diagnostic Archaic shapes and wares, such as bucchero. Similarly, a recent reconstruction of rural infill between Caere, Rome, and Veii, considers the constant presence of tiles and pottery in a red-brown fabric as indicative of a densely settled Archaic landscape (Carandini and others 2007, 546–54). A more concrete example of the likely overestimation of Archaic rural occupation comes from recent work conducted by Jorn Seubers on the countryside around the ancient settlement of Crustumerium, a possibly Latin town situated circa 15 km north-east of Rome (Seubers and Tol 2016; Seubers 2020). The hinterland of this town has been the subject of several archaeological studies. The first surveys were carried out in the mid-

---

24 For the *fibula* see Tol and others 2012, 186.
25 De Haas 2011, ch. 5. The absence of clear Archaic diagnostics was already noted by the original surveyors for both the Ninfa and the Norba area.

26 See for example Quilici 1972 for the area around Collatia; Quilici and Quilici-Gigle 1986 (Fidenae) and 1993 (Ficulae).

1970s as part of the larger Latium Vetus project, and registered 128 Archaic-period rural sites, half of which were new foundations (Quilici and Quilici-Gigli 1980). This reconstruction clearly linked the success of the urban centre of Crustumerium to an intensive and successful (agricultural) exploitation of its surrounding countryside. Subsequent work in the same area by the Suburbium project, a large-scale mapping project of La Sapienza University in Rome, corroborated these results and confirmed the strong peak of rural habitation in the Archaic period (e.g. Fraioli 2016). In stark contrast with this picture, recent surveys by the Groningen Institute for Archaeology found very little evidence for rural infill that can be chronologically linked to Archaic Crustumerium. Covering several parts of its hinterland anew, it could in one sample area confirm an Archaic date for only one of the eight Archaic sites previously mapped in this area; in a second none of the original eleven 'Archaic' sites provided clear datable materials, and overall only three Archaic sites were mapped over an investigated area of *c.* 1.6 km² (Seubers and Tol 2016). Also here, the radical reinterpretation of Archaic rural infill was the result of advances in ceramic knowledge analogous to those outlined for the Pontine region. Where earlier work relied strongly on the broad date ranges of generic ceramic classes (such as red-firing coarse wares) and even building materials (for example, *rosso-bruno* tiles) to identify Archaic occupation, recent work established that these red-firing pottery and tiles were consistently associated with early and mid-Republican diagnostic pottery shapes and wares such as black gloss ware. The partial excavation of one of the 'supposed' Archaic sites, mapped during the Latium Vetus surveys, confirmed the complete absence of Archaic materials, instead exposing a small early to mid-Republican structure (Di Napoli 2016).

Concluding Observations and Future Directions

In this chapter, I have problematized the adoption of high-count models for Archaic ruralization in Latium Vetus. Perhaps inspired by examples from Etruria and Magna Graecia (with the classic example of Metapontum),[27] for too long there has been an optimistic assessment of the degree of rural infill that accompanied the settlement nucleation process taking place across this area. For many parts of the region, traditional reconstructions of the diffusion of

small farms are so rapid and drastic that they simply cannot be explained by any theory of demographic expansion but are more likely to be the result of a strong identification bias. Assuming an impaired visibility of Archaic finds in surface assemblages, many projects, including our own, have adopted very flexible criteria for the documentation of rural Archaic activity. Based on advances in ceramic knowledge and the excavation of a good (and growing) corpus of rural farms, we can now, with some confidence, adjust these criteria and set the identification parameters for Archaic rural activity. These include the presence of both construction materials (either *grumi* or tiles) and a wide range of distinct utilitarian pottery shapes, weaving utensils, and fine wares such as bucchero that circulated widely in both urban and rural areas. There is no reason to allow for a large contingent of destitute, and materially almost invisible, farmers sitting under a tiled roof without access to other forms of durable material culture or consuming only friable and poorly made coarse wares without any access to the wider market. It follows that we cannot simply assign an Archaic date to assemblages without unequivocal Archaic materials.

Based on a detailed reassessment of the evidence, we can start to reimagine rural infill around the Archaic centres Antium and Satricum. The degree of ruralization appears to be much more modest than in previous reconstructions, perhaps more befitting centres that were of relatively small size compared to the much larger Etruscan city-states (and the Greek colonies in Magna Graecia). Rural infill mainly takes place at some distance from these centres, suggesting that both Antium and Satricum — despite displaying urban characteristics — were principally agricultural settlements, inhabited by farmers who worked the surrounding fields.

Despite questioning earlier reconstructions of the degree of rural infill and its fit with standardized models of state formation, the essence of the settlement system presented in earlier works does remain largely valid. In line with developments across Tyrrhenian central Italy, the Early Iron Age presumably saw the initial settling of both centres, as well as the foundation of several smaller satellite villages that — at least in time — must have assumed a role in the demarcation, control, and exploitation of the territories (and their natural resources) of the expanding principal centres (Fulminante 2014, 215). During the Archaic period, significant changes occurred in this settlement configuration, when individual farm sites were founded in the territories of both Antium and Satricum, constituting the kernel of what in later times would grow into the famous Roman villa/farm system.

---

27 For Metaponto see, for example, Carter 2006.

Although it is difficult to speculate on the inhabitants of these rural abodes, it is likely that this populating of the countryside was the initiative of elites previously residing in the main towns or satellite villages. Elites are likely to have been the only ones able to muster sufficient manpower and resources for a shift towards isolated rural settlement that must have entailed the construction of durable farmhouses, the development of surrounding lands for agricultural exploitation, and infrastructural works to connect their farms to the outside world. Further indications of the prosperity of those inhabiting the earliest farms in our case study area are the fact that they — with the exception of one site — in later periods grew into Republican *villae rusticae*, whilst recorded assemblages suggest a high degree of market integration through the consumption of goods (such as bucchero) and surplus agricultural production (as indicated by the presence of *dolia*). At the same time, one of the recorded villages (site 15143) in our area was abandoned after the Archaic period, whereas in the wider area several others appear to contract or disappear (such as L'Altare and Colle Rotondo along the coast between the Archaic centres of Antium and Ardea), perhaps suggestive of a tighter and more direct control exerted by the principal centres over their territories (see also Carandini and others 2007, 542–43; Terrenato 2019, 249–72).

Although we must be cautious in extrapolating the above scenario, and we must reckon with a certain degree of localized variation in the scale of ruralization, I have demonstrated through various additional examples that the overestimation of Archaic rural occupation is a more widespread problem across Latium Vetus. A reassessment of the available evidence — based on data from the Pontine region and Crustumerium — suggests that the model of a sudden and dense settling of the countryside during the Archaic period needs to be replaced with one emphasizing a more gradual development of rural infill, characterized by initial small-scale occupation that accelerated in subsequent centuries (particularly the fourth and third centuries BCE) into a system of intensive agricultural exploitation of rural territories (see Terrenato 2019). The stark revision of the scale of Archaic rural occupation in Latium Vetus proposed in this contribution highlights that state-formation in (central) Italy more generally should not be seen as a uniform process, but rather one that exhibits significant regional (and perhaps even local?) variation. Although general developments across this area appear similar, the differing scale and pace of ruralization between Etruria and Latium Vetus suggests an important role for local factors and negotiations in the process (Terrenato this volume).

At the same time, the outlined uncertainties about the degree of Archaic rural infill and the different criteria that seem to have been adopted by our project, as well as others, to identify Archaic rural activity clearly demonstrate some of the limitations inherent to survey investigations. In the end the new reading of the evidence proposed in this contribution, is also a call for additional research (and especially excavations) into the Archaic countryside. Only by repeated excavations on Archaic rural sites will we be able to reveal the more detailed nature of, and local differences between, Archaic rural practices in Latium Vetus and begin to answer basic queries such as: What do Archaic rural sites look like? What agricultural exploitation strategies did they employ? And what are the links between these isolated rural settlements and nearby secondary settlements and towns?

Works Cited

Alessandri, Luca, Katia F. Achino, Peter A. J. Attema, Majoi de Novaes Nascimento, Maurizio Gatta, Mario F. Rolfo, Jan Sevink, Gianluca Sottili, and Wouter Van Gorp. 2019. 'Salt or Fish (or Salted Fish)? The Bronze Age Specialised Sites along the Tyrrhenian Coast of Central Italy: New Insights from Caprolace Settlement', *PLoS ONE*, 14.11: e0224435

Amoroso, Angelo. 2016. 'Settlement Patterns in South Etruria and *Latium Vetus*', in *Early States, Territories and Settlements in Protohistoric Central Italy*, ed. by Peter Attema, Jorn Seubers, and Sarah Willemsen, Corollaria Crustumina, 2 (Eelde: Barkhuis), pp. 83–100

Attema, Peter A. J. 1993. 'An Archaeological Survey in the Pontine Region' (unpublished doctoral thesis, University of Groningen)

Attema, Peter A. J., A. Beijer, Marianne Kleibrink, Albert Nijboer, and Gerard van Oortmerssen. 2002. 'Pottery Classifications: Ceramics from Satricum and Lazio, Italy, 900–300 BC', *Palaeohistoria*, 43/44: 321–96

Attema, Peter A. J., Tymon C. A. de Haas, and Albert J. Nijboer. 2003. 'The Astura Project, Interim Report of the 2001 and 2002 Campaigns of the Groningen Institute of Archaeology along the Coast between Nettuno and Torre Astura (Lazio, Italy)', *BABESCH: Annual Papers on Mediterranean Archaeology*, 78: 107–40

Attema, Peter A. J., Hendrik Feiken, Tymon C. A. de Haas, and Gijs W. Tol. 2008. 'The Astura and Nettuno Surveys of the Pontine Region Project (2003–2005), 1st Report', *Palaeohistoria*, 49/50: 415–516

Attema, Peter A. J., Tymon C. A. de Haas, and Gijs W. Tol. 2010. 'The Astura and Nettuno Surveys of the Pontine Region Project (2003–2005), 2nd and Final Report', *Palaeohistoria*, 51/52: 169–327

Attema, Peter A. J., Gert-Jan L. M. Burgers, and P. Martijn van Leusen. 2010. *Regional Pathways to Complexity: Settlement and Landscape Dynamics in Early Italy from the Bronze Age to the Republican Period*, Amsterdam Archaeological Studies, 15 (Amsterdam: Amsterdam University Press)

Attema, Peter A. J., Tymon C. A. de Haas, and Gijs W. Tol. 2011. *Between Satricum and Antium: Settlement Dynamics in a Coastal Landscape in Latium Vetus*, Babesch Supplement, 18 (Leuven: Peeters)

Attema, Peter A. J., Tymon C. A. de Haas, Jorn F. Seubers, and Gijs W. Tol. 2017. 'In Search of the Archaic Countryside. Different Scenarios for the Ruralisation of Satricum and Crustumerium', in *The Age of Tarquinius Superbus: Central Italy in the Late 6th Century*, ed. by Patricia S. Lulof and Christopher J. Smith, Babesch Supplement, 29 (Leuven: Peeters), pp. 195–203

Bedini, Alessandro. 1981. 'Edifici di abitazione di epoca arcaica in località Acqua Acetosa Laurentina', *Quaderni del Centro di studio per l'archeologia etrusco-italica*, 5: 253–57

——. 1984. 'Scavi al Torrino', *Quaderni del Centro di studio per l'archeologia etrusco-italica*, 8: 84–90

——. 1993. 'Insediamento arcaico a Casal Brunori. Problemi connessi ai tipi di insediamento ed al paesaggio agrario fra periodo arcaico e periodo repubblicano nel suburbio di Roma', *Quaderni del Centro di studio per l'archeologia etrusco-italica*, 21: 99–107

Bouma, Jelle, and Elisabeth van 't Lindenhout. 1997. 'Light in Dark Age Latium: Evidence from Settlements and Cult Places', in *Papers on Mediterranean Archaeology*, ed. by Maaskant Kleibrink, Caeculus, 3 (Groningen: University of Groningen), pp. 91–102

Borgers, Barbara, Gijs Tol, and Tymon C. A. de Haas. 2018a. 'Roman Cooking Vessels (*ollae*): A Preliminary Study of the Material from the Pontine Region, Central Italy', *Science and Technology of Archaeological Research*, 3.2: 314–25

——. 2018b. 'Reconstructing Pottery Technology and Distribution, Using Thin Section Petrography: A Pilot Study of Roman Pottery Production in the Pontine Region, Central Italy', *Journal of Archaeological Science: Reports*, 21: 1064–72

Buonfiglio, Marialetizia, and Maria L. D'Annibale. 2009. 'Le strutture di Casal Brunori: relazione preliminare', in *Suburbium*, II: *Il Suburbio di Roma dalla fine dell'età monarchica alla nascita del sistema delle ville (V–II secolo a.C.)*, ed. by Vincent Jolivet, Carlo Pavolini, Maria A. Tomei, and Roberto Volpe, Collection de l'École française de Rome, 419 (Rome: École francaise de Rome), pp. 241–59

Carafa, Paolo. 1995. *Officine ceramiche di età regia: produzione di ceramica in impasto a Roma dalla fine dell'VIII alla fine del VI secolo a.C.* (Rome: L'Erma di Bretschneider)

Carandini, Andrea, Maria T. D'Alessio, and Helga Di Giuseppe (eds). 2007. *La fattoria e la villa dell'Auditorium* (Rome: L'Erma di Bretschneider)

Carter, Joseph C. 2006. *Discovering the Greek Countryside at Metaponto* (Ann Arbor: University of Michigan Press)

Ceccarelli, Letizia. 2019. 'Analisi archeometriche e statistiche per la caratterizzazione di produzioni di bucchero', *Archeologia e calcolatori*, 30: 387–404

Cifani, Gabriele. 2002. 'Notes on the Rural Landscape of Central Tyrrhenian Italy in the 6th–5th Centuries and its Social Significance', *Journal of Roman Archaeology*, 15: 247–60

——. 2008. *Architettura romana archaica: edilizia e società tra monarchia e repubblica* (Rome: L'Erma di Bretschneider)

——. 2010. 'State Formation and Ethnicities from the 8th to 5th Century BC in the Tiberine Valley (Central Italy)', *Social Evolution and History*, 9.2: 53–69

——. 2015. 'Osservazioni sui paesaggi agrari, espropri e colonizzazione nella prima età repubblicana', *Mélanges de l'École française de Rome: antiquité*, 127: 429–37

De Haas, Tymon C. A. 2011. *Fields, Farms and Colonists: Intensive Field Survey and Early Roman Colonization in the Pontine Region, Central Italy*, Groningen Archaeological Studies, 15 (Eelde: Barkhuis)

De Haas, Tymon C. A., and Gijs W. Tol. Forthcoming. 'The Analytical Potential of Intensive Field Survey Data: Developments in the Collection, Analysis and Interpretation of Surface Ceramics within the Pontine Region Project', in *Fields, Sherds and Scholars: Recording and Interpreting Survey Ceramics*, ed. by Anna Meens, Margarita Nazou, and Winfred van de Put

Di Napoli, Andrea. 2016. 'Exploratory Trenches in the Southern Territory of Ancient Crustumerium (Tenuta Inviolatella Salaria)', in *Early States, Territories and Settlements in Protohistoric Central Italy*, ed. by Peter J. Attema, Jorn Seubers, and Sarah Willemsen, Corollaria Crustumina, 2 (Eelde: Barkhuis), pp. 33–49

Egidi, Roberto, and Alessandro Guidi. 2009. 'Anzio: saggi di scavo sul Vallo Volsco', *Lazio e Sabina*, 5: 355–61

Fraioli, Fabiola. 2016. 'The Southern Ager of the Ancient City of Crustumerium', in *Early States, Territories and Settlements in Protohistoric Central Italy*, ed. by Peter Attema, Jorn Seubers, and Sarah Willemsen, Corollaria Crustumina, 2 (Eelde: Barkhuis), pp. 17–31

Fulminante, Francesca. 2014. *The Urbanisation of Rome and Latium Vetus from the Bronze Age to the Archaic Era* (Cambridge: Cambridge University Press)

Ginge, Birgitte. 1996. 'Excavations at Satricum (Borgo le Ferriere) 1907–1910: Northwest Necropolis, Southwest Sanctuary and Acropolis' (unpublished doctoral thesis, University of Amsterdam)

Gnade, Marijke (ed.). 2007. *Satricum: trenta anni di scavi olandesi* (Leuven: Peeters)

Gran-Aymerich, Jean. 1993. 'Observations générales sur l'évolution et la diffusion du bucchero', in *Produzione artigianale ed esportazione nel mondo antico: il bucchero etrusco*, ed. by Maria Bonghi Jovino (Milan: Edizioni), pp. 19–41

Iaia, Cristiano, and Alessandro Mandolesi. 2010. 'Comunità e territori nel Villanoviano evoluto dell'Etruria meridionale', in *Preistoria e protostoria in Etruria 9: L'alba dell'Etruria; Fenomeni di continuità e trasformazione nei secoli XII–VII a.C.; ricerche e scavi*, ed. by Nuccia Negroni Catacchio (Milan: Centro studi di preistoria e archeologia), pp. 61–77

Leusen, P. Martijn van. 1998. 'Archaic Settlement and Early Roman Colonisation of the Lepine Foothills', *Assemblage*, 4: 48–63

Loon, Tanja van. 2018. 'Defining the Ritual, Analyzing Society. The Social Significance of Material Culture in Pre-Roman Cult Places of *Latium Vetus*' (unpublished doctoral thesis, University of Groningen)

Loon, Tanja van, Sarah Willemsen, and Gijs Tol. 2014. 'Sites and Finds of the Campoverde and Padiglione Surveys of the Pontine Region Project (2005)', *Palaeohistoria*, 55/56: 105–48

Nijboer, Albert J. 1998. 'From Household Production to Workshops. Archaeological Evidence for Economic Transformations, Pre-monetary Exchange and Urbanisation in Central Italy from 800 to 400 BC' (unpublished doctoral thesis, University of Groningen)

Nijboer, Albert, Peter A. J. Attema, and Gerard van Oortmerssen. 2006. 'Ceramics from a Late Bronze Age Saltern on the Coast near Nettuno', *Palaeohistoria*, 47/48: 141–205

Pacciarelli, Marco. 2009. 'Verso i centri protourbani: situazioni a confronto da Etruria meridionale, Campania e Calabria', *Scienze dell'antichità*, 15: 371–416

Patterson, Helen, Robert Witcher, and Helga Di Giuseppe. 2020. *The Changing Landscapes of Rome's Northern Hinterland: The British School at Rome's Tiber Valley Project*, Archaeopress Roman Archaeology, 70 (Oxford: Archaeopress)

Perkins, Philip, and Ida Attolini. 1992. 'An Etruscan Farm at Podere Tartuchino', *Papers of the British School at Rome*, 60: 71–134

Piccarreta, Fabio. 1977. *Astura* (Florence: Olschki)

Quilici, Lorenzo. 1974. *Collatia* (Rome: Consiglio nazionale delle ricerche)

Quilici, Lorenzo, and Stefania Quilici-Gigli. 1980. *Crustumerium* (Rome: Consiglio nazionale delle ricerche)

——. 1986. *Fidenae* (Rome: Consiglio nazionale delle ricerche)

——. 1993. *Ficulae* (Rome: Consiglio nazionale delle ricerche)

Rasmussen, Tom B. 1979. *Bucchero Pottery from Southern Etruria* (Cambridge: Cambridge University Press)

Seubers, Jorn F. 2020. *Scratching through the Surface: Revisiting the Archaeology of City and Country in Crustumerium and North Latium Vetus between 850 and 300 BC*, Corollaria Crustumina, 3 (Eelde: Barkhuis)

Seubers, Jorn F., and Gijs W. Tol. 2016. 'City, Country and Crisis in the *Ager Crustuminus*. Confronting Legacy Data with Resurvey Results in the Territory of Ancient Crustumerium', *Palaeohistoria*, 57/58: 137–234

Szilágyi, János G. 1992. *Ceramica etrusco-corinzia figurata, I: 630–580 a.C.* (Florence: Olschki)

Terrenato, Nicola. 2001. 'The Auditorium Site in Rome and the Origins of the Villa', *Journal of Roman Archaeology*, 14: 5–32

——. 2019. *The Early Roman Expansion into Italy: Elite Negotiation and Family Agendas* (Cambridge: Cambridge University Press)

Tol, Gijs W. 2012. *A Fragmented History: A Methodological and Artefactual Approach to the Study of Ancient Settlement in the Territories of Satricum and Antium*, Groningen Archaeological Studies, 18 (Eelde: Barkhuis)

Tol, Gijs W., Tanja van Loon, Peter A. J. Attema, and Albert J. Nijboer. 2012. 'Protohistoric Sites on the Coast between Nettuno and Torre Astura (Pontine Region, Lazio, Italy)', *Palaeohistoria*, 53/54: 161–93

Volpe, Rita, Marco Bettelli, Silvia Festuccia, and Esmeralda Remotti. 2009. 'Contesti di VI secolo a.C. sul pianoro di Centocelle (Roma)', in *Ceramica, abitati, territorio nella bassa valle del Tevere e Latium Vetus*, ed. by Marco Rendeli, Collection de l'École française de Rome, 425 (Rome: École française de Rome), pp. 125–36

CAMILLA NORMAN

11. Ritual Connectivity in Adriatic Italy

ABSTRACT Our understanding of the religious behaviours of the indigenous populations of pre-Roman Italy is generally quite poor. This is especially true of the south-east, where there is virtually no epigraphic evidence and, prior to the arrival of Greek settlers, people did not typically worship in purpose-built environments, nor use cultic paraphernalia which is readily recognizable in the archaeological record. There can be detected, however, a certain iconographic vocabulary shared across a number of cultures in seventh- to fifth-century BCE peninsular Italy, plausibly intended to recall contemporary ritual practices. The same images can repeatedly be found together on objects, in a range of media, produced in various geographic and social contexts. When taken individually, the vignettes depicted on any one of these items ostensibly come from either the sacred sphere (processing, for example) or the secular (weaving, for example). Yet the selection of images is clearly deliberate. When read together they can be understood as individual moments in time from the same ritual system: a specific phenomenon in indigenous, Archaic Italy, which, judging from evidence from the Hallstatt culture, may well have been transmitted from further north. Using the concepts of 'lived religion' and 'ritual ecology', this chapter posits that certain clusters of ritualized behaviours were common to a wide range of pre- and proto-historic Italic communities.

A distinctive set of images — a procession; a figure with a lyre/handloom; figures weaving at a vertical loom; two figures working at a mortar and pestle; the tripod cauldron; dancing; and illusions to sacrifice — can be found on stelae and pottery produced by indigenous communities in Italy during the seventh to fifth centuries BCE. The images, taken individually, seem eclectic and illustrate both overtly religious behaviours and seemingly mundane tasks, as well as activities from somewhere in between. Their strong mutual association, however, across a range of media, suggests that they can and should be read together, plausibly forming individual moments from a shared 'ritual system' — an interconnected series of elements and activities, which together form an assemblage which is able to be both identified and utilized by participants within a particular sacral context.[1] Whether a 'ritual system' existed or not, a shared iconographic system is clearly visible, and both its longevity, stretching back to the Bronze Age, and extent, reaching far beyond Adriatic Italy, provide vitally important clues about the nature of connective networks within this part of the Mediterranean basin.

This chapter explores the possible timing, routes, and mechanisms by which knowledge of the iconographic system, and possible associated ritual system, may have been transmitted and become variously rooted in place.[2] The geographical spread of the artefacts bearing the imagery, and their places of production, suggest ideas about their form and purpose travelled back and forth within a network of connectivity which largely operated distinct from that generated by contact with the eastern Mediterranean. This network operated along different and localized pathways from that which connected Italy to

---

1 For 'ritual systems' see particularly Bell 1997. Individual features may have had meaning on their own, yet similar or even identical symbols of activities could have had different meanings in different contexts, assuming a greater ritual potential when functioning within this wider, and mutually comprehensible, ritual framework. As an example, one might think of kneeling in the Christian liturgical system. While there are many reasons one might kneel, or be depicted kneeling, once this activity has been activated or understood within a ritual context it is immediately imbued with heightened meaning and importance.

2 As part of a wider project, a recent paper (Norman 2023) presented the material evidence in detail, sought to reconstruct the physical and cognitive spaces in which ritual took place in Archaic non-Greek Italy, and explored the religious, social, and sensorial experiences of the participants.

Corresponding author Camilla Norman (camilla.norman@sydney.edu.au)

Adoption, Adaption, and Innovation in Pre-Roman Italy: Paradigms for Cultural Change, ed. by Jeremy Armstrong and Aaron Rhodes-Schroder, AMW 3 (Turnhout, 2023), pp. 177–192 · BREPOLS 🟊 PUBLISHERS · 10.1484/M.AMW-EB.5.133273

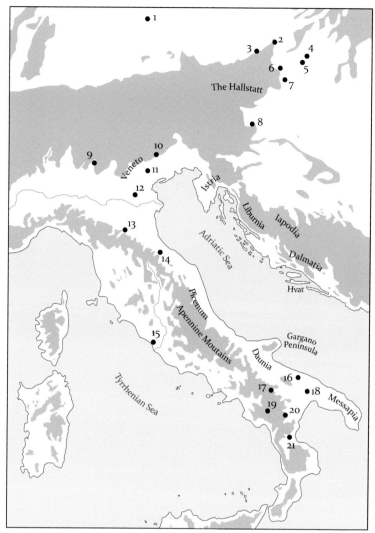

Figure 11.1. Map showing the find-spots, sites, and regions mentioned in the text. 1) Schirdorf; 2) Ernstbrunn; 3) Reichersdorf; 4) Janíky-Dolné Janíky; 5) Nové Košariská; 6) Loretto; 7) Sopron; 8) Kleinklein; 9) Val Camonica; 10) Alpago; 11) Montebelluna; 12) Este; 13) Bologna; 14) Verucchio; 15) Cerveteri; 16) Ruvo di Puglia; 17) Ripacandida; 18) Monte Sennace; 19) Sala Consilina; 20) Guardia Perticara; 21) Francavilla Marittima.

Motifs of a Ritual System in Daunia and Southern Italy

The study takes as its starting point imagery on the statue-stelae of Daunia (northern Apulia), produced from c. the mid-seventh to early fifth centuries BCE (Nava 1980; 1988; Norman forthcoming), which seems to offer the most complete set of the images. The iconography and associated artefacts that form the basis of this discussion have been discussed in more detail elsewhere (see Norman 2023). However, a brief summary of the relevant motifs, and, where pertinent, their object biographies and history of scholastic interpretation is necessary for the argument to follow (Fig. 11.1).

Although there are over 1400 known examples of Daunian statue-stelae, not one has been found in its primary context, and so their exact function is uncertain. A review of other statue-stelae, alongside what little is known of their find-spots, indicates that they were likely intended to both honour the dead — perhaps in general rather than on a one-to-one basis — as well as mark territory (Norman forthcoming, ch. 4). Each stele is comprised of a single slab of limestone, standing anywhere between 30 to 160 cm in height. They are incised on all sides to outline the figure of a human in long, richly decorated robes, with arms held symmetrically across the chest. The male figures feature arms and armour (a 'heart-protector' and sword on the front and circular shield on the back), while the female figures wear aprons, have decorated forearms, and are adorned with jewellery (necklaces, fibulae, and pendants). The heads of the stelae are separate, sitting atop of the slab. They are either carved with facial features or left plain, and are either roughly conical (female) or spherical (male) in shape. All incised elements were further picked out with colour, specifically black, red, and white, of which only faint traces remain today.

Approximately a quarter of the corpus features more extensive decoration. This takes the form of small figural scenes incised within the borders established by the geometric designs of the robes. Many of these scenes, at first, appear mundane in nature, depicting episodes that could simply be drawn from everyday activities. However, when considered within the context of the media, and in relation to the other types of scenes that they commonly appear alongside upon the same stele, patterns emerge which suggest that many of these 'everyday' activities were associated with a greater ritualized or performative significance. In short, the Daunians seem to have depicted their customs, rites, and cosmological views upon these stelae. The Daunians made no use of writing, did

the eastern Mediterranean, often running north/south along the eastern coast of the peninsula and encompassing the full extent of the upper Adriatic basin. The diverse ways in which the imagery was manifested further suggests that these ideas, and the performance of them, evolved and transmuted along the way, being incorporated into ritualized behaviours in varying degrees and configurations as was considered fitting in each locality. All indications are that, by the Archaic period, the imagery was widespread, and the meanings behind it solidly embedded in the cultural fabric of the region.

not typically depict figures upon their pottery nor in wall paintings, and produced only a small number of figurines and even fewer architectural sculptures. As such, the stelae provide essentially the only self-representation we have for the Daunians of this period, and are in fact one of the best sources available for the scrutiny of ritual behaviours in indigenous pre- and proto-historic Italy.

In particular, the imagery on the stelae is vitally important for the light that it can shed on aspects of organized and communal religious practices among the Daunians. The lack of other, more explicit forms of evidence means that the ritual systems of Daunia and their performance are not otherwise readily visible. The context of these images is important, both in relation to other scenes on the same stele and to the stelae themselves, and within the broader context of ritual practices that are found throughout the Italian Peninsula in this period. A number of scenes immediately stand out as strongly suggestive of ritual practices; others can be understood as such only through their frequent association with other image types and their placement upon the stelae. Certain idiosyncratic scenes that also seemingly portray ritual activities imply — by virtue of being found on more than one stele of diverse manufacture, style, and dating — that there was a rich and well-entrenched ritual system in Daunia by the Archaic period. One such notable example is of a rite in which two seated figures face each other, one tending to the outstretched foot of the other, which appears on both Manfredonia 944 (Nava 735; Norman F348)[3] and Manfredonia 25001 (Norman F600; Tunzi 2011, no. 12; Norman 2023, fig. 1a–b).

The most common scene of ritual to be found on the Daunian stelae is that of a procession, perhaps intended to show the exchange of gifts at, or prior to, a wedding (Norman 2011a). The procession, or a shorthand version of it, occurs on approximately seventy of the stelae, the fullest versions of which show two files of women coming together, one of which is headed by a male. The lead female of the other file and this male hold between them what is probably a lyre, or possibly a handloom. There are only

Figure 11.2. Upper half of a female Daunian stele Manfredonia 1008 (55 × 36 × 5 cm) and Manfredonia 1217 (adapted from Nava 1980, pls 256–57, 318).

two renditions that include both files: Manfredonia 1008 (Fig. 11.2: see Nava 775; Norman F368) and Manfredonia 1438 (Nava 1122; Norman F547). More commonly, the man is alone.

A survey of the stelae that carry procession imagery reveals that there is a close link between this scene type and imagery relating to weaving. Thirteen stelae carry a weaving scene, which shows one or more females working at a standing loom (D'Ercole 2000).[4] Eight of these stelae also carry procession imagery. The remaining five are fragments; the stelae they come from may very well have had processions on them also. With a few notable exceptions (for the most part the very few male stelae among the group), stelae with procession and/or weaving imagery rarely carry other scene types. It is posited, therefore, that, under certain circumstances, weaving in Archaic Daunia (as elsewhere) was practised as a ritualized activity, the products of which were worn, gifted, or otherwise associated with a ritual context (Scheid and Svenbro 1996). A good example is the temple of Athena on the Timpone della Motta at Francavilla Marittima in the hinterland of the Ionian Gulf, where Kleibrink Maaskant (2003) has identified a native Italian cult involving the production and dedication of textiles. It is one

---

3   Nava catalogue numbers for the Daunian stelae are from Nava 1980, while Norman numbers refer to Norman forthcoming, in which F = female, M = male, and U = unknown gender.

4   According to my reckoning: Norman F263, F264, F269, F287, F292, F297, F339, F461, F531, F540, F665, M67, U201.

Figure 11.3. Drawing of the mortar and pestle scene on the lower back of a female Daunian stele, F687.

of the very few cults which predate the foundation of Greek colonies in southern Italy for which there is substantial archaeological evidence. Later finds from the site also include terracotta plaques showing a procession of females, terracotta *pinakes* with a seated female holding a folded *peplos*, and votive loom weights and spindle whorls.[5]

A further scene type that can be understood as a part of the ritual system of the Daunians is that of two figures grinding what is probably grain in a vertical mortar with long pestles. The motif appears three times on the stelae: at the far right of the upper register on the back of Manfredonia 1008 (Fig. 11.2), in the lower back panel of Manfredonia 1482 (Nava 1157; Norman F565), and below the skirt pendants in the lower back panel of a stele recently repatriated from Belgium by the Italian authorities (Fig. 11.3). The first stele is one of the two with the complete rendition of the procession; the second is a badly encrusted stele that might also carry a lone horse in the upper, more damaged panel of the back; and the third is devoid of a substantial portion of its imagery. The upper back panel of this stele is largely missing, a zone on the female stelae that tends to carry the most important image(s) of its iconographic programme. Only the lower half of a vignette, showing two women seated in high-backed chairs on either side of a tripod cauldron, remains. It is a scene type found on some twenty of the stelae, although some include variations such as the purification/libation found on Manfredonia 1013 (Nava 781; Norman F371). It is highly likely that the lost imagery on F687 would have been of a ritual nature. Next to the two figures working at the mortar on Manfredonia 1008 is a third working at a saddle quern, confirming the identification of this scene as the preparation of food — almost certainly destined for ritual consumption and/or offering. Neils (2004, 56) and Villing (2009, 326–32) have both concluded that images of the processing of grain in Greek art does not necessarily reflect a mundane domestic activity, but rather alludes to the important, sometimes sacred task of making cakes for certain religious festivals and rites. In pre-Roman Italian communities, the situation was likely fluid, with such daily activities being infused with ritual to varying degrees dependent upon circumstances. The representation is not necessarily of a significant specific act, but rather a general reminder of the specialness of the process to material and spiritual life.

Interestingly, both the example of the mortar and pestle scene on F687 and that on F371 are accompanied by what can be identified as an ithyphallic ritual dancer, not dissimilar to a *komast* dancer.[6] There are seven instances of the figure in the corpus, found on six stelae.[7] The figure is typically shown with one arm raised, the second draped behind their back in an arc, hand pointing towards their buttocks, a gesture prompting the unfortunate moniker of *masturbator analis* by Ferri (1967, 216). Excepting the examples on Manfredonia 1008 and F687, all are in strict profile, with only one leg depicted. The leg is, unusually, bent so that the figure appears semi-crouched. All have an erect penis, except that on F687: the stele has been restored and, not surprisingly, the conservator did not know to include it.

The ithyphallic dancers on the remaining four stelae are again found associated with images of ritual. Manfredonia 1438, mentioned earlier, has the second full procession. Another stele, previously of the collection in Belgium (Norman F686), also has procession imagery, in the form of a man with a lyre/handloom (in the very worn upper back panel). The small fragment Manfredonia 561 (Nava 510; Norman U198) preserves, on the other side from the dancer, three women with long plaits walking in file to the right, another telltale sign of the same rite. Manfredonia 1061–7 (Nava 826; Norman M78), the only male stele in the group, is dominated by an image of martial (funerary?) games.

Glimpses of commensal feasting can also be seen on the stelae. The tripod cauldron scenes suggest the preparation of food for ritual consumption, while on Manfredonia 810 (Nava 621; Norman M53) there

---

5 For further evidence of textile tools used as votives in pre-Roman Italy see Gleba 2008, 178–86; 2009.

6 Ferri (1962, 107) believed the two left-most figures in this scene on F371 to be shown engaging in a sexual act and the quern to be an animal, and the image is still frequently referred to as erotic.

7 Norman F368, F547, F687, M78 × 2, F868, U198.

Figure 11.4. Daunian matt-painted *kernos*, provenance unknown. Princeton, Princeton Museum, inv. no. y1990-4.

Figure 11.5. North Lucanian matt-painted *askos* from Ripacandida T.46. Melfi 118615.

Figure 11.6. Oenotrian matt painted *kanthoros* from Guardia Perticara T.115. Potenza 214825.

is a vignette of people seated at a long table with a smaller figure in attendance (on the front, below the heart protector). The stele is incomplete, preserving only the mid-section, yet it is dense with figurative imagery, which includes the figure with a lyre/handloom, a string of dogs or boar (indicative of a hunt), two warriors in crested helmets sparring (martial games), and numerous fantastic creatures alluding to mythology and local folklore. What is possibly a bull being led to sacrifice by a man holding a large spear appears on Manfredonia 800 (Nava 610; Norman U233). It is a small fragment that otherwise retains only the legs of a chair such as those used around the tripod cauldron.

In addition to being depicted on statue-stelae, this particular array of motifs — the procession, a figure with a lyre/handloom, weaving, the two-person mortar and pestle, the tripod cauldron, dancing, and sacrifice — can be found depicted in various combinations on a variety of media from throughout contemporary peninsular Italy. Such artefacts represent a wide range of object types from differing socio-political and geographic contexts, demonstrating the existence of a shared system of ritual behaviours across non-Greek Archaic Italy.

A Daunian matt-painted *kernos* of the early sixth century BCE has on it, amongst bands of the more typical geometric patterning, registers of female figures with raised, clasped hands between men on horseback (Fig. 11.4). At the head of one of these

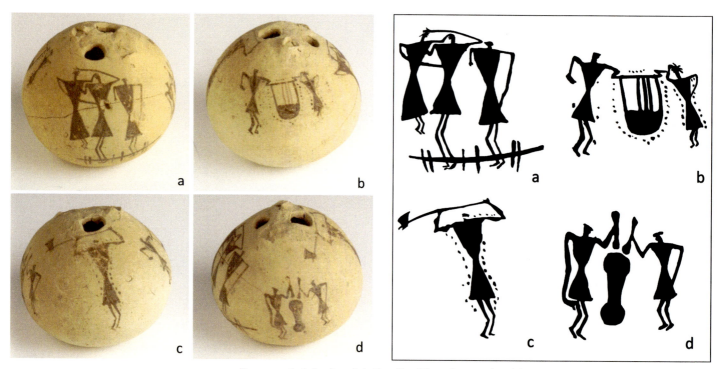

Figure 11.7. *Aryballos* from Sala Consilina T.B.27, Certosa di Padula (after Romito 2006, fig. 8; drawings by E. G. D. Robinson).

Figure 11.8. Roll-out of the imagery on a Campana *dinos*. Boston, Museum of Fine Art, inv. no. 13,205. (Photo courtesy of the Museum of Fine Arts, Boston).

files, a woman holds an enlarged lyre/handloom. There is a man holding it with her from the other side.[8] Similar files of women can be seen on a slightly later matt-painted *olla* of Peucetian manufacture from Monte Sennace (Bari 5083) (Ciancio 2006, 121–22 fig. 10). Both renditions presage the late fifth- to mid-fourth-century BCE depiction of the file of women in brightly coloured robes with joined hands from the Tomb of the Dancers in Ruvo, who are accompanied by a male aulist and a female figure playing a lyre. They are clearly in movement, going forward at some pace. It is a cross between a dance and a procession (Gadaleta 2002).

A matt-painted askos (c. 500–450 BCE) of local production found in the tomb of a women at Ripacandida, a North Lucanian site, carries on its belly a lone female(?) figure, again holding a lyre/handloom (Fig. 11.5). Heitz (2014–2015, 115) counts very few other instances of figural iconography at the site: a jug from tomb 14, small male amber effigies from tomb 48, and dog- and ram-shaped bronze pendants from graves 34 and 102. Like the Daunians, the North Lucanians used geometric decoration almost exclusively on their pottery, long after other peoples in Italy had begun using pictorial designs and made very little figured art besides. This is true also of the Oenotrians, whose territory lay to the south and east of the North Lucanians', stretching across the southern part of modern-day Basilicata and into

---

8 Standing looms would be flat-bottomed and not as readily portable. The lack of loom weights is not necessarily relevant: as Roth (2007, 72–76) points out, none of the depictions of looms on the Daunian stelae have loom weights. This and the fact that the weavers are seated point to them being double-beamed looms. The enhanced size of the object on the Princeton *kernos*, and elsewhere, was presumably for emphasis.

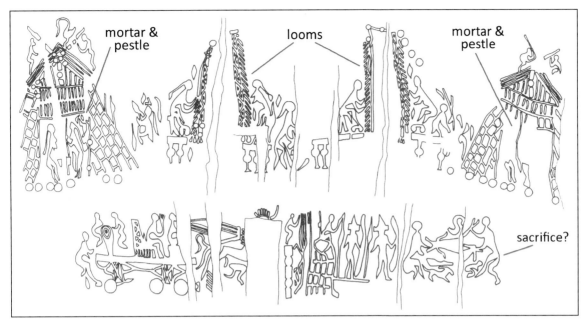

Figure 11.9. Drawing of a detail of the Verucchio Throne (adapted from Haynes 2000, 42).

Calabria. In what can now be seen as something of a pattern, one of the few figural images they produced is of a man(?) with a large lyre/handloom. It is on the handle of a mid-sixth-century BCE matt-painted *kantharos* from the tomb of a male in Guardia Perticara and is otherwise covered in geometric patterning (Fig. 11.6) (Bianco 2002, 67).

A spherical *aryballos* with related figural motifs was also found in the tomb of a male dating to the second half of the sixth century BCE at Sala Consilina, in the Vallo di Diano in Etrusco-Campanian territory (Fig. 11.7). It is thought, by virtue of its fabric and unique shape and decoration, to be an import to the site (de La Genière 1961, 36 n. 1). Whether locally produced or not, it is still unquestionably of Italian manufacture. It carries four rather crudely drawn images in a roughly geometric style. Neutsch (1961) interpreted them as a series of funeral dances: a) between boxers; b) with a lyre; c) with an axe; d) with a bi-lobed shield. Cerchiai (1997) later went on to draw Corinthian parallels for the ball (which is missing what was probably a stirrup handle), offering a slightly different interpretation of the scenes, but still in keeping with a funerary rite. Instead of pugilists he saw *komast* dancers, instead of a dance with an axe he saw an indication of animal sacrifice, and instead of two men with a shield he saw two figures with rhyta held above a 'filler'. Roncoroni (Romito 2006, 68) posited that this final scene (d) represents two people beating a type of tambourine. It is more plausible, however, that this image is in fact of two people with a vertical mortar and pestles, exactly as can be seen on the Daunian stelae. Rocco (2002,

14) has come to the same conclusion. This and the other images — which I read as two figures with a lyre/handloom, three figures dancing, and a figure with an axe (indicative of an animal sacrifice) — all fit the iconographic lexicon we have come to see as representative of a particular ritual system in Archaic southern Italy.

Northern Connections

Intriguingly, reflections of the ritual system depicted on these items can be found further north as well, hinting at a connective zone with shared iconography and practice which encompassed far more of the peninsula than just Daunia and its immediate vicinity. A Campana *dinos* of *c*. 530 BCE in Boston repeats similar imagery to that seen on the stelae and the Sala Consilina aryballos: dancing males (in or close to the *komast* position), the couple with mortar and pestles (this time a man and woman),[9] two auletes, a tripod cauldron, a man with a jug and basket, and another with a jug and bucket-shaped vessel (Fig. 11.8). Gregory Warden (2008, 126–27, 129) posits that the scene may be one of Dionysian celebration, with a secondary symbolism pertaining to the afterlife, whose visual text is Etruscan rather than Greek, the precise meaning of which 'has become

---

9 Villing (2009, 326–27) notes that it is only in a cultic setting that men are ever seen working the pestle and that some have argued this particular scene shows the preparation of the heroic and cultic drink *kykeon*.

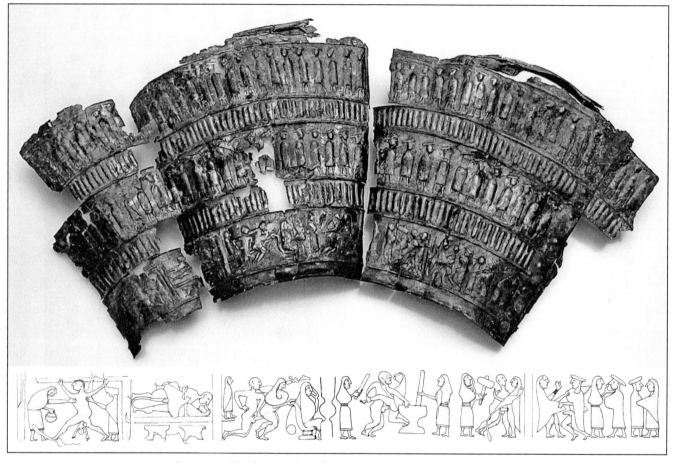

Figure 11.10. The Alpago situla, Belluno (after Gangemi 2015, pl. 16 and pp. 114–15).

ambiguous to the modern viewer for etiological reasons'. Rather than depicting an actual event, he believes, discreet vignettes from a shared cultural vocabulary were used to build up 'symbolic structures that would have evoked to the ancient viewer both the ritual and its meaning, the articulation of a social and religious landscape that connected all the participants in the ritual to divinity'. The pot was likely made by an artisan of eastern Greek origin who is thought to have migrated to Cerveteri, or at the very least to have had the Etruscan market squarely in mind (Osborne 2001; Hemelrijk 2007). It was manufactured in a style, and with techniques, common in the eastern Mediterranean, but, despite the Etruscans' accepted connections with the Greek world, the ritual system alluded to remains firmly Italian. Caeretan cylinder-stamped braziers of the mid-sixth century BCE carry images of banqueting and animal sacrifice at an altar (for example, British Museum GR 1978.5–11.6; Cerveteri 116029), helping to complete the picture.

The imagery can also be traced back earlier, into Villanovan times, having been found on the Verucchio Throne (von Eles 2002). The throne was discovered in an exceptionally wealthy male grave of the mid-seventh century in the mountainous hinterland behind Rimini. It is made from a single tree trunk, studded with bronze. The inside of the throne's backrest is carved with two registers of imagery (Fig. 11.9). The top tier shows, at the centre, two sets of women working at standing looms, and the similarities between the high-backed chairs here and on the Daunian stelae are striking. The weavers are framed by figures who are spinning, and couples working with pestles in a tall mortar inside a hut. In the lower tier, there is a procession involving two enthroned figures, one female and the other male, being conveyed inwards in carriages towards what has been identified as an animal sacrifice. It has been suggested that the Verucchio Throne is a female's chair and was originally a wedding present from a man to his bride, and that the carriages depicted are part of a wedding procession, while the whole scene refers to the exchange of gifts between elite families at a marriage (Torelli 1997, 63–65), an interpretation I have also posited for the Daunian procession (Norman 2011a). Others see it as an extended scene of textile manufacture, interpreting the activity of the figures at the mortar as the dying of fabric rather than the grinding of grain, and the 'animal sacrifice' as individuals making a tunic.[10] Given the pattern of imagery seen elsewhere, the former reading seems more likely, with weaving being but one element of the proceedings. Irrespective of the exact ceremony being depicted, the vignettes must surely have been intended to illustrate ritualized behaviours, and imply a larger system of mutually comprehensible customs and beliefs. Conversely, imagery on the late seventh-/early sixth-century BCE bronze *tintinnabulum* (a bell) from the Arenal necropolis (Bologna) is dedicated entirely to textile production (Gleba 2008, 30 fig. 8). Four of the seven women depicted, who are variously carding, spinning, preparing the warp, and weaving, are seated in chairs not dissimilar to the Verucchio Throne itself. The participants are splendidly dressed and evidentially performing a task of high regard, very possibly in a ritual context.

Finally, further to the north, a bronze situla from the Pian de la Gnela, Alpago (Belluno) has a frieze at the bottom which seemingly shows episodes from the life of a woman, beginning and ending with childbirth (Fig. 11.10). Included among the vignettes of courtship and sexual liaison is a woman seated at a standing loom and another working with a long pestle at a large mortar. A second woman stands to the other side, separated from the mortar by a couple using it as a support for sex. The implement she holds has been described as a baton, but is surely the second pestle. Another woman (or another version of the same woman) holds up an axe, perhaps symbolizing sacrifice. Standing on a shelf is a small female figure, considered to be a statuette of a deity who watches over proceedings, indicating that the space was likely sacralized and the activities that took place within performed ritualistically. The upper two registers of the situla each contain a continuous file of figures, this time men, the lower one processing to the right and the upper to the left. The situla, which shows signs of repair in antiquity, was found in a cremation dating to the fifth century BCE; the situla itself is dated to the late sixth century. Findings from the Venetian sanctuary of the goddess Rietia in Este (Padua) confirm that spinning and weaving were among the activities that took place there, the tools for which were used as votive offerings as far back as the late seventh century (Gambacurta 2017). Another situla from nearby Montebelluna dated to 525 BCE also has, among other vignettes, an image of two women spinning, as well as figures process-

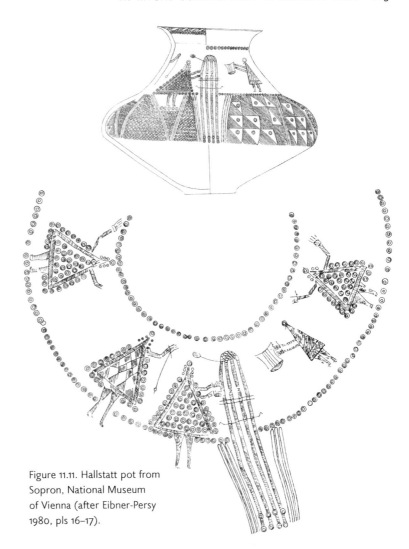

Figure 11.11. Hallstatt pot from Sopron, National Museum of Vienna (after Eibner-Persy 1980, pls 16–17).

ing (some in chariots or on horseback), scenes of libation, two people at a pedestalled cauldron, and a seated man playing what in this case is clearly a lyre (Bianchin Citton 2014).

Interestingly, five standing looms are also found alongside 'worshippers' (dancers?) and deer hunters on the Great Rock of Naquane in the Valcamonica, carved by the Cammuni in the Late Bronze Age or Early Iron Age (Gleba 2008, 29 fig. 5), while a seventh-century BCE Hallstatt pot from a tumulus tomb at Sopron on the Austro-Hungarian border shows women variously at a standing loom, with the lyre/handloom, spinning, and with arms raised in a gesture of worship/dance (Fig. 11.11). A smattering of contemporary ceramic pots and bronze items from modern-day Austria (Kleinklein, Ernstbrunn, Loretto, Reichersdorf), Germany (Schirndorf), and Slovakia (Janíky-Dolné Janíky, Nové Košariská) are also decorated with a figure with lyre/handloom (Rebay-Salisbury 2016, 144–45 fig. 6.18). In all probability, the ritual system identified through this repeated confluence of images has a deep his-

---

10 For a full bibliography and discussion of previous interpretations, see Bonfante 2005, 4–5.

tory and is the result of a broader tradition, in which localized responses based on variant socio-political structures and ecologies saw the gradual development of parallel ritual practices around the upper Adriatic basin and its inland contact zones, both in peninsular Italy and to the north.

Connectivity and Ritual Practice

It is instructive for our understanding of cultural relations in Archaic Italy to consider how and when the ideas for the processes were enacted, and how the instruments utilized in this specific ritual system moved about. It is increasingly clear that pre-Roman Italy consisted of a complex and fluid mixture of populations. While we can sometimes identify broad regional norms in the material cultures that developed in certain areas, seemingly in response to the immediate environment, local societal norms and needs, and ideas transmitted with the movement of people (Bradley and others 2009; Bourdin 2012), one must always remember the axiom 'pots are pots, not people'. In an ancient Mediterranean world (and especially Archaic Italy), where mobility and connectivity have increasingly moved to the fore of our interpretations, we must find ways to explain the emergence and continuity of local traditions within a dynamic human landscape. As such, the labels we use for local populations, such as 'Daunian' or 'Etruscan', should not be understood as ethnic descriptors for stable populations, and certainly not as discrete political entities. Many were not formulated until later in the Archaic or Classical periods and were likely the invention of others, precisely when the notion of 'otherness' and territorial belonging came into being (Malkin 1988; Dzino 2014; Isayev 2019, 87–107). The period in which we are currently interested is largely prior to this, when an individual would have likely identified first and foremost with their kinship group, or perhaps local community or settlement, and had little concept of the greater cultural entity to which they were later ascribed. Accepting that labels and 'borders', such as they were, were permeable and fluid, it is nonetheless convenient to apply some sort of labelling convention across this region as a recognizable method to broadly categorize material culture and geographies. For the remainder of the chapter, therefore, the analysis will use terms like 'Daunian' and 'Etruscan' to denote the populations typically associated with the regions traditionally known as Daunia and Etruria, etc. As Armstrong and Rhodes-Schroder discuss in the Introduction to this volume, however, it must be remembered that these labels

are at best heuristic and neither static nor absolute. Indeed, we must always be wary of any terms becoming reified, and actively mitigate against that. In the present context, these labels can be understood to indicate some aspects, although not all, of a wider connective system in Italy during the period, and nothing more.

The extent to which the ritual system was embedded within the networked society of pre-Roman Italy is demonstrated by the range of cultures in which imagery relating to it can be detected, the diversity of objects the imagery is found upon (in function, form, and medium), and the various ways in which it was presented. These variations, in part, result from the differing affordances of the shapes, sizes, materials, and manufacturing techniques of the objects themselves (Rebay-Salisbury 2016, 110–36). Also a factor is the complexity of the artistic traditions of the producers, with more abstracted and schematic motifs, often displayed alone or paired with only one or two other motifs being found in southern Italy, where figurative art is relatively rare, and more detailed narratives offered in Etruria and the Veneto, where figurative art is more prevalent and has a longer history. Although seemingly related to the same activities, and likely mutually comprehensible, they were clearly shaped by local traditions. Even so, this is not to say that the exact nature of the ritual system being alluded to was stable, clearly defined, or universal. As Kyriakidis (2007, 12–13) stresses, the execution of, and meaning behind, any given ceremony with similar aesthetics was not necessarily the same from one setting to another, as there is a tendency in rituals, especially if well established, to borrow behaviours, paraphernalia, and symbols from one another. Additionally, the distances and multiple stages over which the knowledge was transferred and circulated would have created a 'transmission chain' effect, as ideas are adjusted to fit local customs and conventions (Rebay-Salisbury 2016, 24). This was not a rigid dogma or set of holy scriptures being transmitted, but an agreed and mutually comprehensible way of expressing relationships between individuals, groups, and (perhaps) the gods. It was an adaptive ritual vocabulary.

The particular distribution of the objects' place of manufacture and final deposition, along the Apennine spine and Adriatic side of Italy, indicates a phenomenon that is distinct from other cultural processes occurring in the peninsula at the time. Namely, the changes in socio-political constructs, technologies, and material culture catalysed by contact with people and things from the eastern Mediterranean. The existence of glimmers of the ritual system in the rock art of the Valcamonica further suggests its use, and that regional transmission predates the increased connections with the eastern Mediterranean associated with the Archaic and Classical periods, and is arguably quite separate from the concepts and goods disseminated via interaction with Greek or Phoenician traders and settlers — active networks which were current at the time of the objects' making, but which seem to have functioned primarily on the Ionian and Tyrrhenian coasts. Moreover, images on the Early Iron Age Hallstatt pots and bronzework suggest that the behaviours were also practised to the north, and across the Alps. Again, these were cultures in which decorative schemes consisted mostly of geometric and linear designs rather than figuration. Only a limited amount of figurative art was produced by the Early Iron Age Illyrian tribes of Istria, Liburnia, Iapodia, and Dalmatia. However, we may still speculate, for reasons outlined below, that a version of the same ritual system was extant there also.

Using Social Network Analysis, supplemented by Path Dependence theory, Blake (2014) looked at the spread of recognizable imports and specialized products in Recent and Final Bronze Age peninsular Italy (*c.* 1300 to 900 BCE) to study local and regional connections, with the intention of examining identity formation over an extended period of time. The focus was on the development of regional groupings, framed by the author as ethnic groups. The study was perhaps overly ambitious, and not without problems, many of which are known to the author (Wijngaarden 2015). However, it does provide a basic grounding for conceptualizing the possible routes and nodes via which information regarding a ritual system may have travelled, and when that may have begun. Blake looked at land-based networks, as well as riverine and coastal pathways, with an eye to detecting zones of intensified circulation between neighbouring sites, but also over longer distances. A number of her conclusions regarding the Final Bronze Age are of interest here: in the south there was a distinction between what was happening on the coast (where the vast majority of the Daunian stelae were likely located), suggesting a maritime network heavily influenced by individuals and contacts from outside the region, and in the interior, positing a terrestrial network controlled by locals; the strongest networks are to be found in the Veneto and what was to become southern Etruria, the weakest in Basilicata and the south; much of the peninsula showed little signs of connectivity until the Iron Age (Molise, Liguria, Campania, and Calabria). In general, she determined that 'the RBA networks are distinct from the groupings of the first millennium BCE, and therefore, what we can say is, whether these groups were new or not, it is in the first part of the FBA that the process of regional identity formation is under way' (Blake 2014, 243). It is therefore plausible that this was the period in which information regarding our ritual system first came to be circulated.

Meanwhile, using representations of the human body to interrogate notions of identity in Early Iron Age Hallstatt culture, Rebay-Salisbury (2016, 244–48) has identified a number of 'motif networks' between central Europe, northern Italy, and the upper Adriatic (including Istria), arguing for strong interregional ties across the entire area that were continuously enacted over time through art. In tracking the spread of individual motif types, in an attempt to reconstruct the nature and structure of social systems, her underlying premise was that, even though people as actors are rarely recoverable in the archaeological record, things, people, and places are all linked, and so the connections between elements of material culture are able to reveal relationships that must have existed. There is an understanding that relationships between things, people, and places are both material and semiotic (Rebay-Salisbury 2016, 22).

Combining the work of both scholars, it transpires that the spread of objects carrying imagery relating to the proposed ritual system maps incredibly well onto the FBA networks Blake has identified for early Italy, not a single one having been found in the zones which she saw as disconnected and potentially self-contained, as well as to those detected in art by Rebay-Salisbury for the Hallstatt regions of central Europe. The cross-over region for these networks is the Veneto, which seems to have acted as a vital connective node in this wider communicative system, with particularly important overland networks. There is also reason to believe that the inhabitants of Liburnia also played a prominent role in spreading and regularly activating knowledge pertaining to it, this time by sea. Thus, while the mobility and connectivity which increasingly defines Italy may be more evident in the Archaic and Classical periods, it was not solely a product of this time, and can also be seen clearly along the eastern side of Italy in the FBA as well. Further, and intriguingly, these early networks seem to align remarkably well with the extent and iconographic evidence for the ritual system, and were likely encouraged and developed by ongoing economic activity as well as migration.

Goods, People, and Ideas

One of the best illustrations of connectivity between Italy and the north is the presence of amber from the Baltic, first seen in the peninsula in the early second millennium BCE and across its entirety by the end of the Early Bronze Age. From *c.* 1000–500 BCE, it is found in significant quantities, especially in Villanovan, Etruscan, Picenean, and indigenous Apulian contexts. Numerous riverine routes used to transport the amber have been identified, snaking through Europe and eventually reaching northern Italy and the Adriatic, from where it was taken overland and down river valleys to centres in north-eastern and inland central Italy and by sea to the coasts of central Italy, south-eastern Italy, and beyond (Bouzek 1993; D'Ercole 2002, 120–51; Negroni Catacchio and Gallo 2017). The wealth of Verucchio, a major hub for the distribution of amber and amber-decorated products from the eighth century, was likely generated by this trade. It is said that the Liburnians operated a thalassocracy in the upper Adriatic, beginning in the Late Bronze Age and continuing until the end of the sixth century BCE when Etruscan influence is significantly amplified in the region with the establishment of Adria and Spina, which in turn allowed Greek merchants to take advantage of the pre-existing network. The Liburnians were famed for their ship-building skills and had established a maritime trading route based on the sea currents, circling the coast anticlockwise and crossing between the Gargano peninsula in Daunia and Hvar on the Dalmatian side using a chain of islands, a route in use since the Neolithic (Kirigin and others 2010). At this point the upper Adriatic meets the lower, and the currents are such that it is possible to travel in either direction. Amber was by no means the only material transported, with raw and worked metals from the Balkans and wheat, livestock, and salt from Daunia likely constituting the bulk of the cargo.

Details etched upon the Daunian stelae suggest that it was not only objects that travelled across the Adriatic, but people. The markings on the forearms of the female stelae can be understood as tattoos, a custom that is well documented among female Illyrian elites from the Archaic and Classical periods in representational imagery and ancient literary sources, and that can be traced also in later historical documentation of the area (Norman 2011b). The same is true of the string skirts the female stelae are shown wearing, a tradition that is evident as far back as the fifth millennium BCE in the Balkans and still lingers in modern-day central Europe (Norman 2018). These details are so precise, the tattoos especially not being attested anywhere else in Italy until Roman times and then only as punitive or chattel markings, that migration from Illyria can be confidently argued for. It is one origin story of the Iapygians (the Apulian tribes to which the Daunians belonged) given by later Greek and Roman authors, and there is a certain

amount of archaeological evidence to back up the claim, such as similar metallurgic traditions on both sides of the Adriatic (De Juliis 1988, 10–15; D'Ercole 2002, 152–214). The migrations likely began in the Late Bronze Age when we see shifting settlement patterns in Daunia and a slow repopulation after a period of seemingly sparse habitation. The first people perhaps came south-westward in waves searching for superior agricultural land; once established they may then have continued to move in both directions as individuals, for example to intermarry and help preserve trading relations and community ties.

The distribution of Daunian Subgeometric I matt-painted pottery (*c.* 650/625–550/525 BCE) is telling, as it shows mobility in the other direction, to the north and north-east, throughout the Caput Adriae (north-eastern Italy, central and western Slovenia, and north-western Croatia). The pots can also be found along the Adriatic coast of Italy, in the Po Valley, Etruria, Campanian Etruria, and North Lucanian and Oenotrian territory (Yntema 1990, 234–48; D'Ercole 2002, 291–310; Turk and Murgelj 2008 (2010); Poli 2008). That is, its distribution mirrors the areas that imagery for the ritual system has been located, plus Liburnia and Dalmatia where, due to a lack of figurative art in Archaic times, the regions' inclusion in the network can at this stage only be inferred by its inhabitants' pivotal role in Adriatic seafaring and other indicators such as outlined in these case studies. Daunian pottery of the time was of a high quality, seemingly exchanged for its own perceived worth rather than any contents it may have held. It can be found in elite graves in Istria and in settlement contexts in both ports and trading hubs servicing inland routes. It is also found throughout the entire heel of Italy, where the remaining Iapygian tribes lived (the Peucetians and Messapians), thinning out towards the south where there was greater interaction with residents of the Greek cities of Magna Graecia. The ritual system may, of course, have been practised by the other indigenous populations of Apulia, but simply not be symbolically reproduced in their artistic output, or we are yet to find it. This is almost certainly true for Picenum, situated on the Adriatic coast of central Italy, which was well connected in the region by both sea and land (Riva in Bradley and others 2007, 79–113).

Textiles were an eminently important commodity in the ancient world, used not only for clothing but all manner of soft furnishings and even sail cloth. The labour and skill that went into producing them, and their prominent visual role in society, meant that they could also act as status markers. Textiles moved as objects of trade, as gifts and offerings, in dowries and bride prices, in ransoms and booty. Sometimes they moved over vast distances and through many pairs of hands. They could take on biographies and, in a pre- and proto-literate world, tell stories through their accumulated past and, on occasion, woven pictorial designs. By the Archaic period, the standing loom had been around for millennia. However, technological advances and innovations continued to be made through the circulation of both the cloth itself — an experienced weaver would have been able to reproduce it by observation alone — and the people who made it. As is well attested, textile production was overwhelmingly the domain of females in antiquity, often constituting a source of pride and personal economic worth. When women moved — be it through migration, intermarriage, gifting, purchase, or capture — they passed knowledge of their ways of doing to other women, often also taking their textile tools with them (Gleba 2014).

Links are visible in the textile traditions of Italy and the Hallstatt culture, in terms of production methods and the tools used, but also the fabrics themselves (Gleba 2008; Grömer 2017). Similar costumes for the elite and serving classes are worn by persons represented on situla art from both the Veneto and the western Hallstatt region; not surprising given their close connections and the shared art-form. Yet it goes deeper. For example, Etruscan and Etruscan-inspired distaffs made of luxury materials can be found in indigenous Italian tombs throughout the peninsula but are also to be found in graves as far north as Austria (Gleba 2014, 91). There are very few surviving textile fragments from ancient Italy. One notable exception is a number of high-status, intricately woven Villanovan garments from Verruchio, discovered in the same tomb as the throne. Certain techniques used to make them reflect those used in the Hallstatt regions, such as the tablet woven borders (von Eles 2002, 192–234). These borders, with very similar patterning, are seen again on the robes incised on the Daunian stelae, confirming that knowledge of their construction and design potential was shared also in the southern, seemingly less connected areas of Italy (Nieling 2007; Norman forthcoming, ch. 6. II). A recent find of textile fragments from an early fourth-century BCE grave in Ordona, a major Daunian centre, carries the exact same patterning, demonstrating that it was true in practice as well as theory (Catalli and others 2018).

The stance of the ritual dancer seen on the Daunian stelae is specific to the genre of the *komast* dancer (Fig. 11.3, far right figure). It is one commonly known from a variety of iconographic sources, first on Corinthian pottery of about 630 BCE, and perhaps even earlier in Cyprus and Anatolia (Smith 2010, 14–16). Its image was reproduced on Etrusco-

Corinthan vases, and in all probability was first transmitted across peninsular Italy via the central Tyrrhenian rather than Magna Graecia. There is no doubting, for example, that the Daunians and Etruscans were in contact, as can be seen by the presence in Daunia of Etruscan pearl-rimmed bronze bowls (D'Ercole 2002, 278–83) and Etrusco-Campanian nimbus head antefixes (Mazzei 2011, 190–94). It has become clear in recent times that, in Greece, *komast* imagery reflects a widespread cultural phenomenon that found its roots at least in part in ritual and was not simply the invention of playwrights and painters (Hedreen in Csapo and Miller 2007, 150–95; Steinhart in Csapo and Miller 2007, 196–220; Smith 2010, 27–32). Such a character — a dancer who performed ecstatically within a ritual context, sometimes with a mega- or ithyphallus — could have been endemic to many societies; the aesthetics of it were, however, likely refined with the spread of *komast* imagery.

The procession is an activity commonly associated with *komast* dancers in Greek art, but also in Etruscan. The context is mainly interpreted as 'Dionysian', as per the Boston *dinos* (Fig. 11.8), but at times the setting is more sombre, such as on a Middle Corinthian *pyxis* in Berlin (Antikensammlung, inv. no. 4856) that juxtaposes a series of dancing *komasts* with a sedate file of women not unlike those seen on the Daunian stelae. One might compare this type of scene with those depicted in Etruscan tomb painting, for instance on the rear wall of the T. del Morente at Tarquinia (Brandt 2014), where a dancer is juxtaposed next to a funerary bed with the deceased upon it.[11] Again, ideas regarding the performance of ritual dancing and its appropriateness for inclusion in ceremonies may have been honed and adjusted in accordance with wider trends communicated via imagery and any ensuing discussions around it.

Conclusions

The work of Blake and Rebay-Salisbury, in addition to the material presented above, serve to further illuminate a network of connectivity that, due to the absence of data, can otherwise only be hypothesized by the spread and style of the objects that carry imagery relating to what can be identified as a shared ritual system. The network was no doubt open-ended, and connected with other networks, such as those centred upon the Aegean, Magna Graecia, eastern Sicily, and the Tyrrhenian coast

---

11 Interpretations of this sort of image, in an Etruscan context, are explored by Rhodes-Schroder in this volume, pp. 109–12

of Italy, and that in the Baltics and central northern Europe. Its core, however, covered the Hallstatt regions (Austria, western Slovakia, western Hungary, and Slovenia), parts of Illyria (coastal Croatia), and much of peninsular Italy (the north-east, the Po Valley, Etruria, Etruscan-Campania, the Adriatic coast, the Apennines, and Apulia). An inland hub in the Veneto can be posited, from where ideas from the north would have spread with goods and people overland to the upper reaches of the Italian sector of the network, and vice versa. Maritime trade around the upper Adriatic, likely instigated and controlled by the Liburnians, took knowledge of the system to the ports of Picenum and the Po River delta from where it was transmitted into the hinterlands, to places such as Verucchio, and down the Tiber Valley to the heartland of Etruria. Boats would also have docked in Daunia, which acted as the hub from where information spread down the line, further south in Apulia, into Basilicata via the Bradano and Agri Valleys, and over the Apennines into Etruscan-Campania.

The proposed network, as it stood in the Archaic period, might be characterized as being based primarily on economic relations. However, the existence of the shared ritual system, evidence for earlier migrations from Illyria into Italy, the longevity of the amber trade, and the breadth and depth of common technological know-how regarding weaving suggest something more: that the network developed over a very long period, when regional identities were in flux, and that it served to transmit not only goods, but also culture and modes of cognition. The exist-

ence of this network in Archaic Italy is often overlooked, as later historical events obscure it from view and scholarly attentions traditionally focus on contemporaneous interaction with the eastern Mediterranean, so visible in the material record of the time (and given positive bias by modern preferences, such as for Greek and Greek-inspired ceramics). The northern network is not impervious to external developments, as evidenced by the incorporation of *komast* aesthetics into the ritual dancing of Etruria and Daunia. Nor was it necessarily strong: although entrenched, it was seemingly not robust enough to effect significant change in the other directions or withstand the growing pressure exerted by the increased presence and economic interests of outsiders in Italy. In fact, the network may already have begun to contract in the Archaic period, with the inhabitants of areas such as Messapia in southern Apulia having to turn their attentions towards Magna Graecia.

Further work is required to properly trace both the network and the ritual system and to understand their ramifications in time and place. The next logical steps are 1) to look at the archaeological remains to examine, for example, when and where standing looms were used in a ritualized context, such as those found in the Sanctuary in Este; and 2) to conduct a thorough cross-survey of motifs from Archaic Hallstatt and indigenous Italian representational art. For now, I hope that this brief overview has added something more to our appreciation of the multivariant strata of cultural connectivity at play in Archaic Italy and some of the less visible forces driving it.

Works Cited

Bell, Catherine. 1997. *Ritual: Perspectives and Dimensions* (Oxford: Oxford University Press)

Bianchin Citton, Elodia. 2014. 'Topografia e sviluppo di un centro preromano della fascia pedemontana veneta. Il caso di Montebelluna', in *Amore per l'antico: dal Tirreno all'Adriatico, dalla Preistoria al Medioevo e oltre; studi di antichità in ricordo di Giuliano De Marinis*, ed. by Gabriele Herausgeber Baldelli and Fulvia Lo Schiavo (Rome: Scienze e lettere), pp. 999–1005

Bianco, Salvatore. 2002. 'Immagine e mito nel mondo enotrio', in *Immagine e mito nella Basilicata antica: Potenza, Museo Provinciale, dicembre 2002- marzo 2003* (Venosa: Osanna), pp. 63–72

Blake, Emma. 2014. *Social Networks and Regional Identity in Bronze Age Italy* (Cambridge: Cambridge University Press)

Bonfante, Larissa. 2005. 'The Verucchio Throne and the Corsini Chair: Two Status Symbols of Ancient Italy', in *Terra marique: Studies in Art History and Marine Archaeology in Honor of Anna Marguerite McCann on the Receipt of the Gold Medal of the Archaeological Institute of America*, ed. by John Pollini (Oxford: Oxbow), pp. 3–11

Bourdin, Stéphane. 2012. *Les peuples de l'Italie préromaine: identités, territoires et relations inter-ethniques en Italie centrale et septentrionale (VIIIe-Ier S. av. J.-C.)* (Rome: École française de Rome)

Bouzek, Jan. 1993. 'The Shifts of the Amber Route', in *Amber in Archaeology: Proceedings of the Second International Conference on Amber in Archaeology, Liblice 1990*, ed. by Curt W. Beck and Jan Bouzek (Prague: Institute of Archaeology), pp. 141–46

Bradley, Guy, Elena Isayev, and Corinna Riva (eds). 2007. *Ancient Italy: Regions without Boundaries* (Exeter: Exeter University Press)

Brandt, Johann. 2014. 'Passage to the Underworld. Continuity or Change in Etruscan Funerary Ideology and Practices (6th–2nd Centuries BC)?', in *Death and Changing Rituals: Function and Meaning in Ancient Funerary Practices*, ed. by J. Rasmus Brandt, Håkon Roland, and Marina Prusac (Exeter: Exeter University Press), pp. 105–84

Catalli, Emiliano, Marisa Corrente, Antonella Di Giovanni, Maria Rita Giuliani, Maria Concetta Laurenti, and Monica Pastorelli. 2018. 'Spinning and Weaving by Herdonia Women', in *Purpureae Vestes*, VI: *Textiles and Dyes in the Mediterranean Economy and Society*, ed. by Maria Stella Busana, Margarita Gleba, Francesco Meo, and Anna Rosa Tricomi (Zaragoza: Libros Pórtico), pp. 157–66

Ciancio, Angela. 2006. 'L'introduzione di schemi figurative nella ceramica geometrica di produzione peuceta', in *L'image antique et son interpretation*, ed. by Françoise-Hélène Pairault-Massa, Collection de l'École française de Rome (Rome: École française de Rome), pp. 117–29

Cerchiai, Luca. 1997. 'L'aryballos della Tomba B. 27 di Sala Consilina', in *Iconografía Iberica, Iconografía Itálica: propuestas de interpretación y lectura*, ed. by Ricardo Olmos Romera and Juan A. Santos Velasco (Madrid: UAM-Universidad Autónoma), pp. 129–36

Csapo, Eric, and Margaret C. Miller (eds). 2007. *The Origins of Theater in Ancient Greece and Beyond: From Ritual to Drama* (Cambridge: Cambridge University Press)

De Juliis, Ettore. 1988. *Gli Iapigi: storia e civiltà della Puglia preromana* (Milan: Longanesi)

D'Ercole, Maria Cecelia. 2000. 'Immagini dell'Adriatico arcaico. Su alcuni temi iconografici delle stele daunie', *Ostraka*, 9: 327–50

——. 2002. *Importuosa Italiae litora: paysage et échanges dans l'Adriatique méridionale à l'époque archaïque* (Naples: Centre Jean Bérard)

Dzino, Danijel. 2014. '"Illyrians" in Ancient Ethnographic Discourse', *Dialogues d'histoire ancienne*, 40.2: 45–65

Eibner-Persy, Alexandrine. 1980. *Hallstattzeitliche Grabhügel von Sopron (Ödenburg): Die Funde der Grabungen 1890–92 in der Prähistorischen Abteilung des Naturhistorischen Museums in Wien und im Burgenländischen Landesmuseum in Eisenstadt*, Wissenschaftliche Arbeiten aus dem Burgenland, 62 (Eisenstadt: Amt der Burgenländischen Landesregierung)

von Eles, Patrizia (ed.). 2002. *Guerriero e sacerdote: autorità e comunità nell'età del ferro a Verucchio; la Tomba del Trono* (Florence: All'insegna del Giglio)

Ferri, Silvio. 1962. 'Stele "daunie": un nuovo capitolo di archeologia protostorica', *Bollettino d'arte*, 47.1–2: 103–14

——. 1967. 'Stele daunie VII', *Bollettino d'arte*, 52.4: 209–11

Gadaleta, Giuseppina. 2002. *La tomba delle danzatrici di Ruvo di Puglia* (Naples: Loffredo)

Gambacurta, Giovanna. 2017. 'A Loom for the Goddess – Tools for Spinning and Weaving from the Sanctuary of the Goddess *Reitia* in Este (Padua)', *Origini*, 40: 211–26

Gangemi, Giovanna. 2015. 'Le situla istoriata', in *Le Signore dell'Alpago: la necropoli preromana di 'Pian de la Gnela'; Pieve d'Alpago (Belluno)*, ed. by Giovanna Gangemi, Michele Bassetti, and Diego Voltolini (Treviso: Canova), pp. 113–17

Gleba, Margarita. 2008. *Textile Production in Pre-Roman Italy* (Oxford: Oxbow)

——. 2009. 'Textile Tools in Ancient Italian Votive Contexts', in *Votives, Places and Rituals in Etruscan Religion: Studies in Honour of Jean MacIntosh Turfa*, ed. by Margarita Gleba and Hilary Becker (Leiden: Brill), pp. 69–84

——. 2014. 'Cloth Worth a King's Ransom. Textile Circulation and Transmission of Textile Craft in the Ancient Mediterranean', in *Knowledge Networks and Craft Traditions in the Ancient World: Material Crossovers*, ed. by Katharina Rebay-Salisbury, Ann Brysbaert, and Lin Foxhall (New York: Routledge), pp. 83–103

Grömer, Karina. 2017. 'Textile Products, Consumers and Producers in the Hallstatt Culture', *Origini*, 11: 95–112

Haynes, Sybille. 2000. *Etruscan Civilization: A Cultural History* (Los Angeles: J. Paul Getty Museum)

Heitz, Christian. 2014–2015. 'Ripacandida. An Indigenous Cemetery and the Greek Periphery', *Accordia Research Papers*, 14: 103–21

Hemelrijk, Jaap M. 2007. 'Four New Campana Dinoi, a New Painter, Old Questions', *BABESCH: Annual Papers on Mediterranean Archaeology*, 82: 365–421

Isayev, Elana. 2017. *Migration, Mobility and Place in Ancient Italy* (Cambridge: Cambridge University Press)

Kirigin, Branko, Maja Miše, and Vedran Barbarić. 2010. 'Palagruža. The Island of Diomedes. Summary Excavation Report 2002–2008', *Hesperia*, 25: 65–69

Kleibrink Maaskant, Marianne. 2003. *Dalla Lana all'Acqua: culto è identità nell'Athenaion di Lagaria, Francavilla Marittima* (Rossano: Grafosud)

Kyriakidis, Evangelos. 2007. 'Finding Ritual: Calibrating the Evidence', in *The Archaeology of Ritual*, ed. by Evangelos Kyriakidis (Los Angeles: Cotsen Institute of Archaeology, University of California), pp. 9–22

La Genière, Juliette de. 1961. 'La céramique géometrique de Sala Consilina', *Mélanges de l'École française de Rome: antiquité*, 72: 7–67

Malkin, Irad. 1998. *The Returns of Odysseus: Colonization and Ethnicity* (Oakland: University of California Press)

Mazzei, Marina. 2010. *I Dauni: archaeologia dal IX al V secolo a.C.* (Foggia: Claudio Grenzi)

Nava, Maria Luisa. 1980. *Stele Daunie*, I (Florence: Sansone)

——. 1988. *Le stele della Daunia* (Milan: Electa)

Negroni Catacchio, Nuccia, and Veronia Gallo. 2017. 'L'ambra in Italia. Le vie di penetrazione e la diffusione durante la protostoria', in *The Amber Roads: The Ancient Cultural and Commercial Communication between the Peoples*, ed. by Cellarosi, Pier Luigi, and CIVIA (Florence: Museo fiorentino di preistoria 'Paolo Graziosi'), pp. 313–35

Neils, Jenifer. 2004. 'Kitchen or Cult? Women with Mortars and Pestles', in *Greek Art in View: Essays in Honour of Brian Sparkes*, ed. by Simon Keay and Stephanie Moser (Oxford: Oxbow), pp. 54–62

Nieling, Jens. 2007. 'Brettchengewebte Borten der späten Hallstattzeit im Prunkgrab von Hochdorf und auf den sog. Daunischen Stelen in Apulien', in *Zweiundvierzig: Festschrift für Michael Gebühr zum 65. Geburtstag*, ed. by Stafan Burmeister, Heidrun Derks, and Jasper von Richthofen (Rahden: Leidorf), pp. 159–66

Neutsch, Bernhard. 1961. 'Tonball mit Totenkultszenen aus der italische Nekropole von Sala Consilina', *Apollo*, 1: 53–66

Norman, Camilla. 2009. 'Warriors and Weavers: Sex and Gender in the Daunian Stelae', in *Gender Identities in Italy in the First Millennium BC: Papers from the Conference Held at the Institute of Classical Studies, University of London (June 2006)*, ed. by Kathryn Lomas and Edward Herring, British Archaeological Reports, International Series (Oxford: Archaeopress), pp. 37–54

——. 2011a. 'Weaving, Gift and Wedding. A Local Identity for the Daunian Stelae', in *Communicating Identity in Italic Iron Age Communities*, ed. by Margarita Gleba and Helle W. Horsnæs (Oxford: Oxbow), pp. 33–49

——. 2011b. 'The Tribal Tattooing of Daunian Women', *European Journal of Archaeology*, 14.1–2: 133–57

——. 2018. 'Illyrian Vestiges in Daunian Costume: Tattoos, String Aprons and a Helmet', in *Realtà medioadriatiche a confronto: contatti e scambi tra le due sponde*, ed. by Gianfranco De Benedittis, Considerazioni di storia ed archeologia (Campobasso: Università degli studi del Molise), pp. 57–71

——. 2023. 'The Ritual Ecology of Archaic Italy', in *Sanctuaries and Experience: Knowledge, Practice and Space in the Ancient World*, ed. by Ilaria Bultrighini, Camilla Norman, and Greg Woolf (Stuttgart: Steiner)

——. Forthcoming. *People of Archaic Daunia: Voicing the Statue-Stelae* (Los Angeles: Cotsen Institute of Archaeology, University of California)

Osborne, Robert. 2001. 'Why Did Athenian Pots Appeal to the Etruscans?', *World Archaeology*, 33.2: 277–95

Poli, Nicoletta. 2008. 'Rapporti circumadriatici in età preromana. La diffusione della ceramica di produzione daunia in alto Adriatico', in *Terre di Mare: l'archeologia dei paesaggi costieri e le variazioni climatiche; atti del convegno internazionale di studi (Trieste, 8–10 novembre 2007)*, ed. by Rita Auriemma and Snježana Karinja (Trieste: Università degli Studi di Trieste, Pomorski muzej Piran), pp. 431–34

Princeton. 1991. 'Acquisitions of the Art Museum 1990', *Record of the Art Museum, Princeton University*, 50.1: 16–69

Rebay-Salisbury, Katharina. 2016. *The Human Body in Early Iron Age Central Europe: Burial Practices and Images of the Hallstatt World* (New York: Routledge)

Rocco, Guilia. 2002. 'Il repertorio figurato delle stele della Daunia: iconografie e temi narrativi tra Grecia e Adriatico meridionale', *Prospettiva*, 105: 2–28

Romito, Matilde (ed.). 2006. *Vecchi scavi, nouvi studi* (Salerno: Arti Grafiche Sud)

Roth, Ulrike. 2007. *Thinking Tools: Agriculture and Slavery between Evidence and Models*, Bulletin of the Institute of Classical Studies, Supplement, 92 (London: Institute of Classical Studies)

Scheid, John, and Jesper Svenbro. 1996. *The Craft of Zeus: Myths of Weaving and Fabric*, Revealing Antiquity (Cambridge, MA: Harvard University Press)

Smith, Tyler Jo. 2010. *Komast Dancers in Archaic Greek Art* (Oxford: Oxford University Press)

Torelli, Mario. 1997. *Il rango, il rito e l'immagine: alle origini della rappresentazione storica romana* (Milan: Electa)

Tunzi, Anna Maria (ed.). 2011. *Pagine di pietra: i Dauni tra VII e VI secolo a.C.* (Foggia: Claudio Grenzi)

Turk, Peter, and Ida Murgelj. 2008 (2010). 'Ponovno najdeni apulski kraterji iz Stične. Die wiederaufgefundenen apulischen Kratere aus Stična', in *Stična*, II.2: *Gomile starejše železne dobe: Grabhügel aus der älteren Eisenzeit*, ed. by Stane Gabrovec, Biba Teržan, and Hermann Born, Katalogi in monografije, 38 (Ljubljana: Narodni muzej Slovenije), pp. 159–72

Villing, Alexandra. 2009. 'The Daily Grind of Ancient Greece: Mortars and Mortaria between Symbol and Reality', in *Shapes and Uses of Greek Vases*, ed. by Athéna Tsingarida (Brussels: CReA-Patrimoine), pp. 319–33

Warden, P. Gregory. 2008. 'Ritual and Representation on a Campana Dinos in Boston', *Etruscan Studies*, 11.1: 121–33

Wijngaarden, Gert-Jan van. 2015. 'Emma Blake, *Social Networks and Regional Identity in Bronze Age Italy*. Cambridge; New York: Cambridge University Press, 2014', *Bryn Mawr Classical Review*, 16 September 2015

Yntema, Douwe. 1990. *The Matt-Painted Pottery of Southern Italy* (Lecce: Congedo)

KEELY ELIZABETH HEUER

12. Face to Face

Isolated Heads in South Italian and Etruscan Visual Culture

ABSTRACT Traditionally, scholarship has tended to approach Etruscan and South Italian red-figure vase-painting as entirely separate phenomena, while still acknowledging their common Athenian technical and iconographic roots in the late fifth century BCE. However, Etruscan vases share a striking number of parallel motifs with their South Italian contemporaries, many of which are infrequent or otherwise unknown on Attic painted ceramics. This shared imagery can only be explained by the existence of strong cross-cultural ties between southern and central pre-Roman Italy — linking Greeks, Etruscans, and a wide variety of Italic populations, the latter of which were the primary market for South Italian vases. I argue that this shared iconography hints at important connections and networks that are not otherwise preserved in surviving literary and epigraphic sources. For this chapter, I present the isolated human head as an iconological case study. This image is the most predominant subject on South Italian vases, occurring as the primary or secondary decoration on over 7500 pieces (more than one-third of the published corpus). By the second quarter of the fourth century BCE, similar heads appear on Etruscan and Alto-Adriatic red-figure vases, concurrent with the use of the motif in all five South Italian wares. By observing the consistent patterns of the image's use on ceramics as well other media, including stone carving, moulded terracottas, and wall painting, these heads appear to have been closely associated with eschatological beliefs of peoples throughout the Italian peninsula in the late Classical and early Hellenistic periods.

Despite acknowledging their common Athenian technical and iconographic roots, scholars have preferred to discuss South Italian and Etruscan red-figure vase-painting in isolation from one another, and have not recognized their striking number of paral-

lel decorative motifs, some of which are infrequent or unknown on Attic painted ceramics. This shared imagery can only be explained through the existence of strong cross-cultural connections between southern and central pre-Roman Italy — linking Greeks, Etruscans, and a wide variety of Italic populations, the latter of which were the primary market for South Italian vases. I argue that this shared iconography hints at important connections and networks that are not otherwise preserved in surviving literary and epigraphic sources. In this chapter, I highlight the isolated human head as an iconological case study because of the motif's frequency and consistency of use on ceramics, and in other media produced on the Italian peninsula and Sicily, including stone carving, moulded terracottas, and wall painting. A striking feature of ancient Italian and Sicilian visual culture is the proclivity to represent the human head alone, in contrast to mainland Greece, where the human body was generally conceptualized holistically (Heuer 2015, 71–72). The motif's copious appearance in pre-Roman visual culture is so underexplored that it is essential to provide first a broad overview of its use before embarking on theoretical interpretation, which I offer in my conclusion. The contexts in which these heads occur indicate that they are a manifestation of the sacral and eschatological beliefs of many peoples throughout pre-Roman Italy during the late Classical and Hellenistic periods, embodying desired or anticipated outcomes.

Around 450 BCE, the technique of red-figure vase-painting, along with its respective shapes and imagery, was transmitted from Athens to Greek settlements on Italy's Ionian coast, first appearing at Metaponto.[1] By 380 BCE, workshops of potters and

---

1   See Heuer 2015, 81 n. 1 for a summary of the various hypotheses regarding the transfer of red-figure technique between Athens and southern Italy.

Corresponding author Keely Elizabeth Heuer (heuerk@newpaltz.edu)

Adoption, Adaption, and Innovation in Pre-Roman Italy: Paradigms for Cultural Change, ed. by Jeremy Armstrong and Aaron Rhodes-Schroder, AMW 3 (Turnhout, 2023), pp. 193–219   BREPOLS PUBLISHERS   10.1484/M.AMW-EB.5.133274

painters were active in all regions of southern Italy and Sicily (Denoyelle and Iozzo 2009, 238). Nearly simultaneously, the same technique was mastered by pottery ateliers in Etruria, such as at Vulci, perhaps also the result of itinerant Athenian potters and painters seeking out new, profitable markets.[2] Red-figure vase production in pre-Roman Italy peaked between c. 350–320 BCE before decreasing in quantity and quality until the early third century.

Isolated heads are not original to South Italian and Etruscan red-figure vases. In fact, the motif has a long history in the wares of mainland Greece and the Aegean, dating as early as the Late Geometric period.[3] The motif occurs erratically and not in large numbers, often concentrated within specific workshops where the subject was favoured for yet unclear reasons. During the seventh century BCE, profile heads of bearded men, women, youths, and warriors in outline and black-figure technique were painted on Corinthian and Melian vases, at times with inscriptions naming them.[4] In the first quarter of the sixth century, early Attic black-figure vase painters in turn borrowed the isolated head from the Corinthian vase painters they imitated. Later that same century, Attic potters also produced plastic vases in the form of human heads, and Athenian painters continued using the subject on red-figure vases of the fifth and fourth century BCE.[5] Strikingly, heads seem to have been intentionally selected for export goods in the Athenian Kerameikos, especially towards Italy, where roughly half of Attic vases of known provenience decorated with the motif were discovered. The earliest examples were found near Greek settlements, such as Paestum and Taranto, but nearly three-quarters are from Etruscan and Italic contexts, demonstrating the image's particular resonance for the indigenous population well before its transference with the red-figure technique from Athens to pre-Roman Italy (Heuer 2014).

Isolated Heads in South Italian and Etruscan Vase-Painting

On over 7500 South Italian vases, more than one-third of the published corpus, an isolated head appears as a primary or secondary decorative motif, making it the most common and characteristic subject of South Italian vase-painting.[6] It occurs in all five wares, named for the regions in which each was manufactured and used: Lucanian, Apulian, Campanian, Paestan, and Sicilian (Heuer 2015, 65). The earliest appearance of heads on South Italian vases occurred as South Italian vase-painting departed from its Athenian prototypes and adapted to local needs, c. 410–400 BCE (Trendall 1990). The motif's application as a primary or secondary decorative feature was often dictated by vase shape. Before 340 BCE, heads were the main decoration on small-scale pieces and played a secondary role on large vases, typically found on the neck, shoulder, or in a central band around the belly (Heuer 2015, 65).[7]

Such remarkable statistics confirm the motif's meaning within a south Italian context, especially in Italic burials where these vases are most frequently discovered. Until recently, however, while scholarship has noted the heads' frequency, it primarily concentrated on labelling them as specific mythological figures.[8] Identification has proven challenging, as few heads offer clear iconographic clues, except those of satyrs and Pan (Fig. 12.1).[9] The only inscribed example is a frontal head wearing a polos on the neck of an Apulian volute-krater in London labelled as 'Aura' (Breeze) by incision, possibly indicating a post-production addition.[10] The paucity of inscriptions is surprising, as South Italian vase painters were at times

---

2   On early Etruscan red-figure vase-painting: Beazley 1947, 25–69; Brendel 1978, 343–47; Haynes 2000, 319–20.

3   See Buchner 1953–1954, 37–39 and 48–51; Brock 1957, 122, 144, 164, and 214; von Vacano 1973, 17. Von Vacano notes that the emergence of the isolated head motif at this time may have been driven by the increasing interest in representing facial features, seen also in the drawing of heads in outline with a single dot for the eye, as well as the presence of animal-head protomes in contemporary visual culture of the Near East. Von Vacano 1973, 32–33.

4   For example, London, British Museum, inv. no. 1865,12–13.1, a Corinthian aryballos with a female head on the back of the handle with the inscription, 'I am Aineta'. For further information on heads in Corinthian and Melian vase-painting, see Heuer 2011, 21–25.

5   For further discussion of isolated heads on Attic black- and red-figure vases and relevant bibliography, see Heuer 2011, 25–41.

6   This statistic is derived from the vases in the works of A. D. Trendall and A. Cambitoglou as well as all *CVA* volumes published prior 2015. Undoubtedly, there are many more extant examples that have yet to be published.

7   Heads are sometimes painted on the feet of volute-kraters, such as on St Petersburg, Hermitage, inv. no. 420 (Trendall and Cambitoglou 1982, 863–64 no. 18).

8   On the challenge of identifying heads in South Italian vase-painting: Heuer 2015, 68–70.

9   I am aware of ten heads of Pan on south Italian vases, for example Vatican City, Musei Vaticani, AA 2 inv. no. 18255 (Trendall and Cambitoglou 1978, 194 no. 13) and Rizzo collection, Mandelieu, France (Trendall and Cambitoglou 1992, 507 no. 40-B). Heads of satyrs of varying ages are the most common type of heads on South Italian vases other than those of women. For example: Copenhagen 88 (Trendall and Cambitoglou 1982, 651 no. 12; *CVA* Copenhagen 6 (Denmark 6) 198, pl. 254, 2a–b), Trieste 1836 (Trendall and Cambitoglou 1982, 653 no. 38), and Zurich 2548 (Trendall and Cambitoglou 1982, 653 no. 42; *CVA* Zurich 1 (Switzerland 2) 55, pl. 40, 3–4).

10   London, British Museum, inv. no. F 277: Trendall and Cambitoglou 1978, 193 no. 5. On incised inscriptions: Cohen 1991.

12. FACE TO FACE 195

Figure 12.1. Campanian red-figure bell-krater attributed to the Painter of Oxford 1945 with head of a satyr in profile. New York, Metropolitan Museum of Art, inv. no. 41.162.263, c. 360–330 BCE (photo courtesy of the Metropolitan Museum of Art).

Figure 12.2. Apulian red-figure skyphos with female head in profile, New York, Metropolitan Museum of Art, inv. no. 76.12.15, c. 325–300 BCE (photo courtesy of the Metropolitan Museum of Art).

Figure 12.3. Campanian red-figure neck-amphora attributed to the Pilos Head Group. On the neck, head of youth wearing a *pilos*; on the body, a young warrior seated on an altar facing a bearded warrior. New York, Metropolitan Museum of Art, inv. no. X.21.19, c. 350–325 BCE (photo courtesy of the Metropolitan Museum of Art).

Figure 12.4. Apulian red-figure volute-krater by the Painter of Copenhagen 4223. On the neck, head wearing Phrygian cap; on the body, a youthful warrior and mature male wearing a himation and leaning on a staff in a *naiskos* surrounded by women and youths. Chicago, Art Institute of Chicago, c. 340 BCE (photo courtesy of the Art Institute of Chicago).

Figure 12.5. Lucanian red-figure *nestoris* attributed the Painter of New York 52.11.2. On the neck, head in profile flanked by wings; on the body, a standing youth offering a bird to a seated woman. New York, Metropolitan Museum of Art, inv. no. 52.11.2, c. 360–350 BCE (photo courtesy of the Metropolitan Museum of Art).

Figure 12.6. Etruscan (Caeretan) red-figure Genucilia plate (name plate of the Genucilia ware) with female head in profile. Providence, Rhode Island School of Design Museum, inv. no. 27.188, c. 340–300 BCE (photo courtesy of the Rhode Island School of Design Museum).

Figure 12.7. Etruscan (Caeretan) red-figure *oinochoe* attributed to the Populonia Torcop Painter. On the neck, female head in profile; on the body, confronted male head wearing wolf-skin cap and female head. Paris, Musée du Louvre, inv. no. K 471, second half fourth century BCE (photo courtesy of the RMN Grand Palais, Musée du Louvre).

Figure 12.8. Detail of Hades and Persephone on the Torre San Severo Sarcophagus. Orvieto, Museo Claudio Faina, final decades of the fourth century BCE (photo by author).

Figure 12.9. Campanian red-figure epichysis produced by the Cassandra-Parrish workshop with confronted male and female heads. Bonn, Akademisches Kunstmuseum der Universität Bonn, inv. no. 200, c. 380–360 BCE (photo courtesy of Akademisches Kunstmuseum).

Figure 12.10 (right). Etruscan (Caeretan) red-figure Torcop Group *oinochoe* with female heads in profile on the neck and body. New York, Metropolitan Museum of Art, inv. no. 91.1.465, c. 300 BCE (photo courtesy of the Metropolitan Museum of Art).

Figure 12.12. Campanian red-figure stemless *kylix* attributed to the Rhomboid Group with female head in profile surrounded by laurel leaves in the tondo. Edinburgh, National Museum of Scotland, inv. no. 1956.405, c. 330–320 BCE (photo courtesy of the A. D. Trendall Research Centre for Ancient Mediterranean Studies).

Figure 12.11. Campanian red-figure bell-krater by the Seated Nike Painter with female head in profile. Cambridge, Museum of Classical Archaeology, University of Cambridge, inv. no. GR 14/1963, c. 380–360 BCE (photo courtesy of the A. D. Trendall Research Centre for Ancient Mediterranean Studies).

Figure 12.13. Etruscan red-figure Tondo Group skyphos from Chiusi with female heads in floral surround. New York, Metropolitan Museum of Art, inv. no. 07.286.33, c. 340–300 BCE (photo courtesy of the Metropolitan Museum of Art).

quite lavish with naming labels in mythological and theatre-inspired scenes.[11] Study of the heads is further confounded by the paucity of literary works from pre-Roman southern Italy, which might assist in recognizing who they represent. The heads are overwhelmingly female, often wearing diadems, veils, or polos headdresses, as well as necklaces and earrings (Fig. 12.2).[12] Female heads are rendered identically to those of their full-length mortal and divine counterparts. Unlike in Attic vase-painting, where heads are frequently given clear attributes, such features are rare on South Italian vases — such as Erotes around a female head (possibly Aphrodite?),[13] horns (Io?),[14] or a quiver emerging from behind (Artemis?)[15] — and do not reliably identify the attribute-less majority. Even those feminine heads with indicators of immortal status, such as polos-crowns or a nimbus, are too indeterminate to afford concrete conclusions.[16] Heads of youths and bearded men are similarly ambiguous (Fig. 12.3).[17] Attributes repeatedly occur with heads of indeterminate sex, resulting in a variety of interpretations. For instance, heads wearing Phrygian caps have been labelled as Amazons, Orpheus, and even Paris, who wears this headdress in South Italian vase-painting (Fig. 12.4).[18] Winged

Figure 12.14. Apulian red-figure volute-krater by the Patera Painter. Detail of neck with female head emerging from flower in floral surround. Malibu, J. Paul Getty Museum, inv. no. 77.AE.115, c. 330 BCE (photo courtesy of the J. Paul Getty Museum).

heads are recognized as Nike or the hermaphrodite/effeminate form of Eros, a common full-length figure in all South Italian wares (Fig. 12.5).[19]

In the mid-fourth century BCE, heads first appear on Etruscan red-figure vases. These were produced in multiple centres, including at Cerveteri, Civita Castellana (ancient Falerii), Chiusi, and Volterra.[20] The motif most often serves as the primary decoration on vases of all sizes, although it is more frequent on smaller shapes.[21] Heads in Etruscan vase-painting share many parallels with their South Italian counterparts, from an overwhelming preference for female heads to a general lack of attributes that

11 For inscriptions on Apulian vases, see Carpenter 2016; Oakley 2016.

12 Cambitoglou 1954, 111–21; Schauenburg 1957, 210–12; Smith 1976, 50–51; Lehnert 1978; Trendall and Cambitoglou 1982, 445, 447–48, 456, 462–63, 473, 486, 601–02, 604–05, 647–49; Kossatz-Deißmann 1985, 229–39; Schauenburg 1989, 36–37.

13 For example, Bari, Museo Archeologico, inv. no. 872 from Canosa (Trendall and Cambitoglou 1982, 497 no. 43) and Lecce, Museo Sigismondo Castromediano, inv. no. 855 from Canosa (Trendall and Cambitoglou 1982, 975 no. 186; *CVA* Lecce 2 (Italy 6) 35, pl. 59, 1–2).

14 For example, Milan, Collezione Banca Intesa, inv. no. 115 (once 'H.A.' Collection 306 — Trendall and Cambitoglou 1982, 728 no. 16) and Ruvo, Museo Nazionale Jatta, inv. no. 1092 (Trendall and Cambitoglou 1982, 753 no. 226).

15 Such as on the volute-krater by the Painter of Copenhagen 4223 formerly on the New York market at Ariadne Galleries (Trendall and Cambitoglou 1991–1992, 121 no. 39–4).

16 Examples of a nimbus around a female head: Bologna, Museo Archeologico Civico, inv. no. 567 (Trendall and Cambitoglou 1982, 728 no. 19; *CVA* Bologna 3 (Italy 12) 6, pl. IV Dr 7, 3–4) and St Petersburg, Hermitage, inv. no. 354 (Trendall and Cambitoglou 1982, 728 no. 21). Female heads wearing polos crowns appear on Atami, Moa Museum, inv. no. 1729 (*CVA* Japan 2, 59–62 pls 51, 3–4, 52, and 53) and Parma, Museo Archeologico Nazionale, inv. no. C. 96 (Trendall and Cambitoglou 1978, 408 no. 64; *CVA* Parma 2 (Italy 46) 3–4, pl. 3, 1–2).

17 For example, the heads of youths on Zurich 2636 (Trendall 1967, 432, no. 518; *CVA* Zurich 1 (Switzerland 2) 50–51, pl. 33, 7–9) and Frankfurt ß 607 (Trendall 1967, 411, no. 343; *CVA* Frankfurt am Main 3 (Germany 50) 25–26; pl. 33).

18 On identifying heads wearing Phrygian caps: Schauenburg 1974, 171–72, 174–85; Schmidt 1975, 130–32; Schauenburg 1981, 468; 1982, 253–55; 1984, 364; and Kossatz-Deißmann 1990,

517–20. Examples include St Petersburg, Hermitage, inv. no. 406 (Trendall and Cambitoglou 1982, 490 no. 21) and Warsaw, National Museum, 198951 (Trendall 1967, 235, no. 59; *CVA* Warsaw 5 (Poland 8) 26–27, pl. 32, 1–2).

19 For example, Ruvo, Museo Nazionale Jatta, inv. no. 425 (Trendall and Cambitoglou 1978, 403 no. 15) and Brussels, Musées Royaux des Beaux-Arts de Belgique, inv. no. R 252 (Trendall and Cambitoglou 1982, 886 no. 220; *CVA* Brussels 2 (Belgium 2) 6, IV D b pl. 7; 1a–b). On the ambiguity of winged heads in South Italian vase-painting: Cambitoglou 1954, 121; Schauenburg 1957, 212; 1962, 37; 1974, 169–86; 1981, 467–69; 1982, 250–55; 1984, 155–57.

20 For example: Berkeley, Phoebe A. Hearst Museum of Anthropology, inv. no. 8/992 made in Cerveteri; Princeton, Princeton University Art Museum, inv. no. y1945-187 produced in Civita Castellana; Paris, Louvre, inv. no. H 101 created in Chiusi; and Florence, Museo Archeologico Nazionale, inv. no. 4035 made in Volterra.

21 Occasionally, heads serve as secondary decoration on Etruscan vases, such as the heads of youths flanking a plastic lion-head spout on the shoulder of a late Etruscan hydria in London (British Museum, inv. no. F 487 — Beazley 1947, 172 no. 1 pl. 34, 4). They appear above a scene of chariot racing, a theme that occurs in Etruscan and Italic tombs in Campania (for example, Paestum, Laghetto tomb 64/1954 and Paestum, Gaudo tomb 7/1972 — Andreae 2007, 52–67).

would allow for certain identification (Fig. 12.6).[22] An exception is a Torcop Group *oinochoe* in the Louvre (Fig. 12.7).[23] On the body is a pair of male and female confronted heads. The female head, on the left with her hair pulled up in a reticulate *sakkos*, is analogous to those on other Etruscan and South Italian vases. However, the male head wears an animal skin reminiscent of the wolf-skin cap worn by Aita (Greek: Hades) in Etruscan tomb painting, such as in the Tomba dell'Orco II at Tarquinia, and on the Torre San Severo Sarcophagus at Orvieto (Fig. 12.8) (Del Chiaro 1970, 293). If the male head on the jug is Aita, then the female head is likely his consort, Phersipnai (Greek: Persephone). Confronted heads occur repeatedly in Etruscan red-figure (Heuer 2011, 202–04), and there are earlier parallels on Campanian and Sicilian vases (Fig. 12.9).[24]

The division of the *kekryphalos* (a headdress with an opening tied at the crown of the head) with double lines flanked by rows of dots, perhaps representing stylized folds, worn by the female heads on the Torcop Group *oinochoai* lends strength to the argument that Etruscan vase painters adopted the confronted head motif from Campania (Fig. 12.10).[25] This detail is characteristic of many female heads in Campanian vase-painting, appearing as early as the work of Cassandra Painter (*c.* 380–360 BCE) (Fig. 12.11).[26] The net-*sphendone* headdress that is

a consistent feature of female heads on Caeretan Genucilia plates[27] (Fig. 12.6) appears on female heads in the tondi of contemporary Campanian *kylikes* of the Rhomboid Group (*c.* 330–320 BCE) (Fig. 12.12).[28] This similarity must be an instance of south Italian artisans borrowing from their northern neighbours, as del Chiaro (1957, 308–13; 1974, 122) demonstrated that the headdress was derived from the work of the Athenian Meidias Painter and appears on Falisco-Caeretan plates of the first half of the fourth century.[29] Heads on Etruscan vases are sometimes associated with flowers and floral surrounds (Fig. 12.13),[30] a common feature of Apulian vase-painting starting in the third quarter of the fourth century BCE that also, occasionally, appears on Campanian vases (Fig. 12.14).[31] Few South Italian vases have been uncovered in Etruria, but presumably Etruscans could well have been exposed to the motif on vases in Campania, an area that exhibited strong connections with Etruria as early as the ninth century BCE (d'Agostino 2004). It is also the closest southern Italian region to Etruria that produced red-figure pottery. In fact, the main Campanian workshops were heavily concentrated in Capua, a community with strong Etruscan influences from the very start (Trendall 1967, 190–91). A substantial number of Campanian and Paestan vases decorated with heads were also discovered at Pontecagnano, another important settlement with Etruscan links in the region.[32]

---

22 The majority of isolated heads in Etruscan vase-painting appear on Torcop Group *oinochoai* and Genucilia plates. See Beazley 1947, 168–69, 175–77, 302–03; del Chiaro 1957; 1960; 1974, 63–86; and Pietilä-Castrén 1999.

23 Paris, Louvre, inv. no. K 471, likely from Cerveteri — del Chiaro 1970; 1974, 70–71, pl. 8; Lehnert 1978, 96–97.

24 I know of eighteen Campanian vases with confronted heads, the earliest of which date to the second quarter of the fourth century BCE (for example, Berlin, Antikensammlung, inv. no. F 3017 — Trendall 1967, 233 no. 53). Confronted heads are more popular in Sicilian vase-painting (twenty-five examples), where they appear almost exclusively on *olpai* and *lekanides*, starting around 350 BCE (see Syracuse, Museo Archeologico Regionale Paolo Orsi, inv. no. 46883 — Trendall 1967, 629 no. 286). Usually there is an object between the heads, most often a vegetal element, although *phialai*, bunches of grapes, suspended bead pendants with floral finials, and an altar also occur. See Heuer 2011, 200–02.

25 For example, Lille, Palais des Beaux-Arts, inv. no. Ant. 2 (*CVA* Lille 1 (France 40) 98–99 pl. 39, 1–6); New York, Metropolitan Museum of Art, inv. no. 91.1.465 (Beazley 1947, 169, pl. 38, 4; De Puma 2013, 214–15); and Edinburgh, National Museums of Scotland, inv. no. 1944.15 (*CVA* Edinburgh 1 (Great Britain 16) 48, pl. 56, 5–7).

26 See the reverse of Philadelphia, Penn Museum, inv. no. 31.36.18 (Trendall 1967, 229 no. 18). Other later examples include Zurich, Universität Archäologische Sammlung, inv. no. 2636 (Trendall 1967, 432 no. 518; *CVA* Zurich 1 (Switzerland 2) 50–51, pl. 33, 7–9) and Warsaw, Państwowe Muzeum Archeologiczne, inv. no. 147273 (Trendall 1967, 235 no. 60; *CVA* Warsaw 5 (Poland 8) 27, pls 32, 3–4 and 34, 5).

---

27 Del Chiaro 1957, 255–68. The earliest Genucilia plates were produced in Civita Castellana (Falerii) at the start of the fourth century BCE. Soon thereafter, some artisans who produced these vases set up a workshop in Cerveteri (Caere), which operated until at least the middle of the century (del Chiaro 1957, 312–13). Examples include Providence, Rhode Island School of Design, inv. no. 27.188 (Beazley 1947, 175 pl. 38, 17–19); Naples, Museo Archeologico Nazionale, inv. no. 86015 (del Chiaro 1957, 256 pl. 19a); and Paris, Louvre, inv. no. CA 3187 (del Chiaro 1957, 258 pl. 19c).

28 As on Edinburgh, National Museums of Scotland, inv. no. 1956.405 (Trendall 1967, 543 no. 810 pl. 214, 2) and Birmingham, City Art Gallery, inv. no. 1297.85 (Trendall 1967, 543 no. 812).

29 See also Trendall 1967, 538–39.

30 For example, New York, Metropolitan Museum of Art, inv. no. 07.286.33 (De Puma 2013, 211–12) and on the amphora found in the Golini I tomb at Orvieto (*c.* 350–325 BCE), now in the Museo Archeologico Nazionale, Orvieto. This floral decoration is concentrated in the Clusium Group: Beazley 1947, 116–18; Harari 1980, 158–83.

31 For example, floral tendrils flank a female head in three-quarter view to left on the shoulder of the Campanian hydria Louvre K 276 (Trendall 1967, 406 no. 301 pl. 160, 1). On floral tendrils in South Italian vase-painting: Heuer 2019.

32 Trendall records twenty-seven pieces, such as Salerno, Museo Archeologico Provinciale, inv. no. 170 (Trendall 1967, 324 no. 730), Salerno, Museo Archeologico Provinciale, inv. no. Pc

Despite the inclusion of attributes, the vague identities of the isolated heads on South Italian and Etruscan vases leads to two conclusions: either the meaning of the heads was so readily recognizable to the ancient viewer that further iconographic or written identifiers were unnecessary, or the ambiguity was intentional (see also Rhodes-Schroder in this volume), perhaps to allow for a greater interpretive and functional flexibility dependent upon the user's ethnic and religious background in the cultural melting pot of pre-Roman Italy and Sicily. Imagery with broad, cross-cultural appeal would give potters and painters a wider client base and increase profits. While Etruscan workshops presumably catered to an Etruscan audience, we must remember that in southern Italy, red-figure vases were mainly produced in areas not under the political control of the Greek colonies by the mid-fourth century BCE. In Apulia, it is generally assumed — with some objections — that red-figure vases were first made in Taranto,[33] but by 340–330 BCE, the workshops of the Patera and Baltimore Painters, two of the most prolific and influential *ateliers* of their generation, were active in the Italic settlements of Ruvo and Canosa, respectively.[34] Similarly in Lucania, production began in the Greek colony of Metaponto (D'Andria 1980; De Juliis 2001, 176–80), but moved into the indigenous hinterland *c*. 380–370 BCE (Trendall 1989, 58; Denoyelle and Iozzo 2009, 114–17).[35] Cumae and Capua, the centres of Campanian vase-painting, were dominated by Italic peoples in the final quarter of the fifth century BCE. Capua traditionally fell to the Samnites in 426 BCE, and Cumae, the earliest Greek settlement on the Italian mainland, was captured by Campanians in 421 BCE.[36] Paestum, too, seems to have been governed by Lucanians from around 400 BCE.[37] Thus, Greek ceramicists working in Magna Graecia logically would have taken into consideration the iconographic interests of Italic clientele, as much as those of their fellow Greeks, to create products that yielded a healthy profit margin.

A more successful tactic in understanding the isolated heads' significance is to consider *what* they embody, as opposed to *who* they represent. In Attic vase-painting, heads are repeatedly flanked by full-length figures, implying an *anodos* (Fig. 12.15).[38] By contrast, the motif rarely plays a narrative function on the red-figure wares of pre-Roman Italy. Of the thousands of extant South Italian vases decorated with isolated heads, less than forty examples feature heads in the presence of full-length figures, and no instances are known to me in Etruscan vase-painting. On South Italian vases, such scenes most often take the form of a female head emerging from a flower and flanked by Erotes, such as on the shoulder of Bari 872, a composition with no parallel in Athenian vase-painting, nor an explanation in extant ancient literature (Trendall and Cambitoglou 1982, 497 no. 43). An exception is found on a *pelike* in Amsterdam attributed to the Darius Painter's workshop. On the obverse, a female head rising from an acanthus calyx on the ground gazes at a standing woman with a lyre and open cista beside her and a seated woman in three-quarter view (Fig. 12.16).[39] Comparable tableaux occur occasionally on Etruscan bronze mirrors and engraved gems, where the full-length figures often look towards the isolated head, typically male or that of a satyr. Nancy de Grummond (2006, 26–27, 32–37; 2011) persuasively argued that heads in these contexts represented oracular voices, and has noted similar scenes with the head of Orpheus on Attic vases.[40]

The iconographic meaning of isolated heads becomes clearer by observing the consistent types of figural scenes paired with them on South Italian vases, as they regularly depict mortuary cult practices, mythological scenes involving death, and divine figures with clear eschatological associations. Beginning in the work of the Iliupersis Painter (active *c*. 370–355 BCE), heads often occur in conjunction with scenes of mourners bringing offer-

---

1317 (Trendall 1987, 171 no. 367 pl. 116a–c), and Salerno, Museo Archeologico Provinciale, inv. no. 1319 (Trendall 1987, 223 no. 836 pl. 142g).

33 Trendall and Cambitoglou 1978, xlvii. For dissenting views, refer to Carpenter 2003, 5–6; 2009, 29–31; Thorn 2009.

34 Trendall and Cambitoglou 1982, 450; Robinson 1990; Carpenter 2003.

35 Trendall 1989, 58; Denoyelle and Iozzo 2009, 114–17.

36 Red-figure vase-production in Campania began *c*. 380 BCE. Cerchiai and others 2004, 44; Denoyelle and Iozzo 2009, 181.

37 The earliest Paestan red-figure workshops were established *c*. 390 BCE. Trendall 1987, 2–3; Cerchiai and others 2004, 62.

---

38 Anodoi become increasingly popular in Attic vase-painting between *c*. 375–325 BCE, particularly on *pelikai*, *hydriai*, stemless cups, *lekanides*, *pyxides*, *kylikes*, and *kraters*. For examples, refer to Paris, Cabinet des Médailles, inv. no. 472 (Beazley 1963, 1489 no. 156) and London, British Museum, inv. no. F 18 (Beazley 1963, 1481 no. 1). Regarding anodoi on Athenian vases: Metzger 1951, 72–73; Langlotz 1954, 7–8; Brommer 1959, 52–53, 56; Bérard 1974; Simon 1989; Sgouropoulou 2000.

39 Amsterdam, Allard Pierson Museum, inv. no. 2578: Trendall and Cambitoglou 1982, 521 no. 215.

40 Trendall interpreted the unusual scene on a *pelike* connected in style with the Trieste Owl Group (Honolulu, Academy of Arts, inv. no. 2164 — Trendall and Cambitoglou 1982, 752 no. 224) as the head of Orpheus emerging from a flower between two initiates (one male, one female), who either worship it or seek an oracular consultation.

ings to funerary monuments of various types, most often in the form of a stele or *naiskos* (a small, temple-like shrine usually containing a statue of the deceased, sometimes accompanied by family members or servants) (Fig. 12.4).[41] The head typically emerges from a flower or a leafy base — usually an acanthus calyx, a plant with lengthy sepulchral associations in the Graeco-Roman world[42] — placed directly above the grave marker on the neck or shoulder of the vase.[43] It is enveloped by roughly symmetrical spiralling tendrils, from which various flowers blossom. The juxtaposition of the heads and lush plant life connotes a link between the motif and the regenerative powers of nature, and its placement on the same vertical axis over the funerary monument visually implies the emergence of new life from death.

Around 370–360 BCE, heads began to be painted above mythological subjects that involved the demise of one or more individuals[44] like the death of Hippolytos due to the startling of his horses by a Fury and the white bull of Poseidon rising from the sea on the obverse of an Apulian volute-krater by the Darius Painter in London.[45] Heads also appear together with mythological narratives involving the rescue of a figure from certain death, either through the granting of immortality,[46] forcible abduction by a deity, or heroic intervention, such as the rescue of Andromeda by Perseus (Fig. 12.17).[47] Heads are

also painted in connection with underworld scenes, exemplified by the Apulian volute-krater in Toledo (Fig. 12.18).[48] On the obverse, Persephone stands next to enthroned Hades, who shakes hands with Dionysos, the vegetation god of wine, theatre, and rebirth. Surrounding the infernal palace are members of Dionysos's entourage (two maenads, a satyr, and a *paniskos*), along with familiar characters of the underworld: Hermes, the escort of souls to the afterlife, and Kerberos, the three-headed guard dog. Above, to the left of the palace, Aktaion and Pentheus, two mortals divinely punished for their hubris with gruesome deaths, converse. Below, leaning against a white laver, is Agave, Pentheus's mother, who helped tear her son to pieces in a fit of madness brought on by Dionysos. Dionysian imagery is the most common mythological iconography paired with isolated heads in South Italian vase-painting.[49] Dionysos earned his immortality with the return of Hephaistos to Mount Olympus and retrieved his mortal mother, Semele, from the underworld. He was a resurrected being, according to certain variants of his mythology, and the mystery aspect of his cult seems to have significant popularity in Magna Graecia, in connection with Orphism, ostensibly due to its promises of providing benefits in the hereafter to the faithful.[50]

---

41 For example, Bari, Museo Archeologico, inv. no. 1394 (Trendall and Cambitoglou 1978, 203 no. 101 pl. 65, 1); Milan, Collezione Banca Intesa, inv. no. 108 (once 'H.A.' Collection 275 — Trendall and Cambitoglou 1982, 458 no. 8; *CVA* Milan H.A. Collection 1 (Italy 49) 9–10, IV D pl. 15–16); and Basel, Antikenmuseum, inv. no. S 25 (Trendall and Cambitoglou 1982, 797 no. 7). On funerary monuments in South Italian vase-painting: Lohmann 1979.

42 Between 450–425 BCE, acanthus occurs on Attic marble anthemia stelae and funerary monuments painted on contemporary Attic white-ground *lekythoi*, such as on Berlin 2680 (Oakley 2004, 123) and Athens, National Museum, inv. no. 14517 (Beazley 1963, 1373 no. 13; *BAPD* 217642). On grave stelae with acanthus: Kurtz and Boardman 1971, 124 and Froning 1985. Jucker (1961) argued for the funerary connotations of Roman portrait busts emerging from acanthus calyxes.

43 Heads were also painted under the handles of *hydriai* decorated with grave markers, and the motif may even serve as decoration on the *naiskos*'s base or be placed inside of it (Heuer 2015, 73).

44 An early example is the Cassandra Painter's name vase depicting Ajax dragging Cassandra from the altar (Trendall 1967, 225 no. 1; *CVA* Capua (1) 10–11, pl. 22).

45 London, British Museum, inv. no. F 279: Trendall and Cambitoglou 1982, 487 no. 17; Taplin 2007, 137–38.

46 Such as Aphrodite and Persephone appealing to Zeus for the life of Adonis on New York, Metropolitan Museum of Art, inv. no. 11.210.3 (Trendall and Cambitoglou 1982, 489 no. 20).

47 Heads appear above the rescue of Andromeda on Naples, Museo Archeologico Nazionale, 3225 (inv. no. 82266; Trendall and Cambitoglou 1982, 500 no. 58); Taranto, Museo Archeologico

Nazionale, inv. no. 194764 (once Malibu, J. Paul Getty Museum, inv. no. 84.AE.996 — Trendall and Cambitoglou 1991–1992, 144 no. 16g pl. 34, 3–4); and Fiesole, Collezione Costantini (*CVA* Fiesole 2 (Italy 58) 19–20, pls 20, 2–3, 21).

48 Toledo, Museum of Art, inv. no. 1994.19, *c.* 330 BCE, attributed to the Darius Painter (Trendall and Cambitoglou 1992, 508 no. 41a1; Johnston and McNiven 1996. Other examples of vases with underworld scenes painted below isolated heads are Naples, Museo Archeologico Nazionale, Stg. 11 (inv. no. 80854; Trendall and Cambitoglou 1978, 424 no. 54); London, British Museum, inv. no. F 332 (Trendall and Cambitoglou 1982, 733 no. 45 pl. 271, 1); and Munich, Antikensammlungen, inv. no. 3297 (Trendall and Cambitoglou 1982, 533 no. 282 pl. 194).

49 Nearly one-quarter of the published monumental Apulian vases decorated with Dionysiac scenes as part of their primary imagery also feature isolated heads. Some male heads on South Italian vases may depict Dionysos, as four masculine heads on Paestan vases wear ivy wreaths, such as on New York 65.11.18 (Trendall 1987, 223 no. 834) and Cleveland 1989.73 (Trendall 1992; Denoyelle and Iozzo 2009, 132).

50 On the cult of Dionysos in southern Italy and Sicily: Casadio 2009; Isler-Kerényi 2009; Cinquantaquattro and others 2010; and Lombardo and others (eds) 2011. On Orphism: Rohde 1907, 335–61; Mead 1965; *Orfismo in Magna Grecia* 1975; Detienne 1979; Guthrie 1993; and Edmonds 2013. Ancient writers repeatedly link Orphism in Magna Graecia with the Pythagorean movement (Hdt. II. 81; Diogenes Laertius VIII. 8). Orpheus's presence in underworld scenes on Apulian vases has been interpreted as evidence of Orphic beliefs in the region (Schmidt 1975; Pensa 1977).

Figure 12.15. Attic red-figure hydria attributed to the Herakles Painter with female head flanked by Erotes and satyrs holding pickaxes. Brussels, Musées Royaux d'Art et d'Histoire, inv. no. R 286, c. 370 BCE (photo courtesy of the Royal Museums of Art and History, Brussels).

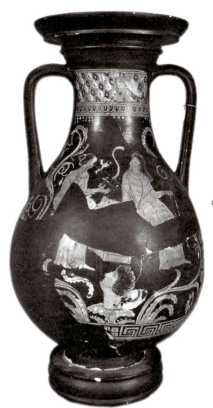

Figure 12.16. Apulian red-figure *pelike* attributed to the Darius Painter with head emerging from flower gazing at two seated women above. Amsterdam, Allard Pierson Museum, inv. no. 2578, c. 340–320 BCE (photo courtesy of Dr Willem van Haarlem, Allard Pierson Museum, Amsterdam).

Figure 12.17. Apulian red-figure volute-krater by the Darius Painter. On the neck, a head wearing a Phrygian cap; on the body, the death of Hippolytos. London, British Museum, inv. no. 1856,1226.1, c. 340–320 BCE (photo courtesy of the Trustees of the British Museum).

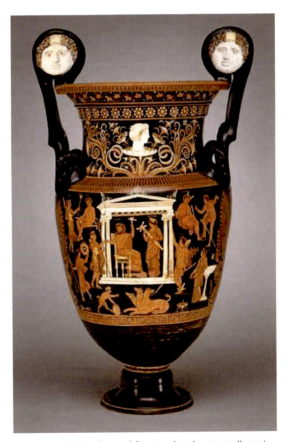

Figure 12.18. Apulian red-figure volute-krater attributed to the Darius Painter. On the neck, profile female head emerging from flower in floral surround; on the body, Dionysos visiting Hades and Persephone in the underworld. Toledo, Toledo Museum of Art, inv. no. 1994.19, c. 330 BCE (photo courtesy of the Toledo Museum of Art).

Figure 12.19 (left). Etruscan (Volterran) *kelebe* from the Portone Necropolis at Volterra. On the neck, female head in three-quarter view to left between horse protomes; on the body, pygmy fighting crane. Florence, Museo Archeologico Nazionale, inv. no. 4035, late fourth century BCE (photo courtesy of Museo Archeologico Nazionale, Firenze).

Figure 12.20. Lecce, Ipogeo Palmieri: entry passage frieze with female head in floral setting, late fourth–early third centuries BCE (photo courtesy of the Istituto per i Beni Archeologici e Monumentali Information Technologies Lab, Lecce).

The connection between the heads and the sepulchral realm is further underscored by the many heads on Volterran *kelebai* (column-kraters) which were used as ash urns in multiple locations across northern Etruria (Fig. 12.19).[51] Nearly all Etruscan and South Italian vases decorated with the motif were uncovered either in or above a tomb, with a few exceptions in civic spaces and votive deposits in sanctuaries (Heuer 2015, 82 n. 35). The predominantly funerary function of vases decorated with heads is also supported by the motif's prevalence on the monumentalized Apulian vases (mainly volute-kraters, amphorae, and *loutrophoroi*), with intentionally perforated lower bodies, rendering them useless as containers for the living. In the necropoleis of Taranto, they served as grave markers through which libations could be poured to reach the remains of the deceased below (Lippolis 1994, 109–28; Fontannaz 2005, 126), but most surviving examples have come to light in the Italic chamber tombs of central and northern Apulia (Carpenter 2003, 6–7).

---

51 On Volterran *kelebai*: Beazley 1947, 123–32; Bocci 1964; Pasquinucci 1968. Examples of heads on *kelebai*: Berlin, Antikensammlung, inv. no. V.I. 3986 (Pasquinucci 1968, 58); Berlin, Antikensammlung, inv. no. V.I. 3988 (Pasquinucci 1968, 60); and Bologna, Museo Archeologico Civico, inv. no. 410 (Pasquinucci 1968, 73).

Isolated Heads beyond Italian Red-Figure

Heads in other media are abundant in pre-Roman funerary contexts. As early as the tenth century BCE, globular stone heads were placed above tombs in northern Apulia at Monte Saraceno, Troia, and Arpi (De Juliis 1984, 142–45; 2009, 61–64). Female heads, often with vegetal surrounds, decorate fourth-century BCE south Italian rock-cut *hypogeum* tombs. Examples of these relief carvings include heads rising from acanthus calyxes on pilaster capitals in a tomb in the Cristallini district of Naples (Pontrandolfo 1996, 470), and the Medusa tomb at Arpi (Mazzei 1984, 197; Pontrandolfo 1996, 470) as well as a female head centred between floral scrolls in the entry passage frieze to the underground sepulchre in the Palazzo Palmieri garden at Lecce (Fig. 12.20) (Bendinelli 1915, 10–11, 18–19, 23–24; L'Arab 1991, 476–79). Among the famous painted tombs of Paestum, a frontal head with short curly hair is between a panther and a lion in Spinazzo necropolis tomb 29 (Rouveret and Pontrandolfo 1983, 125; Rouveret 1990, 339; Andreae 2004, 31, 56; Buranelli 2004).

Heads are also a regular decorative feature in contemporary Etruscan tombs, a practice that continued until the second century BCE. The earliest known examples are in the François Tomb at Vulci (*c*. 330–310 BCE). Centred above three of the doorways leading to side chambers is an isolated fron-

12. FACE TO FACE 203

Figure 12.21a. Vulci, François Tomb: virtual view of the right chamber of the 'atrium' using copies of Carlo Ruspi's reconstruction paintings, c. 330–310 BCE (after Buranelli 2004, 175 fig. 12).

Figure 12.21b. Vulci, François Tomb: female head above central doorway in the right chamber of the 'atrium', c. 330–310 BCE (after Roncalli 1987, 106 fig. 20).

Figure 12.22. Vulci, François Tomb: moulded cement central coffer of the 'tablinum' with the head of Charun, c. 330–310 BCE (after Andreae 2004, 56).

Figure 12.23. Cerveteri: Tomb of the Reliefs, second half fourth century BCE (photo by author).

Figure 12.24. Sovana: Tomba del Tifone, late fourth–early third centuries BCE (photo by author).

Figure 12.25. Figured capital with isolated heads of the central column in Tomba Campanari at Vulci. Florence, Museo Archeologico Nazionale, inv. no. 75279, late fourth–early third centuries BCE (photo courtesy of Museo Archeologico Nazionale, Firenze).

Figure 12.26. Perugia, Tomba dei Volumnii: 'tablinum' with two male isolated heads in the gable, third–second centuries BCE (photo by author).

tal female head on the scale-patterned torus that runs along the top of the walls. The heads above the doors to the lateral vestibules in the so-called 'atrium' have an additional red and blue floral ornament below them (Fig. 12.21). They are not the only isolated heads to occur within the François Tomb; a head of Charun made of moulded cement decorated the central coffer of the rear portion of the central chamber, or the 'tablinum' (Fig. 12.22) (Cristofani 1967, 194–96 and Roncalli 1987, 81–83). Similar in date are the two heavily damaged busts of moulded stucco, one female and one male, flanking the central *kline* in the Tomb of the Reliefs at Cerveteri (Fig. 12.23) (Blanck and Proietti 1986, 20–21). Given the funerary context, it has been suggested that they represent Aita (Hades) and his consort Phersipnai (Persephone). Alternatively, they might depict the couple whose remains were placed on the carved stone bed.

In the early third century BCE, sculpted isolated heads are found primarily on the exteriors of rock-cut tombs in the southern Etruscan interior. The Tomba del Tifone at Sovana, an aedicula tomb cut out of the cliff face, is one of the first (late fourth/early third century). Two projecting anta walls support a pediment filled with a heavily weathered veiled female head in relief, rising from a background of tendrils and flowers (Fig. 12.24).[52] Two other major funerary monuments at Sovana — the Tomba (or Grotta) Pola and the Tomba Ildebranda, both dated to the late third or early second century BCE — have isolated heads on the column capitals of their facades (Rosi 1925, 48–50; 1927, 93–94; Oleson 1982, 49–50, 52–54). A single column still stands at the Tomba Pola, a female head on each side of the capital, placed between the volutes springing up from a base of acanthus leaves at the corners. Related capitals appear on the twelve columns of the Tomba Ildebranda, where the heads on each side of the capitals are not exclusively female, but are occasionally those of youths and bearded males. An example of a figured capital with heads inside an Etruscan tomb chamber is the central column in Tomba Campanari at Vulci (first half of the second century BCE) (Messerschmidt 1930, 49, 60–62). The capital, now in Florence, has a female head on three of its sides and a head wearing a Phrygian cap on the fourth, each emerging from an acanthus calyx and flanked by volutes (Fig. 12.25). At Norchia, another site where rock-cut tombs flourished between the fourth and second centuries BCE,

Figure 12.27. Perugia, Tomba dei Volumnii: coffer with frontal female head in right side-chamber, third–second centuries BCE (photo by author).

frontal human heads in relief are on the low, wide metopes of the so-called Doric tombs of the third or second century BCE (Rosi 1925, 42–43; 1927, 93; von Hesberg 1981, 192; Oleson 1982, 50–51). The Doric friezes of these adjacent tombs appear over a false *porta dorica*.

Frontal heads in relief also occur above false doors of cube tombs, the most common type of Etruscan rock-cut tomb from the Archaic to the Hellenistic period. The Porta della Maschera at San Giuliano formed part of a facade with three doors, two of which are now in ruins. The preserved door, with its simple frame, has an abraded frontal human head a few centimetres above it, and perhaps the other doors to the left had similar reliefs (Rosi 1925, 57). The central head above the false door on the Tomba (Porta) delle Tre Teste in Norchia, a false-cube tomb, is larger and has a low disc on top, perhaps a polos-crown (Rosi 1925, 57). A stele, believed to have once stood above the doorway of a late fourth-century Tarquinian tomb excavated in 1888, features a frontal female head with shoulder-length corkscrew curls and deep-set eyes in a *naiskos* (Haynes 2000, 295–97). She wears two torques, a necklace with bulla pendants, inverted pyramidal earrings, and a polos-like headdress. Sculpted relief heads also occur throughout the Tomba dei Volumnii in Perugia (third–second century BCE), in one of the gables of the 'tablinum' and in the central coffers of the side chambers (von Gerkan and Messerschmidt 1942). In the 'tablinum', the male head on the left has a kithara beside it, leading to its being identified as both Apollo and Orpheus, although it may simply be a member of the elite Volumnii family (Fig. 12.26). The short-haired

---

52 George Dennis (in Oleson 1982, 55–56) and Gino Rosi (1925, 48) were inclined to interpret the head as a gorgoneion, the curious tendrils representing snaky hair.

Figure 12.28. Volterra: Porta dell'Arco with sculpted heads on the keystone and imposts, fourth–third centuries BCE (photo by author).

Figure 12.29. Cinerary urn of Vel Rafi with isolated heads flanking an arched doorway. Perugia, Museo Archeologico Nazionale dell'Umbria, inv. no. 26.291, 150–100 BCE (photo by author).

Figure 12.30. Sarcophagus of Ramtha Visnai and Arnth Tetnies from Vulci. Boston, Museum of Fine Arts, inv. no. 1975.799, late fourth–early third centuries BCE (photo courtesy of the Museum of Fine Arts, Boston).

Figure 12.31. Etruscan terracotta cinerary urn with an isolated head with bovine ears and wearing a Phrygian cap with wings, likely produced in Chiusi. New York, Metropolitan Museum of Art, inv. no. 96.9.221a,b, second century BCE (photo courtesy of the Metropolitan Museum of Art).

Figure 12.32. Terracotta female protome from Ospedale Civile necropolis, tomb 67 in Syracuse. Syracuse, Museo Archeologico Regionale 'Paolo Orsi', c. 550–525 BCE (photo by author).

head of the youth on the right carries a curved stick over his right shoulder from which a container, perhaps a situla, is suspended. This attribute, with its Dionysian connotations, suggests he is a servant or slave. The central decorative coffers in the side chambers are decorated with a frontal female head or gorgoneion, much like the head of Charun in the 'tablinum' of the François Tomb (Fig. 12.27).

It is striking that many heads in Etruscan tombs are placed above doorways, both functional and false. Sculpted heads are found on the keystone or imposts of arched gates of Etruscan city walls built between the fourth and second centuries BCE: the Porta dell'Arco at Volterra, the Porta di Giove at Falerii Nova, and the Porta Marzia in Perugia (Fig. 12.28) (Haynes 2000, 363–64, 377). It has been argued that the heads on gates represented either tutelary deities (such as Tin/Tinia and the Dioscuri or the Capitoline Triad) or the severed heads of enemies displayed as a military trophy. Comparable arches with heads are found on cinerary urns of the period from cities with such structures, such as the urn from Volterra showing a siege[53] or the ash urn of Vel Rafi from Perugia (Fig. 12.29).[54] Arched doorways, opened and closed, have strong associations with the funerary realm, appearing in late Etruscan tomb paintings,[55] on cinerary urns,[56] and on sar-

Figure 12.33. Terracotta tomb slab from tomb 117 at Metaponto, decorated with a mould-made antefix featuring a frontal head wearing a Phrygian cap. Metaponto, Museo Archeologico Nazionale, inv. no. 319201, late fourth century BCE (photo courtesy of the Ministero per i Beni e la Attività Culturali, Direzione Regionale per i Beni Culturali e Paesaggistici della Basilicata, Soprintendenza per i Beni Archeologici della Basilicata).

cophagi,[57] as the entrance to the underworld, either guarded by Vanth or Charun (Jannot 2000, 92–94). Although heads are not placed above arched doorways in or on Etruscan tombs, they may have been intended to be apotropaic, or to distinguish a symbolic threshold between the living and the dead.

During the second half of the fourth century BCE, isolated heads were deemed suitable iconography not only for tombs, but also for stone sarcophagi. On the corners of the lid of the Sarcophagus of Ramtha Huzcnai from Tarquinia, female heads with blond hair are flanked by horizontal palmettes,[58] and short-haired frontal heads emerge from flowers in the gables of the lid of Ramtha Visnai and Arnth Tetnies's sarcophagus from Vulci (Fig. 12.30).[59] A plethora of frontal heads, some replicating terracotta antefixes, are found on all four sides of the sarcophagus from Bomarzo, including one at the middle of the floral

---

53 Volterra, Museo Etrusco Guarnacci, inv. no. 371 (second century BCE).
54 Perugia, Museo Archeologico Nazionale dell'Umbria, inv. no. 26.291 (c. 150–100 BCE): Haynes 2000, 378–79; Jannot 2000, 93.
55 Such as in Tarquinia, tomb 5636 (Steingraber 1986, 371, pl. 180; Jannot 1993, pl. 10, 1; 2005, 64–65) and Tarquinia, Tomba della Querciola II (Steingraber 1986, 339–40; Jannot 1993, 69, fig. 2).
56 Such as on a cinerary urn from Chiusi in Palermo, Museo Archeologico Nazionale 'Antonino Salinas' (Jannot 2005, 69).

57 For example, Tarquinia, Museo Archeologico Nazionale, inv. no. 1424 (Herbig 1952, 60 no. 116 pl. 74c; Jannot 1993, pl. 10, 2) and the sarcophagus of Hasti Afunei in Palermo, Museo Archeologico Regionale 'Antonino Salinas' (Herbig 1952, 41 no. 76 pls 55–57a; Colonna 1993, 358–59, 364–65 pls 21–23; Jannot 1993, pl. 9,1).
58 Florence, Museo Archeologico: Herbig 1952, 26–27.
59 Boston, Museum of Fine Arts, inv. no. 1975.799: Herbig 1952, 13–14.

208 KEELY ELIZABETH HEUER

Figure 12.34. Terracotta bust of a woman wearing a polos from the rock sanctuary below San Biagio at Agrigento. Syracuse, Museo Archeologico Regionale 'Paolo Orsi', inv. no. 16085, c. 400–350 BCE (photo courtesy the Assessorato ai Beni Culturali e dell'Identità Siciliana della Regione Siciliana, Palermo).

Figure 12.35. Terracotta Etruscan female votive head, possibly from Veii. Chicago, Art Institute of Chicago, inv. no. 1975.342, c. 500 BCE (photo courtesy of the Art Institute of Chicago).

Figure 12.36a. Terracotta *pinax* with overlapping male and female profile heads to left from Francavilla di Sicilia. Syracuse, Museo Archeologico Regionale 'Paolo Orsi', inv. no. 85663, c. 475–470 BCE (photo by author).

Figure 12.36b. Line drawing of the terracotta *pinax*, after Spigo 2000b, 34 fig. 48 (by Rita Musumeci, used with permission).

Figure 12.37. Terracotta *arula* from Taranto with a frontal female head surrounded by spiralling tendrils. Taranto, Museo Archeologico Nazionale, inv. no. 208342, second half of the fourth century BCE (photo courtesy of the Ministero per I Beni Culturali, Soprintendenza per i Beni Archeologici della Puglia, Archivo fotografico, Taranto).

band on each of its long sides.[60] Bearded, horned heads, presumably those of Acheloös, are framed by reclining males on the short ends of the lid of the sarcophagus from Torre San Severo.[61] The motif continues until the first century BCE on cinerary urns produced in Chiusi, Volterra, and Perugia, usually appearing on the long sides of the chest and often emerging from a leafy base (Fig. 12.31).[62] Some of the heads on ash urns are gorgoneia, but others are clearly human, sometimes wreathed, veiled, flanked by wings, or wearing a Phrygian cap.

Moulded terracottas of various forms featuring isolated heads were used as grave goods, including *arulae* (portable altars).[63] Protomes have been uncovered in tombs at Syracuse (Fusco and Guardino di Spagna necropoleis), Megara Hyblaia, and Paestum, among others (Fig. 12.32).[64] Protomes, which originated in Ionia during the mid-sixth century BCE, likely travelled from Miletus to Sicily with exported perfume vases.[65] Soon thereafter, Sicilian coroplasts modelled protomes after their East Greek counterparts, and the practice was speedily replicated in various Greek settlements of Magna Graecia, such as at Locri Epizephyrii. During the late fifth century, protomes were lengthened to include the upper torso and arms, which may carry attributes or offerings like cross-bar torches, flowers, piglets, and *phialai* (Kilmer 1977, 95, 98; Lo Porto 1991, 84–85; Kurz 2005, 229–45). Terracotta shoulder busts are also found in mortuary contexts like the remarkable janiform bust of a young woman wearing a polos and a bearded man from a tomb at Locri Epizephryii, possibly representing Persephone and Hades (Orsi 1911, 68–70). Terracotta busts may also have served as cenotaphs, seen in the so-called 'pot-burial' at Locri, dating to the Classical period (Kurtz and Boardman 1971, 259). This terracotta sculpture type was probably derived from experimentation with protomes in southern Italy, where the earliest examples were discovered at Metaponto and Taranto, dated to the sixth century (Lo Porto 1991, 88–89; Bernabò Brea and Cavalier, 2000, 115–17). Busts were produced in Sicily in the following decades, perhaps beginning at Agrigento (Kilmer 1977, 77–78), and by the end of the century they were made in Etruria and other areas in the Etruscan sphere of influence, such as Latium and Campania.[66]

Terracotta isolated heads also served to decorate tombs. Semicircular terracotta antefixes with various types of heads were frequently used as roofing elements on tomb monuments in Taranto and other

---

60 London, British Museum, inv. no. 1838,06–08.12 (*c.* 325–250 BCE): Herbig 1952, 35–36.
61 Now in Orvieto, Museo Claudio Faina: Herbig 1952, 40–41; de Azevedo 1970.
62 For example, Volterra, Museo Etrusco Guarnacci, inv. no. 41, New York, Metropolitan Museum of Art inv. no. 96.9.221, and Perugia, Necropoli del Palazzone, inv. no. 152. Refer to Körte 1916, 199–200, 214–18; Dareggi 1972, 47–48; Sclafani 2010, 92–96. A series of silvered terracotta stands in the form of female heads that appear to have been produced in Civita Castellana are also found in central Italian tombs (Ambrosini 1994).
63 See van Buren 1918, 41–44; Jastrow 1946; van der Meijden 1993, 71, 177–81, 293–95, 309. *Arulae* are found in tombs and chthonic sanctuaries, and the subjects of their moulded reliefs are popular funerary motifs, such as sirens and sphinxes.
64 For protomes and busts as grave goods, refer to Kilmer 1977, 75–76; Lehnert 1978, 135; and Uhlenbrock 1988, 125, 129. For examples from tombs at Syracuse, see Graepler 1997, 256, 259, 262, 273.
65 Zuntz 1971, 142; Kilmer 1977, 65; Croissant 1983; Uhlenbrock 1988, 19–20, 109, 146–50; 1989, 9.

66 The oldest votive heads were found at Veii, where they were produced in significant amounts by the fifth century BCE (Steingraber 1980, 226). Most terracotta busts made in Lazio date after the early fourth century BCE and appear to have been inspired by the coroplasty of Magna Graecia and Sicily, such as the bust of Demetra from the Ariccia Valley (località Casaletto) of the late fourth–early third centuries BCE (Rome, Museo Nazionale Romano, Terme di Diocleziano, inv. no. 112376).

Greek settlements.[67] A mould-made antefix with a frontal head wearing a Phrygian cap was attached to the large terracotta slab that closed the short end of tomb 117 at Metaponto, a late fourth-century BCE burial covered with a large, semicircular 'barrel' of roof-tiles (Fig. 12.33).[68] Similar reliefs depicting a truncated, veiled woman with holes for suspension have been discovered in burials in and around Nola (Claes 1981).

Because terracotta protomes and busts have been found in tombs, it was once erroneously assumed that when comparable items were found in votive deposits in sanctuaries — where most surviving examples have been uncovered — the cult was chthonic in nature (Zuntz 1971, 143; Uhlenbrock 1988, 139–56; and Lippolis 2001). In certain instances, sanctuaries containing terracotta votives in the form of heads or busts do have clear structural or epigraphic evidence for a cult of Demeter and/or Persephone/Kore, such as the Thesmophorion of Bitalemi near Gela, the Sanctuary of the Chthonic Deities at San Biagio in Agrigento, and the Mannella sanctuary at Locri Epizephyrii (Fig. 12.34).[69] Nevertheless, a significant number of these objects were dedicated to goddesses without chthonic associations, such as Athena and Hera (Uhlenbrock 1988, 141, 146–48; Uhlenbrock 1989, 9–10).

The earliest moulded terracottas featuring heads discovered in sacral contexts of central and southern Italy are antefixes, a practice that dates back to *c.* 640 BCE in Etruria.[70] Ex voto heads and 'half-heads' (moulded profile heads in profile with a flat back) were popular offerings at Etruscan, Faliscan, and Latin healing sanctuaries from the late sixth or early fifth century BCE (Fig. 12.35).[71] The early central Italian votive heads share stylistic features with Sicilian protomes of the period. Although mostly mould-made, their variety in gender, age, headdress types, jewellery worn, etc. is remarkable, with the finest examples bordering portraiture (Steingräber 1980, 231–33). They are frequently associated with other anatomical votives in the form of limbs and organs.[72] Thousands of these objects survive, and they are interpreted as requests or thank-offerings for medical cures, with the dedicator providing an image of the affected part of the body (Edlund 1987; Turfa 1994; 2006, 104–06; Oberhelman 2014). Initially, the votive heads were believed to represent maladies associated with that part of the body, like migraine headaches (Stieda 1899, 236. Theory disputed in Steingräber 1980, 235–36). However, the votive heads significantly predate the proliferation of anatomical votives, which began in the last quarter of the fourth century BCE, indicating that they were an independent practice, at least at first, and perhaps referred to the general well-being of an individual

---

67 The production of these antefixes intensified and diversified in Taranto during the fourth century BCE. Favoured head types include the head of Pan and a female type that sometimes has bovine horns emerging from her temples, probably Io. Other recognizable heads of mythological figures include the river god Acheloös and Aphrodite, identified by the winged Eros beside her. Male heads may wear a petasos (Hermes?) or Phrygian helmet. Other heads of uncertain gender are covered by a lion skin (Herakles or Omphale, queen of Lydia?) or have short tousled hair. See Laviosa 1954, 217–50. The Etruscans also used antefixes with heads in funerary contexts, but of a different stylistic type, as seen in the small building adjacent to the necropolis of Grotta Porcino at Vetralla, near Viterbo (Winter 1974, 151–54).

68 Metaponto, Museo Archeologico Nazionale, inv. no. 319201: Pugliese Carratelli 1996, 651–52.

69 For isolated heads on terracotta votives found at Agrigento, see Marconi 1929, 579–80; 1933, 47; Kilmer 1977, 83–84, 101–09; and Uhlenbrock 1988, 125–26. For those at Locri Epizephyrii, refer to Zuntz 1971, 160–61; Kilmer 1977, 74, 89–91, 133–34; Barra Bagnasco 1986; Lattanzi 1987, 54–59; and Croissant 1992. For those at Gela, turn to Kilmer 1977, 65, 75; Uhlenbrock 1988; Bertesago 2009, 55–57.

70 The earliest antefixes are from Poggio Civitate (Murlo). During the sixth century BCE, female heads on antefixes were framed by a 'shell' and began wearing tall diadems and disc earrings. During the late sixth century, Capua (the most important Etruscan

settlement in Campania) became an important manufacturing centre for architectural terracottas, particularly antefixes decorated with various types of heads, including those of women and satyrs, which were exported into Etruria and influenced antefixes in the Greek colonies of southern Italy. In the Greek settlements of Magna Graecia and Sicily, the earliest antefixes with human and mythological heads date to *c.* 600 BCE. They became common in the mid-sixth century BCE and remained popular until the close of the fourth century. See Andrén 1940, cxxx–ccxlii; Winter 1974; 1978; Wohl 1984, 117; Mertens-Horn 1994; Marconi 2005; Winter 2009, 49–54, 85–88, 147, 157, 169–74, 223–36, 245–50, 311–17, 321–24, 344–50, 395–96, 400, 425–44.

71 Brendel 1978, 393–94; Steingräber 1980, 217–22; Turfa 1994; Edlund-Berry 2008, 88–90. The earliest votive heads were discovered at the Portonaccio and Campetti sanctuaries in Veii and seem to have been influenced by architectural terracottas (Torelli and Pohl 1973, 227–48; Steingräber 1980, 238; Comella and Stefani 1990, 18–37; Turfa 2006, 98, 101; Nagy 2011, 117–19). True shoulder busts were a rarer phenomenon in central Italy compared to Magna Graecia and Sicily. See Kilmer 1977, 203–54, 260–62, 265–67. On votive 'half-heads': Steingräber 1980, 216, 222, 231.

72 Steingräber 1980, 235. Examples of sanctuaries where this phenomenon occurs include the Ara della Regina in Tarquinia (Turfa 2006, 96–97; Comella 1982, 23–101, 104–61, 173–82, 186–91), a sanctuary at the necropolis of Sovana (Bianchi Bandinelli 1929, 36–37, 126–27, pl. 30; Steingräber 1980, 237; Pellegrini and Arcangeli 2007, 40–46), the Porta Nord at Vulci (Steingräber 1980, 237; Pautasso 1994), the Manganello sanctuary at Caere (Mengarelli 1935, 38–41; Steingräber 1980, 238; Nagy 2011, 121–24), and the Punta della Vipera sanctuary in Santa Marinella (Comella 2001, 25–51).

rather than a particular ailment (Smithers 1993, 14; Turfa 2006, 105).[73]

In southern Italy, mid-fifth-century BCE *pinakes* from Francavilla di Sicilia feature three designs with male and female isolated heads in profile (Fig. 12.36).[74] These dedications are clearly related to their better-known counterparts from the sanctuary of Persephone on the slope of the Mannella hill at Locri Epizephyrii, as plaques made from the same moulds appear at both sites, but the plaques with heads are unique to Francavilla di Sicilia. The repertoire of terracottas featuring heads and busts offered at Italic and Greek sanctuaries of Magna Graecia expanded during the fourth century to include *thymiateria* (incense burners),[75] *arulae*,[76] and *oscilla* (discs) (Fig. 12.37).[77]

There are clear iconographic connections between the painted isolated heads and their three-dimensional terracotta and stone counterparts.[78] Their identities are similarly ambiguous, as are the types of heads that appear. In all media, most heads are female with comparable headdresses and jewellery. Heads

of youths, satyrs, Pan, Dionysos, Io, and those wearing Phrygian caps also appear in two- and three-dimensional formats. Comparable vegetation to the lush spiralling tendrils around heads on vases occurs on some *arulae* and floral *thymiateria*, as well as those carved in tombs and on sarcophagi and cinerary urns.[79] The occasional appearance of Erotes beside female heads is a further commonality across media, as is the presence of a hand, either empty or holding an object, in front of the face, implying a body out of the viewer's sight.[80] The commonalities between the painted heads and those in terracotta are not surprising as coroplasts, potters, and vase painters would have worked in close proximity, using many of the same natural resources and perhaps even sharing kilns.

Heads of Hope?

The head is a human's most uniquely recognizable body part, capable of encapsulating one's fundamental essence, probably leading to its prominence in portraiture and the development of the bust as a sculptural type that flourished in ancient Italy. The correspondences between the plastic and painted heads in funerary and sacral environments raise the question of whether the motif's iconographic function changed depending on context, or if there was a fundamental underlying principle that made the image appropriate in both scenarios. I propose that in pre-Roman Italy and Sicily the isolated head — as an incomplete figure — was chosen as an effective visual symbol for scenarios involving a transition from one state into another, and thus could have embodied hope for a desired outcome during a state of flux, such as during major life changes (weddings, funerals, etc.) or at times of ill health.

Despite the many personifications in Classical art, the concept of hope (Greek: *Elpis*, Latin: *Spes*) was not commonly anthropomorphized. *Spes* first appears on coins minted under Claudius. She is portrayed as a young woman holding up her chiton in

---

73 The production of votive heads dramatically increases at the time anatomical votives come into use in the late fourth and early third centuries BCE (Steingräber 1980, 226–27).

74 On the sanctuary at Francavilla and its votive deposits: Spigo 2000a. Syracuse, Museo Archeologico Regionale Paolo Orsi, inv. no. 85663 (Spigo 2000b, 33–35) and inv. no. 85664 (Spigo 2000b, 39) are examples of *pinakes* decorated with two overlapping heads, with a female head in the foreground. In some instances, the male head is beardless and wears a wreath with a central rosette over the forehead. On other *pinakes*, the male head is bearded and wears an oak wreath. The sole example of a *pinax* with a single head is Syracuse, Museo Archeologico Regionale Paolo Orsi, inv. no. 85666.

75 Stoop 1960, 3–13; Uhlenbrock 1988, 291–92, 309–10; Dewailly 1997. Floral *thymiateria* have been found at Foce del Sele, Capua, Naples, Timmari, and Macchia di Rossano (Uhlenbrock 1988, 292). Similar floral figurines were discovered in an extramural sanctuary at Predio Maggiore on Lipari, the only examples of this terracotta type from Sicily (Bernabò Brea and Cavalier 2000, 118–21).

76 Wuilleumier 1939, 434; Jastrow 1946; van der Meijden 1993, 71, 293–95, 309.

77 Bedello Tata and others 1990, 19–33, 39–52, 59–69.

78 Bronze *balsamaria* (cosmetics containers) in the form of heads were produced in Etruria between the fourth and second centuries BCE and have been uncovered in burials. Most are female, with elaborate hairstyles, necklaces, earrings, and diadems, which may have small wings or doves attached. It is believed that they represent either generic women, the Etruscan love goddess Turan, or Lasa, the nymph-like companion of Turan and patroness of lovers. Sometimes the heads wear a Phrygian cap or are janiform with the head of a satyr, suggesting Dionysian connotations. For examples, see Boston, Museum of Fine Arts, inv. no. 98.682; New York, Metropolitan Museum of Art, inv. no. 11.91.3 (female); London, British Museum, inv. no. 1868,0601.3 (Phrygian cap); and London, Freud Museum, inv. no. 3029 (janiform).

79 Such as on the *arulae* Taranto, Museo Archeologico Nazionale, inv. no. 208342 and Capua, Museo Archeologico, inv. no. 530 as well as the floral *thymiaterion* Paestum, Museo Archeologico Nazionale, inv. no. 56492.

80 For the presence of Erotes, compare the neck of the Apulian volute-krater Ruvo, Museo Nazionale Jatta, inv. no. 1092 with the fragmentary terracotta bust from the area of the Basilica at Paestum (Paestum, Museo Archeologico Nazionale, inv. no. 2630). For the presence of a hand in front of the face, see the Apulian plate in the Field Museum of Natural History in Chicago (inv. no. 182636 — Trendall and Cambitoglou 1983, 120 no. 462a) and the Campanian plaque in the British Museum (inv. no. 1867,0508.646).

Figure 12.38a–b. Red-figure amphora attributed to the Owl Pillar Group depicting the creation of Pandora in the presence of Hephaistos (?), Zeus (?), and the *pithos*. London, British Museum, inv. no. F 147, *c*. 450–425 BCE (photos courtesy of the Trustees of the British Museum).

Figure 12.40 (below). Terracotta plaque from Grotta Caruso at Locri depicting three female heads above Euthymos in bull form next to an altar. Reggio Calabria, Museo Archeologico Nazionale, inv. no. 110, fourth century BCE (photo by author).

Figure 12.39 (below). Terracotta grotto model from Grotto Caruso with female isolated head above cave entrance. Reggio Calabria, Museo Archeologico Nazionale Locri, inv. no. Gr. Car. 356, third–second centuries BCE (photo by author).

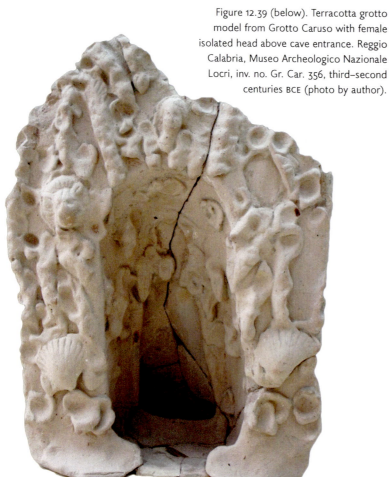

one hand, reminiscent of the pose of Archaic Greek *korai*, and a flower in the other (Clark 1983, 83). In Greek art, the only strongly plausible depiction of *Elpis* appears on a small red-figure neck-amphora found in Campania and now in London, where the concept is represented as a tiny female head, her hair bound up in a *sakkos*, emerging from the mouth of a curious vessel on a low, rectangular base (Fig. 12.38).[81] The inscriptions in a nearly identical scene (without the jar) on an Athenian volute-krater in Oxford reveals that the piece made in southern Italy depicts the *anodos* of Pandora, observed by Hephaistos, who created her from earth and water.[82] On the other side of the London vase, Zeus gazes at the infamous *pithos*, presumably commanding Elpis to remain inside when Pandora could no longer resist her curiosity. Despite the hasty brushwork, this innovative vase painter solved, simultaneously, the dilemma of representing something inside a container, otherwise out of the viewer's sight, and created an image reflecting the definition of hope itself — an incomplete desire or expectation — by depicting the notion as a truncated figure.[83]

In the case of heads on South Italian and Etruscan vases, the referenced transition might be the journey between mortality and the afterlife through death, as they are uncovered almost exclusively in funerary contexts, at times even serving as grave markers. As noted above, isolated heads are frequently painted on the same vases as scenes of figures at grave monuments, mythological tableaux featuring the demise or rescue from certain death of the main protagonists, representations of the underworld, and depictions of the realm of Dionysos — a deity who gained immortality and gave the same gift to his mortal mother. The concept of life beyond the grave is further implied by the rich vegetation repeatedly painted in conjunction with heads, alluding to the regenerative cycle of nature. This interpretation is corroborated by the repeated appearance of heads in explicitly funerary art, including the decoration of tombs and burial containers. Even the types of heads on vases and other media in sepulchral settings could allude to cults practised in pre-Roman Italy known to have promised a blissful hereafter. The female heads could represent Persephone/Phersipnai

or chthonic Aphrodite, while male heads might have been interpreted as Hades/Aita or Dionysos/Fufluns. Those wearing Phrygian caps may have been read as Orpheus, the eponymous author of the now-lost poems that were the doctrinal foundation of the mystic religion. Winged heads might have been understood as Nike, symbolizing victory over death, or as Etruscan death demons like Vanth assisting in the safe passage to the hereafter or even Eros, whose place in the underworld is confirmed by an Apulian volute-krater in the Hermitage, may have served as a guarantor of love's bonds beyond the grave.[84]

Similarly, terracotta isolated heads offered as votives in sanctuaries are regularly found in locations associated with the continuation of mortal life through transitions, whether from illness to health — in the case of healing sites — or the preparation of young women for marriage and motherhood at sanctuaries dedicated to a variety of goddesses including Hera, Aphrodite, and Kore-Persephone. For example, the votive deposits of the fourth and third centuries of the Heraion at Foce del Sele near Paestum contain multiple busts, *protomes*, and floral *thymiateria* that take the form of a female bust with a large open flower on the head, a reversal of the heads emerging from flowers on Apulian vases.[85] The cult seems to have revolved consistently around women's lives, but subsequent to the Lucanian conquest of Paestum in the late fifth century BCE, a new structure, the so-called 'Square Building', was built in the sanctuary (Zancani Montuoro and others 1965; Greco and de La Genière 1996). Inspired by domestic architecture, the building contained objects associated with the feminine sphere, including hundreds of loom weights that are believed to have been used to weave the *peplos* given to Hera annually at her festival, possibly created by aristocratic girls who lived in the structure as part of a period of initiation preparatory to marriage (Cerchiai and others 2004, 80). It is in this structure that most of the few South Italian vases decorated with isolated heads outside of a mortuary context were discovered.

Isolated heads regularly appear among the terracotta votives at Grotta Caruso outside the curtain walls of Locri Epizephyrii, another sacred site connected with the matrimonial and chthonic spheres (Barra Bagnasco 2001, 29–32; MacLachlan 2012, 345). This cave containing a spring was enlarged

---

81 London, British Museum, inv. no. F 147: Trendall 1967, 667 no. 3.

82 Oxford, Ashmolean Museum, inv. no. G 275: *BAPD* 275165; Beazley 1963, 1562 no. 4; Neils 2006. Pandora's creation is recorded by Hesiod (*Works*, 60–105). On the *anodos* of Pandora: Harrison 1900, 106–08; Harrison 1908, 276–83; Robert 1914; Bérard 1974, 161–64.

83 On the complex nature of *elpis* in Archaic and Classical Greek literature: Cairns 2016.

---

84 St Petersburg, Hermitage, inv. no. 1717 = St 424: Trendall and Cambitoglou 1982, 930–31 no. 117.

85 Stoop 1960, 3–13; Uhlenbrock 1988, 291–92, 309–10; Dewailly 1997. Similar offerings have been discovered at the Peucetian sanctuary at Timmari in Apulia (Lo Porto 1991, 69, 75, 84–85, 88–89).

and monumentalized during the fifth and fourth centuries BCE for a cult of the nymphs and perhaps other deities related to nature, the underworld, and regeneration such as Dionysos, Persephone, and Aphrodite, based on the votive terracottas found there. Due to the double meaning of *nymphe* as the term in ancient Greek for 'bride' and a demi-goddess associated with the natural world, the veneration of local nymphs at springs may well have led to the creation of purificatory rites done prior to marriage. A staircase cut into the rock led to a large basin of water, roughly 30–40 cm deep, in the centre of which was a submerged block of stone and an altar.[86] It is believed that young women would descend into the pool and sit upon the block, where they were washed in the spring's water and may have been symbolically married to a chthonic groom.[87] The girls' journey in and out of the cave's pool might have been viewed as a parallel to the *katabasis* and *anodos* of Persephone. One can easily imagine these young brides-to-be's hopes for a happy and fruitful marriage as they brought gifts to the shrine, including female heads and busts as well as grotto models (Fig. 12.39), sometimes decorated with isolated heads in relief, and a distinctive series of terracotta plaques, often called 'herms', with three frontal female heads across the top, assumed to represent the nymphs worshipped at the shrine (Fig. 12.40).[88] Some of these 'herms' refer to the Dionysian realm with images of *thyrsoi* and Pan seated in a cave.[89] On many south Italian vases, heads are paired with scenes of women, youths, and Erotes, a number of which depict explicit bridal preparation, or are associated with water through the inclusion of fountain houses or *louteria*.[90] Perhaps the iconographical combination was inspired by coming-of-age activity like that at Grotta Caruso, where terracotta heads in various forms were dedicated.

Terracotta votive heads are also a common feature of sanctuaries associated with healing and fertility across Italy, exemplified by the thousands discovered during the mid-nineteenth-century excavations at Fondo Patturelli outside ancient Capua (modern Santa Maria Capua Vetere). A mother goddess was revered at this site, often identified as Mater Matuta. The heads — now unfortunately lacking precise provenance — are dated stylistically to two primary phases of production, the first between 423–304 BCE and the second between 304–211 BCE, with their manufacture significantly increasing in the mid-fourth century.[91] The heads are comparable to the numerous others dedicated in Etruscan, Faliscan, and Latin sanctuaries. Their presence among the terracotta statues of babies and swaddled infants resembling those children held by statues of the goddess carved from local stone at the Fondo Patturelli sanctuary strongly imply the desire for future successful pregnancies and deliveries of healthy children. (Steingräber 1980, 235; Smithers 1993, 13–14, 29–30; Turfa 2006, 104). Arguably, the votives were a *pars pro toto* for the supplicant seeking medical assistance, and were offered to the divine as a reminder to the deity of the dedicator's hopeful request, a possible explanation for the many types of heads found at cult locations throughout central and southern Italy (Steingräber 1980, 236).

Isolated heads did have a place, albeit limited, in the visual culture of the Aegean. However, it is in pre-Roman Italy that the motif truly flourished. The many thousands of painted and plastic isolated heads of overwhelmingly enigmatic identity produced in this part of the Mediterranean demonstrate the motif's widespread appeal, transcending ethnic, geographic, and religious boundaries. Whether given as a gesture of religious devotion and gratitude, offered in hopes of a divinity's future benevolence, or placed in a tomb to express expectations of life beyond the grave, the consistent patterns of the image's use across various media strongly imply that the isolated head expressed a similar concept in sacral and funerary contexts, thereby fulfilling an analogous need faced in life and death in which a hoped-for outcome was not yet assured.

---

86 Costabile and others 1991, 7–13; Larson 2001, 251–53.

87 Costabile and others 1991, 103–05; Larson 2001, 254, 256; MacLachlan 2009, 206–07.

88 Costabile and others 1991, 95–103; Larson 2001, 253–54.

89 Costabile and others 1991, 156, 159–61; MacLachlan 2009, 212.

90 For example, Paestum, Museo Archeologico Nazionale, inv. no. 20296 (Trendall 1987, 239 no. 965) and Tampa 1987.37 (Trendall and Cambitoglou 1991–1992, 353 no. D8, pl. 92, 3–4).

91 Bonghi Jovino 1965, 14–16, 21–25; Bedello 1974, 11, 19–25; Steingräber 1980, 241–42; Riis 1981, 18–24. Terracotta *arulae, oscilla*, and *thymiateria* decorated with isolated heads are also found in the votive deposits at Capua, although not nearly in the same amount as votive heads. Refer to Tata 1990, 19–33, 39–52, 59–69.

Works Cited

Ambrosini, Laura. 1994. '"Sostegni" a testa femminile in ceramic argentata. Analisi di una produzione falisca a destinazione funeraria', *Archeologia classica*, 46: 109–68

Andreae, Bernard. 2004. 'La Tomba François', *Forma urbis*, 9.1: 8–57

——. 2007. *Malerei für die Ewigkeit: Die Gräber von Paestum* (Munich: Hirmer)

Andrén, Arvid. 1940. *Architectural Terracottas from Etrusco-Italic Temples*, 2 vols (Lund: Gleerup)

Barra Bagnasco, Marcella. 2001. 'Il culto delle acque a Locri Epizefiri: contesti e documenti', in *Zona archeologica: Festschrift für Hans Peter Isler zum 60. Geburtstag*, ed. by Sabrina Buzzi, Daniel Käch, Erich Kistler, Elena Mango, Marek Palaczyk, and Olympia Stefani (Bonn: Habelt), pp. 27–40

Beazley, John D. 1947. *Etruscan Vase Painting* (Oxford: Oxford University Press)

——. 1963. *Attic Red-Figure Vase Painters*, 2nd edn, 3 vols (Oxford: Clarendon)

Bedello Tata, Margherita, Simone Baroni, and Valeria Casolo. 1990. *Capua preromana: Terrecotte votive; catalogo del museo provinciale campano*, IV: *Oscilla, Thymiateria, Arulae* (Florence: Olschki)

Bendinelli, Goffredo. 1915. 'Un ipogeo sepolcrale a Lecce con fregi scolpiti', *Ausonia*, 8: 7–26

Bérard, Claude. 1974. *Anodoi: essai sur l'imagerie des passages chthoniens* (Neuchâtel: Attinger)

Bernabò Brea, Luigi, and Madeleine Cavalier. 2000. *Meligunìs – Lipára*, X: *Scoperte e scavi archeologici nell'area urbana e suburbana di Lipari* (Palermo: Flaccovio)

Bertesago, Silvia M. 2009. 'Figurine fittili da Bitalemi (Gela) a dalla Malophoros (Selinunte): appunti per uno studio comparator di alcune classi della coroplastica votiva', in *Temi selinuntini*, ed. by Claudia Antonetti and Stefania De Vido (Pisa: ETS), pp. 53–69

Bianchi Bandinelli, Ranuccio. 1929. *Sovana* (Florence: Rinascimento del libro)

Blanck, Horst, and Giuseppe Proietti. 1986. *La tomba dei rilievi di Cerveteri* (Rome: De Luca)

Bocci, Piera. 1964. 'Crateri volterrani inediti del Museo di Arezzo', *Studi etruschi*, 32: 89–103

Brendel, Otto. 1978. *Etruscan Art* (New York: Penguin)

Brock, James King. 1957. *Fortetsa: Early Greek Tombs near Knossos* (Cambridge: Cambridge University Press)

Brommer, Frank. 1959. *Satyrspiele: Bilder griechischer Vasen* (Berlin: De Gruyter)

Buchner, Giorgio. 1953–1954. 'Figürlicher bemalte spätgeometrische Vasen aus Pithekussai und Kyme', *Mitteilungen des Deutschen Archäologischen Instituts: Römische Abteilung*, 60/61: 37–55

Buranelli, Francesco. 2004. 'Die Kopien des Gemäldezyklus der Tomba François von Carlo Ruspi im Museo Gregoriano Etrusco des Vatikan', in *Die Etrusker: Luxus für das Jenseits, Bilder vom Diesseits, Bilder vom Tod: Eine Doppelausstellung des Bucerius Kunst Forums und des Museums für Kunst und Gewerbe Hamburg, 13. Februar bis 16. Mai 2004*, ed. by Bernard Andreae, Andreas Hoffmann, and Cornelia Weber-Lehmann (Munich: Hirmer), pp. 168–75

Buren, Douglas van. 1918. 'Terracotta Arulae', *Memoirs of the American Academy in Rome*, 2: 15–53

Cairns, Douglas. 2016. 'Metaphors for Hope in Archaic and Classical Greek Poetry', in *Hope, Joy, and Affection in the Classical World*, ed. by Ruth R. Caston and Robert A. Kaster, Emotions of the Past (Oxford: Oxford University Press), pp. 13–44

Cambitoglou, Alexander. 1954. 'Groups of Apulian Red-Figured Vases Decorated with Heads of Women or Nike', *Journal of Hellenic Studies*, 74: 111–21

Carpenter, Thomas H. 2003. 'The Native Market for Red-Figure Vases in Apulia', *Memoirs of the American Academy in Rome*, 48: 1–24

——. 2009. 'Prolegomenon to the Study of Apulian Red-Figure Pottery', *American Journal of Archaeology*, 113: 27–38

——. 2016. 'Some Observations on Apulian Vase-Inscriptions with a Particular Focus on the Darius Painter', in *Epigraphy of Art: Ancient Greek Vase-Inscriptions and Vase-Paintings*, ed. by Dimitrios Yatromanolakis (Oxford: Archaeopress), pp. 135–42

Casadio, Giovanni. 2009. 'Dionysus in Campania: Cumae', in *Mystic Cults in Magna Graecia*, ed. by Giovanni Casadio and Patricia A. Johnston (Austin: University of Texas Press), pp. 33–45

Cerchiai, Luca, Lorena Jannelli, and Fausto Longo. 2004. *The Greek Cities of Magna Graecia and Sicily* (Los Angeles: J. Paul Getty Museum)

Cinquantaquattro, Teresa, Mario Lombardo, and Arcangelo Alessio. 2010. *La vigna di Dioniso: vite, vino e culti in Magna Grecia*, exhibition catalogue, Museo nazionale Taranto (Taranto: Scorpione)

Claes, Marie-Christine. 1981. 'Masques féminins de terre cuite d'usage funéraire en Italie méridionale à l'époque hellénistique', *Revue des archéologues et historiens d'art de Louvain*, 14: 7–29

Clark, Mark Edward. 1983. 'Spes in the Early Imperial Cult: "The Hope of Augustus"', *Numen*, 30: 80–105

Cohen, Beth. 1991. 'The Literate Potter. A Tradition of Incised Signatures on Attic Vases', *Metropolitan Museum Journal*, 26: 49–95

Colonna, Giovanni. 1993. 'I sarcophagi chiusini di età ellenistica', in *La civiltà di Chiusi e del suo territorio: atti del XVII Convegno di studi etruschi ed italici, Chianciano Terme, 28 maggio – 1 giugno 1989* (Florence: Olschki), pp. 337–74

Comella, Annamaria. 1982. *Il deposito votivo presso l'Ara della Regina* (Rome: Giorgio Bretschneider)

——. 2001. *Il santuario di Punta della Vipera: Santa Marinella, Comune di Civitavecchia*, I: *I materiali votive* (Rome: Giorgio Bretschneider)

Comella, Annamaria, and Grete Stefani. 1990. *Materiali votive del Sanctuario di Campetti a Veio: scavi 1947 e 1969* (Rome: Giorgio Bretschneider)

Costabile, Felice, Elena Lattanzi, and Paolo Enrico Arias. 1991. *I ninfei di Locri Epizefiri* (Soveria Mannelli: Rubbettino)

Cristofani, Mauro. 1967. 'Ricerche sulle pitture della tomba François di Vulci. I fregi decorativi', *Dialoghi di archeologia*, 1.2: 186–219

Croissant, Francis. 1983. *Les protomés féminines archaïques* (Paris: De Boccard)

d'Agostino, Bruno. 2004. 'The Etruscans in Campania', in *The Etruscans outside Etruria*, ed. by Giovannangelo Camporeale (Los Angeles: J. Paul Getty Museum), pp. 236–51

D'Andria, F. 1980. 'Scavi nella zona del Kerameikos', in *Metaponto*, I, ed. by Dinu Adamesteanu, Dieter Mertens, and Francesco D'Andria (Rome: Accademia nazionale dei Lincei), pp. 355–452

Dareggi, Gianna. 1972. *Urne del territorio Perugino: un gruppo inedito di cinerari etruschi ed etrusco-romani* (Rome: De Luca)

de Grummond, Nancy. 2006. *Etruscan Myth, Sacred History, and Legend* (Philadelphia: University of Pennsylvania Museum of Archaeology and Anthropology)

——. 2011. 'A Barbarian Myth? The Case of the Talking Head', in *The Barbarians of Ancient Europe: Realities and Interactions*, ed. by Larissa Bonfante (Cambridge: Cambridge University Press), pp. 313–45

De Juliis, Ettore M. 1984. 'L'etá del Ferro', in *La Daunia antica: dalla preistoria all'altomedioevo*, ed. by Marina Mazzei (Milan: Electa), pp. 137–84

——. 2001. *Metaponto* (Bari: Edipuglia)

——. 2009. *La rappresentazione figurata in Daunia* (Bari: Edipuglia)

del Chiaro, Mario A. 1957. *The Genucilia Group: A Class of Etruscan Red-Figured Plates* (Berkeley: University of California Press)

——. 1960. 'Etruscan Oinochoai of the Torcop Group', *Studi etruschi*, 28: 137–64

——. 1970 'Two Unusual Vases of the Etruscan Torcop Group: One with Head of Aita', *American Journal of Archaeology*, 74: 292–94

——. 1974. *Etruscan Red-Figured Vase-Painting at Caere* (Berkeley: University of California Press)

De Puma, Richard. 2013. *Etruscan Art in the Metropolitan Museum of Art* (New Haven: Metropolitan Museum of Art)

Denoyelle, Martine, and Mario Iozzo. 2009. *La céramique grecque d'Italie méridionale et de Sicile: productions coloniales et apparentées du VIIIᵉ au IIIᵉ siècle av. J.-C.* (Paris: Picard)

Detienne, Marcel. 1979. *Dionysos Slain*, trans. by Mireille Muellner and Leonard Muellner (Baltimore: Johns Hopkins University Press)

Dewailly, Martine. 1997. 'L'Héraion de Foce del Sele: quelques aspects du culte d'Héra à l'époque hellénistique d'après les terres cuites', in *Héra: images, espaces, cultes; actes du colloque international du center de recherches archéologiques, de l'Université de Lille III et de l'Association P.R.A.C., Lille 29–30 novembre 1993*, ed. by Juliette de La Genière (Naples: Centre Jean Bérard), pp. 201–10

Edlund, Ingrid. 1987. '*Mens sana in corpore sano*: Healing Cults as a Political Factor in Etruscan Religion', in *Gifts to the Gods: Proceedings of the Uppsala Symposium 1985*, ed. by Tullia Linders and Gullög Nordquist, Acta Universitatis Upsaliensis, 15 (Uppsala: Almqvist & Wiksell), pp. 51–56

Edlund-Berry, Ingrid. 2008. 'Temples and the Etruscan Way of Religion', in *From the Temple and the Tomb: Etruscan Treasures from Tuscany*, ed. by Alex Ross (Dallas: Meadows Museum), pp. 67–93

Edmonds, Radcliffe G. 2013. *Redefining Ancient Orphism: A Study in Greek Religion* (Cambridge: Cambridge University Press)

Fontannaz, Didier. 2005. 'La Céramique proto-apulienne de Tarente: problèmes et perspectives d'une "recontextualization"', in *La Céramique apulienne: bilan et perspectives*, ed. by Martine Denoyelle, Enzo Lippolis, Marina Mazzei, and Claude Pouzadoux (Naples: Centre Jean Bérard), pp. 125–42

Froning, Heide. 1985. 'Zur Interpretation vegetabilischer Bekrönung klassischer und spätklassischer Grabstelen', *Archäologischer Anzeiger*, 1985: 218–29

Gerkan, Armin von, and Franz Messerschmidt. 1942. 'Das Grab der Volumnier bei Perugia', *Mitteilungen des Deutschen Archaeologischen Instituts: Römische Abteilung*, 57: 122–235

Graepler, Daniel. 1997. *Tonfiguren im Grab: Fundkontexte hellenistischer Terrakotten aus der Nekropole von Tarent* (Munich: Biering & Brinkmann)

Greco, Giovanna, and Juliette de La Genière. 1996. 'L'Heraion alla foce del Sele: continuità e trasformazioni dall'età greca all'età lucana', in *I Greci in Occidente: Poseidonia e i Lucani*, ed. by Marina Cipriani and Fausto Longo (Naples: Electa), pp. 223–32

Guthrie, Kenneth Sylvan. 1993. *The Pythagorean Sourcebook and Library: An Anthology of Ancient Writings which Relate to Pythagoras and Pythagorean Philosophy* (Grand Rapids: Phanes)

Harari, Maurizio. 1980. *Il 'Gruppo Clusium' della ceramografia etrusca* (Rome: L'Erma di Bretschneider)

Harrison, Jane Ellen. 1900. 'Pandora's Box', *Journal of Hellenic Studies*, 20: 99–114

——. 1908. *Prolegomena to the Study of Greek Religion*, 2nd edn (Cambridge: Cambridge University Press)

Haynes, Sybille. 2000. *Etruscan Civilization: A Cultural History* (Los Angeles: J. Paul Getty Museum)

Herbig, Reinhard. 1952. *Die jüngeretruskischen Steinsarkophage* (Berlin: Mann)

Hesberg, Henner von. 1981. 'Die Aufnahme der dorischen Ordnung in Etrurien', in *Die Aufnahme fremder Kultureinflüsse in Etrurien und das Problem des Retardierens in der etruskischen Kunst* (Mannheim: Vorstand des Deutschen Archäologen-Verbandes e.V. and Archäologischen Seminar der Universität Mannheim), pp. 189–97

Heuer, Keely. 2011. 'The Development and Significance of the Isolated Head in South Italian Vase-Painting' (unpublished doctoral thesis, New York University)

——. 2014. 'Facing West: Isolated Heads and Attic Vases in Etruscan Contexts', in *Athenian Potters and Painters*, III, ed. by John Oakley (Oxford: Oxbow), pp. 63–71

——. 2015. 'Vases with Faces: Isolated Heads in South Italian Vase Painting', *Metropolitan Museum Journal*, 50: 63–91

——. 2019. 'Tenacious Tendrils: Replicating Nature in South Italian Vase Painting', *Arts*, 8.2, special issue: *Ancient Mediterranean Painting*, 1: 71 <https://doi.org/10.3390/arts8020071>

Isler-Kerényi, Cornelia. 2009. 'New Contributions of Dionysiac Iconography to the History of Religions in Greece and Italy', in *Mystic Cults in Magna Graecia*, ed. by Giovanni Casadio and Patricia A. Johnston (Austin: University of Texas Press), pp. 61–72

Jannot, Jean-René. 1993. 'Charun, Tuchulcha et les autres', *Mitteilungen des Deutschen Archäologischen Instituts: Römische Abteilung*, 100: 59–81

——. 2000. 'Etruscans and the Afterworld', *Etruscan Studies*, 7: 81–99

——. 2005. *Religion in Ancient Etruria* (Madison: University of Wisconsin Press)

Jastrow, Elisabeth. 1946. 'Two Terracotta Reliefs in American Museums', *American Journal of Archaeology*, 50: 67–80

Johnston, Sarah Iles, and Timothy J. McNiven. 1996. 'Dionysos and the Underworld in Toledo', *Museum Helveticum*, 53: 25–36

Jucker, Hans. 1961. *Das Bildnis in Blätterkelch: Geschichte und Bedeutung einer römischen Porträtform*, 2 vols (Lausanne: Urs Graf)

Kilmer, Martin F. 1977. *The Shoulder Bust in Sicily and Central Italy: A Catalogue and Materials for Dating* (Göteborg: Åström)

Körte, Gustavo. 1916. *I rilievi delle urne etrusche*, III (Berlin: Reimer)

Kossatz-Deißmann, Anneliese. 1985. 'Nachrichten aus Martin-von-Wagner-Museum Würzburg', *Archäologischer Anzeiger*, 1985: 229–39

——. 1990. 'Nachrichten aus Martin-von-Wagner-Museum Würzburg: Eine neue Phrygerkopf-Situla des Toledo-Malers', *Archäologischer Anzeiger*, 1990: 505–20

Kurtz, Donna C., and John Boardman. 1971. *Greek Burial Customs* (Ithaca: Cornell University Press)

Kurz, Ute C. 2005. 'Büstenprotomen und Büste aus S. Maria d'Anglona', *Jahreshefte des Österreichischen Archäologischen Institutes in Wien*, 74: 225–45

Langlotz, Ernst. 1954. *Aphrodite in den Gärten* (Heidelberg: Winter)

L'Arab, Gilda. 1991. 'L'Ipogeo Palmieri di Lecce', *Mélanges de l'École française de Rome: antiquité*, 103: 457–97

Larson, Jennifer. 2001. *Greek Nymphs: Myth, Cult, Lore* (Oxford: Oxford University Press)

Laviosa, Clelia. 1954. 'Le antefisse fittili di Taranto', *Archeologia classica*, 6: 217–50

Lehnert, Pamela A. 1978. 'Female Heads on Greek, South Italian, and Sicilian Vases from the Sixth to the Third Century B.C. as Representations of Persephone/Kore' (unpublished master's thesis, Michigan State University)

Lippolis, Enzo. 1994. *Catalogo del Museo nazionale archeologico di Taranto*, III.1: *Taranto, la necropolis: aspetti e problem della documentazione archeological tra VII e I sec. a.C.* (Taranto: La Colomba)

——. 2001. 'Culto e iconografie della coroplastica votiva: problemi interpretative a Taranto e nel mondo greco', *Mélanges de l'École française de Rome: antiquité*, 113: 225–55

Lohmann, Hans. 1979. *Grabmäler auf unteritalischen Vasen* (Berlin: Mann)

Lombardo, Mario, A. Siciliano, and Arcangelo Alessio (eds). 2011. *La vigna di Dioniso: vite, vino e culti in Magna Grecia; atti del quarantanovesimo Convegno di studi sulla Magna Grecia; Taranto, 24–28 settembre 2009* (Taranto: Istituto per la storia e l'archeologia della Magna Grecia)

Lo Porto, Felice Gino. 1991. *Timmari: l'Abitato, le necropolis, la stipe votive* (Rome: Giorgio Bretschneider)

MacLachlan, Bonnie. 2009. 'Women and Nymphs at the Grotta Caruso', in *Mystic Cults in Magna Graecia*, ed. by Giovanni Casadio and Patricia A. Johnston (Austin: University of Texas Press), pp. 204–16

——. 2012. 'The Grave's a Fine and Funny Place: Chthonic Rituals and Comic Theater in the Greek West', in *Theater outside Athens: Drama in Greek Sicily and South Italy*, ed. by Kathryn Bosher (Cambridge: Cambridge University Press), pp. 343–64

Marconi, Clemente. 2005. 'I Theoroi di Eschilo e le antefisse sileniche siceliote', *Sicilia antica*, 2: 75–94

Marconi, Pirro. 1929. 'Plastica agrigentina', *Dedalo*, 3.10: 579–99

——. 1933. *Agrigento arcaica: il santuario della divinità chtonie e il tempio detto di Vulcano* (Rome: Società Magna Grecia)

Mazzei, Marina. 1984. 'Dall'ellenizzazione all'età repubblicana: IV e III sec. a.C., il panorama storico archeologico', in *La Daunia antica: dalla preistoria all'altomediooevo*, ed. by Marina Mazzei (Milan: Electa), pp. 185–211

Mead, G. R. S. 1965. *Orpheus* (London: Watkins)

Meijden, Hellebora van der. 1993. *Terrakotta-Arulae aus Sizilien und Unteritalien* (Amsterdam: Hakkert)

Mengarelli, R. 1935. 'Il tempio del Manganello a Caere', *Studi etruschi*, 9: 83–94

Mertens-Horn, M. 1994. 'Antefissa', in *Enciclopedia dell'arte antica classica e orientale, secondo supplemento*, I (Rome: Istituto della Enciclopedia italiana), pp. 242–52

Metzger, Henri. 1951. *Les representations dans la céramique attique du IVe siècle* (Paris: De Boccard)

Nagy, Helen. 2011. 'Etruscan Votive Terracottas and their Archaeological Contexts: Preliminary Comments on Veii and Cerveteri', in *The Archaeology of Sanctuaries and Ritual in Etruria*, ed. by Nancy Thomson de Grummond and Ingrid Edlund-Berry, Journal of Roman Archaeology, Supplementary, 31 (Portsmouth, RI: Journal of Roman Archaeology), pp. 113–25

Oakley, John H. 2004. *Picturing Death in Classical Athens* (Cambridge: Cambridge University Press)

——. 2016. 'Inscriptions on Apulian Red-Figure Vases: A Survey', in *Epigraphy of Art: Ancient Greek Vase-Inscriptions and Vase-Paintings*, ed. by Dimitrios Yatromanolakis (Oxford: Archaeopress), pp. 121–33

Oberhelman, Steven M. 2014. 'Anatomical Votive Reliefs as Evidence for Specialization at Healing Sanctuaries in the Ancient Mediterranean World', *Athens Journal of Health*, March 2014: 47–62

Oleson, John Peter. 1982. *The Sources of Innovation in Later Etruscan Tomb Design (ca. 350–100 B.C.)* (Rome: Giorgio Bretschneider)

Orfismo. 1975. *Orfismo in Magna Grecia: atti del quattordicesimo convegno di studi sulla Magna Grecia, Taranto, 6–10 ottobre 1974* (Naples: Arte tipografica)

Orsi, Paolo. 1911. 'Locri Epizephyrii', *Notizie degli scavi di antichità*, suppl.: 3–76

Pasquinucci, Marinella Montagna. 1968. *Le kelebai Volterrane* (Florence: La Nuova Italia)

Pautasso, Antonella. 1994. *Il deposito votivo presso la Porta Nord a Vulci* (Rome: Giorgio Bretschneider)

Pellegrini, Enrico, and Lara Arcangeli. 2007. *Gli etruschi a Sovana: percorsi culturali e riti magici* (Pitigliano: Laurum)

Pensa, Marina. 1977. *Rappresentazioni dell'oltretomba nella ceramica apula* (Rome: L'Erma di Bretschneider)

Pietilä-Castrén, Leena. 1999. 'Genuculia Plates – Common *Agalmata* or Depictions of the Myth of Persephone', *Arctos*, 33: 93–110

Pontrandolfo, Angela. 1996. 'Wall-Painting in Magna Graecia', in *The Western Greeks*, ed. by Giovanni Pugliese Carratelli (Milan: Bompiani), pp. 457–70

Pugliese Carratelli, Giovanni (ed.). 1996. *The Western Greeks*, exhibition catalogue, Palazzo Grassi, Venice (Milan: Bompiani)

Robinson, Edward G. D. 1990. 'Workshops of Apulian Red-Figure outside Taranto', in *Eumousia: Ceramic and Iconographic Studies in Honour of Alexander Cambitoglou*, ed. by Jean Paul Descoeudres (Sydney: Meditarch), pp. 179–93

Rohde, Erwin. 1907. *Psyche: Seelencult und Unsterblichkeitsglaube der Griechen*, 4th edn (Tübingen: Mohr)

Roncalli, Francesco. 1987. 'La decorazione pittorica', in *La Tomba François di Vulci*, ed. by Francesco Buranelli (Rome: Quasar), pp. 79–110

Rosi, Gino. 1925. 'Sepulchral Architecture as Illustrated by the Rock Facades of Central Etruria: Part I', *Journal of Roman Studies*, 15: 1–59

——. 1927. 'Sepulchral Architecture as Illustrated by the Rock Facades of Central Etruria: Part II', *Journal of Roman Studies*, 17: 59–96

Rouveret, Agnès. 1990. 'Tradizioni pittorische magnogreche', in *Magna Grecia: Arte e artigianato*, ed. by Giovanni Pugliese Carratelli (Milan: Electa), pp. 317–50

Rouveret, Agnès, and Angela Pontrandolfo. 1983. 'Pittura Funeraria in Lucania e Campania puntualizzazioni cronologiche e proposte di lettura', *Dialoghi di archeologia*, 3rd ser., 1.1: 91–130

Schauenburg, Konrad. 1957. 'Zur Symbolik unteritalischer Rankenmotive', *Mitteilungen des Deutschen Archäologischen Instituts: Römische Abteilung*, 64: 198–221

——. 1962. 'Pan in Unteritalien', *Mitteilungen des Deutschen Archäologischen Instituts: Römische Abteilung*, 69: 27–42

——. 1974. 'Bendis in Unteritalien?', *Jahrbuch des Deutschen Archäologischen Instituts*, 89: 137–86

——. 1981. 'Zu unteritalischen Situlen', *Archäologischer Anzeiger*, 1981: 462–88

——. 1982. 'Arimaspen in Unteritalien', *Revue archéologique*, 1982: 249–62

——. 1984. 'Unterweltsbilder aus Grossgriechenland', *Mitteilungen des Deutschen Archäologischen Instituts: Römische Abteilung*, 91: 359–87

——. 1989. 'Zur Grabsymbolik apulischer Vasen', *Jahrbuch des Deutschen Archäologischen Instituts*, 104: 19–60

Schmidt, Margot. 1975. 'Orfeo e Orfismo nella pittura vascolare italiota', in *Orfismo in Magna Grecia: atti del quattordicesimo convegno di studi sulla Magna Grecia, Taranto 6–10 ottobre 1974* (Naples: Arte tipografica), pp. 105–37

Sclafani, Marina. 2010. *Urne fittili chiusine e perugine di età medio e tardo ellenistica* (Rome: Giorgio Bretschneider)

Sgouropoulou, Chrisi. 2000. 'Η εικονογραφία των γυναικείων κεφαλών στα αγγεία Κερτς', *Αρχαιολογικόν Δελτίον*, 55: 213–34

Simon, Erika. 1989. 'Hermeneutisches zur Anodos von Göttinnen', in *Festschrift für Nikolaus Himmelmann: Beiträge zur Ikonographie und Hermeneutik*, ed. by Hans-Ulrich Cain, Hanns Gabelmann, and Dieter Salzmann (Mainz: Von Zabern), pp. 197–203

Smith, Henry R. W. 1976. *Funerary Symbolism in Apulian Vase-painting* (Berkeley: University of California Press)

Smithers, Stephen. 1993. 'Images of Piety and Hope: Select Terracotta Votives from West-Central Italy', *Studia Varia from the J. Paul Getty Museum*, 1: 13–32

Spigo, Umberto. 2000a. 'I pinakes di Francavilla di Sicilia (parte 1)', *Bollettino d'arte*, 6th ser., 85.1: 1–60

———. 2000b. 'I pinakes di Francavilla di Sicilia (parte 2)', *Bollettino d'arte*, 6th ser., 85.3: 1–78

Steingräber, Stephan. 1980. 'Zum Phänomen der etruskisch-italischen Votiveköpfe', *Mitteilungen des Deutschen Archäologischen Instituts: Römische Abteilung*, 87: 215–53

———. 1986. *Etruscan Painting* (New York: Johnson Reprint Corporation)

Stieda, Ludwig. 1899. 'Ueber alt-italische Weihgeschenke', *Mitteilungen des Deutschen Archaeologischen Instituts: Römische Abteilung*, 14: 230–43

Stoop, Maria Wilhelmina. 1960. *Floral Figurines from South Italy* (Assen: Van Gorcum)

Taplin, Oliver. 2007. *Pots and Plays: Interactions between Tragedy and Greek Vase-Painting of the Fourth Century B.C.* (Los Angeles: J. Paul Getty Museum)

Thorn, Jed M. 2009. 'The Invention of "Tarentine" Red-Figure', *Antiquity*, 8: 174–83

Torelli, Mario, and Ingrid Pohl. 1973. 'Veio. Scoperta di un piccolo santuario etrusco in Località Campetti', *Atti della Accademia nazionale dei Lincei: notizie degli scavi di antichità*, 28: 40–258

Trendall, Arthur Dale. 1967. *The Red-Figured Vases of Lucania, Campania, and Sicily* (Oxford: Clarendon)

———. 1987. *The Red-Figured Vases of Paestum* (London: British School at Rome)

———. 1989. *Red Figure Vases of South Italy and Sicily* (London: Thames and Hudson)

———. 1990. 'On the Divergence of South Italian from Attic Red-Figure Vase-Painting', in *Greek Colonists and Native Populations*, ed. by Jean-Paul Descoeudres (Canberra: Humanities Research Centre), pp. 218–30

———. 1992. 'A New Early Apulian *phlyax* Vase', *Bulletin of the Cleveland Museum of Art*, 79: 2–15

Trendall, Arthur Dale, and Alexander Cambitoglou. 1978. *The Red-Figured Vases of Apulia*, I: *Early and Middle Apulian* (Oxford: Clarendon)

———. 1982. *The Red-Figured Vases of Apulia*, II: *Late Apulian* (Oxford: Clarendon)

———. 1983. *First Supplement to the Red-Figured Vases of Apulia* (Oxford: Clarendon)

———. 1991–1992. *Second Supplement to the Red-Figured Vases of Apulia* (London: University of London, Institute of Classical Studies)

Turfa, Jean MacIntosh. 1994. 'Anatomical Votives and Italian Medical Traditions', in *Murlo and the Etruscans: Art and Society in Ancient Etruria*, ed. by Richard Daniel De Puma and Jocelyn Penny Small (Madison: University of Wisconsin Press), pp. 224–40

———. 2006. 'Votive Offerings in Etruscan Religion', in *The Religion of the Etruscans*, ed. by Nancy Thomson de Grummond and Erika Simon (Austin: University of Texas Press), pp. 90–115

Uhlenbrock, Jaimee. 1988. *Terracotta Protomai from Gela: A Discussion of Local Style in Archaic Sicily* (Rome: L'Erma di Bretschneider)

———. 1989. 'Concerning Some Archaic Terracotta Protomai from Naxos', *Xenia*, 18: 9–24

Vacano, Otfried von. 1973. *Zur Enstehung und Deutung gemalter seitenansichtiger Kopfbilder auf schwartzfigurigen Vasen des griechischen Festlandes* (Bonn: Habelt)

Winter, Nancy A. 1974. 'Terracotta Representations of Human Heads Used as Architectural Decoration in the Archaic Period' (unpublished doctoral thesis, Bryn Mawr College)

———. 1978. 'Archaic Architectural Terracottas Decorated with Human Heads', *Mitteilungen des Deutschen Archäologischen Instituts: Römische Abteilung*, 85: 27–58

———. 2009. *Symbols of Wealth and Power: Architectural Terracotta Decoration in Etruria and Central Italy, 640–510 B.C.* (Ann Arbor: University of Michigan Press for the American Academy in Rome)

Wuilleumier, Pierre. 1939. *Tarente: Des origines à la conquête romaine* (Paris: De Boccard)

Zancani Montuoro, Paolo, Helmut Schlaeger, and Maria W. Stoop. 1965. 'L'edificio quadrato nello Heraion alla foce del Sele', *Atti e memorie della Società Magna Grecia*, 2nd ser., 6: 23–195

Zuntz, Günther. 1971. *Persephone: Three Essays on Religion and Thought in Magna Graecia* (Oxford: Clarendon)

WILLIAM M. BALCO

13. Feasting Transformed

Commensal Identity Expression and Social Transformation in Iron Age and Archaic Western Sicily

ABSTRACT Late Iron Age and Archaic western Sicily was a nexus of social interaction, entangling indigenous Elymian populations with Phoenician and Greek colonists economically, socially, and, in some cases, biologically. Such complex social interaction facilitated the exchange of ideas and goods, transforming not only socially constructed power structures, but also the material expressions of wealth, power, and prestige. This paper explores the transmission and reception of displays of status and identity as expressed by indigenous Elymian populations in western Sicily. Feasting vessels are studied as a proxy representing such displays, demonstrating the creation of new identity expressions incorporating stylistic elements borrowed from foreign cultures. The selective adoption of mixed-style commensal vessels among indigenous Sicilian sites, yet the scarcity of such vessels at Greek colonial sites, attests to differential reception of such material culture within the feast.

The arrival of Greek colonists and Phoenician merchants in Sicily during the eighth century BCE resulted in significant transformations amongst the indigenous Iron Age Sicilian polities (Mühlenbock 2015; De Angelis 2016; Balco 2018). Western Sicily is one of the few locations in the western Mediterranean where indigenous cultures encountered, through direct contact, permanent Greek and Phoenician settlements (Morris and Tusa 2004, 36; Kolb and Speakman 2005, 795; Montana and others 2009, 87; Balco 2018, 184). This provides a unique opportunity to explore the resulting social, political, and economic impacts upon all three cultures, due to their mutual and competing interests. This paper will focus on the Elymi, an indigenous population inhabiting fortified hilltop settlements throughout

western Sicily during the Iron Age and Archaic periods (Castellana 1989; Spatafora 1997; Vassallo 2000; Gargini and others 2003; Kolb and Speakman 2005; Albanese Procelli 2005). Elymian settlements were subjected to significant social, political, and mercantile stresses introduced by Greek and Phoenician colonists in the first millennium BCE. The establishment of *apoikiai* at Selinus and Himera, as well as *emporia* at Mozia, Panormus, and Solunto in the areas surrounding the Elymi (Fig. 13.1) thrust the indigenous population into a period of significant social transformation. As this contact became sustained interaction, new ideas, behaviours, and material culture emerged. Indigenous and colonial populations then began to adopt some of them, possibly with direct or indirect encouragement from their new neighbours. Barring widespread participation in feasts among the Greek colonists, indigenous Sicilian persons may not have fully understood the function, social context, or social implications of the behaviour and materials associated with the Greek-style feast from the perspective of Greek or Phoenician cultures. The same could be said of the colonists who may have participated in indigenous feasts. Consequently, the degree to which feasting behaviours common in one culture were then understood by members of other contemporary cultures remains unknown, particularly in ancient western Sicily. Such diverse feasting behaviours may have led to mutual misunderstandings, where the reception of foreign feasting equipment and behaviours led to the adoption, adaptation, rejection, or reimagination, of their uses and meanings.

Contextualizing feasting behaviours among these entangled populations and cultures is challenging. Few sites have been extensively excavated, particularly indigenous Elymian ones, and relatively few macrobotanical or residue analyses have been con-

Corresponding author William M. Balco (wmbalco@uwm.edu)

Adoption, Adaption, and Innovation in Pre-Roman Italy: Paradigms for Cultural Change, ed. by Jeremy Armstrong and Aaron Rhodes-Schroder, AMW 3 (Turnhout, 2023), pp. 221–233   BREPOLS ✹ PUBLISHERS   10.1484/M.AMW-EB.5.133275

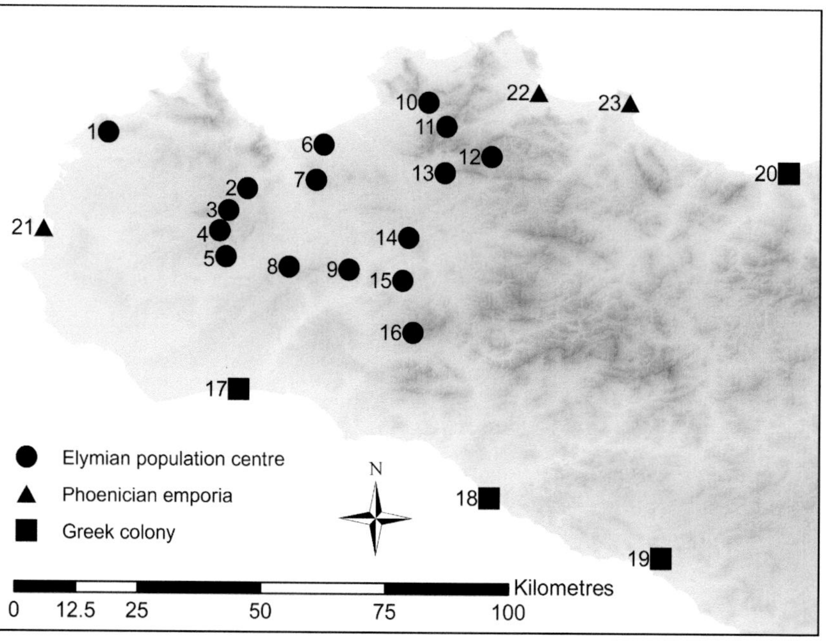

Figure 13.1. Map showing locations of key sites in Iron Age and Archaic western Sicily. 1. Eryx; 2. Segesta; 3. Poggio Roccione; 4. Monte Polizzo; 5. Salemi; 6, Calatubo; 7. Monte Bonifato; 8. Monte Finestrelle; 9. Monte Castellazzo di Poggioreale; 10. Conca d'Oro; 11. Castellaccio di Sagana; 12. Cozzo Paparina; 13. Monte Iato; 14. Monte Maranfusa; 15. Entella; 16. Monte Adranone; 17. Selinus; 18. Eraclea Minoa; 19. Akragas; 20. Himera; 21. Mozia; 22. Panormus; and 23. Solunto (by author).

ducted on material from Sicilian contexts at large (Tanasi and others 2018). The present study attempts to explore Elymian feasting behaviours before, during, and after colonization, contextualizing the transformation of the commensal feast with the available data. Feasting was one social behaviour that individuals engaged in while displaying symbols of status and identity (see for example contributions in Dietler and Hayden 2001; Aranda Jiménez and others 2011). Changes to feasting behaviours, I argue, occurred concomitant to changes in the symbolic representations of status and wealth as communicated through the possession and use of prestige goods. Consequently, the social significance of such changes to feasting behaviours were couched within broader indigenous responses to the social entanglements that enveloped Elymian, Greek, and Phoenician populations in ancient western Sicily.

Social Entanglement and Feasting

Any discussion of feasting behaviours, couched within complex social entanglements, requires a robust theoretical perspective capable of thoroughly examining social changes experienced by the cultures involved — especially indigenous ones. Social entanglements are often complex relationships of dependence (*sensu* Hodder 2012), sometimes born from relationships of circumstance, in this case colonial expansion. For example, colonial contexts facilitated complex, inter- and intra-cultural relationships of interaction, entangling people and cultures through 'an array of rights and obligation' (Thomas 1991, 14) that were reproduced, negotiated, and redefined. Consequently, indigenous and colonial populations and networks coexisted tangentially within complex social entanglements.

One theory in particular, Cultural Hybridity, disentangles processes of cultural 'borrowing' and the creation of an archaeologically visible 'other' during complex social entanglements. Drawing from the works of White, Bhabha, and others, this theory characterizes the 'other' as a figure in the 'social middle ground' (White 1991; Malkin 2005) or 'third space' (Bhabha 1990). Cultural Hybridity breaks from the binary opposition typical of previous theories surrounding complex social interaction. The concept of the social middle ground accommodates the 'other' by characterizing social boundaries as porous rather than impermeable, subject to the ebb and flow of cultural interaction. Consequently, it recognizes the actions of individuals and populations to transform their identities (plural), to break from the established social order and forge a new social frontier. The application of Cultural Hybridity to archaeological case studies involving people, things, and networks has been critiqued (see Pappa 2013 and Silliman 2015), demonstrating how the concept of hybridity has become, in some cases, an explanation, rather than a theoretical tool. In this paper, hybridity is considered a concept and a process explored through a postcolonial lens. Postcolonial perspectives are particularly well suited to explore the nuance of social entanglement, recognizing the complexities and the power inequalities of colonial situations while finding space for indigenous voices.

Navigating through a social entanglement can afford the individual and/or community the agency to modify behavioural responses and to incorporate or reject elements of other culture(s) as they see fit, repurposing concepts, traditions, and materials in the process. Attempting to understand the agency of actors inhabiting a complex social middle ground is difficult at best, requiring epistemological reflection and an impartial theoretical approach. Here, postcolonial approaches intersect with symmetrical archaeology, an approach that emphasizes 'methodological impartiality' in the study of people and things (Shanks 2007, 589). Symmetrical approaches recognize and explore the complex entanglements between people and things (material culture along with the natural and built environment), as well as the network of agents interacting with and affecting them (Whitmore 2007, 547). By emphasizing the use of a flat ontology (Thomas 2022), symmetrical approaches respect analytical neutrality, avoiding assumptions of significance or centrality (DeLanda 2016). Identifying and interpreting complex social entanglements, as well as the social middle grounds that developed concomitant to them, requires the use of a flat ontology to understand and contextualize the social choices and material expressions of all participants.

Consequently, postcolonial and symmetrical approaches can be alloyed to explore complex social entanglements and the networks within and amongst them. This establishes the means to account for the transformation of material culture, as well as the synthesis of new purposes, expressions, and physical forms within multi-scalar social interactions. For these reasons, it is well suited to the study of feasting behaviours and material culture among complex social transformations.

Evidence of such interactions within a social middle ground, and any consequent social transformations, are best observed materially, as changes to a site's material assemblage can represent significant social transformation and behavioural changes. As a result, studying the material culture of social entanglements is essential to understanding the transformation of social behaviour. This is readily accomplished in Iron Age and Archaic western Sicily, the period spanning from approximately 900 BCE to 480 BCE, through a detailed contextual and morphological study of pottery. Fired-clay vessels, ubiquitous as both utilitarian objects and displays of power, wealth, and prestige, arguably represent archaeologically visible evidence of social transformations. Although indigenous Iron Age populations imported a wide variety of fired-clay vessel forms, commensal vessels — those associated with the social consumption of food or drink — were paramount to all others (Walsh 2014a, 125). Such is the case at Monte Polizzo (Mühlenbock 2008, 122) and Eryx (Montana and others 2019, 606) in western Sicily. The importation of high-status commensal hardware has also been observed more generally across the central Mediterranean (Fletcher 2007) as well as further afield, including at the minor sites in the Heuneburg (Shefton 2000, 31). This is not surprising, as feasting behaviours, popular among Greek colonists, may have been likened to extant indigenous traditions, just with new flavours, in both a literal sense (such as with imported wine) and a figurative one (the feasting behaviour itself).

Many diverse activities gather people together to interact and exchange ideas; however, one of the most successful of these is the feast. Commensal activities can bridge social boundaries to engage and integrate participants who otherwise might avoid intimate public contact. Feasts amplified the social aspects of the commensal meal, strengthening social bonds and creating new ones (Wells 1980). They provided a forum in which diverse cultural practices were exercised, adopted, and modified. Feasting behaviours and traditions served as catalysts of social interaction between colonists and indigenous populations. They offered the opportunity to 'create social relationships beyond the family' (Wills and Crown 2004, 153), energizing communication and interaction among the community and non-local actors.

Every component of the feast was culturally significant. For example, the food and drink served at the feast were culturally defined within rubrics of 'proper consumption' (Dietler 2010, 185). Concepts of what constituted proper feasting behaviour varied from culture to culture and extended beyond just social behaviour. As colonial interaction introduced exotic foods — and more especially beverages — local populations 'indigenized' (Dietler 2010, 186) these over time, eventually reconfiguring them as components of local cuisine. As demonstrated in Iron Age southern France, local Gauls transitioned from consuming beer and animal fats to consuming wine and olive oil following contact and intense interaction with their colonial neighbours (Dietler 2005; 2010). Local Iron Age populations in the Rhône basin then incorporated Attic drinking vessels alongside their own cream-ware ones, suggesting that indigenous wine consumption 'was the result of choices made by consumers to which traders responded' (Dietler 2010, 195). The adoption of foreign commensal vessels thus corresponds with 'what was being consumed by the aristocracy as a status beverage' (Arnold 1999, 75). In this way, feasts were (and remain) social functions where participation communicated status and power between and among the participants. The possession of specific feasting hardware could communicate cultural affiliation, status, or economic connections. Concepts of what constituted 'proper use' of such hardware must have varied, particularly when considering the adoption of imported feasting vessel forms both novel and previously unknown to local populations.

The choice to use one particular commensal vessel form over another was an important decision. The social consumption of certain beverages is frequently associated with particular vessel forms (Sherratt 1987), resulting in the development of emic associations that constitute social concepts of proper, or improper, use of such material. As a result, commensal vessels are active products of social reality (Hodder 1982, 27; 1986, 64; Shanks and Tilley 1987, 251; 1992, 15; Miller 2005, 8; Boivin 2008, 10), constructed from the intersection of utility and sociality. They are more than simply temporary containers; they are symbolically charged attestations of identity, wealth, and status readily displayed for others to see.

Feasting in Ancient Sicily

Despite an increased focus on ancient human diets over the past several decades, few projects have holistically explored the topic in ancient Sicily. Those that have done so, have utilized a variety of methods and data to infer ancient dietary patterns. This includes the study of macrobotanical remains (Stika and others 2008; Ramsay and Wilson 2013; Speciale and others 2020), the analysis of domesticated faunal remains (Wilkins 1997; Bedini 1998; Cultraro 2004; Oma 2006), explorations of butchered vertebrate zooarchaeological remains (Garilli and others 2020), isotopic studies of human remains (Mannino and others 2011; Reitsema and others 2020), and even spectroscopic analysis of a kidney stone recovered from a human burial (D'Alessio and others 2005, 135). These studies provide broad characterizations of past dietary patterns, yet parsing the foods and beverages consumed during feasts from those consumed on a regular basis remains a monumental challenge. Here, organic residue analyses have the potential to identify compounds belonging to foods and beverages once contained within, and now preserved on, feasting hardware. For example, these methods have begun to identify the contents of feasting vessels from Early Bronze Age eastern Sicily (Mentesana and others 2018; Tanasi and others 2018; Spiteri and others 2020), and the contents of cooking pots and transport containers from the medieval period

(Carver and others 2019). Such studies of beverage residues are a welcome addition, but unfortunately, they remain few and far between, leaving us to rely on circumstantial evidence to posit what foods and beverages may have been available and consumed during Iron Age and Archaic feasts in western Sicily.

The identification of the beverages consumed by indigenous western Sicilian populations before and after the establishment of the colonies is difficult. A wide range of recent scientific studies have confirmed that indigenous Italian peoples cultivated grapes long before the arrival of Aegean and Levantine colonists (see for example De Angelis, this volume). A similar case for early grape cultivation in Sicily can be made. For example, Iron Age contexts at Monte Polizzo and Archaic contexts at Salemi and Monte Iato have yielded remains of grapes (including unsquashed seeds of *vitis vinifera*) (Stika and others 2008; Kistler and Mohr 2015). This could suggest the presence of cultivated varieties in western Sicily; however, unsquashed seeds could equally suggest the importation of whole grapes from afar (see Kistler and Mohr 2015). Regardless, wine was present at Iron Age and Archaic Elymian sites, either locally produced or imported from Greece or the eastern Mediterranean, the latter suggested by the presence of imported wine amphorae recovered at these sites. In addition to wine, it is possible the Iron Age Sicilian populations fermented something akin to beer. Macrobotanical evidence from numerous Iron Age and Archaic sites in western Sicily confirm that the Elymi cultivated a wide array of grains, including barley, emmer, and free-threshing wheat. These grains could then have been transformed into an alcoholic beverage to be consumed at social functions. Kistler and Mohr's (2015) study of Archaic Sicilian vessel forms from interior sites propose that their functions were associated with fermentation, suggesting that indigenous populations such as the Elymi produced fermented beverages for consumption during commensal rituals and/or everyday meals. Identifying *what* was being fermented is more difficult. Given the archaeobotanical evidence, it is equally likely that such beverages were fermented from grains as they were from grapes. Evidence of the manufacture and consumption of other alcoholic beverages, such as mead and/or fermented milk is, at present, entirely absent. Barring extensive residue testing, this is currently the best evidence of the broad types of beverages indigenous Sicilians in the Iron Age and Archaic period were manufacturing and consuming.

Feasting Hardware and Status Display

In addition to food and drink, feasts required socially appropriate accoutrements, some of which remain archaeologically visible. Feasting hardware was socially charged, constituting an essential component of what was considered a proper execution of the feast. The possession and use of feasting vessels was a visible display of status and identity, whether accompanying the feast or when deposited in sanctuary contexts. For example, among the Celts of west-central Europe (Arnold 1999, 85), the possession and display of foreign-style drinking equipment likely served to indicate social status. Likewise, the material that feasting hardware was constructed from also communicated status, as vessels made of gold, silver, or bronze were costlier than fired-clay cups. The appearance of fired-clay skeuomorphs, vessels that took the shape of costlier metal forms, has been interpreted as evidence of the utility of public displays of the vessels (Walsh 2014b).

Feasting and sympotic behaviour energized communication and interaction, facilitating social and material transformations. Such feasts amplified the social aspects of the commensal meal, strengthening social bonds and creating new ones (Wells 2012, 80). Feasts were, and still remain, social functions where participation communicated status and power between and among the participants. The consumption of alcoholic beverages during the feast animated communication by 'facilitating social interaction and channelling the flow of social relations' (Dietler 1990, 361).

Indigenous Sicilian populations have a long tradition of feasting behaviours marked by specific hardware. Deposits of stylized cups dating from the Neolithic (Natali and Forgia 2018), Copper (Maniscalco 2007; Adamo and Gulli 2008; Giannitrapani 2009), Bronze (Tusa 1994, 1997; Copat 2020), and Iron (Spatafora 1996; Oma 2006; Mühlenbock 2008) Ages have been identified at numerous sites across Sicily. Such vessels are material evidence attesting to feasting behaviours among ancient Sicilian populations long before the arrival of Greek colonists and Phoenician merchants. Just as vessel forms and decorations varied from period to period, so too did the social use of those vessels. For the indigenous Iron Age Elymi, the variety of cup and bowl forms they manufactured and used reflected the societal repertoire of vessels associated with the consumption of food and drink in everyday use and/or feasting contexts.

Iron Age Elymian commensal vessels were likely multifunctional, employed as dippers to ladle beverages and as cups from which to imbibe. Some Iron

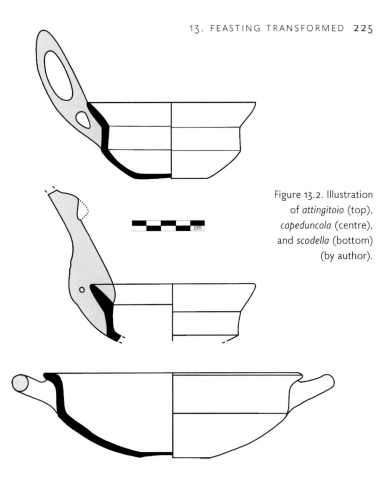

Figure 13.2. Illustration of *attingitoio* (top), *capeduncola* (centre), and *scodella* (bottom) (by author).

Age forms, such as the *capeduncola* and *attingitoio* (Fig. 13.2, top and bottom) were derived from earlier Bronze Age antecedents (Spatafora 1996b, 101; Mühlenbock 2008, 111). Others, such as the *scodella* (Fig. 13.2, centre), are unlike earlier Bronze Age Sicilian vessels, attesting the development of new forms that likely accompanied a significant transformation in feasting rituals, including behaviours, food, and drink.

Many, but not necessarily all, Elymian commensal vessels were decorated with complex impressed and incised geometric motifs. One of the more frequent of these motifs to be recovered archaeologically is known as *denti di lupo*, or 'teeth of the wolf' (Kolb and Speakman 2005; Oma 2006; Kolb and others 2006) (Fig. 13.3). Additionally, some commensal vessels were decorated with brown and black painted horizontal bands and vertical bars atop tan or cream coloured slips. Vessels with such decorative motifs are ubiquitous at Iron Age settlements in western Sicily, suggesting the presence of a feasting tradition shared among numerous indigenous polities (Kolb and others 2006).

As social interaction and entanglement with Greeks and Phoenicians increased, indigenous populations incorporated imported material culture within their feasting assemblages with increasing frequency. Forms such as the *kylix*, lip-cup, *kantharos*, and krater,

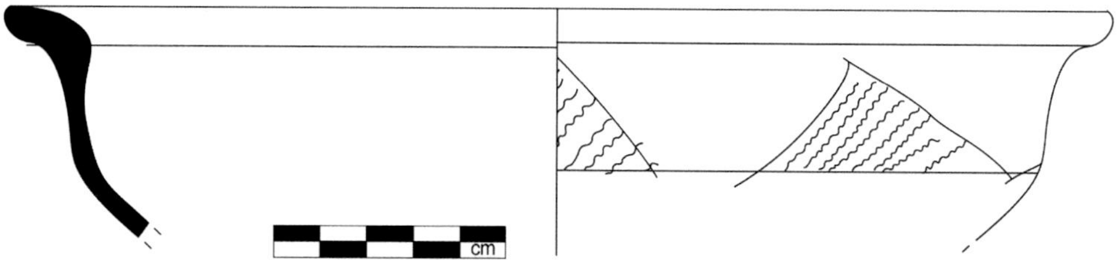

Figure 13.3. Line drawing of *scodella* decorated with *denti di lupo*. Recovered from Salemi (by author).

all directly associated with Greek feasting behaviour, may have been afforded special attention as 'exotic' vessels from afar. Possessing, or even using, such vessels would have visibly associated an individual with the wealth, power, prestige, or connections required to obtain them. As a result, using such imported vessels likely became a means to establish, maintain, or exert one's status within the group (Vives-Ferrándiz 2008, 265). Objects (in this case, sympotic vessels) manufactured or influenced by foreign cultures can 'increase the ideological power and political prestige of those who acquire them' (Helms 1988, 263). Acquiring these objects demonstrates an individual's status, because possessing such exotica testifies to the 'personal characteristics of the acquirer, who has had to deal [...] with a conceptually distinctive foreign realm' (Helms 1993, 101). Not all foreign objects are inherently prestigious, but the possession of high-quality vessels directly associated with the Greek-style feast may have elevated the perceived social and economic connections of indigenous users. Among the Iron Age Elymi, feasting vessels may have served a similar function, displaying an individual's power, wealth, and prestige. The frequency of typically undecorated *attingitoi* and cup forms (Fiorentini 1985–1986, 49; Trombi 1999, 281; Mühlenbock 2008, 113) and the scarcity of elaborately incised anthropomorphic vessels (Leighton 1999, 266) suggests the latter form may also have functioned to communicate status.

The highly stylized *capeduncola* (*capeduncole* (pl.)) serves as an excellent proxy for status display. These vessels, elaborately decorated with incised designs and an anthropomorphic handle (Fig. 13.4), are often found in association with other indigenous feasting hardware. The function(s) of the *capeduncola* remains unknown and contested; Ferrer-Martin (Ferrer 2010) argues that *capeduncole* are vessels for measuring fixed volumes of grain, while Mühlenbock (2008) classifies them as commensal vessels adorned with images of a female deity. Their highly stylized nature, coupled with variation among the decorative elements adorning the anthropomorphic representation on them, suggests that they served a significantly different role from other commensal vessels. Their potential function as a status display may not have been restricted to the feast. The handle and rim of these vessels were typically pierced during the manufacturing process, prior to being fired. The locations of the piercings suggest that the vessels may have been suspended or tied to a post, facilitating a display function in a multitude of social and ritual contexts, not only during the feast. The relative scarcity of *capeduncole* compared to other commensal forms suggests that they may have served as visible communicators of status, power, and identity, possibly as an integral component of a particular, infrequent ritual activity. As a result, the use of one vessel over another was a conscious choice, serving as a display of wealth or status among a structured indigenous social hierarchy.

Transforming the Feast

After social interaction with foreign Greeks and Phoenicians intensified, Sicilians adopted some elements of the Greek feast alongside their own feasting behaviours, diversifying their choices of foods, beverages, and commensal hardware. This modification of feasting traditions did not mean an abandonment of earlier indigenous foods and commensal hardware; instead, the selective adoption of foreign elements redefined feasting traditions culinarily, behaviourally, and materially. For the indigenous Elymi, this was done through an indigenous lens, just the same as Aegean and Levantine colonists would have interpreted and redefined their own, respective, feasting traditions on their own terms. In the Late Iron Age and Archaic periods, indigenous Sicilians encountered elaborately decorated commensal vessels imported from the east through sustained contact and interaction with Greek and Phoenician settlers and merchants. Through trade with their new neighbours, these populations were capable of acquiring Phoenician calotte cups and any of the plethora of Greek cup forms imported from the east. At first, these novel and exotic cups were only available to Sicilians with the means to sustain mercantile interaction with the colonies and *empo-*

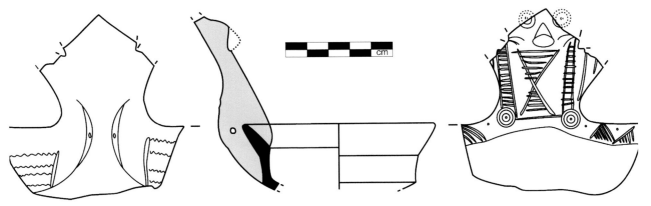

Figure 13.4. Illustration of *capeduncola* with details of exterior (left), profile (centre), and interior (right) (by author).

ria. As a result, relatively few Sicilians possessed the imported vessels and, much like the indigenous *capeduncole*, their possession and use became visible displays of wealth, status, and connections/affiliations. In this manner, the indigenous populations incorporated foreign material culture among their own feasting practices, imbuing these vessels with new meanings and status associations particular to their own cultures.

To reach the Sicilian populations, these imports first had to be transported to the Greek colonies or Phoenician *emporia* where many were consumed by the colonists. The popularity of commensal feasts among the Greek settlers at Selinus and Himera is evident from the number of drinking vessels recovered from sixth- and fifth-century BCE contexts. The Gaggera necropolis at Greek Selinus provides an excellent proxy for Greek imports during this period. Imported sympotic vessels account for 67 per cent of all fired-clay vessels deposited in tombs there during the sixth century (Kustermann Graf 2002, 33), and increased to 77 per cent in the fifth century (Kustermann Graf 2002, 48), suggesting that the consumption of these imported vessels was important to the populations living in the Greek colonies, emphasizing their social status as well as their colonial, Greek-derived identity.

This voracious colonial appetite for imported feasting hardware, driven by conspicuous consumption among feasting and mortuary contexts, would have left few available for exchange with indigenous populations. Consequently, imported commensal vessels would have been scarce among indigenous consumers. The relative infrequency of imported feasting vessels among sixth- and fifth-century BCE indigenous contexts, coupled with evidence for the repair of broken vessels, attest scarcity rather than a lack of interest in the vessels. For example, a fragment of an Attic cup preserving evidence of a repair was recovered during excavations in Salemi, Sicily (Balco 2012). The repair, consisting of a perforation used to 'stitch' fragments together, likely made the vessel ill-suited for use with liquids; however, it preserved the vessel's ability to communicate social status through display. Interestingly, indigenous western Sicilians appear to have avoided Phoenician-style commensal vessel forms. Despite their overwhelming presence at the Phoenician *emporia* at Mozia, Panormus, and Solunto, calotte cups and other Phoenician forms remain absent from Elymian assemblages.

In the sixth century BCE, the scarcity of imported commensal vessels stimulated the appearance of cups mixing Greek, indigenous, and even Phoenician potting techniques, vessel forms, and decorative motifs. One could imagine enterprising potters attempting to turn a quick profit making and selling pottery that, to the untrained eye, appeared to be an imported vessel. Communities of potters, working with their own conceptual models and techniques, expressed their creative license through shared ontologies of style, transforming their products — either actively or passively — in response to the changing social environment (Balco 2018). By incorporating foreign forms and motifs alongside those already familiar to the potter, a new type of pottery was synthesized, one which was not indigenous, mainland Greek, colonial Greek, or Phoenician.

Indigenous western Sicilian populations actively transformed their feasting traditions, adopting and repurposing foreign materials and behaviours amongst their own, reflecting their transforming social identity. Two phenomena demonstrate this. First, indigenous western Sicilians incorporated imported East Greek vessels, but not Phoenician-style vessels, into their feasting assemblages. Second, indigenous western Sicilian potters, and possibly potters of unknown ethnic background at Mozia, manufactured mixed-style cups displaying elements of Greek, indigenous Sicilian, and to a lesser degree Phoenician forms and decorative styles together. These phenomena suggest that the Elymi purposefully selected socially and functionally appropriate commensal vessels for their use. Imported Greek forms, but not Phoenician ones, were chosen as appropriate additions to the indigenous feasting assemblage, demonstrating an intentional incorporation of some foreign vessels and the exclusion of others.

Interestingly, indigenous potters incorporated Phoenician decorative motifs alongside their own, but the indigenous Elymi did not incorporate imported Phoenician vessels or even Phoenician vessel forms into their feasting assemblage. This could suggest that the transfigured feasting behaviours culminated from a mixture of Greek and indigenous proxies, with little incorporation of Phoenician feasting traditions. Perhaps the indigenous populations found the sympotic feast more appealing than the Phoenician-style feast. Perhaps Greek sympotic behaviour was more akin to indigenous feasting behaviours than Phoenician ones, facilitating the incorporation of imported Greek hardware among indigenous assemblages within a slightly modified form of the indigenous feast. Conversely, the Greek colonists might have more actively promoted their own feasting traditions by inviting members of the indigenous populations to participate, facilitating political and mercantile alliances through the exchange of gifts such as valuable imported vessels. Regardless, the selective preference for Greek-style, but not Phoenician-style, feasting hardware, coupled with the retention of indigenous forms, demonstrates that the indigenous Elymi actively preserved their indigeneity in the face of social transformation.

The adaptation of imported commensal vessels was not limited to western Sicily; an interest in Greek material, namely Attic pottery, was also identified among Sicilians living at Morgantina in central Sicily (Walsh and Antonaccio 2014). This has been interpreted functionally, where imported vessels were status signals, visibly communicating social identity and status (Walsh and Antonaccio 2014, 61).

Contextualizing the Feast

The social significance of the feast was context driven — each feast differed in purpose, execution, duration, and flavour, nuances that reflected the culture(s) of the organizers and participants. Amongst western Sicilian Iron Age and Archaic sites, these feasting contexts were also likely associated with cultic behaviours practised by extended family units (Öhlinger 2015, 421). Consequently, the exercise of feasting behaviours would have reinforced familial and social identities through shared food and drink.

No matter its purpose, every feast required three components: food/drink, feasting hardware, and participants. Feasting hardware, specifically commensal vessels, remain the most archaeologically visible of these components. Classifying these vessels archaeologically is difficult at best. Disassociating any blatant cultural affiliation in favour of a morphological description such as 'mixed-style' better suits their contextualization and interpretation (Balco 2018). The mixed-style classification is an objective methodological tool, divorced from the social behaviours and processes affiliated with the manufacture, use, meaning, and discard of the object. Cups that blended Greek and Elymian decorative styles together have previously been classified as hybridized, yet this term implies a behavioural connotation rather than a descriptive one. Such subjective behavioural classifications introduce biases that affect our interpretations. Classifying an artefact objectively reduces theoretical biases inherent in subjective classifications such as 'hybrid' or 'imitation', facilitating a more robust interpretation of the material culture within its context of use.

Mixed-style vessels were frequent components of Elymian feasting assemblages in the Iron Age and Archaic periods (Balco 2018). These vessels typically assumed a form similar to an Ionic cup with painted fields and bands emulating those seen on the highly sought-after imports. Rather than have a glossy, highly polished appearance, these decorative motifs were often dull and flat, applied expediently and without the use of a potter's wheel as indicated by the undulating limits of the paint. To the trained archaeologist, the lacklustre decorations on these vessels appear in stark contrast to the crisp glossy lines typically applied to the imported vessels. Despite the disparities in decorative skill and quality, these vessels were important components of indigenous feasting assemblages.

Discussion

Socially entangled interactions elicit multifaceted behavioural responses projected upon people and objects, transforming their form, use, and meaning. This is particularly true of feasting contexts, where objects and behaviours communicate and reinforce status and identity. Unlike the clothing and jewellery that adorned participants at the feast, commensal vessels visibly communicated social status through a repetitive action; drawing the vessel to one's mouth connected the individual to visible displays of status and identity — drinking literally put a status to the face of the individual. The behaviours associated with feasting within each chronological phase were probably not static, they must have transformed with the ebb and flow of societal change. Likewise, feasting behaviours were likely not executed uniformly; seasonal and functional variation may have been reflected through the ritual execution of the feast.

Mixed-style cups are a proxy for the behavioural response to socially entangled interaction — they attest to the process of cultural hybridity in action. In central and western Sicily, these began to appear at indigenous and Phoenician sites in the sixth century BCE. Recovered from domestic and mortuary contexts, they are often found alongside imported ones, yet they appear to outnumber the imports, particularly among indigenous contexts. Their absence from colonial Greek centres is a stark reminder of the social significance of commensal hardware. Consumers in the colonies may have had ample access to imported and colonial vessels, precluding the need to consume vessels manufactured in indigenous or Phoenician workshops. Perhaps also, colonial Greeks may have regarded indigenous or Phoenician commensal vessels as inferior to colonial or imported vessels, or simply not suitable for their commensal activities. Indeed, the absence of mixed-style vessels in colonial Greek contexts could be a consequence of the colonists' agency, as they forged their own expression of Greek identity. In this case, the colonists may have avoided mixed-style vessels altogether as they did not convey the image of the developing colonial Greek identity.

Interpreting who manufactured commensal vessels, particularly mixed-style ones, remains an important consideration. Because indigenous Sicilian, Phoenician, and Greek potters employed potting techniques that differed from each other, a study of the potting techniques employed to manufacture a vessel can unveil the general social identity of the potter or potters. Interestingly, mixed-style commensal vessels do not appear to have been the product of Greek or colonial Greek potters. Paste characterizations, resulting from quantitative and qualitative petrographic analysis, suggest that the techniques employed to manufacture these mixed-style vessels are similar to those employed by indigenous and/or Phoenician potters (Balco 2012). Indigenous potters employed the techniques they were most familiar with, resulting in a moderately sorted paste with infrequent coarse inclusions and a profile generally more robust than the imported vessels. In this same manner, Phoenician and Greek potters are each generally distinguished by their pastes as these reflect traditions learned through communities of practice. Such communities of practice are 'network[s] of relations among people and objects mediated by actions they conduct' (Joyce 2012, 150). They are communities of experiential learners that practice shared methods and structure meanings (Kohring 2013). Accordingly, the manufacture of these vessels with pastes common among indigenous and Phoenician, but not Greek, potters suggests that indigenous Sicilians and Phoenicians manufactured these vessels, perhaps to take full advantage of the entrepreneurial opportunity resulting from the social entanglement.

For indigenous and Phoenician populations in Sicily, the consumption of mixed-style cups served important social functions. Rather than continuing to use *attingitoi*, *capeduncole*, and/or *scodelle* exclusively, these populations chose to incorporate foreign-style vessels, or vessels with foreign elements, into their extant feasting traditions. This choice was but one component of the transformation of the feast, yet it might have served as one of the most significant choices. Just as the possession and use of an indigenous *capeduncola* may have communicated status, so too did an imported Ionic cup. Mixed-style cups were apparently employed in the same manner as the imports, suggesting that they may have taken on a role as a status display, albeit possibly in a reinvented manner. To the indigenous individual who wished to signal wealth, power, prestige, and connections, the mixed-style cup was an attractive alternative, signalling an association with indigenous heritage and social links to colonial Greek culture. The purposeful inclusion of indigenous forms and decorative elements suggests that mixed-style vessels, and the commensal assemblage, retained a visible indigenous quality to it. Possessing such vessels likely objectified the social acumen of the individual as a cultural agent navigating between distant and local social boundaries.

While this possession and display of mixed-style feasting hardware may have worked at first, the increasing frequency of these vessels must have diluted any status association the vessels portrayed. Had everyone possessed a mixed-style cup, any status that it was meant to convey, real or imagined, associated with the possession and use of such a symbol, then became relatively equal. At that point, only those with real imported commensal vessels would have stood out among the crowd. In this way, mixed-style commensal vessels were a short-lived trend. Coming into vogue among Late Iron Age populations, these mixed-style vessels were a product meant to elevate the social status of some, but their widespread use reduced the appearance of all but those who possessed genuine imports. The popularity of these vessels waned in the mid-fifth century BCE, likely due to the sudden influx of imports to indigenous populations. Once the indigenous western Sicilian populations allied themselves with Athens against Syracusa, mercantile relations with the colonies intensified, flooding the market with imports. As colonial and imported vessels became more readily available, the status associations of commensal vessels changed yet again, diminishing the demand for locally manufactured products. At that point, the function of mixed-style commensal vessels also changed. So highly desired several generations earlier, they became just another surrogate vessel in a tomb, a stand-in for a costlier import from Athens.

Concomitant to transformations of indigenous feasting behaviours was a transformation of the symbolic representation and execution of displays of wealth, power, and prestige as understood by the participants. As social structures were 'both the medium and outcome of (individual) motivated practices' (Shanks 2007, 590), the feast was an important locus of social interaction that reinforced the social structure among the populace, as well as the social identity/identities of the participants. By incorporating Greek-style vessels and foods, but not Phoenician vessel forms, among feasting behaviours, indigenous communities redefined social displays of status. In this way, the appearance of foreign-style commensal hardware attests to the exchange of ideas between diverse cultures. The initial appearance of Greek-style vessels, followed by the emulation of such vessels at indigenous Elymian and Phoenician centres occurred because of the transformation of symbols of power and their display. Consequently, Iron Age and Archaic western Sicilian feasts were loci of supralocal interaction that facilitated social transformation and the concomitant displays of wealth, power, and prestige. Without competition and a continual redefinition of power and status, the mixed-style cup serves almost no purpose. Such objects were situated in the liminal space between cultures. The display of one, through its possession and use, allowed individuals to compete on the visible social stage, to express their own identity and status, actual or projected, as needed at a particular moment.

In Iron Age and Archaic western Sicily, feasting functioned to reinforce social status and identity. Within the context of a social entanglement, the indigenous Elymi borrowed elements of Greek ritual, fitting them into their own indigenous narrative. Indigenous populations, expressing their agency, put their own spin on the possession and use of foreign behaviours and material culture. The absence of a total adoption of Greek elements attests to the power of indigenous agency; what the Elymi borrowed and what they ignored are equally important. Elymian feasting behaviours reflected social entanglement through an indigenous lens, demonstrating the preservation of social identities and status among new means to express them.

Works Cited

Adamo, Ornella, and Domenica Gulli. 2008. 'Il tipo della coppa quadrilobata nell'ambito dell'Eneolitico siciliano. Recenti acquisizioni', *Rivista di scienze preistoriche*, 58: 191–200

Adams, Ron L. 2004. 'An Ethnoarchaeological Study of Feasting in Sulawesi, Indonesia', *Journal of Anthropological Archaeology*, 23: 56–78

Albanese Procelli, Rosa Maria. 2005. 'La ricezione dei modelli dell'architettura greca nel mondo indigeno: le strutture abitative', in *Urbanistica e architettura nella Sicilia Greca*, ed. by Patrizia Minà (Palermo: Regione Siciliana, Assessorato dei beni culturali ambientali e della pubblica istruzione), pp. 167–70

Aranda Jiménez, Gonzalo, Sandra Montón-Subais, and Margarita Sánchez Romero. 2011. *Guess Who's Coming to Dinner: Feasting Rituals in the Prehistoric Societies of Europe and the Near East* (Oxford: Oxbow)

Arnold, Bettina. 1999. '"Drinking the Feast": Alcohol and the Legitimation of Power in Celtic Europe', *Cambridge Archaeological Journal*, 9: 71–93

Balco, William M. 2012. 'Material Expressions of Social Change: Indigenous Sicilian Responses to External Influences in the First Millennium B.C.' (unpublished doctoral dissertation, University of Wisconsin-Milwaukee)

——. 2018. 'Thinking beyond Imitation: Mixed-Style Pottery in Ancient Western Sicily', *Journal of Mediterranean Archaeology*, 31.2: 180–202

Bedini, Elena. 1998. 'I reperti faunistici del deposito votivo del Bronzo Antico di Monte Grande', in *Il Santuario Castellucciano di Monte Grande e l'Approvvigio Namento dello Zolfo nel Mediterraneo nel'Età del Bronzo*, ed. by Castellana Giuseppe (Palermo: Regione Sicilia, Assessorato beni culturali ed ambientali e della pubblica istruzione), pp. 431–54

Bhabha, Homi. 1990. 'The Third Space', in *Identity: Community, Culture, Difference*, ed. by Jonathan Rutherford (London: Lawrence & Wishart), pp. 207–21

Boivin, Nicole. 2008. *Material Cultures, Material Minds: The Impact of Things on Human Thought, Society, and Evolution* (Cambridge: Cambridge University Press)

Carver, Martin, Alessandra Molinari, Veronica Aniceti, Claudio Capelli, Francesca Colangeli, Léa Drieu, Girolamo Fiorentino, Fabio Giovannini, Madeleine Hummler, Jasmine Lundy, Antonino Meo, Aurore Monnereau, Paola Orecchioni, Milena Primavera, and Alica Ughi. 2019. 'Sicily in Transition: New Research on Early Medieval Sicily, 2017–2018', *The Journal of Fasti Online*, 437 <https://www.fastionline.org/docs/FOLDER-it-2019-437.pdf> [accessed 24 January 2023]

Castellana, Giuseppe. 1989. 'Un progetto per riappropriarci della nostra identità culturale', in *Gli Elimi*, ed. by Sebastiano Tusa and R. Vento (Trapani: Associazione nazionale 'Ludi di Enea'), pp. 11–12

Copat, Valentina. 2020. 'On Pots, People and Cultural Landscape: The Hyblean Mountains (Sicily) in the Early Bronze Age', *Journal of Archaeological Science: Reports*, 30: 102219

Cultraro, Massimo. 2004. 'Food for the Gods: Animal Consumption and Ritual Activities in the Early Bronze Age Sicily', in *PECUS: Man and Animal in Antiquity; Proceedings of the Conference at the Swedish Institute in Rome, September 9–12, 2004*, ed. by Barbro Santillo Frizell, Projects and Seminars, 1 (Rome: Swedish Institute in Rome), pp. 201–11

D'Alessio, Aldo, Emilia Bramanti, Marcello Piperno, Giuseppe Naccaroto, Piergiorgio Vergamini, and Gino Fornaciari. 2005. 'An 8500-Year-Old Bladder Stone from Uzzo Cave (Trapani): Fourier Transform-Infrared Spectroscopy Analysis', *Archaeometry*, 47.1: 127–36

DeLanda, Manuel. 2016. *Assemblage Theory* (Edinburgh: Edinburgh University Press)

De Angelis, Franco. 2016. *Archaic and Classical Greek Sicily: A Social and Economic History* (Oxford: Oxford University Press)

——. 2023. 'Mixing up Mediterranean Innovation: The Case of Viticulture and Wine', in *Adoption, Adaption, and Innovation in Pre-Roman Italy: Paradigms for Cultural Change*, ed. by Jeremy Armstrong and Aaron Rhodes-Schroder (Turnhout: Brepols), pp. 47–58

Dietler, Michael. 1990. 'Driven by Drink: The Role of Drinking in the Political Economy and the Case of Early Iron Age France', *Journal of Anthropological Archaeology*, 9: 352–406

——. 2005. *Consumption and Colonial Encounters in the Rhône Basin of France: A Study of Early Iron Age Political Economy*, Monographies d'archéologie méditerranéenne, 21 (Lattes: Édition de l'Association pour le développement de l'archéologie en Languedoc-Roussillon)

——. 2010. *Archaeologies of Colonialism: Consumption, Entanglement, and Violence in Ancient Mediterranean France* (Berkeley: University of California Press)

Dietler, Michael, and Brian Hayden. 2001. *Feasts: Archaeological and Ethnographic Perspectives on Food, Politics, and Power* (Tuscaloosa: University of Alabama Press)

Ferrer, Meritxell. 2010. 'Raciones de solidaridad: mujeres, alimentos y *capeduncolas* en Sicilia Occidental (ss. VII–V A.C.)', *Sagvntvm Extra*, 9: 209–18

Fiorentini, Graziella. 1985–1986. 'La necropolis indigena di età greca di Valle Oscura (Marianopoli)', *Quaderni dell'Istituto di archeologia della Facoltà di lettere e filosofia della Università di Messina*, 1: 31–54

Fletcher, Richard N. 2007. *Patterns of Imports in Iron Age Italy*, British Archaeological Reports, International Series, 1732 (Oxford: Archaeopress)

Gargini, Michela, Chiara Michelini, and Maria A. Vaggioli. 2003. 'Nuovi dati sul sistema di fortificazione di Entella', in *Guerra e pace in Sicilia e nel Mediterraneo antico (VIII–III sec. a.C.)*, ed. by Chiara Michelini (Pisa: Scuola Normale Superiore di Pisa), pp. 327–78

Garilli, Vittorio, Gerlando Vita, Angelo Mulone, Laura Bonfiglio, and Luca Sineo. 2020. 'From Sepulchre to Butchery-Cooking: Facies Analysis, Taphonomy and Stratigraphy of the Upper Palaeolithic Post Burial Layer from the San Teodoro Cave (NE Sicily) Reveal Change in the Use of the Site', *Journal of Archaeological Science: Reports*, 30: 102191

Giannitrapani, Enrico. 2009. 'Nuove considerazioni sulla diffusione del Bicchiere Campaniforme in Sicilia', *Rivista di scienze preistoriche*, 59: 219–42

Hammond, Debora. 2003. *The Science of Synthesis: Exploring the Social Implications of General Systems Theory* (Boulder: University of Colorado Press)

Helms, Mary W. 1988. *Ulysses' Sail: An Ethnographic Odyssey of Power, Knowledge, and Geographical Distance* (Princeton: Princeton University Press)

——. 1993. *Craft and the Kingly Ideal: Art, Trade, and Power* (Austin: University of Texas Press)

Hodder, Ian. 1982. *Symbols in Action: Ethnoarchaeological Studies of Material Culture* (Cambridge: Cambridge University Press)

——. 1986. *Reading the Past* (Cambridge: Cambridge University Press)

——. 1992. *Theory and Practice in Archaeology* (London: Routledge)

——. 2012. *Entangled: An Archaeology of the Relationships between Humans and Things* (Chichester: Wiley-Blackwell)

Joyce, Rosemary. 2012. 'Thinking about Pottery Production as Community Practice', in *Potters and Communities of Practice: Glaze Paint and Polychrome Pottery in the American Southwest, A.D. 1250–1700*, in Linda S. Cordell and Judith Habicht-Mauche (Tucson: University of Arizona Press), pp. 149–54

Kohring, Sheila. 2013. 'Conceptual Knowledge as Technologically Materialised: A Case Study of Pottery Production, Consumption and Community Practice', in *Embodied Knowledge: Historical Perspectives on Belief and Technology*, ed. by Marie L. S. Sørensen and Katharina Rebay-Salisbury (Oxford: Oxbow), pp. 106–16

Kistler, Erich, and Martin Mohr. 2015. 'Monte Iato: Two Late Archaic Feasting Places between the Local and the Global', in *Sanctuaries and the Power of Consumption: Networking and the Formation of Elites in the Archaic Western Mediterranean World*, ed. by Erich Kistler, Birgit Öhlinger, Martin Mohr, and Matthias Hoernes (Wiesbaden: Harrassowitz), pp. 385–415

Kolb, Michael J., Sebastiano Tusa, and Robert J. Speakman. 2006. 'La decorazione a "Denti di lupo": identità sociale e interazione nell'Età del Ferro in Sicilia occidentale', *Sicilia archeologica*, 104: 33–46

Kolb, Michael J., and Robert J. Speakman. 2005. 'Elymian Regional Interaction in Iron Age Western Sicily: A Preliminary Neutron Activation Study of Incised/Impressed Tablewares', *Journal of Archaeological Science*, 32.5: 795–804

Kustermann Graf, A. 2002. *Selinunte, Necropoli di Manicalunga: le tombe della contrada Gaggera* (Catanzaro: Rubbettino, Soveria Mannelli)

Le Roux, Ronan. 2007. 'L'homéostasie sociale selon Norbert Wiener', *Revue d'historie des sciences humaines*, 16: 113–35

Leighton, Robert. 1999. *Sicily before History: An Archaeological Survey from the Paleolithic to the Iron Age* (Ithaca: Cornell University Press)

Luaces, Max. 2017. 'The Late-Punic Amphorae as Reflections/Actants: An Example of the Contribution of the Symmetrical Archaeology to the Analysis of Artifacts?', *Forma revista D'estudis comparatius*, 16: 31–51

Malkin, Irad. 2005. 'Herakles and Melqart: Greeks and Phoenicians in the Middle Ground', in *Cultural Borrowings and Ethnic Appropriations in Antiquity*, ed. by Erich S. Gruen (Stuttgart: Steiner), pp. 238–58

Maniscalco, Laura. 2007. 'Considerazioni sull'età del rame nella media valle del Platani (Sicilia)', *Rivista di scienze preistoriche*, 57: 167–84

Mannino, Marcella A., Rosaria Di Salvo, Vittoria Schimmenti, Carolina Di Patti, Alessandro Incarbona, Luca Sineo, and Michael P. Richards. 2011. 'Upper Palaeolithic Hunter-Gatherer Subsistence in Mediterranean Coastal Environments: An Isotopic Study of the Diets of the Earliest Directly-Dated Humans from Sicily', *Journal of Archaeological Science*, 38: 3094–100

Mentesana, Roberta, Giuseppe De Benedetto, and Girolamo Fiorentino. 2018. 'One Pot's Tale: Reconstructing the Movement of People, Materials and Knowledge in Early Bronze Age Sicily through the Microhistory of a Vessel', *Journal of Archaeological Science: Reports*, 19: 261–69

Miller, Danny. 2005. 'Introduction', in *Materiality*, ed. by Danny Miller (Durham, NC: Duke University Press), pp. 1–50

Montana, Giuseppe, Ioannis Iliopoulos, Valeria Tardo, and Caterina Greco. 2009. 'Petrographic and Geochemical Characterization of Archaic-Hellenistic Tableware Production at Solunto, Sicily', *Geoarchaeology*, 24.1: 86–110

Montana, Giuseppe, Luciana Randazzo, and Chiara Blasetti Fantauzzi. 2019. 'Archaeometric Characterization of Late Archaic Ceramic from Erice (Sicily) Aimed to Provenance Determination', *International Journal of Conservation Science*, 10.4: 605–22

Morris, Ian, Trinity Jackman, Brien Garnand, Emma Blake, and Sebastiano Tusa. 2004. 'Stanford University Excavations on the Acropolis of Monte Polizzo, Sicily, IV: Preliminary Report on the 2003 Season', *Memoirs of the American Academy in Rome*, 49: 197–279

Morris, Ian, and Sebastiano Tusa. 2004. 'Scavi sull'acropoli di Monte Polizzo, 2000–2003', *Sicilia archeologica*, 37.102: 35–90

Mühlenbock, Christian. 2008. *Fragments from a Mountain Society: Tradition, Innovation, and Interaction at Archaic Monte Polizzo* (Gothenburg: Gothenburg University)

——. 2015. 'Expanding the Circle of Trust: Tradition and Change in Iron Age Communities in Western Sicily', in *Tradition: Transmission of Culture in the Ancient World*, ed. by Jane Fejfer, Mette Moltesen, and Annette Rathje, Danish Studies in Classical Archaeology: Acta Hyperborea, 14 (Copenhagen: Museum Tusculanum Press), pp. 239–68

Natali, Elena, and Vincenza Forgia. 2018. 'The Beginning of the Neolithic in Southern Italy and Sicily', *Quaternary International*, 470: 253–69

Öhlinger, Birgit. 2015. 'Indigenous Cult Places of Local and Interregional Scale in Archaic Sicily: A Sociological Approach to Religion', in *Sanctuaries and the Power of Consumption: Networking and the Formation of Elites in the Archaic Western Mediterranean World*, ed. by Erich Kistler, Birgit Öhlinger, Martin Mohr, and Matthias Hoernes (Wiesbaden: Harrassowitz), pp. 417–30

Oma, Kristin. 2006. 'Human-Animal Relationships: Mutual Becomings in the Household of Scandinavia and Sicily 900–500 BC' (unpublished doctoral thesis, University of Southampton)

Ramsay, Jennifer, and Roger J. A. Wilson. 2013. 'Funerary Dining in Early Byzantine Sicily: Archaeobotanical Evidence from Kaukana', *Mediterranean Archaeology*, 26: 81–93

Reitsema, Laurie J., Britney Kyle, and Stefano Vassallo. 2020. 'Food Traditions and Colonial Interactions in the Ancient Mediterranean: Stable Isotope Evidence from the Greek Sicilian Colony Himera', *Journal of Anthropological Archaeology*, 57: 101–44

Shanks, Michael. 1992. *Experiencing the Past: On the Character of Archaeology* (London: Routledge)

——. 2007. 'Symmetrical Archaeology', *World Archaeology*, 39.4: 589–96

Shanks, Michael, and Christopher Tilley. 1987. *Social Theory and Archaeology* (Albuquerque: University of New Mexico Press)

Shefton, Brian B. 2000. 'On the Material in its Northern Setting', in *Importe und Mediterrane Einflüsse auf der Heuneburg*, ed. by Wolfgang Kimmig, Heuneburgstudien, 11 (Mainz: Von Zabern), pp. 27–41

Sherratt, Andreas. 1987. 'Cups that Cheered', in *Bell Beakers of the Western Mediterranean*, ed. by William H. Waldren and Rex C. Kennard, British Archaeological Reports, International Series, 331 (Oxford: BAR), pp. 81–106

Spatafora, Francesca. 1996a. 'Gli Elimi e l'età del ferro nella Sicilia occidentale', in *Early Societies in Sicily: New Developments in Archaeological Research*, ed. by Robert Leighton (London: Accordia Research Center, University of London), pp. 155–66

——. 1996b. 'La ceramic indigena a decorazione impressa e incisa nella Sicilia centro-occidentale: diffusione e pertinenza etnica', *Sicilia archeologica*, 29: 91–110

——. 1997. 'Tipologie abitative arcaiche nei centri indigeni occidental: il caso di Monte Maranfusa', in *Wohnbauforschung in Zentral- und Westsizilien / Sicilia occidentale e centro-meridionale: ricerche archeologiche nell'abitato*, ed. by Hans-Peter Isler, Daniel Käch, and Olympia Stafani (Zürich: Archäologisches Institut der Universität Zürich), pp. 151–64

Speciale, Claudia, Ilhem Bentaleb, Nathalie Combourieu-Nebout, Gian Pietro Di Sansebastiano, Filippo Iannì, François Fourel, and Enrico Giannitrapani. 2020. 'The Case Study of Case Bastione: First Analyses of 3rd Millennium cal BC Paleoenvironmental and Subsistence Systems in Central Sicily', *Journal of Archaeological Science: Reports*, 31: 102332

Spiteri, Cynthianne, Matthias Belser, and Anita Crispino. 2020. 'Preliminary Results on Content Analysis of Early Bronze Age Vessels from the Site of Castelluccio, Noto, Sicily', *Journal of Archaeological Science: Reports*, 31: 102355

Stika, Hans-Peter, Andreas G. Heiss, and Barbara Zach. 2008. 'Plant Remains from the Early Iron Age in Western Sicily: Differences in Subsistence Strategies of Greek and Elymian Sites', *Vegetation History and Archaeobotany*, 17: 139–48

Tanasi, Davide, Enrico Greco, Valeria Di Tullio, Donatella Capitani, Domenica Gulli, and Enrico Ciliberto. 2017. '¹H NMR, ¹H-¹H 2D TOCSY, ATR FT-IR and SEM-EDX for the Identification of Organic Residues on Sicilian Prehistoric Pottery', *Microchemical Journal*, 135: 140–47

Tanasi, Davide, Enrico Greco, Radwan Ebna Noor, Stephanie Feola, Vasantha Kumar, Anita Crispino, and Ionnis Gelis. 2018. '¹H NMR, ¹H-¹H 2D TOCSY and GC-MS Analyses for the Identification of Olive Oil in Early Bronze Age Pottery from Castelluccio (Noto, Italy)', *Analytical Methods*, 10: 2756–63

Thomas, Julian. 2022. 'Steps toward an Archaeology of Life', *Trabalhos de antropologia e etnologia*, 62: 197–211

Thomas, Nicholas. 1991. *Entangled Objects: Exchange, Material Culture and Colonialism in the Pacific* (Cambridge, MA: Harvard University Press)

Trombi, Caterina. 1999. 'La ceramic indigena dipinta della Sicilia dalla seconda metà del IX sec. a.C. al V sec. a.C.', in *Magna Grecia e Sicilia: stato degli studi e prospettive di ricerca*, ed. by Marcella Barra Bagnasco, Ernesto De Miro, and Antonino Pinzone (Messina: Di. Sc. A.M.), pp. 275–93

Tusa, Sebastiano. 1994. *Sicilia preistorica* (Palermo: Dario Flaccovio)

——. 1997. 'Considerazioni tipologico-cronologiche sui corredi tombali', in *L'Insediamento dell'età del bronzo con bicchiere campaniforme di Marcita*, ed. by Sebastiano Tusa (Trapani: Soprintendenza per i beni culturali e ambientali), pp. 57–70

Vassallo, Stefano. 2000. 'Abitati indigeni ellenizzati della Sicilia centro-occidentale della vitalità tardo arcaica alla crisi del V sec. a.C.', in *Atti delle Terze giornate internazionali di studi sull'area Elima, Gibellina – Erice – Contessa Entellina, 23–26 Ottobre 1997* (Gibellina: Centro studi e documentazione sull'area Elima), pp. 985–1008

Vives-Ferrándiz, Jaime. 2008. 'Negotiating Colonial Encounters: Hybrid Practices and Consumption in Eastern Iberia (8th–6th Centuries BC)', *Journal of Mediterranean Archaeology*, 21.2: 241–72

Walsh, Justin St Pierre. 2014a. *Consumerism in the Ancient World: Imports and Identity Construction* Routledge Monographs in Classical Studies, 19 (London: Routledge)

——. 2014b. 'Skeuomorphic Pottery and Consumer Feedback Processes in the Ancient Mediterranean', in *Knowledge Networks and Craft Traditions in the Ancient World: Material Crossovers*, ed. by Katharina Rebay-Salisbury, Ann Brysbaert, and Lin Foxhall (London: Routledge), pp. 147–59

Walsh, Justin St Pierre, and Carla Antonaccio. 2014. 'Athenian Black Gloss Pottery: A View from the West', *Oxford Journal of Archaeology*, 33.1: 47–67

Wells, Peter S. 1980. *Culture Contact and Culture Change: Early Iron Age Central Europe and the Mediterranean World* (Cambridge: Cambridge University Press)

——. 2012. *How Ancient Europeans Saw the World* (Princeton: Princeton University Press)

White, Richard. 1991. *The Middle Ground: Indians, Empires, and Republics in the Great Lakes Region, 1650–1815* (Cambridge: Cambridge University Press)

Whitmore, Christopher L. 2007. 'Symmetrical Archaeology: Excerpts of a Manifesto', *World Archaeology*, 39.4: 546–62

Wilkens, Barbara. 1997. 'Resti faunistici provenienti da alcuni siti dell'area di Milena', in *Dalle Capanne alle Robbe: la storia lunga di Milocca-Milena*, ed. by Vincenzo La Rosa (Caltanissetta: Pro loco, Milena), pp. 127–33

Wills, Wirt Henry, and Patricia L. Crown. 2004. 'Commensal Politics in the Prehispanic Southwest: An Introductory Review', in *Identity, Feasting, and the Archaeology of the Greater Southwest: Proceedings of the 2002 Southwest Symposium*, ed. by Barbara J. Mills (Boulder: University of Colorado Press), pp. 153–72

PETER ATTEMA, CARMELO COLELLI, MARTIN GUGGISBERG,
FRANCESCA IPPOLITO, JAN KINDBERG JACOBSEN,
GLORIA MITTICA, WIEKE DE NEEF, AND SINE GROVE SAXKJÆR _____

14. The Deep Past of Magna Graecia's Pottery Traditions

Adoption and Adaption at Timpone della Motta and in the Sibaritide (Northern Calabria, Italy) between the Middle Bronze Age and the Archaic Period

ABSTRACT Since the postcolonial turn in Classical archaeology, the relationship between indigenous populations and Greek settlers in southern Italy has increasingly received attention. This is particularly true, notably and importantly, in fieldwork and related material culture studies focusing on the period of mobility, migration, and early settlement that preceded Archaic Greek colonization. Such studies have brought Aegean connections to light, anticipating the historical Greek colonial movements that resulted in the poleis of Magna Graecia. At the same time, an increased interest within field archaeology in the later phases of protohistory, notably the Final Bronze and Early Iron Ages, has highlighted the continuity of Bronze Age Aegean influences on the material record of southern Italy. While we cannot argue (yet) for actual continuity between protohistoric and early historical indigenous and Aegean interactions in terms of mobility and migration — as the time gap between protohistoric and early historical Aegean connections is still considerable — it is the longer-term processes of adoption, adaption, and innovation of ideas and the symbiosis in material culture that is a striking element of the socio-economic and cultural context of the indigenous communities. This not only holds for the more well-known wares such as Aegean-influenced pottery, but is just as relevant for developments in the handmade impasto tradition. In this chapter, we review the evidence for the deep past of pottery traditions in Magna Graecia, in the Sibaritide in northern Calabria, and reflect on the consequences for the current Hellenocentric paradigm surrounding indigenous and (early) colonial interactions prior to Archaic Greek settler colonization.

Since the postcolonial turn in Classical archaeology in the 1980s, the relationship between indigenous populations and Greek settlers in southern Italy has increasingly received attention, with a particular focus on the period of mobility and migration that went ahead of Greek colonization.[1] An important project in this area was undertaken by Kleibrink in the early 1990s called 'Dominant versus Nondominant, Enotrians and Greeks on the Timpone della Motta and in the Sibaritide' (Kleibrink 2017). This excavation project focused on the interaction between the indigenous community of Timpone della Motta, located on a prominent foothill overlooking the coastal plain, and the nearby Greek community of Sybaris, located in the plain on the shore of the Ionian Sea (Fig. 14.1).

Founded at the end of the eighth century BCE, according to ancient writers (Bérard 1965, 149),[2] Sybaris likely started out as a small trading post (*emporion*) at the confluence of the Rivers Crathis (Crati) and Sybaris (Coscile) (Fig. 14.1).[3]

---

1 See recent contributions in Donnellan and others 2016a and 2016b, and contributions in Lucas and others 2019. For an earlier geographically broad-ranging study see Hodos 2006.

2 Strab. VI. 1. 13; Diod. XII. 9. 2; Plin., *HN*, III. 97; see also Pseudo-Skymnos 357–60 (probably deriving from Ephorus) and Eusebios (ed. Helm, pp. 91, 183). According to Eusebios, Sybaris was founded 709/708 BCE, though Pseudo-Skymnos (360) dates Sybaris to 721–720 BCE while Strabo (VI. 2. 4) makes Croton contemporary with Syracuse, traditionally founded in 733 BCE. The Eusebian date is also found in Dion. Hal., *Ant. Rom.*, II. 59. 3.

3 See for a recent synthesis of archaeological and literary data, Guzzo 2016. See for archaeological evaluations Kleibrink 2001; Yntema 2000; Vanzetti 2013.

Corresponding author Peter Attema (p.a.j.attema@rug.nl)

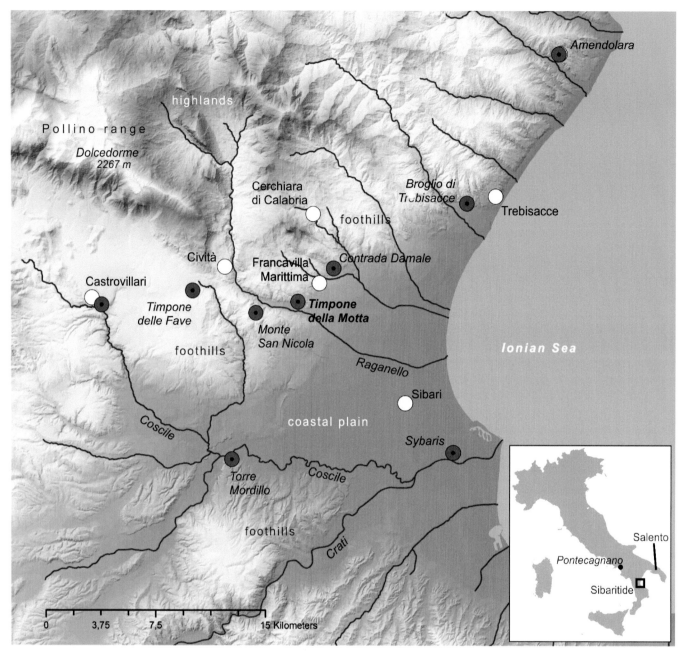

Figure 14.1. Map of the Sibaritide with location and toponyms of sites, rivers, and landscape zones mentioned in the text (by Wieke de Neef).

The archaeological evidence for the earliest occupation phases of Sybaris is extremely scarce, due to a combination of superposition by the Classical city and the difficulty of excavating below the water table. Despite this, the existence of an early *emporion* in the lagoonal and riverine environment of the plain of Sybaris fits the general Mediterranean trading model of the period (Attema 2017). However, it was Sybaris's legendary history as an Archaic city that promoted both the archaeological 'Search for Sybaris' and long-term excavation (Attema 2003). This work happened at the expense of archaeological investment in the indigenous settlement of Timpone della Motta, where, coeval with the 'Search for Sybaris', the Iron Age necropolis of Macchiabate was being excavated by Paola Zancani Montuoro while Maria W. Stoop worked to reveal the Greek sanctuary on the summit of Timpone della Motta and houses on its lower slopes. As it turned out, the necropolis revealed the existence of an advanced Iron Age community that predated Sybaris's historical foundation date. Furthermore, Timpone della Motta, besides evidence for Archaic cult activities that are indicative of close relationships with Sybaris, proved to have

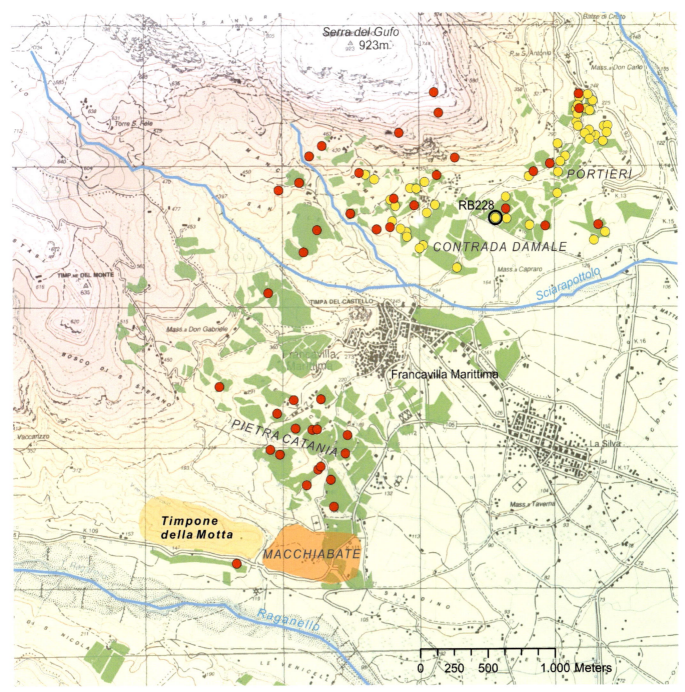

Figure 14.2. Overview map of Timpone della Motta, Macchiabate, and immediate surroundings. Red dots: protohistoric sites without corded pithoi, yellow dots: sites with *doli cordonati*, green areas: fields investigated by the Raganello Archaeological Project (by Wieke de Neef).

a long occupational history starting in the Bronze Age (Fig. 14.2).[4]

Although Greek–indigenous relationships had been a subject of discussion prior to the postcolonial turn, Kleibrink's research programme put the spotlight on implicit and explicit assumptions of asymmetry between colonizers and indigenous populations in terms of material culture, technology, and socio-political organization. In this period of paradigm change, characterized by theoretical papers often based on limited case studies, the 'Dominant versus Nondominant' programme was based on a longer-term, theory-laden excavation project. The result was exceptional insight into the long-term dynamism and complexity of interaction, including

---

4 Kleibrink 2001; Zancani Montuoro 1966; 1970–1971; 1974–1976; 1977–1979; 1980–1982; 1983–1984; Stoop 1974–1976; 1979; 1983; 1988; 1989; 1990.

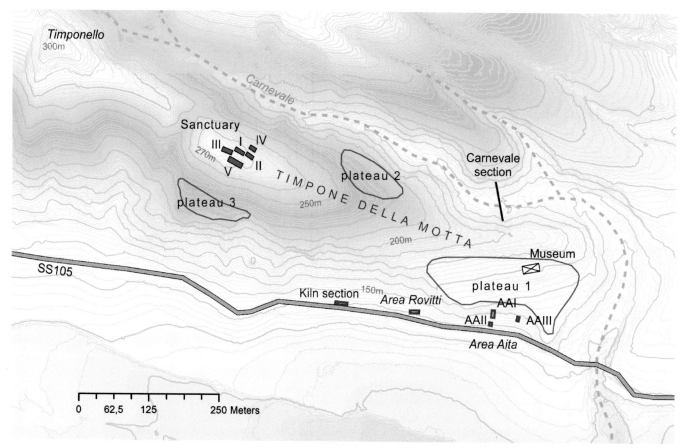

Figure 14.3. Overview map of the site of Timpone della Motta and contexts mentioned in the text (sanctuary, plateaus, excavation areas) (by Wieke de Neef).

hybrid architectural innovation, gradual adoption and adaption of the indigenous ceramic repertoire, and changes in religious socio-economic organization of settlement and landscape. Kleibrink dedicated a range of publications to the Iron Age roots of the Greek-style, but architecturally hybrid, sanctuary on Timpone della Motta and its associated material culture (Fig. 14.3).[5] The new data corroborated the existence of early Mediterranean connections running through the indigenous community of Timpone della Motta that were already evident from the grave inventories of the Macchiabate necropolis.[6] Her new and (at least from the perspective of Magna Graecia's Classical tradition) slightly controversial insights were, on a material level, further elaborated by Dutch and Danish researchers who had participated from the start in the research environment created by Kleibrink. Over the past two decades, this next generation of scholars published their own results on the basis of landscape archaeological work, new excavations, and specialist studies on several categories of material culture.[7] The focus of these studies was not only Timpone della Motta, but also the wider, regional, proto-urban settlement configuration of the Sibaritide in which this settlement functioned. These studies, including the regional surveys carried out in the framework of the University of Groningen's Raganello Archaeological Project, support the main hypothesis of Kleibrink's initial research that the Greek seafarers would have encountered a well-developed society of comparable complexity to societies elsewhere in the Mediterranean, and indeed comparable to those in the Aegean.[8]

In the programme 'Dominant versus Non-dominant' the hurdle of the traditionally assumed subordination of the indigenous community at Timpone della Motta to Greek cultural norms had

---

5 Kleibrink 2006a; Kleibrink and others 2012a; Kleibrink and Weistra 2013; Kleibrink 2015a; 2015b; 2017.
6 Zancani Montuoro 1970–1971; 1974–1976; 1977–1979; 1980–1982; 1983–1984; for a synthesis of the recent excavations carried out by the University of Basel see: Guggisberg and others 2012; Colombi and Guggisberg 2016. For the report of the most recent published research campaign see: Guggisberg and others 2020.

7 Jacobsen 2007; Colelli 2012; Feiken 2014; Ippolito 2016; Fasanella Masci 2016; Crudo 2023.
8 See Peroni and Trucco 1994; Bettelli 2002; 2009. See for the Raganello Archaeological project Attema and others 2010, 81–102.

been cleared, supported by the paradigmatic change brought about by postcolonial theory (Ippolito 2016). In subsequent years, research has revealed much about the intricate and long-term background of the long-term interconnectedness of the community living at Timpone della Motta. The growing awareness of a deeply interconnected Bronze and Iron Age world before Greek colonization is a part of the current paradigmatic change taking place in Classical archaeology, captured in buzzwords such as 'connectivity', 'cultural and technological transfer', 'hybridity', and 'creolization'. These developments find a useful tool in formal network analysis (Blake 2014; Donnellan 2016). It is, however, worrying to note how, in Classical archaeology, this welcome change from a Hellenocentric attitude towards mobility, migration, and colonization, in spite of having evolved in the more general model of Mediterraneanization (Morris 2005), still does not take into consideration the already long-standing awareness of a connected Mediterranean world among pre- and protohistorians. While this may be an overstatement in the case of the highly visible Aegean material culture connections evident in the Late Bronze Age cultures of Italy, such connectedness is also present in the even longer-term traditional handmade impasto tradition, reflecting connections with remote parts of the Italian peninsula from very early on in the Bronze Age.[9]

Two aspects have promoted our knowledge on longer-term Mediterranean connectivity in the Sibaritide. The first aspect is the fieldwork that followed up on the 'Dominant versus Nondominant' research programme within the framework of the International Francavilla Project.[10] This resulted in the detection of additional ritual spaces in the sanctuary on the summit of the hill dating to the sixth century BCE and of pottery workshops on the lower slopes of Timpone della Motta. The remains of these have shed light, not only on pottery production in the sixth century BCE, but also well before that, testifying to influences brought about by cultural contacts predating Greek colonization. Moreover, the restudy of materials and new field research has brought to light earlier phases of occupation on the hill, link-

ing the Early Iron Age with Final Bronze Age occupation. At the same time, fieldwork was taken up again in the Macchiabate cemetery by the University of Basel, resulting in novel high-resolution data on burial practices at the site and new insights in the association of imported and local pottery. The second aspect is the material knowledge produced in the series of dissertations and publications by individual researchers who participated in the ongoing work at Timpone della Motta, within the framework of the International Francavilla Project. These studies explore both technological and typo-chronological aspects of the prehistoric, early colonial, and colonial ceramic record of Timpone della Motta and its surroundings, taking into account both impasto and fine wares, tracing local and imported manufacturing methods, as well as decorative traits, and how these may blend. In combination, these two aspects reveal the longer-term patterns of cultural interaction in the Sibaritide and offer new insights into the tangled question of indigenous and introduced features of material culture in the context of the south Italian settled landscape.

In this chapter, instead of looking back from the period of Greek colonization, we propose to begin with the Middle Bronze Age based on the longevity of Timpone della Motta's occupation history and work forward. Throughout, we will discuss the adoptions and adaptions within the material culture in the context of a connected culture through the entire period. In doing so, we will not solely highlight Aegean pottery connections but also draw attention to other culturally influenced pottery wares, including cultural connections evident from the indigenous handmade Italic impasto tradition. While the time gap between protohistoric and early historical Aegean connections is still considerable, it is, in our opinion, the longer-term adoption, adaption, and innovation of ideas and symbiosis in material culture revealed therein, that is a striking element of the socio-economic and cultural context of the indigenous communities.

We will therefore set ourselves the task to review the evidence for the deep past of Magna Graecia's pottery traditions in the Sibaritide in northern Calabria, and to reflect on the consequences for the currently changing paradigm concerning indigenous and (early) colonial interactions, prior to and including Greek settler colonization.[11] Below, we review the evidence

---

9 Ippolito and Attema forthcoming (a); Jacobsen and others 2018; Ippolito 2016, section 4.11. See for a broader view on south Italy van Wijngaarden 2002.

10 The University of Groningen, the Danish Institute at Rome, and the University of Basel collaborate on respectively landscape archaeology, excavations in the sanctuary and settlement of Timpone della Motta and the Macchiabate necropolis under the umbrella of the International Francavilla Project with their own independently financed research programme.

11 In doing so, we fully realize the specialist nature of the topic in terms of typo-chronological knowledge, the high versus low chronology debate on the Final Bronze Age–Early Iron Age transition, and the issue of radiocarbon versus typo-chronological dating in general, as well as the fact that archaeometric

for the connected nature of production and consumption of pottery at Timpone della Motta and in its surroundings in the context of the settled landscape. First, we present the ceramic evidence of the various ceramic productions present at Timpone della Motta and in its surroundings, after which we evaluate this evidence in the light of adoption and adaption of the local pottery traditions.

Settlement Archaeology and Material Culture Studies at Timpone della Motta and in its Surroundings

Since 1963, archaeological excavations of the settlement and sanctuary of Timpone della Motta, and in the Macchiabate necropolis, have unearthed pottery from different contexts with distinct cultural and functional characteristics belonging to domestic, funerary, religious, and pottery production contexts, and within a chronological framework between the Middle Bronze Age and the late sixth century BCE, when the settlement was virtually abandoned (see Table 14.1 for the chronological framework).[12] Excavation reports and specialist pottery studies have been published since the 1970s, with an increased output from the late 1990s onwards (Jacobsen 2007; Colelli and Jacobsen 2013; Fasanella Masci 2016).

Table 14.1. Table showing periodizations as used in the text (after Dickenson 2020 and Ippolito 2016) (by Francesca Ippolito).

Central Aegean	Date BCE	Southern Italy (Calabria)
LH IIIA1 LH IIIA2	1425–1400	MBA2
LH IIIB1 LH IIIB2	1300	MBA3
LH IIIC Early	1200/1190	RBA1
LH IIIC Middle	1150/1140	RBA2
LH IIIC Late and Submycenaean	1100/1090	FBA1
EPG and MPG	1025	FBA2
LPG	950	FBA3
EG I–II	900	PF1
MG I	850	
MG II–LG Ia	800	PF2
LG Ib–IIb	750 725–700	

studies informing on clay provenance and manufacturing techniques are only now maturing, mainly because of the fact that evidence on actual pottery workshops until recently was very scarce. See Nijboer 2016 on the C14 debate in relation to early colonization. See, for an overview of C14 dates from settlement contexts on the Timpone della Motta, Jacobsen and others 2018. For archaeometric research on ceramics from the Timpone della Motta, see Andaloro and others 2011, 445–53; De Francesco, Andaloro, Mittica, and Jacobsen 2009, 33–34; De Francesco, Andaloro, Jacobsen, and Miriello 2009, 273; De Francesco, Andaloro, Jacobsen, Mittica, and De Stefano 2012, 1–9; Andaloro and others 2012, 112; De Francesco, Andaloro, and Jacobsen 2012, 145–62. In 2020 a NAA research programme of the Danish Institute in Rome has started, aimed at a systematic mapping of cultural contacts and exchange of goods between indigenous groups in Calabria, Basilicata, and Puglia. The programme is part of the research initiative 'A Clay Science Approach to Indigenous and Greek Cultural Dynamics in Southern Italy' supervised by Gloria Mittica. The investigations area carried out in collaboration with Atominstitut, TU-Wien (Prof. Johannes H. Sterba). Additional XRF-analysis and petrological analysis will be conducted in collaboration with the University of Amsterdam within the framework of the NWO-project 'What Went into the Melting Pot? Land-Use, Agriculture, and Craft Production as Indicators for the Contributions of Greek Migrants and Local Inhabitants to the So-Called Greek Colonization in Italy (c. 800–550 BCE)' (NWO-project code: VC.GW17.136). This NWO-project is directed by Jan Paul Crielaard and supervised by Xenia Charalambidou.

12 For an overview De Lachenal 2007, 17–81; Kleibrink 2011; Jacobsen and Handberg 2010.

Reports and pottery studies have, however, predominantly been focused on specific excavation areas and distinct classes of pottery, leading to fragmentation of what must have been an organic process of innovations within pottery production and consumption at the site. So far attempts at longer-term approaches to the site's pottery record are scarce (although see Jacobsen and others 2018; Kleibrink 2020). Of the recent excavations, the stratigraphical evidence from trenches dug on the slopes of Timpone della Motta facing the Raganello River signifies a breakthrough, as it allows the creation of a chronological framework for the occurrence of the various classes of pottery present at Timpone della Motta that bridges the Late Bronze Age/Early Iron Age divide, including Italo-Mycenaean ware and Early and Middle Geometric matt-painted pottery.[13] In combination with the ceramic evidence from the sanctuary, the necropolis, and our field surveys, the new stratigraphical evidence has enabled us to draw up a chronological table of overlapping classes of pottery covering the

13 We refer here to Area Rovitti with dwelling structures A and B, the complex stratigraphy exposed in Area Aita and more in general the zone SW of Plateau III.

period from the Middle Bronze Age to the end of the Archaic period (see below, Figure 14.31). To set the scene, we will first discuss the Aegean ceramic evidence in the Sibaritide, which occurs in the form of imports of Mycenaean wares, local productions of Italo-Mycenaean ware, as well as Grey Ware and a specific class of large storage jars, known in the Italian literature as 'doli cordonati', originating from Aegean pottery traditions.[14] This allows us to trace Aegean connections back to the Middle Bronze Age as a starting point in our discussion of adoption and adaption in the ceramic record.

The Ceramic Record of the Sibaritide and Timpone della Motta

Aegean and Aegean-Influenced Productions of the Bronze and Early Iron Age in the Sibaritide

Evidence for contacts with the Aegean world in the Sibaritide consists of Mycenaean painted pottery (both imports and imitations), Grey Ware, and corded *pithoi*, mostly from Late Bronze Age contexts. These classes of pottery are found in association with local handmade pottery, the so-called impasto pottery. Based on the ceramic evidence, contacts between the Aegean area and southern Italy had a modest beginning, as early as the Late Helladic I–II, which saw a slight intensification during the LH IIIA–B, when Aegean pottery is mostly found along the southern Adriatic coast. In the LH IIIB, new areas, including Calabria, became more clearly connected with the Aegean, displaying a continuity of contacts throughout the period of Italo-Mycenaean production. At Broglio di Trebisacce, it has been noted that LH IIIB–C pottery production shows clear Mycenaean LH IIIA stylistic features (Vagnetti and Panichelli 1994, 411–13). Stylistic influences continue in the LH IIIC, when the production of Italo-Mycenaean pottery is upscaled along both the Adriatic and Ionian coasts. It follows that, after the collapse of the Mycenaean palaces, exchanges between the Aegean and the central Mediterranean region continued. This indicates that, while palatial elites may have managed local productions during the earliest phase of interaction, after the LH IIIB local communities were responsible for the high production level recorded.

In the Sibaritide, most of the Aegean materials come from the sites of Broglio di Trebisacce, Torre Mordillo, and, as we will show below, now also from Timpone della Motta. Based on archaeometric analyses of Aegean and Aegean-type pottery at Broglio di Trebisacce (Jones and others 2014, site 32, 34), ten fragments of Mycenaean pottery at this site were found to be imported from Greece and fifty-eight fragments locally made (Italo-Mycenaean). The evidence dates to the LH IIIA–C, in Italy corresponding to the period between the Middle Bronze Age and the Final Bronze Age (MBA3–FBA1). From the settlement of Torre Mordillo, there are about 280 fragments of Aegean and Italo-Mycenaean pottery. Based on archaeometric analysis, four Mycenaean fragments are likely of imported vases and thirty-three fragments of local Italo-Mycenaean production (Jones and others 2014, site 34, 34–35). These productions are dated to the LH I–II and LH IIIA–C, therefore between the MBA1–2 and the FBA.

So far, Mycenaean decorated pottery in the Sibaritide has only been attested in stratigraphic contexts, and has not been found in surveys, neither in the surroundings of Timpone della Motta nor in the Raganello Archaeological Project area (Middle and Upper Raganello basin) (Attema and Ippolito 2017). In combination with the data from sites, including Broglio di Trebisacce, Timpone della Motta, and Torre Mordillo, the data from the surveys provide a long-term settlement framework showing how the hinterland was predominantly inhabited until the end of the Middle Bronze Age, after which settlement declined there. The foothills around the Sybaris plain, however, continued to be settled in the Late Bronze Age. It is in this area that Timpone della Motta and the other major excavated sites of the Sibaritide — Broglio di Trebisacce and Torre Mordillo — are located. Intensive surveys around Timpone della Motta have shown that its surrounding territory in the foothill zone was densely settled in the Final Bronze Age. We can therefore distinguish two types of Late Bronze Age sites: hilltop sites overlooking the plain, and a complex network of smaller sites spread across the sloping land of the lower foothills surrounding the plain. Although Mycenaean decorated pottery has not yet been found associated with the latter type of settlement, the pottery found does show clear Aegean influences, as many of these sites feature the presence of corded *pithoi*. This class has been defined a 'true hybrid production' (Jones and others 2014, 456–57), as it includes both local and Aegean technological and stylistic features. These *pithoi* are both hand- and wheel-made, and their shape is generally new within the Bronze Age ceramic repertoire but refined (and decorated) according to Aegean influences (Fig. 14.4).

---

14 We will refer to this class in this paper as 'corded *pithoi*'.

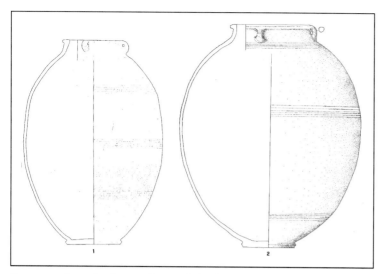

Figure 14.4. Example of a complete corded *pithos* from Broglio (after Tenaglia 1994, tav. 66).

Most of the *pithos* fragments from the site of Timpone delle Fave are characterized by wide horizontal grooves, similar to fragments found at Broglio di Trebisacce, from Sector B West, level S3 and level H (Tenaglia 1994, pl. 63.2, 4–11, 13–14 and pl. 62.1–8, 10–13), and dated to the late Final Bronze Age (Ippolito 2016; Ippolito and Attema forthcoming (b)). The type of fabric of most of the *pithos* fragments from Timpone delle Fave resembles impasto pottery of an orange/brown colour contrary to the *pithoi* from Broglio, the fabric of which is mostly pale pink and depurated (Levi and others 1999, 328). In our surveys of the Contrada Damale we found many pottery scatters with corded *pithoi* fragments of different fabrics, both depurated and coarse (de Neef 2016; de Neef and others 2017).

The use of coarse ware *pithoi* evolved in the Late Bronze Age and continued, uninterrupted, into the Iron Age. In both the settlement of Timpone della Motta and in the necropolis of Macchiabate fragments of yellow-orange coarse ware *pithoi* have been found.[15] In the necropolis, fragments of these vessels were used as lids of impasto *pithoi* generally thought to have contained the burials of neonates and babies (Zancani Montuoro 1980–1982, 56 no. 24; Guggisberg and Colombi 2021, 50–52 cat. nos S4/4 and S4/5 pl. 19 (S. Billo)).

A third class of pottery that shows influences from the Aegean world is Grey Ware, primarily found at the larger sites of Broglio di Trebisacce, Torre Mordillo, and Timpone della Motta (Fig. 14.5). Grey Ware was produced in the Sibaritide from the advanced Middle Bronze Age, but was mostly produced during the Recent Bronze Age; only few fragments are known from the Final Bronze Age (Belardelli 1994, 319–25; Trucco and Vagnetti 2001, 271–72). Production of Grey Ware also took place during the Iron Age. However, there is a major technological distinction with this later material since the early production is wheel-thrown and the later production is coiled. Only a few Bronze Age fragments, coming from carinated cups, are known from Timpone della Motta (Colelli 2012; Colelli and Jacobsen 2013; Ippolito 2016). Along the southern slope of Timpone della Motta, in the Area Rovitti, and also in the sanctuary on top of the hill, fragments dating to the Final Bronze Age have also been found.[16] Moreover, the find of a burnished ware cup from the acropolis of Timpone della Motta (Southern Sector), similar in shape to a Grey Ware specimen from Torre Mordillo and dating to the Final Bronze Age, points to the hybrid nature of production (Ippolito 2016, pl. LIV.586 cat. no. 586) (Figs 14.6 and 14.7). The Late Bronze Age contexts in Area Aita A did not contain Grey Ware fragments and so far, the majority of Grey Ware in the excavations has come to light in Iron Age contexts. The origin of the Iron Age Grey Ware production remains uncertain. It might be possible that the later Iron Age production was a continuation of the Bronze Age tradition, however, the difference in techniques and the rare presence of Grey Ware pottery from Final Bronze Age contexts in the Sibaritide[17] speaks against this. At this point, it thus seems prudent to consider a hitherto unknown external source of influence.

The longue durée *of the Impasto Production and its Relation to Fine Ware Classes*

The productions discussed above occurred alongside an enduring and gradually evolving tradition of the local handmade impasto pottery. Impasto production at Timpone della Motta can be traced back to the Middle Bronze Age and beyond in its formal and technological development, and it continues well into the Iron Age, after which it is replaced by wheel-turned coarse wares. In this chapter we do not have the space to go into any typo-chronological details nor cultural influences on the production in

---

15 For a brief preliminary of Early Iron Age *pithoi* from the settlement and sanctuary of Timpone della Motta see Elevelt 2001.

16 Final Bronze Age fragments are from Area Rovitti (Colelli 2012, 210–12; Ippolito 2016, section 4.10).

17 For a typology of Grey Ware in Broglio di Trebisacce between the Late and Final Bronze Age, see Belardelli 1994a. For Torre Mordillo see Belardelli 1994b and Arancio and others 2001, 197–202. For Timpone della Motta, see Colelli 2012, 208–19.

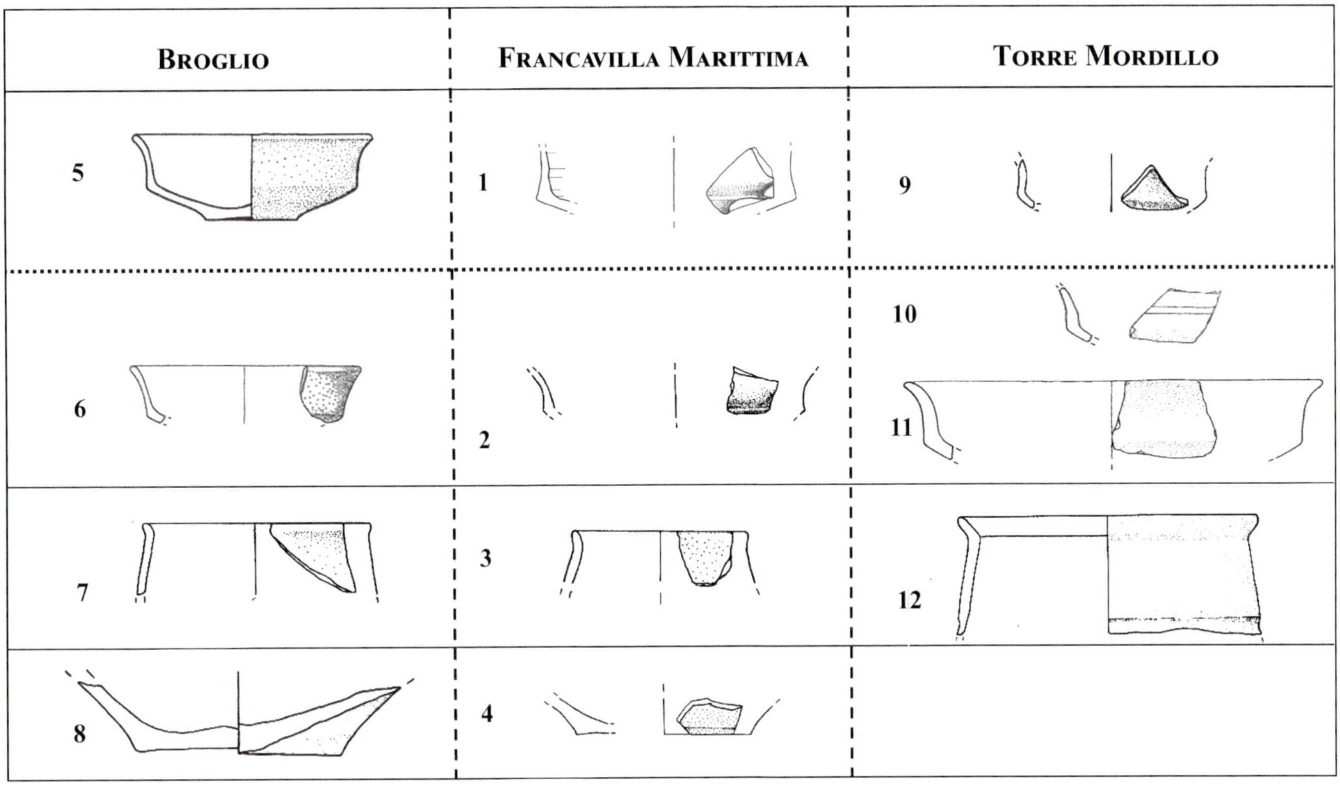

14. THE DEEP PAST OF MAGNA GRAECIA'S POTTERY TRADITIONS 243

Figure 14.5. Grey Ware shapes from Francavilla Marittima and parallels from Broglio di Trebisacce and Torre Mordillo (by Carmelo Colelli).

Figure 14.6. Orthophoto of the lower slopes of Timpone della Motta showing, from left to right, excavation locations Area Rovitti and Area Aita I–III (photo and elaboration by Giovanni Murro).

Table 14.2. Table showing similarities in shapes between various classes of pottery during the Bronze Age (by Francesca Ippolito).

Shapes from TdM	Impasto shapes from the RAP sites	Grey Ware shapes from Broglio di Trebisacce
Cat. 67, impasto, RBA1		
Cat. 586, impasto, FBA		
Cat. 94, impasto, FBA		Belardelli 1994, forma 51, RBA
Cat. 520 (Rovitti), grey ware, FBA		Ric. 1, Pl. 13,5, Sect D, RBA
Cat. 27, 13 (Carnevale), impasto, RBA1		
	Cat. 444 (Timpone delle Fave), FBA	
Cat. 8 (Carnevale), impasto, RBA1	Cat. 478, 464 (Timpone delle Fave)	Ric. 1, 13.3, Sect. D, RBA
	Cat. 212 (Mandroni di M.), RBA	
	Cat. 301 (Timpa del Castello)	Ric. 1, Pl. 13,6, Sect D, RBA

Grey Ware shapes from Torre Mordillo	Mycenaean decorated shapes
Trucco, Vagnetti 2001, type 40, RBA1	
Trucco, Vagnetti 2001, type 15, FBA	
	Fig. 75, FS 225 LIIIA1 (Mountjoy 1986); Fig. 366.50, LHIIB (Mountjoy 1999)
Trucco, Vagnetti 2001, Unicum 3, FBA	
	BdT Myc Forma 11, RBA, tav, 79.9

the Sibaritide;[18] we limit ourselves here to mentioning how impasto and fine ware productions underwent mutual technological and stylistic influences.

Grey Ware drinking cups from Broglio di Trebisacce (Belardelli 1994a), Torre Mordillo (Arancio and others 2001, 197–202), and Amendolara, show similarities with impasto counterparts and, to a lesser extent, Mycenaean cups (Table 14.2). With the emergence of matt-painted productions during the Late Bronze Age, impasto became a class of pottery that was largely destined for cooking and storage functions (Fig. 14.8). Also, the production of Grey Ware forms did not undergo any further substantial innovations (Fig. 14.8, 1, 2, 3 5). In contrast, the matt-painted and Oinotrian-Euboean productions, which we will discuss in detail below, underwent comprehensive stylistic and typological developments during the Iron Age. In fact, it is only at the very end of the eighth century BCE that we find some wheel-made impasto vessels that imitate Greek shapes: this is the case, for example, with a cup from Timpone della Motta (Fig. 14.8, 8), the shape of which resembles Thapsos *skyphoi* (Colelli and Jacobsen 2013, 276–78). Alternatively, a type of fine ware impasto bowl (*scodella*) remained part of the impasto repertoire during the Iron Age alongside the newly introduced matt-painted *scodelle* (Fig. 14.8, 4). This suggests that the impasto version must have retained a recognizable functional or indigenous cultural significance. One-handled impasto cups — so-called *attingitoi* (Fig. 14.8, 9) — must have had a comparable significance, as they remained in production during the Iron Age. Both *scodelle* and *attingitoi* can be seen as Iron Age continuations of Bronze Age potters' traditions. The vessels are elegantly coiled, the *attingitoi* often down to a wall thickness of a few millimetres, and the surface is polished to a clear shine. In comparison, the Iron Age impasto is produced in a different manner. The clay employed is less depurated, and while the shapes are generally well executed, little attention is given to the appearance of the surface — although a hasty polishing has occasionally been carried out. The technical execution of decorative elements also reflects two different methods. On the polished *attingitoi* and *scodelle*, decorative elements have been included by forming the exterior surface in the desired pattern while decorative elements on the coarse impasto are attached to the surface.

---

18 The impasto production is exceptionally well-studied in the Sibaritide on account of the studies carried out by Renato Peroni and his research group (Peroni and Trucco 1994; Trucco and Vagnetti 2001). Specifically, for Timpone della Motta, see Colelli 2012 and Ippolito 2016.

Figure 14.7. Early Geometric matt-painted closed vessels from Area Aita (photo by Mikkel Jørgensen, drawing by Camilla Poulsen).

The two impasto production modes clearly indicate the existence of workshops with different degrees of specialization. The production of the finer polished impasto — typical of local productions in north-Ionian Calabria, Ionian Basilicata, and southern Apulia — is coherent with the Iron Age impasto productions of Campania at sites such as Pontecagnano.[19] While we can be certain that the bulk of the impasto cooking and storage pottery found at Timpone della Motta and in its surroundings was produced locally,[20] we have indications from our stratigraphic excavations that also finer impasto wares may have been produced locally.

Late Bronze Age and Early Iron Age Pottery Production at Timpone della Motta

Excavations in Area Aita between 2018 and 2020 offer the possibility of addressing pottery production at Timpone della Motta during the Late Bronze Age and Early Iron Age through stratigraphical contexts that allow us to make conjectures on possible pottery production on the slopes of Timpone della Motta.

While Italo-Mycenaean pottery was previously only found in secondary contexts, or as sporadic surface finds, excavation of an area of about 2 m² in Area Aita I already has brought to light thirteen fragments of Italo-Mycenaean pottery in a context underneath an Iron Age floor level (Fig. 14.9).[21] A sporadic wall fragment of a closed-shaped vessel decorated by painted running spirals was found in the excavation in Area Rovitti (Fig. 14.10).[22] Finally, a possibly imported Mycenaean fragment was found in a secondary context in the sanctuary in 2018 (Fig. 14.11).

Italo-Mycenaean pottery is well attested at Broglio di Trebisacce and at Torro Mordillo. Jones and oth-

---

19 Colelli and Jacobsen 2013, 40–42, 273–76; Colelli and Ippolito 2017, 24–27; Ippolito 2016, ch. 4.
20 For results of archaeometric analysis see Colelli and Jacobsen 2013, 291–319.

21 Several scholars have reported on a fragment of a stirrup jar from Timpone della Motta found by M. Stoop in the 1960s. See Lattanzi 1984, 157; Vagnetti 1984, 159–60. Van Wijngaarden 2002; Jacobsen 2007.
22 Ippolito 2016, cat. no. 361; Jacobsen and others 2015, fig. 1.3. The decoration is of Motive Type FM 46. This is a common decoration both on Crete and mainland Greece on open and closed shapes dating to the LH IIIB–C, see Settis and Parra 2005, 307; Vagnetti and Panichelli 1994, tav. 71.2, Broglio di Trebisacce, Sett. B Ovest, liv. 1A, FBA1, Vagnetti and Panichelli 1994, tav. 72.5, Broglio di Trebisacce, Sett. D Est, liv. 1 Est, RBA2. RBA2–FBA1. The study on this new material is still preliminary and NAA analyses have not yet been conducted.

14. THE DEEP PAST OF MAGNA GRAECIA'S POTTERY TRADITIONS   247

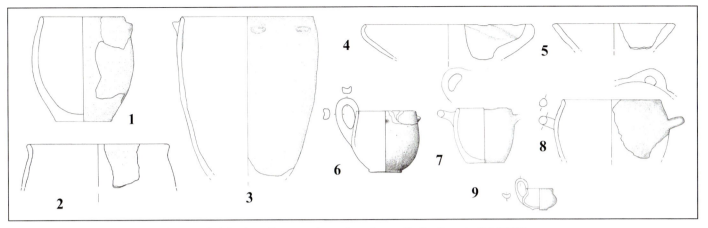

Figure 14.8. Selection of impasto shapes from Francavilla (by Carmelo Colelli/GIA).

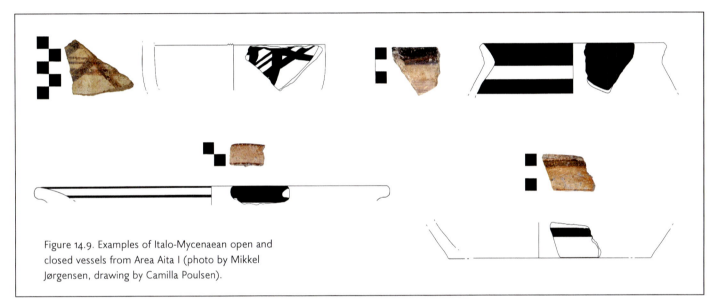

Figure 14.9. Examples of Italo-Mycenaean open and closed vessels from Area Aita I (photo by Mikkel Jørgensen, drawing by Camilla Poulsen).

ers (2021, 13–15, 24–29) observe that there is no evidence for notable exchange of Italo-Mycenaean pottery between the two sites. Overall comparison between the Italo-Mycenaean pottery from these two sites shows differences in vessel shapes and decoration, indicating the existence of two individual productions, supported by clay analyses from both sites (Jones and others 2021, 13–15). Regional exchange apparently only happened occasionally. Taking into account the observations by Jones and others, we hypothesize that the Italo-Mycenaean fragments found in the excavations on the lower slopes of Timpone della Motta also resulted from locally produced pottery.[23]

Figure 14.10. Wall fragment of a closed shaped vessel decorated by painted spiral motifs from Area Rovitti (photo by Jan Kindberg Jacobsen).

Figure 14.11. A possibly imported Mycenaean fragment found in a secondary context in the sanctuary in 2018 (photo by Jan Kindberg Jacobsen).

---

23 The currently known fragments from Area Aita belong to large, closed vessels decorated with simple bands. This renders the definition of a local stylistic characterization difficult for the time

Figure 14.12. Proto-Geometric matt-painted fragment from a closed jar from Area Aita I (photo by Mikkel Jørgensen, drawing by Camilla Poulsen).

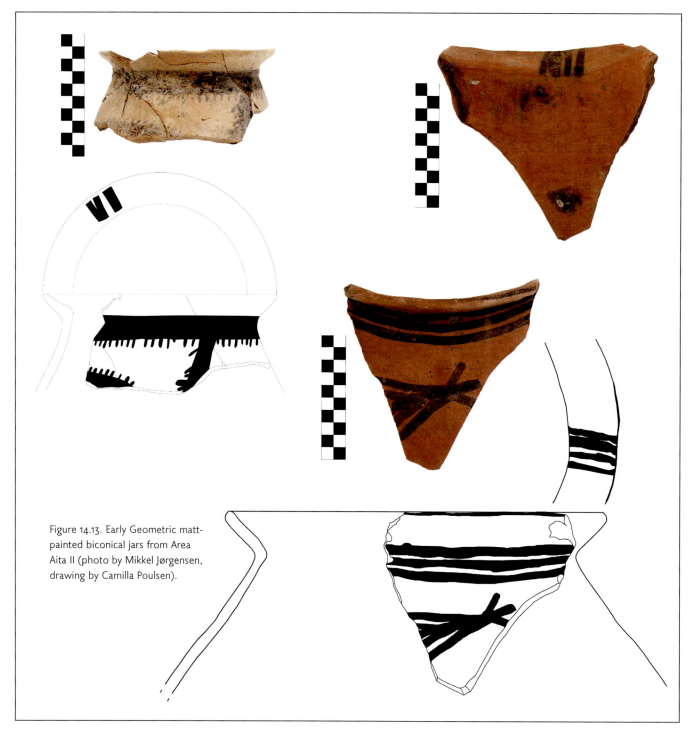

Figure 14.13. Early Geometric matt-painted biconical jars from Area Aita II (photo by Mikkel Jørgensen, drawing by Camilla Poulsen).

In addition to the described Italo-Mycenaean pottery, the Late Bronze Age contexts in Area Aita have produced several impasto fragments from large, closed vessels, cups, and large shallow bowls with a characteristic wave decoration below the rim. The shallow bowl type became a frequently used vessel during the Iron Age, but in a smaller version with a distinct black colour, whereas the excavated Late Bronze Age specimens are notably larger with a reddish-brown colour. Finally, several Proto-Geometric matt-painted fragments were found in the same contexts. They will be discussed in the following section, as they are forerunners for the production of matt-painted pottery during the ninth and eighth centuries BCE.

Early Matt-Painted Pottery Production

The stratigraphic sequences of the recent excavations in Area Aita and Area Rovitti have yielded a substantial number of sherds belonging to the class of matt-painted pottery. The stylistic development of geometric decorations on matt-painted pottery during the Iron Age offers the chance to investigate the chronology for its local production and revise some of the traditional views on the development of the local pottery production from the late ninth and eighth centuries BCE.[24]

Until recently, only two fragments of Early Geometric matt-painted pottery were attested at Timpone della Motta, whereas it was well known from sites nearby such as Monte San Nicola (van Leusen and Ippolito 2018; 2021) and Castrovillari, as well as Torre Mordillo and Broglio di Trebisacce.[25] The 2020 excavations in Area Aita have fundamentally changed this picture: in fact, not only has Early Geometric pottery come to light, but also Proto-Geometric matt-painted pottery. The latter was excavated from the above-mentioned Late Bronze

Age contexts in trench AAI.A, where it was found together with Italo-Mycenaean and indigenous impasto pottery (Fig. 14.12). The matt-painted fragments found so far pertain to large, closed vessels and are decorated with closely set, three-line triangles. The paint colour is dark grey and visibly different from that of the matt-painted pottery from the eighth century BCE at the site. The results from the NAA analyses are still pending, but a preliminary visual observation of the fabric shows frequent large calcareous inclusions, together with sand and a very frequent occurrence of medium-sized yellow mica particles. Interestingly, the Italo-Mycenaean pottery from the same context has a visibly similar clay fabric to that of the Proto-Geometric matt-painted pottery. This suggests the same source of raw clay material and similarities in clay tempering methods. In a superimposed context (US60B), Early Geometric fragments from large, closed matt-painted vessels were found. These have a decoration composed of closely set three-lined triangles, which on one occasion occur as two superimposed rows of triangles.

A second context (AAII.US209) containing Early Geometric matt-painted pottery was excavated in trench AAII, to the east of AAI.A (Fig. 14.13). Among others, three rim fragments from large biconical shaped vessels came to light. The fragments are decorated with large triangular motifs and bands with hanging dots. Interestingly, all three rim fragments have a decoration composed of groups of closely set vertical lines on the interior part of the rim. This decoration has, so far, not been attested on other large matt-painted vessels found at Timpone della Motta, but a similar decoration is seen on Early Geometric matt-painted vessels from Torre Mordillo and Castrovillari,[26] hereby supplying additional evidence for an Early Geometric date for the fragments from the described context US209. The Early Geometric matt-painted pottery is still under study, but it is already clear that a recurring decorative feature of closely set triangles in single and superimposed rows, is characteristic of the period (Fig. 14.7).

Returning to the excavation trench AAI.A, the above-mentioned Early Geometric context US60B was sealed off by a floor. On the floor, a large quantity of fragments, of which several can be joined into almost complete vessels, were excavated from contexts US60A and US60. The matt-painted pottery consistently belongs to the Middle

---

being. NAA analyses are planned to investigate whether we deal with a local production.

24 The matt-painted pottery of southern Italy was first studied as a coherent pottery class by Yntema (1990). Despite an increase in the available material his chronological stylistic framework still largely stands. Kleibrink studied the matt-painted pottery from Timpone della Motta cf. Kleibrink 2015b with reference to earlier publications.

25 Ferranti 2014, 87–88; Fasanella Masci 2016, 22. In recent excavations in the vicinity of Civita a few Early Geometric matt-painted fragments have been recovered (van Leusen and Ippolito 2018, fig. 5.b). A single Early Geometric fragment was excavated on Timpone della Motta in relation to building Vb, cf. Fasanella Masci 2016, 308 n. 12c. A second Early Geometric fragment is from the lower western slope of Timpone della Motta below Plateau I, cf. Jacobsen and others 2018, 29–30; 65 fig. DA1/5.

26 See, for instance, Peroni and Trucco 1994, II, tav. 137.2 (Belloluco), also in Fasanella Masci 2016, cat. no. BL 11C.

Geometric 'Undulating Band Style', termed by Kleibrink (Fig. 14.14).[27] No other decorative styles can be observed from US60A and US60, despite the quantity of ceramics, which shows that undulating bands were the predominant stylistic preference of the indigenous community at the end of the ninth century and early part of the eighth century BCE. This offers, for the first time, insight into how the 'Undulating Band Style' was introduced to the potters active at Timpone della Motta and other indigenous sites in the Sibaritide. Rather than an indigenous adaption from imported Euboean Greek or locally produced Oinotrian-Euboean pottery, as suggested by Kleibrink, Barresi, and Fasanella Masci (2012a, 29), the Middle Geometric 'Undulating Band Style' would have developed out of earlier preferences for wave-like decoration in southern Italy.

On the basis of the stratigraphy of Area Aita (US60A and 60), the 'Undulating Band Style' production dates between the late ninth century BCE to c. 760 BCE, whereas contexts containing indigenous material in association with imported Middle Geometric Euboean pottery and Oinotrian-Euboean pottery date from c. 760 BCE to 730/720 BCE. Contexts containing indigenous material in association with Late Geometric Corinthian and Early Proto-Corinthian imported pottery, as well as Oinotrian-Euboean ceramics, date to the period from 730/720 to 690 BCE.

In the following, we will discuss the development of the indigenous matt-painted production and the introduction of locally produced Greek-inspired Oinotrian-Euboean productions after c. 760 BCE, when the first Late Middle Geometric Greek import ceramics reached Timpone della Motta, giving rise to local Greek-inspired pottery production.

Indigenous Matt-Painted Production and the Introduction of Locally Produced Greek-inspired Oinotrian-Euboean Productions after c. 760 BCE

The pottery record from the excavation contexts AAII US258 and US259 from Area Aita gives evidence for a new class of Oinotrian-Euboean pottery that was added to the local production of decorated pottery featuring Greek shapes and decorations. At the same time, the matt-painted pottery devel-

oped further into several different distinct decorative styles. The 'Undulating Band Style' continued, but, after 760 BCE, in a more refined manner with thinner lines (Fig. 14.15). In the same contexts we now find the first Iron Age ceramics imported to the site, namely Euboean chevron *skyphoi* and indigenous matt-painted pottery produced in the Salento region, some 130 km north of Timpone della Motta (Fig. 14.16).[28]

The Oinotrian-Euboean pottery was first identified at Timpone della Motta in 2007 and has been viewed by the second author as strong evidence for the presence of immigrant Greek potters of Euboean origin within the indigenous settlement at Timpone della Motta during the eighth century BCE.[29] This hypothesis is based on typological, stylistic, and technological comparisons between the production of Oinotrian-Euboean and indigenous matt-painted pottery, which revealed two fundamentally different manufacturing techniques. It also demonstrates how indigenous typological and stylistic traits were adopted in the production of Oinotrian-Euboean pottery (Jacobsen and Handberg 2012, 702–05). Perhaps the most indicative examples for this adoption are the indigenous vessel shapes, such as biconical vessels and *scodelle* (Fig. 14.17); whereas the shapes are indigenous, the decoration of concentric circles and other geometric motifs has an origin in contemporary Greek Geometric pottery production. The decorations on these vessels are sometimes executed in a Greek-mannered glossy paint, but a conspicuous part of the vessels is decorated with a matt dark grey-to-black paint, which has a clearly visible connotation with the indigenous matt-painted pottery. Within this group, we find numerous *skyphoi* with a simple decoration consisting of a single wavy line, but also larger vessels with complex geometric and figure-decoration which find precise parallels in Greek-Euboean models (Fig. 14.18).

---

27 Kleibrink and others 2012a; 2012b. Kleibrink identified the 'Undulating Band Style' at the time as the earliest production of matt-painted pottery in Francavilla Marittima based on contextual evidence from building Vb and the earliest known graves at the Macchiabate necropolis.

28 Fragments of imported Euboean Middle Geometric II *skyphoi* were already known from secondary contexts and as sporadic surface finds at the Timpone della Motta; Jacobsen and Mittica in press. For Salentine matt-painted pottery in Francavilla, see Jacobsen and others 2009, 98; Kleibrink 2015a, 17–33. For additional finds of Salentine matt-painted pottery in Area Aita, see Jacobsen and Mittica 2019, 92–98.

29 Jacobsen 2007, 39–68. Petrological analysis has shown that Oinotrian-Euboean and local manufactured matt-painted wares were made of the same clays extracted close to present-day Lauropolis located 2.9 km to the south of Timpone della Motta (Andaloro and others 2011).

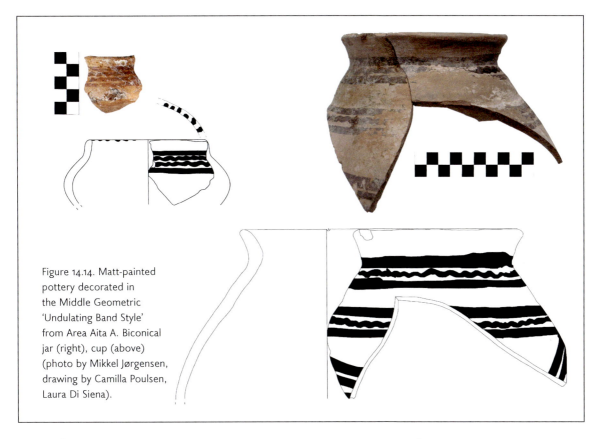

Figure 14.14. Matt-painted pottery decorated in the Middle Geometric 'Undulating Band Style' from Area Aita A. Biconical jar (right), cup (above) (photo by Mikkel Jørgensen, drawing by Camilla Poulsen, Laura Di Siena).

Figure 14.15. Matt-painted jar with decoration in the 'Undulating Band Style' with thinner lines (photo by Mikkel Jørgensen).

The use of indigenous shapes by the potters working at Timpone della Motta in the Greek-Euboean style might be seen as an attempt to respond to the demand of the indigenous community at Timpone della Motta. It has previously been proposed that the Oinotrian-Euboean vessels had little general appeal to the indigenous community, but this is no longer sustainable, for two reasons.[30] First, the recent excavations conducted by the University of Basel in the Macchiabate necropolis have brought to light a series of Oinotrian-Euboean vessels, among which are lidded kraters.[31] On one occasion, a Greek–indigenous hybrid shape might even have been specially commissioned by an indigenous individual.[32] Second, the excavations in Area Aita (among others, contexts AAII 258 and 259) have shown that Oinotrian-Euboean vessels were frequently used in the indigenous domestic sphere. As Oinotrian-Euboian vessels also occur in the sanctuary, the

---

30 Jacobsen 2013, 20. Subsequent to this statement by Kindberg Jacobsen the Basel excavations at the Macchiabate necropolis and the recent excavations in Area Aita showed a general reception of Oinotrian-Euboean vessels in indigenous contexts, cf. Guggisberg 2018; Jacobsen and others 2018, 37–40.

31 Grave De Leo 1: Guggisberg 2018, 168–70 fig. 4; Guggisberg and Colombi 2021, 97, 101–04 cat. no. DL1/1 pl. DL1/1 (M. Guggisberg). See also a second krater found accidentally in the area of the Cerchio Reale: Quondam 2014, 28–30 fig. 8; Guggisberg and Colombi 2001, 104 fig. 3.83.

32 Guggisberg 2018, 167–68, fig. 2; Guggisberg and Colombi 2021, 49, 104–05 cat. no. S2/1 pl. 13 (S. Billo, C. Colombi).

Figure 14.16. Context US 258 in Area Aita. 1: Imported Euboean Middle Geometric *skyphos*. 2–3: Imported Iapyrgian matt-painted cups. 4: Oinotrian-Euboean *amphora*. 5: Local matt-painted cup. 6: Local matt-painted jar (photo by Mikkel Jørgensen, drawing by Camilla Poulsen, Laura Di Siena).

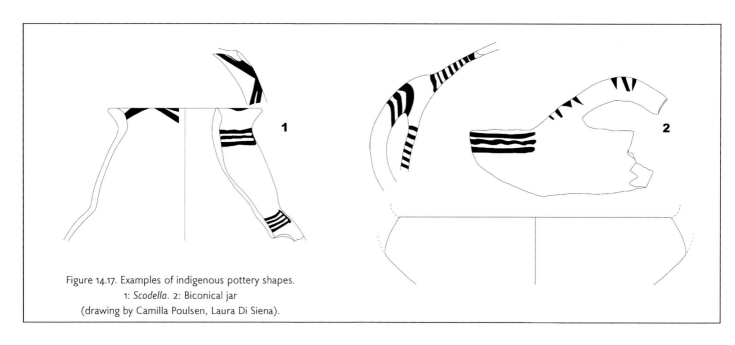

Figure 14.17. Examples of indigenous pottery shapes. 1: *Scodella*. 2: Biconical jar (drawing by Camilla Poulsen, Laura Di Siena).

Figure 14.18. Stand from large vessel in Greek-Euboean style (photo by Jan Kindberg Jacobsen, drawing by Helle Thusing).

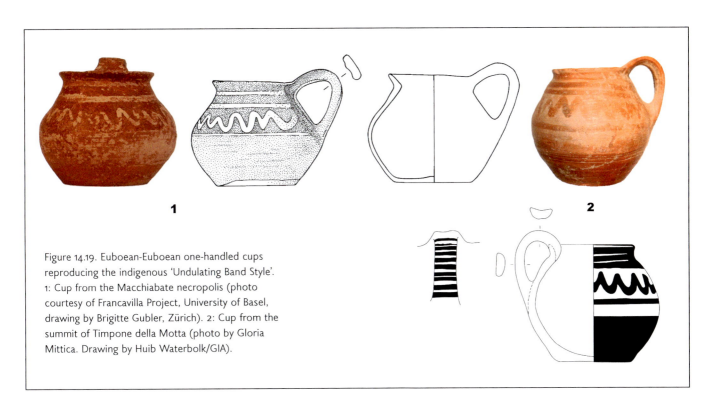

Figure 14.19. Euboean-Euboean one-handled cups reproducing the indigenous 'Undulating Band Style'. 1: Cup from the Macchiabate necropolis (photo courtesy of Francavilla Project, University of Basel, drawing by Brigitte Gubler, Zürich). 2: Cup from the summit of Timpone della Motta (photo by Gloria Mittica. Drawing by Huib Waterbolk/GIA).

Oinotrian-Euboean vessels appear to have been an integrated part of the site's material culture.

Interestingly, alongside this innovation, the production of indigenous matt-painted pottery remains remarkably immune to the characteristics of the Oinotrian-Euboean production. Kleibrink and others (2012a, 27–31) credited the Oinotrian-Euboean production with stimulating the stylistic development of the wavy band decorations on the indigenous matt-painted 'Undulating Band Style', but this seems unlikely. The production of matt-painted vessels with undulating bands was already well established in the decades before the emergence of the Oinotrian-Euboean production, and stylistic transformations would therefore have been initiated prior to any potential Greek inspiration. In line with the scenario proposed above of a high demand by the indigenous community for Oinotrian-Euboean vessels, we suggest that the wavy line decoration was applied in order to stylistically align some types of

Figure 14.20. Imported one-handled bowl with simple matt-painted decoration (photo by Giovanni Murro).

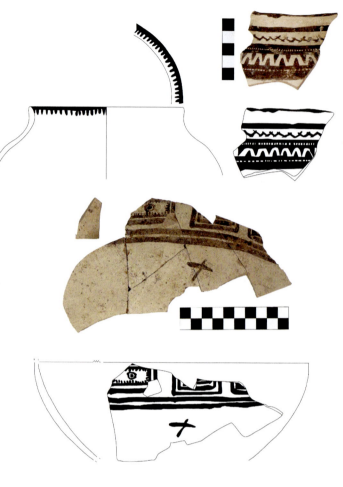

Oinotrian-Euboean vessels with the contemporary indigenous vessels decorated in the 'Undulating Band Style'. Support for this hypothesis is provided by, for example, two wheel-made cups (*attingitoi*), one from building V on the Timpone della Motta (Jacobsen 2007, 45 no. 38 pl. 17; Kleibrink and others 2012a, 12 fig. 16), the other from grave Strada 5 in the Macchiabate necropolis (Guggisberg and Colombi 2021, 110–11 cat. no. S5/2, pl. 26). Both are decorated with a regular set of wavy lines similar to the 'Undulating Band Style'-decoration applied to numerous handmade *attingitoi* from Timpone della Motta (Fig. 14.19).

During the second half of the eighth century BCE, the matt-painted pottery of Timpone della Motta developed into a variety of style groups (Kleibrink 2006). Part of this production was imported, likely from the Salento — as is the case with the pottery excavated from US258 and US259 in Area Aita. Here we again meet the 'Undulating Band Style', but in an advanced and refined version, as well as matt-painted vessels decorated in the new 'Fringe Style' and 'Cross-Hatched Band Style' (Kleibrink and others 2013; Kleibrink 2015b). These local and regional styles were already observed by Yntema and other scholars dealing with matt-painted pottery in southern Italy.[33] The evidence shows that the influx of Salentine matt-painted pottery and its distribution over the various contexts excavated at Timpone della Motta was more consistent than previously thought (Jacobsen and others 2008, 89–91). Moreover, the evidence in Area Aita shows that matt-painted pottery was not only used in the sanctuary, from which it was already known, but also in the settlement.

Figure 14.21. Imported, Salentine, matt-painted pottery from Area Aita (photo by Mikkel Jørgensen, drawings by Camilla Poulsen, Laura Di Siena).

Figure 14.22. Misfired bichrome fragment from structure B, Area Rovitti (photo by Gloria Mittica).

---

33 Kleibrink and others 2012a; Kleibrink and Weistra 2013; Kleibrink 2015a; 2015b; Herring 1998; De Juliis and others 2006.

The excavations at Area Aita have now added fragments of sixty individual vessels to the existing corpus (Fig. 14.20). The complex geometric decorative schema and a pale whitish coloured clay make Salentine pottery easily distinguishable from other matt-painted ceramics. It has already been argued that the occurrence of Salentine matt-painted pottery in Francavilla Marittima proves the existence of long-range, inter-indigenous trade connections during the second half of the eighth century BCE (Jacobsen and others 2008, 89–91). In all likelihood, these trade connections also brought imported Corinthian Late Geometric pottery to the Sibaritide.[34] The Salentine–Sibaritide matt-painted connection may, however, be part of a broader south Italian network. NAA analysis of a one-handled bowl with simple matt-painted decoration indicates a Campanian origin, even though, upon visual inspection, clay, paint colour, and manufacturing technique do not differ from most matt-painted ceramics found at the site. While this type of bowl was certainly not in widespread use at Timpone della Motta, nevertheless fourteen specimens are known from the summit of Timpone della Motta and from Area Aita (Fig. 14.21). While the analysis is preliminary, and only based on one sample of a rare form, it does emphasize the need for NAA examination of the full repertoire of matt-painted pottery from Timpone della Motta in order to test our assumptions of locally manufactured and imported pottery. Vice versa, a possible output of matt-painted pottery from Timpone della Motta to other sites should also be considered.[35]

Local Productions between c. 760 BCE and 730/720 BCE

Between c. 760 and 730/720 BCE in the Sibaritide, the coiling technique of the matt-painted pottery improves, the decorations become more complex, and red and black bichrome paint is introduced. The

Oinotrian-Euboean pottery remained in production. It appears that Euboean potters were joined by potters from Corinth and other Greek areas. The period coincides with the foundation of the Greek colony of Sybaris some 12 km south-east of Timpone della Motta, but the impact of the colony on the material culture of the site was not felt until later in the seventh century BCE. Sealed contexts dating to this period have been excavated in the sanctuary on the summit of Timpone della Motta, in the area immediately to the south of building Vc, in Area Rovitti structure B, and in a partly excavated indigenous hut on Plateau I.[36] Relevant contexts have also been excavated in Area Aita, but their interpretation is problematic on account of subsequent use of the area during the sixth century BCE. The assemblages from these areas are remarkably similar and well dated thanks to the presence of Corinthian Late Geometric and a few specimens of Early Proto-Corinthian pottery, of which globular *pyxides* and drinking cups are the dominant shapes. Most of the material consists, however, of matt-painted ceramics and impasto vessels. The matt-painted vessels now occur in both monochrome black and bichrome red and black.

Previous studies argued that the bichrome style developed in the period slightly prior to the foundation of the first Greek colonial cities along the Ionian coast (Castoldi 2006, 1–5; 2009). The evidence from Timpone della Motta supports this theory, since the Corinthian pottery in the assemblages slightly predates the earliest known Corinthian pottery from Sybaris.[37] Both the monochrome and the bichrome matt-painted vessels show that the local artisans now could produce complex and thin-lined decorations on vessels which were coiled to a wall thickness as delicate as 2 mm (Kleibrink 2006b). External influences on the local workshops may have played a part in this rapid transformation. A source of inspiration could well have been the Corinthian Late Geometric pottery which reached the site. The panels, with closely set chevrons and lozenges, form a recurring feature on the matt-painted vessels, and the same

---

34 Alongside typochronological analysis, the identification of Salentine matt-painted pottery of Timpone della Motta is now also based on NAA analysis. The first sample confirms a Salentine origin, see Posamentir, Geißler, Riehle, and Mommsen (in print). Also a group of unpublished matt-painted fragments from nearby Castrovillari in the collection of the Museo Civico Archeologico di Castrovillari holds several fragments of Salentine origin.

35 Kleibrink, Barresi, and Fasanella Masci (2012a, 19) propose that matt painted pottery produced at Timpone della Motta arrived at nearby Torre Mordillo. Colelli and Jacobsen (2013, 284–85 fig. 67 with bibliography) postulate the presence of a workshop at Timpone della Motta, nearby Torre Mordillo, or at Castrovillari that produced a type of *askòs* found in Sala Consilina and Pithekoussai.

36 For the contexts south of building Vc, Kleibrink 2006b (context AC22A.11/15); Mittica 2010, 21–33 (context SM215). For structure B in the Rovitti Area, Jacobsen and others 2018, 34–35. For the hut remains on Plateau I Kleibrink 2006a, 77–110.

37 Jacobsen 2007, 35–37. A recent study argues for the presence of some Middle Geometric Greek fragments from the Sibari excavations among these Euboean black cups and so called proto-*kotylai*, see Luberto 2020, 61–62, 118. On account of a partial discrepancy between the decoration on the fragments in question and Middle Geometric Greek pottery it is however evident that the fragments in question belong to well-established Ionian-inspired cup types and Corinthian *kotyle-pyxides*, both datable to the seventh century BCE.

decoration is found on Corinthian Late Geometric ceramics from Timpone della Motta. However, the indigenous potters did not attempt to imitate Greek geometric decorative schemes, but instead merely inserted Greek motifs into otherwise local decorations. The same use of Greek motifs is found on the numerous Salentine matt-painted fragments found on Timpone della Motta.[38] As shown above, these Salentine vessels were well known to the local potters in Francavilla Marittima and hence offered a direct source of inspiration (Kleibrink 2015a, 7–10). The current absence of NAA results calls for caution, and we should not automatically attribute matt-painted ceramics to local productions. The mere quantity of matt-painted pottery at the site points, however, to a substantial local production. Also, much of the pottery from the settlement and necropolis constitutes stylistically refined continuations of pre-existing styles, such as Kleibrink's 'Fringe Style' or the 'A Tenda Style' as originally defined by Yntema.[39] The presence of a few clearly misfired fragments, including a bichrome misfired fragment from structure B, offers direct evidence for local production (Fig. 14.22).

The Oinotrian-Euboean production continued, which is evident from the frequent finds of fragments at structure B in Area Rovitti and the sanctuary, where it occurs in closed contexts. This also holds for the production of Oinotrian-Euboean vessels with locally inspired matt-painted decoration. A few fragments from *scodelle* and *skyphoi* even show that the new bichrome technique was adapted to the Oinotrian-Euboean production (Fig. 14.23).

New Greek Resident Potters?

As described above, pottery workshops were established in Area Rovitti, just before the middle of the eighth century BCE, that produced pottery that was technically, typologically, and stylistically distinct from the indigenous matt-painted production. The strong links with Euboean pottery hint at the presence of immigrant potters of Euboean background at Timpone della Motta. During the period between 730/720 BCE and 690 BCE, distinctly Greek-mannered vessels appear that point to the presence of potters from other Greek backgrounds as well. Two new

classes of pottery are significant here: the 'Ticino Group' and Sub-Thapsos ware.

The Ticino Group has Geometric decorations with new motifs, such as human figures. This group consists of a series of vessels now in public and private collections. They are generally believed to have been illegally excavated in Francavilla Marittima. Several fragments and complete vessels from Timpone della Motta and the Macchiabate necropolis can be added to the Ticino Group (Fig. 14.24) (Guzzo 2020). Various scholars have already published exhaustive stylistic analyses of individual vessels, as well as observations on the group as a whole, and we shall therefore, in this context, only focus on the evidence for attributing the group to a local production and the consequent implications for the argument of the presence of Greek resident potters.[40] The group takes its name from a figure-decorated *pyxis*, previously kept in a private collection in Ticino, Switzerland. The vessel is decorated with figure-friezes on each side. One depicts a row of female dedicants approaching a seated goddess, whereas a row of male dancers is found on the opposite side of the vessel. The style of the Ticino vase is closely related to figure-decorations on Attic vases of the Late Geometric IIb period.[41] A similar, closely related vessel in the Antikenmuseum Basel und Sammlung Ludwig has a similar panel with dancing males on each side (Descoeudres 1981, pl. 4, 1). A third stylistic parallel, excavated on the summit of Timpone della Motta, is a lid fragment decorated with a male and a female holding hands (Fig. 14.25) (Guzzo 2020). The stylistic coherency between these decorations is striking and links these types of vessels to Timpone della Motta. Other vessels belonging to the Ticino Group are decorated with birds or scenes recalling the Euboean Cesnola style. The vessels of the Ticino Group have either glossy paint or are matt-painted, a modus operandi well known from the Oinotrian-Euboean workshops. The style is, however, different from the Geometric-dominated Oinotrian-Euboean production, and the introduction of human figurative decoration is new. Nevertheless, the Oinotrian-Euboean pottery and the Ticino Group have stylistic similarities, as can be seen in fragments from the excavation in Area Rovitti with secondary Geometric decoration resembling those of the vessels in the Ticino Group. The most likely conclusion is that the Oinotrian-Euboean workshops were joined by potters working in different Greek traditions dur-

---

38 For the incorporation of Greek motifs in Salentine matt-painted pottery, Yntema 1990, 51–53.

39 Yntema 1990, 310–11; for a reassessment Quondam 173–74 fig. 3. For good examples of the Late Geometric subgroup *stile vuoto* of the *a tenda vuota* style see: Guggisberg and Colombi 2021, 51, 69, 100 cat. nos S4/1 and S11/1 pl. 19. 47.

40 Kleibrink 2020; Jacobsen and others 2017, 178–82; Granese and Tomay 2008, 141–44.

41 Jacobsen and others 2017, 179. Guzzo 2020 considers the Ticino Group the product of a Greek workshop from Sibari.

14. THE DEEP PAST OF MAGNA GRAECIA'S POTTERY TRADITIONS 257

Figure 14.23. Example of bichrome technique applied in the Oinotrian-Euboean production. 1: *Kantharos*. 2: *Scodella* (photos by Mikkel Jørgensen and Gloria Mittica).

Figure 14.24. Ticino Group. 1: Globular *pyxis* (after Cahn and Cahn 1998, fig. 6). 2: Lidded globular *pyxis* (photo courtesy of Antike Kunst, Freiburg). 3–5: Krater (photo courtesy of Antikenmuseum Basel und Sammlung Ludwig).

Figure 14.25. Lid fragment decorated with a male and a female holding hands related to the Ticino Group (photo by Gloria Mittica).

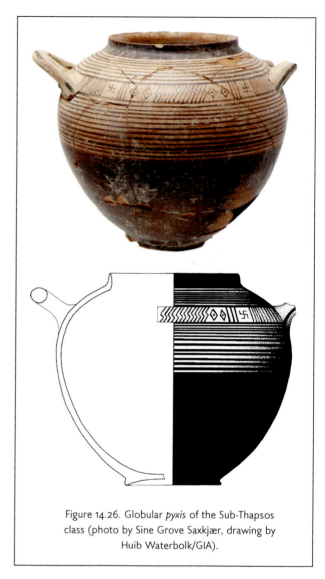

Figure 14.26. Globular *pyxis* of the Sub-Thapsos class (photo by Sine Grove Saxkjær, drawing by Huib Waterbolk/GIA).

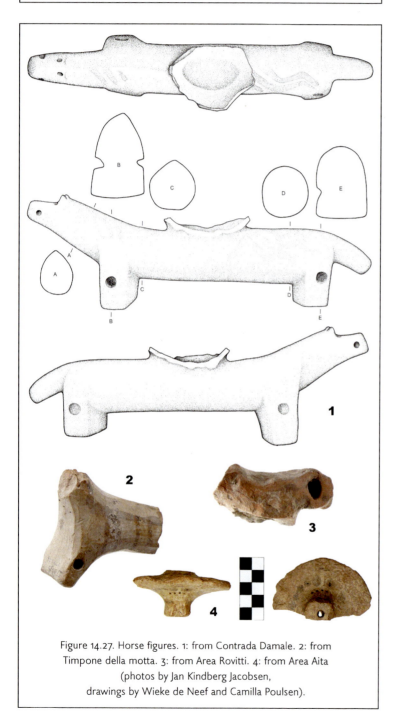

Figure 14.27. Horse figures. 1: from Contrada Damale. 2: from Timpone della motta. 3: from Area Rovitti. 4: from Area Aita (photos by Jan Kindberg Jacobsen, drawings by Wieke de Neef and Camilla Poulsen).

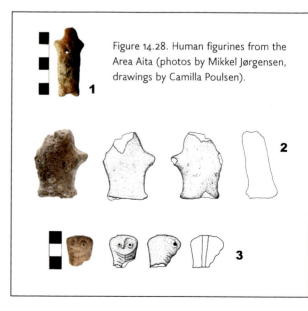

Figure 14.28. Human figurines from the Area Aita (photos by Mikkel Jørgensen, drawings by Camilla Poulsen).

ing this period. Resident Greek potters of various origin working in Italy during the Iron Age have, for instance, also been proposed for the island of Ischia, Incoronata, Canale-Janchina, and Etruria.[42]

A second class of locally produced pottery, the so-called Sub-Thapsos pottery (a local production of Thapsos Ware pottery, Fig. 14.26), suggests the presence of Corinthian potters in Francavilla Marittima towards the end of the eighth century BCE and the beginning of the seventh century BCE (Saxkjær forthcoming). The Thapsos Ware production is traditionally ascribed to Corinth, due to the uniformity of the fabric of Proto-Corinthian pottery and Thapsos Ware (Bosana-Kourou 1984; Coldstream 1998, 327–28). That workshops producing Thapsos Ware existed outside Corinth as well is now becoming increasingly clear. This means that it should be viewed as part of a Late Geometric *koine* rather than a 'genuine production' limited to one particular area (Gadolou 2011, 47; 2017, 193–96). At Timpone della Motta, both imported Thapsos Ware pottery, most likely from Corinth, as well as a local production of Thapsos-style pottery, termed 'Sub-Thapsos pottery', has been identified. In total, fragments of about one hundred individual Sub-Thapsos vessels have so far been recorded among the material from Timpone della Motta. Recently, a *skyphos* of the Sub-Thapsos group came to light in a grave context at the Macchiabate (Strada 16).[43] The Sub-Thapsos ware is hard-fired and contains silver mica and calcareous inclusions, similar to that of the local clay. The Sub-Thapsos group includes three shapes — *pyxides*, *skyphoi*, and *kotylai* — of which the *skyphos* constitutes the prevailing type, making up more than half of the vessels. As noted above, imported and locally manufactured Oinotrian-Euboean drinking cups and *pyxides* were already in use on Timpone della Motta. The novelty of the Sub-Thapsos production seems to have been a response to changing stylistic preferences rather than the introduction of new pottery uses. The same overall decoration scheme can be observed across the three shapes: a monochrome field on the lower part of the vessels followed by horizontal bands, interrupted by a panel or a frieze. Motifs within the panels and friezes recur on *pyxides* and *skyphoi*.

Production of Terracotta Figurines between the Final Bronze and the Iron Age

From Timpone della Motta, the Macchiabate necropolis, and adjacent sites, many terracotta figurines are known, pointing to local production from the Late Bronze Age onwards. Two types exist: a) human figurines, singular or in couples; and b) figurines of horses on four wheels. Both types make use of a local figurative language also known from bronze figurines, incisions on clay objects, and vase-painting (Kleibrink 2016a, 47–61). A largely intact and painted horse figurine was recently excavated in Contrada Damale, some 4 km to the north-east of Timpone della Motta (de Neef 2013; 2016, 316–17). The figure was found in association with Late Bronze Age material in what is most likely a settlement context (van Leusen and Ippolito 2021). Remains of a vessel are visible on the back of the horse, and similar vessel-equipped horse figurines are known from Greece during the Bronze and Iron Age.[44] The legs of the horse have horizontal perforations accommodating the four (now lost) wheels. Timpone della Motta has not yielded horse figurines in Late Bronze Age contexts, although they occur in Iron Age contexts, both in Area Rovitti and Area Aita, where wheels as well as horse fragments have been found. Parts of horse figurines have also been found at Timpone della Motta, but without context — one is currently in the collection of the Museo Civico di Cosenza (Kleibrink 2016b, 58 fig. 26b). The decoration of the latter suggests a date in the Proto- or Early Geometric Period, whereas a horse element from Area Rovitti came to light in an Iron Age context in association with early Proto-Corinthian pottery, indicating a date during the latter part of the eighth century BCE. The Contrada Damale figurine and the fragments from Timpone della Motta suggest that horse figurines were in use from at least the Late Bronze Age and throughout the Iron Age. All horse figurines have horizontal perforations for wheel attachments. The wheels, of which several examples have been found in Area Aita, have matt-painted decorations. Some wheels have vertically impressed holes around the horizontal perforation with a depth of *c.* 0.5 cm and a diameter of *c.* 1 mm. These holes originally held decorative elements in a different material (organic, metal?). In Greece, these types of wheeled horse figurines are predominantly found in children's graves and the same may

---

42 Neeft 1987, 59–65 (Ischia); Denti 2018 (Incoronata); Mercuri 2004, 127–34; 2012, 977–79 (Canale-Janchina); Canciani 2000, 9–15 (Etruria).

43 C. Colombi in: Guggisberg and Colombi 2021, 84, 111–12 (cat. no. S16/2) pl. 66. Given its close resemblance to vessels from Pithekoussai both a local and a Bay of Naples production is possible.

---

44 De Neef 2013, 54–56. A fragment from the head of a similar horse figurine is known from Torre Mordillo (Colburn 1977, 483 fig. F 1, 'periodo geometrico'). A similar bronze horse from Torre Mordillo is exhibited in the Museo Civico di Castrovillari.

be noted in Italy.[45] Interestingly, all known examples from Timpone della Motta have come to light in domestic contexts, and the fragments from Broglio are also associated with habitation layers. To date, horse figurines are not known from the Iron Age graves in the Macchiabate necropolis or from the sanctuary (Fig. 14.27).

Terracotta figurines depicting humans are found in several Macchiabate graves, in the sanctuary and in Area Aita. A recently discovered figurine from Area Aita indicates that human terracotta figurines were already present at the site during the Late Bronze Age (Fig. 14.28, 1). It is handmade and extremely basic: arms and legs look short and raised, the head is very simple. Because of the shape of the legs and the absence of feet, this figurine could not stand on its own. The figurine's chest is perforated; probably it held a chain or a rope so it could be used as a pendant. The figurine was found without context in the vicinity of trench AAI.A in Area Aita and can therefore not be dated on the basis of a find context. However, the figurine finds clear parallels in Final Bronze Age figurines from Campomarino (Molise) (Babbi 2008, n. 13; Cassola Guida 2013, 1.7), Roca Vecchia (Puglia) (Babbi 2008, nn. 18–19; Cassola Guida 2013, 243 fig. 5, 6–7), and Frattesina (Veneto) (Babbi 2008, 33–34 n. 4 with bibliography), indicating a contemporary date for the figurine from Area Aita (Bietti Sestieri 2008, 39 fig. 1, 52 fig. 17).

A second figurine from Area Aita, AAI (Fig. 14.28, 2) lacks its head. The profile is very simple: legs and arms are abstract; it is more squat than the one discussed above. The shape is simple and the similarity with other figurines (see, for example, the one from Campomarino, Babbi 2008, 44–45, tav. 5,A, fig. 4,A) suggests a date in the Final Bronze Age or beginning of the Iron Age. The head of a third figurine from trench AAII in Area Aita is preserved (Fig. 14.28, 3). It has a long neck with incised horizontal lines and applied and inlaid eyes. The shape and decorative features are of the southern Italian Iron Age; the closest parallel is the figurine recently found in Macchiabate, grave Est 10 (see below) (Jung and Pacciarelli 2019, 35).

From the Macchiabate burial ground, several terracotta anthropomorphous figurines are known. Three were excavated in the 1960s from children's graves by Paola Zancani Montuoro in the so-called Temparella area and represent single figures (T. 69,[46]

T. 78[47]) a fourth one, from T. 2, represents a couple.[48] In recent excavations, the Swiss team found additional figurines in the eastern part of the necropolis. One, representing a couple, comes from the area of a destroyed grave (Settore 82) (Guggisberg and others 2016, 63 pl. 7, 6). Another, representing a single figurine, was found in a double burial nearby (grave Est 10) (Guggisberg, and others 2018, 79 fig. 2). A final figurine, a more elaborately executed but partially preserved specimen, stems from the Bern-Malibu-Copenhagen collection of illicitly excavated objects from the acropolis of Timpone della Motta (Kleibrink and Weistra 2013, 46 fig. 16).

Figurines began to occur in graves at the Macchiabate burial ground during the first half of the eighth century BCE and are found in contexts in Area Aita from the second half of the eighth century BCE. Although iconographically related to the bronze figurines and pendants of anthropomorphic couples, so well attested at Francavilla Marittima and elsewhere in northern Calabria, the terracotta human figurines clearly relate to an independent stylistic tradition. With their compact body, their stretched out or uprising arms, their long neck, and birdlike face they not only form a coherent group, so far unique among the Oinotrian communities on the Ionian coast of south Italy, but also show several stylistic features relating them to external productions. Links have been established, in particular, with the Aegean, where a series of bell-shaped figurines from the Dodecanese show similar features, such as elongated necks, upraised arms, and thin triangular or birdlike faces.[49] In the absence of imported figurines from the Aegean in the Sibaritide, so far it is difficult to clearly assess the relationship between these two traditions, all the more so since there are local terracotta traditions in other areas of Early Iron Age Italy too (such as Pontecagnano). Regarding the figurines, it should be kept in mind that, in contrast to most pottery, they were closely linked to their specific ritual function as a grave good or votive offering and therefore less apt to be part of economically motivated trade and exchange of goods.[50] Nevertheless, the possibility of contacts

---

45 De Neef 2013, 56. For Italy cf. Bianco and others 1996, 41, 51–56. Grave 21 at Tursi-Valle Sorigliano (first half eighth century BCE).

46 Zancani Montuoro 1974–1976, 51–55 fig. 14; Babbi 2008, 67–68 n. 34 pl. 23; figs 18, B–C; 19, A.

47 Zancani Montuoro 1974–1976, 53, 55 pl. XXV, b; Babbi 2008, 66–67 n. 33 pl. 24; figs 19, B–C; 20, A.

48 Zancani Montuoro 1966, 202–08 figs 1–4; Babbi 2008, 339–40 pl. 89; fig. 60. Human pairs in bronze were used as pendants in northern Calabria and elsewhere; Timpone della Motta has the largest collection of such finds (recently Taliano Grasso and Pisarra 2019).

49 Babbi 2008, 371–75, 402; 2012, 295–96; Kleibrink and Weistra 2013, 35–55 especially 44–47.

50 Kleibrink 2016b suggests a relationship between figurines and bride rituals on the Timpone della Motta, cf. Kleibrink 2016b.

Figure 14.29. 1: Misfired *hydriskai* from the sanctuary.
2: Misfired *kernos* from the sanctuary
(photos by Søren Handberg).

with the Aegean should not completely be ruled out, considering the stylistic connections to the Dodecanese. For want of imported figurines from the East, other media might be taken into account as a means of transmission of the specific iconographic and stylistic features. Among them anthropomorphic north Syrian perfume bottles could be possible candidates, given their well-known presence as far west as Pithekoussai. According to a hypothesis by J. N. Coldstream, these perfume bottles were imitated locally on the island of Rhodes, in proximity, thus, of the production centres of the bell-shaped figurines mentioned above and with which they share a number of stylistic features, such as the globular body, the tub-like elongated neck, and the stylized head.[51]

Local Pottery Production during the Archaic Period

The foundation of Sybaris did not have an immediate fundamental cultural or material impact on Timpone della Motta, but towards c. 680 BCE the situation changed, and from there on local material culture becomes increasingly difficult to detect (Handberg and Jacobsen 2011, 179–80). From the beginning of the seventh century BCE, the settlement started to depopulate and in this period, there is also little activity in the Macchiabate necropolis. The vast majority of ceramic evidence for the seventh century BCE comes from the sanctuary, which seems to have been frequented by many visitors. Misfired pottery excavated from seventh-century contexts in the sanctuary suggests that part of the pottery needed for the rituals was locally produced. The fragments shown in Figure 14.29 belong to miniature *hydriskai* and *kernos* rings. Both shapes are ritual vessels, and they were used and deposited within the sanctuary in tens of thousands during the seventh century BCE. The misfired pottery should, however, not be seen as an indication for pottery production within the limits of the sanctuary, but rather as a result of the large-scale use of these vessels for ritual purposes. Misfired or otherwise defective vessels accidently reached the sanctuary from time to time (Mittica and others 2006, 29–32). Apart from the miniaturist shapes, a broad variety of shapes and stylistic variations associated with the colony of Sybaris was in use in the sanctuary during the seventh century BCE (van der Wielen-van Ommeren and De Lachenal 2008). Notable are the many drinking cups, among which *skyphoi* and *kantharoi* are dominant (Fig. 14.30). The *skyphoi* belong to the so-called *coppa a filletti* type. Their shape derives from imported Proto-Corinthian *skyphoi*, commonly used along the Ionian coast (Berlingò 1986). The colonial *kantharoi*, on the other hand, closely follow the shape and decoration of imported Akhaian *kantharoi*.[52] In general, the non-miniature

---

51 Coldstream 1969, 3 pl. 2a–f; Papapostolou 1968, 85–86. The particularly elaborate figurine from grave Temparella 69 was found together with the well-known north Syrian stone seal of the lyre player group.

52 Papadopoulos 2001; 2003; Tomay and Granese 2002; Kleibrink and others 2004.

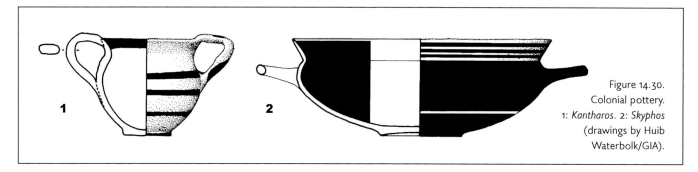

Figure 14.30. Colonial pottery. 1: *Kantharos*. 2: *Skyphos* (drawings by Huib Waterbolk/GIA).

shape repertoire is in line with that of the imported ceramics of the period. The colonial ware therefore appears to be a local response to accommodate a need for Greek shapes, which could not be met by imported ceramics alone. On stylistic grounds, differences are clear between the colonial ware and the imported Greek pottery. The Greek pottery, which mainly originates from Corinth, is equally divided between sub-Geometric and figurative decoration (silhouette style and black-figure technique), whereas the colonial ware is almost exclusively decorated in the sub-Geometric manner. Only in a few instances does figure decoration occur on colonial ware vessels (Saxkjær 2013). The misfired fragments mentioned above, together with the sheer amount of colonial miniature vessels deposited in the sanctuary, indicate that a pottery production area was located in the vicinity of Timpone della Motta. Whether the production of indigenous matt-painted pottery continued is less certain. Matt-painted pottery does occur in seventh-century BCE contexts in the sanctuary, but in very limited amounts. This suggests that a Greek-inspired material culture was prevailing over the original local one. A sharply decreasing demand for local matt-painted pottery may have obliterated local production. The most recognizable import group that filled the gap consists of a series of wheel-thrown, narrow-necked jugs, decorated in bichrome matt-painted style. The vessels reached Timpone della Motta from the north and numerous identical vessels are known from graves at Amendolara. These date to the seventh and sixth centuries BCE (Saxkjær 2021).

From the end of the seventh century BCE the site became repopulated. By the sixth century BCE the slopes of Timpone della Motta were again inhabited and a more frequent use of the Macchiabate necropolis is noted. Graves of the sixth century BCE are constructed within the tumuli of the Iron Age. The continuation in the use of the indigenous family burials suggests that the deceased had maintained cultural relations with the site. Colonial pottery continued to be used and deposited in the sanctuary in great quantities. The shapes dominant during the seventh century BCE remained *hydriskai* and drinking cups. The discovery in 2019 of a pottery kiln in association with an accumulation of misfired pottery in Area Aita gave direct evidence of local colonial pottery production. The misfired pottery shows that the production was destined for the sanctuary, as well as for the settlement and Macchiabate necropolis. Most of the misfired fragments belong to Ionian type drinking cups and coarse ware cooking pots of the Greek *chytra* type. Similar Ionian type cups are known throughout the site and *chytra* cooking pots are known from sixth-century BCE contexts in the sanctuary and from the houses on the slopes of Timpone della Motta.[53] While we have evidence for continued activities at Timpone dell Motta during the period following the Archaic period, this currently does not add to our knowledge about pottery traditions at the site.[54] Therefore, we will now turn to the discussion of the data presented so far.

Adoption, Adaption, and Local Pottery Traditions in the Sibaritide and at Timpone della Motta

In the sections above, we have given an overview of current knowledge concerning classes of pottery that we have come across in surveys and excavations in the foothills of the Sibaritide and in the excavations at Timpone delle Motta. This has had the aim to detect continuity and change in pottery production and consumption over a period of about eleven centuries, from the Middle Bronze age, around 1600 BCE, to the end of the Archaic period around 500 BCE. The approximate time ranges of the occurrence of these classes are indicated in Figure 14.31. Actual and circumstantial evidence for pottery production and their find contexts is listed in Figure 14.32.

---

53 For a preliminary report on the pottery kiln and misfired pottery see Mittica and others 2021.
54 For an overview of the Classical and Hellenistic remains cf. Kleibrink 2011, 7, 115–26.

In the following discussion, we highlight the processes leading to adoption and adaption of pottery traditions in the Sibaritide as well as the implications of these dynamics for our understanding of socio-economic developments in a context of mobility and migration. We take a chronological approach, starting in the Bronze Age, followed by the Early Iron Age, and concluding with the Late Iron Age and Archaic periods.

Mechanisms of Adoption and Adaption and their Socio-economic Implications during the Bronze Age

Of the classes discussed, that of impasto has the longest continuity, bridging the Bronze and Iron Ages. Its production constitutes a strong local ceramic tradition and continued to be present in domestic, funerary, and ritual contexts until the start of the Archaic period, when it is replaced by colonial ware. Although conservative, it did undergo technological, functional, formal, and stylistic changes over time. These changes have been studied in detail in a range of typo-chronological works, some of which we have referred to in the footnotes. While predominantly locally produced, it would be wrong to believe that the local impasto did not show influences of traditions from elsewhere in Italy (Ippolito 2016). In a recent paper, Ippolito and Attema (forthcoming (a)) showed how the local impasto repertoire in our fieldwork area absorbed formal influences from Sicily, northern Italy, and the Dalmatian coast, and how these relationships show patterning in time and space related to the waxing and waning of cultural core areas over time, such as, for instance the Terramare.

The mechanism of adoption and adaption in ceramic production is, in our view, best analysed using Mesoudi and O'Brien's cultural transmission concept, which they define as 'the process by which information (for example, knowledge, skills, or beliefs) is passed from individual to individual via social learning' (Mesoudi and O'Brien 2008, 4). Cultural transmission is different from diffusionism, as it emphasizes reciprocity, agency, and the reconstruction of connectivity between areas, even if far apart. On a macroregional scale, these three factors imply long-distance mobility of people, goods, and information, and may even include migration of individuals or small groups whose presence accelerated processes of adoption and adaption, in our case regarding pottery production. As to the prehistoric and early protohistoric impasto repertoire of Timpone della Motta and its hinterland of the

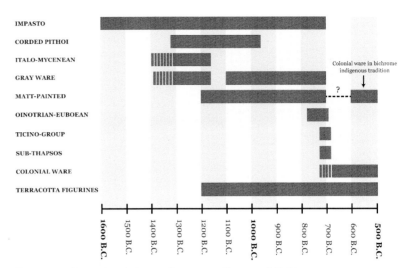

Figure 14.31. Longevity of classes of pottery at Timpone della Motta (by Mikkel Jørgensen).

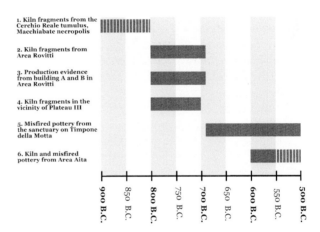

Figure 14.32. Actual and circumstantial evidence for pottery production at Timpone della Motta (by Mikkel Jørgensen).

Raganello basin, Ippolito's 2016 typochronological studies indicated that adoption and adaption came about through a persistent form of cultural connectivity involving a range of subsequent cultural areas from the Early Bronze Age to the Iron Age, in which imports also played a role.[55] The *longue durée* perspective taken in this paper reveals how, from a pottery perspective, cultural connectivity between Timpone della Motta and other cultural areas was a continuous process bridging the Final Bronze Age and Early Iron Age divide and extending into the Archaic period. The introduction of new classes of pottery from outside, both imported and locally adopted, while a subject in itself, can also serve as a

---

55 See for the typochronological studies see Ippolito 2016. For the cultural analysis see Ippolito and Attema forthcoming (a).

proxy for mobility and migration, highlighting individuals or groups acting as agents of technological and aesthetic transfer. Being the most widespread and continuously present commodity in the archaeological record, pottery plays an eminent role in the reconstruction of the social and functional significance of processes of adoption and adaption, first of all in the modes and organization of pottery production itself, but also related to both social and ritual practices (commensality, cult and funerary ritual), as well as subsistence modes and trade (agricultural and storage practices, transport) associated with the actual product. Even if we should realize that at Timpone della Motta the intensity of cultural links with the Aegean and Greek world, on account of the 'otherness' of its pottery production, is magnified at the expense of cultural links with areas with more similar material culture expressions in Italy itself, the Aegean and Greek links were still instrumental in the long-term processes of demographic, socio-economic, and cultural changes.

To summarize briefly, the production of Italo-Mycenaean pottery around 1400 BCE was based on depurated wheel-turned Mycenaean wares and was completely different from that of impasto in production process, shapes and stylistic features. Grey Ware, introduced slightly later than Italo-Mycenaean ware, was likewise an innovative product, which moreover proved highly receptive to stylistic influences from the local impasto tradition. The introduction of these new classes set the scene for the pluriformity that characterizes the local pottery traditions at Timpone della Motta during the Late Bronze Age and the Early Iron Age. In Figure 14.31, the longevity and perdurance of Italo-Mycenaean pottery and Grey Ware productions is striking, while Table 14.2 demonstrates the mutual influences between Bronze Age Aegean and local ceramic production practices in the Sibaritide. While we do not have any physical evidence yet for actual production of Italo-Mycenaean and Grey Ware pottery (Figure 14.32), we pointed out that archaeometric research on Italo-Mycenaean pottery from Torre Mordillo and Broglio di Trebisacce by Jones and others 2014, points to local production facilities at major sites. The local demand for these fine ware classes highlights their social function in the context of ceremonial practices, and especially the introduction of wine drinking (Iacono 2015). Its adoption is reinforced by the fact that shapes related to drinking were executed in impasto as well as in Grey Ware and thus had become part of indigenous consumption habits. That cultural transmission in the manufacturing of Aegean-type pottery in the later Bronze Age may have been brought about by the actual presence of potters with an Aegean background, at least at an initial stage of contacts, at sites such as Torre Mordillo, Timpone della Motta, and Broglio di Trebisacce seems increasingly realistic (Jones and others 2014, 453–54). Interaction between potters from various backgrounds will have occurred in the *kerameikoi* of these settlements.

A scenario of *in situ* cultural transmission is supported by the widespread presence of the class of the corded *pithoi*, large storage jars modelled on Aegean prototypes, that we must relate to novel agricultural practices demanding bulk storage, such as grain and olive oil. The map in Figure 14.2 above showed how the foothills near Timpone della Motta in the Final Bronze Age were dotted with small sites characterized by the presence of sherds of the corded *pithoi* class. These are found in association with surface scatters of impasto pottery which can be plausibly interpreted as pertaining to farmsteads. Recent geophysical research and excavations have indeed revealed that these scatters can be linked to subsurface architecture (de Neef 2016). The storage practices using these large *pithoi* started in the Recent Bronze Age at the end of the fourteenth century BCE and lasted into the tenth century BCE. The presence of these corded *pithoi* in the landscape has two important implications. One relates to the internalization of technologically advanced Aegean pottery practices in local workshops to produce these huge vessels in tempered clays as well as in depurated clays. The other relates to socio-economic structure.

The first implication is based on the complex production of corded *pithoi*. In a recent paper on economy and storage strategies at Troy, Diane Thumm-Doğrayan and others discuss the production, transport, and use of *pithoi*, which they classify as 'the most difficult among ceramic production requiring the knowledge of complicated procedures' (Thumm-Doğrayan and others 2019, 183). The adoption of the corded *pithos* in the agricultural economy of the Sibaritide is therefore an achievement that could only take place in a social learning environment that was receptive to advanced pottery technology, knowledge of modes of transport, and in an economic system geared towards surplus production. From this perspective, the corded *pithoi* can be considered part of a locally adopted Aegean ceramic package.

The second implication is based on the storage capacity of these vessels. On account of their dimensions and their occurrence in designated storage spaces, Bronze Age *pithoi* are often related to redistributive economic forms in the world of the Aegean palatial economies (Iacono 2016). However, our recent surveys in the foothills of the Sibaritide have shown that the corded *pithoi* are associated with small domestic sites in the countryside.[56] At the same time, storerooms — albeit of modest size if compared to Aegean examples — are also known to have existed at larger settlements, as at Broglio di Trebisacce.[57] While the presence of surplus storage capacity, in proto-urban and rural contexts in Late Bronze Age Sibaritide, implies that economic complexity was already established by the Final Bronze Age, and therefore acquired earlier, the contexts of the corded *pithoi* do not fit a centralized redistributive model, such as that found in the Aegean. In fact, the palatial redistributive model, as famously put forward by Colin Renfrew (1972) in his *Emergence of Civilization*, is currently being criticized for being too restrictive, based on fieldwork results of the last decades. The picture that emerges of Crete's Bronze Age economy — as put forward in a recent paper by Christakis (2011), for instance — is one of socio-economic diversity and multi-scalar complexity. We also refer to Alberti and others' (2019) study of the food economy of the town of Malia and its hinterland on Crete. They state that families involved in primary food production made up the greater part of the population, by a significant margin, producing food in very different rural and urban situations. Also, they note how the status of farmers varied, from wholly dependent on the palatial economy to entirely independent of it. In this vein, we may also interpret the complex socio-economic patterns that appear from the archaeological record now available for the Sibaritide and southern Italy more generally.

In the absence of palace economies in the Sibaritide, we can either follow Peroni's model of a strong nexus between proto-urban settlements with local elites and a dependent productive countryside, where peasant families produced olive and wine for redistribution, or think in terms of a hybrid economy as proposed by Alberti and others with a more independent role for farming families. In both cases, storage practices would have been supported by specialists who produced *pithoi*. The fact that the latter were produced in various fabrics suggests the existence of several production places providing for the needs of the population in the major and long-duration sites, but also of dispersed rural settlements, such as the large cluster of such sites at Contrada Damale found in the surveys of the Raganello Archaeological Project.[58] It also shows the longer-term effect of the mechanism of cultural transmission. The agents responsible for the initial knowledge transfer of the manufacturing of *pithoi* must have either been potters of Aegean background or local potters who had been in contact with specialists from the Aegean. Evidence that the production of Aegean-type *pithoi* was initially triggered by the introduction of wine and/or oil production is still thin and what was actually stored in the *pithoi* needs further research.[59]

The end of the Late Bronze Age in the Sibaritide saw the emergence of one further important kind of pottery production, that of matt-painted ceramics. Bridging the Late Bronze Age from 1200 BCE into the Early Iron Age, the production of matt-painted pottery would grow into a highly specialized indigenous enterprise. During the following centuries it was the preferred choice of potters for both domestic and fine ware purposes up to the Archaic period. As can be seen in Figure 14.31, the matt-painted pottery tradition overlaps with the Aegean package. While already known from other sites in the Sibaritide, the prototype of this class in the Proto-Geometric style has now also been found at Timpone della Motta in stratigraphic context, bringing the site in line chronologically with regional developments in pottery production. The mechanism behind this development must be sought in the intensification of connectivity along the Ionian coast, perhaps due to trade and exchange, implying increased regional mobility.

Mechanisms of Adoption and Adaption and their Socio-Economic Implications during the Early Iron Age

Continued receptiveness to innovations in pottery production in the Sibaritide by local workshops is evident from the adoption of the matt-painted tradition between the Late Bronze Age and the late ninth century BCE (Figure 14.32). When, in the eighth century BCE, Euboean pottery reached Timpone della Motta, this resulted in the production of the local derivative of the so-called Oinotrian-Euboean class. The increase, by the eighth century BCE, in the quantity and diversity of ceramics points

---

56 De Neef 2016, de Neef and van Leusen 2016; de Neef and others 2017.

57 Another famous example from south Italy, and more readily comparable to palatial capacity is Roca Vecchia in Puglia (Scarano and Maggiulli 2014 and related literature).

58 De Neef 2016 discusses the various fabrics of the *pithoi* found in the survey of the Contrada Damale.

59 The residue analysis on the *pithos* fragment from Broglio di Trebisacce pointed to vegetable fat, but the laboratory of Tübingen could not distinguish between hazelnut or olive oil. Peroni 1994, 855 n. 59. On the debate on oil production in protohistoric south Italy, Lentjes and Semerari 2016.

to the upscaling of local ceramic production and the existence of multiple specialized workshops, while the frequency of imports testifies to intensification of regional trade. Both were needed to satisfy the increased demand for pottery for various uses: domestic, funerary, and ritual. The latter two domains are particularly well represented by the sanctuary on Timpone della Motta, and the needs of the Macchiabate necropolis increased a specialized demand and presupposes the growth of a market mechanism with multiple stakeholders (artisans, middlemen, and consumers). Combined, these socio-economic developments created a cultural environment in which adoption and adaption in ceramic production may have aligned with economic choices. Indeed, as outlined above, the Oinotrian-Euboean and matt-painted classes of pottery were the result of two fundamentally different production modes, based respectively on a distinct Greek and a distinct indigenous workshop tradition. While the Oinotrian-Euboean products show several indigenous traits, the matt-painted production seemingly remained immune to Greek influences. Only during the second half of the eighth century BCE did the matt-painted potters begin to incorporate Greek-inspired motifs. However, this was not in the Euboean tradition but in the Corinthian geometric tradition with which local matt-painted potters had become familiar through Salentine matt-painted and Corinthian Late Geometric imports. The inclination of the Oinotrian-Euboean workshops to incorporate aspects of indigenous material culture falls within a tradition of targeting non-Greek markets. This was already apparent in the production of Euboean pottery in Greece itself where, for instance, Euboean workshops produced plates with geometric decoration for Phoenician markets in Cyprus and as far away as southern Spain (Boardman 2004). Euboean pottery workshops were apparently versatile in trying to satisfy the demands of their many (overseas) customers. A parallel situation might be drawn in the case of the production of Oinotrian-Euboean vessels at Timpone della Motta. Incorporation of indigenous shapes (*scodelle* and biconical jars) adapted the production to a familiar local repertoire; moreover, the emphasis on wavy line decorations brought it stylistically in line with the decoration scheme on matt-painted vessels; finally, the application of a matt-like paint resembled that of the indigenous matt-painted pottery.

Our studies have shown that, during the eighth century BCE, pottery workshops existed on the lower slopes of Timpone della Motta that produced Oinotrian-Euboean pottery (Figure 14.32). In the Rovitti area, structure A and B have been inter-

preted as potters' dwellings based on the finds of instruments, misfired pottery, and pottery test pieces (Jacobsen and Handberg 2012, 710–11). Currently, we also have evidence for three different kiln sites. Immediately to the west of the Rovitti area, a high concentration of kiln fragments has been recorded and indeed an Iron Age kiln had been partly exposed during road construction of the mid-nineteenth century. As recently as August 2020, a second concentration of kiln fragments was identified at a distance of *c.* 300 m north-west of the Rovitti area. Iron Age pottery fragments found in association with the kiln fragments indicate that pottery was produced in this area contemporary with the production in the Area Rovitti. Indirect evidence for a third kiln site derives from a number of kiln fragments excavated during the 1960s from the Cerchio Reale tumulus on the Macchiabate necropolis. The kiln fragments found here were reused for grave construction and probably collected in the near surroundings of the Macchiabate necropolis (Kleibrink and others 2012a, 8–10). As stated above, further excavations on the slopes of Timpone della Motta may reveal the *kerameikos* that could substantiate our hypotheses on the socio-economic and ethnic complexity of pottery production during the period prior to the Archaic Greek colonial productions.

Before discussing the Archaic period, we need to recall two other Greek-inspired pottery productions dating to the latter part of the eighth century BCE and the beginning of the seventh century BCE, both of which stayed unreceptive to the traditional indigenous material culture. The Ticino Group, as we saw, closely reproduces figure scenery from Attic and Boeotian vase-painting on Greek shapes, uncommon in indigenous matt-painted pottery. In fact, the only hints of indigenous influence can be seen in the application of matt-like paint on some of the vessels belonging to the Ticino Group. The Sub-Thapsos production, on the other hand, was Greek both in shape and lustrous paint and decoration. It was, moreover, executed on a technical level matching the most advanced productions in Greece itself. The introduction of this 'all-Greek' production marks the start of the decline of traditional indigenous pottery production. As such, the Sub-Thapsos group can be regarded as the first truly colonial production in the Sibaritide, starting at the end of the eighth century BCE. However, during all this period, the impasto tradition was kept alive by the potters, as we can see in Table 14.2. We note, however, that a functional diversification developed between the production of table wares, and cooking/storing wares. The former became exclusively manufactured from depurated clays, while the latter could still be executed in impasto.[60] The evidence thus points to an amalgamation of potters with different cultural and technological backgrounds that coexisted at Timpone della Motta and who produced various classes of pottery to satisfy an apparently very diverse demand depending on purpose (domestic, funerary, ritual), social status, and possibly ethnic background. Workshops continued to produce terracotta (horse) figurines, a tradition that started around 1200 BCE and which lasted to the end of the Archaic period (Figure 14.31). Their persistence will have been due to an embedded cultural meaning and/or a function that escapes us, as they appear in domestic, funerary, and ritual contexts.

Mechanisms of Adoption and Adaption and their Socio-economic Implications during the Late Iron Age and Archaic Period

With the beginning of the seventh century BCE, the colonial ceramics began to dominate the previous productions and, in consequence, it becomes increasingly difficult to identify local traits in the pottery productions. It is currently unclear if production of matt-painted pottery continued at Timpone della Motta, but, if it did, it must have been on a much-reduced scale. By now the demand was focused on Greek-style products to cater to the pilgrims visiting the temples on its summit. Misfired pottery from the sanctuary indicates that vessels meant for ritual use were produced in its near vicinity (Figure 14.32). The colonial production is nevertheless to be regarded as a new phenomenon and not as a transformation of previous local productions and traditions. The depopulation of the settlement in the seventh century BCE caused a stop to indigenous productions, which had been shaped by centuries of local and regional vessel traditions and stylistic preferences.[61] The colonial production, now largely replacing the indigenous material culture, was introduced via a permanent and expanding Greek presence in the colonies along the Ionian coast and operated at an increased scale. Consequently, a strong

coherence is notable between the colonial pottery production of Sybaris, the Sibaritide, and the major sites along the Ionian coast in general (Mater 2005; Luberto 2020). We recall here how, towards the end of the seventh century BCE, Timpone della Motta was gradually repopulated; the archaeological record again shows activity in the Macchiabate necropolis and on the settlement plateaus in the first part of the sixth century BCE. It is also from the beginning of the sixth century BCE that we find renewed direct evidence for pottery production in the form of a pottery kiln and misfired pottery from the excavation in Area Aita (Figure 14.32). The caesura in activities on Timpone della Motta may be related to the successful development of the Greek settler colony of Sybaris, that may have at first disrupted and then changed the activities on Timpone della Motta, that in the sixth century BCE centred on the new Greek-style sanctuary replacing the indigenous cult buildings. The local market for pottery production started to expand again to include pottery destined for domestic and funerary purposes, in addition to a, now truly massive, demand for pottery meant for the sanctuary. The repopulation caused, we suggest, a renewed demand for vessels with traits from indigenous material culture.[62] As we have shown, indigenous bichrome matt-painted vessels remained in use in the sanctuary during the seventh century BCE, albeit limited. A part of it appears to have been imported to the north in Calabria, possibly at Amendolara (Saxkjær 2021). These imports continued to reach Timpone della Motta in limited numbers during the sixth century BCE where we find them in non-pottery production related contexts in Area Aita and in the sanctuary.

By the sixth century BCE, the production of matt-painted pottery in southern Italy had undergone fundamental changes through the inclusion of Greek shapes in the indigenous repertoire and the introduction of the fast potter's wheel. One indigenous aspect — the matt-like paint — however, remained unchanged from the Late Bronze Age to the sixth century BCE. We believe the visual appearance of the paint was of cultural importance for the indigenous communities over a vast south Italian area. An importance that, as we have argued, caused Oinotrian-Euboean potters to create a matt paint-looking version of the Oinotrian-Euboean pottery to exploit indigenous market possibilities. The same cultural importance can be seen in the vast

---

60   Currently there is no evidence for impasto workshops. Local impasto production may have remained on household level although there are signs of specialization after 760 BCE.

61   The depopulation is evident from the number of graves that can be assigned to respectively the eighth and seventh centuries BCE, see Luppino and others 2012, 649–50. Outside the sanctuary, limited numbers of burials datable to the first half of the seventh century BCE have been found in Area Aita (unpublished). A discussion of the causes of the depopulation and repopulation of the Timpone della Motta is beyond the scope of the current article.

62   Handberg and Jacobsen 2011, 190–94 suggest that the settlers revitalizing the settlement in the sixth century BCE came from families that had kept on burying their members in the family tumuli at the Macchiabate.

group of miniature vessels with matt bichrome decoration which were probably produced at Timpone della Motta and used in the sanctuary. In the sixth century BCE, Sybaris had become the centre of colonial pottery production, and such pottery was also produced at Timpone della Motta, where, however, local traditions in pottery production were kept alive to meet the demand of the local population. This continuous visibility of different styles and productions throughout the centuries highlights a constellation of diverse groups of people within the area, all of which had a strong connection to Timpone della Motta.

Conclusions

In this chapter, we have, for the first time, discussed the pottery traditions in the Sibaritide from a holistic and *longue durée* perspective, primarily from the viewpoint of local production and with a focus on Timpone della Motta. This we have done in an attempt to clearly elucidate the long-term development and interconnectedness of the main classes of pottery that were introduced and produced in the Sibaritide, and subsequently used in various contexts ranging from domestic to cultic and funerary. Similarities in shapes of different classes, as shown in Table 14.2, indicate how, already in the course of the Bronze Age, a technological environment had developed in which local potters learned about, absorbed, and reproduced traits of foreign productions. While it seems feasible that Aegean artisans were active in Italy producing Italo-Mycenaean pottery, the local makers of impasto pottery were able to imitate Aegean products. Besides indicating the origin of the process of manufacturing new classes of pottery that significantly differed from the impasto tradition, this also points to the changing demographic composition of the communities in southern Italy as melting pots in which local and foreign knowledge came together to form the pottery assemblages that we, as archaeologists, document in our surveys and excavations.

In a recent, posthumously published, paper, Sebastiano Tusa has remarked how knowledge about

Sicily's external contacts, after the end of the first half of the second millennium BCE, helps in the interpretation of the complex historical situation of colonization during the historical period. In the same vein, we think the complex ethnic situation characterizing the Early Iron Age cultures of southern Italy cannot be understood without studying its Bronze Age roots. We hope that the new excavations on additional sites in the Sibaritide that are underway, as well as the continued excavations at Timpone della Motta, will shed more light on the connectedness between the Final Bronze and Early Iron Age. In both cases, the analysis of ceramic assemblages from closed contexts reinforces the study of the relationship between local and imported cultural components and their developments through subsequent phases, in order to frame both the cultural encounters and the circumstances that from the Late Bronze Age ceramic repertoire led to that of the southern Italian Iron Age. As we have shown, adoption and adaption of features continues to take place in the Sibaritide in later Geometric and matt-painted productions, a tradition bridging the Final Bronze Age and Early Iron Age. The recent excavations on the lower slopes of Timpone della Motta provide ample arguments to posit that local production facilities were instrumental in the processes of adoption and adaption of new techniques, shapes, and decorations. Finally, we remark that the development of urban centres, epitomized in the growth of the city of Sybaris taking off in the sixth century BCE, brought a new factor into play: that of a developed market mechanism which eradicated the impasto tradition and replaced it with the standardized production of coarse wares. This increased the proportion of imported pottery, as well as locally produced Greek colonial pottery, forcing a break in a long and complex tradition of overlapping productions. At the same time, we have shown how local potters did keep the matt-painted tradition alive, even if at Timpone della Motta this pottery style died out earlier than in its place of origin, in the Salento region, where it continued for several centuries in a tradition of pottery production that was less dominated by the Greek colonial workshops.

Works Cited

Andaloro, Eliana, Lorena Belfiore, Anna Maria De Francesco, Jan K. Jacobsen, and Gloria Mittica. 2011. 'A Preliminary Archeometric Study of Pottery Remains from the Archaeological Site of Timpone della Motta in the Sibaritide Area (Calabria Southern Italy)', *Journal of Applied Clay Science*, 53.3: 445–53

Arancio, Maria Letizia, Vittoria Buffa, Isabella Damiani, and Flavia Trucco. 2001. 'La classificazione tipologica', in *Torre Mordillo 1987–1990: le relazioni egee di una comunità protostorica della Sibaritide*, ed. by Flavia Trucco and Lucia Vagnetti (Rome: CNR – Istituto per gli Studi Micenei ed Egeo-Anatolici), pp. 155–213

Attema, Peter A. J. 2003. 'From Ethnic to Urban Identities? Greek Colonists and Indigenous Society in the Sibaritide, South Italy. A Landscape Archaeological Approach', in *Constructions of Greek Past*, ed. by Hero Hokwerda (Groningen: Egbert Forsten), pp. 11–23

——. 2017. 'Sedimentation as Geomorphological Bias and Indicator of Agricultural (Un)Sustainability in the Study of the Coastal Plains of South and Central Italy in Antiquity', *Journal of Archaeological Science: Reports*, 15: 459–69

Attema, Peter A. J., and Francesca Ippolito. 2017. 'Il Progetto Archeologico Raganello (RAP). Sviluppo insediativo di lunga durata nell'hinterland della Sibaritide protostorica', in *Centri fortificati indigeni della Calabria dalla Protostoria all'età Ellenistica: atti convegno internazionale, Napoli, 16–17 gennaio 2014*, ed. by Luigi Cicala and Marco Pacciarelli (Naples: Naus), pp. 69–80

Attema, Peter A. J., Gert-Jan Burgers, and P. Martijn van Leusen. 2010. *Regional Pathways to Complexity: Settlement and Land-Use Dynamics in Early Italy from the Bronze Age to the Republican Period* (Amsterdam: Amsterdam University Press)

Babbi, Andrea. 2008. *La piccola plastica fittile antropomorfa dell'Italia antica: dal Bronzo finale all'orientalizzaznte* (Rome: Fabrizio Serra)

——. 2012. ''Ελα, Ύπνε, και Πάρε το … Clay Human Figurines from Early Iron Age Italian Children Tombs and the Aegean Evidence', in *Aθανασία: The Earthly, the Celestial and the Underworld in the Mediterranean from the Late Bronze and the Early Iron Age*, ed. by Nikolaos C. Stampolidis, Athanasia Kanta, and Angeliki Giannikouri (Herakleion: University of Crete), pp. 287–306

Belardelli, Clarissa. 1994a. 'La ceramica grigia', in *Enotri e Micenei nella Sibaritide*, ed. by Renato Peroni and Flavia Trucco (Taranto: Istituto per la storia e l'archeologia della Magna Grecia), pp. 265–346

——. 1994b. 'Nuovi siti e materiali archeologici, Torre del Mordillo (Spezzano Albanese)', in *Enotri e Micenei nella Sibaritide*, ed. by Renato Peroni and Flavia Trucco (Taranto: Istituto per la storia e l'archeologia della Magna Grecia), p. 736

Bérard, Jean. 1965. *La Magna Grecia: storia delle colonie greche dell'Italia meridionale* (Turin: Piccola Biblioteca Einaudi)

Bergonzi, Giovanna, Andrea Cardarelli, Pier Giovanni Guzzo, Renato Peroni, and Lucia Vagnetti. 1982. *Ricerche sulla Protostoria della Sibaritide*, Cahiers du Centre J. Bérard, 7–8, 2 vols (Naples: Centre Jean Bérard)

Berlingò, Irene. 1986. 'La necropoli arcaica di Policoro in Contrada Madonnelle', in *Siris-Polieion: Fonti letterarie e nuova documentazione archeologica* (Galatina: Congedo), pp. 117–27

Bettelli, Marco. 2002. *Italia meridionale e mondo miceneo: ricerche su dinamiche di acculturazione e aspetti archeologici, con particolare riferimento ai versanti adriatico e ionico della penisola italiana*, Grandi contesti e problemi della Protostoria Italiana (Florence: All'Insegna del Giglio)

——. 2009. 'Le ceramiche figuline dell'età del Bronzo: importazioni, imitazioni e derivazioni locali', in *Prima delle colonie: organizzazione territoriale e produzioni ceramiche in Basilicata e Calabria settentrionale ionica nella prima età del ferro; atti delle Giornate di studio Matera, 20–21 novembre 2007*, ed. by Marco Bettelli, Cecilia De Faveri, and Massimo Osanna (Venosa: Osanna), pp. 17–35

Bianco, Salvatore, Pontrandolfo Bottini Angelo, Russo Angela, Alfonsina Tagliente, and Elisabetta Setari (eds). 1996. *I Greci in Occidente: Greci, Enotri e Lucani nella Basilicata meridionale* (Naples: Electa)

Bietti Sestieri, Anna Maria. 2008. 'L'età del Bronzo finale nella penisola italiana', *Padusa*, n.s., 44: 7–54

Blake, Emma. 2014. *Social Networks and Regional Identity in Bronze Age Italy* (Cambridge: Cambridge University Press)

Boardman, John. 2004. 'Copies of Pottery: By and for Whom?', in *Greek Identity in the Western Mediterranean: Papers in Honour of Brian Shefton*, ed. by Kathryne Lomas, Mnemosyne Supplementa (Leiden: Brill), pp. 149–62

Bosana-Kourou, Nota. 1984. 'Some Problems concerning the Origin and the Dating of the Thapsos Class Vases', in *Annuario della Scuola archeologica di Atene e delle Missioni italiane in Oriente*, 61, n.s., 45 (1983): 257–69

Canciani, Fulvio. 2000. 'La ceramica geometrica', in *La ceramica degli Etruschi: la pittura vascolare*, ed. by Marina Martelli (Novara: Istituto geografico de Agostini), pp. 9–15

Cassola Guida, Paola. 2013. 'Figurine fittili antropomorfe nel Bronzo finale italiano', in *Φιλική Συναυλία: Studies in Mediterranean Archaeology for Mario Benzi*, ed. by Gianpaolo Graziadio, Riccardo Guglielmino, Valeria Lenuzza, and Salvatore Vitale, British Archaeological Reports, International Series, 2460 (Oxford: Archaeopress), pp. 239–48

Castoldi, Marina. 2006. *La ceramica geometrica bicroma dell'Incoronata di Metaponto (scavi 1974–1995)*, British Archaeological Reports, International Series, 1474 (Oxford: British Archaeological Reports)

——. 2009. 'L'esplosione della bicromia', in *Prima delle colonie: organizzazione territoriale e produzioni ceramiche specializzate in Basilicata e in Calabria settentrionale ionica nella prima età del Ferro; atti delle giornate di studio Matera 20–21 novembre 2007*, ed. by Marco Bettelli, Cecilia De Faveri, and Massimo Osanna (Venosa: Osanna), pp. 239–46

Christakis, Kostis S. 2011. 'Redistribution and Political Economies in Bronze Age Crete', *American Journal of Archaeology*, 115: 1–9

Colburn, Oliver C. 1977. 'Torre del Mordillo (Cosenza). Scavi negli anni 1963, 1966, e 1967', *Notizie degli scavi di antichità*, 31: 423–526

Coldstream, John Nicholas. 1969. 'Phoenicians at Ialysos', *Bulletin of the Institute of Classical Studies*, 16: 1–8

——. 1998. 'Achaean Pottery around 700 B.C., at Home and in the Colonies', in *Helike*, II: *Ancient Helike and Aigialeia: Proceedings of the Second International Conference, Aigion, 1–3 December 1995*, ed. by Dora Katsonopoulou, Steven Soter, and Demetrius Schilardi (Athens: Helike Society), pp. 323–34

Colelli, Carmelo. 2012. 'Ceramica d'impasto da Francavilla Marittima. Ceramica grigia e altre produzioni ceramiche, circolazione di merci e modelli nella Sibaritide (e in Italia meridionale) nell'età del Ferro' (unpublished doctoral thesis, University of Groningen)

Colelli, Carmelo, and Jan K. Jacobsen. 2013. *Excavation on the Timpone della Motta, Francavilla Marittima (1991–2004): The Iron Age Impasto Pottery*, II, Bibliotheca archaeologica (Bari: Edipuglia)

Colelli, Carmelo, and Francesca Ippolito. 2017. 'Evoluzioni e trasformazioni nella Calabria settentrionale fra il Bronzo finale e la prima età del Ferro', *Enotri e Bretti in magna Grecia: modi e forme di interazione culturale*, II, ed. by in Giovanna De Sensi Sestito and Stefania Mancuso (Catanzaro: Rubbettino, Soveria Mannelli), pp. 3–44

Colombi, Camilla, and Martin Guggisberg. 2016. 'Indigeni e greci prima e dopo Sibari: nuovi dati sulla continuità d'occupazione della necropoli di Macchiabate di Francavilla Marittima', in *Enotri, Greci Bretti nella Sibaritide: atti della giornata di studi in memoria di Silvana Luppino, Rivista dell'Istituto Nazionale d'Archeologia e Storia dell'arte*, 3rd ser., 69: 53–66

De Francesco, Anna Maria, Eliana Andaloro, and Jan K. Jacobsen. 2009. 'Preliminary Results on Ancient Pottery Fabrics from the Archaeological Site of Timpone della Motta, Francavilla Marittima (Cs) Calabria', in *Book of Abstracts for the XIV International Clay Conference, 14 June 2009* (Castellaneta Marina), pp. 33–34

De Francesco, Anna Maria, Eliana Andaloro, and Jan K. Jacobsen. 2012. 'Undulating Band Style and Fringe Style Matt-Painted Pottery from the Sanctuary on the Timpone della Motta in the Sibaritide Area (CS) Calabria – Southern Italy', *Periodico di mineralogia*, 81.2: 145–62

De Francesco, Anna Maria, Eliana Andaloro, Jan K. Jacobsen, and Domenico Miriello. 2009. 'Matt-Painted Pottery from the Archaeological Site Timpone della Motta – Francavilla Marittima (Cs), Calabria – Southern Italy', *Atti del 7° Forum italiano di scienza della terra GEOITALIA 2009, Rimini 9–11 settembre 2009*, III (Rimini: Epitome), p. 273

De Francesco, Anna Maria, Eliana Andaloro, Jan K. Jacobsen, Gloria Mittica, and Emanuela De Stefano. 2012. 'Confronto di differenti ceramiche matt-painted dal Timpone della Motta di Francavilla Marittima (Cs)-Calabria', in *Atti del VI Congresso nazionale di archeometria scienza e beni culturali, Pavia 2010*, ed. by Maria Pia Riccardi and Elena Basso (Bologna: Pàtron), pp. 1–9

De Juliis, Ettore M., Fabio Galeandro, and Palmentola Paola. 2006. *La ceramica geometrica della Messapia* (Rome: La Biblioteca by ASPPI)

De Lachenal, Lucilla. 2007. 'Francavilla Marittima. Per una storia degli studi', in *La dea di Sibari e il Santuario ritrovato: studi sui rinvenimenti dal Timpone della Motta di Francavilla Marittima*, I.1: *Ceramiche d'importazione, di produzione coloniale e indigena*, ed. by Frederike van der Wielen-van Ommeren, and Lucilla De Lachenal, Bollettino d'arte, special volume (Rome: Poligrafica e zecca dello stato), pp. 17–81

Denti, Mario. 2018. 'Aegean Migrations and the Indigenous Iron Age Communities on the Ionian Coast of Southern Italy: Sharing and Interaction Phenomena', in *The Emporion in the Ancient Western Mediterranean: Trade and Colonial Encounters from the Archaic to the Hellenistic Period*, ed. by Eric Gailledrat, Rosa Plana Mallart, and Michael Dietler (Mauguio: Presses universitaires de la Méditerranée), pp. 207–17

Descoeudres, Jean Paul. 1981. *Corpus vasorum antiquorum: Schweiz; Basel, Antikenmuseum; Schweiz – Faszikel 4; Basel – Faszikel 1* (Bern: Lang)

Dickinson, Oliver T. P. K. 2020. 'Evidence from Archaeology', in *A Companion to the Archaeology of Early Greece and the Mediterranean*, ed. by Irene S. Lemos and Antonis Kotsonas (Hoboken: Wiley-Blackwell), pp. 33–53

Donnellan, Lieve. 2016. 'A Networked View on "Euboean" Colonisation', in *Conceptualising Early Colonisation*, ed. by Lieve Donnellan, Valentino Nizzo, and Gert-Jan Burgers (Rome: Belgisch Historisch Instituut te Rome), pp. 149–66

Donnellan, Lieve, Valentino Nizzo, and Gert-Jan Burgers. 2016a. *Conceptualising Early Colonisation* (Rome: Belgisch Historisch Instituut te Rome)

——. 2016b. *Contexts of Early Colonisation*, Mededelingen van het Koninklijk Nederlands Instituut te Rome, 64 (Rome: Palombi)

Elevelt, Stefan. 2002. 'De Dolia van Francavilla Marittima, Zuid-Italië', *Paleo-Aktueel*, 13: 74–77

Esposito, Arianna, and Airton Pollini. 2016. 'Postcolonialism from America to Magna Graecia', in *Espaces sacrés et espaces de production: quelles interactions dans les nouvelles fondations? Colloque international (Napoli, 21–22 octobre 2016)*, ed. by Arianna Esposito and Airton Pollini (Naples: Centre Jean Bérard), pp. 61–76

Fasanella Masci, Marianna. 2016. 'La produzione della ceramica geometrica enotria nella Sibaritide. Studio comparativo sulle tecnologie di foggiatura' (unpublished doctoral thesis, University of Groningen)

Feiken, Hendrik. 2014. 'Dealing with Biases. Three Geo-archaeological Approaches to the Hidden Landscapes of Italy' (unpublished doctoral thesis, University of Groningen)

Ferranti, Francesca. 2014. 'Il vasellame di ceramica depurata', in *Museo dei Bretti e degli Enotri: catalogo dell'esposizione* (Catanzaro: Rubbettino, Soveria Mannelli), pp. 85–91

Gadolou, Anastasia. 2011. *Thapsos-Class Ware Reconsidered: The Case of Achaea in the Northern Peloponnese; Pottery Workshop or Pottery Style?*, British Archaeological Reports, International Series, 2279 (Oxford: British Archaeological Reports)

——. 2017. 'Thapsos-Class Pottery Style: A Language of Common Communication between the Corinthian Gulf Communities', in *Material Koinai in the Greek Early Iron Age and Archaic Period: Acts of an International Conference at the Danish Institute at Athens, Athens, 30 January – 1 February 2015*, ed. by Søren Handberg and Anastasia Gadolou (Aarhus: Aarhus University Press), pp. 323–42

Granese, Maria Tommasa, and Luigia Tomay. 2008. 'Immagine e rituali nel santuario arcaico di Francavilla Marittima', in *Image et religion dans l'antiquité gréco-romaine: actes du colloque de Rome, 11–13 décembre 2003*, ed. by Sylvia Estienne, Dominique Jaillard, Natacha Lubtchansky, and Claude Pouzadoux (Naples: Centre Jean Bérard), pp. 137–52

Guggisberg, Martin. 2018. 'Returning Heroes: Greek and Native Interaction in (Pre-)Colonial South Italy and Beyond', *Oxford Journal of Archaeology*, 72.2: 165–83

Guggisberg, Martin, and Camilla Colombi (eds). 2021. *Macchiabate, 1: Ausgrabungen in der Nekropole von Francavilla Marittima, Kalabrien 2009–2016: Die Areale Strada und De Leo* (Wiesbaden: Reichert)

Guggisberg, Martin, Camilla Colombi, and Nobert Spichtig. 2012. 'Gli scavi dell'Università di Basilea nella necropoli enotria di Francavilla Marittima', *Bollettino d'arte*, 15: 1–18

——. 2016. 'Basler Ausgrabungen in Francavilla Marittima (Kalabrien). Bericht über die Kampagne 2015', *Antike Kunst*, 59: 53–65

——. 2018. 'Basler Ausgrabungen in Francavilla Marittima (Kalabrien). Bericht über die Kampagne 2017', *Antike Kunst*, 61: 73–87

Guggisberg, Martin, Marta Billo-Imbach, and Nobert Spichtig. 2020. 'Basler Ausgrabungen in Francavilla Marittima (Kalabrien), Bericht über die Kampagne 2019', *Antike Kunst*, 63: 93–104

Guzzo, Pier Giovanni. 2016. *Le Città di Magna Grecia e di Sicilia dal VI al I secolo, 1: La Magna Grecia* (Rome: Scienze e lettere)

——. 2020. 'Su un frammento figurato dal Timpone Motta di Francavilla Marittima presso Sibari', *Mitteilungen des Deutschen Archäologischen Instituts: Römische Abteilung*, 126: 205–15

Handberg, Søren, and Jan K. Jacobsen. 2011. 'Greek or Indigenous? From Potsherd to Identity in Early Colonial Encounters', in *Communicating Identity in Italic Iron Age Communities*, ed. by Margarita Gleba and Helle W. Horsnæs (Oxford: Oxbow), pp. 175–94

Herring, Edward. 1998. *Explaining Change in the Matt-Painted Pottery of Southern Italy: Cultural and Social Explanations for Ceramic Development from the 11th to the 4th Centuries B.C.*, British Archaeological Reports, International Series, 722 (Oxford: British Archaeological Reports)

Hodos, Tamar. 2006. *Local Responses to Colonization in the Iron Age Mediterranean* (London: Routledge)

Iacono, Francesco. 2015. 'Feasting at Roca: Cross-Cultural Encounters and Society in the Southern Adriatic during the Late Bronze Age', *European Journal of Archaeology*, 18.2: 259–81

——. 2016. 'From Networks to Society: Pottery Style and Hegemony in Bronze Age Southern Italy', *Cambridge Archaeological Journal*, 26.1: 121–40

Ippolito, Francesca. 2016. 'Before the Iron Age: The Oldest Settlement in the Sibaritide, Calabria (Italy)' (unpublished doctoral thesis, University of Groningen)

Ippolito, Francesca, and Peter A. J. Attema. Forthcoming (a). 'The Potential of Impasto Pottery Studies for Understanding Regional Settlement Dynamics, Cultural Transmission and Connectivity in Bronze Age Landscapes in Italy', *Proceedings International Mediterranean Workshop 'Field, Sherds and Scholars, Recording and Interpreting Survey Ceramics'* (Athens, 24–25 February 2017)

Ippolito, Francesca, and Peter A. J. Attema. Forthcoming (b). 'Nuovi dati sulla diffusione dei dolii protostorici d'impasto nell'hinterland della Sibaritide', in *Volume in memoria di Renato Peroni* (Rome)

Jacobsen, Jan K. 2007. 'Greek Pottery on the Timpone della Motta and the Sibaritide *c.* 780 to 620 BC. Reception, Distribution, and an Evaluation of Greek Pottery as a Source Material for the Study of Greek Influence before and after the Founding of Ancient Sybaris' (unpublished doctoral thesis, University of Groningen)

——. 2013. 'Consumption and Production of Greek Pottery in the Sibaritide during the 8th Century BC', in *Vessels and Variety: New Aspects of Danish Research in Ancient Pottery*, ed. by Hanne Thomansen, Annette Rathje, and Kristine Bøggild Johannsen, Acta Hyperborea, 13 (Copenhagen: Museum Tusculanum Press), pp. 1–24

Jacobsen, Jan K., and Søren Handberg. 2010. *Excavation on the Timpone della Motta, Francavilla Marittima (1992–2004)*, I: *The Greek Pottery*, Bibliotheca archaeologica (Bari: Edipuglia)

——. 2012. 'A Greek Enclave at the Iron Age Settlement of Timpone della Motta', in *Atti del 50° Convegno di Studi sulla Magna Grecia (Taranto, 1–4 ottobre 2010)* (Taranto: Istituto per la storia e l'archeologia della Magna Grecia), pp. 683–718

Jacobsen, Jan K., Søren Handberg, and Gloria P. Mittica. 2009. 'An Early Euboean Workshop in the Sibaritide', *AION*, n.s., 15–16: 89–96

Jacobsen, Jan K., Francesca Ippolito, Gloria Mittica, and Søren Handberg. 2015. 'Greek and Greek Style Pottery in the Sibaritide during the 8th Century B.C.', in *Early Iron Age Communities of Southern Italy*, ed. by Giulia Saltini Semerari and Gert-Jan Burgers, Papers of the Royal Netherlands Institute in Rome, 63 (Rome: Palombi), pp. 151–75

Jacobsen, Jan K., and Gloria Mittica. 2019. 'L'insediamento abitativo dell'età del Ferro. Area Aita: ricerche e scavi 2017–2018', in *Francavilla Marittima un patrimonio ricontestualizzato*, ed. by Gloria Mittica (Vibo Valentia: Adhoc), pp. 87–95

——. In press. 'Cultural Dynamics and Religious Transformation in the Sibaritide *c.* 800–680 BC', in *AION Proceedings of the 2nd Euboica Meeting (Ischia, 14–17 maggio 2018)*, ed. by Matteo D'Acunto (Napoles: AION)

Jacobsen, Jan K., Sine G. Saxkjær, and Gloria Mittica. 2017. 'Observations on Euboean Koinai in Southern Italy', in *Material Koinai in the Greek Early Iron Age and Archaic Period*, ed. by Søren Handberg and Anastasia Gadolou, Monographs of the Danish Institute at Athens, 22 (Aarhus: Aarhus University Press), pp. 169–90

Jacobsen, Jan K., Peter A. J. Attema, Carmelo Colelli, Francesca Ippolito, Gloria Mittica, and Sine G. Saxkjær. 2018. 'The Bronze and Iron Age Habitation on Timpone della Motta in the Light of Recent Research', *Analecta Romana Instituti Danici*, 43: 25–90

Jones, Richard J., Sara T. Levi, Marco Bettelli, and Lucia Vagnetti. 2014. *Italo-Mycenaean Pottery: The Archaeological and Archaeometric Dimensions*, Incunabula Braeca, 103 (Rome: CNR – Istituto di studi sul Mediterraneo antico)

Jones, Richard J., Sara T. Levi, Marco Bettelli, and Valentina Cannavò. 2021. 'Italo-Mycenaean and Other Aegean-Influenced Pottery in Late Bronze Age Italy: The Case for Regional Production', *Archaeological and Anthropological Science*, 13: 23 <https://doi.org/10.1007/s12520-020-01245-5>

Jucker, Hans. 1982. 'Göttin im Gehäuse und eine neue Vase aus der Gegend von Metapont', in *Απαρχαι: Nuove ricerche e studi sulla Magna Grecia e la Sicilia antica in onore di Paolo Enrico Arias*, ed. by Luigi Beschi, Giorgio Gualandi, Luciano Massei, and Salvatore Settis (Pisa: Giardini), pp. 75–84

Jung, Reinhard, and Marco Pacciarelli. 2016. 'A Minoan Statuette from Punta di Zambrone in Southern Calabria', *Metaphysis: Ritual, Myth and Symbolism in the Aegean Bronze Age; Proceedings of the 15th International Aegean Conference, Vienna, 22–25 April 2014*, ed. by Eva Alram-Stern, Fritz Blakolmer, Sigrid Deger-Jalkotzy, Robert Laffineur, and Jörg Weilhartner, *Aegaeum*, 39: 29–36

Kleibrink, Marianne. 2001. 'The Search for Sybaris: An Evaluation of Historical and Archaeological Evidence', *BABESCH: Annual Papers on Mediterranean Archaeology*, 76: 33–70

——. 2006a. *Oenotrians at Lagaria near Sybaris: A Native Proto-urban Centralised Settlement*, Accordia Specialist Studies on Italy, 11 (London: Accordia Research Institute, University of London)

——. 2006b. 'Athenaion Context AC22A.11. A Useful Dating Peg for the Confrontation of Oenotrian and Corinthian Late and Sub Geometric Pottery from Francavilla Marittima', in *Studi in onore di Renato Peroni*, ed. by Andrea Cardarelli, Marco Pacciarelli, and Alessandro Vanzetti (Florence: All'Insegna del Giglio), pp. 146–55

——. 2015a. *Excavations at Francavilla Marittima 1991–2004: Matt-Painted Pottery from the Timpone della Motta*, IV: *The Miniature Style*, British Archaeological Reports, International Series, 2734 (Oxford: British Archaeological Reports)

——. 2015b. *Excavations at Francavilla Marittima 1991–2004: Matt-Painted Pottery from the Timpone della Motta*, III: *The Fringe Style*, British Archaeological Reports, International Series, 2733 (Oxford: British Archaeological Reports)

——. 2015c. 'Crateri e crateri-pissidi attribuiti al Pittore di Francavilla Marittima e uso rituale di tali recipienti', in *Atti della XIV giornata archeologica francavillese*, ed. by Pino Altieri (Rende: Universal Book), pp. 20–79

——. 2016a. 'Tra mito e storia. Elementi di dibattito sulla realtà archeologica di Francavilla Marittima (Lagaria)', in *Atti della XV giornata archeologica francavillese*, ed. by Pino Altieri (Rende: Universal Book), pp. 18–68

——. 2016b. 'Into Bride Ritual as an Element of Urbanization: Iconographic Studies of Objects from the Timpone Della Motta, Francavilla Marittima', *Journal of the Classical Association of Canada*, 3rd ser., 13.2: 235–92

——. 2017. 'Architettura e rituali nell'Athenaion di Lagaria – Timpone della Motta (Francavilla Marittima)', *Atti e memorie della Società Magna Grecia*, 2: 171–234

——. 2020. 'Crateri e crateri-pissidi attribuiti al Pittore di Francavilla Marittima e uso rituale di tali recipienti', in *Atti XIV giornata archeologica francavillese: omaggio a Silvana Luppino*, ed. by Pino Altieri (Rende: Universal Book), pp. 20–79

Kleibrink, Marianne, Søren Handberg, and Jan K. Jacobsen. 2004. 'I kanthariskoi di Lagaria (Francavilla Marittima)', in *Atti della III giornata archeologica francavillese* (Rende: Universal Book), pp. 21–35

Kleibrink, Marianne, Lucilla Barresi, and Marianna Fasanella Masci. 2012a. *Excavations at Francavilla Marittima 1991–2004: Matt-Painted Pottery from the Timpone della Motta, I: The Undulating Band Style*, British Archaeological Reports, International Series, 2423 (Oxford: British Archaeological Reports)

——. 2012b. 'The "Crosshatched Bands Style" and the "Undulating Bands Style". Two Italic Middle Geometric Matt-Painted Pottery Styles from the Timpone della Motta (Francavilla Marittima)', *Antike Kunst*, 55: 3–24

Kleibrink, Marianne, and Elizabeth Weistra. 2013. 'Una dea della rigenerazione, della fertilità e del matrimonio. Per una ricostruzione della dea precoloniale della Sibaritide', in *Sibari: archeologia, storia, metafora*, ed. by Giorgio Delia and Tullio Masneri (Castrovillari: Il Coscile), pp. 35–55

Kleibrink, Marianne, Marianna Fasanella Masci, and Lucilla Barresi. 2013. *Excavations at Francavilla Marittima 1991–2004: Matt-Painted Pottery from the Timpone della Motta, II: The Cross-Hatched Bands Style*, British Archaeological Reports, International Series, 2553 (Oxford: British Archaeological Reports)

Lattanzi, Elena. 1984. 'Documenti micenei dalla Motta. I. Il rinvenimento', in *Atti e memorie della Società Magna Grecia*, 24–25: 157

Lentjes, Daphne, and Giulia Saltini Semerari. 2016. 'Big Debates over Small Fruits, Wine and Oil Production in Protohistoric Southern Italy (ca 1350–750 BC)', *BABESCH: Annual Papers on Mediterranean Archaeology*, 91: 1–16

Leusen, Martijn van, and Francesca Ippolito. 2018. 'Progetto Pilota Monte San Nicola – Civita (CS), Campagna di scavo 2018', Poster, 58° Convegno internazionale di studi sulla Magna Grecia (27–30 September), Taranto

——. 2021. 'Tracing the Final Bronze Age–Early Iron Age Transition. Groningen Institute of Archaeology Settlement Excavations in the Sibaritide (2018–2019)', *Palaeohistoria*, 61–62 (2019–2020): 141–68

Levi, Sara Tiziana, Salvatore Bianco, Maria Antonietta Castagna, Dora Gatti, Richard Jones, Lorenzo Lazzarini, Emilia Le Pera, Luigi Odoguardi, Renato Peroni, Andrea Schiappelli, Maurizio Sonnino, Lucia Vagnetti, and Alessandro Vanzetti. 1999. *Produzione e circolazione della ceramica nella Sibaritide protostorica: impasto e dolii, Prima di Sibari* (Florence: All'Insegna del Giglio)

Luberto, Maria Rosaria. 2020. *Ceramiche arcaiche da Sibari, Crotone e Caulonia: importazioni e produzioni coloniali tra la metà dell'VIII e la fine del VI sec. a.C.*, Fondazione Paestum, Tekmeria, 19 (Paestum: Pandemos)

Lucas, Jason, Carrie Ann Murray, and Sara Owen. 2019. *Greek Colonization in Local Contexts*, University of Cambridge Museum of Classical Archaeology, Monograph, 4 (Oxford: Oxbow)

Luppino, Silvana, Francesco Quondam, Maria Tommasa Granese, and Alessandro Vanzetti. 2012. 'Sibaritide: riletture di alcuni contesti funerari tra VIII e VII sec. a.C.', *Origini*, 2012: 645–82

Mater, Benoît, and Maria Beatrice Annis. 2002. 'Some Reflections on the Meaning of Pottery within Landscape and Settlement Archaeology', in *New Developments in Italian Landscape Archaeology: Theory and Methodology of Field Survey, Land Evaluation and Landscape Perception, Pottery Production and Distribution; Conference Proceedings, University of Groningen, April 13–15, 2000*, ed. by Peter A. J. Attema, Gert-Jan Burgers, Esther Van Joolen, Martijn van Leusen, and Mater Benoît, British Archaeological Reports, International Series, 1091 (Oxford: British Archaeological Reports), pp. 155–68

Mercuri, Laurence. 2004. *Eubéens en Calabre à l'époque Archaïque: formes de contacts et d'implantation*, Bibliothèque des Écoles françaises d'Athènes et de Rome, 321 (Rome: École française de Rome)

——. 2012. 'Calabria e area euboica', in *Atti del Convegno di studi sulla Magna Grecia, Taranto, 1–4 ottobre 2010* (Taranto: Istituto per la storia e l'archeologia della Magna Grecia), pp. 971–84

Mesoudi, Alex, and Michael J. O'Brien. 2008. 'The Cultural Transmission of Great Basin Projectile-Point Technology I: An Experimental Simulation', *American Antiquity*, 73.1: 3–28

Mittica, Gloria. 2010. 'Produzioni ceramiche ed analisi dei contesti archeologici. L'abitato enotrio di Timpone della Motta, Francavilla Marittima (CS)' (unpublished doctoral thesis, Scuola di Specializzazione in Archeologia Classica, Università del Salento)

Mittica, Gloria, Søren Handberg, and Jan K. Jacobsen. 2006. 'Campagna di studio dei materiali dal Timpone della Motta 2006', in *Atti della V giornata archeologia francavillese*, ed. by Pino Altieri (Rende: Universal Book), pp. 27–29

Mittica, Gloria, Rikke Christiansen, Jan K. Jacobsen, Mikkel W. Jørgensen, Giovanni Murro, and Nicoletta Perrone. 2021. 'Area Aita di Timpone della Motta tra l'età del Ferro ed il periodo arcaico', in *Dal Pollino all'Orsomarso: ricerche archeologiche fra Ionio e Tirreno; atti del convegno internazionale, San Lorenzo Bellizzi, 4–6 ottobre 2019*, Analecta Romana Instituti Danici. Supplementum, 56 (Rome: Quasar), pp. 211–22, 127–36

Morris, Ian. 2005. 'Mediterraneanization', in *Mediterranean Paradigms and Classical Antiquity*, ed. by Irad Malkin (London: Routledge), pp. 30–55

Mountjoy, Penelope A. 1986. *Mycenaean Decorated Pottery: A Guide to Identification*, Studies in Mediterranean Archaeology, 73 (Goteborg: Åström)

——. 1999. *Regional Mycenaean Decorated Pottery* (Rahden: Leidorf)

Neef, Wieke de. 2013. 'Het Paard van Cerchiara', *Paleo-aktueel*, 24: 51–57

——. 2016. 'Surface, Subsurface. A Methodological Study of Metal Age Settlement and Land Use in Calabria, Italy' (unpublished doctoral thesis, University of Groningen)

Neef, Wieke de, Kayt Armstrong, and Martijn van Leusen. 2017. 'Putting the Spotlight on Small Metal Age Pottery Scatters in Northern Calabria (Italy)', *Journal of Field Archaeology*, 42.4: 283–97

Neeft, Cornelis Willem. 1987. *Protocorinthian Subgeometric Aryballoi*, Allard Pierson Series, 7 (Amsterdam: Allard Pierson Museum)

Nijboer, Albert J. 2016. 'Is the Tangling of Events in the Mediterranean around 770–60 B.C. in the Conventional Absolute Chronology (CAC) a Reality or a Construct?', in *Contexts of Early Colonisation*, ed. by Lieve Donnellan, Valentino Nizzo, and Gert-Jan Burgers, Mededelingen van het Koninklijk Nederlands Instituut te Rome, 64 (Rome: Palombi), pp. 35–47

Panichelli, Stefania, and Lucia Vagnetti. 1994. 'Ceramica egea importata e di produzione locale', in *Enotri e Micenei nella Sibaritide*, ed. by Renato Peroni and Flavia Trucco (Taranto: Istituto per la storia e l'archeologia della Magna Grecia), pp. 373–413

Papadopoulos, John K. 2001. 'Magna Achaian Late Geometric and Archaic Pottery in South Italy and Sicily', *Hesperia*, 70: 373–460

——. 2003. 'The Achaian Vapheio Cup and its Afterlife in Archaic South Italy', *Oxford Journal of Archaeology*, 22: 411–23

Papapostolou, I. 1968. 'Παρατηρήσεις ἐπὶ γεωμετρικῶν ἀγγείων ἐξ Ἰαλυσοῦ', *Archaiologikon Deltion*, 23 A: 77–98

Peroni, Renato, and Flavia Trucco. 1994. *Enotri e Micenei nella Sibaritide*, 2 vols (Taranto: Istituto per la storia e l'archeologia della Magna Grecia)

Posamentir, Richard, Leonhard Geißler, Kai Riehle, and Hans Mommsen. In print. 'Ionians East and West: Differences according to the Pottery Evidence', in *Ionians in the West and East: Proceedings of the International Conference 'Ionians in East and West', Museu d'Arqueologia de Catalunya-Empuries, Empuries/L'Escala, Spain, 26–29 October 2015*, ed. by Gocha R. Tsetshkladze, Colloquia antiqua, 27

Quondam, Francesco. 2009. 'La necropolis di Francavilla Marittima tra mondo indigeno e colonizzazione greca', in *Prima delle colonie: organizzazione territorial e produzioni ceramiche spcializzate in Basilicata e in Calabria settentrionale ionica nalle prima età del ferro; atti delle Giornate di Studio, Matera, 20–21 novembre 2007*, ed. by Marco Bettelli, Cecilia De Faveri, and Massimo Osanna (Venosa: Osanna), pp. 139–78

——. 2014. 'Il mondo indigeno della Sibaritide all'alba della colonizzazione greca', *Rivista dell'istituto nazionale d'archeologia e storia dell'arte*, 69: 15–52

Renfrew, Colin. 1972. *The Emergence of Civilization: The Cyclades and the Aegean in the Third Millennium* BC (London: Methuen)

Saxkjær, Sine G. 2013. 'A Figure-Decorated Plate from the Sanctuary on the Timpone della Motta', *Acta Hyperborea*, 13: 179–95

——. 2021. 'Considerations of the Narrow-Necked Jugs from Amendolara and their Cultural Significance', in *Dal Pollino all'Orsomarso: ricerche archeologiche fra Ionio e Tirreno*, ed. by Gloria Mittica, Carmelo Colelli, Antonio Larocca, Felice Larocca, Analecta supplementa (Rome: Quasar), pp. 199–210

——. Forthcoming. 'Greek-Style Pottery', in *Excavation on the Timpone della Motta, 1992–2004*, III: *Oinotrian-Euboean and Greek-Style Pottery*, ed. by Gloria Mittica, Jan K. Jacobsen, and Sine G. Saxkjær, Bibliotheca archaeologica (Bari: Edipuglia)

Settis, Salvatore, and Maria Cecilia Parra. 2005. *Magna Graecia: archeologia di un sapere* (Milan: Electa)

Stoop, Maria Wilhelmina. 1970–1971. 'Santuario di Athena sul Timpone della Motta', *Atti del Convegno di studi sulla Magna Grecia*, 11–12: 37–66

——. 1974–1976. 'Francavilla Marittima, Acropoli sulla Motta', *Atti del Convegno di studi sulla Magna Grecia*, 15–17: 107–67

——. 1979. 'Note sugli scavi nel santuario di Atena sul Timpone della Motta (Francavilla Marittima – Calabria), 1–2', *BABESCH: Annual Papers on Mediterranean Archaeology*, 54: 77–97

——. 1983. 'Note sugli scavi nel santuario di Atena sul Timpone della Motta (Francavilla Marittima – Calabria), 4', *BABESCH: Annual Papers on Mediterranean Archaeology*, 58: 19–52

——. 1988. 'Note sugli scavi nel santuario di Atena sul Timpone della Motta (Francavilla Marittima – Calabria), 8', *BABESCH: Annual Papers on Mediterranean Archaeology*, 63: 77–102

——. 1989. 'Note sugli scavi nel santuario di Atena sul Timpone della Motta (Francavilla Marittima – Calabria), 9', *BABESCH: Annual Papers on Mediterranean Archaeology*, 64: 50–60

——. 1990. 'Note sugli scavi nel santuario di Atena sul Timpone della Motta (Francavilla Marittima – Calabria), 10', *BABESCH: Annual Papers on Mediterranean Archaeology*, 65: 29–43

Taliano Grasso, Armando, and Damiano Pisarra. 2019. 'I pendagli a coppia antropomorfa', *Atti e memorie della Società Magna Grecia*, 5th ser., 3: 261–89

Tenaglia, Paola. 1994. 'I dolii cordonati', in *Enotri e Micenei nella Sibaritide*, ed. by Renato Peroni and Flavia Trucco (Taranto: Istituto per la storia e l'archeologia della Magna Grecia), pp. 347–71

Thumm-Doğrayan, Diane, Peter Pavúk, and Magda Pieniążek. 2019. 'Economy and Storage Strategies at Troy', in *Country in the City: Agricultural Functions in Protohistoric Urban Settlements (Aegean and Western Mediterranean)*, ed. by Dominique Garcia, Raphaël Orgeolet, Maia Pomadère, and Julien Zurbach (Oxford: Archaeopress), pp. 169–87

Tomay, Luigia, and Maria Tommasa Granese. 2002. 'Ceramiche di tradizione achea della Sibaritide', in *Gli Achei e l'identita etnica degli Achei d'Occidente: atti del convegno Internazionale di Studi (Paestum, 23–25 Febbraio 2001)*, ed. by Emanuele Greco, Tekmeria, 3 (Paestum: Pandemos), pp. 331–56

Trucco, Flavia, and Lucia Vagnetti. 2001. *Torre Mordillo 1987–1990: le relazioni egee di una comunità protostorica della Sibaritide* (Rome: CNR – Istituto per gli Studi Micenei ed Egeo-Anatolici)

Yntema, Douwe. 1990. *The Matt-Painted Pottery of Southern Italy: A General Survey of the Matt-Painted Pottery Styles of Southern Italy during the Final Bronze Age and the Iron Age* (Galatina: Congedo)

——. 2000. 'The Ancient Written Sources and the Archaeology of Early Colonial-Greek Southeastern Italy', *BABESCH: Annual Papers on Mediterranean Archaeology*, 75: 1–49

Vagnetti, Lucia. 1984. 'Documenti micenei dalla Motta. II. Descrizione e inquadramento', *Atti del convegno di studi sulla Magna Grecia*, 24–25: 158–62

Vagnetti, Lucia, and Stefania Panichelli. 1994. 'Ceramica egea importata e di produzione locale. Catalogo', in *Enotri e Micenei nella Sibaritide*, ed. by Renato Peroni and Flavia Trucco (Taranto: Istituto per la storia e l'archeologia della Magna Grecia), pp. 373–93

Vanzetti, Alessandro. 2013. 'Sibari Protostorica', in *Sibari: archeologia, storia, metafora*, ed. by Giorgio Delia and Tullio Masneri (Castrovillari: Il Coscile), pp. 11–33

Wielen-van Ommeren, Frederike van der, and Lucilla De Lachenal (eds). 2008. *La Dea di Sibari e il Santuario ritrovato: studi sui rinvenimenti dal Timpone Motta di Francavilla Marittima, 1.2: Ceramiche di importazione, di produzione coloniale e indigena*, Bollettino d'arte, special volume (Rome: Poligrafica e zecca dello stato)

Wijngaarden, Gert-Jan van. 2002. *Use and Appreciation of Mycenaean Pottery in the Levant, Cyprus and Italy (1600–1200 BC)* (Amsterdam: Archaeological Studies)

Zancani Montuoro, Paola. 1966. 'Coppie dell'età del ferro in Calabria', *Klearchos*, 29–32: 197–224

——. 1970–1971. 'Francavilla Marittima: A) Necropoli di Macchiabate, coppa di bronzo sbalzata', *Atti e memorie Società Magna Grecia*, 11–12: 9–37

——. 1974–1976. 'Tre notabili enotri dell'VIII secolo a.C.', *Atti del convegno di studi sulla Magna Grecia*, 15–17: 9–106

——. 1977–1979. 'Francavilla Marittima. Necropoli di Macchiabate: saggi e scoperte in zone varie', *Atti del convegno di studi sulla Magna Grecia*, 18–20: 7–91

——. 1980–1982. 'Francavilla Marittima: Necropoli e ceramico a Macchiabate. Zona T. (Temparella)', *Atti del convegno di studi sulla Magna Grecia*, 21–23: 7–130

——. 1983–1984. 'Francavilla Marittima: Necropoli di Macchiabate. Zona T. (Temparella, continuazione)', *Atti del convegno di studi sulla Magna Grecia*, 24–25: 7–110

Index

Acquarossa: 149–57

adaption: 119, 123–26, 128, 132–34, 138–39, 235, 238–41, 250, 262–68

adoption: 19, 21–24, 27–29, 37, 52, 54–55, 68, 85, 101, 105, 109–12, 117, 119–21, 123–25, 132–35, 137–39, 147–48, 161, 198, 221, 223–24, 226–27, 230, 235, 238–41, 250, 262–68

  of children: 25fn

  of criteria: 161, 164–66, 171–73

Aeneas: 37

agency: 22, 24, 28, 48, 50, 52, 71, 96, 101, 112, 139, 154, 223, 229–30, 263

agriculture/agricultural: 22, 26, 35, 121, 162, 165–66, 169, 172–73, 188, 264

alcoholic: 224–25

Aleria/Alalia: 59–61, 64–66

Alps: 21, 187

amber: 127, 182, 187–88, 190

Amykos: 73–75, 77–79

ancestor worship: 35, 42

antefix(es): 88, 91, 151fn, 189, 207, 209–10

Antium: 162–73

Apollo/Suri: 106–08, 110, 112, 151–2fn, 205

Apennines: 26, 126, 186, 190

Apulia: 25, 56fn, 75, 77, 79, 178, 188, 190, 194–95, 197–202, 211fn, 213fn, 246

archaeobotany: 50–51, 54, 56, 224

Archaic period: 54, 85–86, 93–96, 101, 106–07, 109–11, 117, 119, 121–22, 132–34, 138, 144, 161, 163–66, 168, 170fn, 172–73, 178–79, 189–90, 224, 235, 241, 261–63, 265–67

architecture: 22, 35, 40, 60–61, 71, 85–87, 92, 94–96, 120–21, 133–34, 138–39, 147–52, 154, 156, 213, 264

  architectural design: 95

  architectural energetics 147, 151

  Etrusco-Campanian: 189

  Etrusco-Italic: 92, 149fn

  hybrid architecture: 238

  Tuscanic: 85, 88, 90, 92–93, 95

Argonauts: 74, 77–78

artist(s)/artisan(s): 73–78, 152–53, 184, 198, 255, 266, 268

  artisanal: 38

assemblage: 23, 63–64, 77, 80, 95, 107, 123–26, 128, 133, 138, 161, 165–70, 172–73, 177, 223, 225, 227–29, 255, 268

Athena/Minerva/Menrva: 78, 86, 88–89, 92, 106, 108, 110, 112, 179, 210

Athens: 25, 52, 75, 95, 102, 104, 112–13, 153, 193–94, 200fn, 230,

  Athenian: 52, 54, 74, 78, 104–07, 111–12, 193–94, 198–99, 215

Auditorium (villa): 164, 167

banquet/banqueting: 52–54, 65, 101, 107, 109–10, 123, 125–26, 138, 184

  banqueter(s): 105

Bateson, N.: 40

bricolage: 27, 33–34, 40–43

bronze: 27–28, 35, 62, 64, 72, 75–76, 88, 91, 94fn, 111, 127, 135, 182, 184–85, 189, 199, 225, 259fn, 259–60, 260fn

  bronzework(ing)/bronze casting: 23–24, 72, 187

Bronze Age: 21–23, 28, 34–35, 37–38, 40, 48, 55, 59–61, 63, 68, 118, 154, 163–64, 177, 185, 187–88, 224–25, 235, 237, 239–42, 244–46, 249, 259–60, 262–64, 267–68

burial: 34, 36–38, 40–41, 75, 77, 105, 119–21, 123, 133, 138–39, 167fn, 171, 194, 209–11, 213, 224, 239, 242, 260, 262, 267fn

  grounds: 117, 119–22, 124, 134, 138, 260

  see also funerary archaeology, tomb(s)

Caere/Cerveteri: 52–53, 77, 86–88, 90, 93, 102, 104, 126, 137, 139, 164, 171, 178, 184, 197–98, 203, 205, 210fn

  Caeretan: 137, 184, 195–96, 198

Campania/Campanian: 21, 92, 123, 187, 197–99, 209–10, 213, 246

  Campanian Etruria: 188

  Etruscan-Campania/Etrusco-Campanian territory: 183, 190

Carthage/Carthaginian: 25, 27, 37, 55, 60, 62, 65, 67–68

Castelnuovo Berardegna: 150fn

Centocelle: 167

central Italy: 24, 27–28, 33–34, 36, 38–40, 42–43, 50, 71, 75–76, 78–79, 85–86, 101–02, 117, 124, 126–27, 147–48, 150–52, 154, 156, 158, 161–63, 167, 171, 173, 188, 193, 210, 214

    Central Italic/Italian: 22, 24, 27, 34–36, 38, 75, 78, 80, 85, 92–94, 96, 111, 126, 128, 138, 149, 161, 166, 209–10

    Central Italians: 22, 37, 38, 43, 86, 127,

    Central Tyrrhenian Italy: 119, 123fn, 125–26, 128, 130–32, 138–39, 161, 163–64, 166, 171–72, 189

century/centuries (all BCE)

    eighth: 22–24, 28, 52, 61, 63–64, 71, 123, 128, 133–35, 137, 147, 157, 188, 221, 235, 245, 249–50, 254–56, 259–60, 265–67

    seventh: 22–24, 28, 38, 52–53, 61, 63, 66, 68, 71, 76, 111, 117, 121–23, 125, 127fn, 132–34, 137–38, 147–49, 152–58, 164, 170, 177–78, 184–85, 194, 255, 259, 261–62, 266–67

    sixth: 22, 28, 38, 42, 52–55, 61, 63, 71, 76, 88, 90–91, 93–96, 102, 105, 110–12, 117, 120–21, 123fn, 126, 131, 138, 144, 147–48, 151, 153–55, 157–58, 161, 163–65, 168, 171, 177–78, 181, 183–85, 188, 194, 209–10, 227, 229, 239–40, 255, 262, 267–68

    fifth: 21, 55, 63–66, 71, 76–78, 89, 91, 95–96, 102, 104–05, 107, 109, 111–13, 121, 138, 147–48, 150, 153fn, 168, 177–78, 182, 185, 193–94, 199, 209–11, 213–14, 227, 229

    fourth: 38, 55, 59, 66, 71–72, 74–79, 78fn, 89, 107, 110–11, 168fn, 173, 182, 189, 193–99, 202–07, 209–14

Charu(n): 107, 111–12, 203, 205, 207

chronology: 33, 35–36, 49, 117–18, 121fn, 166, 239fn, 249

cinerary urn(s): 105, 109, 112, 206–07, 209, 211

cista: 71–80, 73–74, 199

Classical period: 21, 59, 68, 102, 107, 186–88, 209

colonial: 67, 126, 221–23, 227, 229–30, 235, 239, 255

    pottery: 261–63, 266–68

colonist(s): 23, 28, 48, 221, 223–29

colonization: 60, 65, 67, 222, 235, 239–40, 268

colony/colonies: 28, 61, 67, 199, 255, 261, 267

community: 26, 35–37, 43, 91, 117, 119–21, 123–28, 130, 132, 139, 154fn, 158, 163, 186, 188, 198, 223, 235–36, 238–39, 250–51, 253

connection(s): 20–21, 23–25, 28, 34, 37, 49, 52, 59, 61–66, 71, 77, 85–86, 90, 92–94, 96, 117, 124, 137, 153fn, 183–84, 187, 189, 193, 198, 200, 202, 211, 224, 226–27, 229, 235, 238–39, 241, 255, 261, 268

    interconnection(s): 40, 125

connectivity: 20, 22–23, 49–50, 59–61, 85, 87, 121, 177, 186–87, 189–90, 239, 263, 265

    see also interconnectivity

conservatism: 26, 34, 38, 40, 126

consumption collective(s): 117–19, 123–32, 138–39

Corinth(ian): 24, 52, 54, 118, 151–53, 183, 255, 259, 262

    Proto-Corinthian: 118, 152

Corsica(n): 21, 28, 59–68

countryside: 161, 164, 170–73, 265

cover tiles/imbrices: 151–52

craft(s)/craftwork: 35, 71, 74–75, 78, 151, 153fn, 240fn

craftsperson/craftspeople/craftsmen: 24, 59, 112, 137, 139, 154,

creole/creolizing: 22, 239

Croton: 235fn

Crustumerium: 28, 117, 119–21, 123–28, 130, 132–35, 137–39, 171–73

cultural: 19–29, 33–35, 37–43, 47–48, 51–52, 54, 56, 59–61, 63, 65, 67–68, 72, 74–75, 77–80, 85, 87, 92–95, 101, 106, 117–21, 123–28, 132–33, 137–39, 178, 184, 186, 189–90, 193, 199, 222–24, 228–29, 235, 238–40, 242, 245, 261–68,

    connections: 117, 137, 193, 239

    exchange: 19, 21–22, 28–29, 139

    hybridity: 22, 222, 229, 239

culture: 19–25, 27–29, 34–38, 40, 47–48, 50–51, 56, 63–66, 71fn, 72–75, 78–80, 85–87, 92, 94–95, 101, 110, 112, 117–20, 123–28, 130, 133–34, 138–39, 154, 161, 164, 172, 177, 186–87, 189–90, 193–94, 214, 221, 223, 225, 227–30, 235, 237–40, 253, 255, 261–62, 264, 266–67

dance/dancing: 78, 109–12, 177, 180–83, 185, 189–90, 256

    Tomb of the Dancers: 182

Daunia(n): 178–84, 186–90

Demaratus: 153fn

diffusionism: 51, 54–55, 86, 263

Dindii (gens): 72, 74, 76–77

Dionysian: 43, 106, 109–12, 183, 189, 200, 207, 211fn, 214

    cult: 109, 111

Dionysius of Halicarnassus: 43, 111, 154

Dionysos/Dionysus/Fufluns: 52–53, 78, 106, 109–12, 200–01, 211, 213–14

Dioscuri: 207

    see also Pollux

discrepancies: 66, 68

Dohrn, T.: 72–76, 78

Dumezil, G.: 34–35

Durkheim, E.: 34fn, 39–40, 43fn

dynamics: 23–24, 26, 28–29, 59–60, 66–68, 117, 154, 156, 240fn, 263

eclecticism: 95–96
ecology: 40, 49–50, 55, 177
    microecology: 49
economic(s), economy: 21–22, 25, 34–35, 47, 50, 52, 54–55, 59–61, 63, 65–68, 85, 87, 119, 128, 133, 147–48, 151, 153, 158, 164, 170–71, 187, 189–90, 221, 224, 226, 235, 258–60, 263–67
Elba: 59, 60, 63–64, 67
elite(s): 22, 26, 35–38, 42, 47, 54, 73, 75–78, 80, 108, 117, 120, 138, 154, 163, 173, 184, 188–89, 205, 241, 265
elpis: 211, 213
Elymi/Elymian: 28, 221–22, 224–28, 230
engrave/engraving: 37, 72, 74–77, 79–80, 199
entanglement: 22, 26, 50, 79–80, 95, 124–25, 221–23, 225, 228–30
Epicharmos: 77
Eryx: 222–23
eschatology/eschatological: 101, 106–08, 110–13, 193, 199
ethnic/ethnicity: 20, 24, 94, 186–87, 199, 214, 227, 266–68
Etruria: 19, 21, 22, 37, 49–50, 52–53, 55, 59, 62–65, 68, 73, 75, 79–80, 85–86, 93–96, 101–02, 104–13, 118, 120, 123–24, 126, 135, 137, 139, 163, 167, 170, 172–73, 186–88, 190, 194, 198, 202, 209–11, 259
Etruscan: 19, 21–22, 25fn, 27, 51–52, 54–55, 60, 62–63, 65–68, 71–75, 77, 79–80, 85–91, 93–96, 101–02, 104–13, 117–18, 123, 126, 133–34, 137, 149fn, 164, 172, 183–84, 186, 188–90, 193–99, 202, 205–11, 213–14
exchange: 19–24, 28–29, 55, 60–61, 66, 72, 75–76, 80, 119, 124–25, 127–28, 139, 179, 184, 188, 221, 223, 227–28, 230, 240–41, 247, 260, 265
    See also cultural

farm(s)/farming/farmstead(s): 161, 164–65, 167–73, 264–65
    farmer(s): 164, 172, 265
feast/feasting: 180, 221–30
fecit: 76
fermentation: 224
field survey: 161, 163–66, 240
floral: 72, 87, 196–98, 201–02, 205, 207, 211, 213
fortification(s): 35–36, 38, 41, 61, 161, 164
Francavilla Marittima: 178–79, 250fn, 255–56, 259–60
François tomb: 202–03, 205, 207
Fustel de Coulanges, N.: 33–34, 38–39, 41fn

Gabii: 36, 123, 133, 157
Gaul (France): 28, 55, 223
gender: 122, 125–26, 128–29, 138, 179fn, 210
Genucilia plates: 195, 198
grain: 180, 185, 224, 226, 264
grapes: 51–53, 55, 198fn, 224
Greece: 21–24, 26–28, 35, 43, 48, 50, 52, 93–94, 96, 105–06, 111, 118, 149, 153fn, 189, 193–94, 224, 241, 246fn, 259, 266
Greek (culture): 19–25, 27–29, 38–39, 47–52, 54–56, 60–61, 65, 68, 71, 74–75, 77–80, 85–86, 90, 92–96, 101, 105–13, 125–26, 130, 132, 134, 138, 147–49, 172, 177, 180–81, 183–84, 187–89, 193–94, 198–99, 209–11, 213, 221–23, 225–30, 235–39, 250, 253, 255–56, 259, 262, 264, 266–68
Greek (language): 211, 214

Hallstatt: 177, 185, 187, 189–90
Hellenistic: 61, 71, 193, 205, 262fn
'Hellenization': 21–22, 25, 28, 47, 49, 54, 85–87, 96, 101, 109
Herakles/Hercules/Hercle: 52–54, 73, 86, 88–90, 93–94, 106, 108–12, 201, 210fn
    Pillars of Herakles: 25
Hermes/Turms: 73–74, 106–08, 112, 200, 210fn
heterarchy: 71
Heuneburg: 223
Himera: 221–22, 227
Horden, P.: 19, 22, 49–50, 59–61
house society: 35
household: 25, 133, 148, 267fn
hut(s)/capanne: 35–36, 41–42, 148–50, 156, 164, 184, 255
hybridity: 22, 222, 229, 239

Iberia (Spain): 21, 49–50, 55
iconography: 28, 47, 52, 54, 65, 73–74, 77–80, 95, 106–07, 109, 111, 178, 182–83, 193, 200, 207
identity/identities: 19–20, 23–27, 35, 39, 41–42, 49, 51, 63, 66, 85, 91, 118fn, 123, 126, 139, 187, 190, 199, 208, 211, 214, 221–22, 224–30
Illyria(n): 187–88, 190
indigenous: 28, 47–49, 51, 56, 60–61, 65–68, 117, 148fn, 153fn, 177, 179, 188–90, 194, 199, 221–30, 235–40, 245, 249–56, 258, 264–67
innovation: 19, 28, 33, 37, 40, 48–49, 52, 54, 56, 59, 68, 80, 85, 124, 137–39, 150, 163, 189, 213, 235, 238–40, 245, 253, 264–65

intentional ambiguity: 199
interconnectivity: 117, 119, 124–25, 127, 139
Iron Age: 21–23, 25–29, 33–35, 37, 40, 48–50, 54, 59–68,
   117–19, 121, 123, 133, 138, 140, 154, 156, 163, 170, 172,
   185, 187, 221–26, 228–30, 235–36, 238–42, 245–46,
   249–50, 259–60, 262–68
iron: 24, 63–64
Isayev, E.: 21, 25–26, 186
island, insular: 28, 54, 59–61, 63–68, 149fn, 188, 259,
   261

Jason: 78

Kainua (Marzabotto): 91, 153fn
Kassope: 153fn
koine: 22–24, 75, 79–80, 120, 126, 259

Latin (language): 51, 55, 59, 67, 76, 79, 91, 152, 211
Latium: 22, 37, 75, 79, 85–86, 93, 108, 118, 123, 133, 137,
   161, 163, 167, 171, 209
   Latium Vetus: 117, 120, 123–27, 132, 134, 139, 161–62,
      171–73
Levi-Strauss, C.: 35, 39–40
Livy: 21, 109, 153–54
longue durée: 242, 263, 268
loom: 177, 179–85, 189–90, 213
   loom weight: 167fn, 170, 180, 182fn
Lucania(n): 75, 77, 79, 181–82, 188, 194, 195, 199, 213
lyre: 177, 179–83, 185, 199, 261fn

Mediterranean (Sea): 49, 59–60, 124fn
metallurgy: 63–64
metaphor: 39–40, 42–43
microregionalism: 49–51
Middle Ground: 222–23
migration/migrant(s): 38, 47, 50, 77, 137, 139, 184,
   187–90, 235, 239–40, 250, 256, 263–64
mobility: 21, 25–26, 29, 49, 50, 64, 186–88, 236, 239,
   263–65
Moknine, Tunisia: 153fn
Mommsen, T.: 39, 43, 77, 255fn
Monte Del Bufalo (burial ground): 121–22, 124,
   133–34, 136–37, 140–43
Monte Polizzo: 222–24
Morgantina: 228
mortar and pestle: 177, 180–81, 183–85
Mozia: 221–22, 227

network: 19–21, 23–25, 28–29, 50, 55, 59–60, 63, 65–68,
   77fn, 87, 117, 119, 121, 124–33, 138–39, 165, 177, 186–90,
   193, 222–23, 229, 239, 241, 255
   network analysis: 117, 119, 121, 125–26, 132–33, 139,
      187, 239
Norba: 171
North Africa: 121
northern Calabria: 235, 239, 260
northern Italy: 187–88, 263

'Orientalizing': 62, 120, 124, 130, 133, 135, 138
Orientalizing period: 21–22, 27, 111–12, 117–18, 121, 123,
   139, 164
Orvieto: 86, 102, 102fn, 104, 109, 198, 198fn

Panormus: 221–22, 227
Papposilenus: 77
peristyle: 86, 88, 91–95
Phari, Thasos: 152
Phoenician(s): 21, 47–52, 54–56, 59, 62, 93, 111, 123,
   125–26, 128, 130, 133, 135, 137, 139, 187, 221–22, 225–30,
   266
Pisè: 149–50
Plautia (gens): 76–77
   Novios Plautius: 73, 75–77
Podere Tartuchino: 164, 167
Poggio Civitate: 149fn, 154, 210fn
Pollux: 74, 78
   See also Dioscuri
Pontine Region: 28, 161–66, 171–73
   Pontine Region Project (PRP): 161–63, 165–66, 168,
      170–71
postcolonial: 19, 22, 222–23, 235, 237, 239
post-structuralism: 34
pottery: 23, 25, 27–28, 51–52, 60, 62–63, 66–67, 101–06,
   109, 111–13, 123, 132–34, 136–39, 152fn, 161, 163–68,
   170–72, 177, 179, 182, 188, 194, 223, 227–28, 235,
   239–42, 244–47, 249–50, 251–52, 254–56, 259–68
   amphora/amphorae: 52–55, 67, 91, 102–12, 135,
      167fn, 195, 198fn, 202, 212–13, 224, 252
   Attic black-figure: 102–10, 112, 194
   Attic red-figure: 102–03, 201
   black gloss ware: 166, 171–72
   bucchero: 52, 91, 120, 126, 128, 130, 137–38, 164–68,
      170–73
   Campanian: 79, 194–96, 198–99, 211fn, 255
   capeduncola: 225–27, 229
   corded pithoi: 241–42, 264–65

Corinthian: 52–54, 110, 183, 189, 194, 250, 255, 259, 262, 266
cup/kylix: 52–53, 55, 102–05, 111, 126, 128, 131–35, 137–38, 196, 199fn, 225–30, 242, 245, 249, 251–55, 259, 261–62
Etruscan red-figure: 193–94, 196–98
Etrusco-Corinthian: 120, 138, 164–65, 167fn, 189
Etrusco-Italic: 134
Greek: 23, 27, 52, 66, 75, 101–02, 110, 131fn, 137–38, 184, 190, 193, 199, 226–30, 245, 250–51, 253, 255–56, 259, 262, 266–68
Grey Ware: 241–45, 264
impasto: 35, 52, 123, 125–26, 128, 130, 132, 134, 137–38, 167fn, 171, 235, 239, 241–42, 244–47, 249, 255, 263–64, 266–68
Impasto Chiaro Sabbioso: 167–68, 171
impasto rosso/red impasto: 135–38, 165–68
Italo-Geometric: 123, 125, 128, 136–37
matt-painted: 181–82, 240, 245–46, 248–56, 262, 265–68
mixed-style: 221, 228–30
Oinotrian-Euboean: 245, 250–57, 259, 265–67
Proto-Corinthian: 250, 255, 259, 261
Sardinian: 55
South Italian red-figure: 193
Tuscanic: 67
Villanovan: 52
Volterran kelebai: 202
White-on-Red: 128, 136–37
pottery studies: 240
power: 24, 35–38, 40–42, 85, 93–94, 96, 108, 111, 133, 151, 153–54, 157–58, 221–26, 229–30
Praeneste: 72, 76–77
prestige: 35, 86, 221–23, 226, 229–30
procession: 106–07, 109–11, 177, 179–82, 184, 189
protome(s): 152fn, 194, 202, 206, 209–10, 213
Purcell, N.: 19, 22, 49–50, 59–61
Pyrgi: 78fn, 85–95, 108, 252

Raganello: 240–41, 263
Raganello Archaeological Project: 237, 238, 241, 265
religion: 22, 34, 40, 42, 85, 90, 94, 107, 177, 213
Roman(s): 19–22, 25–29, 34, 37–39, 41, 47–51, 54, 56, 60–61, 63, 65–68, 71, 73–80, 85, 93–96, 101, 111, 117, 148, 153–55, 161, 164–66, 172, 177, 180, 186, 188, 193–94, 197, 199–200, 202, 211, 213–14
Roman Republic(an): 65–66, 165–66

Rome: 19–22, 25–27, 33–34, 36–37, 41–43, 54, 66–68, 71–77, 79, 85–87, 93, 95, 110, 117, 123, 133, 137–39, 147fn, 149–50, 152–57, 162, 164, 167, 171–72
Forum: 153–55, 157
Largo Argentina: 85, 95
Sacra Via: 152–55
Velabrum: 153
roof/roofing: 61, 86, 88–91, 93, 134, 138, 147–53, 155–58, 163–64, 172, 209–10
roof beams: 90, 149
see also tiles
rural: 28, 161–73, 265
ruralization: 161, 164–67, 169, 171–73

sacrifice: 111, 154, 177, 181, 183–85
Salemi: 222, 224, 226–27
San Giovenale: 148–50
sanctuary/sanctuaries: 64, 85, 87–89, 93–95, 108, 163, 165fn, 185, 190, 202, 208, 209–11, 213–14, 225, 236, 238–40, 242, 246–47, 254–56, 260–62, 266–68
sarcophagus/sarcophagi: 80, 108–09, 196, 198, 206–07, 209, 211
Sardinia: 21, 28, 35, 49–50, 54–55, 59–60, 62–64, 66–68
Sardinian(s): 55, 63
satellite villages: 163, 170, 172–73
Satricum: 36fn, 86, 121, 147fn, 150fn, 162–72
science: 240fn
archaeological: 47, 51
social: 39, 59
Selinus: 221–22, 227
settlement archaeology: 240
Sibaritide: 235–36, 238–39, 241–42, 245, 250, 255, 260, 262–68
Sicily: 21, 28, 35, 59–60, 75, 77, 92, 189, 193–94, 199–200, 209–11, 221–25, 227–30, 263, 268
Sicilian(s): 66, 77, 79, 193–94, 198, 209–10, 221–22, 224–30
slip: 138–39, 150–52, 225
social transformation: 121, 221, 223, 228, 230
Solunto: 221–22, 227
south(ern) Italy: 28, 35, 78, 80, 126, 178, 180, 183, 186, 193–94, 197–200, 209–11, 213–14, 235, 239–41, 249–50, 260, 265, 267
south(ern) Italic/southern Italian: 24, 79, 193–94, 197–200, 202, 210fn, 213–14, 239–40, 254–55, 260, 267–68
state: 19, 24–26, 33, 36–39, 42, 48, 154, 157, 161, 163, 172
formation: 33–34, 36, 161, 163–64, 169, 171–73

status: 54, 94, 96, 101, 106, 110, 120, 128, 133, 137–38, 188–89, 197, 221–29, 265,
  social: 68, 120, 153, 225, 227–29, 267
Sybaris: 28, 235–36, 241, 255, 261, 267–68
Syracuse/Syrcausa: 90, 153fn, 206, 209, 230, 235fn

Tarquinia: 36fn, 86, 101–03, 105–09, 106–11, 118, 148fn, 157, 189, 198, 207, 210fn
Tarquinian(s): 105–06, 109–10, 205
technology: 21, 35, 48, 55, 147, 237, 264
teleology: 33–34, 36–37, 154
temple(s): 28, 85–96, 108, 111, 149, 151–55, 157, 164, 179, 200, 210fn, 267
terminology: 23–24, 51, 152fn
terracotta: 86–87, 89, 93, 147–58, 180, 206–14, 259–60, 267
textile(s): 179–80, 184–85, 188–89
thatch: 148–51, 164
tile(s): 91, 147–53, 155–56, 158, 163–66, 168, 170–72
  pan tiles/*tegulae*: 151–52
  ridge tiles/*kalypteres*: 151–52
  roof-tile(s): 89, 94, 134, 147, 149–50, 152–53, 168fn, 210
Timpone della Motta: 28, 179, 235–43, 245–46, 249–51, 253–56, 258–68
tomb(s): 22, 37–38, 41, 55, 65, 104–07, 109–10, 113, 117, 119–34, 136–44, 168, 182–83, 185, 189, 197–98, 202–07, 209–11, 213–14, 227, 230
  chamber tombs: 106, 120, 122–23, 132, 134, 138, 202
  loculus tomb(s): 132, 134
  rock-cut tomb(s) 205
  Tomb of the Volumnii/Tomba dei Volumnii: 204–05
  see also burial, Francois tomb
trade: 21, 23, 25, 28, 62, 101–02, 105, 113, 117, 119, 124, 126, 139, 188, 190, 226, 255, 260, 264–66
trader(s): 25, 187, 223
transfer: 39, 54–55, 61, 186, 193–94, 264–65
  cultural: 47–48, 239
  economic: 47
  technological: 239, 264
  see also exchange
tripod: 177, 180–81, 183
tufo del Palatino: 150fn
tufo giallo: 150fn

underworld: 108–10, 200–01, 207, 213–14
  scene(s): 200
urban: 22, 26, 28, 33, 35, 37–40, 92, 120–21, 138, 147, 153–54, 156, 161, 163–68, 170, 172, 265, 268
  proto-urban: 258, 265
  urbanism: 66, 96, 147, 157–58
  urbanization: 33, 161, 163, 169
  urban planning: 85fn, 94

Vanth: 111–12, 207, 213
Veii: 77fn, 86, 108, 123, 126, 133–35, 137–39, 151fn, 157, 167fn, 171, 208, 209–10
Vesta: 42
villa(s): 168, 172
  see also Auditorium (villa)
Villanovan: 23, 52, 62–63, 105, 110, 118, 148fn, 184, 188–89
viticulture: 28, 47–52, 54–56
Volterra(n): 94fn, 197, 202, 206–07, 209
votive(s): 96, 133–34, 163, 167fn, 180, 185, 202, 208–11, 213–14, 260
Vulci(an): 52–53, 73, 79, 102, 104, 108–09, 194, 202–07, 210

war/warfare: 26–27, 39, 41, 61, 66
warrior(s): 38, 89, 181, 194–95
  ideology: 37
wattle and daub: 35, 148–50, 164
weapon(s)/weaponry: 24, 27, 64, 120, 125
Weber, M.: 38
wine: 47, 52–56, 105, 109–12, 123, 133–35, 137–38, 200, 223–24, 264–65

ARCHAEOLOGY OF THE MEDITERRANEAN WORLD

All volumes in this series are evaluated by an Editorial Board, strictly on academic grounds, based on reports prepared by referees who have been commissioned by virtue of their specialism in the appropriate field. The Board ensures that the screening is done independently and without conflicts of interest. The definitive texts supplied by authors are also subject to review by the Board before being approved for publication. Further, the volumes are copyedited to conform to the publisher's stylebook and to the best international academic standards in the field.

Titles in Series

Religious Dynamics in a Microcontinent: Cult Places, Identities, and Cultural Change in Hispania, ed. by Alejandro Sinner and Victor Revilla Calvo (2022)

Perspectives on Byzantine Archaeology: From Justinian to the Abbasid Age (6th–9th Centuries), ed. by Angelo Castrorao Barba and Gabriele Castiglia (2022)

In Preparation

New Approaches to the Materiality of Text in the Ancient Mediterranean: From Monuments and Buildings to Small Portable Objects, ed. by Erica Angliker and Ilaria Bultrighini